Liberalism Undressed

Liberalism Undressed

Liberalism Undressed

JETHRO K. LIEBERMAN

OXFORD
UNIVERSITY PRESS

Oxford University Press is a department of the University of Oxford.
It furthers the University's objective of excellence in research,
scholarship, and education by publishing worldwide.

Oxford   New York
Auckland   Cape Town   Dar es Salaam   Hong Kong   Karachi
Kuala Lumpur   Madrid   Melbourne   Mexico City   Nairobi
New Delhi   Shanghai   Taipei   Toronto

With offices in
Argentina   Austria   Brazil   Chile   Czech Republic   France   Greece
Guatemala   Hungary   Italy   Japan   Poland   Portugal   Singapore
South Korea   Switzerland   Thailand   Turkey   Ukraine   Vietnam

Oxford is a registered trade mark of Oxford University Press in the UK and certain other countries.

Published in the United States of America by
Oxford University Press
198 Madison Avenue, New York, NY 10016

© Jethro K. Lieberman 2012

All rights reserved. No part of this publication may be reproduced,
stored in a retrieval system, or transmitted, in any form or by any means, without
the prior permission in writing of Oxford University Press, or as expressly
permitted by law, by license, or under terms agreed with the appropriate
reproduction rights organization. Inquiries concerning reproduction outside the
scope of the above should be sent to the Rights Department, Oxford University Press,
at the address above.

You must not circulate this work in any other form
and you must impose this same condition on any acquirer.

Library of Congress Cataloging-in-Publication Data
Lieberman, Jethro Koller.
Liberalism undressed / Jethro K. Lieberman.
p. cm.
Includes bibliographical references and index.
ISBN 978-0-19-991984-0
1. Liberalism. I. Title.
JC574.L55   2012
320.51—dc23   2011053132

1 3 5 7 9 8 6 4 2

Printed in the United States of America
on acid-free paper

For Charles E. Lindblom

CONTENTS

1. The Liberal Premise   3

2. Constructing Harm from Natural Rights: The Cases of Locke and Nozick   29

3. The Meaning of Harm Derived from Interests: Joel Feinberg's Harm Principle   47

4. Collective Harms and the Market: Problems of Causation   69

5. Taxation, Welfare, and Benefits   97

6. The Duty to Act: Toward the Fiduciary Ethic   127

7. The Forms of Intervention   143

8. What Who?   162

9. Paternalism and the Timeline   180

10. Harm to Norms   207

11. Liberalism Redressed   242

Appendix: Four Liberal Premises and Their Problems   255
Acknowledgments   271
Notes   275
References   343
Index   363

Liberalism Undressed

Liberalism Unleashed

1

The Liberal Premise

Commitments in Search of a Premise

The fundamental human dilemma is how to escape from the jungle without landing in the zoo.

How is it possible to prevent the community from fracturing into fearful and ruinous hostilities while protecting the individual from the heel of an intolerant, superior ruler? Nearly four centuries ago, a beguiling idea seized the western imagination: A just balance between disorder and repression could be achieved if the state withdrew from the business of imposing an ultimate good. Liberalism, the philosophical venture that promoted this apparently simple idea, holds that it is not only possible but also morally proper to govern by refraining from decreeing ultimate ends, and that the state's only business is to prevent people from harming each other, not to engage in moral projects. Laws and political institutions should free us to seek and fulfill our own good as best we can without interfering in the same pursuit by others. Liberalism is thus a common life led at arm's length: We can live together, but not so close that either we must watch our backs or someone else must look over our shoulders. This regime of "ordered liberty"[1] has empowered large numbers of people to shape their own lives, and the release of energy has led to the most astonishing transformation in the human condition known to history.

The liberal venture was audacious, and for two significant reasons. First, it flew in the face of historical evidence. The state had always been an ordainment of God, not an artifact of man. The place of people, families, citizens, subjects, and slaves was fated and fixed—from ancient times through the Renaissance, the state that bound them was thought to be part of the natural order.[2] Although history records many kinds of states, in all of them rulers ruled, they did not serve, and they ruled to promote the good that they commanded. To do otherwise would risk disorder, even chaos and depravity.

The liberal venture was audacious, second, because it required the paradoxical belief, as things worked out, that only in the state and by obedience to law was it possible to be free. Contrived to remove the yoke of the state, liberalism ultimately was tethered to it. Some acclaimed philosophers of liberty went further, arguing that freedom requires wholesale submission—in Rousseau's famous words, citizens "shall be forced to be free."[3] Without a fine balance, liberalism risks devouring itself.

Liberalism did not arrive all at once or anywhere conquer the ground completely.[4] Nevertheless, a set of foundational beliefs took root and ripened into political institutions and practices that today are widely familiar as the hallmarks of liberal regimes. Although no two writers provide the same list—liberalism is a voluminous collection of commentaries without a central scripture[5]—most of these institutions and practices can easily enough be named. "The core practices of a liberal political order," says Stephen Holmes,

> are religious toleration, freedom of discussion, restrictions on police behavior, free elections, constitutional government based on a separation of powers, publicly inspectable state budgets to inhibit corruption, and economic policy committed to sustained growth on the basis of private ownership and freedom of contract. Liberalism's four core norms or values are *personal security* (the monopolization of legitimate violence by agents of the state who are themselves monitored and regulated by law), *impartiality* (a single system of law applied equally to all), *individual liberty* (a broad sphere of freedom from collective or governmental supervision, including freedom of conscience, the right to be different, the right to pursue ideals one's neighbor thinks wrong, the freedom to travel and emigrate, and so forth), and *democracy* or the right to participate in lawmaking by means of elections and public discussion through a free press.[6]

Other practices that belong on this list include freedom of association; a universal franchise; fair hearings; jury trials; an independent bar; public education; universal literacy; civilian control of the military; equal right to pursue occupations; and prohibitions against hereditary privileges, secret and ex post facto laws, group guilt, the selling of public office, and self-exemption (i.e., everyone, including the lawmaker, is to be subject to the law).[7] An additional practice, less often remarked but essential to the notion of fair procedure, is that people are to be held accountable by the norms of scientifically accessible evidence.[8] These, collectively, are the liberal commitments.

Though at this level of generality the liberal institutional and procedural commitments are broadly accepted throughout the western world and increasingly beyond, their descriptive label has been under steady and often heavy attack, from both the right and the left, for many decades (and longer[9]). At the outset of World War II, Ezra Pound put it that liberalism was a "mess of mush."[10] A few years later, in the early days of the cold war, a liberal was said to be "only a hop, skip, and a jump from a Communist."[11] A generation later, an acclaimed conservative philosopher asserted that liberalism has put "morality today ... in a state of grave disorder."[12] Now, in the early twenty-first century, a well-known historian writes that liberalism connotes "something damnable, unhealthy, and odious."[13] On the left, a noted legal scholar proclaimed that "life in modern, liberal society continually denies us the possession of coherent personality."[14] A political philosopher, summarizing a strand of communitarian thought, notes that "liberalism is said to undermine community, to restrict unduly opportunities for democratic participation, to create inegalitarian hierarchy, and to reinforce egoistic social conflict at the expense of the common good."[15]

The less academically inclined, on entering any used bookstore, can find tracts, many by well-known commentators, that proclaim liberalism a "mental disorder," "godless," a "sin," "evil," a "tragedy," an "assault," lacking common sense, "fascist," "death," "a demonic mob," and, more limp, though starkly oxymoronic, wanting liberty.[16] And from the modern medium of the blogosphere comes a jejune complaint about the very sound of it: "The biggest problem with modern American liberalism may be the word itself—it just hits the ear wrong."[17] Cynically, one might suppose the truer claim is that liberalism foments hysteria.

How can these attacks on liberalism (which by its very principles encourages them) be squared with the reality of widespread and deeply rooted liberal political institutions? The most obvious answer is that the word has multiple meanings. "Liberalism" is a confederation of connotations, not all consistent or necessarily conjoined. "Overuse and overextension of [the term] have rendered it so amorphous," Judith Shklar insisted, "that it can now serve as an all-purpose word, whether of abuse or praise."[18] Liberalism, says Raymond Geuss, "has no definition."[19] He means, I should suppose, that it has too many.[20]

In the realm of politics, especially American party politics, liberalism can stand for minimalist government, an expansive welfare state, and everything in between.[21] It is sometimes taken as a synonym for utilitarianism or egalitarianism (moral theories about human ends) or democracy (a theory about means).[22] In a more philosophical vein, it is associated with a general idea about individuality, "the belief that the freedom of the individual is the highest political value, and that institutions and practices are to be judged by their success in promoting it."[23] Individuality itself can be expressed in a multitude of ways.[24] A political-sociological approach has it that "no person may be forcibly imprisoned within the class or clan or even family into which he was born."[25] A political-psychological approach holds that "liberals are committed to a conception of freedom and of respect for the capacities and the agency of individual men and women."[26] And sometimes the political conception is put in moral terms: "[T]he ideal of individual sovereignty . . . holds that the only things that can rightly be required of human beings . . . are those forms of conduct that are necessary to maximizing the scope of everyone's freedom to control his or her life according to his or her own judgments."[27]

Often, liberalism is taken as a rationalist approach to human problems, specifically, the idea that we can and therefore should be social engineers and not rely on tradition. Just after World War II, Chester Bowles put it that "liberalism is an attitude. The chief characteristics of that attitude are human sympathy, a receptivity to change and a scientific willingness to follow reason rather than faith or any fixed set of ideas."[28] A century earlier, John Henry Cardinal Newman, a critic, took it as expressing the philosophical attitude that all change is good.[29] The liberal is thus often characterized as one who believes in the possibility of progress in human affairs, and is less likely than the conservative to be deterred in proposing change for fear that it will result in unanticipated baneful consequences.[30]

Quite separately, liberalism may describe psychological or cultural moods. Max Frankel described these senses in a series of polarities contrasting liberalism and conservatism:

> It is liberal to expect corporations to behave like the government. It is conservative to expect the government to behave like corporations.... It is liberal to risk high-priced failure and costly overruns in almost every federal department, except the Pentagon. It is conservative to risk them only in the Pentagon.... It is liberal to favor government subsidy for the Metropolitan Opera. It is conservative to favor government subsidy for the Mets.... It is liberal to wish to expunge most criminal records, except for those seeking to buy a pistol. It is conservative to keep such records public, except for those seeking to buy a pistol.[31]

The policy judgments expressed in these juxtapositions are not rooted in principle but in preferences and outlook. Although Frankel's pairings relate to political matters, the temperament these terms describe need not be. A fiscal conservative can be socially liberal (or, as in the case of the Republican Congress of the early twenty-first century, socially conservative and fiscally liberal). A cultural liberal might feel inclined to wear his hair long (or she, to wear it extra short or purple); a cultural conservative, to visit the barber weekly. But one's hairstyle does not determine beliefs about gun control or gay marriage: The cultural liberal or conservative is not logically committed to political liberalism or conservatism. Though they may go hand in hand, they do not always: Home-schooling parents tend to be political conservatives. Yet the very point of home schooling is that a family can teach specific members of the next generation, free from the larger community's oversight; this is a form of individualism that one might have supposed would more likely be the creed of liberals. In contrast, liberal proponents of public schooling appear to be advocating forms of community building, not, according to some of its critics, a liberal characteristic. Shortly after William F. Buckley Jr. died in February 2008, his son Christopher Buckley was asked: "Is liberalism dead in New York?" His response—"The key will be how many people start arriving at Lincoln Center in pickups with gun racks."—is a sassy reminder of the important distinction between cultural and political labels.[32]

Just as important, liberalism is a perspective on beliefs about the state of the world and what counts as knowledge. The old joke has it that a conservative is a liberal who was mugged, a liberal a conservative who was arrested: One's experiences of the world are taken to alter or fix one's outlook about policy and even what constitutes fact. In 2008 reports of a bitterly cold winter in many parts of the United States cheered a few Republicans because they thought the freeze disproved global warming.[33] The interpretation of an empirical observation and the factual conclusion they took to follow from it seem oddly placed on a liberal–conservative continuum. Why shouldn't such news cheer Democrats as well? No one could actually want to bear the trouble and expense of repairing the effects of global warming if the threat is empty. Presumably the Democrats refused to read the cold winter as evidence disproving the global warming thesis. That political leanings can account for opinion of this sort suggests that one's philosophical perspectives can determine factual beliefs about the world logically independent of the content of the philosophy.

Attacks on liberalism have much less validity than their combined fierceness might suggest, since they are aimed not necessarily at the philosophical beliefs that sustain our political institutions and practices but at the varied other uses of the word. The United States may seem to be ideologically volatile, in the sense that it swings between the parties to express displeasure at the failure of the governing party to solve difficult problems. But there is no reason to suppose that underlying liberal institutions are spurned by a majority. Indeed, a recent and well-publicized emblematic sign that the public is not ready to jettison liberal institutions was the apparently nonironical warning to a Southern Republican congressman: "Keep your Government hands off my Medicare."[34]

Still, that liberalism has so many meanings should counsel caution. Why use the word at all? The answer is that it remains useful, if appropriately qualified, as the descriptive term for a theory about the metes and bounds of state power. "[H]ardly anyone denies," said the intellectual historian Shirley Robin Letwin, "that the distinctive political issue since the 18th century has been whether government should do more or less."[35] What justifies the power of the state? Over what domains may the state legitimately govern against the wishes of dissenters? Rejecting the long-held Aristotelian belief that man is *zoon politikon* (a political animal whose ultimate good is found only in the state), liberalism is the intuition that not everything in life that matters can or should be shaped or bounded or fixed or cured by politics and law. It names a philosophical system that proposes why limited government, exemplified by the liberal commitments, provides the best chance of striking a livable balance between disorder and repression, from one age to another.

The Harm Principle
The Ends, Means, Reach, and Shape of Government

To understand and justify liberalism, to see why the commitments, institutions, and practices that have been instantiated in its name and refined over the centuries are consistent and valuable to human life, I propose returning to a core principle that is often taken for granted but rarely explored—the principle that the state's legitimacy rests in how it deals with harm.

Many political philosophers reject this focus, not because harm should be ignored but because a preoccupation with the ways we hurt each other seems unglamorous and insufficiently ennobling. Reducing suffering is worthy, to be sure, but there is more to life than that. Surely there are more significant tasks for all of us collectively to take on. We are called to greater things. We should not stay in the trenches when some great good remains to be fought for and won. So perhaps the key to justifying and limiting government power is to assign it to pursue a particular good or set of goods and to judge its performance by its fidelity to the pursuit.

The problem for the theorist is that there is no accepted single, universal theory of the good. Or to put it perhaps more precisely, there are too many possible candidates. Justice? Salvation? Morality? Tradition? God's will? Peace? Community? Efficiency? Prosperity? Growth? Order? Nobility? The ruler's felicity? Human flourishing? Autonomy? Adventure? Security? Glory? Conquest? Liberty? Equality? Choice? Political participation? Personal happiness? Communal satisfaction? Some mixture of all these and more? Society teems with different and often conflicting beliefs about the individual and collective good, and a multiplicity of groups seek disparate ends within single national communities.

Some people are convinced that they know what is the highest good, and they are prepared, or say they are prepared, to live with the consequences of tasking the state with its fulfillment. So, for example, accepting the good of tradition and order supports a foundational principle of at least one strand of conservatism—that what has endured is what is right—and provides the justification for preserving existing institutions, whatever they may be and whoever they may oppress.[36] Others wish a state that will foster fidelity to God's wishes, as manifest in a particular religious tradition; a theocracy results.

If we could agree on a common end, we could seek policies and practices to accomplish it. But many who have thought through this problem—we might as well call them "liberals"—are dubious that any of the many ends on offer will command consensus. It is too late in human history, they suppose, to think that any group committed to a highest good will sacrifice it for a competing but inconsistent good held by a more sizable share of others. Liberalism is thus a response both to pluralism[37] and to the difficulty of persuading dissenters to accept something other than what their tradition teaches them. A final end or highest good, then, is unlikely to provide an acceptable principle for limiting the exercise of governmental power, since in striving to achieve many such ends people would likely cede the state unlimited power or acquiesce in its acquiring such power. We know all too many societies that have found themselves in thrall to just such a claim.

The task, then, is to find a workable principle of state action that is self-limiting, that yields the liberal commitments we generally prize, and that preserves potentially valuable ends. Several candidates have been put forward, but most are complex and controversial (as we will shortly see). There is one function, however, that almost everyone acknowledges government may properly undertake: to reduce, deter, and redress the harms that people cause each other. As a theory of harm, liberalism puts the injuries we cause each other at the center of focus: It is not just an *activity* of government, but the *rationale* of government. Government is necessary in the way that engine oil is necessary: Something needs to keep friction at bay and parts from rubbing together. Engine oil may not be alluring, but without it the vehicle goes nowhere.

Dealing with harm is a venerable task of government, stretching back to the very origins of the state. However adept or inept a particular state may have been in protecting its population from invaders and from each other, few can have rejected its authority to do so, whatever other course or end it may have pursued (as most throughout history have done). It is no revelation that states have safeguarded their subjects unevenly at best. Poor and primitive states, those with feeble administrative capacity, could do little. Hierarchical societies (and historically most have elevated king, clergy, and nobility over the masses) have protected the few to the detriment of the many, actually causing harm to the low-born for the sake of those in charge. So the efficacy and sincerity of states in pursuing their protective function has, in most places and times, not been high. Still, the political arm of many societies pretended to do so and over long periods of time began to do so. And as the liberal impulse took hold in the west, it came to be understood that the state should serve an instrumental purpose: to defend, shield, secure, and protect its people. Though Thomas Hobbes did not come to liberal conclusions, it was the focal point of his 1651 political masterpiece, *Leviathan*, that the people assigned state power to a sovereign for the express purpose of protecting themselves from the war of all against all. In his counterpoint four decades later, John Locke suffused his far more liberal state with the explicit duty to guard against harm. Ever since, the liberal canon has held that the state has a core duty to protect an ever-widening swath of the public.

Today we accept without much thought that, in countries with liberal roots, the state is meant to serve us and not we the state. We take for granted that the state's primary purpose is to keep us safe and to let us go about our business, so thoroughly has the state's harm-repelling function penetrated. But for all our easy familiarity with this principle ("it's a free country," we commonly say, "I should be able to do what I want as long as I don't hurt anybody"), we have not attended deeply to the consequences of supposing that dealing with harm should be not merely the central purpose of government but its only purpose.

This proposition—that the government should occupy itself solely with reducing harm and its effects—has not been deeply understood, in part because its most eloquent proponent, John Stuart Mill, did not explore the meaning of harm, and in part because political theorists have not supposed the harm principle sufficiently powerful to account for all that they want the liberal state to do. To the contrary, I contend throughout this book, the harm principle deserves a closer look than it usually gets because its contours can be filled in, because it is self-limiting, and because from it we can derive all the significant liberal commitments. Since as an explanatory principle it is both less controversial and less complex than the other leading candidates, it is more likely, once explained, to attract support (indeed, it is likely already the basis of widespread unreflective support) for liberal institutions and practices.

Though I postpone to a later section an examination of the liberal conception of human nature, begin for the moment with the uncontroversial notion that some beliefs, behaviors, and activities should be left to individual discretion—and that these deserve state protection from interference. No society can claim to be liberal that does not, as Mill said, draw "a circle around every individual human being which no government, be it that of one, of a few, or of the many, ought to be permitted to overstep," or as Friedrich A. Hayek rephrased it, that does not carve out through publicly declared rules at least some "domain of the individuals (or organized groups) with which others are not allowed to interfere."[38]

It follows that in this domain people must be free to act *regardless of the consequences* both to themselves and others—for example, you do not lose your vote if you cast it for the irresponsible candidate. Otherwise the state will necessarily be concerned to constrain every action to accomplish some consequence of which it approves (or to deter some consequence of which it disapproves), in other words, an end or good. In classical liberal theory, this private domain can be established only by what have come to be called "negative rules." The state declares what we may not do, leaving us free to do whatever is not proscribed. This characteristic has been much noted. Thus, H. L. A. Hart: "The common requirement of law and morality consists for the most part not of active services to be rendered but of forbearances, which are usually formulated in negative form as prohibitions." Lon L. Fuller: "In what may be called the basic morality of social life, duties that run towards other persons generally . . . normally require only forbearances, or as we say, are negative in nature." Hayek: "[P]ractically all rules of just conduct are negative in the sense that they normally impose no positive duties on any one, unless he has incurred such duties by his own actions." The liberal state says: "Thou shalt not do thus and so." It does not say: "Thou must act so as to accomplish this and that."[39]

Accept that the state's authority should be limited to declaring negative duties—duties to refrain. Still, restricting the state in that way will not necessarily ensure usable liberty for the individual to pursue an ultimate good. The state could apply a negative rule—"do not do X, or Y, or Z"—to so many types of conduct that the space in which to roam would shrivel. A rule of forbearance, therefore, must be self-limiting in some way.

Since the seventeenth century, only one criterion has gained the assent of liberals as a self-limiting component of forbearance, and that is the criterion of *harm*. All agree that one ought to avoid harming another, and that the state may intercede to prevent one person from causing another harm or to redress a harm that has occurred—not surprisingly, since a state that frees individuals from the torpor of traditionalism must then cabin the restless energy of the individual "sovereigns" that it releases. John Locke put it that the law of nature teaches "that being all equal and independent, no one ought to harm another in his Life, Health, Liberty, or Possessions." Nearly a century later, Adam Smith opined in *A Theory of Moral Sentiments*:

> Mere justice is, upon most occasions, but a negative virtue, and only hinders us from hurting our neighbour. The man who barely abstains from violating either the person, or the estate, or the reputation of his neighbours, has surely very little positive merit. He fulfils, however, all the rules of what is peculiarly called justice, and does every thing which his equals can with propriety force him to do, or which they can punish him for not doing. We may often fulfil all the rules of justice by sitting still and doing nothing.[40]

Limiting freedom to prevent people from causing harm is, of course, not exclusive to liberalism. Any political theory worthy of the name must at a minimum incorporate some version of a harm principle. What makes the harm principle of peculiar interest here is that liberalism, or at least classical liberalism, proposes that preventing or redressing harm to others is the *sole* basis on which the state may act. In his First Inaugural, Thomas Jefferson perfectly stated this proposition:

> With all these blessings [of geography, religion, character, energy], what more is necessary to make us a happy and prosperous people? Still one thing more, fellow-citizens—a wise and frugal Government, which shall restrain men from injuring one another, shall leave them otherwise free to regulate their own pursuits of industry and improvement, and shall not take from the mouth of labor the bread it has earned. This is the sum of good government.[41]

The classic formulation of the harm principle is that of John Stuart Mill, who in 1859 in *On Liberty* asserted "one very simple principle," which, despite its familiarity, is always worth rereading and which, as a biographer has said, "is so forcibly and memorably argued that it has passed into the public philosophy of all the great Western democracies."[42]

> That principle is, that the sole end for which mankind are warranted, individually or collectively, in interfering with the liberty of action of any of their number is self-protection. That the only purpose for which power can be rightfully exercised over any member of a civilised community, against his will, is to prevent harm to others. His own good, either physical or moral, is not a sufficient warrant. He cannot rightfully be compelled to do or forbear because it will be better for him to do so,

because it will make him happier, because, in the opinions of others, to do so would be wise, or even right. These are good reasons for remonstrating with him, or reasoning with him, or persuading him, or entreating him, but not for compelling him or visiting him with any evil in case he do otherwise. To justify that, the conduct from which it is desired to deter him must be calculated to produce evil to some one else. The only part of the conduct of anyone, for which he is amenable to society, is that which concerns others. In the part which merely concerns himself, his independence is, of right, absolute. Over himself, over his own body and mind, the individual is sovereign.[43]

Mill's harm principle certainly seems to embody a negative rather than a positive claim of political power: The state may interfere with us to prevent us from harming others, even perhaps a tiny harm, but not to force us to do good, even perhaps a great one. The harm principle is rooted in a suspicion of state power and justified by our uncertainty about the good. The smaller the state's power to command, the freer we will be, certainly freer of the state, to seek our own ends. This is a common strategy, not reserved to philosophical inquiry. The approach of many social scientists, Charles E. Lindblom has written, is to identify "ills to escape rather than ideals to approach. . . . Unable to describe an ideal tomato, they identify the inedible."[44]

With the meaning and extent of the harm principle I am concerned in all that follows. For now, observe that Mill's harm principle has five distinct components and that Mill quite incorrectly called it "one very simple principle": (1) *harm* (2) *to others* (3) *caused by* a wrongdoer (4) permits the state to *interfere with* (5) the wrongdoer's *liberty of action*. The most visible component is that dealing with "others." The state may interfere with our liberty only to prevent us from harming *others*; the harm principle rules out, as Mill argues, paternalistic rules. The other components have often been obscured. The first is that the state may use its coercive power only when what one person does to another is actually *harmful*. An action that merely *affects* someone is not, simply by virtue of the effect, a harm that the state may prevent or redress;[45] this component rules out "moralistic" effects. The third, and much more ambiguous, component is that the state may deal only with harm actually caused by *another human being*. Mere suffering, misfortune, or bad luck, therefore, are not ipso facto the types of injuries that permit the state to intervene. Fourth, an important question is the *manner* by which the state may interfere with liberty. What methods, sanctions, and remedies may the state use or impose to deter or redress the harm? Detecting conduct that might (or did) lead to harm, may the state threaten with criminal sanctions or civil fines, issue civil injunctions, award private damages, or otherwise "regulate"? Finally, what is the "liberty of action" with which the state may interfere? Is the state restricted to imposing physical restraints against the person (incarceration), or may it interfere with other sorts of liberties (the liberty to contract, the liberty to possess property)? Whether the harm principle can specify under what conditions the state may limit any or all of the types of liberties is an important part of the issue at hand.

By its terms, the harm principle seems to prescribe a narrow function for government, nothing more. So restricted, it might provide the basis for some of the institutions and practices we associate with liberalism, but not likely all or even most of them. Where, for example, is separation of powers to be found within its contours, or frequent elections, or a universal franchise? As it will turn out, the harm principle cannot serve only to justify and limit the exercise of power. It must also serve to establish and maintain a government that will both adhere to the harm principle and faithfully carry it out.

To be useful as a principle of *government*, then, the harm principle is complex in yet another way. A government, even one that draws its energy from the harm principle, is not just a programmed machine, calibrating its power with a dial that moves from "off" to "full." We cannot simply instruct whoever is in power to sweep away harmful activity and avoid all else. No such machine does or can exist. Government, in any event, is not a machine at all, but a collection of people with their own interests and motives. To expect a harm principle to live up to its name, it must be capacious enough to confront government along a number of dimensions.

First, we must be concerned with the objects of government power. The harm principle must, as Mill observed, exert itself against harm to others. So it is necessary to consider the nature of harm, what it means to harm. Chapters 2 and 3 examine these issues, concluding that while the intent of the harm principle is to narrow the focus of government power, what remains open to it is, while constrained, nevertheless quite sizable. One particularly significant human activity, the economic market, as chapter 4 shows, is subject to policing under the principles developed.

Second, beyond the objects or activities subject to the government's power, the harm principle must specify to some degree the extent of the power to be exercised. When may the government intrude? Must the harm be already manifest? What may it tackle? Is it limited to holding up a stop sign or may it affirmatively undertake various "projects" that might be seen as attempting some good rather than preventing some evil? Chapters 3, 4, and 5 examine these questions, concluding that the government may broadly tailor its efforts to deal with the whole range of actions that under the principle may be characterized as harmful. That to carry out its mission the government may even direct that people carry out affirmative duties, rather than merely refrain from harmful conduct, is the subject of chapter 6.

Third, to be useful as a practical matter, the harm principle must instruct us on the means and methods that the government may use to enforce the principle's precepts. Prescribing the death penalty for most offenses under the penal code, as nearly was the case in eighteenth-century Great Britain, leads to disrespect, disobedience, and a disinclination to follow the ordinances, even if in some way within the outer limits of the governing principle.[46] The modes of intervention, and the limits on the forms and reach of those modes, are the subject of chapter 7.

Fourth, we need some assurance that the harm principle can actually be carried out, without being co-opted or corrupted by the government it means to legitimate. The harm principle, in other words, is not a collection of legal ordinances or even a method of deducing rules that can be enacted into legal restrictions on our conduct. To the contrary, the harm principle is just that—a principle—and it requires explication. The question of who should interpret it and give it concrete form in particular instances is particularly urgent. And not merely who, but subject to what sorts of constraints. So the harm principle must necessarily have much to say about who constitutes the government, how its parts are to be arranged, and the sorts of limitations that can be imposed, not merely theoretically but by virtue of institutional practices, such as separation of powers, frequent elections, and decisions constrained by evidence. In particular, the harm principle implies the right of every person to participate in the political life and have a say in formulating its varied applications to the harms that abound. These issues are considered in chapter 8.

Fifth, the harm principle may seem to embrace all of life. But it does not, as it explicitly proclaims. It is the burden of chapters 9 and 10 to explore the reasons for barring the application of harms that a person may bring upon himself or that arguably befall the culture and the norms of the community.

Sixth, all the considerations just noted imply certain other principles that are not so much adjunct theories about government power and limitations as they are consequences of the harm principle itself. Significant among them are: (1) the principle of equality, which states that in ways to be determined the state must treat each person as it treats all others; (2) the principle of neutrality, which asserts that the state may not impose on people its own notions of their good, if harm is not at stake; (3) the principle of consent, which states that the public has a stake in the functions and outputs of government and each person must therefore be permitted to register consent or disapproval of the government's policies to the extent feasible; and (4) the principle of dialogue, which states that the people must be free to think, believe, associate, and talk to one another and the government, charged as it is to deal with the harms that impede their life's fulfillment.

Saddling a principle with all these tasks may seem a tall order. Perhaps alternative principles can more easily explain the liberal commitments than the complex of considerations that constitute the harm principle.

Liberal Alternatives to the Harm Principle

Beginning in the early 1970s, political theorists raised liberalism into the realm of high theory. As theories these ideas became imaginative (and, one is quickly drawn to observe, imaginary), intricate, sometimes dazzling, but brought to the ground of policy and politics, faint and largely unheeded. Four major strands emerged, all with old roots but none that had ever been developed in such rich and comprehensive ways. Each—consent, dialogue, equality, and neutrality—has been the subject of an extensive literature offered as the basis for understanding a liberal political order. Even if this book were devoted to their themes, rather than to another, I could not begin to do them justice, much less make sense of any of them in a short passage. So although I offer a somewhat more extended critique in the Appendix, here I can only fleetingly assert the essence of each and mention some difficulties.

Consent-based liberalism rests the exercise of political power on the consent of the governed, in the familiar phrase. Social contract theory sees no need to justify consent, since as a practical matter when people freely agree they are unlikely to complain or seek an alternative. Assuming that consent extends to the form and methods of government and its objects and limits, a full-blown theory of government can be spun out. But its defect is immediately apparent: Legitimacy depends on actual consent, and we can be confident that in no state could everyone have consented to the shape and reach of government, which in most lands was in place before anyone thought to question its legitimacy. Social contract theorists are drawn to just-so stories or fanciful constructions of how consent might rationally be achieved. John Rawls, for example, put imaginary people around a table, shorn of most of the characteristics that make us what we are, and inferred how these wraiths and changelings might reason their way to principles of justice. It turns out that to achieve even this consensus, the theorist must specify other principles—for example, the rules that will structure the dialogue in which the conversants will engage. But if what justifies the rules is consent, then the participants are in a vicious circle, for before they can consent they must proceed under rules that can be justified only by prior consent. So the consent is not primary and collapses into other requirements and principles. In any event, whether or not other principles are prior to the practice of consent, hypothetical consent is not consent and cannot reasonably serve as the justification for the exercise of power.

Dialogue as the theoretical basis of political order suffers from a similar difficulty. At its broadest, the theory is that legitimate rules of state will emerge when people sit down to talk things through. They will, say the proponents of dialogue, convince each other of what rules to adopt for the government to which they will be subject. While no one can doubt the usefulness of actual conversation among real people, it is not likely to be effective unless the people proceed under rules that will guide the discussion. But that is the point of the conversation: to hammer out the rules that will guide political debate. So the conversation to construct rules cannot proceed unless such rules are in place to begin with. Again, the theory seems to collapse into a circularity (or into more than one, since one of the questions to be resolved is whether all are to be treated equally in the grand founding dialogue; if so, then perhaps it is equality that is the founding principle). Moreover, there is no theoretical reason to believe that an unconstrained conversation among the people (if that were possible) would have any obvious stopping point (beyond the fatigue of the moment), nor is there any reason to feel confident that the conversation would conclude with normatively valid rules. Unlimited conversation could lead to any outcome: Hobbes's leviathan as well as a worker's council.

The claim of egalitarians is that liberal political theories must begin with equality because we lack a sound basis to assume the entitlement of particular people to priority in governing or in political outcomes. Start, then, with the premise that liberal commitments are justified to the extent that they bind the state to give each person equal respect. But it is unclear whether an equality rule is based, instead, on an antecedent rule of neutrality: The state must pay equal respect to persons because there is no a priori account of which person's end or good is best. (Otherwise, an equality criterion might be paternalistic, allowing the state, in paying equal respect, to deny a given person the ability to live his own life on the ground that his poor choice overlooks his "true" interests.) Moreover, the abstract notion of equality is insufficient by itself to determine what is to be equalized. Perhaps it is liberty, perhaps resources—but a preliminary equality criterion may be compatible with a narrow set of liberties or a meager redistribution for all. Equal respect might require no more than paying careful and sincere attention to each person in determining whether the state should extend the freedom to act or redistribute the social product; it need not compel the state to do so.

A fourth strand, neutrality, holds that liberal institutions and practices are consequences of abstaining from politically pursuing the good. I have already noted the liberal's propensity for just such a rule: the great difficulty, if not impossibility, of ascertaining the proper end amid a welter of conflicting claims. But premising the liberal state on such a foundation, the critic charges, involves a contradiction in terms: Declaring neutrality the state's prime directive is itself the choice of a good. It enshrines a rule of choice, against the preferences of many people not to live in a society in which choice is available. Moreover, the state is open to the same critique whenever it determines on any course of action, since that very choice is to pursue some good, a pursuit that neutrality as the core principle would presumably require it to relinquish.

That these various foundational principles are subject to the reproach that they are circular or self-contradictory, or that they may collapse into each other's domains, does not mean that they play no part in liberal institutions and practices. Each is a significant constituent of the liberal order, not because it starts with them but because, as already noted, they are entailed by the harm principle itself.

The Modesty of the Harm Principle

Mill's version of the harm principle is now 150 years old. Widely acknowledged, it has also been widely dismissed, usually because, its critics assert, the concept of harm is too vague to give the principle any traction.[47] As one political theorist summarizes the objection: "Since any activity may be deemed harmful, the principle has no cutting edge to be employed in the distinction of legitimate and illegitimate interference."[48] But the critiques often stop just there, denying the principle's utility without further examining whether it has bite or reach or can effectively draw the lines that describe a liberal order. It is the burden of much of this book to undertake just that examination.

Still, it may be worthwhile to consider in briefest compass the sort of work a principle is supposed to do—and the modesty of the harm principle in comparison. You might rashly demand that a principle definitively resolve all relevant questions that may be fairly put to it, just as a mathematical formula tells us without fail how to convert a temperature reading from Fahrenheit to Celsius. Some legal rules permit definitive judgments—if the person sitting on the barstool is provably twenty-one, he may legally buy a beer; otherwise, not. But these are not the sorts of problems that fundamental principles are asked to resolve. What we expect to gain from them is not how to decide whether someone is complying with a legal rule but whether there ought to be a law in the first place. The primary question for the legislature is not how to prove a teenager has been tippling but whether the state should prohibit a class of people from drinking at all. A political regime that rests on an external code, like the Bible, will have a relatively easy time of it. If it is a sin to commit adultery than it is simple to see that the legislature may criminalize the prerogative of kings. That is not our situation. The question that has confronted political thinkers for more than three centuries is how to determine the legitimate scope of political power. A principle that could definitively map the state's reach would be as valuable as it is unprecedented, and unlikely.

Some have supposed that a "genuine" political theory must provide "a set of principles that, by themselves, determine what should be done without the need for further ad hoc moral judgment, given any specification of the factual circumstances in which the principles are to be applied."[49] Mill supposed that utilitarianism, which he championed, was such a theory because its fundamental theorem provides a determinate outcome when the facts are known: Individual actions and public policies are morally correct if they maximize total satisfaction or utility across society. If society's total happiness would be increased by assassinating mighty Casey at the Bat after he struck out, thus slaking Mudville's frenzied mob's thirst for revenge, it is right to do so, even though Mrs. Casey might feel sad for a time.[50] There are, of course, two reasons to suspect such a theory of failing its mission. The first is the well-known major theoretical weakness of utilitarianism, that a social maximum need not respect persons, so that a utilitarian regime can sacrifice some people for the greater satisfaction of others.[51] Just this defect fueled Rawls's assault on utilitarianism: "Each person possesses an inviolability founded on justice that even the welfare of society as a whole cannot override."[52] The second weakness is that even accepting the standard, in almost all cases we will find it impossible to apply: How do we know the utility functions at issue and how can we tell, even if the net satisfaction of society is immediately maximized, that the killing will not so frighten other players that the game of baseball will collapse, thereafter decreasing the net social satisfaction? The abstract standard "maximize" contains no workable calculus of decision.

Other theories that purport to derive a determinate rule suffer from similar defects. Thus, to decide under what circumstances the state may interfere with the market distribution of goods, Rawls proposed his "difference principle," which follows a "maximin" rule: Inequalities are to be arranged to maximize the primary goods that go to the worst-off; or, to put it differently, to choose that alternative that is the least worst. But this rule is also far from determinate. For one thing, Rawls cannot specify which persons are the "least advantaged," and so he "plead[s] practical considerations . . . because [s]ooner or later the capacity of philosophical or other arguments to make finer discriminations is bound to run out." The practical consideration leads him to choose an arbitrary and blunderbuss standard that counts as least advantaged "all persons with less than half of the median income and wealth."[53] (Not for Rawls the Shakespearean exaltation in Sonnet 29: "For thy sweet love rememb'red such wealth brings / That then I scorn to change my state with kings.") The maximin rule is also unconcerned with the number who are benefited (it could favor small numbers of the worst-off to the detriment of large numbers of others only slightly better off), and it fails to account for the gains won and lost. "Maximin would prefer the outcome in which a single worst-off person gains a penny's worth of benefit at the cost of the loss of thousands of dollars for each of thousands of the better-off."[54] So the claim that aggregation (maximizing) and priority (ordering) rules are necessary to make theories "genuine" seems suspect. Such calculation rules rarely (most likely, never) provide definitive resolutions to particular issues in the real world because we cannot specify precisely enough the factual circumstances that count. The calculations may be too difficult or the things being counted may be too indistinct.

The harm principle is more modest. It is not an aggregating or prioritizing principle. It does not require the state to maximize liberty by minimizing harm or maximizing the state's response to it. Since most interests are incommensurate, and since few interests can be quantified, maximizing policies, even if they could be made into workable formulas, would yield specious results.[55] The harm principle answers the question whether the state may legitimately act, without specifying a necessarily determinate outcome in each case. It holds that dealing with harm (reducing, preventing, and redressing harm) is a justifiable aim of government. The state may deal with harm in all its guises in appropriate ways. But the consequence of a theory that does not maximize is that the state is not compelled to act in a certain way, or even act at all; prudential concerns of all sorts may counsel caution and forbearance in the face of harms, both high and low. (Nothing in the harm principle decrees a particular jail term for robbery, or even a jail term at all—music downloading, anybody?) The harm principle, then, states a necessary but not necessarily sufficient condition for government to act. If harm is in the air, government may sniff it out, but it need, indeed, ought not, try to diffuse it all. In real societies with limited resources, people face a multitude of misuse and mischief, a kaleidoscope of harm and peril; to demand that the government go this way and that to root it all out is to risk dissipating its strength and making all worse.

That is not a defect in the theory; it is a condition of our world. We face irreducible uncertainty both in the background of events and in our ability to predict accurately what will occur or to determine from measurements and models how to explain a phenomenon. No one can say with ultimate confidence how we should allocate resources to minimize harm. Will there be an earthquake? Very well, spend money to retrofit buildings; or move everyone elsewhere. But in retrofitting buildings, people will die in construction accidents. Very well, allocate resources to building engineers to design safer ways to build. But that will take time and in the meantime an earthquake may strike. And money spent on earthquake prevention is money diverted from health care, traffic safety, and myriad other activities that cause or pose a risk of harm. Does a particular prescription drug have an unsafe side effect? Very well, pull it from the market. But if we do so, many who might have benefited from it will now suffer, perhaps even die. Are illicit drugs harmful? Very well, enforce the laws against them. But drug enforcement is very costly and puts many users in jail who have not harmed and would not harm anyone. The risk of false positives and false negatives attends every potential decision. No algorithm exists, and none can be devised, to avoid them, despite the vague claims of utilitarians and others that their principles can be applied with perfect fidelity and justice to the world at large.[56]

The Self: Autonomous Solitary or Communal Solidary?

Like all political theories, liberalism begins with a conception of human nature. It presupposes a "self," a personality that has moral agency and at least some capacity for autonomous choice. Each person is an individual, with an inner being distinct from all other people, who need not identify herself solely as a fixed member of the community into which she was born. Each person, moreover, behaves in ways about which other people may make moral judgments. Without such a notion of human nature, liberalism, and the harm principle that underwrites it, would make no sense. Why provide a private space around every human being unless each person has a capacity and reason to live and act in it?

This conception of the self, as unexceptionable as it by now may seem, has faced severe, but usually misleading, criticism. In recent years, liberals have been accused of relying on a mythical, impossible being: the "unencumbered self," a self that is "prior to its ends" and that from its own resources somehow cobbles up a destiny to seek. The reality, the critics assert, is quite to the contrary: a "situated self," a self constituted by its ends; that is, a person whose selfhood derives beliefs, desires, and ultimate ends from the social norms of the community in which he was born and raised.[57] The unencumbered self is associated with the anthropologically naive theory of a social contract.[58] However, that the social contract argument, first associated with Thomas Hobbes, is erroneous scarcely undercuts the liberal argument.

Hobbes wrote at the dawn of the scientific revolution. The new scientific method rejected the Aristotelian notion of final cause, an approach to the natural world that had endured for nearly two millennia. Scientists after Galileo no longer expected to understand a phenomenon by deducing its causes from a purpose that itself could only be derived from metaphysical speculation. Instead, scientists resolved the whole of any phenomenon into its elements and then looked for laws that governed them. An early statement of scientific reductionism was made by Francis Bacon, who in his 1620 work *The New Organon* declared that "in nature nothing really exists besides individual bodies, performing pure individual acts according to a fixed law."[59] In physics, this new approach led to Newton's triumph. In social science, this same approach seemed likewise to require repudiating Aristotelianism, specifically the view that human community was prior to any individual.[60]

Applying these principles to the social realm, Hobbes, a friend and admirer of Galileo, asserted that "nothing in the world [is] Universall but Names; for the things named, are every one of them Individual and Singular."[61] Hobbes took the general political phenomenon he wished to explain—political community—and dissolved it into what he conceived to be its elements, disconnected individuals, possessing natural rights, living in an isolated original condition he called the "state of nature." The whole he then reassembled according to the logic by which these atomistic[62] individuals behaved. Hobbes made two assumptions about natural humans not bound by political restraints: that each would seek power over others and that all are fundamentally equal in body and mind (differences from person to person, he held, were contained within narrow limits). From these assumptions Hobbes easily deduced that the state of nature was a state of war, a condition so fearful and uncertain that for the sake of industry, culture, navigation, building, technology, arts, letters, and security, solitary individuals had long ago mutually agreed in a "social contract" to yield their individual rights to a sovereign. Individuals, then, are the enduring reality; the state is their instrument, artificially created to serve their interests.[63]

So ran the argument, quite contrary to preliberal beliefs, and it ran pretty far, straight to the nineteenth-century conclusion that each person ought to be virtually free and independent of the state. Since individuals come first, their rights must come first; the artificial construction of "society" cannot have rights superior to those who constitute it. As the British essayist William Hazlitt put it in 1828:

> Society consists of a given number of individuals; and the aggregate right of government is only the consequence of these inherent rights, balancing and neutralising one another. How those who deny natural rights get at any sort of right, divine or human, I am at a loss to discover; for whatever exists in combination, exists beforehand in an elementary

state. The world is composed of atoms, and a machine cannot be made without materials.⁶⁴

Hazlitt's error is obvious: One might as well say that since spleens exist in combination with kidneys in each person, both spleens and kidneys must have existed beforehand by themselves.⁶⁵

Nevertheless, the apparent scientific premise of this idea of the self has retained a powerful hold on our thinking to this day. Even its detractors seem unable, at times, to avoid it. For example, Stephen Spender, the British poet and critic, denouncing the modern emphasis on the fulfillment of private interests, once argued:

> Throughout history the comparative failure of every human generation has been that of the inability of those living to think of life as a single consciousness of which each separate contemporary person is a minute extension, and not a whole world unto himself or herself. No one is to be blamed for this failure which is indeed the result of the condition of isolation into which each of us is born.⁶⁶

Despite its lineage, this doctrine of the biological and historical primacy of the individual is hopelessly at odds with what we have come to learn about human development and history. That birth itself is an expulsion "into isolation" may be a physical fact, but it is not a sociological, psychological, genetic, or neurological fact, and it is, after all, only a moment, before and after which each person is necessarily connected to others. Spender has confounded a single moment of separation at birth with the socialization of childhood. Studies of psychological and social development⁶⁷ show that the adult personality is not self-created: Individuals do not and cannot precede the community of men and women into which they are born.⁶⁸ It blinks reality to maintain that people shape themselves, that their very desires, preferences, beliefs, enthusiasms, hopes, and fears are rationally chosen, rather than implanted, grown, shaped, and nurtured by parents and family, playmates, neighbors, and even strangers in the community, by the actions they take and the stories they tell—or that this process stops when the child becomes an adult. Family socialization, Michael Walzer has quipped, "is just agitprop with love."⁶⁹ Socialization, though it can take innumerable forms, is universal. Decades before evolutionary psychologists caught up, Lewis Mumford wrote that "man might even be defined as a creature never found in a 'state of nature,' for as soon as he becomes recognizable *as* man he is already in a state of culture."⁷⁰

Considerable evidence suggests that through most of our existence humans have thought of themselves first as players on the community's stage, not as writers of their own lines. Throughout the medieval era, Jacob Burckhardt wrote, "man was conscious of himself only as a member of a race, people, party, family or corporation—only through some general category."⁷¹ Man, it was assumed, had a place in a divinely ordered "great chain of being"[72] and as Tocqueville noted, "every individual necessarily belonged to a group and no one could regard himself as an isolated unit."[73]

Psychologically and historically, then, there is no unencumbered self, and there never was. Human beings are not self-made; no ghostly "I" sits in some control seat in the mind, willing a "me" into existence by assembling a psychological unity from a stockpile of desires, beliefs, and dispositions.[74] Humans are forged from others.[75] They must necessarily be situated selves. The situated self is not a solitary self; it is, rather, a solidary self, constituted by others and responsible to them. In this telling (discussed in more detail in chapter 10), it is the community, not the individual, that is the carrier of value.[76]

Nevertheless, when used to deny liberal premises, the conclusions drawn from the modern account of the self suffer from three fallacies. The first is the non sequitur that derives rights from the creation of a self.[77] There is no necessary or logical connection between rights and the origin of the individual. It does not follow that because my genetic, family, and cultural background determine my dreams and desires the community may dictate the ends I should seek, or that if somehow all on my own I had wished myself into being the community would be bound to permit an autonomous me to do whatever I pleased. In short, it no more follows from the social priority of the community that the individual should have no rights than it follows from the moral priority of the individual that the community, through the state, should have no power. The relationship between individual and community is the very problem to be solved.[78]

The second fallacy is the tacit assumption the antiliberal makes about the nature of the situated self. That the self is shaped by community says nothing about what sort of self the community will create. That depends on the community. There is no single "natural" communal approach to child-rearing and no single communal view about the appropriate relation between individual and community. Why else has there been a philosophical conversation about these issues lasting now more than two millennia?

A community may fashion selves who view themselves solely as part of a general category within the social mass, as Burckhardt characterized the psychological assumption of the Middle Ages. But the acculturated self is not logically and inherently a clone of the community, slavishly adhering to community norms. A community may instead create the sort of individual capable of self-reflection and with the motivation and will to distance himself from the society whence he sprang. A person need not be self-made to feel and exercise at least some degree of autonomy. A belief, however acquired, can be that it is possible to review one's ends and even change them as it becomes apparent it is proper to do so. "What is central to the liberal view is not that we can *perceive* a self prior to its ends, but that we understand our selves to be prior to our ends, *in the sense that no end or goal is exempt from possible re-examination*."[79] Such a self need not feel a compulsion to rethink its ends; it is enough that it has the power and may choose to do so. Thus the warning of a returning Soviet teenager in 1989 about the dangers of Russian youth traveling to capitalist countries:

> I had the chance to go to the United States on an exchange basis. I used to be a true patriot of our country and I turned into something really horrible. I became a human being. I think; I have my own opinions; it's a nightmare. After what I saw in the USA it's impossible to live here.[80]

People change jobs, careers, parties, homes, and spouses (though perhaps fans never stop rooting for the Chicago Cubs). I may originally understand myself as a southwestern American Presbyterian Republican male heterosexual with a certain fetish, but come to understand that I will be better off without one or more of these "constituted" or "embedded" roles or attributes (or that, like the Tin Woodman, I can still be me while ridding myself of one part and adding another). We neither do nor need shed one practice, desire, role, or belief on a whim: We attach value to the changed positions we adopt.

As a basis for determining proper governing rules, the origin of the self is irrelevant, therefore, since the source of the developmental force does not preordain the type of self it will produce.[81] Animals may be unable to escape the ends assigned to them by biology, but for humans even anatomy is no longer destiny. A self constituted by its ends need not be cabined by them. Nothing in the empirical evidence offered by critics suggests that individuals cannot arise above, descend below, or step sideways from their origins and become something other than what, unfiltered by thought, they might have become. A situated self, in other words, can become at the very least a partially unencumbered one.

The third fallacy follows from the second. Just as a particular community can create a partially unencumbered self, so too it can create the conditions for individuality generally, as Emile Durkheim argued more than a century ago.[82] A community, even an extremely stratified community that perpetuates social hierarchy, may change over time, as invention, growth of knowledge, historical circumstance, and self-reflection put custom and convention to the test. In the west, the emancipation (or escape) of individuals from community began a thousand years ago, and continues to this day. A personal sense of the self began to emerge as early as the eleventh century.[83] It was implicit in the Christian idea of personal salvation[84] and took explicit form with the Reformation. Economically and politically, serfs and others from at least the twelfth century could escape their villeinage by residing a year and a day in a city (as the German proverb put it, *Stadtluft macht frei:* city air makes you free).[85] An important part of this history is thus the gradual disappearance of slavery, serfdom, and peonage as justified institutions, and the freeing of people from group responsibility and collective guilt for conduct by members of family, clan, caste, and tribe.[86] Throughout the world selves have become considerably less situated and encumbered than they once were.

If it is incorrect to assume that community is reducible to its individual members, it is no more correct, or at least no more proven, that individuals are reducible to the community in which they live and participate. Community and individual are interdependent, and so the real self does not lie at extremes. A truer conception of humanity is the self standing between the solitary and the solidary, neither the person immovably attached to roles within the community to whom some antiliberals wish to return nor the atomistic individual whom they incorrectly blame liberals for creating and serving. It is the person Jacob Bronowski has called the "social solitary,"[87] at home neither outside society nor submerged within it.[88] This is the person the liberal seeks to protect through a political system that supports liberty to seek the good life, individually accepted as given or modified and refined as each individually has chosen.

A separate critique of the liberal conception of the autonomous self, not from the left but the right, can be dispatched more summarily. Some conservatives contend that the liberal venture must inevitably capsize on the shoals of individuals' proclivity to do evil. Alan Wolfe summarizes one recent conservative claim, by John Kekes, that the roots of liberalism are inherently contradictory:

> If we allow individuals to be autonomous, then they may use their unfettered powers to do evil things. Under such conditions, liberals face an impossible dilemma: if they insist on autonomy, they enhance the amount of cruelty in the world, but if they demand the diminishment of cruelty first, they undermine their commitment to autonomy.... Much of liberal thought, says Kekes, is devoted to unsuccessful attempts to avoid this dilemma. When liberals argue backward from the fact of evil to the view that anyone who commits such an act could not have been "really" autonomous, for no autonomous person would choose an evil course, they are attaching preconditions to agency which, whether they admit it or not, reduce the agent's autonomy to establish his own conditions, and in this way compromising themselves philosophically.[89]

Kekes's view misapprehends the claims of autonomy. Unfettered autonomy of course can lead evildoers to act cruelly, but a theory based on the harm principle need not respect claims to unfettered autonomy. The most doctrinaire libertarian agrees that each person's freedom must be consistent with others' like freedom. Liberalism has never presupposed absolute liberty or "unfettered powers," even of autonomous selves. Indeed, Joseph Raz, a liberal "perfectionist," agrees that "autonomy-based freedom ... does not extend to the morally bad and repugnant." Raz argues, contrary to the liberalism I am defending, that there is an ultimate good that the state should pursue (namely, autonomy for each person). Since autonomy is only valuable if the autonomous person pursues the good, "providing, preserving or protecting bad options does not enable one to enjoy valuable autonomy."[90]

Pointing to the receptivity of American constitutionalism even to those who wish to be Nazis, Stephen Macedo comments that they must nevertheless be "law-abiding Nazis.... They cannot be 'gung-ho' Nazis, in fact they cannot *be* Nazis at all but only play at it."[91] That is neither an accident nor a contradiction. In the liberal theory here proposed, when people cause harm, whatever the nature of their internal selves, the state may act. Containing, moderating, deflecting, redressing, and eliminating harm is the state's central function.[92]

A Few Words about Reason

Much abused, rarely defined, "reason" has been attacked as responsible for liberalism's mistakes and confusions. Conservative critics berate philosophers for relying on intellect to design a new society to correct unsatisfactory conditions in our present one: "Conservatism's enemy... is the attempt to remake society on the basis of formulae, explicit rules that declare the fundamental norms for social life."[93] We should not discount the fear. Entire societies have been brought to ruin by those who deduced their way to abolishing old traditions wholesale, and it is certainly true that reason has not bathed a single way of life in universal assent. So it is a useful caution to be reminded that reason lies yet under the Cartesian spell that we can think our way back to the beginnings of things and then reassemble them to something brighter and more rational. It is not accidental that many liberals, reasoning their way to a better future, often tell founding stories, imagining social contracts, constrained conversations, and disembodied selves. It ought to be obvious that behind those veils sits the solitary thinker who wishes to make sense of things however he can.

That is just the problem, say those who object to the reasoned elaboration of politics. Life is refractory and makes sense, if at all, only long afterward. We should, instead, live in our felt communal traditions and refrain from adjusting them to a set of universal principles that are all-embracing only in the mind of a solitary philosopher. Philosophy—the mind's attempt to discern goodness (or evil), rightness (or wrongness), and order (or disorder) from within—can ignorantly (one hesitates to say thoughtlessly) obstruct and ultimately wreck what works. Philosophy excludes feelings, longings, yearnings, and the complexity of connections forged in the richness of the past, all in a vain attempt to describe or explain events and generate an ordered system of abstract principles. Philosophy, by this account, is soulless, passionless, empty. It gives us nothing to cheer for. In short, philosophy is religion without the football team.

Moreover, the critique continues, reason is merely an option. Those who employ it as a tool intolerantly assume it superior to other alternatives. Liberalism in essence, says Stanley Fish, is a faith in reason, and, so, liberalism is a faith like all the others. Though liberalism purports to be tolerant of other faiths it is not and cannot be, since it necessarily discounts any worldview that does not proceed according to reason: "[L]iberalism depends on not inquiring into the status of reason, depends, that is, on the assumption that reason's status is obvious: It is that which enables us to assess the claims of competing perspectives and beliefs." Liberalism, says Fish, can be

> tolerant only *within* the space demarcated by the operations of reason; any one who steps outside that space will not be tolerated, will not be regarded as a fully enfranchised participant in the marketplace (of ideas) over which reason presides. In this liberalism does not differ from fundamentalism.... [T]he principle of a rationality that is above the partisan fray (and therefore can assure its "fairness") is not incidental to liberal thought; it *is* liberal thought, and if it is "softened" by denying reason its priority and rendering it just one among many legitimate paths, liberalism would have no content.[94]

Liberalism wrongly claims not to be "the program of any particular group or party." But since it is the program of the party of reason, it is no different from any competing vision of the truth, "and therefore in the absence of that difference one can only conclude, and conclude nonparadoxically, that liberalism doesn't exist."[95] Fish appears to be offering this sophistry without a wink and with his tongue planted firmly outside his cheek.

For if there is no *reason* to give reason priority, there is no *reason* to give any competing approach priority either. But Fish is simply wrong, and he knows better. Reason is not a faith but an inescapable part of being human.[96] Edmund Burke did not stamp his foot—he wrote a book. Reason—his reason—told him not to tinker; he did not go out at night, sword drawn, to dispatch his foes without an explanation. No competing faith dispenses with reason. Nor is it the exclusive tool of a particular political perspective: Mass disasters have flowed from "reasoned" policies of both the left and the right.[97] (Even terrorists offer reasons to justify their actions, and reckon strategically that violence and destruction will cause their opponents to reconsider and will perhaps cow their compatriots too.) People of all faiths, who live every way of life, employ reason continuously and broadly in explaining how their assumptions should translate into institutions, practices, and rules. No religious tradition could survive without reason—in an important sense, religion as practiced is the record of reasoned interpretation of tradition (and, for many, of revelation).[98] That people's capacity to reason varies, that fools are unaware of their limitations, that intelligence often strays from reasoned conclusions, that true believers often ignore the facts or fail to assess them, that human cognitive skill may not be sufficiently powerful to understand and explain that at which it aims are no arguments for abandoning reason.[99] As if we could. And abandon it for what? If we have learned that the "role assigned to reason" in reconstructing society can be "too big," we ought not forget that for most of human history it has been too small.[100] The opposite of reason is not some other sort of reason: It is *not reasoning*. It is the Terminator. It is the bullet in Winston Smith's head.[101]

Those sixteenth- and seventeenth-century thinkers who pondered the dislocation and destruction of religious wars did not begin as liberals; they began as worriers. Their concern about social conditions led them to interrogate the assumptions that impelled rulers, armies, and common folk to fight and live (and die) as they did. What they found was belief lodged in superstition, acceptance rooted in authority, life governed by tradition. Armies of states, contending for biblical rectitude, went head to head, brutal slaughter and misery the inevitable result. On the home front, one class of human being lorded over another, asserting prerogatives, privileges, and diktats that astonish us today. In Great Britain, to single out only one culture, the lord of the manor was entitled to bed any woman within his domain, married or single, no matter her wishes. Children were yoked to their parents' trades. A jobless man who strayed from home searching for work was whipped and returned to his parish. Social class determined manner of dress, which was strictly regulated by law. You went to church or you were fined, or worse (in Henry VIII's time, the penalty for denying transubstantiation was to be roasted alive).[102] Though the belief, authority, and tradition seemed reasonable to those who professed the need for things to remain as they were, those who thought about the misery and indignity that these customs and laws fostered saw that there were other possibilities. These other possibilities matured into liberal theories. The theories were enunciated in books, carried over to the street as maxims, and translated piecemeal and never wholly into law by civil servants.

But nothing in liberal reason, skeptical about knowing the ultimate good, has led to human beings being shackled in the service of some Absolute: A political theory of limits and impartiality does not produce a Stalin or a Hitler, religious zealots, or revolutionary despots. Certitude, not doubt, provokes violence and reaction. It was the unreason of antiliberals, not the reason of liberals, that almost destroyed the world in the first half of the twentieth century.[103]

When a political argument is recorded in an essay or a book, it cannot, in the nature of things, aim at or succeed in capturing more than a partial view. Books are not social life, though they may intrude on it; books are not public policies, though they may be partisan; books are not the voices of others than their authors. Whether a book succeeds in prompting the change it advocates depends in large part on whether the author understands the assumptions of its readers. Those who wrote the essays that in time we came to see as liberal shared with their readers more than a gnawing apprehension of power. Those who identify with power-holders and discount abuse are much less likely to suppose that they will ever be abused and are more likely therefore to accept a theory that the old ways have value and should be maintained. But the liberal writers came to feel that people had been abused by power-holders. They sought to uncover the spell that held them in its grip, and in the age when science promised the power to change lives for the better, not surprisingly thought that through the same power of reason they could do so too. Whether they reflected thoughts of the day they distilled in their writings, or prompted the thoughts, liberal theorists saw over time the partial success of their intellectual labor, both in implementing policy and translating their reasoning into the commonplace notions of a later day.

What we know now, what tempered by history reason itself has taught us, is that reason itself is never enough; it cannot work usefully or intelligently without worldly knowledge. "The life of the law," Justice Oliver Wendell Holmes memorably opined, "has not been logic; it has been experience."[104] Liberalism as a system rooted in the harm principle is reason acting upon experience. Government, it began to dawn on people, is the application of reason to social life; that is, as we say, its rationale. Liberals do not suppose they can or should try to change the world in the abstract by following metaphysical precepts dreamed up in the darkness of a closed and isolated cloister. That lawmaking and policy-setting may misfire and substitute now and then a new evil for an existing one, as the great cynic Ambrose Bierce reminds us,[105] is not a reason to despair. It is a reason to work harder, learn more, reason better.

Rawls, the preeminent political theorist of our age, asks the primary political question anew: "When may citizens by their vote properly exercise their coercive political power over one another when fundamental questions are at stake?"[106] His answers are difficult to assess. The complexity of his thought (and prose), and that of other liberal political thinkers, is problematic. One critic has complained that justice theory has "become so specialized and so academic and so utterly unreadable that it has become just another intellectual puzzle, a conceptual Gordian knot awaiting its academic Alexander."[107] Liberalism opens itself for public inspection; it does not hide behind history's veil and should not hide behind the density of abstruse theory. "Like his empiricist counterparts in science, the liberal insists that intelligible justifications in social and political life must be available in principle for everyone, for society is to be understood by the individual mind, not by the tradition or sense of a community."[108] In that spirit, seeking to answer the primary question, this book proceeds.

2

Constructing Harm from Natural Rights

The Cases of Locke and Nozick

The Traditional Neglect of Harm

Remarkably, given the central importance of harm in any account of political legitimacy, political thinkers historically have consigned the concept to a philosophical orphanage where it languishes from neglect. In his foreword to *Western Political Philosophy*, Christopher Morris says: "I have concentrated . . . on thought about the ends of government rather than about its means."[1] Yet his index is miraculously free of any reference to harm, injury, safety, risk, danger, or redress. Now it may be that these omissions simply reflect faulty thinking about what makes an index useful: Much better to see what the author has to say about Aristotle, Calvin, and Vico than about "government, purposes of" or "harm, nature of." If that is so, the shortcoming is widespread: Even those who purport to be talking about the very terms of political discourse appear to ignore harm and its cognates.[2] Yet omission of these terms from the indices is, I think, no mere oversight: It reflects the failure of theorists to give content to their theories.

Rawls disregards almost entirely the problem of defining the harm that one person can do to another.[3] Unlike other liberal thinkers, Rawls at least has an excuse for neglecting harm in Mill's sense: His task is to show that on liberal principles the state has broader powers than usually assumed and may undertake policies aimed at redressing the suffering of the least well off, whatever or whoever conspired to put them at the bottom of the heap. So a large problem for classical liberalism, the distinction between harms caused by individuals and the depredations of nature, simply vanishes in Rawls's account.

Likewise, nonliberal political theorists need not defend their failure to dwell on the difficulties of defining harm, for it has merely an instrumental value in the regimes that they propose. When the polis is defined by and dedicated to a theory of the good, whatever interferes with that good is harmful and is therefore the proper object of state action. In other words, philosophers who profess to know the good are not bound to analyze the harm; what is harmful can be left to lesser thinkers like jurisprudes, the lawyers and judges in whose thought will be embedded the norms of the particular societies in which they live.[4] Moreover, although the ultimate purposes that a particular nonliberal state will serve—salvation, for example—are eternal, the conditions in any society that will thwart the relevant end are variegated. It is impossible to pronounce in advance on specific harms, or even specific types of harms. As Edmund Burke noted in a celebrated passage:

> Government is a contrivance of human wisdom to provide for human *wants*. . . . Among these wants is to be reckoned the want, out of civil society, of a sufficient restraint upon their passions. . . . In this sense, the restraints on men, as well as their liberties, are to be reckoned among their rights. But as the liberties and the restrictions vary with times and circumstances, and admit of infinite modifications, they cannot be settled upon any abstract rule; and nothing is so foolish as to discuss them upon that principle.[5]

The philosophical problem of harm becomes relevant only when *preventing harm itself* is the state's central purpose.

Still another reason that philosophers have felt little compelled to explore the meaning of harm is that simpler societies had relatively few ways to cause injuries, people had less power than today to do so, and the consensus on the nature of harm was strong enough that it did not occur to theorists to contradict it. In a nonmarket society with a crude technology that gave almost no one the power to inflict injury beyond his immediate reach, what point would be served in questioning the conventional definitions? It is not surprising, then, that the problem of defining harm had to await more recent times, for not until individuals had practical power and political freedom to employ that power did a theory of harm as a way of drawing the bounds around individual sovereignty become necessary. That necessity can be seen at the dawning of the Renaissance in the work of the first modern political thinker, Niccolò Machiavelli. In *The Discourses*, Machiavelli blames Christianity for subordinating the common run of humanity to the wicked among them. "Our religion," he said,

> has glorified humble and contemplative men, rather than men of action. It has assigned as man's highest good humility, abnegation, and contempt for mundane things, whereas [Roman paganism] identified it with magnanimity, bodily strength, and everything else that conduces to make men very bold. . . . This pattern of life, therefore, appears to have made the world weak, and to have handed it over as a prey to the wicked, who run it successfully and securely since they are well aware that the generality of men, with paradise for their goal, consider how best to bear, rather than how best to avenge, their injuries.[6]

Here, in the early sixteenth century, is the modern sensibility that injuries should be redressed. Implicit in Machiavelli's apparent solution to the enfeeblement of society by the Universal Church—that the pious should give way to the strong—is the need to limit what the strong may do, else one form of enfeeblement will simply be exchanged for another.

The philosophical study of harm has been neglected also because the issues it raises have long seemed subordinate to the more pressing problem of finding proper governors for mankind. Not *what* should be the limits of power but *who* should rule had always been the primary question. As Locke put it:

> The great Question which in all Ages has disturbed Mankind, and brought on them the greatest part of those Mischiefs which have ruin'd Cities, depopulated Countries, and disordered the Peace of the World, has been, Not whether there be Power in the World, nor whence it came, but who should have it.[7]

It took a long time to understand that settling the question of rulership did not settle the question of ruling. Even as late as the American Revolution, the problem of the extent of government was widely misunderstood. "Who could be more free," asked a Charleston, South Carolina, newspaper, "than the People who representatively exercise supreme Power over themselves?" John Adams agreed: A "democratical despotism is a contradiction in terms."[8] Because they held that people would never vote to deprive themselves of basic liberties, the drafters of the American Constitution did not suppose it necessary to protect *individual* liberty against the state, a position, as it turned out, so mistaken that the leading Federalists had to promise a Bill of Rights just to secure ratification.[9]

But even philosophers such as Locke, who concerned themselves with harm, talk about it through a veil. Locke said that the purpose of government is to protect our property; but despite his celebrated derivation of the origin of private property from natural rights, he devoted almost no attention to the broad range of things that can constitute property, how property may be harmed, or in what ways it may be taken from us. Adam Smith expressly allowed government to deter and punish those who commit harm: "In the race for wealth, for honours, and preferments [every man] may run as hard as he can, and strain every nerve and every muscle, in order to outstrip all his competitors. But if he should jostle, or throw down any of them, the indulgence of the spectators is entirely at an end." But Smith too was silent about what constitutes "jostling."[10]

One reason that the early liberals may have ducked the task of defining harm is that, despite the generality in which they appeared to cast their theories, at bottom they were really defending a specific conception of the good—for example, the protection of property in a narrow sense. Adam Smith proposed "no other object [for law and government] but this; they secure the individual who has enlarged his property, that he may peaceably enjoy the fruits of it."[11] However that may be, once we withdraw political oversight of people's ultimate good, we can no longer rely on a merely intuitive understanding of harm to protect them.

Locke and the Indeterminacy of Harm

Begin, as Locke began, with the proposition that people have certain natural rights. In Locke's state of nature, the law of nature governs: "And Reason, which is that Law, teaches all Mankind, who will but consult it, that being all equal and independent, no one ought to harm another in his Life, Health, Liberty, or Possessions." So we are obliged to preserve ourselves and "the rest of Mankind," unless "to do Justice on an Offender." In the state of nature, every person has a natural right to punish those who violate the Law of Nature, and every person who is injured has the right to reparation. So important is the latter right, Locke argued, that although a magistrate might refrain on his own authority from carrying out punishment for criminal offenses, only the "private Man" may "remit the satisfaction due for the damage he has received." But the right "in the State of Nature" of "every one [to] the Executive Power of the Law of Nature" has certain inconveniences, for there every person can act as a judge in his own case and "ill nature, passion, and revenge will carry [him] too far in punishing others." Moreover, many who are wrongly injured will lack the power to impose a suitable punishment. Most important, nature lacks a "settled, known Law, received and allowed by common consent to be the Standard of Right and Wrong, and the common measure to decide all Controversies between them."[12]

This lack of a "settled, known Law" is Locke's confession that a philosophic theory of harm is impossible. The law of nature, he had said, is Reason, but reason, he now concedes, is incapable of discerning the standard of right and wrong. To overcome this regrettable obstacle, people must relinquish their natural right to redress their injuries and cede to civil society the power to preserve their liberty and property. In the society so formed, the legislature acquires the power to regulate the society by laws and the executive has the power to punish. "Political Power," Locke says, is the

> Right of making Laws with Penalties of Death, and consequently all less Penalties, for the Regulating and Preserving of Property, and of employing the force of the Community, in the Execution of such Laws, and in the defence of the Common-wealth from Foreign Injury, and all this only for the Publick Good.[13]

True, these are not unbounded powers. In a legitimate state:

> [W]hoever has the Legislative or Supream Power of any Commonwealth, is bound to govern by establish'd *standing Laws*, promulgated

and known to the People, and not by Extemporary Decrees; by *indifferent and upright Judges*, who are to decide Controversies by those Laws; And to employ the force of the Community at home, *only in the Execution of such Laws*, or abroad to prevent or redress Foreign Injuries, and secure the Community from Inroads and Invasion. And all this to be directed to no other *end*, but the *Peace, Safety*, and *publick good* of the People.[14]

In this passage, Locke set out two quite different criteria for the legitimate state: a procedural criterion and a substantive one. The procedural criterion encompasses the rule of law. Unless the law is known and impartially applied, no one can be assured of the equal treatment due by virtue of the equal moral worth of every person. Although the rule of law is only rudimentarily formulated here, its broad contours are clear and it is not difficult to see how it can be put to work in any real regime. However, the substantive criterion, that the laws be directed toward the common good, has no contours at all, and cannot be fixed in actual policy by what Locke tells us of it. It is a platitude because, as he has already conceded, no amount of reasoning in the abstract will determine in what that good consists in a real society. That is why the actual rules by which the society is regulated are contingent, dependent on legislative enactment.[15] Nothing in *The Second Treatise* guarantees that a legislature, intent on following Locke's prescriptions, would create a narrow, limited government that would respect the natural rights of individuals to their sovereign space.

Nozick and the Relativity of Harm

This difficulty is not a peculiarity of Locke's theory. To the contrary, it is inevitable in any account of the legitimacy of state action premised on a concept of fundamental rights. Why this should be so may perhaps be best understood by inspecting what remains the most powerful modern libertarian work, Robert Nozick's *Anarchy, State, and Utopia*, which begins with the premise that "individuals have rights, and there are things no person or group may do to them (without violating their rights)." Nozick sets out to demonstrate—counter to claims of anarchists, social democrats, and dictators—that only the "minimal state," one "limited to the narrow functions of protection against force, theft, fraud, enforcement of contracts, and so on," is justifiable. But his conclusion is unwarranted. The state to which Nozick's argument gives birth has far broader powers than he is willing to concede.[16]

Nozick echoes Locke to begin in a mythical state of nature, where people have natural rights to protect themselves against the depredations of others. In Locke's account, the people came to believe a state was necessary to protect their property from theft or injury. The state was justified, Locke argued, because everyone consented to establish it. But this was an awkward fiction. Nozick faces up to the hard problem—that not everyone could have consented to the creation of the state—and purports to show, through a subtle "invisible hand" technique, how a state could nevertheless emerge without invading anyone's rights.

In this state of nature, the people by and by feel the need for some means of preventing and redressing injuries to themselves that are beyond their individual powers to accomplish. Some of them will enter into an agreement with a "protective association." Initially, this agency may consist of nothing more than the stated willingness of each person who joins (a miniature but plausible social contract) to aid any fellow member who is wronged, much as nations sign mutual defense treaties. But this crude first contract will prove burdensome because members of the compact may be called on too often to interrupt daily pursuits to honor their pledges. So they will contract with a specialized service, assigning to it their right to punish those who injure them. The service will carry out its police function full-time.

If the only quarrels that ever arose were between members and nonmembers, the association could disregard any claims of justice and at the call of a member simply wage war against outsiders. But members will also quarrel among themselves, and a protective association that refused to intervene would soon prove itself useless. So in each dispute between members the association must devise a means of judging who is right. If these means are irrational, not well-designed for ferreting out the truth, people will lose patience with the service and quit, or fail to renew their contracts and instead join another service that better serves their purposes. Hence each protective association will tend to perform its duties equitably and rationally. Moreover, any client who thereafter sought his own revenge against nonmembers or even members would be dismissed from the association and would not be protected against counterretaliation. Unless the protective association adopted such a rule it could be drawn into too many battles at times when it would be impossible to sort out the facts underlying the dispute.

In the early days of social life there will be many protective associations. Anyone is free to join one or another or start his own or not join at all. But in time, Nozick reasons, one of them will become dominant. It will acquire this status because the agencies will learn that it is more efficient and less barbaric to follow a common set of rules for determining which of their battling clients is the (wrongful) aggressor. By treaty, merger, or otherwise they will gradually create a new institution, a dominant protective association, that protects all the clients of what had been warring, lesser protective associations. On Nozick's terms, the state has yet to emerge, however, because the dominant agency (so far) has not justified two essential powers of any state: the power to prevent nonmembers from seeking to revenge wrongs done by clients and the power to compel clients to pay for the protection of nonclients. Unless all are in this sense "members" of the association—bound by its rules and guaranteed protection under them—the association cannot claim to be a state. Nozick now proceeds to show how a dominant agency may claim exactly these powers without violating anyone's rights.

If a nonmember, through some other agency, were to judge a member by a standard or a procedure not accepted as fair by the dominant agency, the lesser agency might wrongly punish a member of the dominant agency. The dominant protective association, therefore, would prohibit any procedure it had not approved and would proceed to punish any nonmember who did not abide by its norms. The dominant agency would not deny that any nonmember has the moral right to apply the same rules against its members, but since it would have more muscle its claim of fairness would, as it becomes the dominant agency, inevitably root out all other such claims under different rules. Though it could not claim the moral right to hold a monopoly of power, in time it would acquire such power anyway.

At this juncture, the dominant agency would not yet have claimed the right to compel its clients to help pay for the protection of nonmembers. But if it did not force its clients to do so, nonmembers would be deprived of the right to self-help in cases in which their rules (though deemed unfair by the dominant agency) would have led to the same (and proper) result as the dominant agency had reached under its own rules. Unless nonmembers were to be compensated for this loss, their right to protect themselves would be violated. So, Nozick concludes, members of the dominant agency must provide for or contribute toward a protective service for nonmembers. The only agency that could supply these services would be the dominant association. Payment by members for protection of nonmembers would not be a redistribution of assets but a just compensation for rights taken. The dominant protective association thus would have become the "minimal state."[17]

That no state was ever formed in this way does not refute Nozick's thesis.[18] Nozick does not claim historical validity. His theory of legitimacy hinges only on whether the sequence of events described is logically possible. If so, then a state claiming a monopoly of power to redress injuries and to compel all within its territory to finance it is consistent with the natural rights of mankind.

What do we know about this minimal state? According to Nozick, it can claim for itself no powers beyond the limited functions mentioned: "protection against force, theft, fraud, enforcement of contracts and so on." That is because these are the only rights that each person possesses in the state of nature. The people cannot bootstrap their way collectively to power they do not legitimately possess singly. Presumably, therefore, the state could not raise taxes for cancer research, or demand that children attend public schools, or create monopolies, because no individual has the right to demand payments, attendance, or forbearance from productive activities from others. A state that claimed such powers would be, in Nozick's view, a rogue state.

Despite its ingenuity, Nozick's fable is an illusion, not because it is ahistorical but because it does not continue. It seems to assume that once the unfolding rhythm of rights condition their holders to accept a state, no more unresolved questions about the foundation of rights will arise. Nozick's fallacy lies in his neglecting to articulate the substantive laws the state is entitled to enforce. Though never clearly stated, an assumption runs throughout his argument that the minimal state would act as a court sifting evidence to judge offenders and not as a legislature defining offenses. In his apparent view, the state emerges in a world of preexisting law (namely, the natural rights with which each person is endowed). At its birth, the state is assumed to know the law instinctively, as a gosling knows its mother upon being hatched. Yet we know that a gosling will fix an unshakable but erroneous conviction of motherhood on the first thing that moves past it at birth.[19] Might not the state make the same error? Nothing in Nozick's theory would save it.

It is futile to say that the minimal state has limited functions, just as it is insufficient to say that every gosling has a mother. The gosling's safety depends on recognizing the actual mother, just as the citizenry's well-being depends on devising a means of judging whether in an actual case the state has overstepped its limited powers. But Nozick's philosophical yarn ends in the middle and cannot assure us that the tidy world it built will not unravel. This inability does not stem from any oversight on Nozick's part. The logic of the transformation from protective association to state requires us to accept the legitimacy of *some* institution that can authoritatively settle disputes, an institution that we identify with the state, but that logic cannot provide us with a basis for judging the validity of a particular settlement or decision.

In short, although Nozick derives a state, he can neither deduce the substantive rules that it is obliged to follow nor show that the state acts improperly in recognizing rights that are arguably not found in his (or anyone's) state of nature. Nozick puts the argument about legitimacy backward. The legitimate state does not spring from preexisting legitimate law. Rather, law in Nozick's telling derives its legitimacy from a preexisting legitimate state.[20] Only in a world of perfect certainty would Nozick's conception make sense. In Nozick's world, a world of uncertainty, the task is to create institutions that will judge or legislate according to procedures that are thought to be legitimate. That is not merely the best that can be done; it is the only thing that can be done.[21]

To see more clearly why the minimal state would not be bound to generate substantive rules circumscribed by the original fundamental rights of each citizen and understood in advance to be so circumscribed, recall Nozick's central conclusion: The state brought to life through the invisible hand has limited functions (that is, it is a minimal state). But his painstakingly enumerated premises do not support that conclusion, for two related reasons. He has failed to inspect carefully what is common to the rights that people ostensibly possess in the state of nature, and he has ignored the inherent difficulties in explaining these precisely in the contract that each individual is hypothesized to enter into with his protective association.

What do natural rights have in common that would justify Nozick's (I think proper) use of the *etcetera* ("and so on") clause in naming the functions of the minimal state? Each, fundamentally, is *a right not to be harmed* and, as it turns out, that right is inevitably open-ended.

The first clients of a simple protective association might try to specify precisely the harms they wish to be protected against. For example, "the undersigned is to be protected from theft of his new gold watch, being hit on the head by his neighbor's cane, and diversion of the water in the stream that flows through his land." But such a detailed undertaking would not long remain the preferred method of engaging a protective association's services. Sooner or later people would sign up for protection against sets of ill-defined wrongs, such as "theft of or damage to personal property," "assault," and "breach of contract" (all explicit responsibilities of protective associations). And one day a canny client would insist on a clause that covered him against aggressive acts "including but not limited to" those contained in an enumerated list (a first-year law student's drafting trick). It is necessary to write in generalities because of the unpredictability of events in the real world, the same contingencies that compel us to adopt political institutions in the first place. One might be assaulted in the foot, the thigh, the abdomen, the head. One's axe might be stolen or one's words plagiarized. Protection against each contingency is necessary, but it would be a crippling and ultimately impossible assignment to label each one.

This open-ended right against being harmed necessarily would require the state to make substantive choices about what claimed injuries it would remedy. The need to choose is implied by the state's first duty, to honor its own contract with its clients. But in attempting to honor its commitments, the state will discover that it is necessary to adopt rules for interpreting the vague contract language—"property," "assault," "breach of contract," and so on. These rules, however, would not be the kind of procedures that Nozick says the protective association may choose for itself—in effect, rules of evidence that could be intuited by reason as better or worse suited to glean what happened (e.g., did the accused party actually hit the association's client over the head with his cane?). Rather, these rules would be substantive; in short, legislation, which might mandate duties or forbearances beyond the limited functions of the minimal state. And notice that these are not rules that only a rogue state might adopt. All states would ultimately need to devise them because the same invisible hand that brought the state into being initially would continue to direct events.

Since this is the crucial point, let me underscore it. A real state cannot be confined to deterring or remedying acknowledged harms, that is, harms known a priori. Even in Nozick's model, the dominant protective association could not restrict itself to selecting the fairest rules—those most calculated to be accurate—to determine who *committed* a complained-of injury. Inescapably the dominant protective association, and certainly the state, must divide the frenetic bustle of the world into acts that cause compensable or punishable harms and those that do not. In a world of even minimal complexity, a client would one day come forward and complain that he had been harmed in a new way—for example, "My neighbor wore her skirt above her ankles in plain sight of me and my family." All concerned will agree that the neighbor in question really did show her ankles, but there will be the bitterest dispute whether such a flash of flesh was wrongful—that is, whether the action had unlawfully injurious consequences. It is wrongfulness or unlawfulness of the injury that is at issue, not merely the injury. For we can hypothesize that the plaintiff really did suffer mental distress from observing the neighborly limbs. The question is whether, nevertheless, the neighbor had a right to exhibit herself or the plaintiff had an obligation to avert his eyes.

To whom, if not to the dominant protective agency, could the disputants turn? If to anyone else, then the hegemony of the protective association is threatened. To remain the dominant arbiter it must also be the dominant legislator. It must decide whether the raised skirt is an injury worth preventing. If it so decides, the neighbor's "state of nature" right to flaunt the turn of her ankle will be quashed. And as the dominance of the protective association is transformed into exclusivity as the state emerges, so the power of legislating will pass with it. The legitimate state, therefore, is not merely the institution with a monopoly on coercive power to deter infringement of preexisting rights. Far more importantly, *the state is the final authority for defining harm.*

Just such a power was acquired as nation-states developed out of feudal institutions. In medieval society, a pluralism of contesting powers each claimed a sphere of life in which their writs were superior.[22] These gave way to central states. Though it may allow different institutions discretion to act, the lawmaker (unless bound by constitutional restraints) always possesses ultimate authority to define the nature and scope of injury. As examined below in greater detail, the laissez-faire notion that owners may use "property" as they see fit directly contradicts the rationale of even the dominant protective association. Private property as a sovereign "estate," as an autonomous power center, is a reversion to the old pluralism. No dominant protective agency in Nozick's theory—as no state in real life—can permit any other institution ultimate authority to define injury and hence to commit it.

Now we see why Nozick's failure to articulate a theory of substantive rules cripples his case. Since the power to interpret is the power to legislate, the state inevitably makes rules that give substance to the clients' broadly phrased directives to the original protective associations. The interests and activities of people being wondrously diverse, the state must quickly face up to the *relativity of harm.* In a market society especially, one person's rights are often—perhaps always—another's injuries. There can never be an absolute noninjury, if "injury" or "harm" is conceived broadly enough. Any change in one place will radiate through society. Whether or not any given action that causes change or affects others should be considered legally injurious cannot be answered with certainty nor fixed for all time.

Nozick's derivation of a minimal state suffers from two additional and considerable defects: the cost of knowledge and the relativity of property. The first defect stems from the assumption that people not only are rational actors but also possess or could obtain the knowledge that they need to pursue their ends. The second defect stems from the nature of property: A property right does not inhere in the thing itself but in a rule that cannot always arise "naturally," that is, from the consent of the parties concerned.

Ignorance and Harm

Although the minimal state has authority to use its coercive power to deal with violations of natural right, it is always an open question, unexplored by Nozick, how the victim's state of mind bears on the moral quality of the wrongdoer's act. Summed, Nozick's natural rights are apparently the right to be free of harms resulting from actions to which the victim has not consented or, if he has consented, harms that are not reasonably foreseeable consequences of those actions. A person killed by a stray bullet from a shooter randomly firing into the crowd has been murdered, and the state may act against the killer. But a person who wanders into a target practice area with well-marked signs and is struck by a stray bullet is a casualty of an unfortunate accident. To the anguished cries of the accident victim's family that "there ought to be a law" against target shooting, just to prevent such accidents, Nozick's minimal state would presumably say: "We lack the authority." But murder is the easy case.[23] The effect of inadequate knowledge or negligent failure to provide for one's own self-interest is much more equivocal in a range of other cases.

Consider our ancestors still in their quasi-state of nature, sitting around contemplating what to do after returning from the branch office of the Ur Protective Association, where they signed up for the Deluxe Package: protection against violations of each of their natural rights (against force, theft, fraud, "and so on"). Along comes a stranger, Ponzi, offering a fantastic investment opportunity in local tulip futures. Our newly insured innocents tender the stranger their year's nut hoard, "guaranteed" to double in just six months. Unfortunately, there never was a tulip crop and when this distressing news comes to light, the futures market collapses.

The Ur Protective Association hauls Ponzi before its Theft and Fraud Tribunal and demands that he return the plaintiffs' nuts. Ponzi says that he is not obligated to make restitution since nothing in his deal with the plaintiffs required him to be honest. "I have the liberty to defraud anyone I want," he says, "unless we have agreed that I will not engage in fraud, and of course we agreed to no such thing." The Tribunal quickly rejects this defense, since the Association has undertaken to relieve its clients from any and all sorts of fraud damage under the Deluxe Package. Freedom from fraud is a natural right and does not depend on an agreement between the parties not to defraud. Ponzi looks puzzled. "We're here to redress harm," the Chief Protector says. "It doesn't matter that you didn't agree not to harm. A natural right exists quite apart from any contract. Our deal is to vindicate our clients' rights. We're not concerned about what you think."

"Well, but it was their own fault," Ponzi gamely continues. "You can't expect me to be responsible for everyone's ignorance. It can only be fraud when the victim has no way to detect the deception. Like if I had sold them gold but when they weren't looking substituted brass. In this case, the plaintiffs knew or should have known that futures markets are risky. They could have asked around. If they had, they would have learned that tulips don't grow in our soil, and that, besides all that, I'm known as a shady character against whom *anyone* with half a brain should have been on guard. After all," Ponzi persists, warming to his subject, "it's a tough world out there, and the price to be paid for freedom is, as Jefferson will say in another context, 'eternal vigilance.' So we all have to bone up on the world. Education is a vital necessity. We must know how the world works and what risks we face when we do just about anything. We need to read up on foods and medicines. We need to understand the mechanics of our carts and inquire into whether the barque company is adequately training its crew. I didn't *force* them to invest. They were just greedy and naive. So if under those circumstances they wanted to give me their nuts, it was their risk. And you can't hold the consequences of their risk against me. I thought you fellows had a *minimal* state going here."

The ruffled Protectors turn to their clients, who respond that the benighted Ponzi has gallingly misapprehended the situation. In an *absolutely* simple world, maybe Ponzi would have a point, but this is already the modern age of Protective Associations. Nothing is simple any more. If people spent all their time looking out for themselves, examining all the details of everything that came their way, reading all the latest technical literature, investigating the bona fides of each person who seems honest enough, no one would ever get any work done. Something else always could have been done, some extra step always could have been taken, to ensure that a sales representative is not bent on fraud. But how far must we go to protect ourselves before handing over our basket of nuts: Must we have demanded that people like Ponzi take lie-detector tests or be injected with truth serum? And what if Ponzi had refused? What kind of a miserable world would it be if the Protective Association were to put all the burden on its clients, who, after all, are not the wrongdoers here, and none of the burden on the scalawag against whom the Association is pledged to take revenge? If that were the rule, only deals that came with ironclad guarantees would ever be made, and who ever offers ironclad guarantees? So no one would ever make a deal or take a risk and life would continue to be "solitary, poor, nasty, brutish, and short."[24] It was to avoid just such inconveniences that they were coming in out of the cold state of nature. In any event, the plaintiffs, also warming to their subject, say they knew that tulips did not grow in the local soil, but they thought Ponzi was talking about Dutch bulbs, and the local librarian confirmed that in Holland big crops were the rule and droughts rare.

Relieved, the Protectors reject the argument that the plaintiffs' knowledge of risk negates the defendant's responsibility for harm and turn again to Ponzi. "But surely our contract must mean *something*," Ponzi brashly resumes. "I never said 'guaranteed,' and besides, if I did, I didn't mean 'absolutely guaranteed.' I carefully explained to these fellows sitting under the tree just what the risks were. Why else did they think the payoff would double their nut hoard in six months? I said it was a long shot."

"Did not," say the investors.

"Did too," insists Ponzi.

"Enough!" cry the Protectors. They retire for an unusually long time but at last return and rule against Ponzi. The Chief Protector explains that in an attempt to be fair, they did not assume that the investors' version of the story was true simply because they were Association clients and Ponzi's false simply because of his name. But attempting to be fair has put the Association in quite a pickle, since the Protectors have no other basis on which to determine the facts, there being no witnesses. Of course, in similar future cases, there might be witnesses or other extrinsic evidence. But it's quite a bother to be compelled to undertake hearings when the evidence is likely to be lacking or untrustworthy. Moreover, the natural uncertainty that attends such conversations might prompt all sorts of unscrupulous people falsely to claim that they had disclosed all risks. So the sensible solution, the Chief Protector announces, is to require every seller to distribute a prospectus stating the financial basis of the offer and disclosing all risks. And not just any old prospectus, but one that sets out quite particular kinds of information, in accordance with a scheme to be promulgated later in the week by the Rules and Regulations Tribunal of the headquarters office of the Ur Protective Association.[25]

"But I'll have to hire advisors," Ponzi protests. "That will cost me a bundle. Why, you'll be making me spend my resources to aid buyers. Don't you see? You're making me do research that the buyers could do for themselves. You're using your 'coercive apparatus for the purpose of getting some citizens [me] to aid others.' Nozick won't allow that!"

"And just who might this Nozick be? Your Protector? We suggest you ditch him and sign up with us, who understand how the world really works."[26]

As human society grows complex, the state will be pressed to settle ever more numerous quarrels over increasingly more complex matters than those that obtained in the state of nature. Inevitably, the svelte lady of the state whom Nozick embraces will grow stout as she ages. Because time and resources are limited, making certainty impossible to achieve, regimentation in the name of social order will appear. Dispute settlement will require regulations that restrict the freedom of many and sometimes of all.

The Relativity of Property

Much of the value of the minimal state arises from its claim of authority to protect each person's property rights. But the state will remain minimal only if (1) we can begin with an account of property that locates a thing as property before the state is called on to judge whether a particular person's property has been wrongfully appropriated; and (2) the natural right to the full enjoyment of one's property is not subject to the state's power to prohibit a use because it is causing harm. But neither of these conditions obtains in an even minimally complex world. It is often the case that the state must decide whether a particular concrete thing or abstract conception should be considered property. The very existence of the property right comes from the state; the right does not call the state into existence to protect it. Likewise, since the state is the ultimate authority for defining harm, the full extent of a property right depends on the degree to which the state is willing to refrain from taking steps to ensure against certain consequences of its use. Thus, in many cases at least, there can be no natural right to use property since the state is the agency that defines in the first instance the permissible extent of the use.

Some examples may shed light on these so far rather abstract points. The first, from Augustine Birrell's amusing story about a Belgian book pirate, points to the practical necessity of the state's actually defining property; the second, from nineteenth-century American legal history, to the state's authority to limit its use. In his lectures on copyright, Birrell noted how very different the same act could appear, depending on who was looking at it:

> If your right to turn your neighbour off your premises—to keep your things to yourself—was *property*, and therefore *ex hypothesi* founded on natural justice, he who sought to interfere with your complete dominion was a thief or trespasser, but if your rights were based upon some special concession made to you upon your own merits, you then found yourself dubbed a monopolist, and the brave man who sought to get the better of you was, at the worst, an *infringer* or smuggler. Monopoly is always an odious word. Property is still a sacred one. Marmontel, in his Memoirs, tells us of an interview with Bassompierre, a bookseller, or, as we should now call him in this department of his business, a publisher of Liége. Bassompierre had made such a good thing out of the sale of Marmontel's famous *Bélisaire* that he felt compelled to call upon the author, who was passing through his town, and thank him for the service he had rendered. Marmontel was furious. "What," says he, "you first rob me of the fruits of my labours, and then have the effrontery to come and brag about it under my nose!" Bassompierre was amazed. It had not struck him in that light. "Monsieur," said he, "you forget Liége is a free country, and we have nothing to do with you and your *privileges*."[27]

Had Marmontel been living in the state of nature, it is difficult to understand to what principle he could have pointed in demanding his protective association stop Bassompierre from selling his book in the next village. Bassompierre would have indignantly argued that he had taken nothing from Marmontel of any substance: It was Bassompierre, after all, who paid for everything—typesetting, paper, ink, binding, and shelf space in his store. Nor had he attempted to prevent Marmontel from selling his own copies to the good people of Liége. It is hard to see how Marmontel can claim a property interest in the arrangement of words that preexists the declaration by the state that it will confer a copyright monopoly on authors. And is that not then an infringement of Bassompierre's "natural right" to print what he wishes? Property or privilege? As Birrell commented dryly: "There is a good deal in a name."[28]

To test whether a rule of the forbidden type can be derived, the second example begins with the axiomatic function of the minimal state to safeguard the property of each of us. Can a rule be justified that claims to benefit society by taking from some in order to give to others?

Put yourself in a congested urban area in which hundreds of butchers slaughter cattle on their premises. Live cattle are brought in by rail and parceled out across city streets to the slaughterhouses. The city elders decide that the situation presents worrisome hazards: The congestion is noxious and the danger of disease great. So they enact an ordinance creating a single slaughterhouse near the rail yards and forbidding butchers from continuing to use their shops as slaughterhouses. Three questions arise: (1) May the state legitimately establish a monopoly for the conduct of the slaughtering business to benefit city residents? (2) If it may, does the means selected—prohibiting independent butchers from conducting business on their own premises—constitute a "taking" of private property? (3) If it is a taking, must the independent butchers be compensated for their losses?

In 1873 the United States Supreme Court—an agency, to be sure, far from Nozick's ideal protective association—answered the first question affirmatively and the others negatively. To protect the health and safety of the people of New Orleans, the Court held that the city may control dangerous activity by restricting it to a single spot. This zoning regulation is not a "taking of property" (and, hence, did not require the city to compensate the butchers), the Court said, because unlike land condemned for a public road, the butchers' structures and the land on which they sat were left intact.[29]

If this result seems unjustified, it must be so only because the butchers wished to define property expansively to include all acts that people have been accustomed to doing without objection. But this is not a necessary definition of property. Indeed, it is not even a possible one. Does someone obtain a vested right to commit a harm because the injured party forbears initially from complaining or seeking to deter it? Does acceptance of slight injury shield the commission of greater injury later? If I tap you lightly on the shoulder and you grin and bear it, am I thereby entitled to punch you in the stomach? And must you pay me for the privilege of having me refrain from similar roughhousing in the future? To avoid such obviously absurd conclusions, it follows either that a long-established practice does not of itself constitute a property right or that the state may regulate a property right that harms others. Otherwise the understanding of what is harmful can never be legitimately changed, at least without compensating those who cause it (as feudal lords maintained in insisting on payment to forgo enforcing ancient privileges over their vassals).

The city might have enacted a less restrictive regulation permitting each butcher to continue operating a slaughterhouse—for example, a health inspection system financed by the butchers and limiting transportation of cattle to certain hours of the day. Does the difference between the course chosen and the less restrictive alternative amount to a violation of natural rights? However desirable it may be for a legislature to choose a least restrictive rule, there is no standard by which to know when the "least" point has been reached, nor will it ever be clear whether an alternative would achieve the objectives of the more draconian scheme. Certainly Nozick presented no such standard, and for the reason that Locke gave long ago: Abstract reason cannot extract a code of conduct from natural law. It cannot be discovered. It must be legislated.

It could also be supplied by someone usurping that power—a Platonic guardian, like the Supreme Court after deciding the *Slaughterhouse Cases*. In the late nineteenth century, the Court began to scrutinize regulatory legislation much more closely, holding in several cases that government regulations burdening corporate enterprise unconstitutionally interfered with private property. In some of the cases, the judges voided the regulations (if they deemed the state interference too rank); in others, they sustained the regulations on condition that the government compensate owners for their lost property values.[30]

In this Nozickian experiment in minimal statehood, the Court redefined the property concept, from a property right in possession to a property right in "exchange value," in the words of the economist John R. Commons.[31] The Court assumed that the value of the possessions any business controls lies in the ability of the unregulated enterprise to make them produce revenue. To interfere with that ability was to confiscate. This redefinition led to a paradoxical result: A business that caused an injury had to be compensated for what was lost in being prohibited from continuing to do so.[32]

A property right to use land however its owner sees fit did not pose a dilemma for classical political theorists because the use of land in preindustrial times rarely harmed other landowners, so the need to limit the use of property to avoid injury rarely arose. As long as it did not, the state's duty to protect property was straightforward: It was enough to deter trespassers and punish poachers.[33]

With industrialization, however, the dilemma grew acute. Inevitably new uses stirred new conflicts. Thus an owner of an old estate was said to have an easement for "ancient lights"—the right to enjoy sunlight—and hence could prohibit an adjacent owner from building a structure that reduced the light that fell on his estate. Similarly, those who lived on land through which a stream ran were entitled to a "natural flow" and could prevent others from interfering with the course of the stream, for instance, by building a mill or a dam. "The premise underlying the law as stated was that land was not essentially an instrumental good or a productive asset but rather a private estate to be enjoyed for its own sake."[34]

Early in the nineteenth century in the United States, property was redefined to connote an instrumental good. The courts reconsidered riparian rights to permit reasonable use of streams for mills and manufacturing activities, despite the claim that natural (agricultural) use or even "prior use" (the first mill) should preempt other uses. This transformation, which played a significant role in the development of capitalism, the courts warranted as necessary to promote economic growth. In so doing, the courts explicitly conferred benefits on one group of private individuals at the expense of others. Would a dominant protective association or a minimal state be bound to resist this transformation? Nozick does not provide an answer, for it is unclear why the possession of land or its proximity to a stream could justify a rule that would bar the improvement of still other land. To assert the primacy of the prior use would require a finding in the name of Nozickian principles that capitalism between nonconsenting adults is illegitimate.[35] So it once was thought. Eighteenth-century English courts gave judgments to shopkeepers against established customers who deserted them for more competitive merchants.[36] But the claim that one has a compensable right against loss of patronage seems as absurd as the claim that one can gain a vested right to continue to injure someone because the harm was initially accepted without complaint.

In the minimal state, interfering with property to prevent harm is a redistribution—a taking from some to aid others. To say that someone's property has been illegitimately taken is, in this context, to say that the definition of harm was wrong. But overturning the rule that defines unlawful injury assumes either that some other institution has higher authority or that the minimal state may legislate beyond the minimum. The principle that a person is entitled to protection against aggression toward his person and his property thus affords no help in determining how far the use of his property may be permitted to injure others. Reconciling the claims of property owners with the claims of those who say they are harmed by the owners' use involves ultimately a series of value judgments on which people may reasonably differ.

To quarrel with this conclusion is to imply that a state that assumes more than simple watchman-in-the-night duties is perforce illegitimate. But an industrial civilization does not carry out aggression only during the dark of night; the larger share of injuries by far are committed in the plain light of day. In industrial society, for every owner harmed by theft of bread or silver, thousands have been injured just by working at a job. The outpouring of protective legislation has often been condemned for exceeding the authority of Nozick's minimal state. But against the claim of a factory owner to use his factory as he sees fit and to contract for labor on any terms he likes must be measured the harm that accrues. A state made legitimate by attending to natural rights must now transcend its origins. In a technological age, in other words, the duties of even the watchman-in-the-night (or, more properly, the watchman-around-the-clock) will no longer be simple.

The meaning and boundaries of harm cannot be derived from natural rights. The reason should by now be clear: Harm is the criterion that we wish to put into service to limit the exercise of the rights by which we claim to act; those rights cannot therefore be a limitation on the criterion of harm. Minimalist or ultraminimalist accounts of the state, such as those embodied in Locke's general social contract theory and Nozick's more limited contract theory, establish only that a harm principle cannot be ruled out. They do not provide a method for determining its content and scope. To discover what those might be, we must look elsewhere.

3

The Meaning of Harm Derived from Interests

Joel Feinberg's Harm Principle

The Butterfly Effect

Among the difficulties of a liberalism based on natural rights is the requirement that rights be specified. You do not have to agree with Jeremy Bentham's derision of natural rights as "nonsense upon stilts"[1] to see that a workable harm principle avoids the difficulty. Why search for what we must be allowed to do if the harm principle can specify, rather, what we may be prohibited from doing? The trick, of course, is to give content to the concept of harm.

A careless reading of Mill might suggest that harm may simply be equated with *effect on others*, for Mill sharply distinguishes between conduct that concerns only oneself and conduct that concerns or affects others, the latter subject to control by the state and the former subject to no restraint at all.[2] Similarly, John Dewey suggested that the very origins of the state lay in the recognition of effects beyond the immediate concerns of the parties to a transaction and that the effects may serve as the basis for control.[3] But it cannot be the case that any change in position whatsoever is a harm when brought about by human agency. In an interdependent society, whatever we do affects others—and in ways that are rarely foreseeable. A now familiar concept, the "butterfly effect," holds that a tiny disturbance in a system sensitive to initial conditions, such as the weather, can quickly lead to major and unpredictable fluctuations: "A butterfly stirring the air today in Peking can transform storm systems next month in New York."[4] If a butterfly, so too the wiggling of a finger. And the rains mean that you stay home when you preferred to go on a picnic, so because I wiggled my finger someone else is frustrated. Likewise, my demand for a product, expressed when I purchase it, has an effect on price and supply. But should that effect, considered by itself, permit the state under a harm principle to prohibit me from purchasing a quart of milk or a loaf of bread?[5] If you move from your old home to a new one in a different town, and enroll in the local school system, your presence may affect the distribution of grades awarded to the students who had been living there. Should the state, for that reason, be empowered to declare that you may not move? By such a logic every change is harmful (rather than sometimes merely indifferent or even beneficial). But a relationship so universal is useless, since to be workable a harm principle must allow us to discriminate between that which we may prevent or redress, on the one hand, and that which we are free to do, on the other.

No more useful is the suggestion that the gravity of the effect should determine harm (direct or strong effects being considered harmful but not weak or indirect effects). Mill distinguished between conduct that directly or primarily affects oneself and that which only indirectly affects others, but the distinction described the area of *impermissible* paternalistic regulation, since Mill recognized that no conduct is entirely "self-regarding."[6] Indeed, it was in the face of this very point—that every action in some way affects others—that Mill insisted that each person must have a domain within which to act freely. So the distinction between direct and indirect effects on other people may be a way to determine the bounds of paternalism, but it will not serve to fix the meaning of harm. In this same vein is Bentham's proposition that any act causing pain, even a small amount of pain, is an injury that the state may take measures to prevent.[7] Whether to allow the pain to be inflicted, and to what degree, depends on the consequences at large of easing or eliminating it. Under Bentham's general happiness principle, the state should balance the sum total of pains and pleasures.[8] But not every experience of a pain is an injury, and many pleasures *are* injurious (in the sense that they can do bodily damage); for example, cholesterol-rich foods. So reducing pains and enhancing pleasures cannot be a good test of what the legislator may prohibit. To be useful, the concept of harm must be grounded in a rule capable of discrimination.

The most comprehensive account of the harm principle is that of Joel Feinberg, in his magisterial four-volume work, *The Moral Limits of the Criminal Law*, completed in 1988.[9] Feinberg ranges across an immense number of issues, providing an extended commentary on Mill's claim that protecting others is the sole justification for public interference with another's liberty of action. Feinberg's strategy is to locate harm in a particular effect on people's *interests*, not on *people* themselves.[10] By considering types of interests that can be affected, and the manner in which they are affected, Feinberg anchors the concept of harm in a principle of considerable power, accessible to reason and intuition.

Feinberg proposes that a liberalism serious about protecting people's liberty to seek their own end recognizes only two liberty-limiting principles, by which he means principles that justify limitations on liberty *through the prohibitions of criminal law*: These are the harm and offense principles. Feinberg's version of the harm principle holds that it "is always a good reason in support of penal legislation that it would probably be effective in preventing (eliminating, reducing) harm to persons other than the actor (the one prohibited from acting) *and* there is probably no other means that is equally effective at no greater cost."[11]

To set the stage for what follows, recall that Mill's harm principle has five strands: (1) harm (2) to others (3) caused by a wrongdoer (4) permitting the state to interfere with (5) the wrongdoer's liberty of action. Unlike Feinberg, Mill did not explicitly restrict the state's interference to the criminal law.[12] In what follows, I suggest that if we take "interference" in its broadest sense, meaning any interference with or power over liberty of action, then Feinberg's discussion of these five components, comprehensive as it is within the realm for which he intended it, is nevertheless incomplete and artificially restricts the range of state action consistent with a plausible reading of the harm principle. Confining the investigation to criminal law, it will turn out, distorts the analysis of the "caused by" component. But broadening the range of state action makes the harm component indeterminate in the most intractable and the most interesting cases—as we shall see, the liberal state must leave to voters the question not merely how much harm prevention to pay for but also whether particular conduct constitutes harm at all.[13]

Wrongful Harmdoing: Harm as Wrongful Setback to Interest

Feinberg defines "harm" as a wrongful setback to a person's interest.[14] His definition thus contains three variables, to the elucidation of which Feinberg devotes several chapters. What follows is necessarily a highly abbreviated summary in reverse order of the fundamental terms as he uses them.

The Interest Criterion

Feinberg distinguishes four classes of interests: (1) passing wants (eating an ice cream cone); (2) instrumental wants (to get exercise); (3) welfare interests (the congeries of conditions and goods, such as physical health and economic sufficiency, that make it possible for us to achieve our ulterior or ultimate or focal aims); and (4) focal aims (our ultimate aims, that is, what we see as our good, such as building a dream house, running a restaurant, seeking religious salvation, promoting a cause, raising a family).[15] Although focal aims may seem the more important, they are rarely invaded directly: It is difficult to conceive of a malefactor who points a gun and says, "Desist from leading a holy life." Rather, interference is almost always with those welfare interests that serve us as means to our more ultimate ends.[16] Welfare interests "are the very most important interests a person has, and cry out for protection, for without their fulfillment, a person is lost."[17] There is another sense in which welfare interests and focal aims should be distinguished. We have an interest in our focal (or ulterior) aims only to the extent we want them; it is incorrect to say that we want them only to the extent that we have an interest in them. We have no interest in writing a book or running a restaurant if we don't want to do so, but even if we did not *desire* to be healthy we have an *interest in* good health, since it is a crucial means to all other ends.

An interest is not just a want. In some sense, any strong desire for something can be said to result in a gain if the desire is satisfied or a loss if not. But by itself the desire is not sufficient to establish an interest. Feinberg distinguishes between loss constituted entirely by disappointment and disappointment caused by personal loss—"between the 'gain' that consists entirely in satisfaction at some outcome and the satisfaction that occurs *because* there has been some personal gain." Hence, "an interest in, and desire for, some development Y does not imply an interest in or desire for a satisfied state of mind, or for the avoidance of a disappointed state of mind in respect to Y. What we have a stake in is Y itself, not the avoidance of disappointment."[18] In other words, our interest is in something happening other than the mental states of satisfaction or frustration if it does or doesn't happen.

Moreover, you must have a *stake* in Y to say that you have an interest in it that is protectible under the harm principle. You may be the most devoted baseball fan in the nation, with the strongest desire imaginable to see your team win the World Series. If the players strike and the Series is canceled, you may suffer ghastly agony, perhaps even to the point of long-term incapacitating nausea. But you may not demand the state redress your sufferings, because you had no stake in the game. Now you *can* have a strong enough desire for something that its fulfillment is an ultimate interest, even if it would not advance any of your other interests, but even then you must have *done* something to have a stake in it—for example, by underwriting the cost of music lessons to enable your child to become a great musician. It's not enough merely to *desire greatly* (but silently and passively) that the child become a great clarinetist: You have no interest to be defeated, should someone thwart your child's musical career, if you have done nothing to advance the possibility of your child's success.[19]

Ordinarily, you do not have an interest in the ultimate ends of another human being. That you may greatly desire the company of a friend does not entitle you to that companionship unless the friend wishes to give it. That you deeply love your fiancé and are looking forward to a lifetime of wedded bliss will not allow you to compel a marriage should he change his mind, even if you will suffer deep emotional distress, everlasting regret, and somatic effects at the parting. Nor, without a special relationship (such as between spouses or a parent and a minor child), do you have an interest in another's welfare interests. That is why one person may not assert an interest in causing another to suffer, so that what Feinberg terms "morally disreputable interests" (of the psychopath, for example) may not be counted as an interest to be protected by the harm principle.[20] Otherwise, application of the harm principle would become a vicious circle: My very wish to harm you would be an interest protected under the harm principle. Under the circumstances of special relationships a person may have an interest in taking some action that will cause another distress. For example, a parent may decide that a child must take medicine the child would rather refuse or force the child to suffer the torment of unwanted music lessons. But a special relationship will not serve to justify every invasion of the other's welfare interests. A parent may spank a child, but at some point (very poorly spelled out in American law) corporal punishment will slide over into child abuse that may be barred under the harm principle.[21] Another important special relationship is the contract, by which you gain through my consent an interest in my performing under it, entitling you to compensation should I default and even, under some conditions, to force my actual performance. But without a relationship that justifies the mutuality of interest, one person does not have an interest in another's interests.

Finally, as Feinberg notes, "not everything that we dislike or resent, and wish to avoid, is harmful to us." He distinguishes harm proper from conditions or states of mind or being that are merely annoying, distressing, or offensive but that do not adversely affect our interests. These latter phenomena he labels "hurts and offenses," depending on whether they have a physical effect (a jostling in a crowd) or a mental effect (disgust at seeing something revolting on a street corner). These are passing inconveniences: "They come to us, are suffered for a time, and then go, leaving us as whole and undamaged as we were before." It is unlikely, therefore, that anyone would have as a focal aim of his life to be free of the passing annoyances that come from living among others.[22]

Feinberg acknowledges one class of persons who have just such an ultimate interest. The Epicurean's highest aim in life is to avoid pain and emotional turbulence; hence any hurt or offense, no matter how slight, impairs this ultimate aim. Nevertheless, says Feinberg, the criminal law cannot be brought to bear against someone who causes such a minor hurt: "It is improper to use coercion to protect [the Epicurean] from these invasions, not because his negative goals are not real harms to him, but rather because by falling short of harm to the interests the law ascribes to the standard person, they are deemed to be less serious harms than those that would come from restricting the liberty of others."[23]

Although this conclusion sounds plausible—what kind of a world would it be if we were forbidden from doing anything that might offend the most squeamish recluse?—Feinberg's solution does not avoid a significant difficulty. In saying that some at least of what the Epicurean wants prohibited does not amount to a harm (merely a minor hurt or offense), Feinberg is forced to contemplate that mythical "standard" person whose good is the one protected (that is, the standard person's liberty to act free of a restraint against causing minor hurts and offenses). Now it is no doubt a practical necessity for the state to decline to punish acts of *minimal* effect on others. But the state, then, is weighing conflicting interests and choosing one person's good over another's. Harm, therefore, cannot be known a priori. The state will have discretion to determine when it should intervene. Feinberg responds that since some balance is inevitably necessary, lest every action be criminalized, he is simply providing a plausible reason to distinguish true harm from passing hurts, and that, moreover, criminal law in particular must be written in general terms and could not possibly "accommodate the whole range of idiosyncratic vulnerabilities." But a real state provides more than a system of criminal justice. Tort law is adequate to redress at least those actions that are knowingly and deliberately intended to cause even the most minor hurt to the Epicurean, though the knowledge requirement might seriously limit the number of successful actions that an Epicurean could bring.[24]

An interest need not be specific to an individual to be cognizable under the harm principle. Many interests, usually labeled "public interests," are simply interests that many or all individuals have in common: for example, a community secure from invasion by a foreign enemy, courtrooms free from perjury, and a public revenue system spared tax fraud.

The Setback Criterion

Without listing every possible interest that may be harmed, we may assume consensus on the most important ones, in particular a range of welfare interests the interference with which might doom our ultimate aims. It remains to spell out in what way a harmful act must affect an interest to invoke the state's intercession. Not every effect on or interference with an interest can plausibly be supposed to do so. For example, if someone steals your watch, permanently depriving you of it, your interest has been sufficiently affected that the state may legitimately prosecute the thief and you may sue to recover its value. But suppose your watch is sitting on your desk at work, and a wandering colleague happens to spot it (your door being open) and "borrows" it for an hour to time a project he is finishing. You are not in your office, do not recall that you left the watch there, and do not miss it during the time your colleague has it. He replaces it as he found it, none the worse for wear. Although the interest you have in the watch may somehow have been affected, it was not affected sufficiently to make criminal prosecution plausible or sensible (though, had this been your home, the law of trespass would apply).[25]

Feinberg's solution to the "affects" problem is to limit state interference to actions that *set back* an interest. A setback includes such related concepts as impairing, defeating, thwarting, blocking, impeding, frustrating, and dooming an interest. So if a person deprives me of my possessions, physically injures me, or causes me mental distress such that I am in some way incapacitated from doing, even for a time, some of the things that I ordinarily do, or otherwise invades one of my welfare interests, making it impossible or simply more difficult for me to continue a normal life or strive to fulfill one of my ulterior interests, even temporarily, then this person has affected my interests sufficiently for the state to enact or invoke a relevant criminal law. This understanding of setback is consistent with the distinction above between hurt or offense and harm. To turn the criminal law against those who commit transitory hurts that do not set back interests (threatening prosecution for the slightest bit of jostling, for example) would do more damage than it would mend, by paralyzing us in indecision, hesitation, and fear.[26]

Once it is determined that an act is within a class that does set back an interest, the actual *quantum* of setback does not matter. For example, any theft, no matter how small, is nevertheless a criminal offense because the act is in its nature a setback to interest. So if my colleague had stolen a broken (hence almost worthless) watch from my desk, the harm principle would permit prosecution, even though a prosecutor would not be obligated to indict or try the case.[27]

One critic of the harm principle argues that the setback criterion is faulty because it does not clearly define the baseline from which a person's interest is changed.[28] Set the baseline as the victim's situation before the miscreant acts. Suppose the victim was in pain and the miscreant acts to continue the pain. If the pain would have gone away but for the miscreant's intervention, we intuitively understand that the victim's interest was set back, even though by the proposed baseline no harm was done, since the pain remains just what it was. Pick, instead, a "counter-factual" baseline: "An event harms an individual if and only if it renders her worse off than she would otherwise have been."[29] Suppose now that a mother decides to pay the cost of a ticket for her daughter to take a trip to Paris, but I persuade the mother to give the money to charity. Has the daughter's interest been set back? Perhaps so, if it is fair to conclude that by losing the chance at the free ticket she is worse off than she would have been (had she had the ticket). And if that is so, the harm principle would unreasonably put many people in jeopardy. So neither the factual nor the counter-factual baselines seem to work. But the examples are contrived, and the proposition that a single baseline must be the measure in all cases is unjustified. Another rejoinder is that for at least certain kinds of setbacks the miscreant's action must be wrongful. Suggesting to a friend that a charity deserves the mother's largesse more than the daughter does is not necessarily wrongful. Moreover, it is far from clear that the daughter's interest has been set back at the counter-factual baseline. If she actually had the ticket in hand, perhaps; but to measure a loss against what "would otherwise have been" opens up a timeline to all sorts of intervening circumstances that could be unfairly invoked against the putative harmdoer.

Consider the following scenarios and ask whether you have been harmed by a setback to interest:

1. I have been thinking of giving you a ticket to Paris but I change my mind before I tell you what I've been contemplating. (This might be a setback under a counter-factual baseline, but only if there was an interest to be set back. You knew nothing of my thoughts so have suffered no defeat of any expectation. Your hopes weren't aroused so they could not have been dashed. Otherwise, the state could enforce our every kind thought or intention.)
2. I tell you I'm thinking of giving you a ticket but I eventually decide not to, and tell you that. (You can claim disappointment but cannot establish a stake in my contemplated generosity.)

3. I tell you I've bought you a ticket to Paris but in the end I don't give it to you because I decide not to spend the money. (This scenario seems the same as the previous one, since the ticket was not yet yours.)
4. I tell you I've got a ticket in hand but a friend talks me out of giving it to you because he would prefer I take him to a lavish dinner instead. (The friend is now the miscreant and he cannot hide behind my argument that I may do as I wish with my money. But your interest is no stronger at this point than in the previous example.)
5. I tell you I'll give you the ticket but only on the understanding that you'll let me accompany you to Paris. (You may have been counting on a solo trip, but you have no interest that permits you to dictate the terms of my gift.)
6. I give you the ticket but then while you're thanking me I take it right back out of your hand and say I've changed my mind. (Have I crossed some sort of line here? Your interest in the ticket as property cannot have greatly ripened, and you could scarcely have acted to your detriment assuming it to be yours.)
7. I give you the ticket but then go into your wallet the next day when you are not looking and take it back. (Does a gift convey a vested property interest so that you now have an interest in the ticket and the trip?)
8. I give you the ticket but then steal it back weeks later on the eve of your trip. (Is there a difference in kind between this scenario and the previous one? You've certainly had more time to make plans, spend money, and otherwise rely on the belief that you would be going to Paris.)

What, if anything, has changed from hypothetical to hypothetical? This set of scenarios contemplates what contract doctrine calls a reliance interest. The later examples are setbacks to that interest. No particular principle of any political theory can state with certainty that (6) does not cause harm but (7) does; what the examples show is that a body of contract law must come not from natural law but from the policy-making agencies of the state—the legislature or the courts or both—to determine where the lines are to be drawn, taking into account the variability of the situations and interests with which contract law must deal. The harm principle amply permits the enactment and development of contract law but must necessarily leave the details to the state.

The Criterion of Wrongfulness

In Feinberg's telling, a setback to interest does not yet legitimate state interference with the actor. The setback must be wrongful. In the simple cases it is easy to see why. Agree that the loss of your car is a setback to interest. Now it obviously makes a difference if the car is gone because (a) someone stole it or (b) you gave it to me. In (a) the setback is wrongful, since it is wrong to steal. But in (b) the setback is not wrongful, since you consented to the transaction. It would make no sense to conclude that

I could be prosecuted for the crime of "receiving a gift." Similarly, consent provides the answer to setbacks of interest in sporting contests. If my lifelong aim has been to win an Olympic track meet, and you beat me, my interest has been severely set back. But you had the same aim and interest, and we have each consented to take part in a competition in which only one will win. Indeed, without the likelihood that my interest will be defeated, I will be unable to achieve my end, which is to show that I am a better runner than all other serious contenders.

The problem remains how to provide stable content to the meaning of "wrongful." An intuitive sense that a murderer or thief's actions are wrong does not carry us beyond commonly acknowledged crimes. How can we assign moral culpability to actions that set back interests? Feinberg gives four possibilities:[30]

1. Harm *simpliciter*. But causing injury cannot by that fact alone be wrongful, because then things that I have a sound reason to do could be barred, as we have already seen. Indeed, if mere injury were sufficient to constitute a wrong, we would not need to inquire into the meaning of wrong in the first place.

2. Illegal act. It is circular to extract the wrongfulness of an act from its illegality: "We cannot know which harms may properly be prevented by the criminal law until we know which harms when inflicted indefensibly are wrongs."[31] We are trying to uncover whether a particular action is wrongful *in order to decide* whether the action can be outlawed; that is, the purpose of the harm principle is to determine when in the first instance the state may interfere with our liberty.

3. Violation of a moral right. To say that a wrong violates a "moral right," as opposed to a law, avoids circularity, but it then requires recourse to a theory of natural rights. How would we establish what natural rights we possess or show that they are specific enough to be useful? Moreover, if there were such things as moral rights antecedent to the law, then the state would have an independent reason to step in and legislate, even if violation of the right did not inflict a harm in the sense of setback to interest. The harm principle would thus paradoxically require a condition for its enforcement that would permit the state to sidestep it altogether. This problem looms large in claims that there is a natural right to live in a society in which certain "harmless" moral wrongdoing is outlawed and punished—for example, homosexuality. This seems an unpromising road to take, as chapter 10 establishes.[32]

4. Unjustified or inexcusable act. These considerations lead to a fourth possibility: that "*any interest at all* (apart from the sick and wicked ones) is the basis of a valid claim against others for their respect and noninterference. Then it will follow that *any* indefensible invasion of another's interest (excepting of course the sick and wicked ones) is a wrong committed against him as well as a harm."[33] But this fourth understanding of the wrongfulness criterion sounds very much like harm *simpliciter*, already rejected. Feinberg argues here that it is not setback to interest per se that constitutes wrong but an *indefensible* or *unexcused* setback to

interest. Feinberg relies on a "burden of proof" strategy. The one whose interest has been set back need not demonstrate that the actor did wrong; rather, the actor bears the burden of showing that he had a justifiable reason for doing what he did. As long as there is a genuine interest, its setback is wrongful *unless* the actor can show that the setback is "defensible" (that is, excused or justified in some way). The state, then, may criminalize setbacks to interest, without further regard to what is wrongful, as long as it provides an "escape" clause for those who can justify or excuse their conduct.

For acts that we know as "conventional" crimes, this burden-of-proof approach to wrongfulness is familiar and plausible. Causing the death of another is insufficient to support a conviction for murder. The prosecutor must always prove intention (hence an accidental death is not murder). The defendant always has the opportunity to demonstrate excuse—for example, the death resulted from self-defense.

But Feinberg's solution to the problem of determining wrongfulness does not really avoid the difficulty he set out to resolve for most of the interesting cases that life in a complex society presents. The difficulty, to repeat, is to avoid circularity: to fix what is "wrongful" without pointing to a prior decision of the state to outlaw the action. To say that a setback to interest is a wrong unless the action that set it back is defensible or excusable still requires, in all but the most intuitively obvious cases, some method for determining whether the action was defensible or excusable.

A simple example may help. In the state of nature, a dairy farmer milks his cow and offers the milk for sale. Milking cows and selling the milk are justifiable activities. Failure to pasteurize is not, per se, a wrongful act. The buyer bears the risk of contamination—or, at most, once the theory of pasteurization is worked out, the farmer is obliged to affix a warning label to the milk: "The milk in this bottle comes straight from the cow; it is not pasteurized." If a customer dies from drinking contaminated milk, it is difficult to see how the farmer can be guilty of murder from these facts alone. To sustain a murder charge, there must be, at a minimum, a law requiring pasteurization. But in enacting it, the state will have used its coercive powers against the farmer's liberty of action, even though the action itself is not wrongful unless the law declares it so. Let me be clear. I am not arguing that it is illegitimate for the state to enact a mandatory pasteurization law. I am arguing that a lack of intrinsic wrongfulness does not defeat the state's authority to act. But this same lack also requires the state to determine in the first instance whether or not an action is defensible.

Feinberg is right to dismiss the problem of defining defensibility or justifiable excuse in the context in which he sets the problem. As his general title explicitly states and as he repeatedly notes, his concern is for moral limits to the *criminal law*.[34] Criminal law imposes one highly significant restriction on prosecutors that does not impede other forms of state action. That is the burden of proving *intent*. In most cases in which the state saddles our liberty of action with criminal penalties, the state must show that the wrongdoer intended to set back an interest before it can lock him up.[35] But in many other circumstances, the harm caused may not have been impelled by an intention to injure anyone. My actions, like selling milk or building a house, are undertaken for reasons entirely independent of causing damage, injury, or suffering. The morality of stabbing you with a sharp knife is quite different from the morality of selling you a knife with which you might injure yourself.

I conclude, then, that the meaning of harm cannot be restricted to morally wrongful setbacks to interest, because many classes of harms that we will want to prevent cannot be said to involve indefensible actions unless and until the state first declares them to be such. I postpone a fuller discussion of the reasons for this conclusion until after briefly considering the problem of harmless wrongdoing and after considering further the distinctions between criminal and civil process.

Harmless Wrongdoing

We have seen that harmful actions need not be wrongful in some predetermined sense: "Wrongful harmdoing" is not the only type of harming that the state may regulate. In this section I consider briefly whether the converse—"harmless wrongdoing"—is subject to state intervention. Here it is necessary to distinguish two types of harmless wrongdoing: (1) wrongdoing that is wrong because it is immoral, but harmless in Feinberg's sense because it does not set back anyone's interests; and (2) wrongdoing that is wrong because it violates a law premised on something other than morality, even though it does not harm or even necessarily affect anyone. The first type of harmless wrongdoing I consider in chapter 10, in which the argument, consistent with Feinberg's, is that the state may not interfere with our liberty of action on the pretext that what we are doing, though harmless, is wrong.

The second type of harmless wrongdoing is a narrow class of cases that arise when a particular kind of law in the "derivative" sense is violated. As Feinberg uses the term,[36] a derivative crime is an act that must be sanctioned to enforce a command of the legal system. A classic example is "contempt of court": Failing to follow a court's order is punishable only because it is sometimes the only way to ensure that a litigant will obey a decree or order directed at upholding an underlying right. The aim of a contempt decree is not to make the particular litigant jump to a judge's orders but rather to encourage him do the thing that justice requires (handing over a document, making restitution, refraining from violating an injunction). It is easy to spot the harm that would flow if the state were unable to punish these sorts of derivative crimes, crimes that interfere with the orderly processes of government or of a system that the government has the authority to enact (for example, the state's authority to criminalize counterfeiting derives from the government's legitimate power to regulate the money supply).

Related to these "process"-derivative laws is the set of enactments that constitute the government itself. Most importantly but by no means exclusively, these laws are embodied in the Constitution, which directs how the government is to be organized, who may serve in it, how the governors are to be appointed or elected, and the limits of their powers. Violations of many of these commands may be thought harmless, at least in the sense that it would be extremely difficult to detect or trace any actual setback to the interest of a citizen. In what sense could a twenty-nine-year-old senator be shown to have harmed his constituents by his age, despite the Constitution's command that he be at least thirty?

On rare occasions a question has arisen in the courts about a claimed violation of one of these structural laws. In one notable instance, the Supreme Court dismissed a suit largely on the grounds, though it did not put the matter quite in these words, that violations of these laws constitute harmless wrongdoing and hence are not actionable. Article I of the Constitution forbids persons "holding office under the United States" from serving in Congress. This Incompatibility Clause is the constitutional embodiment of one aspect of separation of powers. It has long been supposed by competent legal authority that officers in the United States military "hold office under the United States."[37] It has also long been the habit of members of Congress, sometimes as many as a fifth of the whole body, to hold military commissions. (Not surprisingly, these members tend to cluster on committees with jurisdiction over the military, including, especially, the subcommittees dealing with compensation and pensions of veterans.) A suit was filed to force these members of Congress to resign their commissions on the obvious ground that holding them was unconstitutional. The Supreme Court never reached the constitutional issue, reasoning that citizens lack "standing" to contest the point. In effect, the Court said that citizens suffer no "harm" from the practice that the Court was willing to recognize.[38] But it is unclear why this sort of harmless wrongdoing should be ruled out of court. The wrongdoing is the violation of the Constitution's plain command. The "harm" is the failure of the government to uphold the Constitution, a setback to the people's interest in orderly government and liberty. Although in form the citizen-plaintiffs were not charging a violation of a derivative criminal statute, their claim was qualitatively the same. Fidelity to the Constitution is in everyone's interest, and governmental infidelity ought to be remediable.[39]

That "abstract" violations of the Constitution may be cognizable harms does not mean that every conceivable such complaint should be heard in court. The Supreme Court has long been unfriendly, for example, toward claims that Congress has unconstitutionally spent public money. In a well-known 1923 case, the Court held that taxpayers could not contest a federal maternity program because no taxpayer has a "direct injury." Though the characterization is incorrect (a taxpayer has a direct injury if his claim is true, although the impact on him is slight), the decision in this case seems merely a convenient way to avoid hearing the complaint of every hothead against a government project he detests; it was not, or ought not to have been, a ruling that the constitutionality of *raising* of a tax (which is more directly the concern of a taxpayer) may not be contested because a taxpayer's interest is too dilute.[40]

Harm in Criminal and Civil Contexts

In an interesting analysis of the puzzling concept of "wrongful conception,"[41] Feinberg concludes that it is a wrong but not a harm and since criminal liability depends on both harm and wrong, the state may permit civil damages but not impose criminal sanctions:

> The harm principle does not permit criminal liability for "wrongful conception" since the act causing the conception does not cause harm in the special narrow sense that requires both set-back interests and violated rights.... But since infant-rights are violated in the case where inherited impairment is severe, there is no reason why the wrongful progenitors (or other wrongful facilitators—doctors, pharmaceutical companies, earlier partners transmitting venereal diseases, etc.) should not be held civilly liable to pay damages to the child.[42]

From the defendant's perspective the interference with liberty appears the same whether the state permits suit for civil damages or imposes a criminal sanction in the form of, say, a monetary fine (the amount to be awarded or decreed after a trial). Why should the harm principle prohibit a fine labeled "criminal" yet apparently permit an award labeled "compensation," which for argument's sake could be equal dollar amounts? One answer is that Feinberg has built into the harm principle a "no other means" criterion—that a criminal sanction is permissible to redress harm but only if "there is probably no other means that is equally effective at no greater cost." If a civil suit would just as likely and just as cheaply redress the harm and serve as a deterrent to similar future harms, the civil suit should be preferred. I see no reason to quarrel with this modest limitation on criminal jurisdiction, for the criterion merely holds that even though the state may legitimately enact criminal laws, it should if it can find less intrusive and draconian means of dealing with harm. In other words, once it is seen to be permissible to enact criminal laws, it is no less legitimate to construct other tools by which to intervene—indeed, it may even be morally requisite that the state try to do so.

But in the wrongful conception case, Feinberg does not argue for what we might call the "lesser-included remedy." Mill's version of the harm principle does not distinguish between civil and criminal intervention and so would include civil rules and remedies in the state's armamentarium. But Feinberg's version of the harm principle does distinguish between civil and criminal liability, since nothing in the setback-to-interest formulation appears to allow the state to intervene at all in the absence of harm. Since wrongful conception produces no harm in his sense, the harm principle ought to be wholly inapplicable, and yet Feinberg is willing to entertain a civil suit, but not as a lesser-included remedy within the harm principle.

To take another example, Feinberg says that we should not criminalize the behavior of the inane passenger on a bus who engages in voluble, boring, nonstop chatter, but that it might be permissible to regulate him into silence (by promulgating an ordinance forbidding loud talking, talking at all, radio playing, etc.). From the perspective of liberty, I fail to see the difference. In either case the state interferes with the chatterer's liberty. Why the state may intervene civilly when there is only wrong, but not criminally unless there is both harm and wrong, Feinberg does not explain.

Throughout, Feinberg invokes civil processes of government because, he says, they are less onerous to the individuals caught up in them. Civil remedies should be allowed to deal with evils that fall short of harmful wrongdoing. Speaking of the distinction between harm and mere offensiveness, for example, Feinberg says:

> The law should not treat offenses as if they were as serious, by and large, as harms. It should not, for example, attempt to control offensiveness by the criminal law when other modes of regulation can do the job as efficiently and economically. For the control of uncommon and transitory forms of offensiveness, for example, reliance can be placed on individual suits for injunctions, or by court orders initiated by police to cease and desist on pain of penalty, or by licensing procedures that depend on administrative suspension of license as a sanction. These alternatives would not entirely dispense with the need for punishment (which is almost always a disproportionately greater evil to the offender than offended mental states are to his "victims"), but punishment would be reserved as a back-up threat, not inflicted for offending others so much as for defying authority by persisting in prohibited conduct. It may well be that the ordinary criminal law need not concern itself at all with defining crimes of offensiveness, even though offensiveness is the sort of evil it could in principle be used legitimately to combat. It is more likely, however, that for various practical reasons, reliance on injunctions, administrative orders, and license withdrawals would be insufficient to control *all* properly prohibitable offensive conduct.[43]

But this lesser-regulation-mode thesis amounts to an argument that because the person whose liberty the state proposes to infringe did not commit as great an evil as the wrongful harmdoer, the state needs a lesser justification to interfere with him, as long as the process used and the sanction meted out are likewise less onerous than the full measure of criminal law. I cannot fault this proposition as a normative description of how the state should best deal with the entire range of evils in the world, once it is agreed that the state may act at all.[44] But the question before us remains how to justify the intervention in the first place. In building a *general* theory of the harm principle, encompassing *all* the ways a state may act, the "no other means" clause is no longer available. It makes no sense to say that the state may not act at all if there is some less intrusive way the state may act.[45] If "criminal law is only a part of a more comprehensive system of rules and remedies,"[46] the question is what justifies that entire system.

The only practical way out of the dilemma is to acknowledge that in limiting his concerns to the criminal law, Feinberg has given us only one-half of the harm principle—or only one version, a weak version, of the meaning of harm. To impose criminal sanctions, it is necessary that the setback to interest be wrongful—in setting back the victim's interest the actor must have acted indefensibly or without excuse. In most cases that will mean the actor intended to cause the harm, either as the sole end or as a means to some other end. But there is another reading of "harm," a strong version, which permits the state to intervene whenever there is a setback to interest, regardless of the actor's intention, in a wide range of cases often involving *aggregative* and *accumulative* harms. Although in these cases the state may justify its intervention on the basis of the actor's wrongful actions, the wrong is ascribed to the act only because the state wishes to control the action in the first place, and it wishes to do so only because the act tends to set back a victim's interests. If I am correct about this conclusion, then Feinberg's claim "that no plausibly interpreted harm principle could support the prohibition of actions that cause harms without violating rights"[47] is either incorrect or must be reinterpreted. Although aggregative and accumulative harms constitute the major class of cases to which the weaker version of the harm principle applies, they are not the only kind. Before turning to the major class, consider the following.

You own a house with a scenic view. I buy an empty lot next to yours and construct a home that blocks your view. I do not do so intending to defeat your interest in the view; I do it to gain the view myself. This conflict between interests does not lend itself to a determinable analysis of wrongdoing because there is no obvious state-of-nature rule governing the use of land. My desire for the view may be defensible, but not conclusively so. That you were there first may imply an obligation by the second-in-time to spare your view. But since you knew that later construction on the adjacent parcel could block your view, you may have been obliged to obtain the parcel to preserve the status quo, and otherwise to allow the owner to build as he wishes. The harm principle is in equipoise. This sort of dispute can be settled only by an authoritative rule—a set of zoning regulations—that establishes expectations. It is the zoning regulations that determine who is wrong, not the wrongful conduct that writes the code.

Feinberg accepts the strong version of the harm principle when he acknowledges that the hard cases are those in which an activity harms people affected by it but prohibitions against the activity "would tend to cause harm to those who have an interest in engaging in it . . . because . . . substantial interests of these persons are totally thwarted." Hence it is essential for the legislator to "compar[e] the relative importance of conflicting interests."[48] In granting the legislature the authority to determine the balance of interests, Feinberg is agreeing that an a priori understanding of harm is not decisive, indeed, may not even exist. Again, it is the state's power to act that determines the wrong, not the wrong that determines the state's power to act.

This conclusion should not be unsettling. State actions do not arise in a vacuum. The state is called upon when interests conflict, in situations that require a rule to avert clashes that will inevitably occur without an authoritative declaration of rights in the circumstances. Thwarted homeowners, each confident of the rightness of his view, may come to blows. The state need not wait so long.

In prohibiting particular conduct the state often acts to avert risks. The actor may not intend harm, and may have a perfectly proper aim in mind in pursuing his activity, but the risk that lurks in the background will color a conclusion about whether the activity is justifiable. Consider an urban helicopter service. May a city refuse to permit helicopter flights under the harm principle? Lifting off from the roof of a tall building is harmless, we may suppose, and as long as the helicopter is airborne, it is hurting no one. Its passengers and crew may have consented to the risk of failure and crash, but those who live and work on the ground will not have consented to the omnipresent risk of death and destruction. Whether the state may prohibit flights altogether depends, for Feinberg, on whether it was wrong to send it aloft (since it is a setback to interest of whoever has been injured). If the chopper was knowingly or negligently maintained or piloted, then a crash was wrongful. But it may have been superbly maintained. Perhaps it fell, through no fault of its pilot or maintenance crew, because it inadvertently and unavoidably ran into a flock of birds. Still, few would suppose that the legislature, foreseeing the possibility of such an accident, ought to be barred from enacting a criminal ordinance against municipal overflights because the company's operators and pilots had a nonwrongful reason for their service. So either wrongfulness cannot be a necessary condition for operation of the harm principle—or we must conclude that exposing people to the risk of injury through a demonstrable chain of causation is, in its very nature, at least sufficiently "quasi-wrongful" to permit the state to regulate when the risks are too high. Risk regulation, not limited to the instance of a single action or activity, probably comprises the largest branch of state engagement with the harm principle.

Aggregative Harms and the Problem of Risk

An aggregative harm is one that manifests itself only if enough people engage in certain conduct, since any particular act may not set back anyone's interest and may not be wrong. If there is only one car on the road, it cannot crash into another; if there are thousands of cars on the road, sooner or later two will collide. The aggregation of conduct creates danger. The risk of harm quintessentially calls forth the state's power to make rules of the road.

Suppose that a (pollution-free) automobile has just been invented in the Nozickian state of nature. Since driving down the lane does not violate anyone's natural rights (assuming the driver is careful not to bump into a pedestrian), the owner of the first car is perfectly free to crank up and drive away, on the left or the right side of the road, as he pleases. To the cry of a prophetic observer that "there should be a rule of the road," the driver responds that the dominant protective association has no authority to intervene, for he is harming no one. Even as more cars take to the roads, they will not crowd each other, and on the rare occasions when they are driving toward each other on the same side of the road they can easily avoid colliding. It is not inherently wrong for a driver to be on one side or the other.

When the roads do finally congest, drivers will likely follow a particular stream of traffic: Some days the lead car will drive on the left, some days the right, but in general it will be sufficient for the day's lead driver to establish a traffic flow. Some accidents will doubtless occur, but they will result from the failure of a driver to follow the leader, and in claims for damages the dominant protective association will hold against the negligent fellow. But relying solely on damage suits to deter and redress the ensuing harms is inefficient, especially if people do not widely understand the appropriate rule. Eventually, when too many cars are on the roads to make practicable this fluctuating daily creation of the appropriate "rule," the dominant protective association will accept the left or right side as the sole custom of the community and will hold accountable anyone involved in an accident who drove on the incorrect side. Even the minimalist, then, must be prepared to accept that the courts, by acceding to the common custom, will have given the force of law to the predominant social fact about driving, to govern the outcome in private damage suits. But since the underlying justification for this rule, as for all such rules, is that it will serve to minimize the harm that would ensue from an unregulated, chaotic highway—even though any single driver on the wrong side of the road might harm no one—there can be no sound objection to the legislature's having enacted it in the first place. The very existence of rules, if widely publicized, will set back fewer interests and make more efficient the assessment of damages when an injury occurs. So the state must have the authority to decree rules of the road to prevent, lessen, or redress aggregative harms. The trigger for the exercise of state power is not a wrongful setback of someone's interest but the probability of a setback without the regulation. The weak version of the harm principle does not create rights or entitlements; it simply punishes when harm is committed. But the strong version, the only one competent to deal with aggregative harms, does not merely punish; it also and necessarily enacts regulations that establish wrongfulness. Once the power to devise rules of the road is granted, the power to enact derivative criminal penalties for failing to abide by the rules necessarily follows. The state may therefore deal with driving-related harms under either a civil or a criminal law system. Feinberg acknowledges the problem of risk but, again, views it through the lens of the criminal law.[49]

An important consequence of the rule-making function is that limitations on liberty can be justified not merely to prevent or reduce harm but also to foster administrative convenience. A slight loss of liberty (you must drive on the right side of the road) is amply repaid by the savings in court time in trying to determine, in the absence of a rule, who was at fault.

Now it might be supposed that premising the state's rule-making authority on the aggregative principle will permit the state to regulate without end. For anything can be aggregated. The first million people to own sharp knives may do no harm with them; the million-first person may stab his enemy. To prevent this last berserk act, may the state regulate knife ownership by the first million people? Putting the question this way misses an essential difference between aggregative harm and crime. The state criminalizes not the preliminary *acts* (buying a knife, storing poison) but the *consequences* of a particular action. A rule against murder is a rule against an *outcome*; we do not attempt to delineate and outlaw everything in the chain of actions that might lead to murder. The law does not ban possession of all the types of instruments that could cause someone's death. Many actions and instruments are harmless in themselves. For instance, to shoot at a target is harmless (unless the shooter fails to see that someone has mistakenly wandered onto the target range). So in criminalizing the consequences of the action, the state says that you have committed a murder only if you intended the death (unless, of course, you have a justified excuse).

For aggregative harms the state, in general, does the reverse: It criminalizes (or otherwise burdens) your liberty to do a particular act, even though the consequence of your action may not be harmful. A classic example is speeding. A single car on the road might hit no one, no matter how fast it was driven. But when many cars take to the highways, it is a certainty that some cars will cause damage that would not have occurred but for the speeding. So the law imposes speed limits, even though the actual act of speeding is not itself injurious. In contradistinction to the law against murder, here the law penalizes an act, in order to avoid the consequences. (Hitting someone while you were speeding is separately punishable.) That is why the potential misuse of knives is not an aggregative harm to be dealt with by regulating their purchase. Unlike the speeder, whose *act* of speeding can be regulated and penalized, the knife buyer's *act of buying the knife* is not a risk. It is the entirely separate action of, say, waving the knife around that poses the danger.

Aggregative harms cannot be reckoned with abstractly. Controlling them depends on circumstances. A modern example in the United States is gun control. Like the knife buyer, the gun buyer, it might be supposed, poses no risk to anyone merely by buying the gun.[50] An empty gun, on a back closet shelf, poses no danger akin to that of the speeder in a school safety zone. But it seems indisputable that gun possession is an aggregative harm in at least one clear sense: Just as one of the speeding cars will inevitably hit someone, so one of the guns inevitably will be loaded and go off. The difference in regulatory treatment between knives and guns stems from the complex sociological differences between the cultures of knives and guns and their relative power and degree of dangerousness. The gun has a longer range, works more quickly, and incites use in different communities according to different perceived dangers. Some guns have nonlethal uses, but many are designed only to kill or maim.[51]

The problem that risk of any sort poses for the legislator, then, is to know how to recognize when assorted, apparently unrelated, actions have risen to the level of an aggregative harm that can be practically dealt with. Once in people's hands, guns cannot easily be regulated (except post-facto in prosecutions when they have done their damage). So if statistical evidence suggests an aggregative problem, the question for the legislature is not *whether* it has legitimate authority to deal with it but *how* to do so. The legislature does not regulate kitchen-knife-buying because there is no evidence that it poses an aggregative harm. Once it is clear that the legislature may regulate an aggregative harm, the choice of method is itself a policy matter. So, for example, it is not necessary to conclude that mere ownership of cars and guns pose aggregative harms for the legislature to require both to be registered; registration systems may be seen as a means of holding users accountable for damages they may later cause.[52]

Such regulations are justifiable under the strong version of the harm principle, which holds that unreasonable risks of certain types, probability, and magnitude are wrongful, even though the conduct regulated, taken individually, is neither wrong nor injurious. Still, as Mill noted, the principle of aggregative harm (which he called "social harm"), knowing no limits, can in the name of preventing harm swallow all liberty. If unregulated driving sooner or later will cause sufficient damage for us to enact speed limits, then surely we can regulate and even ban the consumption of alcohol for the same reason:

> If anything invades my social rights certainly the traffic in strong drink does. It destroys my primary right of security, by constantly creating and stimulating social disorder. It invades my right of equality, by deriving a profit from the creation of a misery I am taxed to support. It impedes my right to free moral and intellectual development, by surrounding my path with dangers, and by weakening and demoralising society, from which I have a right to claim mutual aid and intercourse.[53]

Mill decried the tendency of this belief to harden into an absolute: "that it is the absolute social right of every individual, that every other individual shall act in every respect exactly as he ought."[54] The fallacy of those who would comprehensively outlaw liquor lies in the false analogy between speeding and Prohibition: We do not prohibit driving, only speeding. As the sorry experiment of the Eighteenth Amendment in the United States demonstrated, draconian liberty-limiting laws against products that have nonharmful uses create black markets and may ultimately be unenforceable. Today we understand that we ought not to have banned drinking, though the reasons for not legislating generally do not preclude banning drinking while driving.

But Prohibition should remind us that the harm principle, which narrows liberty limitations to only those required to deter or redress harm, grants a power that is not easily curbed, except by practical judgment and the experience that comes from taking a long view. The harm principle is a principle of legitimacy, not a principle of utility or prudence. Although the state may properly seek to avert risks of danger to our various interests, nothing in the harm principle tells policy-makers when it is time to act or what they should do. We do not position police on every street corner twenty-four hours a day to await the possibility that someone might commit a crime or be injured, not because doing so is ruled out by the harm principle but because it is too costly.[55] Resources devoted to one risk diverts them from others. Living is a balance of risk that no philosophy of legitimacy can properly or usefully set.

Accumulative Harms and the Problem of Causation

A cousin of aggregative harm is accumulative harm. An individual instance of particular conduct may be deleterious in only a minor, insubstantial way. Accumulated, the conduct may constitute material and significant harm to many or even to the whole society. A simple case is tax evasion: One tax evader hurts no one (or hurts in a way too tiny to measure), but tens of millions of evaders would cause the government to collapse. The paradigmatic example of an accumulative harm is pollution. The exhaust from a single car, if there were no other cars, would damage the environment only minimally, if it would do any damage at all, since the ecosystem is resilient enough to rid itself of an occasional plume of smoke. But as more cars spew fumes, natural ecological processes might be overwhelmed. The question is: Who caused the harm? Not the first person, for he may have done no harm at all. Not the tenth, or hundredth, or even possibly the thousandth. But when the ten-thousandth or the millionth person's fumes spill into the open roadway, and the incidence of lung disease increases, or a hole in the ozone layer develops, it is not the millionth person who finally caused the harm but everyone.[56]

The complex problem of dealing with pollution is beyond my scope but not beside the point, for it shows once again that only the strong version of the harm principle justifies state intervention. In dealing with tax evasion, as Feinberg notes, the law can subject particular evaders to prison and monetary fines directly, since the cheater cannot advance any defensible interest in cheating. No such simple solution is available to regulate acts of pollution, however. The legislature cannot simply say "stop polluting," for we all pollute in some ways, and the acts that cause the pollution are extremely useful to us. Taken together, our myriad individual acts comprise a vast network of pollution activities, so that a blunderbuss prohibition would cause more far more harm than it would cure. So in the context of pollution, Feinberg concedes that what is wrongful "must mean unlawful as judged by a regulative agency applying rules for allocating permits in accordance with specified requirements of fairness and efficiency. In these contexts, no prior standard of wrongfulness exists."[57]

Not only do aggregative and accumulative harms differ sharply from traditional crimes in the wrongfulness of the acts from which they spring. They differ sharply also in both the identity of the victims and the distinctiveness of causation. Anticipating harm, the state promulgates a rule (drive on the right, do not go more than forty miles per hour). The aggregative harm thus derives from risk: The regulating principle permits liberty to be limited even though a particular act may cause no harm at all to anyone. Punishment for violating the prohibitory regulation, such as a speeding law, is not for causing harm to an identifiable person but for taking a forbidden risk. The loss of liberty entailed in the prohibitory regulation, while perhaps annoying, is in everyone's interest, even though a particular speeder, say, may benefit by violating the law.[58] But when the risk materializes, when the particular damage is done, it is caused by a specific person and settles on an identifiable victim. Many cars may speed down the road before one of them finally has an accident. When that one speeder finally does crash into his victim, the driver harms a known person.

By contrast, in accumulative harm, it is impossible to discern who was harmed by a particular actor. The causal link between specific wrongdoers and identifiable victims has been snapped. The environmental police can prove that noxious fumes are spewing from my exhaust pipe, but not who may be hurt by them. The doctor can prove that my neighbor's emphysema is aggravated by smog, but no one could prove that it was my car that caused or worsened his disease.

The "caused by" component of the harm principle, then, comes in two distinct forms. In its direct form, we link an identifiable actor as the cause of harm to (setback to interest of) an identifiable victim. In its indirect form, we can at best merely *impute* responsibility to one or more actors because we cannot link identifiable victims (though we know who such victims are) to identifiable actors (though we know also who some of these are). Under the weak version of the harm principle, both actor and victim must be identified for the state to have legitimate authority to impose criminal sanctions. A person's liberty may not be curtailed because he merely might be guilty or because, being among the class of potential actors, he is likely the wrongdoer. He must *be* the wrongdoer to suffer punishment. In the usual case there will be, as well, a known victim, else against whom can it be said that the actor committed a wrong? The wrongdoer need not know his victim—a madman shooting into the crowd is guilty of murder when his bullet finds its mark. But there must be a clear connection between his action and the harm suffered by the victim.

In the case of accumulative harms, however, the state imposes liberty-limiting regulations by imputing culpability to the class of harmdoers, because it is impossible to demonstrate that any one of them harmed any identifiable victim. To justify such regulations under the strong version of the harm principle, the lawmaker must show that the acts prohibited plausibly contribute to a harm that will be suffered by some people if sufficient numbers of other people were to continue to do the acts. Such proof can be difficult and politically controversial, as the long and continuing story of the attempt to curb smoking in America attests. But once the case is made, once it can be shown that particular acts, if multiplied, will likely cause others harm, the power to intervene is complete.[59] In each case, the problem for legislators is to determine how far along the chain of causation the law should extend.[60]

I conclude, then, that a setback to interest, *simpliciter*, may serve as the basis for limitations of liberty in appropriate cases, as discussed, as long as the setback was caused by human agency, whether or not the harm to others can be attributed to particular members within the group of harmdoers. This conclusion is significant because, as the next chapter demonstrates, it legitimizes particular types of government intrusions in what has long been considered the inner domain of freedom—the market.

4

Collective Harms and the Market

Problems of Causation

The Market as Natural Force

One of the most significant long-term historical trends is the lengthening shadow of human causation, in fact if not in perception. Ages ago, people supposed they bore responsibility for the forces of nature: The gods sent storms and earthquakes to punish.[1] But in those days the actual human reach was slight: What happened in one village was unlikely to affect things in the next, and nothing that anyone did could significantly affect nature herself. These days, things seem reversed. Our reach is global: Motion radiates from one remote corner of the world to another, affecting societies and the very entrails of the planet. Yet many persist in the belief that we are not responsible for what actually happens. We are caught in the grip of an "iron law of necessity," "laws of history," "social forces," or an "invisible hand." Whatever happens it's not what we planned and not our fault.

The idea that we are captives of an order larger than all of us is a familiar one. Here is David M. Kennedy, writing on Franklin and Eleanor Roosevelt during World War II:

> Behind that historical debate lurks a philosophical question about the relationship of will and fate: does conscious human striving, as represented in the deliberate policies of the New Deal, count for more in determining the human condition than unwilled events, like the war, that simply befall us? Are we the masters of our own souls or the creatures of historical forces beyond our control?[2]

But the commonplace that we are victims of unwilled events or beset by forces beyond our control—war, depression, and other sweeping events that just seem to happen—masks a basic ambiguity.[3] On the one hand it could mean that they are impersonal forces, like sunspots and tides. If they are, then it is in the first place pointless to oppose them, and in the second, perhaps illegitimate to try. For things that "just happen" are misfortunes. To relieve the suffering from calamitous nature would permit one person to help himself to the goods or services of others despite the lack of human causation. The harm principle appears to extend only to those instances of adversity, hardship, and distress that are *caused by* people. We do not hold anyone to account for God's handiwork: The gale that sinks the boat, when no sailor's skill could save it, is a misadventure but not an injustice.[4]

On the other hand, that we are beset by social forces beyond our control might mean only that they are beyond our skill to control, at least for now, but not necessarily forever, and certainly not that they are morally beyond our reach. On this reading, social forces are no more than uncoordinated activities that have consequences not easily channeled in another direction by passing a law that says: "Stop."

Of all the social forces in whose grip we personally feel ourselves on a daily basis, none is more impressive or apparently stronger than the force of the market. The "market" is actually no thing at all, "only" a system of customs, rules, and organizations that seem naturally rooted in the basic premise of the liberal order—that we are to be free to strive for our own ends. "It is not from the benevolence of the butcher, the brewer, or the baker that we expect our dinner, but from their regard to their own interest," Smith famously said. "We address ourselves, not to their humanity but to their self-love."[5] If everyone were free to acquire, use, and trade property without state interference, resources would be most efficiently allocated and goods most efficiently distributed. From politically uncoerced acts, without conscious design, private interests and social good would be harmonized.[6]

For Smith's successors in the nineteenth century, two related features of the market stand out: It is the embodiment of a universal law of supply and demand, and any attempt to interfere with the working of this law will be futile or worse. But if the free market leads to general social harmony, why would anyone wish to interfere? We now know that the harmony thesis is false (because of a plenitude of faulty assumptions), and in a world that adheres to the market, not only do great calamities periodically blow—inflations, recessions, depressions, economic dislocations—but even in normal times employment conditions can be distressingly hostile to the health and even the very lives of workers.[7] In England of the nineteenth century, the plight of laboring children was dreadful:

> The system imposed on children more work and longer hours than human nature could bear, and somebody had to wring it out of them. Everywhere this cruel necessity hemmed in the life of the new society, and the new system wore a more inexorable face just because it made workmen, or even parents, the agents of its iron rule. In some cases, of course, not involuntary agents, for there have always been parents ready to exploit their children, and the factory system offered a powerful incentive to that spirit. One witness before a Lords Committee boasted that he

had broken his child's arm for disobedience in the mill. A system such as this was bound to find parents, and bound to make parents, callous to their children's sufferings, and no charge more bitter could be brought against it.[8]

From the sexual abuse of women and children to the most ironclad discipline of adults (a spinner near Manchester in the early nineteenth century who worked in 84 degrees Fahrenheit heat was subject to fines of a shilling if his window was open or if he was dirty, found washing himself, or heard whistling[9]), the worker became a productive object, harnessed to and increasingly, as the market's most famous critic charged, an "appendage of the machine."[10] And what was the attitude of liberals who trumpeted the virtues of freedom? By and large, it was to accept the conditions, requirements, and degradations as necessary, inevitable, and even, astonishingly, to argue that the whole charge of worker injury was a chimera.

Injuries necessary. In 1786 Joseph Townsend, whose description of the principle of the survival of the fittest was transmitted through Malthus to Darwin, wrote in his "Dissertation on the Poor Laws, by a Well-Wisher to Mankind" an admirably succinct objection to providing welfare to the poor:

> It seems to be a law of nature, that the poor should be to a certain degree improvident, that there may always be some to fulfil the most servile, the most sordid, and the most ignoble offices in the community. The stock of human happiness is thereby much increased, whilst the more delicate are not only relieved from drudgery, and freed from those occasional employments which would make them miserable, but are left at liberty, without interruption, to pursue those callings which are suited to their various dispositions, and most useful to the state. As for the lowest of the poor, by custom they are reconciled to the meanest occupations, to the most laborious work, and to the most hazardous pursuits; whilst the hope of their reward makes them cheerful in the midst of all their dangers and their toils. The fleets and armies of a state would soon be in want of soldiers and of sailors, if sobriety and diligence universally prevailed: for what is it but distress and poverty which can prevail upon the lower classes of the people to encounter all the horrors which await them on the tempestuous ocean, or in the field of battle? Men who are easy in their circumstances are not among the foremost to engage in a seafaring or military life. There must be a degree of pressure, and that which is attended with the least violence will be the best. When hunger is either felt or feared, the desire of obtaining bread will quietly dispose the mind to undergo the greatest hardships, and will sweeten the severest labours. The peasant with a sickle in his hand is happier than the prince upon his throne.[11]

Innumerable disquisitions since then have expressed no more concisely the belief that the poor are necessary to society and that the poor must be kept so, regardless of their suffering. Bernard Mandeville, whose *Fable of the Bees or Private Vices, Publick Benefits* first asserted that society would most benefit from letting every person seek his own ends, held that "[i]t is manifest, that in a Free Nation where Slaves are not allow'd of, the surest wealth consists in a multitude of Laborious Poor." Not only materially poor: Mandeville insisted "it is requisite that great numbers ... should be ignorant as well as poor."[12] In 1807, the president of the Royal Society, the premier scientific body, argued in the House of Commons:

> However specious in theory the project might be, of giving education to the labouring classes of the poor, it would in effect be found to be prejudicial to their morals and happiness; it would teach them to despise their lot in life, instead of making them good servants in agriculture, and other laborious employments to which their rank in society had destined them; instead of teaching them subordination, it would render them factious and refractory, ... it would enable them to read seditious pamphlets, vicious books, and publications against Christianity; it would render them insolent to their superiors.[13]

Injuries inevitable. That the status of the poor was inevitable became clear in the half century after Townsend wrote. The science of economics was refined: Thomas Malthus discovered an inexorable natural law that caused population to increase faster than the food supply. Nothing that enlightened men tried to do could reverse this law. The poor were condemned to their fate: Higher wages would simply breed more of them, pressing them faster against the edge of famine. The ineluctable immiserization of labor was systematically developed by David Ricardo, who concluded that the total wages available to labor would be just sufficient to cover the subsistence of each; any interference with the economic system would be an injustice, not toward the rich, but as between one poor man and another.[14]

Expressed in its most extreme form, this was the individualist, laissez-faire philosophy of Herbert Spencer, who elevated the inevitability of suffering to a biological principle. In his widely read *Social Statics*, first published in 1851, Spencer said that whoever survived (and prospered) deserved to survive (and prosper) and whoever failed or died likewise deserved to fail or die. This was the way of nature, which rid the world of the poor, the ill, the ignorant, and the incompetent because they are unfit; any interference, such as through poor laws or "sanitary supervision," would simply lead to social disaster:

> The whole effort of nature is to get rid of such, to clear the world of them and make room for better. Nature demands that every being shall be self-sufficing.... Nature just as much insists on fitness between mental

character and circumstances as between physical character and circumstances; and radical defects are as much causes of death in the one case as in the other. He on whom his own stupidity, or vice, or idleness entails loss of life must, in the generalizations of philosophy, be classed with the victims of weak viscera or malformed limbs. . . . Beings thus imperfect are nature's failures, and are recalled by her laws when found to be such. Along with the rest they are put on trial. If they are sufficiently complete to live, they *do* live, and it is well they should live. If they are not sufficiently complete to live, they die, and it is best they should die.[15]

Injuries chimerical. Finally, since it was perhaps embarrassing to concede that the best of all possible social systems appeared to generate and tolerate misery, an argument came to fashion in England early in the nineteenth century, echoes of which were heard in the Southern slave states in America, that the employer (like the slave-owner) naturally had the best interests of his worker (slave) at heart: "The first discovery, that the State could not really protect the workman, was followed by another, even more interesting, that the employer could not really injure him."[16]

Underlying all these rationalizations was the fundamental belief that the conditions in which workers and the poor found themselves, no matter how awful, were not harms brought about by human agency but simply misfortunes that sprang from a concatenation of forces arising from the existing economic and material circumstances. That being so, it would be as futile as it would be wrong for the state to try to ameliorate the lot of the maimed, the poor, or the sick.

The climate of opinion in which these beliefs flourished was general. No less a thinker than Oliver Wendell Holmes Jr. saw no moral relationship between people who set conditions in motion and the victims of those conditions who would suffer fatalities and grisly maiming at work or on the streets. Summarizing the common law at the time, Holmes held that unless the chain of causation was extremely short—directly between tortfeasor and victim—accidents were just that, accidents, for which no one, except perhaps the worker, could be blamed. "The general principle of our law is that loss from accident must lie where it falls, and this principle is not affected by the fact that a human being is the instrument of misfortune," Holmes declared in his Lowell Institute Lectures in 1881.[17]

Though the law has undergone revolutionary changes, the argument that the market is not an agency that can or should be reformed by the state, that it is rather the result of spontaneous forces resulting from free choices of consenting players, continues to be pressed. Perhaps the most elegant modern formulation is that of Friedrich A. Hayek, who has expressed it this way: "Justice is not concerned with those unintended consequences of a spontaneous order which have not been deliberately brought about by anybody."[18] As Judith N. Shklar sums up Hayek's thesis:

His market is neither fair nor unfair; it knows only winners and losers. It has no will, no purposes, no personality. We cannot hold it responsible for anything at all. Because the market is an impersonal force of nature, those who are injured by it cannot claim that they have suffered an injustice, although many of their normal expectations may have been shattered. The sense of injustice has no place here, no more so than in cases of earthquakes or volcanic eruptions.[19]

By "spontaneous order" Hayek has in mind something like a highway on which, let's suppose, we drive in the morning to work. We do not intend to make someone else late or arrive tardily ourselves. The more cars on the road, the greater the probability that the trip will take longer, thus disserving drivers who will be penalized for arriving late. But in the spontaneous order of the freeway, in which drivers zoom as fast as they can, cutting in and out of lanes to acquire an advantage, entering and leaving the freeway as their plans require, no one has deliberated on harming anyone. Each driver is simply trying to push ahead. Lateness (and even car crashes) are an unintended consequence of all the driving on the road that day. It would not do, Hayek would say, for a police cruiser to pull certain cars at random to the side of the road so that others might pass. Nor would it make sense to enact a law requiring drivers to "let others get to work on time." As Hayek says:

> Rules of conduct cannot simply prohibit all actions that cause harm to others. To buy or not to buy from, and to serve or not to serve, a particular person, is an essential part of our freedom; but if we decide not to buy from one or not to serve another, this may cause great harm if those affected have counted on our custom or our services; and in disposing of what is ours, a tree in our garden, or the façade of our house, we may deprive our neighbour of what to him has great sentimental value. Rules of just conduct cannot protect all interests.[20]

That rules of conduct cannot prohibit all actions, however, does not mean they cannot prohibit some. No rule of conduct is written to say: "Desist from all harm."[21] In a market economy, we would not say: "Do not impoverish anyone," because that "rule" does not describe conduct from which the actor could know to refrain. A sensible rule picks out an action that can be linked to harmful consequences or an action that creates certain types of risks. Thus we can point to certain kinds of actions that contribute to impoverishment, and constrain them in some way (for example, "Do not fix prices"). Just so, stoplights, one-way streets, and other devices can prompt people to drive in more orderly ways to minimize confusion on the roads. Moreover, that the highway serves as a medium for the spontaneous ordering of transportation does not mean that the conduct that causes every unintended consequence may not be regulated. A careless driver who causes a multiple-car crash should not be absolved from responsibility for injuries caused to the last driver in line, simply because the collision was mediated through several intermediate cars and the wrongdoer himself was never near the last car to be hit.

Historical forces, invisible hands, and other such constructs are the vectors of the various consequences of human activities. There are no historical forces apart from humanity. We think so, or wish to call them "forces," because it is often difficult or impossible to agree on how to curb or tame them. The question is whether government policies are more harmful to other objects of our desires and ambitions than helpful to us in preventing the particular disaster we wish to avoid. The problem is how to recognize what constitutes a remediable harm in a market society, and to understand how it is that in affecting people in harmful ways, the market is not an impersonal mechanism but a human agency legitimately subject to certain kinds of intervention by the state.

The Market as Human Agency

To understand the market as human agency, we need to consider a historic but uncompleted transformation: the fitful substitution of human systems for natural systems in the daily life of our species.[22] Conflicts in nature are "resolved" by force—mayhem, death, extinction. In humanity's nonage, when people devoted their time to activities closely related to animal survival, existence depended on a social system that knit the community together and in which everyone had a place. Tradition, not considerations of fairness or individual equity, was the controlling principle. It made no more sense to inquire whether a rule of the community was just than to inquire whether gravitation was moral. The customs of the community were simply rules of nature. In such a time, only the most obvious—and preventable—injuries would be recognized as coming from the hands of their fellows. By far the larger share of harms was naturally caused—storms, fires, disease, famine—for which remedies were excruciatingly difficult to find. So when something went wrong the grounds for complaint were narrow. If your spouse died from eating poisoned food that you had plucked from the ground, you could blame a witch[23] perhaps, but who else could you name as defendant—surely not the food?[24]

In such a society custom had a double consequence. It prescribed the place and function of every person and ensured for that very reason against drastic change. From generation to generation people might suffer from famine and even murder, but community custom decreed how to cope. However rudely or unequally, each person was taken care of according to his place in the family and society into which he was born. And in that society, each person was educated to the degree required to understand the things that needed to be understood. The child would learn early which mushrooms were safe to eat—or he would die. Once enlightened, he could then evaluate mushrooms for himself. If he relied on others for comfort and help in the hunt or in planting, the chain through which passed the things that counted in daily life was very short. He did not sign contracts for flint stones to be delivered a year hence or call in an engineer to consult on the foundations of the hut he was building.

A short while ago in historical terms, all this changed. The Church lost its grip on Europe, petty princes consolidated territories into larger kingdoms, long-distance trade fostered business methods and increased the money supply, inflation drastically reduced the value of feudal privileges that local nobles held over their vassals' heads, inventions and towns with jobs grew apace, plague depopulated the countryside, printing and literacy spread, open land was enclosed and peasants lost their birthright, manufacturing and commerce became a growing part of the economy. When all this and more came to be, traditional society could no longer mediate change and regulate itself. Too much happened too fast for customary processes to adapt human behavior and belief to the necessities of an industrial age.

This Great Transformation[25] created circumstances for which traditionalism was helpful to neither the agents of change nor those whom change injured. Change in customary societies is measured in generations; the process of unconscious adaptation to small changes could no longer suffice to protect the mass of individuals uprooted from their traditional place in the community. A society that liberated people from the suffocating group order in which most of humanity had always lived required at the same time new institutions that would provide the security that in theory the social classes owed and sometimes paid each other. Individuals truly alone in the world were no better, indeed were worse off, than those smothered by tradition. But custom as man's means of brokering change was not only too slow in providing remedies for those injured by the destructive engine of industrialism. It was also too parsimonious to allow much play to the creative capacity of that same industrialism. Custom enslaved both servants and masters. But custom could not simply be shed. Something had to replace it to cope with the one singularly successful and novel transformation in human life that was budding: the conquest of nature. The emerging society would require comprehensive political oversight to tame it.

To conquer the natural world and direct it to their advantage, to reduce natural disasters and misfortunes, people have learned to substitute themselves, through social institutions, for nature. More people devoted less time to mere physical survival. Instead, they confronted not nature but social institutions that managed increasingly more powerful technologies. The specialization that allows us as a species to accomplish more permits us to do less for ourselves individually, drawing us closer together. Time, knowledge, and other resources are limited. We desire things we cannot do for ourselves, so we necessarily turn to others to provide them. Where once we could turn only to people within our hilltop or village, now, in the burgeoning market society, people reached out ever farther.[26]

But as each person's reach grew, so did his dependence. Once I knew for myself whether my mushrooms were safe to eat; now I must depend on the skill and care of someone else. Once I could swim across the stream; now I must depend on the knowledge of the engineer and the skill of the builder to ensure the safety of the bridge or the ferry across the river. Human mastery of nature through technology and industry has thus richly multiplied the connections between injury and human undertaking—and severed the controls every person once had over his own life.[27]

In switching allegiance from nature to human institutions, we are at the mercy of systems far too powerful to control directly—and this, in two ways: I cannot easily assess what they do or oversee them to ensure that they do it right. A manufacturing system in a factory a thousand miles away may have developed a glitch, unnoticed or disdained by the managers, or the production crew, or several other layers of intermediaries. When the canned mushrooms reach me, I am defenseless against the poison inside. The birth of the corporation greatly multiplied these glitches, for a single company may now be spread out geographically and consist of numerous units performing specialized tasks—procurement, production, marketing, distribution, accounting, research—so that no single person can control all that is being done or be held unequivocally responsible for the general actions of the firm. Of course, the head of the firm may knowingly approve or even direct a corrupt act, like failing to use sufficient safety devices or to give crews adequate training. Such harms awakened public attention dramatically in early railroad disasters. In 1868, an observer noted in his diary of an accident on the Erie line:

> Scores of people smashed, burned to death, or maimed for life. We shall never travel safely until some pious, wealthy, and much beloved railroad director [like Cornelius Vanderbilt] has been hanged for murder, with a conductor on each side of him.[28]

But few market activities, including, perhaps, the Erie accident, are corrupt in the sense of harms deliberately caused. This problem was not well understood, or perhaps understood at all, at the dawning of the market system. In 1755 in his *Discourse on Inequality*, Rousseau said: "[A]s long as [a man] does not resist the inner impulse of commiseration, he will never harm another man or even another sensitive being, except in the legitimate case where, his preservation being concerned, he is obliged to give himself preference."[29] But commiseration does not save us when acts and consequences are dissociated. As Reinhold Niebuhr noted, "[a]n increasing tendency among modern men [is] to imagine themselves ethical because they have delegated their vices to larger and larger groups."[30] A century ago, E. A. Ross insisted that the new "social sins" were difficult to confront precisely because they were impersonal:

> The hurt passes into that vague mass, the "public," and is there lost to view. Hence it does not take a Borgia to knead "chalk and alum and plaster" into the loaf, seeing one cannot know just who will eat that loaf, or what gripe it will give him.[31]

Embracing the weak version of the harm principle—that the law should deal only with crimes or omissions that one person directly caused another—implied that business entities and those who ran them were beyond regulation. "The moral and legal codes inherited from the 18th Century," the historian Henry Steele Commager wrote, "were adequate to detect and punish cruelty to children or misappropriation of funds or poisoning; they were incompetent to detect and punish child labor, stock watering, and the adulteration of foods."[32]

To conclude, as Hayek did, that because the lines of responsibility cannot be traced the market is therefore a wholly impersonal agency is to miss a central feature of the market. Through the market we have not merely transformed communal life, we have wholly supplanted it. We have created benefits and corresponding burdens that are not just tonier versions of the artifacts and customs of the primeval village. The market has given us the modern world. It has blessed and cursed us. Even if the market organizes action spontaneously, it does so through human agency. It is only because the market works through human agency—that is, because we entrust our lives to so many people—that it works at all.[33] The market is not a machine or an earthquake. It is a collection of people. Things that happen to people are caused by people. When people harm each other, the state may always do something about it.

This claim is often denied. Opponents of regulation assert that the market renders us powerless to effect sensible changes. This durable argument comes in two forms, which Albert O. Hirschman has identified as the "perversity" and the "futility" theses. The perversity thesis holds that "any purposive action to improve some feature of the political, social, or economic order only serves to exacerbate the condition one wishes to remedy. The futility thesis holds that attempts at social transformation will be unavailing, that they will simply fail to 'make a dent.'"[34] Hirschman traces these theses and a related jeopardy thesis (that reform will endanger hard-won principles or policies[35]) to late-eighteenth-century rhetoric that borrowed in turn from the prestige of Newton's third law of motion (that every action produces an equivalent reaction) and that was then fueled by the French Revolution. These theses regularly resurface when reform is in the air. The perversity thesis, for example, reemerged in the 1980s in Charles Murray's bestselling *Losing Ground*. Murray argued that "we tried to provide more for the poor and produced more poor instead. We tried to remove the barriers to escape from poverty and inadvertently built a trap."[36] Hayek remains the most renowned modern exponent of the jeopardy thesis, warning for forty years around mid-century that a society attempting to redress outcomes of market transactions will wind up enslaved.[37]

These grand abstractions bristle with difficulties that would take me far afield to consider at any length, though their sweeping contentions are almost surely false (reformers can point to any number of successes through purposive legislation). But in any event they largely miss the point. Public policy may be a difficult art, but it is not an illegitimate one. In a market society, the very means by which people live is to connect with one another. They cannot leave each other alone. Most of us cannot say that we will refuse to deal, that we will not shop for food, that we will work our land, that we will homestead and entail our property, free of king and bank, to the succeeding generations. We cannot opt out of the market. And in the society that it has created, to seek relief from harms, we cannot depend, like Tennessee Williams's Blanche DuBois, on the kindness of strangers. Here, if you like, is the working of a different perversity thesis: The unintended consequence of the market itself—that invisible coordinator of freely chosen economic decisions—was the phenomenal increase of interdependence, which multiplies collisions, frauds, and other disturbances that the market does not regulate. The market thus bred the very conditions that subject it to the state's oversight under the harm principle.

Precisely for this reason has come the seeming paradox that every student of liberalism has noted, that from the nineteenth century on

> [m]ore and more aspects of economic and social life came under legal regulation and restriction. Much of this legislation had been the work of liberal governments; yet liberals could not avoid feeling uneasy about these developments. They ran counter both to their belief in the minimal state, and to their belief that freedom consisted essentially in the absence of all but a minimum of law, regulation and compulsion. Was not the historic task of liberalism to abolish restrictions, limitations and obstructions?[38]

What emerged from the legislatures was not inconsistent with the liberal premise, if the laws were aimed at the harms that industrialism scattered about in its wake. Indeed, this singular power of the market to produce great good and great evils accounts for liberalism's transformation from its crabbed nineteenth-century minimalism to its twentieth-century expansion (leading Democrats for four decades to duck for cover because they cannot figure out how to persuade voters that it is only logical to pay for the protection programs that voters otherwise desire).[39]

Addressing Market Harms

We must now face up to the difficulty of specifying the sorts of market effects that the liberal state may redress, for not every deleterious outcome traceable to the market is a harm. To say that the market works through human beings and that the chain of causation is longer than once was possible does not mean that we should trace indefinitely back along the chain to find a putative wrongdoer or that we must discount the plaintiff's own contribution to his suffering. For that is to play the "victim" game: Everything that happened to me happened because of something that someone else did (it's my parents' fault, my teachers' fault, my boss's fault; fault is in the stars, my genes, the culture). The problem is to locate the harms and their causes for which redress is appropriate.[40]

Lack of space and imagination preclude, in what follows, anything like a full accounting of the types of effects that have been proposed over the years as remediable. Here I consider only what appear to be the major targets of reform or methods of attack, not necessarily in order of importance: (1) competition harms (i.e., policies to reduce or alter losses engendered by competition); (2) investment harms (i.e., policies to rationalize investment decisions); (3) market harms and harms to the market (i.e., policies to protect people from market "disturbances" and policies to protect the market itself); (4) production harms (i.e., policies to restrict uses of property); (5) employment harms (i.e., policies affecting hours, wages, safety, and other working conditions); and (6) welfare harms (i.e., policies to provide for the "losers").

Competition Harms

At common law in preindustrial England, ferry owners and mills could maintain actions against competing newcomers under the right of "ancient usage."[41] Indeed, even the loss of customers was held to be a compensable injury. As the legal historian Morton J. Horwitz has written:

> [W]ell into the eighteenth century English courts allowed damage actions against consumers who departed from long-standing business relationships to take their trade elsewhere. Even in the nineteenth century, English courts entertained damage actions for competitive injury to markets by prescription.[42]

Mill insisted that the logic of such a policy is unsound:

> Whoever succeeds in an overcrowded profession, or in a competitive examination; whoever is preferred to another in any contest for an object which both desire, reaps benefit from the loss of others, from their wasted exertion and their disappointment. But it is, by common admission, better for the general interest of mankind, that persons should pursue their objects, undeterred by this sort of consequence.... society admits of no right, either legal or moral, in the disappointed competitors to immunity from this kind of suffering.[43]

Feinberg agrees: Whoever loses the competition has no grounds to complain because whatever the injury, no wrong was done.[44] But as we saw in chapter 3, whether a wrong is committed when interests conflict may depend on the state's prior declaration. The question is why the state may not, under the harm principle, decide whether the first in town should be spared the competition?

It seems intuitive that if the state were to be granted the power to prevent competition, the very premise of liberalism would be undercut. In other words, competition is definitional for liberalism. If, believing that I can make a better mousetrap than you, I were barred from trying, I would be denied the very thing that the liberal state had promised: the right to attempt to carry out my purposes. Of course, intuition is often faulty, and this argument may be seen as circular. Under the harm principle, I may carry out my purposes only if they are not harmful, and whether they are harmful depends in turn on whether the state has declared that the business that is first in time has a right against competitors. For unlike in a sports competition, the first mousetrap seller will protest that he did not consent to the newcomer's opening shop or engaging in the contest; if he loses the competition, his interest will have been wrongly set back. Circularity can be defeated only if there is some reason to believe that economic competition by itself is not wrongful. It is not an answer to say that society will prosper from fair economic competition; no doubt it does, but it might also prosper by killing the elderly who consume without paying for medical resources. What we want is an argument that the state may not undertake to ban competition. That it would not use the power if the harm principle bestowed it may be a practical but not a theoretical solace.

Two additional answers seem plausible. First, that others are allowed to compete with an existing producer does not by that fact alone set back the first producer's interest. The others, too, must leave each other free to compete. My selling competing goods does not automatically defeat your right to do so nor does it imply that you will lose the race. I may believe I have a better mousetrap but it may be worse, or I may not have the knowledge or skill to manufacture it cheaply enough or put it into the pipeline in an efficient way. None of that can be known the instant I open up for business. To block me from the outset implies a forecast that I will inevitably be better than my predecessor without any proof that that will be so. Moreover, when others discover a booming market in mousetraps they may offer supporting goods and services (electronic add-ons that will signal that a mouse has been caught, in-home trap removal) that may lead to an increase in total sales. Rather than harm, competition may profit us both. Nor is it clear what would constitute competition for purposes of protecting the first in time. I sell blacksmith services; you sell cars. You run an old-fashioned diner; I operate a fast-food counter in a department store. You sell to people on the north side of town; I sell to new customers, who have never been to your store and who have moved into the new condominiums on the south side of town. Even if your business declines, it is unclear to what degree the competition I offer contributed toward your misfortunes.

Second, a more intractable problem for the first in time seller is the nature of his claim. He might lose money, without any competition at all, if he makes an inferior product that no one wants or that goes out of fashion. Under any version of the harm principle, his claim cannot be that he is entitled to the patronage of his previous customers come what may. Such a claim amounts to the contention that every business "owns" the customer or has a stake in his patronage. But one cannot have an interest in the interest of someone else (unless there is a special relationship, such as a contract between the supplier and customer to purchase goods). The customer's interest is in obtaining the best product or service for the price, or purchasing it most conveniently, or buying it or subscribing to it because the customer trusts the supplier. The seller cannot override the customer's interest by asserting that the customer's pocketbook, convenience, ease of mind, or desire for the product do not count. If he could, the harm principle would be defeated as wholly circular (and the buyer could then demand that the seller stay in business; stock what he first stocked, even if demand for it decreases; and otherwise do what it would be unprofitable to do, just because he had once done it that way).

Investment Harms and the Problem of Planning

The critic of the market says that it is an irrational process; it leads to overmanufacture of many goods, no development of some important goods, maldistribution of necessary goods. In an important way, the criticism is but a tautology, for the market is precisely a mechanism for ordering activities without central direction, that is, without the application of a rational plan for the entirety of the process. To demand central planning is, quite plainly, to wish to dismantle the market itself. So it should be clear that comprehensive planning is the antithesis not only of the market but of a liberal order.

To dispatch the argument that the market, of itself, does harm, two responses tailored to the harm principle are sufficient. The first is that planning requires an authoritative command to the investor about where to devote his resources. The essence of such a command is that the investor may not freely choose to compete (or to make business contracts). As we have just seen, the state may not issue such commands under the harm principle. The second response is the other side of the same coin: The outcome of the market, at any slice of time, is not of itself a condition that can be called a setback to interest since it is not a single condition. It is a complex outcome of trillions of decisions that can have variable effects on millions, even billions, of people. There is no ultimate state (the vector of all decisions in the market) the interest of which can be said to be set back, since only individual people's interests can be set back. To suppose otherwise is to hypothesize an ultimate good, or set of goods, that is inconsistent with the reason for employing the harm principle in the first place. So while the market will favor some people and frustrate others, the condition in which they find themselves (a person's "interest network") should not be characterized, in Feinberg's terminology, as a "harmed condition,"[45] because there is no knowable baseline or alternative outcome to which it can be compared. If X shoots Y, the inference is almost certainly correct (in the absence of strong contradictory evidence) that but for the shooting Y would still be living. So the change in Y's condition from before the shooting to after is quite obviously a harm. But if as a result of market conditions, the chip manufacturers do not deliver a breed of faster chips that Y would prefer to have in his computer this year, there is no way to show that a planned alternative would have put him where he wanted to be. Moreover, Y has an interest in not being shot, but no stake in someone else's inventing and manufacturing a new product.

Nevertheless, not all market outcomes are harmless. The critique of central planning is that it is erroneous to brand as harmful individual labor and investment decisions that constitute the market process *as a whole*. But the actions of many people within that system will produce redressable harms. That is what an "externality effect" or accumulative harm is. To say that the market "produces" pollution is to say, in economic terms, that because air is a free good, there is no cost to polluting. Individuals are not charged what they would be if air were owned or otherwise capable of exacting a price from those whose activities damage it. Harmful effects are within the state's legitimate reach.

The liberal can provide a different sort of response to the advocate of central planning. It is the practical response that wholesale planning would derail the harm principle. Although it is possible to imagine a central planning institution concerned solely with economic decisions, it is difficult to conjure a limited central planning mechanism into being. If at first the planner wants merely to direct the largest automobile manufacturers to build smaller (or larger) cars, it will discover soon enough that it also needs to concern itself with steel production, and then with all the other users of steel, and by and by it will realize that its real task is to turn out citizens who will more efficiently respond to the commands of the planning agency. To protect the deserving the state must create the worthy. Long before then, the planner will have swallowed up the state's other political organs and will have substituted its vision of the good for the multitude of visions that led to the "mess" that called it into being. To guard against instability of a legislature bowing to changing public opinion, an ultimate decision-maker would emerge, and all decisions would ultimately flow up the line. But power over everything is, finally, power over very little, because the press of business would paralyze any single person or agency.[46] In such a regime, the possibility of preserving individual liberty, guided by a harm principle, is nil. That this projection is not merely theoretical we have the history of the twentieth century and much of the globe to bear witness.[47]

Although central planning is incompatible with the harm principle, specific regulation of industries to lessen particular harms is not. Intervening to deal with aggregative and accumulative harms is a staple of the modern state. That such intervention may "distort" the market does not render the regulations illegitimate. Well-designed regulations, in fact, can even enhance efficiency. That is because private companies are not immune from the inefficiencies of their own central planning. They are prone to the same difficulties that confront hierarchically arranged production and decision-making by the state. Government, it turns out, can spur private industrial concerns to greater efficiencies, not by centrally planning but by regulating in ways that require manufacturers and others to respond. So, for example, an environmental law affecting the chemical industry prompted companies to redesign their production, reducing pollution and saving on average three and a half times the cost of the redesign.[48] Regulating harms generated by market players is not tantamount to market control.

Market Harms and Harms to Market

Fidelity to the market is not adherence to anarchy. The market is not chaos but a means of organizing unplanned activity, a method of coordinating without design, and insofar as that is possible the market is a mechanism. Like all mechanisms, it must be kept in good repair. A "free" market is not an unconstrained one, therefore. This distinction is sometimes lost on its defenders. T. H. Huxley lambasted extreme individualists like Spencer for their brutal indifference, on the one hand, to the fate of the "weak" and poor who might die of starvation, and their self-absorbed failure, on the other, to acknowledge their dependence on other people for their own survival. He ironically contrasted "men who are accustomed to contemplate the active or passive extirpation of the weak, the unfortunate, and the superfluous; who justify that conduct on the ground that it has the sanction of the cosmic process, and is the only way of ensuring the progress of the race" with men "who, if they are consistent, must rank medicine among the black arts and count the physician a mischievous preserver of the unfit."[49] When inconvenient, the individualists ignored the rules that grounded their ethical preconceptions, denying them effect or recalling them as useful. The market, too, exists as a system of rules, which cannot be applied or discarded at whim if we are to preserve it. Without the state's aid the market itself would fail.

The state's involvement is most obvious in the realm of contract law. The market would collapse if the courts were unavailable to enforce contractual commitments, for anyone could then walk away from a disadvantageous deal. It is possible that in the absence of contract law certain kinds of contracts would be kept, even if unprofitable, since those with a continuing relationship would rather swallow an occasional loss than jeopardize, say, an ongoing source of supply.[50] But no liberal supposes that life would be worth living without a law of contracts. The moral obligation to honor commitments is ancient, and all modern political philosophers insist on it. For Hume, the obligation to honor promises is one of the three principles of justice; for Hobbes, a law of nature; for Locke, who refused to set down the principles of natural law, it is implicitly a law of nature; for Nozick, contract enforcement is a primary responsibility of government. So entrenched in any liberal theory of the state (indeed, probably in any theory) is the power to declare and enforce the law of contracts that I do not bother here to defend it.[51]

But the rules governing the existence and enforcement of contracts are not the same as those governing their substance. You cannot immunize yourself from prosecution by entering into a contract with another to commit a crime. So the state need not uphold every agreement just because it is called a contract. Some contracts are inimical to the very existence of the market. The price-fixing contract, for example, undercuts or destroys the efficient allocation of goods by artificially raising or lowering prices. So, too, a range of other economic maneuvers, of special importance to a particular firm, need not be tolerated—monopolistic behavior, contracts among competitors to divide geographic markets, requirements that the purchase of one good be tied to the purchase of another. These, and many other anticompetitive restrictions, are barred in antitrust and trade regulation laws that in one form or another have the venerable support of Adam Smith himself.[52] I do not assert that current antitrust policy is sound, only that antitrust policy itself is compatible with the liberal theory of the state. Likewise, the state may police economic institutions—banking and securities regulations, for example—to minimize fraud and to ensure that the market is not rigged to favor one set of interests over another. Many other economic laws similarly may be understood as a means of supporting and enhancing the market—for example, federal deposit insurance, which in minimizing runs on failing banks ensures that the entire system does not collapse. That these laws and regulations impede the efficiency of the market is not the issue: "Liberalism is committed to markets, not to efficiency as such."[53]

Sometimes the market itself gets "stuck." Inflation reduces the value of assets and existing obligations; contractions in the form of recession eliminate jobs and employment possibilities, among other things. These and other market disturbances should be seen as the consequences of aggregative and accumulative harms that the government may seek to curb. To prevent runs on banks, the government guarantees deposits. To stimulate the economy, the Federal Reserve system acts to lower interest rates, and Congress lowers the tax rate or provides tax rebates. How well these and other economic measures work is a policy question—that the government may pursue them consistent with the harm principle is no question at all.[54]

Production Harms and Restrictions on Property

Voicing a representative viewpoint about the rights of property in the nineteenth century, Benjamin Constant said that people must have "unlimited freedom" in using their property; that is, "the inherent right, the essential requirement of all those who own property."[55] He could not have meant by "property" any physical possession to which we have title, since it is patent that my ownership of a gun does not entitle me to the unlimited freedom to shoot you with it. In this sense of the word, much of the harm redressable under the harm principle is mediated through physical possessions that are owned—the knife, the gun, the car, the polluting smokestack. Constant was referring to the use of property for productive purposes—the decision of what to invest, produce, sell. We have just seen that stated this broadly, the liberal answer is that Constant is correct if market order is to mean anything at all. But that answer does not take us very far.

In feudal times, the most important form of property, land, was burdened with obligations. "Owners" of the major estates could not alienate their land; it belonged to their families in perpetuity, and it was the source of reciprocal obligations between lords and vassals, whose descendants inherited both the rights and obligations of vassalage. But by the end of the sixteenth century, those had become unstuck. Land was no longer a bundle of rights and obligations. The ameliorating effects of status—the reciprocity of obligation—was shaved clean away when the lord of the manor no longer merely possessed his estate but owned it. With land no longer burdened by responsibilities and with money-making the primary goal, a person was now free to do with it as he wished. He could sell it from underneath his children to strangers. He could graze his sheep, lease his castle, erect a mill, or invest in new industry. So much is explicit in the liberal premise: If it is yours, use it as you will.

But that cannot be the end of the story. When traditional morality was sapped, when the restraints of the old culture dissolved in the pressure cooker of capitalism, the state had inevitably to move in, if only to lower the heat. For the range of human activity had broadened immeasurably, and property could now be used in ways that would have been unfathomable to those gone not so many generations. Inevitably, these uses set back others' interests.

But as already noted, difficulties arise when two interests conflict. Two owners seek to view the river. Only one can. To resolve the conflict, some rule is necessary. Sooner or later, the state must choose a rule of property that will settle the matter. Who else can do it? It does not avail to suggest that the parties bargain. The first owner, whose view will be blocked when the second owner builds a house, could offer to compensate his rival to refrain. But that is already to concede the issue. Why should the first owner, if he has a right to the view, pay the second owner anything? And what if the second owner refuses the offer? As we have seen, only an authoritative rule issued by the state can determine the answers. Thereafter, bargaining can proceed against the backdrop of law.

Whether a property right can arise without a state's first having to declare a rule, whether, that is, property is a "natural" rather than "conventional" right, is a question of no importance, despite the immense attention it has generated in the literature since the late seventeenth century when Locke proposed in *The Second Treatise* that he had succeeded in answering it affirmatively. As discussed in chapter 5, a natural right to the fruits of one's labor quickly runs up against the barrier of uncertainty. No one will quarrel with my scooping up and eating a nut from a field, except the person who claims he owns it. The practical problem for all societies is not whether any of us could theoretically have a right to things without the sanction of the state, but whether we have a right to the actual things we claim are ours. It is the great practical function of the state, then, not merely to resolve quarrels that turn on conflicting uses of property, but to lay down rules that define property rights in the first instance. As Hayek says: "The rules of just conduct thus delimit protected domains not by directly assigning particular things to particular persons, but by making it possible to derive from ascertainable facts to whom particular things belong."[56] A conflict between rights is resolved or resolvable not by arguing over abstract natural rights but by judging the merits of assigning a right to a particular interest among the set of interests that conflict.

Some of these rules are evidentiary. A handshake conveys no enforceable right to the buyer to move into his new home or to the seller to collect the purchase price. Even though everyone may agree that the deal actually was struck, the contract exists (that is to say, will be enforced) only if a written agreement can be provided to the court. Other property rules are more substantive. Bankruptcy laws, which might at first glance appear to contradict the right to enforcement of contracts (the state says you may not extract more from a promisor than he has paid on a valid debt beyond what he has when he is bankrupt), in fact give body to the risk to be run when contracting with anyone. A known, stable bankruptcy law makes society less risk-averse (hence more productive) because it sets boundaries to the magnitude of the loss should the gamble go sour. The law sets ground rules for every transaction, balancing the risk of recovering the full debt against the risk that an unlucky or improvident person will be hounded for life, perpetually unable to care for himself because all future earnings could be garnished. Knowing the rules, the would-be creditor can demand collateral. Bankruptcy law is a formal limitation on remedy, the necessity of which Locke acknowledged and which, he held, only the state can make.

Likewise, the most fundamental business unit of the modern world, the corporation, is a construct of the law and would not be possible without it. People can, of course, pool their resources and agree to create an entity that will carry out a particular business without the permission of the state. But they could not obtain the one primary advantage the state confers over the operation of an unincorporated proprietorship: limited liability. If a proprietor harms another through the course of his business, the victim may seek recompense under ordinary liability laws that are a staple of the harm principle. It is likewise the province of the legislature to determine how far those liability laws will extend and whether to immunize a class of persons who might otherwise be subject to suit. In the corporate case, the law conventionally limits liability to the assets of the business and immunizes the owners of the corporation's stock. To pretend that the corporation is but a "person," as has been the fiction since the nineteenth century, is to ignore the laws that call it into being and determine the relationships among the various classes of people (capital owners, managers, directors) without which it could not exist.

In sum, property and the state are inextricably bound. Property in the liberal sense is meaningless without a state that not only enforces but also defines property rights.

Employment Harms and Working Conditions

Perhaps nothing brought greater reproach to the nineteenth-century orthodox liberals than their cold indifference as a matter of political philosophy to the suffering of the masses. They professed an inability to resolve the plight of the poor; it was nature's way to weed out the unfit or to ensure the necessary labor force for the few who were destined for luxury. They were adamant that no relief was possible even in times of emergency—in the name of liberal economic principles the British government refused to relieve Ireland in the wake of the potato famine in the 1840s that left more than a million dead.[57] And they could find no rationale for dealing with the unhealthful and unsafe conditions of the factories and mines where backbreaking labor led to grisly injuries and early deaths. In all cases, the problem the liberals could not work around was this: Injuries are part of the inevitable price to be paid for progress; since no one forced the workers to put themselves in harm's way, there was no one against whom to lay the blame and from whom an accounting could be sought. To demand it from the taxpayer, or the employer, would be, in the much later words of Robert Nozick, to "use [the state's] coercive apparatus for the purpose of getting some citizens to aid others."[58]

Suppose I am in the market for cheap labor for my bakeshop and devise a novel scheme. I hang around marinas hoping to encounter people who have fallen into the water. When I spot someone who is drowning, I row over and extract a promise that, if I spare his life, he will work twelve-hour days for me in a windowless room in perpetuity for subsistence-level food and housing in company barracks. Not very healthy, I agree, but since I did not push him into the water nor was I in any way responsible for his capsizing, he cannot accuse me of coercing him or forcing the deal. By and by I have a large stable of indentured servants, whose indenture, in a society truly dedicated to free markets and contracts, I can enforce in court. I now begin to undersell my competitors and am on my way to riches. But my competitors counterattack by rowing around in other marinas and rescuing their own supply of cheap labor. The market for high-priced labor has collapsed now that we have a plentiful supply of "wets." Moving into town, new and more humane bakeshop owners would like to pay their bakers a living wage but realize they will fail if they do, so they offer "drys" the same miserable terms. Down on their luck, jobless, the drys accept. Now entrepreneur employers are all prospering—on the backs of bakers, to be sure, but only on the backs of those who have consented. Appalled at what looks to her like peonage, the governor proposes a law to raise the bakers' wages, shorten their hours, and ventilate their workrooms. The employers remind the governor that relief is barred under sound liberal principles.

What is wrong with this little tale? A reform-minded New Liberal, Leonard T. Hobhouse, writing a century ago, had an answer:

> The majority of employers in a trade we may suppose would be willing to adopt certain precautions for the health or safety of their workers, to

lower hours or to raise the rate of wages. They are unable to do so, however, as long as a minority, perhaps as long as a single employer, stands out. He would beat them in competition if they were voluntarily to undertake expenses from which he is free. In this case, the will of a minority, possibly the will of one man, thwarts that of the remainder. It coerces them, indirectly, but quite as effectively as if he were their master. If they, by combination, can coerce him no principle of liberty is violated. It is coercion against coercion, differing possibly in form and method, but not in principle or in spirit.[59]

But the employers have a ready response. Hobhouse is misusing the concept of *coercion*. The employee may be driven to extremes by biological cravings, parentally conditioned needs, mistaken wants, or personal mishap, but these are misfortunes not of our making. He is *free* to decline, so he is not coerced. Only *harm* is redressable: setbacks to interest *caused by* a *wrongdoer*. Suffering that results from misfortune is not remediable by the state.[60]

Is it possible to spare the workers, while remaining faithful to the harm principle? The answer, in several parts, proceeds as follows. First, consider the plight of the original near-drowning victim. He is flailing about, almost sinking. At this moment, he could have one of four relationships to his rescuer: (1) the owner was trying to drown him in order to extract the employment agreement; (2) the owner was not trying to drown him but did close off other rescue options, perhaps by sending the lifeguards away on a pretext; (3) the owner's plan to find a drowning man was premeditated, and he was searching for a victim; (4) the owner just happened along at the right moment, a pure opportunist, and the idea of the employment contract popped into his head spontaneously.[61] If the first relationship holds, then the contract need not be enforced; the baker was coerced. He was probably coerced in the second relationship as well, since the owner eliminated alternatives that might have saved him. The third relationship suggests intent to exploit any potential drowning victim; that is, to take advantage of the natural peril that awaited. For the owner to expend his time and resources in this way to trap the victim in an exploitive deal seems far more gratuitous than the fourth relationship in which the coercion, if any, did not come from the man in the rowboat. To the owner's argument that in the third relationship he did not himself create the circumstances of the peril, the state might reasonably respond that a man who has the time on his hands to go around searching out a drowning person to "make him an offer he can't refuse" is one who is trafficking in other people's misery, and that is not an interest that the state has any reason to uphold. The state might point out, moreover, that a diligent rowboater patrolling the marina might be mistaken for a legitimate rescue operation, thus thwarting the drowning person's chances for a genuine rescue when others turn back. Only if the fourth relationship holds (only if the rescuer was a chance opportunist) is it probably fair to say that the rescuer was not implicated in the coercion.

that the victim suffered no setback to his interest, and that he genuinely consented. But this relationship holds only for the first victim; for all others, at best the third relationship holds, since the rescuer has understood that harvesting drowners is the road to riches.

What justifies the state's invalidating the contract between the owner and the first baker, rescued on the spur of the moment as the owner happened along in his rowboat? Feinberg suggests that in these narrow circumstances the rescuer has a duty to rescue: When the potential rescuer has the opportunity and knowledge of the danger, knows that he has both, and the inconvenience and danger to himself would be slight, the state could impose a legal requirement that the rescue attempt must be made.[62] The law would not be requiring the rescuer to confer a benefit on the victim but to return the victim to the "baseline" where he would have been but for his mishap in the water. If there is a duty to rescue, then refusal to do so until the victim assents to the employment deal is coercive and the exploitive agreement need not be enforced. I do not develop this argument further, because there is another general justification for rejecting the contract.[63]

The law does not, because it cannot, deal in certainties. Only philosophers can evade reality with the claim that "it really happened just this way because I'm making up the story and I say so." In any world to which the story relates, it is always reasonable to inquire how we can be so certain of the facts. Claims that we should draw rules from hypothetical stories, with exceptions when the "real" facts are otherwise, depend on what might be called the "facts are known exactly" (FAKE) argument. A FAKE argument asserts that the facts are known and counsels us not to contradict them as we construct a rule from its implications. For example, we might be told, in the context of an argument justifying otherwise reprehensible conduct, to "assume that God has told a perpetrator P to kill a victim V." The question then is whether P is justified in killing V if he has no other reason. Relying on the assumption, we would grant P's right to kill V (if we are also correct in assuming that it is "always right to carry out an instruction from God"). But, of course, we do not live in the realm of the FAKE argument, where essential facts are stipulated. We live in the "real world," where such knowledge is always difficult to come by. No doubt most of us, even those who are deeply religious, are unwilling to credit the claims of people like P to have received God's instructions to kill V. Political theory ought to inhabit the real realm. The question is how the state should act given the world as it is. In the world as it is, we do well to be skeptical of claims about God's instructions and arguments that derive from similar sorts of hypothetical facts. The state must always be concerned with the means of proof and their degrees of difficulty. Much flows from this point.[64]

A legal system must provide procedures for sifting through evidence to determine whether claimed events were real events. Some legal "facts," such as state of mind, are impossible to prove directly; others are extremely difficult to substantiate, especially when the evidence offered is a statement of a witness with a strong motive to lie or under circumstances in which the accuracy of an observation is suspect (the baker in the rowboat might have interpreted "glug glug" to mean "sure, I consent to your terms"). To avoid the uncertainties of this kind of evidence, the law often prescribes formalities to which the parties must adhere to give their claims credence — for example, a written contract or a notarized signature. It cannot plausibly be maintained, then, that the state must accept the bakery shop owner's word that the drowning baker just happened to volunteer to submit to a lifetime of unhealthy peonage. So onerous a condition suggests the presence of coercion. The state might demand a notarized agreement, and since that is obviously impossible, the rescuer's claim may simply be disregarded.[65]

In the story so far, the baker's justification for treating his workers callously appears to be based on one of two possible lies: (1) that he had nothing to do with the victim's head being under water (one successful rescue attempt is believable, but dozens? especially when they all turn out to be working in his bakery?); and (2) that he and the baker actually discussed the terms of an employment contract while the victim was drowning. Neither is plausible and need not be the basis for sustaining his right to treat his workers miserably.

Another escape from the unscrupulous contract is to condition the remedy for breach on the likelihood that such a deal was actually made. Just as the bankruptcy laws are a remedial limitation on the right to collect on a debt, so the law here might say that the probability that the baker and his employee actually reached agreement in the water is so low that it will not enforce more than, say, three days' work against the rescued victim.

We are halfway to a general solution to covering working conditions under the harm principle. Having resolved the work situation in favor of the "wets," what can a liberal state offer the "drys"? In our scenario, working conditions had become so depressed that the only deal available for out-of-work bakers was to work alongside the drowning victims under unsafe and unhealthy conditions for too many hours a day. This time the new owner (one who has newly arrived in town and who wishes to do right by his employees) was involved in no prior exploitation. The owner did not recruit these bakers; they walked in off the street. He offered them a look at the sweatshop and said, "I wish I could do better but I cannot, so take it or leave it." They were free to walk out. Unlike the bakers pulled into rowboats, he was not going to enforce a contract made under some suspicious deal.

The down-and-out employee concedes that the employer did not force him to accept such a miserable job. But, he says, it was the only job for which he was qualified, and he had no more choice than that of the man whose head was going under water. Moreover, he points out, no one can deny that his health and vitality will deteriorate from working in the bakery. The owner may be honest enough to agree, but he will point out that for him to do what the employee asks will cause him in turn to suffer a setback to his interest in maintaining his business. He cannot overbid the market wage or his competitors will run him into the ground.

Nor can he improve working conditions because the extra expense will likewise price him out of the market. This deplorable situation is not the fault of either employers or employees. There are no alternatives if one wants to bake the bread and the other to sell it. They were brought to their present situation by *the market*. It just worked out that way. They are in a market trap, and they cannot escape it. This is the story that the early-twentieth-century Supreme Court told,[66] and it is what the owners now press on the governor in their plea that he not sign the reform bill.

But this case differs from that of the drowning men because here the harm occurs at the hands of other people, through the market, a human agency, and not through the impersonal eddies of the water in the marina. The bakers who accept employment because they must eat and feed their families are given unventilated, unhealthy kitchens in which to work not by an impersonal "social" or "historical" or "market" force but by human beings, the owners. The owners who claim that they do not wish to harm will argue that they have no choice.[67] And yet they do have a choice. They are free, in the fullest political sense of the word, not to mistreat their employees. In enacting health and safety laws and laws limiting the length of the workday, the state is simply recalibrating the market. A uniform safety requirement eliminates the sole reason that the employer can point to for refusing to improve conditions—the economic detriment should other employers not follow suit. The law commands all to abide by the new minimum. It is not so much, as is sometimes claimed, that laws regulating working conditions are redressing the imbalance of bargaining power[68] as it is that it is removing the employer's only justification for setting back the interests of the employees. Under the harm principle a setback to interest is a harm if no plausible justification for the action can be offered. When interests conflict, the justification is often that refraining from setting back someone's interest is to set back one's own interests. Laws governing injuries in the workplace eliminate the condition that sets back the employer's interests. The readjustment of the starting position does not interfere with liberty, only the terms of a bargain that continues to be set by the market. Employers may grumble but they will not pay: The market will see to that, since in general operating costs will be passed on to consumers. Although particular people directly cause the harm by providing an unsafe workplace, they do so (they say) because of market conditions, so it is the collective actions of all that led to the danger, and the collective method is to pay for it through the market. It is no more wrong to make the public pay to deter harm to workers who benefit them than it is to make the public pay for police who deter other harms. Harm prevention costs. It is the cost of a liberal society. Even Mill, who supposed that laissez-faire "should be the general practice," acknowledged, as early as 1848, contrary to the opinions of many other liberals, that there was no practical way that workers can protect themselves aside from legislation, so that laws limiting workers' hours are of necessity an exception to his principles and do not violate them.[69]

A Note on Market Socialism

One claimed answer to market-induced harms, though not a liberal one, is state socialism. It is clear that the historical regimes that abolished the market system and private ownership of the means of production were profoundly illiberal. The "dictatorship of the proletariat" was just that—a totalitarian power in the hands of party elites who had little concern for the proletariat in whose name they governed and who perpetrated massive crimes in the name of historical "inevitability." Central planning institutions and practices, it is now conceded, were failures, causing widespread misery in several countries over the better part of a century. The Communist "solution" to the harms of capitalism was a decidedly wrong turn. None of this is news and only the naive should express surprise that this political-economic system took the trajectory that it did and collapsed as it has in most of the nations in which it held sway. That it has not disappeared altogether may be attributable to the economic turn it has taken toward a market-based system, generally known as "market socialism." Is market socialism a plausible alternative to the liberal state's increasing reliance on regulation to curb market harms? Although the question sweeps largely beyond my purview, it may be worthwhile to reflect briefly on the claim that some structural changes in economic relations could alleviate a significant source of harm and to consider whether those changes are consistent with the harm principle.

An immediate difficulty is that there is no consensus on the meaning of "market socialism." Like liberalism, it has many variants, though all reject the notion of central planning at the national level.[70] One of its core ideas is to elevate workers from their position as wage laborers and to give them a share in the management of the enterprise for which they work. This is not a new idea. Mill pointed to the advantages of worker cooperatives in his 1848 *Principles of Political Economy*. In the same essay he "utterly dissent[ed]" from the socialists' "vehement . . . declamations against competition,"[71] so perhaps Mill was a proto–market socialist. For decades economists considered the idea of market socialism wholly theoretical, but in the early 1950s Yugoslavia began to experiment with a form of market (but not democratic) socialism, and some of the other European Communist nations toyed with introducing it. Those economic systems have vanished; today, China remains the most significant example of nondemocratic market socialism.[72]

One modern proposal for democratic market socialism, that of John Roemer, would put management of corporate enterprises in the hands of a board consisting of representatives of the firm's lending bank, its workers, and its stockholders. Each citizen at birth would be given a share of the nation's corporate stocks, but the shares, though tradable, could not be sold and would have to be returned to the state when the shareholder dies. All banks would be nationalized and lend to business enterprises from private savings on deposit. Although a private entrepreneur might start a business, it would be nationalized when it grew to a certain size. The government would prompt investment decisions by influencing interest rates. Each enterprise would remain free to compete in the market for sales of its goods and services, and prices would be set in the market, not by government. Another scheme, that of David Schweickart, would give workers the power of self-management; each worker would have a vote in electing the top managers. The enterprise would be taxed on its assets, and the resulting pool of funds would be sent back to communities on a per capita basis and invested in local enterprises according to their "projected profitability and employment creation."[73] These and other proposals aim to avoid what their proponents see as the basic sins of Communism—central planning and the absence of democratic government—and the basic evils of capitalism—depressed wages for workers and lack of worker control over their productive lives, vast inequalities between the capitalist and labor classes, and the "hypermobility of capital," which leads to "job insecurities, destruction of communities, and mass migrations."[74]

Putting aside whether these problems are harms in the liberal sense and whether, if they are, they can be dealt with directly by liberal democracies, the analyses of market socialism as the cure rely heavily on economic speculation and stint mightily on how the necessary institutional changes would play out. In Schweickart's model, for example, worker councils select and oversee management. But overseeing management requires sophisticated skills. Who will teach them to the workers? What prevents the usual petty factionalism, personal likes and interests, from taking hold? Can worker councils overrule management or only fire the managers? By what criteria? If the managers do not have tenure, then what protection do they have (or why would they want such a job if they are subject to political and psychological whims of the workers council)? What if the council is factionalized? The problem resembles, perhaps not surprisingly, the same difficulty as that of Nozick's theory of the protective association. It is taken to be an automaton that runs smoothly and correctly without human intervention, when of course it would be subject to all the vagaries of humans working together, subject to stresses, incentives, inducements, bribes, extortion, fatigue, free-rider instincts, and everything else that keeps corporate, nonprofit, and other institutions from running smoothly and according to the "rules." The idea of worker control is to give every employee a share of the profits, but an unregulated workers council could distort the pay differences in enterprises much as competitive labor conditions do in the capitalist economy. To prevent it, the state would need to sharply limit pay differentials. What else would it need to rein in?

In Schweickart's model, funds for new investment come from flat taxes on capital assets. Who sets the taxes? Will those taxes be the source of funds for government infrastructure like police departments, tax collectors, and all the rest? If so, how will taxes be allocated? If instead other taxing schemes, like an income tax, must be employed, why should we suppose that a system as complex as the Internal Revenue Service code would not emerge? Taxes are to be plowed back "to communities on a *per capita* basis."[75] Who determines what constitutes a community? Who sets the boundaries? What would prevent voters from electing politicians who would skew the tax rates to the advantage of some communities over others, as happens now?

Many of these issues, and the innumerable others that I am not competent to raise and discuss, turn on economic theory that may not have deep implications for the liberties of the citizenry. So, at least, it is claimed.[76] But one problem intimately affecting the interests of a wide swath of the public is that of the transition to market socialism. Though acknowledging that the "the likelihood of an abrupt transition from advanced capitalism" to his scheme for market socialism is "remote," Schweickart proposes that if somehow a socialist party came to power with popular support to impose a new economy, only four laws would be necessary. The first is dramatic: "Henceforth, all income entitlements based on property are null and void." Dividends, interest, and rental payments would cease. Private enterprises would be turned over to their workers. Banks would be nationalized. If this "transition" were to happen in the United States, and the Constitution remained intact, such a law would require compensation for the accumulated losses of tens of millions of people. Schweickart says, rather phlegmatically, that his few laws would require some "adjustments," including separate treatment for home mortgages, residential rentals, consumer loans, and pension and retirement benefits, in addition to "small stockholders and bondholders." So one thing is clear: This four-law transition would be a revolution indeed, and would cause massive harm as we understand the term in light of the harm principle.[77]

Whether democratic market socialism would truly be an enlightened and workable alternative to a capitalist economy is beyond the capacity of any theorist to say, though it seems prudent to doubt. It is equally impossible to see through the haze of abstract schemas to determine whether the resulting politics would or could remain faithful to the harm principle. Perhaps such a regime could do so, assuming that a rule against controlling a productive enterprise as owner or profiting from an innovation as far as the market will take you are not within the ambit of interests that the harm principle protects. However that may be, it seems highly unlikely that a new market-socialist order could arise without at the least seriously denting the liberalism I am defending in this book. It is just as unlikely that market socialism, as an economic system cohabiting with a constitutional political order, would solve any of the problems that robust competition throws up all too often as harms. Nothing in worker control of their businesses can guarantee outcomes different from those that are dealt with by regulatory and litigation systems in capitalism.

Welfare Harms

That leaves us with the capitalist market system. Unfortunately, that system can harm in ways that cannot be remedied as theoretically easily as a worker safety law or a prohibition on destruction of air rights. Sometimes the economy sinks into depression and millions lose their jobs; sometimes inflation wipes out the retired prudent investor living on an annuity that once seemed sufficient. The question is whether these and other sorts of suffering too are harms that the state may redress, not by demanding that certain people in a particular relationship with others do something to lessen the pain but by taxing us all to provide the unfortunate with benefits they would not otherwise have. This subject is sufficiently distinct to deserve separate discussion in the next chapter.

5

Taxation, Welfare, and Benefits

The Problem of Charity

Preventing and redressing harm is important, noble, and consuming work, but human beings have many other needs (and varying talents for satisfying them): food, shelter, health, education, work, companionship, art, play, worship, relief from disasters, care in old age. Will all these needs be supplied by institutions other than the state? The question is important because if the state may do no more than eradicate harm in the sense so far defined under the harm principle, then furnishing benefits that might satisfy these needs cannot be the work of government.

Many seventeenth- and eighteenth-century theorists—including Hobbes, Locke, Hume, Smith, and Kant—explicitly advocated welfare policies, though their reasons were rooted in different traditions.[1] The most general argument was the reciprocity required by the social contract: People give up their sovereignty for security and having done so cannot be left to starve to death. Though he limited a right to charity to those incapacitated by accident, Hobbes declared that the sovereign had a moral responsibility to assist those who could no longer work:

> Whereas many men, by accident unevitable, become unable to maintain themselves by their labour; they ought not to be left to the Charity of private persons; but to be provided for, (as farforth as the necessities of Nature require), by the Lawes of the Common-wealth. For as it is Uncharitablenesse in any man, to neglect the impotent; so it is in the Soveraign of a Common-wealth, to expose them to the hazard of such uncertain Charity.[2]

Locke more broadly burdened the right of ownership with the proviso that there be "enough and as good left in common for others"; when that proviso failed, "every man [has] a Title to so much of another's Plenty, as will keep him from extream want, where he has no means to subsist otherwise."[3] Smith, too, defended redistribution; his was grounded in the contribution of all to the social weal. Justice requires "that they who feed, clothe, and lodge the whole body of the people, should have such a share of the produce of their own labour as to be themselves tolerably well fed, clothed and lodged."[4]

But toward the end of the eighteenth century, other powerful voices dissented. The conservative Edmund Burke was broadly hostile to the idea that the state should help a poor working man subsist: "[T]he impossibility of the subsistence of a man, who carries his labour to a market, is totally beside the question.... The only question is, what is it worth to the buyer?" The government may not help to relieve poverty, Burke said, because doing so would interfere with "the laws of commerce, which are the laws of nature and consequently the laws of God."[5] By the nineteenth century, libertarian liberals such as Herbert Spencer had adopted Burke's outlook and upped the ante. Not only do the poor laws interfere with the workings of commerce, but they also injure the wealthy by substituting for the natural human faculty of sympathy, and in so doing they "diminish the demands made upon [that faculty], limit its exercise, check its development, and therefore retard the process of adaptation" to a higher civilization.[6] This sense that the government's sole responsibility is to preserve people's rights against harm, and not to provide benefits, began to harden into policy about the time Spencer was writing. It was perhaps most brutally manifested by the British government in the 1840s during the Irish potato famine when the new prime minister, Lord John Russell, withdrew much of the relief efforts and adopted policies that exacerbated the suffering, leading to death by starvation and disease of more than a million people. But these harsh conclusions and results led other theorists, less dogmatic and more charitable, to become acutely uncomfortable at the corner into which they supposed their principles painted them.[7]

Thomas Paine, liberal champion of the "rights of man" and a proponent of minimal government, said in 1776 on the very first page of *Common Sense* that society

> is produced by our wants, and government by our wickedness; the former promotes our happiness *positively* by uniting our affections, the latter *negatively* by restraining our vices. The one encourages intercourse, the other creates distinctions. The first is a patron, the last a punisher. Society in every state is a blessing, but government even in its best state is but a necessary evil.[8]

Yet responding to Burke in 1791–1792 in *The Rights of Man*, Paine was concerned to ensure that the state would provide for the needs of a broad range of people, including children, the poor, and the elderly, and not merely for subsistence but also for a variety of purposes, including, especially, education.[9] One historian says that Paine's writings

> may be the first appearance of that contradiction between an antiinterventionist theory and an increasingly interventionist practice....

Paine stands at the very point where the divide between radical democrats and the more cautious and conservative liberals begins. He helps to create the radical democratic tradition, but retains in his thinking much of bourgeois liberalism, which associated taxation with tyranny, and freedom with free trade.[10]

Mill, also, had two moods: in one, a libertarian (laissez-faire, he said, "should be the general practice: every departure from it, unless required by some great good, is a certain evil"); in the other, a more generous liberalism, he held that one of the great goods was state provision of sustenance to the needy. This was a fair trade for the obedience of citizens down on their luck. If someone is jailed for stealing, then the state provides his subsistence. "Not to do the same for the poor who have not offended is to give a premium on crime."[11]

Beginning early in the twentieth century, the New Liberals such as L. T. Hobhouse sought a way out of the bind in which they believed the rigid libertarians had been caught, suggesting that a destitute man was a cornered man who was not free and needed to be liberated in some fashion by the state itself. This argument retains its force even today. Donald Moon says that "[t]he standard argument for welfare rights begins with the observation that, without access to certain basic resources, it is impossible to exercise the powers of agency." A slightly different line of reasoning became in due time an argument, in the hands of R. H. Tawney, for a state-mandated equality, a socialist liberalism. In its modern form, says Will Kymlicka, the egalitarian argument is essentially that "[i]t is unjust if people are disadvantaged by inequalities in their circumstances." Recent liberal theorists such as Rawls and Ronald Dworkin press redistribution according to powerful but complex and different ideas about foundational rights and moral desert. Still others have put the onus for the suffering of the poor on the government's failure to manage the economy. Since the state has a monopoly on force and authority over every other institution, one argument runs, "therefore the state is ethically responsible for the operations of the entire economic system," meaning, principally, that the state is obliged to redress its failures measured by the poverty of some.[12]

To all this, some modern libertarian liberals adhere to a stern, uncompromising, even austere position. Robert Nozick bluntly asserted that "redistribution is a serious matter indeed, involving, as it does, the violation of people's rights."[13] But others, troubled by the outcome of theoretical purity, have offered a safety net, even if it is otherwise incompatible with their theories. Thus, Hayek consistently maintained the necessity of providing "a certain minimum income for everyone, or a sort of floor below which nobody need fall even when he is unable to provide for himself."[14] Charles Fried held that "[a] person has a claim on his fellows to a standard package of basic or essential goods—housing, education, health care, food: i.e., the social (or decent) minimum—if by reasonable efforts he cannot earn enough to procure this minimum for himself."[15] Loren E. Lomasky proposed that in cases of "extreme exigency," everyone has a claim to the residual surplus of others' property (beyond their need).[16]

Are we simply stuck with a political theory that seems to point us one way and a desire to alleviate human suffering that points us somewhere else? If we allow an exception to our theory here, what other holes must we be prepared to poke into it, until all content has rushed out? Since taxation and redistribution of tax revenues in modern democratic states have become major activities, the question is whether the democracies are no longer liberal or whether their intentions, if not all the practices they employ, can be explained under the harm principle.

Positive and Negative Rights

The harm principle justifies money taken from me to compensate one whose interests I have wrongfully set back. But what can justify taxation, money taken from me to be used by someone else? We began with the proposition that the state may interfere with me solely to prevent me from harming another. In the conventional phrase, the right not to be harmed is a "negative right." A negative right is simply your right against my interfering with you. A positive right, in contrast, is your right to have my assistance—or, put in the form of corresponding duties, my (negative) duty to refrain from interfering with you and my (positive) duty to do something for you, to assist you in some way.[17] Negative rights appear tidy, coherent, expressible in a principle; positive rights do not. Every negative right has the same fixed end: Thou shalt not. A positive right—Thou must—appears to have no logical stopping point, only infinite gradations. That you may not eject me from my home is certain and simple; that I must provide you with shelter could imply anything, including an obligation to sell my own home to afford the means to build yours and to keep repairing it because you do not know how.[18]

What makes a negative right especially attractive to the moral philosopher is that it can always be stated categorically. As Fried puts it: "Rights are categorical moral entities such that violation of a right is always wrong."[19] One can always refrain from violating a negative right, but no one, individually or collectively, can guarantee positive rights. This inability has been called the scarcity problem. It is not merely a practical difficulty; it inheres in the nature of the distinction between positive and negative rights: "The relevant duties corresponding to negative rights are duties of abstaining from actions of interference, and as such, because they imply *not* doing certain things, do not suffer from a scarcity limitation."[20] Or as Fried says:

> A positive right is a claim to something—a share of a material good or to some particular good like the attention of a lawyer or a doctor, or perhaps to a result like health or enlightenment. . . . Positive rights are always asserted to scarce goods and consequently scarcity implies a limit to the

claim. Negative rights, however, the rights not to be interfered with in forbidden ways, do not appear to have such natural, such inevitable limitations. If I am let alone, the commodity I obtain does not appear of its nature to be a scarce or limited one. How can we run out of not harming each other, not lying to each other, leaving each other alone?[21]

Claims to negative rights, on this view, do not violate our individual autonomy, because a negative right is that which recognizes our autonomy, whereas claims to positive rights necessarily infringe someone else's autonomy, since they will always compel us to give up something and to work for others, against our will if necessary. "It is logically possible to respect any number of negative rights without necessarily landing in an impossible and contradictory situation" produced by scarcity.[22] That is, the duty to refrain from interfering with a person however defined by the correlative right is not impeded or thwarted by the existence of several people with the same rights or by the existence of several different negative rights. Logically I can refrain from killing X, Y, and Z and also from robbing each of them. But it is not reasonable to suppose that I can satisfy a positive right to aid X, Y, and Z in the different ways that they need assistance, especially since A, B, and C might also have such rights, and I have only so many assets and so much time. The quantitative dimensions to negative rights and positive rights thus appear quite different. We need not pause over "how much" I am entitled not to be robbed of: I am entitled to be robbed of nothing, universally. We very much must pause over the question of "how much" shelter or food a positive-rights theory will allow us. Hence "negative rights can be claimed by all rights holders simultaneously just because they are not claimed against a background of scarcity. They are categorical in a way that positive rights are not."[23]

But what good is a negative right? It is not enough to suppose we are protected if people would just refrain from harming us (or, in the language of rights, if potential attackers are saddled with duties to refrain from doing so). A society in which we had only negative rights, as a statement to others about what they must forbear from doing, would be workable only if it were a society of saints. We want not merely a statement painted on a sign and held up for all to see, but a claim for protection when the right on the sign is violated. "To have a right," Mill said, "is, I conceive, to have something which society ought to defend me in the possession of."[24] A negative right, in other words, is a claim of *justification* for the state's acting. "To have a right is to have a justification for societal protection—not merely a request for potential violators to pay attention to. It is to have a justification to demand (and get) protection from society against potential and actual violators."[25] That justification is, of course, the harm principle.

For this reason, it is conventional to speak of a negative right as a double claim—against all others to refrain from harming me and against the state to protect me.[26] But the claims are different. The claim to noninterference from all others is a claim that justifies my calling on the state to enforce. But there is no corresponding claim-right against the state itself. The claim against the state for protection is a demand that the state may justifiably meet, not a right that it must meet. Otherwise we would be involved in a paradox, and philosophers, not legislators, would make the laws. For if we had a *right* to government protection, then we would have a right that somebody do something *for us*, not merely that somebody refrain from doing something *to us*, and it is only this latter kind of right that we are prepared to accept. If we have some right to compel the government to do something for us, then we could demand that courts order the government to act in any instance in which it is alleged a negative right has been violated. It would no longer be the legislature but philosopher-judges to whom would be vouchsafed the obligation to define the scope of the right to be enforced. The only way out of this paradox is to accept the inherent limitation of our premise. If the only categorical right is negative, then the state is justified in enforcing the harm principle against a rights violator, but it is not required do so. Or, to put it another way, the state does not harm us should it fail to entertain a legal claim for a harm that it would be justified in recognizing under the harm principle, as long as it impartially declines to entertain the claim by all who assert it. The claim for protection is not so much a claim of right as a demand for aid.[27] What this rather abstract consideration leads to is this: Every action of a liberal government established to give meaning to the harm principle is the application of a *positive* right, not a negative one.

Two consequences follow. First, the state necessarily may demand from citizens the means to pay for the discharge of its justified responsibilities under the harm principle. In other words, it is a legitimate function of the state to tax.[28] Second, as noted, positive rights are subject to the limits of scarcity. Protecting our right not to be harmed is costly, and it will be the state's difficult job of determining just how much protection the people can afford. Protection is a need, like food and shelter. And just as a needs-based positive right has no definable end point (how much food or shelter?), so the degree of protection that the state will offer cannot be assigned by any principle or agency outside the state.

If the state, then, is justified in taxing us to carry out its protection function, which we now understand to be a positive right, why may it not tax us to provide other positive rights? A quick answer is that the positive right to protection is a right to the enforcement of a negative right—enforcement, that is, of a demand that a wrongdoer respect a person's categorical right not to be interfered with in particular ways. By contrast, the proponent of other positive rights wants a claim on resources to satisfy a need based in something other than a categorical duty to refrain from acting. In other words, the state may tax me to provide itself with the means to stop me from robbing my neighbor, because I am duty-bound not to do so, but it may not tax me, the argument runs, to provide my neighbor with housing, because the neighbor's "right" to housing corresponds to no duty of mine. So, it seems, liberalism, strictly construed, cannot allow the state to provide benefits even to those who need them.

But the problem of positive rights is not so easily avoided. Those who would deny positive rights encounter a telling difficulty when we observe that the standard account generally presupposes a present world of human beings entitled to equal concern, but who do not necessarily possess equal resources. How they came to occupy this world is never stated. And yet any realistic account of rights must consider not only the present moment but all the past ones. If you see two people fighting on the street your impulse may be to pull them apart to stop the altercation. But merely from witnessing the fight you cannot logically determine culpability for the fight: Necessarily you must inquire into what started it (perhaps one of them was merely defending himself against a wholly unprovoked attack). With this problem in mind, and with the understanding that taxation as such is a necessary function of the liberal state, I turn to the task of defending welfare benefits under the harm principle.

Welfare Benefits

Suppose a man, call him Job, who has retired on a disability and is unable to work, is robbed of all his possessions by an archfiend, call him Moriarty, a clever computer hacker. Moriarty drains Job's bank accounts, hires an arsonist to burn down his house, and dials "M" for a contract killer to murder his wife and family. Moriarty, the arsonist, and the killer are all extremely careful, are unknown to Job, and leave no evidence the police can use to track them down. To make matters worse (and to show that Job was no irrational or ignorant slacker), Job's insurance company has gone bankrupt. So there stands Job, returned from his family's funeral, staring at the lump of ashes that was once his home, destitute and without prospect of earning a living. Suppose further that the local private homeless shelters and soup kitchens are overcrowded and can offer him no room. Are we to leave Job on the corner begging? Do we demand that a neighbor take him in and, failing that, order the neighbor to do so? Or may the state itself give Job a handout? To get at the problem I turn to Nozick's entitlement theory to see whether the minimalist state can accommodate people's misfortunes (or some of them, at any rate).

Nozick distinguishes three kinds of property distributions: distributions based on "end results" (or "end states"), "historical" principles, and "patterns."[29] An end-result theory asserts some criterion by which the social product ought to be apportioned, regardless of how any particular array of wealth in society came to be held at any particular time. Under an end-result principle, the social product would be subject to constant redistribution because the just distribution under this criterion decays over time. One example of such a distribution is equality. Another is embodied in utilitarianism: the greatest happiness for the greatest number. In a society of ten people, where one is productive (creating wealth and becoming rich) and the others (who could work if they chose to) are idle and unhappy, an equality distribution requires that we take nine-tenths of the rich person's wealth and donate it in one-tenth lots to the others. In a utilitarian distribution, the rich person's assets would be given to the poor only to the degree that the increase in happiness of the nine offsets the decrease in the unhappiness of the one whose property is seized (and perhaps only to the degree that it will not interfere with his continuing production of wealth). Under a patterned distribution, a distribution is just if it accords with some "natural dimension" or attribute; for example, moral merit, intelligence, or usefulness to society. By contrast, a historical theory of just distribution of the social product inquires how property came into a person's possession. Nozick's own theory—the entitlement theory—is historical. It declares that "a distribution is just if everyone is entitled to the holdings they possess under the distribution."[30]

Nozick rejects end-state and patterned theories because they require a person's property to be seized for another's benefit, implying that those who are beneficiaries of the redistribution are in effect partial owners of those whose property is confiscated. Such an ownership right contradicts the original absolute-rights hypothesis that people are individuals whose rights are limited to protecting themselves against the depredations of others. No one in this hypothesis can have an ownership right in someone else.

Even if we rejected this hypothesis and accepted an end-result or patterned distribution as just, it would be difficult, Nozick suggests, to avoid falling back on an entitlement theory. Consider, he says, the case of basketball star Wilt Chamberlain. Assume any distribution of wealth in society you consider just.

> Now suppose that Wilt Chamberlain is greatly in demand by basketball teams, being a great gate attraction. . . . He signs the following sort of contract with a team: In each home game, twenty-five cents from the price of each ticket of admission goes to him. . . . The season starts, and people cheerfully attend his team's games; they buy their tickets, each time dropping a separate twenty-five cents of their admission price into a special box with Chamberlain's name on it. They are excited about seeing him play; it is worth the total admission price to them. Let us suppose that in one season one million persons attend his home games, and Wilt Chamberlain winds up with $250,000, a much larger sum than the average income and larger even than anyone else has. Is he entitled to this income?

If the first distribution was just, Nozick asks, on what ground can the reshuffling of the community's wealth be unjust? "If the people were entitled to dispose of the resources to which they are entitled (under the original distribution), didn't this include their being entitled to give it to, or exchange it with, Wilt Chamberlain?"[31] Nozick assumes that they do have this right and concludes that liberty thus upsets patterns and that the entitlement theory is thus impossible to avoid, if we wish to respect the claims of liberty.

Two rejoinders, one weak and one strong, are possible. The weak rejoinder says that Nozick has proved nothing; rather, he has made visible a usually hidden tautology. For it does not follow that a person is entitled under an assumed end-result distribution, say, to dispose of his property as he sees fit. If we reject the entitlement theory initially in favor of another distribution, as Nozick expressly invites us to do, why import the entitlement theory under the guise of the liberty of the individual? A nonentitlement theory of distribution, in other words, need not carry with it the freedom of the individual to contribute to a deviation from the ideal distribution. Indeed, it cannot carry such freedom, or we will necessarily be stuck with the very paradox Nozick presents us in the Wilt Chamberlain story.

This is a weak rejoinder because it does not destroy the force of the argument, even if the argument is tautological rather than deduced. Nozick chooses to equate a premise of individual rights and self-fulfillment with the liberty to dispose of property as we each see fit, and this seems more than intuitively plausible. It is the heart of the liberal premise. How have I harmed anyone by giving Wilt Chamberlain twenty-five cents? How has he harmed anyone by keeping the money?

The strong rejoinder is that even if we accept the entitlement theory, it does not necessarily lead where Nozick would have it go. The force of this rejoinder can be appreciated only by inspecting the entitlement theory more closely. For a holding (that is, possession or ownership of property) to be just, it must have been legitimately acquired. If the property was originally unowned by anyone, then the person who lays claim to it must have acquired it according to the "principle of justice in acquisition." If the property was already owned, then it can legitimately come into another's possession only through the "principle of justice in transfer." The entitlement theory says that "no one is entitled to a holding except by (repeated) applications of these two principles."[32]

"If the world were wholly just," says Nozick, then by following these two principles we would have to conclude that the grossest disparities in holdings would be entirely legitimate.[33] But the world is not wholly just. People do steal; they do commit fraud. Consequently, says Nozick, there is need for a third principle, "rectification."

Here we encounter a startling admission: Nozick forthrightly declares that he has not (cannot?) set down concretely any of the three constituent principles of the entitlement theory. He does not (cannot?) give substance to the three rules. We thus have no statement of how to recognize when property was acquired legitimately, whether it was transferred legitimately, or how to rectify the situation if it was not. The entitlement theory, in other words, is operationally infirm. It cannot be applied to the real (historical) world.[34]

But let us not give up so easily. For the sake of argument, suppose that the principle of justice in acquisition is simply that anyone may rightfully acquire that which has never before been owned or which has been abandoned, and that the principle of justice in transfer is that anyone who acquires from a rightful owner is a rightful transferee, if the owner (with or without payment) knowingly consented to the transfer.[35] These two principles create two problems. How can we determine whether someone was a rightful owner? How can we determine whether the owner knowingly consented to the transfer? Together these two problems will lead to the indeterminacy of entitlement and to a social uncertainty principle.

Fanciful invisible-hand theories to the contrary notwithstanding, it is inescapable that the distribution of possessions did not arise through repeated applications of the principles of justice in acquisition and transfer. Usurpations, conquest, chicanery, fraud, theft, and other wrongful dispossessions are commonplace in every time and every place.[36] In the absence of written records, how could someone prove beyond the lifetime of those living that he was the legitimate possessor of land against which a claim of misappropriation was being asserted? Are the wealthy living today descendants of those who wrongfully threw peasants out of the commons? Of slave holders? Of merchants who conspired against competitors, suppliers, customers? Of gangsters who robbed their way to riches? Of corporate insiders and stock manipulators who cheated their way to the top?[37] The fundamental objection to a pure theory of entitlement is thus the indeterminacy of entitlement. In the real world we do not know, and we can never know, who originally had legitimate possession and whether transferees took through lawful transfer. The effects of past crimes are beyond tracing.

That we cannot untangle the depredations of the past does not mean that we must leave them unrectified. To the contrary, under an entitlement theory we must rectify violations of the principles of justice in acquisition and transfer. On that much Nozick is clear. What might a principle of rectification be? We could, perhaps, enact a statute of limitations. For example, (1) after January 1, 2015, no one may sue to recover what was rightly his; or (2) no one may sue to recover his property one year after the date of enactment; or (3) no one may sue to recover any property of which he claims to have been unjustly deprived more than four years earlier than the date of the suit. But this is weaseling. A statute of limitations blinks at injustice. Such a statute may be a practical necessity but it is not a moral virtue to refuse redress in the face of actual injustice. A principle of rectification should do more.

Looking forward, rectification might couple a moratorium on examining past holdings with a rigorous inspection of future transfers. But any attempt to determine for the future who is entitled to a particular property would run up against a social uncertainty principle. For the elaborate bureaucracy necessary to examine motives, intent, reliance, value, knowledge, and accidents (all of which contribute to the acquisition and alienation of property) would defeat the possibility of many, if not most, activities. Such a bureaucracy would be asked to trace and value each element of property through every possible transfer. It could do so with certainty only if the very act of transfer were halted and then allowed to proceed at the snail's pace of bureaucracy. Long before anything like this could happen, human interaction on any social scale would have ceased. Alexis de Tocqueville provides an entertaining proof of this difficulty in his report of eighteenth-century French administration in the pre-Revolutionary period:

> Long before the Revolution, Ministers of State had made a point of keeping a watchful eye on everything that was happening in the country and of issuing orders from Paris on every conceivable subject.... Towards the close of the eighteenth century it was impossible to arrange for poor-relief work in the humblest village of a province hundreds of miles from the capital without the Controller-General's insisting on having his say about the exact sum to be expended, the site of the workhouse, and the way it was to be managed.... Owing to this system of centralizing information and controlling everything from Paris, a most elaborate machinery had to be set up for coping with the flood of documents that poured in from all sides, and even so the delays of the administration were notorious. On studying the records I found that it took a year at least for a parish to get permission to repair a church steeple or the priest's house. Oftener than not the time required was much longer: two or three years. The Council itself took notice of this regrettable state of affairs in one of its minutes (March 29, 1773). "The transaction of public business is delayed to an almost incredible extent by administrative formalities and the public has all too often just cause for complaint. Nevertheless," the writer makes haste to add, "all these formalities are indispensable."[38]

Moreover, the cost of maintaining such social machinery would take so much away from the property it sought to safeguard that the bureaucracy would have forfeited its purpose at the outset. This uncertainty principle of property (or, more broadly, of justice) says that we cannot observe both the absolute protection of property and an absolute right to its free use. If we try to fix private property too closely, noting its location in the social universe, we will prevent it from moving, from being used and transferred. And if we allow it, and therefore ourselves, freedom of action, we will be unable to pin down its location in the principles of acquisition and transfer. Inevitably, therefore, usurpations will follow. Even in theory, then, it is impossible to assure "pure justice in rectification" in all cases. And if it is impossible even in theory—because the only conceivable mechanisms will interfere with the goal—then the only remaining way to rectify these injustices in the real world is by some sort of approximation, even if that approximation is both too narrow and too broad.

Since we cannot pinpoint how someone has been deprived of property because last year, a generation ago, ten generations ago, or thousands of years ago someone wrongfully took what belonged to his ancestors (and since we are equally unable to prove that his entire genealogy would have handed the property on to him had they but possessed it), we might suppose that the rectification principle is empty, that there can be no means by which the state may legitimately and broadly rectify wrongs of the past that cannot be explicitly proven under rules of evidence that tie the wrongdoer to the victim. Such a conclusion is as dismal as it is unwarranted. We can escape it by recalling that the state has legitimate authority not only to determine what constitutes a wrongful taking but also to determine the means that it will employ to redress the injury. Restoring to the dispossessed rights that were extinguished by slavery, by legally mandated discrimination, by enclosure acts, by the systematic exploitation of factory hands, by the unequal enforcement of the laws, by bribes that siphoned off public property to powerful corporations and individuals through the offices of the state itself, by all the arts of chicanery practiced through history, requires at the very least some sort of compensation. Many people suffering from harms committed against them who cannot prove their specific claims in court might reasonably be thought to be entitled to redress simply by lacking possessions, being down and out, being at the bottom of the heap, being desperate.

A means of providing for these people commonly goes by the name *welfare*.

As usually conceived, welfare is a principle of distributive justice—a redistribution of the social product to those who need or merit it for some reason other than that they were wrongly deprived of it. I am proposing that we consider welfare, at least in part, as a principle of *compensatory* justice—recompense to those who were harmed. To provide this kind of welfare will require, for reasons of efficiency and administrative convenience (to avoid the indeterminacy of entitlement and the social uncertainty principle that led us to this pass), some sort of patterning or end-result criterion. Because we cannot say definitively that Mr. X was wronged we must look to some other criterion for judging the entitlement to compensation. Obvious criteria are assets, income, and prospects for employment—living below the poverty line or being jobless will entitle the luckless to some sort of welfare or other assistance drawn from the taxes that the rest of society must pay. Such assistance is not a patterned or end-result redistribution in a Nozickian sense. Nozick concedes as much, in a passage mostly overlooked. In a short conclusion to his discussion of the entitlement theory, he notes that "an important question for each society will be the following: given *its* particular history, what operable rule of thumb best approximates the results of a detailed application in that society of the principle of rectification." Nozick expressly states that without knowing the rules of rectification or the need for them, the theory he sketches *cannot* (his emphasis) use the entitlement theory "to condemn any particular scheme of transfer payments," although introducing "socialism as the punishment for our sins would be to go too far."[39] Thus the principle of rectification may require some set of policies close to those actually practiced in the social democracies, however these policies are currently justified.

Let me be clear on what this sort of rectification redistribution principle holds. Under a state-mandated criterion (perhaps a version of Rawls's notion of the least advantaged, such as relative poverty), people are entitled to tax-financed payments to compensate for the deprivation they may have suffered as a result of unjust transfers in the past. No doubt this principle is both too narrow and too broad. For example, penurious people from other countries may wish to emigrate to a welfare state to receive payments that they would not be entitled to, even on the rectification principle, because neither they nor their ancestors were members of the society and hence depredations that justify welfare payments cannot be justified for them. On Nozickian principles, the proper means of reducing claims from this class of recipient is better control of the borders.[40] Other sorts of people who arguably should not be included in the class of welfare recipients are those who squandered money their family passed on to them and those whose families squandered the money (but not because of fraud). Those who arguably should be included are people who, although relatively comfortable, would have had even more wealth but for crimes committed against their ancestors long ago. The answer in all these cases is simply that the practicalities of administration require a system in which these issues need not be determined.[41]

The indeterminacy of entitlement and the social uncertainty principle not only justify welfare benefits of some sort but make clear why a welfare system must be a continuing policy. Harm prevention is neither easy nor foolproof. Lots of crimes and other harms will slip through the state's harm-preventing and harm-redressing machinery, so that there will be no end to cheating, fraud, and other harms that will require social redress through welfare systems.[42]

Let us return to Job on the street corner where we left him. He is, we have assumed, the victim of actual harms wrongfully inflicted on him. Yet the state is powerless to provide him with redress against the evildoers. That is because Moriarty's cleverness would have cost the state too much to take defensive steps. If everyone's every move were monitored (perhaps we could all wear GPS tracking devices), it would be easy to see that Moriarty was the culprit, and he could be dealt with in the ordinary way. The cost of administering this scheme, however, would be prohibitive, certainly for the benefits to be gained, and we have other important reasons for rejecting such monitoring. But it seems unfair to say that the state may decide to spend tax dollars to go after one type of crook and leave others alone, to provide the means of redress to those suffering some harms and to leave others unrequited. That it seems unfair does not mean that the state can be forced to redress all harms. Scarcity remains, and no amount of theorizing will wish it away. But neither is it inherently improper for the state to settle on a cheaper means of providing redress for those situations in which traditional prosecution and civil suits would be prohibitively expensive or unlikely to succeed. In recognizing the limitations of the social uncertainty principle the state may legitimately expend its resources more efficiently, as long as the spending redresses harms cognizable under the harm principle. The state may, if it chooses, provide Job unemployment and welfare assistance.

This conclusion is generalizable. Many public expenditures that today are derided as illegitimate transfers of property are what might be called "pseudo-welfare" payments. During the hotly debated federal crime bill in 1994, one provision was repeatedly attacked: public funds for inner-city night basketball games. The idea was that by providing youths with an activity they would enjoy, they could be enticed off the streets and inveigled out of gangs that prey on the public.[43] Such a program is surely no mere handout if the cost in crime, police, prosecutors, court systems, and jail would be far higher. Those confounded by pseudo-welfare payments have confused the choice of remedy with the justification for providing one (chapter 7).

Suppose Job was not beset by evil Moriarty. Perhaps he is a diligent worker who loses his job when his employer "downsized" because of a sudden downturn in the economy. While it is rarely feasible to single out the perpetrators of a souring business cycle, transfers such as unemployment assistance serve as props to sustain the market. If enough people are suddenly thrown out of work, the decline in purchasing power could force the entire system into recession or worse, to the great misery of all. Thus unemployment benefits and the like are means of preventing an accumulative harm from building beyond the danger point.[44] Providing assistance to the unemployed may also be seen as pseudo-welfare, in the sense that it prevents outbreaks of crime by those desperate to feed themselves and their families. But any redistributive scheme could be justified by the assumption that but for it people would riot at a cost higher than that of the program. It seems sensible to avoid a justification for transfer payments that amounts to a conclusion that it is always just to buy off people who threaten us with disorder.[45]

That the state may tax to provide public assistance is the answer to two rhetorical flourishes often aimed at undermining the legitimacy of welfare. One is that providing welfare to the indigent or others in need is akin to enslaving the taxpayer. In speaking of the income tax, Nozick declares that it "is on a par with forced labor."[46] He adds that if

> people force you to do certain work or unrewarded work for a certain period of time, they decide what you are and what purposes your work is to secure apart from your decisions. This process whereby they take this decision from you makes them a part owner of you. Just as having such partial control and power of decision, by right, over an animal or an inanimate object would be to have a property right in it.[47]

These remarks are more provocative than cogent. Though it may be small consolation to the grumbling taxpayer, welfare payments do not force anyone to work or to take any particular job. The state must tax, and Nozick does not deny it.[48] He may have relished stoking the antitax cause by branding us all slaves for paying it, but it seems better to use the proper word—"citizen." A second flourish is that providing public assistance directly burdens the rest of us. A libertarian might argue that

> it is too much of a burden for me to drop my gardening every time some positive action would set someone else up in gardening. If I spend too

much time and energy helping others (on this model such actions are seen merely as helping others, not as part of duty fulfillment), then my own talents and projects suffer. There are likely to be many such interruptions, so no one is ever left in peace to garden.[49]

This argument, too, is tendentious. The state does not draft people individually to become gardening instructors. We help others in distress collectively by establishing public institutions that provide relief, undertake education and retraining, and the like. Taxation for welfare benefits does not interrupt our gardening, even if it arguably provides us less time to put our hands in the soil.

If welfare distributions as recompense for harm are consistent with other remedies warranted by the harm principle, natural disasters as the reason for public assistance seem more troublesome. The range of calamities to which we are prone is wide—hurricanes, tornadoes, floods, earthquakes, fire, disease, genetic defects—and the extent of the damage inflicted and the pain suffered can, of course, be colossal. But these disasters are, at first glance, instances of misfortune. Under the harm principle, only harms people cause each other, not bad luck, may be redressed. Yet a closer look, as always, suggests that it is misleading to rely on a word or a phrase to explain an underlying reality. At least six justifications for various forms of governmental disaster planning and relief present themselves.

First, public assistance is often and understandably spent on disaster relief—measures designed to forestall worse injuries than might be suffered or have already been suffered from the primary disaster. Measures may be taken after the fact or even during the event. To forestall the chaos of unregulated evacuations and dampen the spread of disease in the wake of a flood or storm, public agencies may establish relief centers, temporary housing, cleanup efforts, overtime pay for police and fire fighters, and other measures to alleviate the consequences of mass disruptions. The natural event may not have resulted from human agency, but human activity, sometimes intentional, more often the consequence of the dislocation, always contributes to the turmoil that surrounds it, and may thus be the object of government intervention.

Second, not every class of "natural" disaster *is* attributable entirely to nature. Did the dam break because God's storm was particularly violent or because it was poorly engineered?[50] In almost any conceivable disaster in our interdependent world, we can detect some human involvement—that is the consequence of the transformation from natural to human systems. Lightning can cause fires all on its own, but many fires have human origins, and we establish fire departments to deal with the whole range of fires and their consequences. It would be neither efficient nor effective to require fire departments to assess before putting fires out whether people contributed to the cause or spread of the fire. Likewise, even if the causative agent of a disease is natural (perhaps a mutation of a previously harmless pathogen), most epidemics are driven either by direct human contact or by patterns of living (sewage conditions, farming practices, animal and pest control) that require government coordination and oversight to contain. Private actors (sellers of tainted foods, for example) might hesitate to take precautions or stop the harm in a timely fashion, prepared to risk that a contagion will die out on its own or seek to contain their own liability in lawsuits filed long after the fact.

Third, given the costs of on-the-scene relief and of restoring the living patterns of the uprooted community (including, not incidentally, welfare benefits for child care, food, and drugs), it is financially sound to anticipate and plan for such events. So research into the causes of storms, floods, earthquakes, fires, and other natural disasters and public agencies that forecast them may considerably lessen the brunt of damage before it occurs. People who know what to expect can undertake to safeguard themselves, their families, and their homes from what might have been a worse catastrophe. Likewise, public funding of research to cure and prevent disease seems equally obvious: If we can expend public resources to fight the disease on the ground, we ought to be able to support research that one day might avoid the trouble altogether. Much research is mixed, in the sense that it is intended to ferret out not merely biological causes but also the sorts of human activities that contribute to diseases.

Fourth, the consequences of natural disasters are frequently abetted by human failures, sometimes intentional, usually negligent or inadvertent, but nonetheless harmful. Only 20 percent of the damage from the San Francisco earthquake of 1906 was the direct result of the earthquake itself; four-fifths of the destruction has been attributed to the secondary effects of fires that were caused and spread because of poor engineering. Modern-day flooding in many locations is traceable not merely to an overeager atmosphere but crucially to farming and other human activities that have destroyed wetlands, "nature's antidote to floods," and to bridge and highway construction that in interfering with tidal waters bottled up downpours that might have been swept out to sea.[51]

Fifth, the aftermath is often misrepresented: People are told (by private developers and government agencies) that it is safe to relocate to the very earthquake zones, floodplains, and storm centers that flattened their homes and caused them to flee. They come to believe through a variety of misrepresentations and omissions that the new buildings and levees are safe.[52]

Sixth, even misfortunes that seem wholly natural and to which it is difficult to attribute wrongful human causation may still have partial remedies housed in the harm principle. Consider one of the most intractable of such misfortunes: genetic defects that leave human beings disabled or handicapped. While not every instance of such ill fortune is attributable solely to nature,[53] some surely are, and people are handicapped in addition by accidents and other misadventures not socially caused. What justifies enactments that, for example, demand builders and developers spend their money to accommodate people whom they could not possibly be accused of having harmed? It sounds callous to say that people are free to stay at home without the sights and services that make life worth living, but no society can accommodate to the characteristics of every individual. Nevertheless, standard building codes aim at reducing and eliminating potential harms by conforming buildings and other constructed environments to the reasonably foreseeable hazards that attend the average characteristics of human beings. For example, a code might mandate so many stairways for a given number of occupants and limit each step to a height determined on average to be safe. A building code for the handicapped amounts to an assessment of what is reasonably safe for a wider pool of human beings likely to use buildings and public spaces. So, for example, because people who must climb stairs in wheelchairs are bound to have accidents, codes will require elevators or other devices to transport them.

None of the foregoing is meant to suggest that particular remedial activities of government, short- or long-term, are effective and positive. No one who watched the rapid unfolding of misery in the wake of Hurricane Katrina in 2005 can suppose that our actual government is a benign presence rather than often a bungling mischief-maker. One of the tragedies of that catastrophe is how frequently the same agencies have been prone to the same incompetence, intellectual errors, and political malfeasance. But not all government programs suffer from the defects of emergency management systems, and in any event, the answer to bad government is not no government, but better government.[54]

Projects

In *The Wealth of Nations*, Adam Smith called for government to engage in projects to enhance national commerce, among other things.[55] Mill agreed. In *On Liberty* Mill said that a person may be compelled to perform "many positive acts for the benefit of others," including "his fair share in the common defence, or in any other joint work necessary to the interest of the society of which he enjoys the protection."[56] In *Principles of Political Economy* Mill was quite specific about how far-reaching these powers might be:

> There is a multitude of cases in which governments, with general approbation, assume powers and execute functions for which no reason can be assigned except the simple one, that they conduce to general convenience. We may take as an example, the function (which is a monopoly too) of coining money. This is assumed for no more recondite purpose than that of saving to individuals the trouble, delay, and expense of weighing and assaying. No one, however, even of those most jealous of state interference, has objected to this as an improper exercise of the powers of government. Prescribing a set of standard weights and measures is another interest. Paving, lighting, and cleansing the streets

and thoroughfares, is another. . . . Making or improving harbours, building lighthouses, making surveys in order to have accurate maps and charts, raising dykes to keep the sea out, and embankments to keep rivers in, are cases in point. . . . The admitted functions of government embrace a much wider field than can easily be included within the ring-fence of any restrictive definition, and that it is hardly possible to find any ground of justification common to them all, except the comprehensive one of general expediency.[57]

Today, these and many other functions are classed as public goods. As generally understood, public goods are beneficial undertakings that the government must fund because a market system cannot exclude from their benefits those who will not pay for them. A classic example is military security. If you and your friends agree to pay for it, I will benefit too, even though I do not contribute to the cost. Since everyone could be a free rider to the same extent, no one has an incentive to pay for a public good.

Public goods, as Mill suggests, are not restricted to a narrow category of beneficial undertakings. The scope given to government to carry out these projects thus seems to contradict the main tenor of *On Liberty*, in which Mill asserts that the sole reason the state may interfere with our liberty is to prevent harm to others. Writing in 1873, shortly before Mill's death, James Fitzjames Stephen argued that taxation for subsidies to various public projects (such as symphony orchestras and scientific research) is impermissible on Mill's principles:

> None of these can in the common use of language be described as cases of self-protection or of the prevention of harm to persons other than those coerced. Each is a case of coercion, for the sake of what the persons who exercise coercive power regard as the attainment of a good object, and each is accordingly condemned . . . by Mr. Mill's principle. Indeed, as he states it, the principle would . . . condemn, for instance, all taxation to which the taxed party did not consent, unless the money produced by it was laid out either upon military or upon police purposes or in the administration of justice; for these purposes only can be described as self-protective. To force an unwilling person to contribute to the support of the British Museum is as distinct a violation of Mr. Mill's principle as religious persecution. He does not, however, notice or insist on this point, and I shall say no more of it than that it proves that his principle requires further limitations than he has thought it necessary to express.[58]

Feinberg agrees with Stephen's assessment, explaining the state's engagement in projects of this sort as simply what will inevitably emerge from a legislature and justifying that result on the legitimacy of the democratic legislature:

Individual tax-supported programs win their moral legitimacy (though in specific instances they may not be ideally wise, fair, or useful), and are in that sense justified (legitimized), by virtue of being the end product of a legitimate procedure, a complex institutional practice without which, in turn, everyone would be a net loser. That is the sort of justification for legally compelling people to pay for particular programs, like the British Museum, which they do not want, and from which they may not benefit. Citizens pay their money and take their chances, knowing that they will not win all the time, but also that they may be protected from harm to some of their own vulnerable ulterior interests which are not widely shared.[59]

In essence, Feinberg is arguing that democratic procedures may be sufficient to legitimate state actions not otherwise justifiable under the harm principle. In the civil arena, in other words (at least according to Feinberg), the harm principle is not the whole show.[60] A separate principle of democratic regularity may provide an independent ground for legislation.[61]

The difficulty with this kind of justification is that, unanchored to the harm principle or for that matter to *any* principle, there appears to be no limit on the type of project on which the state might embark. By this logic, may the state establish a church, or at least contribute to the construction of major cathedrals? If so, have we not abandoned the fundamental principle with which we began? The answer, I think, is that many of the ordinary public goods that governments around the world provide can, with little stretching, be shown as permissible, if not necessary, implications of the harm principle. I do not pretend to a comprehensive demonstration of this point, but even the cursory remarks that follow indicate the directions in which one who desired to build the point should go.

In general, many projects of government that appear to provide benefits rather than deter harm can be subsumed under the harm principle nevertheless in one or more of four categories: (1) self-provisioning; (2) rule making; (3) preventing incipient harms; and (4) duty to rescue.

Self-Provisioning

In most discussions about liberty, the existence of the state is inferred or deduced but only as an abstract entity. Theory does not delineate the merely contingent. That we must have a legislative power says nothing about the place where that legislative power may be exercised or the kind of building in which the representatives are entitled to legislate. That theory does not spell out the details does not mean that we can dispense with details *in theory*. Details must look to policy, finance, architecture, geography, and even the character and dispositions of the population for their provenance. Government must function. Implementing the harm principle requires a government in being: a police force, a judicial system, public prosecutors, courtrooms, and a near (or seeming!) infinity of other parts. The police need uniforms. Why? Perhaps they can perform their duties sufficiently by wearing ordinary clothing, which they can be expected to provide themselves. Perhaps, but a philosophy of political legitimacy has no basis to assert so. Whether uniforms will make for more effective, safer policing is an empirical question that can be determined only by the experience of a government in place. If the government determines that uniforms are necessary, their purchase and use can scarcely be condemned as inconsistent with the harm principle. On this principle, that the government may provision itself and furnish what is necessary to proper functioning, rest many of the projects that various commentators have ascribed to mere convenience. If we imagined a government being built from scratch, its citizens would conclude, among other things, that their government could not function without roads (how else could officials travel between branches or citizens find their way to the seat of government?) and without a postal service or some other means of communication; that the Navy could not very well guard the nation without lighthouses to guard its ships; and that the whole could not function without a stable money supply enforced by a central monopoly on the definition of legal tender. So much, and much more, is implied by the fundamental need to provision the government.[62]

Rule Making

Mill puzzles rhetorically over the state's accepted function of declaring rules, wondering "under which of these heads, the repression of force or of fraud, are we to place the operation, for example of the laws of inheritance?" He muses similarly over other sorts of laws, primarily laws defining property generally and the law of contracts:

> Non-performance does not necessarily imply fraud; the person who entered into the contract may have sincerely intended to fulfill it; and the term, fraud, which can scarcely admit of being extended even to the case of voluntary breach of contract when no deception was practiced, is certainly not applicable when the omission to perform is a case of negligence.[63]

But we have already found the key to this supposed dilemma. Without ground rules, society must always be, if not in a state of war, at least in a state of perpetual doubt. Who is the rightful owner of the intestate's belongings? How far does the domain of one's property extend—if I plant a flag on the moon, do I own the whole moon? If I own the whole moon, must you desist from flying around it? From gazing at it? If the state were called upon to answer these questions every time they were raised, in an ad hoc proceeding, the expense and the uncertainties would be intolerable, and much wrongful self-help would in the meantime have ensued. The state's dispute-resolving function is not supererogatory but ensues directly from the harm principle, for in any dispute over property or contract, the disputants will claim a wrongful setback to their interests. To forestall the endless bickering that a regime without any sort of rules would engender and the injustice that would follow from inconsistent judgments, the state will define the extent of these rights and the procedural rules by which such claims can be proved. For the same reason, establishing a common money supply and a standard of weights and measures obviates claims of fraud and other disputes that would arise in their absence.

It is no more difficult to comprehend contract law under this same principle. The question that might be raised is this: Grant the basic proposition that in a society dedicated to self-fulfillment people may carry out joint plans to which they consent, why should an undertaking be enforced when one of the parties no longer consents? The answer is that the defeat of expectations is a classic setback to interest. From this starting point, the remainder of contract law, substantively and procedurally, can be justified, though I make no effort to do so here. Among its provisions a general contract law will contain evidentiary rules and presumptions about the validity of claimed consent.[64] To prevent disputes over claims of entitlement that could otherwise be settled only by force, the state will legitimately engage in the foundational task of prescribing rules to which all must repair in determining which of conflicting claims must be upheld and which, I think more importantly, will materially lessen the probability that people will act toward each other in ways that will prompt the claims.[65]

Preventing Incipient Harms

In a sense, it is fair to say that provisioning and rule making are but methods of preventing incipient harms. But here I mean the term in a narrower sense: The state may establish and fund certain positive programs to minimize particular harms that one person or set of persons will inflict on others. A simple example is garbage collection. Of course it is true that people could agree among themselves to remove noisome and disease-ridden garbage to safe disposal sites, and private companies engaged in that task obviously do exist. But that a task may be privately carried out does not defeat the state's authority to do likewise if the activity falls within the harm principle. If I burn garbage in heaps on the corner or throw it through my window and let it splatter on the street I am probably harming (certainly I am potentially harming) many people. The state will be warranted in prescribing rules for garbage disposal, despite a contrary agreement between neighbors; and the governing authority may judge that in the absence of any effective means of eliminating the hazard it must take on the task itself. If boats are in the habit of colliding because it is too dark for the lookouts to see clearly, the state will inescapably develop rules for determining the degree of culpability between two vessels that have struck each other. It may also prescribe affirmative duties, for example, requiring boats to carry lights, and it seems difficult to understand why, if these alternatives are available, it may not also construct a lighthouse.

Sometimes the incipient harm is more subtle or indirect. Consider public funding for dams, used to control flooding, produce energy, aid navigation, and provide irrigation for crops. How is a dam a response to harm? It seems to be quintessentially a public good. But the need for dams is prompted in large part by expanding population and increasing population density that require more efficient means of transporting water, and more of it, for agriculture. Without technologies that can provide water, the chances increase that people will feud over the available water and the means of obtaining it. The utility of the dam does not diminish its importance in avoiding long-term suffering that might be caused not only by the lack of water but also by the violence that would attend the difficulty of putting it to use.

On a smaller scale, even such public goods as municipal boosterism may be explained in part as a response to potential harm. I have in mind the myriad activities—from municipal parades to beautification projects to marketing campaigns to scare up tourists—that villages, towns, regions, and even states undertake every day. These public expenditures are usually explained as ways of benefiting business, as they certainly are. But what often underlies them (no doubt, not always: municipal graft and corruption play their part too) is the desire to maintain tax revenues to support essential government functions. Daily headlines make us painfully aware of the difficult choices that must be made when municipal budgets are cut and public services, starved for funds, are reduced or eliminated.

Duty to Rescue

Imagine a tiny frontier town being built from the wood of surrounding forests. Fire is the deadly enemy. The founding families organize themselves into a fire brigade whenever anyone is threatened, for the risk to one is risk to all. A fire brigade resister (the economist's free rider) cannot be fined because there is no government, just families building their homes in the wilderness. But the shirker would likely be shamed or shunned until he relented or left town. Such a society would act on a moral obligation to aid those in distress, whether or not prompted by a rational calculation of each person's self-interest. But as the town grew, and neighbors became no longer family or friends, but just those who happened to live next door, the moral bonds, we might suppose, would loosen. In that town, the gradually emerging government might impose upon each "able-bodied" person the obligation to shoulder fire-fighting duties. Eventually, as the town became wealthier, it would assign that obligation to a publicly funded fire department. Whether this unfolding of the community's response to fire is grounded in the harm principle depends on whether it can be shown that there is an underlying duty to rescue. If so, there can be no principled objection to public funding of injury- and damage-prevention institutions, such as fire departments, ambulance services, and hospitals.

It might seem odd to doubt a duty to rescue. Surely an army and a police force are paradigmatic examples of rescue institutions: funded by taxes to prevent one person or community from preying on another. But there is an essential distinction. Police enforce a person's duty not to harm—they uphold the negative right not to be harmed. The fire-fighting function, by contrast, might be viewed as providing a benefit—to prevent destruction not caused by another.[66] No negative right has been violated, unless a duty to act is itself mandatory. But an obligation to act implies a positive right to a benefit, and the difficulty with positive rights is that there is no persuasive stopping point.

Feinberg, as we saw in chapter 4, argues for a limited duty to rescue, under circumstances in which the rescuer faces no danger to himself or outlay of funds. The usual case is the passerby's obligation to lift a drowning baby out of a pool of water; in general, this duty is confined to those circumstances in which it is easy to pull the victim out of harm's way. But Feinberg was pursuing the limits of criminal law—penalizing the passerby for failing to perform the easy rescue should be sharply distinguished from sanctioning someone for failing to "adopt a child" by sending a check for famine relief abroad or for dodging the opportunity to spend a few hours working in a soup kitchen here at home.[67] It may be that the reasons to oppose a more extensive duty to rescue vanish (or are likely to make us far less apprehensive) when the rescue is to be effected by socializing the duty and funding the operation from the public treasury. Feinberg urges that the very reason we need not impose a legal obligation directly on someone to come to another's aid is that we have already socialized the responsibility, and we have done that because it would be very difficult to know how to allocate the blame were we not to do so:

> Part of the reason why I don't have a duty to maximize the harm-preventing I can achieve on my own is that society collectively has preempted that duty and reassigned it in fair shares to private individuals [i.e., those paid to discharge the duty, such as fire departments]. *Collectively* there *is* hardly any limit to how far we are prepared to go to prevent serious harms to individuals.[68]

That may be a sound policy, but it takes supplemental arguments to show that it follows from the harm principle.[69] A child falls into a well. Whether the child's predicament is a harm depends on why the well is where it is, and what accounts for the child's wandering into it. The law of attractive nuisance is designed to ascribe responsibility in just such situations, and although I do not attempt to develop the idea here, it is plausible that many of the common hazards the overcoming of which we today routinely assign to public functionaries are risks wrongfully put in place by others. Such a rationale, suitably extended (an increasing proportion of injuries that afflict us today come from complex human systems that extend the capacity to injure to every corner of the world), might justify many public expenditures to reduce human suffering, for example, public funding of cancer research. Cancer, it might be assumed, is an accumulative harm: the consequence of metastasizing technologies.[70] Another reason for assigning rescue duties to government is that we rightly doubt the capacities or motivations of potential casual individual rescuers, especially since we cannot easily assign particular rescue duties by law. We will want to rely on a rescue team to try to pull the child from the well, since we could not depend on a neighbor to assist the parents and fear that they may cause more damage in the attempt. In any event, the duty to rescue, socialized as it is in municipal agencies, presents only slight impediments to liberty, for ultimately it reduces to a duty to pay taxes; we are obliged to do no more. The modern state poses more direct infringements on liberty in affirmative obligations to carry out particular assignments. This problem, the duty to act, is the subject of the next chapter.

But before addressing it, one public project remains to be considered. It is not simply one among many projects. It is, most people will readily agree, the one indispensable project: ensuring the development and well-being of the next generation.[71]

Education and Families

Nowhere does the difficulty of consigning the pursuit of the good to the private realm and the administration of the harm principle to the state come into sharper focus than in the problem of the state's relation to the family and the rearing of children. Liberalism is a theory of what is here now, of people as they actually are, and of the societies in which they live. So the liberal has a significant problem when the issue is *what sort of person shall a new human being become?* What things should this person value? How can this person be brought to moral awareness to value those things? And who should decide?

That parents have the right to nurture their children according to their conception of the good is, I will assume, a fundamental aspect of personal liberty. Still, raising children is not a hobby like stamp collecting, in which you are free to neglect stamps from Peru and fasten instead on those from Belgium. Raising children is the quintessentially other-regarding activity. You may not say that, preferring the older to the younger child, the boy to the girl, the handsome to the ugly, or the smart to the dumb one, you may therefore ignore the disfavored. Many of the quandaries of the harm principle, when applied to adults, disappear when the issue is protection of children. For example, providing welfare to destitute adults, while justifiable, as we have just seen, depends on assumptions about tracing harms to unknown and usually unknowable agents. In the case of children who are destitute, the agent is always identifiable: the parents.

Parents obviously cannot secure consent from children to be born,[72] but bearing children obligates parents to care for them, and the state may intervene if they are harmed. So much is clear in easy cases such as physical abuse and abandonment.[73]

Perhaps the most important consequence of this conclusion is the state's role in education. If a parent beats a child senseless, no one doubts the state may intervene to save the child's life. Can anyone suppose it less a harm for a parent to make a child senseless, literally, by starving the child of an education? No argument against paternalism can defeat the state's interest in seeing to the education of each generation—seeing to the welfare of children is what paternalism is for. The child without an education is a stunted adult. The child cannot be heard to say: "Trust me, I won't need an education when I grow up." Neither should the parent. The liberal rationale for compulsory education is that "it leaves all of a child's occupational alternatives open so that the matured informed student can later select his future path himself."[74] There simply is no way around the involvement of others in the raising of children. Overseeing that involvement is, next to security, perhaps the most significant project the state can undertake.

Though this conclusion is unexceptionable today, it has only fairly recently been accepted as universally applicable. In cultures in which children can learn from their families all that is needed for self-sufficiency, formal schooling has not seemed vital. The Enlightenment's fathers, who valued learning and knowledge, saw no use in educating the masses. Confounding his own theories about the nature of the human mind, Locke granted education only for the sons of gentlemen because the bulk of mankind is governed by superstition. In *Emile*, Rousseau said that "the poor have no need of education." Kant held that the *Volk* "consists of idiots." For many years, even Voltaire denounced the project of educating the people: "We have never pretended to enlighten the shoemakers and servants; that is the job of the apostles." Voltaire, at least, later changed his mind, but many who followed, and well into the nineteenth century, hewed to this basic contempt for everyman and to this basic misunderstanding of education itself. Spencer was dead-set against state-funded schools.[75] In 1859 Mill ironically observed that no one denies "that it is one of the most sacred duties of the parents . . . after summoning a human being into the world, to give to that being an education. . . . But while this is unanimously declared to be the father's duty, scarcely anybody, in this country, will bear to hear of obliging him to perform it."[76] Those who saw children as fully formed or as parental property, rather than as beings becoming human, could not see that depriving children of an education is to harm them.

The question today is not whether education, but what kind. Broadly understood, education is more than book learning. Educated adults will have acquired not only testable skills, like reading, writing, and arithmetic, as important as those skills are, but also character—appropriate dispositions, social skills, habits, preferences, tastes, beliefs, sentiments, and other virtues—that permit them to lead lives that are not designed and ordered by the state. Virtues are not innate. All may agree that character formation is essential, but what sort? The state may legitimately mediate (and ultimately resolve) disputes that arise over the clash of personal interests, but wouldn't it be cheaper in the long run to mandate and provide for the character that would reliably maintain order without invoking the state's heavy hand?[77]

Among the virtues requisite for a well-ordered society are sympathy for others, cooperation, restraint and courage in the face of provocation, dispositions both to obey and question the law, and the ability to think through means and ends—what once was, and in some quarters still is, known as a moral sense. But the moral sense can develop through a myriad of beliefs and stories; no one in a pluralistic society need be told about the variable content that is imparted by different cultural norms, religious beliefs, ethnic customs, and communal traditions. It is just here, in the very creation of human spirit, taste, intellect, and feeling, that the liberal can run aground.[78]

Human beings need instruction in the good; a failure to equip one's children to pursue some version or tradition of or ambition for the good is surely a very great harm. But followed carelessly such a line of reasoning would allow antiliberals to commandeer the state over the long run by choosing a particular good in which to instruct, or it would permit liberals to abandon liberalism, like a snake swallowing its tail, by insisting that only those educated to be psychological liberals are unharmed—or even worse, to yield to a dystopian *Brave New World* future of genetically induced workers with predetermined interests who have no motive or desire to resist the illiberal society that their efforts support. The liberal disposition tolerates differences. It celebrates the ability and welcomes the opportunity to reflect on one's own beliefs about one's life goals and one's sense of the good. But precisely because liberalism eschews official versions of the good, those very differences, which the liberal insists must be tolerated, mean that many other people will disagree, often vehemently. So-called perfectionist views—that there is a particular correct good that must be pursued—impel adherents of various religious and non-scientific cultural outlooks to reject at least some and perhaps many of the subjects taught in public schools.

During the 1980s, parents in Tennessee and Alabama asked the courts to direct public schools to excuse their children from reading secular texts in several courses because the very exposure to these readings, they insisted, conflicted with the parents' religious beliefs. In the Tennessee case, parents objected to teaching their children to exercise critical judgment or choice "in areas where the Bible provides the answer." One mother asserted that mere exposure to readings about evolution and feminism violated her religious beliefs and that exposure to other philosophies and religious ideas should be permitted only if the schools professed that these ideas were fallacious. In the Alabama case, parents opposed a home economics textbook that they said taught that moral choices should ultimately be made by students rather than determined by the parents' religious doctrines. Federal appeals courts rejected the parents' First Amendment challenges, holding that the texts neither required religious practices nor promoted or endorsed religion. School boards must have authority, said the court in the Alabama case, to teach the values of "independent thought, tolerance of diverse views, self-respect, maturity, self-reliance and logical decision-making."[79]

The courts' rulings suggest, unsurprisingly, the impossibility of settling these issues on grounds that both sides would accept as neutral. As one commentator wrote about the Tennessee case, the plaintiffs

> viewed seemingly neutral exposure to varying beliefs as a mechanism for undermining religious absolutes in favor of personal opinion. Mere exposure to other viewpoints itself implies that beliefs are simply subjective opinions. . . . In my view, the core issue raised by [the Tennessee case] is whether the diversity protected by liberalism extends to the right to hold one's beliefs in a particular manner. The [Tennessee] parents feared not only that their children might reject their own values, but also that even if they remain attached to these, they would view them as merely subjective, or as contestable matters of opinion. Their beliefs and worldview would represent just one possible life narrative among others, rather than one that transcends all others. From a fundamentalist standpoint, then, consciousness of alternatives is a harm which, once introduced, can never be mended.[80]

A partial answer to the parents may be that, whether or not the children are exposed to the idea in school (unless they are kept in a closed community apart from others), it is difficult to conceive of anyone living in a pluralist society who will not sooner or later come to see that many people view a fundamentalist belief as "just one possible life narrative among others." It is also unclear how to separate "critical thinking" from any sort of education, whether or not the subject is values as such. Parents may wish their children excused from "values" thinking to avoid learning about the view that religious beliefs can be challenged by critical thinking. But most of the rest of education is also about such things as thinking, evidence, relevance, even if not so labeled, and we may surmise that these ways of approaching the world will eventually seep into the child's views on those ideas that matter the most.

There seem to be two choices. One is to permit parents to keep their children in a community closed off as much as possible from the wider society. The Supreme Court once endorsed something like this approach in permitting the Old Order Amish in Wisconsin to withdraw their children on religious grounds from public schools at age fourteen, rather than at sixteen, as state law required. In reaching this surprising decision, the Court relied in no small part on the relatively closed, "highly successful social unit" of the Amish religious community that permitted the children, despite the lack of additional schooling, to enter a secure adulthood in the life of the community. This resolution assumes that the point of education is to provide value, as determined by parents, for the child, not for the larger society.[81] In many, if not most such instances, however, parents seek to shield their children from intellectual influences but not to withdraw from the general society or political communities in which they live. Indeed, even the Old Order Amish are not wholly separate from the state where they reside, nor could they be—indeed, to obtain their goal they necessarily went to the public courts of the state (and relied on public education through the eighth grade).

The other choice is to recognize the independent value of education to the democratic community in which all, including the Old Order Amish, live. Without the state itself, committed to the central role of the harm principle, parents could not for long maintain their freedom to shape their children's moral and intellectual development, including the possibility of withdrawing into separate enclaves. Like anything of value, the liberal state that makes these freedoms possible comes at a cost. Working out the political norms and laws that support a free society in which people may seek after their different conceptions of the good requires a participating citizenry. The harm principle is neither neutral toward itself, nor self-defining. Striking an appropriate balance between freedom and harm requires political attention to the issues of the day. No one can wholly withdraw from a contemporary nation-state. We can all be expected, as citizens, to abide by the law, pay our taxes, and answer the state's call to the extent the state is warranted in summoning us. But the content of the law, the amount of our taxes, and the extent of the call are ultimately of our making.

To guard against a fatal inattention to the requirements of political order, citizens must have certain knowledge and abilities, which the state would be utterly remiss in failing to inculcate in each generation. It is not simply for each individual's private benefit, but to make possible social cooperation, that the state undertakes to teach its principles to its citizens. Chief among what must be taught is ability to reason, to sift and weigh evidence, to comprehend the nature of a pluralistic culture, to understand one's history and the mechanics of the civil order, and to appreciate the nature of obligations and freedom. If that raises in a child's mind, ultimately to be fortified by what the adult discovers, the idea that there are other claims than their parents' about moral worth and truth, that is the cost of living in a state in which parents may shape their children to follow their faith. It remains open to parents to contradict the teachings of the schools, should they choose to guide their children on a different path. Parents may always educate to benefit their children as persons. But the right to do so cannot override the state's simultaneous entitlement to teach the political knowledge and skills necessary for living in the society that the state supports and defends.[82]

By its nature, the liberal conception of education, that neither the family nor the state can have exclusive jurisdiction in how children are educated, leaves many conflicts open to continuing debate. In teaching about rights, the state may need to concern itself not only with what families are teaching about the good but how they model themselves for their children. As Kymlicka poses the question: "[W]hat ensures that children are learning about equality rather than despotism, or reciprocity rather than exploitation?"[83] Among the Tennessee parents' various objections to the public school curriculum was its teaching about the role of women in the family and in society. The schools may teach a nonbiblical view that adapts to changing social norms about sex equality, but fundamentalist families (and many others) may persist in subordinating women in traditional roles. Learned early enough, children of either sex may not absorb the schools' later teaching. May the state intervene? The issue is highly contested, and even liberals predisposed to seeking an end to all discrimination draw back against government interference in the constitutive relations of the family.[84]

Some place the family in a domain sharply distinct from the mundane concerns of politics. Michael Sandel has proposed that forcing families to consider lesser issues of justice will only reduce the bonds of love and benevolence, which, he says, are the appropriate guides to relations within the family realm.[85] In response, Susan Moller Okin has pointedly inquired why we should "suppose that harmonious affection, indeed deep and long-lasting love, cannot co-exist with ongoing standards of justice?"[86] In the relationship between the family as the creator and nurturer of values and the values of the outside world that affect the means and ends toward which the family works, cause and effect run in both directions simultaneously. Barred from high-paying jobs and interesting work, women lower their expectations of finding employment and become more likely to accept unremunerative work in the home. That lesson reinforces itself on both boys and girls, who from their earliest years absorb the model of the complex division of work and responsibility between men and women. "The way we divide the labor and responsibilities in our personal lives seems to be one of those things that people should be free to work out for themselves, but because of its vast repercussions it belongs clearly within the scope of things that must be governed by principles of justice," Okin insists.[87]

It is difficult for a legal system to oversee the fulfillment of obligations within the family, especially one that has been created in a liberal order that cedes to mothers and fathers and husbands and wives the attitudes and beliefs they will inculcate in their children. But the liberal state can play a significant role in reforming the background that contributes to family relationships. It can insist on equal pay for equal work. If parents separate or divorce, it can insist on properly valuing the marital assets (understanding that the husband's earning potential is not his but theirs) and also properly valuing the contribution that wives have made through the work that women do within the family in the raising of children and the daily routines of the household. More, it can insist that husbands and fathers pay their obligations, and construct and fund machinery to ensure that they do. In taking on these tasks, the state does not breach its obligation to permit individuals to seek their ends. Perhaps a woman may commit to serving her new husband in all his endeavors, but obligations to the children are not fulfilled simply by whatever relationship between themselves a husband and wife claim to be following. They have independent obligations to children to see that they are nurtured, educated, clothed, housed, and fed. They ought not—or at least the state need not let them—insist that children are at the mercy of their daily whims or even their long-term plan to maltreat them.

Finding the appropriate line between parents' rights to transmit their values to their children and the state's interest in ensuring that children are respected and properly raised within the moral, cultural, and economic norms of the family is not easy—it is perhaps the most difficult of all tasks that the state engages in. To remain faithful to its principles, the liberal state must educate its citizens to consider that regardless of the parents' personal views and relations within the family, there remains an independent civic ground to reassess those relations, and people's powers and capacities, in the public realm. Throughout much of history, the state has failed to ask probing questions about family relations. It may seem but should not be a paradox that the liberal state is empowered to do just that.

6

The Duty to Act

Toward the Fiduciary Ethic

Proximity and the Duty to Act

Historically, liberal states have located in two general circumstances the authority to order a person to act—when he has agreed to do so; and when he has a special relationship with another, who will be harmed unless the first person acts. The apparent extension of an affirmative obligation to act can largely be accounted for by a progressively more generous interpretation of what people have agreed to do and what constitutes a special relationship. Of the rules of "just conduct," Hayek said

> that practically all . . . are negative in the sense that they normally impose no positive duties on anyone, unless he has incurred such duties by his own actions. . . . [This feature of negativity] applies to most rules of conduct but not without exception. Some parts of family law impose duties which do not result from a deliberate action (such as duties of children toward parents) but from a position in which the individual has been placed by circumstances beyond his control. And there are a few other rather exceptional instances in which a person is deemed by the rules of just conduct to have been placed by circumstances in a particular close community with some other persons and in consequence to incur a specific duty towards them. It is significant that the English common law appears to know only one such case, namely the case of assistance on the high seas. Modern legislation tends to go further and in some countries has imposed positive duties of action to preserve life where this is in the power of a particular person. It may be that in the future there will be further developments in this direction; but they will probably remain limited because of the great difficulty of specifying by a general rule on whom such a duty rests.[1]

Hayek might have added that even when people have obliged themselves to perform a particular service for others, modern American constitutional law, at least, views their agreements with strong misgivings. A person who promises to work for another may always renege or quit, since employment contracts are one-sided: The employee may demand his salary be paid if he is let go, but the employer may not force a worker to continue who wishes to resign. To hold the worker to his agreement would amount to involuntary servitude. That is a thoroughly liberal interpretation of the Thirteenth Amendment.[2] Yet the Supreme Court has consistently denied that the antislavery provision applies to coerced military service and even to conscripted labor for road maintenance, forms of positive acts that Hayek unaccountably missed and never discussed.[3] Although forced highway labor has been abandoned, the law does compel those without excuse to serve on juries, sometimes for onerous lengths of time and even at personal risk (when a particularly unsavory defendant might threaten to retaliate). And the state in times of crisis calls on young men (and in some nations young women) to risk their very lives in defense of the homeland. On what grounds can these affirmative acts be justified?

From one perspective, jury duty and military service are viewed as obligations of citizenship. As Mill said, a person has a duty to "bear his fair share in the common defence, or in any other joint work necessary to the interest of the society of which he enjoys the protection."[4] But for all that they are nonetheless interferences with liberty for the sake of others with whom the juror or the soldier cannot be said to have a special relationship. On just such grounds one could be impressed into a road gang to build a highway, deputized in a posse to catch cattle rustlers, or ordered to dam a riverbank to prevent a flood. These are not duties to refrain, and they therefore appear to be exceptions to the harm principle.

A possible answer is to analogize these directives to participate in certain activities to the state's power of eminent domain. In every country, the state retains power to seize land to put to public use as long as (at least in the United States) it pays for what it has taken. One could argue, therefore, that since a person's labor is property, as long as the state pays the juror and the soldier the state is entitled to the service. The argument is unpersuasive, in part because the very idea of eminent domain is illiberal. It is a holdover from earlier ages and its basis in the harm principle is rarely plausible, since the state is usually demanding the property for positive purposes and not to prevent any harm that the land is causing.[5] Moreover, the very vice of positive duties is evident in such an argument, since *any* demand for service could be made on these grounds.

From another perspective, the obligation to serve on the jury seems distinct from the obligation to answer the draft call, which may be a special form of the duty to rescue. Unlike other forms of impressment, which are intended to serve particular positive needs or interests of people in the community, jury duty is the obligation to serve a unique need of the state itself. As an institution, the jury serves the harm principle derivatively by permitting the community to pass judgment on those accused of committing harms.[6] In this sense, the jury is unique, and its uniqueness lies in representing the community. To assemble a representative selection, the state must summon individual citizens. There simply is no other way to constitute a jury. To make jury service entirely voluntary would be to run up against the free-rider problem: Many whom one would want to serve on juries would simply opt out.[7]

Military service is something else again.[8] Feinberg suggests that under certain circumstances, which he calls the "garrison threshold," a person might not be entitled to withdraw from defense of the community. He imagines a "beleaguered garrison of settlers under attack from warlike Indians." In the midst of a fierce battle, in which the loss of even a single man might be enough to "tip the balance," John Wayne suddenly announces that he is "bored and depressed" and intends to kill himself. There is "no distinction in these circumstances ... between not helping and positively harming."[9] If a nation is at war and young men do not respond to the lure of a soldier's pay and military adventure, great harm may befall the people. But still the harm is extrinsic: It comes in the first instance from the enemy, not from the young men who decline to be inducted. They are in somewhat the position of the bank president whose employees are held at gunpoint and who is told that if he does not open the vault, the ensuing massacre of the employees by the gunmen will be his fault. The solution to the problem, if there is one, must be sought in the underlying notion of the duty to rescue.

The principal objection to a duty to rescue, that is, to a duty to act affirmatively rather than negatively, is, as we have seen, that there is no obvious stopping point. The celebrated example is that of Lord Thomas Macaulay, writing in 1837 on revisions to the Indian penal code. Here is Lord Macaulay's dilemma:

> A omits to tell Z that a river is swollen so high that Z cannot safely attempt to ford it, and by this omission voluntarily causes Z's death. This is murder if A is a person stationed by authority to warn travellers from attempting to ford the river. It is murder if A is a guide who had contracted to conduct Z. It is not murder if A is a person on whom Z *has no other claim than that of humanity.*
>
> It is true that none but a very depraved man would suffer another to be drowned when he might prevent it by a word. But if we punish such a man where are we to stop? How much exertion are we to require? Is a person to be a murderer if he does not go fifty yards through the sun of Bengal at noon in May in order to caution a traveller against a swollen river? Is he to be a murderer if he does not go a hundred yards?—if he does not go a mile?—if he does not go ten? What is the precise amount of trouble and inconvenience which he is to endure? The distinction between the guide who is bound to conduct the traveller as safely as he can, and a mere stranger, is a clear distinction. But the distinction

between a stranger who will not give a halloo to save a man's life, and a stranger who will not run a mile to save a man's life, is very far from being equally clear.[10]

To say that we cannot promulgate a rule because of a line-drawing problem is to err in favor of one class of people over another. Macaulay sees two classes about whom we are concerned: (a) those who may die as the result of others' failing to come to their rescue, and (b) those who may be penalized for failing to act when they had no obligation to do so. Macaulay's solution is to sacrifice group A to group B, but he offers no reasons for the choice. If it is the drowning man (group A) whom we must sacrifice, the rationale must be that the injury he is about to suffer is due to natural causes, whereas the potential rescuer (group B) can suffer an injury only if we impose a duty on him, which by our initial premise we are not allowed to do. The drowning man ran into bad luck; it should not be shifted to the potential rescuer. But I do not see exactly why: Is it not equally the bad luck of the potential rescuer that he happened along when he did? If one of them must suffer bad luck, it seems more prudent to let it rest on the rescuer, who after all must merely try to save the drowning man, than on the man who then will surely drown. Any lingering objection must relate to the difficulty of drawing the line rather than the lack of a special relationship between the two. For the claim on the man with knowledge is not, at the point it would do the drowner any good, merely that of humanity, as Macaulay insisted; it is, rather, the claim on a man who is in a position to help—in short, the claim of proximity. If, with a simple "halloo," I can save a man, I am no longer one in the mass of humanity, no longer a stranger.

That logic cannot draw a line does not mean that it is illogical or wrong to have it drawn somewhere. The difficulty lies in knowing *where*, not *whether*, to draw it. But in this case the duty is not open-ended; it is not one mile or ten. The duty springs from the proximity of the rescuer to the victim. To fix the boundaries—to determine how far justice requires beyond "quite close"—requires a choice. But it is the type of choice that legislatures and juries commonly make: legislatures when they choose between incommensurable conflicting interests; juries when they decide whether someone acted reasonably under the circumstances.

If, then, there is *some* kind of duty to rescue, albeit limited to a compact vicinity that rescuer and victim just happen to inhabit, what ground can there be for the apparently much less bounded obligation to serve one's country, quite possibly at the risk of dying? Surely there is no special relationship between a young citizen, any young citizen, and all the rest of the community. Surely the young man to be drafted is to me but a stranger, over whom my claim can be but that of humanity. But if the draftee's reluctance is universalized and the enemy invades, sooner or later the relationship will turn out to be as proximate as the shouted advice that can save the drowning man. For sooner or later, when the enemy shoots at me, he is shooting also at the people just next to me, and when I repel the enemy for myself, I repel him for them.[11]

In the absence of an agreement that creates the obligation, the duty to rescue does not extend beyond a reasonable proximity between rescuer and victim. It is fundamentally illiberal to demand that certain people or members of certain groups have obligations to serve other members of the public just because they possess a special skill that would aid these others in their moments of distress. A common example is the demand that lawyers be required to provide pro bono publico (free) services to the indigent (particularly indigent criminal defendants and prisoners). Proponents of this donation of free time and knowledge look to justify their position on an obligation reciprocal to the lawyers' monopoly position—licensed by the state, they alone can practice law; in return for this advantage, it is suggested, they owe society a favor of helping those whom the market has overlooked.[12] The fallacy is the supposition that the licensing requirement that creates the monopoly is a favor, a fallacy that confuses the political *cause* of licensing (often, sophisticated lobbying by the professional group) with the *justification* for it. Licensing is imposed on lawyers, as on at least some other professionals,[13] not as advantage but as regulation. Licensing is an application of the harm principle, to assure the public that some minimum standard of competence will be available. Lawyers may be prevented from doing harm, but they, no more than others in society, may be ordered to do good. Liquor stores are regulated, but that is not an argument to hand out free liquor; medicine is regulated, but that is not an argument to perform operations at the expense of a particular doctor. However, when a relationship between a lawyer and client is particularized, this objection does not apply. So, for example, a lawyer in the middle of a trial may be prohibited from resigning just because the client has run out of money, not because the lawyer is being forced to do good but because he is prevented from doing harm. To secure a public end, the public must be willing to pay for it, not to suppose that everyone with something to offer must offer it to humanity in general. That may be a wonderful idea, but it is not a liberal one.

Special Relationships and the Duty to Act

We live in a world where almost unimaginable powers cause harms beyond an individual consumer's capacity to control and out of all proportion to the producer's capacity to redress. Years later, names such as Thalidomide, Bhopal, Chernobyl, Exxon Valdez, and Deepwater Horizon[14] still call to mind their special horrors— misery and destruction of thousands from the marketing of a tiny pill, the collision of a single ship, a gas leak, and the explosion of a single generator. We now know that millions have suffered cruel deaths because they became habituated to tobacco products, the addictive powers of which they did not comprehend.[15] And the power to inflict damage and distress bears no relation to the ease or difficulty with which the destructive act may be performed. Small, seemingly innocuous errors can cause catastrophes: "At Cape Kennedy, the omission of a hyphen by a programmer made it necessary to destroy a rocket costing $18,500,000."[16]

Against such disasters as these and a multitude of other risks less severe but scarcely negligible, applying a rule excusing the drug manufacturer, the master of the supertanker, and the operators of the reactor and oil rig because they did not intend the consequences of their actions would be to disable the harm principle in all but a tiny portion of cases. Yet so it occasionally continues to be argued on apparently liberal principles. Thus a libertarian writes that regulating "the manufacture or offering for sale of toys and drugs that no one is compelled to purchase" is "a species of initiatory coercion, a moral authoritarianism that robs individuals of their sphere of moral autonomy."[17] To excuse the producer from the responsibility for creating a harmful condition because the consumer is not compelled to purchase is to saddle the consumer with the burden of every injury, for it is axiomatic to the libertarian that the consumer is never *compelled* to purchase. Economic and psychological "wants" and physiological "needs" are not politically coercive. Even the starving man is free to refrain from stealing. The libertarian argument is thus that the state may deal with only those harms caused by a producer who has guaranteed against them. A producer may avoid all responsibility, then, by the simple expedient of warning customers that "the product is sold as is, and no warranty of fitness or safety is expressed or implied." Since no one is coerced into buying, any consumer must be assumed to have consented to the disclaimer. In essence, the argument is that producers and consumers are strangers to each other, too remote for the law to demand that one watch out for the other or for any special relationship to be imposed that is not of their own making. Beyond proximity or a special relationship, it is argued, the harm principle does not run.

This ethic of caveat emptor is understandable in the romantic strain of liberalism that believes true freedom possible in a society in which all people are producers and so deal with one another independently and not subserviently. This is the image, for example, of Hilaire Belloc in *The Servile State*.[18] In Belloc's society, a liberal rule of caveat emptor might be sufficient as a rule of redress, since no one would have the knowledge or power to fundamentally harm another, at least not in any way that would be beyond the capacity of the other to avoid. In such a world, the individual manufacturer and seller would be one and the same. Products would be simple; their defects, if any, apparent; their strengths and weaknesses testable. Buyers could exercise a reasonable degree of precaution before settling on anything that looked too dangerous, faulty, or unworkable. In any event, the product would not likely injure or affect anyone beyond the immediate purchaser. But we do not live in such a world, so justifications based on it will not avail. The question is whether the world we do live in will justify the state's imposing affirmative obligations rather than merely negative duties.

If while walking in a woods you are hit on the head by a falling tree limb the burden of the injury must lie on you. It is an "act of God," we say, and no one must blame God or, in any event, could hold him responsible. There is no one in the woods who can be called upon to care for your well-being by pruning the branches. But if you are hit on the head by a tile falling from a roof, the law, by imposing a duty to keep one's roof in good repair, can attempt to influence behavior so that the passerby will be spared the risk of a considerable injury. In the name of preventing harm, then, a law of negligence can impose affirmative duties. The question is what justifies this interpretation of the harm principle against the charge that rules of just conduct in a liberal society must always be negative. To understand the argument, a bit of history is instructive.[19]

Until the mid-nineteenth century negligence, as we know it today, "was the merest dot on the law."[20] In our terms, negligence is the absence of due care, the unreasonable doing of something one has a right to do. But the term took on this meaning only some 150 years ago. Before then, when referred to at all, negligence meant the failure of someone (usually a sheriff or other official) to do something he was supposed to do (like keeping imprisoned debtors locked up). Negligence did not carry with it connotations of reasonableness. It was as strict as any modern strict liability, perhaps more so. Thus a 1795 New Jersey court imposed liability on a sheriff who demonstrated not only that he had exercised every precaution but that even had he observed extraordinary precautions the prisoner would have escaped through completely unforeseen circumstances.[21]

Likewise, the notion of fault was only fitfully a part of the more general legal action for injuries. The most ancient torts, like assault, battery, conversion (theft in a variety of degrees), and trespass, have survived today as wrongs deliberately caused. Suits directed against intentional wrongdoers lie at the heart of the harm principle. No one argues that such suits are morally wrong or impose an undue burden on society. When the odor of malice is in the air, retribution, deterrence, and compensation are quickly sniffed.

But malice is not the only kind of fault, and fault is not easy to parse. Before the nineteenth century, the question was not so much whether the defendant intended the *consequences* of his act but whether he intended to *commit* his act; whether, that is, he acted *deliberately*, of his own free will. Thus, the common law imposed liability on the trespasser, though innocent of any intent to do damage. A man might walk through a woods, thinking it wild land; but no matter how reasonable, his mistaken belief would incur liability. Though intent to injure the owner was absent, the law concluded that by his direct actions in causing the damage—a felled tree, trampled flowers, slaughtered game—the defendant must pay compensation. The preindustrial mind disregarded blameworthiness in our sense. The moral sense was that a victim's redress was more important than the wrongdoer's intent to do harm. Even when the act caused harm only indirectly (for example, by setting on one's own property a fire that escaped and did damage next door), the law did not inquire into the foreseeability of the consequences. If damage occurred, liability attached to him who did it.

Why the concept of negligence—unreasonable carelessness from which damage results—was not yet part of the law is easy enough to see. In a preindustrial world, harmful contact between people resulted much more from deliberate than negligent activity. A gun that can store several shells and is easy to fire is more likely to be operated carelessly than a gun that requires a good deal of attention before it can be fired (and much more likely than a bow and arrow). Moreover, the range of destructiveness of any particular action in an agrarian society was likely to be small. A railroad train or a car will wreak more havoc than a horse. Horses rarely killed people; the automobile subjects thousands to grisly death every year. Before the nineteenth century, transportation was limited, the machine's multiplication of muscle power feeble, the factory nascent. Most personal injuries in the old days were, therefore, of the kind we today consider intentional, like assault and battery. Negligence—the law governing the reasonableness of a person's behavior—was not a necessary concept.

But in the late eighteenth century, the increasing frequency of collisions between private ships at sea and between horse-drawn carriages on the public roads led to new inquiries: Did the alleged tortfeasor have a *reason* to be doing that which led to harm? And which party had *caused* the injury? These were never questions in assault and battery or trespass cases because the defendant acted intentionally and the plaintiff was plainly the victim. But the collision cases required the courts to consider that both ships had the right to be at sea, and so the real question was one of causation: Who was responsible for the accident? If one crew was careless, it should pay for the damage. But if the victim had been careless, then the other party could be excused. The careless victim had only to have stepped out of the way.

It was in this context that Justice Holmes advanced his rule against liability for accidents. Pondering the conundrum whether a person could be held liable for striking another with a stick if the other person came up unannounced from behind just as the stick was being raised to separate two fighting dogs, Holmes concluded that the stick-wielding person could not be blamed since it was as if he had had a "spasmodic muscular contraction," rather than a "chance to guard against the result which has come to pass." So, Holmes concluded in the sentence I have already quoted: "The general principle of our law is that loss from accident must lie where it falls, and this principle is not affected by the fact that a human being is the instrument of misfortune."[22]

The trend from strict liability toward negligence is usually assumed to have begun around 1840, with the development of the locomotive. As a commentator put it a half century later, "the quiet citizen must keep out of the way of the exuberantly active one."[23] Strict liability would have put all risk on the train. A rule of negligence liberates the railroad, because it condemns only that which is unreasonable. Now to minimize or eliminate *strict* liability does not logically abolish *all* liability. Negligence need not be an empty concept; it need not give advantage to movers rather than watchers, to trains rather than the houses they hit. Yet during the nineteenth century, individualism became the talisman that decided controversies. The liberal idea of the autonomous, self-seeking individual, answerable to no one save himself, led to a radical shift. Before, the status quo was preserved at virtually any cost; now, the man of action was freed to take risks. Before, the duty of care ran to the whole world; now, a duty of care would run only to those to whom one directly obligated oneself. Freedom for enterprise demanded that the entrepreneur not be saddled with liability for the effects of the enterprise. If a contractual relationship existed or could be implied, a duty of care (drawn as narrowly as the contract) could be enforced. But the law would impose no independent duty. Let him be protected who looks out for himself. In the absence of contract, a social duty to others shrank, often to the vanishing point. A host of legal doctrines contained for decades the explosive pressure of the industrial age, which saw an inexorable rise in human carnage. Among the doctrines were these:

Fellow-servant rule. First announced in 1842, it said that injury to a worker was not recompensable if brought about through the negligence of a fellow employee. Recovery against a corporate enterprise was possible only if the owner or manager was personally at fault—not very likely, since owners and managers did not spend much time in factories or railroad yards.

Contributory negligence. A plaintiff's carelessness mooted his suit against the defendant, no matter how slight the plaintiff's negligence or how great the defendant's.

Assumption of risk. A person was assumed to have accepted the risks inherent in a situation he willingly entered, like the taking of a dangerous job.

Proximate cause. The more indirect the connection between act and injury, the less inclined the courts were to order compensation. In one famous case, a fire in a railroad woodshed in Syracuse, New York, spread by heat and sparks and burned down several houses 130 feet away. Despite clear proof that the railroad's careless operation of an engine caused the fire, the New York court in 1866 denied recovery with these words:

> To sustain such a claim . . . would subject [the railroad] to a liability against which no prudence could guard, and to meet which no private fortune would be adequate. . . . In a country . . . where men are crowded into cities and villages . . . it is impossible [to] guard against the occurrence of accident or negligent fires. A man may insure his own house . . . but he cannot insure his neighbor's. . . . To hold that the owner . . . must guarantee the security of his neighbors on both sides, and to an unlimited extent . . . would be the destruction of all civilized society. . . . In a commercial country, each man, to some extent, runs the hazard of his neighbor's conduct.[24]

Standard of care. Whether a defendant acted reasonably is not mathematically determinable; it is entirely judgmental and was frequently left to juries as a factual issue (as it is today). But the courts imposed outer limits on the standard, so that a railroad, for instance, was not thought to be a "dangerous instrumentality" for which a higher degree of care would be required.

Prohibition against wrongful death suits. The common law has always considered a tort to be personal to the victim. Illogical in 1848 when it was first imposed in America, the ban on wrongful death actions made it "more profitable for the defendant to kill the plaintiff than to scratch him."[25]

These and other rules added up to a golden age, brief though it may have been, for industrial enterprises. The law permitted producers to shift the burden of an enormous number of accidents onto the victims. By the beginning of the twentieth century, "industrial accidents were claiming about 35,000 lives a year and inflicting close to 2,000,000 injuries."[26] Few who were harmed were recompensed; virtually none adequately.[27] So harsh were the consequences of this minimal law of negligence that even during its heyday courts made some attempts to sharpen its dull edges. By 1881, when Holmes penned his famous lines, *fault* was not limited to acts willfully calculated to injure. Though people would not be held liable for many consequences of their actions, they could be brought to account for some consequences of careless acts. But the judges did not at first attack the premises of the laissez-faire liability system they had created, so they piled on "exception[s] to an exception to an exception."[28] The actual law was, therefore, never quite as hard and indifferent to suffering as the summaries render it, but for a long time most plaintiffs discovered that the old idea of people owing socially defined duties to others (as opposed to duties they contracted for) had, if not all but vanished, become quite faint.

The reform of the negligence concept came when the courts understood not merely the costs of caveat emptor and its corollaries but the faulty assumption on which they rested. The romantic world of Belloc's imagination required equal knowledge, or equal ability to secure the knowledge, of risk. If such a world ever existed, it cannot exist in an industrial age. But even in the world of idyll, we might wonder whether one must always shoulder the burdens when the burdens fall on one's shoulders. Picture Herbert Spencer strolling of an afternoon with Mrs. Spencer.[29] As they pass by a row of lovely London townhouses, some loose roof tiles suddenly dislodge from their perch and clatter down upon Mrs. Spencer's head, killing her instantly.[30] The owner of the house, let us suppose, knew that they were loose but did not want to incur the expense of repair. A wroth Spencer files a wrongful death suit. The owner, he charges, has killed poor Mrs. Spencer. But the owner's canny lawyer cracks open a copy of *Social Statics* and tells the judge that Spencer himself had said that if people "are sufficiently complete to live, they *do* live, and it is well they should live. If they are not sufficiently complete to live, they die, and it is best they should die."[31] So was Mrs. Spencer a stupid or imprudent woman "insufficiently complete to live"? One hopes Spencer would have neither thought nor said so. The responsibility for this deplorable accident should not be imputed to Mrs. Spencer, for she could not have been expected to look upward at every roof as she walked along, much less to have inspected beforehand the structural soundness of every building that she might encounter.[32] Imposing liability on the negligent homeowner means that one does owe some duty of care toward strangers, if the strangers are as likely to cross your path as they are unlikely to possess the means to protect themselves against traps that lie in wait.

In an industrial age, an age of science and complexity, we reject caveat emptor not because the ideal of rugged individualism is any less valuable, not because people have lost their free will, and not because we no longer treasure personal liberty, but because its essential prerequisite—knowledge of risk—cannot be maintained. The classic justification for the rule of caveat emptor is that of Chief Justice Holt in 1703: "We are not to indict one for making a fool of another."[33] The flaw in this rule, however, is that "to be always on guard against [trickery is] a terrible bother."[34] But it is more than a bother. Ours is an age of intricate specialization before which every person is individually helpless.

That this helplessness has paralleled the growth in knowledge generally is not as paradoxical as it sounds, for each individual's ability to comprehend the whole varies inversely with the total amount of knowledge produced. The more *we* know, the more mankind knows, the less you or I know. If more certainty resides somewhere about a particular aspect of the universe, in some book or mind, the less likely that any one of us possesses it. No single person can any longer control his environment.

This difficulty has not always been apparent. In the early years of the twentieth century, the great sociologist Lester Ward taught a course at Brown University titled "A Survey of All Knowledge."[35] But by then the claim was preposterous. The development of the machine tool industry; the division of labor into an ever-widening circle of industrial occupations; the requirements of capital accumulation for efficient production; the advancement of higher mathematics, physics, chemistry, and agricultural science; the old learned professions and the proliferating new ones—all this specialization was rampant and no one could halt the wave. The vice of specialization has squeezed hard even within single "professions," splitting every major field into minute subspecialties, so that those who a century ago might have met on common ground can do so no longer. Marx's well-known dream that in the time when the state has withered away it will be

> possible for me to do this today and that tomorrow, to hunt in the morning, to fish in the afternoon, to carry on cattle-breeding in the evening, also to criticize the food—just as I please—without becoming either hunter, fisherman, shepherd or critic[36]

is all very well as a description of simple hobbies in an age of great leisure when the economic problem of scarcity is "solved," but it is significant that the avocations he listed did not include nutritionist, immunologist, or environmentalist. In an age of technological innocence, when the soil is fertile, time is not pressing, but in an age of multiple choices amid an abundance of knowledge and material goods, we feel the final scarcity: the scarcity of time. There is not enough of it to master more than the tiniest fraction of one corner of one room of the house of knowledge.

The problem for the consumer follows. If we can barely master the art of producing, of making, of acting, we cannot hope at all to evaluate personally all the skills, products, and services that we draw upon to sustain us in life. In a complex world, the individual is helpless. The ordinary consumer does not and cannot understand the engineering and safety aspects of most modern goods. Thus, one design study of the lowly tricycle concluded that

> it is often unreasonable to expect consumers to know what it is about a product that is dangerous, and thus to be able to demand appropriate safety features. It required a morphological study of children's weights, applied to an engineering study calculating the center of gravity of children sitting on tricycles, to determine what design characteristics make tricycles unstable when turned around a corner. A parent could hardly judge the safety of competing tricycle designs even if he wanted to.[37]

Few risks are obvious. It may once have been efficient to have a legal rule that burdened the buyer to inspect before purchasing, but in our world quite the reverse is true. Efficiency lies in putting designers and builders to the test, not in forcing each individual to master several lifetimes' worth of technical specialties. In this world, we may each be capable of knowing our desires and forming a life plan, but we are incapable of looking out for ourselves. Hence our ability to fulfill our plan on our own is small. We need help. The image of the autonomous, rational, calculating human being, responsible for himself at every turn, is simply false.[38]

We have encountered this problem before. It is the same conflict of interests that arises whenever X's refraining from setting back Y's interest in Z would instead set back X's interest in W.[39] A producer, say, asserts an independent interest in manufacturing cheaply; to be required to watch out for the consumer's interests would set back that interest. But the question always is whether the producer is justified in setting back the consumer's interest in safety. He might be justified if it were reasonable to put the burden of inspection on the consumer. Under the harm principle, then, the inescapable issue is where it is reasonable to put the burden. The harm principle itself neither weighs the competing interests nor prescribes the outcome. Under the harm principle, it is the state that may do both.

Just so, courts in the twentieth century reversed direction and extended the law of negligence. No point would be served to outline that change here, but one particular stop along the way is worth pausing over, for it highlights how the meaning of "stranger" has been reinterpreted to permit the scope of liability to expand. The stop is in 1916, when Benjamin N. Cardozo, then chief judge of the New York Court of Appeals, overthrew the doctrine of "privity." A wooden wheel of an automobile collapsed and injured its driver, MacPherson, who sued Buick Motor Company, the manufacturer, which had negligently failed to inspect and thus to discover the tire's defect. The company said that it had no relationship (no privity of contract) with MacPherson because he had purchased the car from an independent dealer, not directly from Buick. Cardozo said that it did not matter: The manufacturer owes a duty of care to those who will ultimately use the product.[40] In a simpler world, when people bought directly from the manufacturer, the privity requirement little mattered, since there were no strangers. But in an industrial age, there are only strangers, until we understand that it is the very fact of our market-bred *interdependence* that makes our relationships proximate enough for the state to define duties of care as an inescapable part of the right not to be harmed.[41]

The Fiduciary Ethic

The standard of care contained in the law of negligence is one of ordinary reasonableness. You must take reasonable precautions against harm befalling someone who foreseeably will cross your path. In fact, since the 1960s in the United States, the law has gone beyond negligence and returned to a strict liability standard for many forms of productive activity: If a defective product emerges from your assembly line, no matter how well you maintain the production process and how vigorously you inspect your output, you will be responsible for injuries that occur. This is obviously a more stringent requirement. To minimize its legal exposure a manufacturer will spend more than it might under a negligence standard on research, quality control, and inspection. Even during the heyday of laissez-faire liberalism, the courts imposed strict liability on certain classes of activity, namely, particularly dangerous activities that posed a significant risk of serious harm.[42]

In singling out dangerous activities, the courts can be seen as discerning a special relationship between the dangerous instrumentality and the potential victim. Not surprisingly, that relationship turns on the impossibility of adequate knowledge or power to protect oneself from the risk posed. In our world, the exemplar of such a relationship is that between the expert and the client, for by definition the expert possesses knowledge that the client does not and cannot be expected to have. We turn to experts because we need the assistance that only they can give. But we must be protected from them because they possess knowledge and skills that only they can judge.[43]

For centuries, certain skilled professionals have been held to the high standard of the *fiduciary*. To cabin many of the destructive forces let loose in a technological society, the law is moving toward what I have termed a *fiduciary ethic*;[44] its legitimacy under the harm principle is thus at issue. In its legal sense, a fiduciary is one who stands in a special relationship to another, as a trustee of an estate stands toward the estate's beneficiaries. I borrow the term to reflect the growing number of special relationships to which the state may attach a fiduciary duty. The fiduciary owes a high standard of care; the standard is inherent in the relationship. The fiduciary ethic values not just any goods but safe goods; not just any work but healthy work; not just any service but beneficial service; not just any contract but a fair and honest one. So in mandating a fiduciary ethic, the state is imposing a duty to act; it is not an illegitimate interference with liberty if there is a sound reason for assuming that a special relationship exists.

The concept of the fiduciary is not new. The term itself comes from Roman law, and doctors today still subscribe to the Hippocratic Oath to devote their skills to the care of the sick and suffering. From an early time the persons who exercised a skill or office—like the lawyer and the doctor—were understood to be employing it on behalf of others. In such a relationship, the rule of caveat emptor cannot be invoked, for it is the buyer's very inability to beware that prompts him to seek out the professional.

Consider the alarming case of the patent attorney who repeatedly refused to consult with his clients about the status of their application pending in the U.S. Patent Office. After having paid more than $2,100 (in 1970s dollars) for interim services meaningless to them unless a patent was eventually issued, and their demand to discuss with the lawyer how the application was proceeding having been rebuffed, the inventors refused to pay more. As a consequence the lawyer failed to follow through and the inventors forfeited patent rights for all time. The lawyer subsequently declined to render an itemized accounting unless also paid to do that. At proceedings before the Kansas Supreme Court that resulted in the lawyer's disbarment, the hearing record contained the following exchange:

> Q: Well, did you not feel some obligation after undertaking this work to secure the patent?
> A: No. My—I'm a contract worker. They pay me to do something, I do it, and that's it.
> Q: They had already paid you or you had been paid $2,185 from these people?
> A: It has been accounted for. It is contract work. . . . For the work I did, I got paid in advance. I got paid my fee for preparing and filing the patent application, and that was it. I have no obligation to them other than what I contracted to do. That is the way the patent business is run, and she's a toughie.[45]

It is the heart of the fiduciary ethic that the relationship of skill is not to be a "toughie" imposed on the unwitting, that the skill employed in the service of another must be employed beneficially. Fiduciaries may not contractually limit their obligations; they may not refuse, like Lord Macaulay's stranger, to go an extra mile. It may even be a breach of the fiduciary's responsibility to resign the case or refuse further treatment, at least if the only reason for doing so is the client's or patient's refusal or failure to tender further payment.

Although the fiduciary ethic imposes an affirmative obligation to act, it is not an open-ended obligation. It is tied to the object that called the relationship into being. So the usual objection to the positive duty is at least partially met by the limiting principle of the fiduciary. You are free to choose what it is you wish to take on; once having chosen, you must do well whatever it is you are doing. If a lawyer is working on a case, then her fiduciary obligation is to subordinate personal feelings and ambitions and defer to the client's needs with respect to the case. She need not sacrifice her life for the client, nor her bankbook for the client's comfort, but she may need to sacrifice her vacation, say, to the exigencies of the case at hand. Similarly, the standard of strict liability in manufacturing is not a requirement that the manufacturer make "uplifting" toys rather than, say, "unwholesome" ones; it is a requirement that whatever comes from the factory be safe and fit for the use intended. The fiduciary standard is imposed because the harm that can flow from the failure to perform the particular skill in a punctilious manner will often be irremediable.

The fiduciary ethic is subject to a large difficulty—or misinterpretation. We wish a person who undertakes some activity on behalf of other people to act responsibly toward them: not to cheat or defraud them, not to injure them, not to use less than best efforts on their behalf. Insofar as the person for whom some action is undertaken is either identifiable (the particular client) or a group whose interest in not being harmed is itself identifiable (the class of people purchasing lawnmowers), there will be no difficulty in knowing on whom the duty must be placed or what the duty must be. The difficult question arises when there is no readily identifiable person or group of persons—when, in short, the presumed duty is to the public or society as a whole. Then the individual actor, professional, or producer is in an untenable position because he can no longer be a fiduciary for a particular person. Instead, he is the servant of many interests, and unless some authority spells out how the balance is to be struck, he will necessarily be called on to resolve an unresolvable conflict of interests or to settle a matter unilaterally that ought to be referred to public institutions for resolution. A legal demand that one act in the "public interest," without more, is therefore illiberal. To this degree, the fiduciary ethic is negative: It may bar private institutions from harming the particular interest that is the object of protection, but it ought not direct them to accomplish some public good.

So it is illiberal to require, as has sometimes been proposed, that since lawyers are "officers of the court" or because they are in a position to play a public role, they must seek the public good.[46] In particular, the argument has been made that lawyers ought not represent particular clients accused of socially reprehensible habits (large, actively polluting corporations or tobacco companies, for example) or that they ought to temper their representation in the interests of the public. Requiring counsel for a party to represent another interest as well is simply to force the lawyer into an unresolvable conflict of interest. The law may prohibit the lawyer from participating in fraud or perjury, but these and like prohibitions are not a ban on advocacy itself when employed to advance a client's sense of the good.

That the state may impose affirmative obligations on particular people under the harm principle is an important advance over an entirely negative conception of interference with liberty. But it is not enough to say that affirmative obligations are legitimate. An equally important question is whether, once it justifies the power to act (whether positively or negatively), the state may act in any manner it pleases. Does the harm principle limit the forms of intervention? To this question I now turn.

7

The Forms of Intervention

How far may the state intrude on our lives once the legitimacy of intrusion is accepted? May the state do whatever it thinks effective in eliminating or redressing harm, or does the very principle that animates the state's function limit its means of realizing its objective? Does every wrong logically entail a particular remedy or is the choice of remedy at the state's discretion?[1]

Locke certainly supposed that it would be wrong for the state to shoot guns at gnats. In the state of nature, Locke asserted, everyone

> has a right to punish the transgressors of that Law [of nature] to such a Degree, as may hinder its Violation.... Each Transgression [of the law of nature] may be *punished* to that *degree*, and with so much *Severity* as will suffice to make it an ill bargain to the offender, give him cause to repent, and terrifie others from doing the like.

How to recognize or define the "measures of punishment" was incidental to Locke's purpose; he declined to "enter ... into the particulars" but opined that they were "intelligible and plain."[2] Mill did not directly propose a rule of proportionality, though he recognized that other significant reasons might weigh against punishing the harmdoer, reasons arising "from the special expediences of the case: ... because the attempt to exercise control would produce other evils, greater than those which it would prevent."[3] As we have seen, Feinberg proposed for enacting criminal law what in effect is a principle of least intrusion: The state may criminalize a harmful action if there is "no other means that is equally effective at no greater cost to other values."[4]

No formula can spell out the limits of remedy. We might examine different types of harm, measured by their intrinsic nature (for example, death is different from loss of reputation). Or we might inspect the gravity or quantum of harmfulness (death vs. bodily injury; "serious" embezzlement vs. pinching office supplies to use at home), the relative value of the harmful action (dumping toxins in the river vs. driving to work), the degree of intention to cause the harm (desire vs. inadvertence), or the directness of causation (through how many other people was the action filtered?).

Each of these comparisons implies a principle of balance but not one that in its particulars is logically entailed. Unless the harm principle imposes no limit at all, therefore, the problem is to determine whether there are principled types of balances to be struck, for it is not a part of the present inquiry to assess the soundness of *allowable* penalties and remedies. Whether a life sentence, the death penalty, or some other penalty is best dealt to murderers is a question for criminologists, unless it can be shown that one of these, or other particular, penalties is not legitimately within the state's power at all. So this chapter seeks to establish principles of intervention; principles, that is, that vindicate the types of interference with liberty the state may actually practice for any particular type of harm.

Modes and Types of Intervention

I distinguish here between *modes* of intervention the state may employ and *types* of intervention intended to be accomplished. Modes of intervention have to do with technique, such as criminal law or taxation. Types of intervention have to do with function and timing; they reflect what the state hopes to achieve by its intrusion—deterrence (before the harm occurs), reduction or elimination (during), or redress (after). There are at least eight modes of intervention and three types of intervention.

Modes of Intervention

1. *Criminal law.* Through criminal law the state threatens and imposes direct loss of liberty (incarceration) and, in extreme cases, death and loss of property (fines). Criminal law has four major functions: It serves to (a) deter harm (crime), (b) punish when the deterrence fails, (c) incapacitate (isolate the criminal), and (d) rehabilitate (theoretically).

2. *Redress.* Primarily through the system of private or civil law, the state makes available a court system in which people can redress harms actually committed. The principles of redress are available not only to private parties but also to the state itself in enforcing a range of regulatory statutes with civil penalties attached.

3. *Direct compulsion.* To assure that some tasks are carried out, the state may order individuals directly to undertake them. These tasks include defense (military draft, posse comitatus), justice (compulsory jury service), privately bargained services (specific performance for the sale of a house), and publicly mandated private duties (requirement to bargain in good faith in labor negotiations). Some direct compulsions are seen as payments rather than as orders to perform: for example, the requirement that automobile registrants purchase insurance. Other apparent compulsions may be more like a tax (social security). Direct compulsion

is reinforced by the threat of criminal sanctions: If a conscript refuses to register or heed the draft call, if a citizen shirks a jury summons, if a seller or buyer disobeys the order of specific performance, the penalty may be jail or a fine.

4. *Direct prohibition.* To prevent certain kinds of harm, the state (usually acting through courts) will issue orders directly prohibiting particular acts. Neighbors may be enjoined from storing dynamite on their premises. Picketers may be ordered to stand back from abortion clinics. Again, these orders are ultimately enforceable by criminal sanctions.

5. *Licensing.* The right to carry out an activity may be conditioned on the actor's meeting various requirements, such as training, skill, knowledge, and financial security. In its strict form, these requirements are enforced through a license: the actor may not go forward without showing that he has complied with the requirements (driver's license, admission to the bar).[5] In its lesser form, the actor is prohibited from proclaiming to the world that he is qualified unless he has met certification requirements, though he may be free to carry on the activity whether or not he has been certified.

6. *Regulation.* As ordinarily understood, a regulation is an order that a particular activity be carried out in a definite or special way. Although closely related to direct compulsion and often enforceable directly against an individual, a regulation strictly does not require anyone to undertake the general activity. Rather, the regulation declares that whoever does carry out a specified task must adhere to guidelines or accomplish it by certain means and not by others. You need not field a fleet of airplanes, but if that is your business then you must maintain your aircraft in specified ways.

7. *Taxation.* To operationalize the harm principle, if for no other reason, the state transfers money from private pockets into public coffers. We generally think of taxation as a means of funding programs, but since taxation by definition is a cost, it can be used to affect particular activities. Mill was prepared for the state to control the use of deleterious substances through taxation:

> It must be remembered that taxation for fiscal purposes is absolutely inevitable; that in most countries it is necessary that a considerable part of that taxation should be indirect; that the State, therefore, cannot help imposing penalties, which to some persons may be prohibitory, on the use of some articles of consumption. It is hence the duty of the State to consider, in the imposition of taxes, what commodities the customers can best spare; and *a fortiori*, to select in preference those of which it deems the use, beyond a very moderate quantity, to be positively injurious. Taxation, therefore, of stimulants, up to the point which produces the largest amount of revenue (supposing that the State needs all the revenue of which it yields) is not only admissible, but to be approved of.[6]

The Supreme Court has essentially endorsed Mill's principle, refusing to speculate on the motives that led Congress to enact a taxing scheme, as long as the tax measure is aimed at producing revenue.[7]

8. *Funding.* The state uses public revenues to purchase goods and services, to establish and operate programs, and to declare the extent to which others will be allowed to compete with these programs (so the postal system, through mailboxes at the door, is an exclusive franchise of the federal government).[8] The major publicly funded service is the government itself, to breathe life into the harm principle; another major form is the transfer payment to people meeting certain conditions (e.g., social security).

Types of Intervention

However the state chooses to intervene, it will do so to accomplish one or more of three goals: (1) to deter or prevent harm from occurring (or to reduce it), (2) to bring a harmful activity to an end, and (3) to redress or compensate for harm that has already occurred. Deterrence and prevention have three categories, and these are not mutually exclusive but overlapping and combinatory: (a) rules declarations (rules of the road); (b) threats (criminal law, civil injunctions); and (c) policies and programs intended to divert the potential for harm into harmless or less harmful activity (recreation programs to keep gang members off the streets; retraining programs to lessen the threat of criminal activity by people made desperate by starvation or other unfortunate circumstances; maintaining homeless shelters). The state deals with ongoing harms through investigations and inspections and a mix of modes aimed at turning individuals away from their course of conduct. Understood in the most general sense, there are three categories of redress: (a) civil suits—procedures that permit the government and private litigants at their discretion to exact restitution and compensation from the harmdoer;[9] (b) criminal prosecution to punish the wrongdoer, and equivalent civil suits by the government to enforce statutory regimes;[10] and (c) publicly funded programs that provide relief against harms that cannot easily be redressed by charging wrongdoers directly (for example, disaster relief).

Types of harm and modes and types of intervention have no a priori connection or correlation. The state deals with wrongful death, for example, in many ways: It criminalizes murder, opens courts to tort suits for compensation, creates insurance-compensation systems (for example, workers' compensation programs), enacts regulations to ensure airplane safety and to reduce pollution that could cause fatal illnesses, funds programs to entice some people away from a life of crime, registers and taxes guns, regulates drug use, licenses hospitals and medical personnel, and drafts people into the army, to list but a few modes of action. Whether any particular mode is appropriate depends on a complex calculus of circumstances. Perhaps the only theoretical relationship between types of harm and modes and types of intervention is that which lies along the chain of causation. The greater the causal distance between the perpetrators and the harm, the less warrant the state will have to impose a sanction or intervene against a particular person and the less intrusive the sanction should be. So intervention runs from direct criminal sanctions, to rules of the road, to welfare payments. The murderer may pay with his life; drivers must heed speed limits; the polluting factory must limit its emissions; the system as a whole funds assistance programs for orphans.

General Limiting Principles of Intervention

The harm principle warrants some intrusions on liberty to guard against still greater interferences. It would be counterintuitive, therefore, to suppose no limitations on the state's acknowledged power. We ought not burn down villages to save them. Five general limiting principles suggest themselves. These are principles of proportionality, least intrusion, retroactivity, equality, and procedural fairness.

Proportionality Principle

The ancient principle of proportionality has been expressed in many ways. A familiar, harsh form is the *lex talionis* or law of retaliation, best known in the biblical injunction to take a "life for life, eye for eye, tooth for tooth, hand for hand, foot for foot, burning for burning, wound for wound, stripe for stripe."[11] However expressed, the idea that distress to a wrongdoer should be equivalent to the victim's suffering or to the wrongdoer's degree of culpability is at bottom a narrow jurisprudential maxim and not always coherent.[12] Its intuitive plausibility derives from an innate sense of balance or justice, but it is a principle notoriously difficult to apply, since there is no clear standard by which to judge the equivalence of harms to which penalties will be attached. The infamous "Black Act" of eighteenth-century England mandated capital punishment for more than fifty offenses against property and even for methods of committing offenses, so that the mere act of "blacking" one's face was punishable by death.[13] While we can agree that death for overtime parking is excessive and unjust (except in my neighborhood), it is less clear that a thief is proportionately dealt with by being incarcerated for twenty years rather than by losing his hand and being sent on his way. In the realm of criminal law, then, the proportionality principle is at best an abstraction that cannot be applied without an understanding of cultural norms. Locke to the contrary notwithstanding, there is no obvious or logical proportionality map.

Moreover, apart from penalty, the degree of harm caused by the wrongdoer in any given instance of a particular type of wrongdoing (theft, for example) cannot plausibly be the basis for determining how much protection the state should offer against the commission of the harmful act:

> The law of burglary protects not only the pauper who would be ruined by the theft of his welfare check, but also the millionaire for whom a thousand-dollar bill has less utility than a penny has for a child. There would be enormous practical difficulties in attempting to apportion degrees of protection according to the actual seriousness of harm. Moreover, protection of the wealthy person from minor thefts does not interfere with the normal everyday exercise of [other people's] individual liberty.[14]

In other words, we must distinguish between two types of proportionality: (1) between the nature of the harm and the nature of the state's corresponding interference with liberty; and (2) between the quantum of harm caused and the quantum of interference with the wrongdoer. In the first type, it does not matter that the thief managed to make off with a piece of candy from the dime store instead of the cash register contents; the state may employ criminal law to punish either act.[15] But it might not be justified in limiting every sort of liberty interest that the thief has (for example, punishment for theft should presumably not result in a loss of the legal power to enter into an enforceable contract).[16] In the second type of proportionality argument, the gravity or amount of harm does bear on the outcome. We would not expect the judge to sentence a thief who takes candy to as onerous a sentence as a thief who robs the cash register.[17] It is this second kind of proportionality that informs our disapproval of the Black Act's assigning the death penalty to so many acts of varying degrees of harmfulness.

Principle of Least Intrusion

Besides its use in assessing *penalties* to be applied, proportionality also bears on the *types* of state oversight and control to be applied to particular types of conduct. Consider contractual default. A homeowner engages a worker to paint his house and then refuses to pay when the job is done. That the painter has suffered a harm is patent, but what may the state do about it? Among the conceivable options are incarceration, a fine payable to the public treasury, a suit instigated by the attorney general for the agreed price, and a similar suit by the homeowner. A quite different possibility would be to establish a Painters' Protective Escrow Agency, to which all payments for house painting would be made before work can begin. Under this arrangement, the painter would not start the job until the payment had been deposited in escrow along with a notarized copy of the contract. To ensure that painters do not negotiate separately with homeowners, the courts would be barred from enforcing a contract between owners and painters. A refinement might be to subject painters to loss of licenses for negotiating with owners, followed by fines or jail terms for painting without a license. Again, it seems intuitively obvious that valuing liberty requires the state to follow some principle of least (or lesser) intrusion, preventing or redressing harms by whatever means will least interfere with the wrongdoers' liberty. What is least intrusive depends, again, on many factors that cannot be lexically ranked; that is, modes will not invariably follow the same priority of ranking.[18] Is it less intrusive to subject the homeowner to an escrow scheme than to the rigmarole of a private contract battle in civil court? Moreover, a principle of least intrusion cannot focus exclusively on the liberty of the defendant. It must always include what Feinberg has expressed as the criterion of equal effectiveness. It may be less intrusive to the owner to adopt one scheme or another, but we should not favor a scheme that would be much less likely to make the plaintiff whole. So while a principle of least intrusion is useful as a general guide, it will avail only in cases so obvious that the state would not likely have chosen to proceed otherwise. Finally, the principle will not serve when more than one type of intrusion is necessary to deal with a particular harm—as, for example, the act of causing someone's death may be both a criminal offense (murder or manslaughter) and civil offense (wrongful death).

Retroactivity Principle

As a limiting principle of intervention, the retroactivity principle is unlikely to be controversial. That the harm principle does not mandate intervention[19] means that the state has power over its timing. The state may decide to intervene in some limited way, to postpone intervention until some condition is reached, or under some circumstances not to intercede at all. But it may not interfere with a person's liberty because of conduct not declared to be unlawful or wrongful at the time the person acted, for the obvious reason that the insecurity of punishment would chill all sorts of activities and make it impossible for a person rationally to follow a life plan.[20]

Equality Principle

In its earliest incarnation, liberalism (or, at any rate, a proto-liberalism) knew nothing of equality. The earliest liberals justified a liberalism of inequality: Certain people were entitled to be free, and their freedom consisted in part of the power to dominate all the rest. An absolute monarch might as well have argued that he believed in liberalism, too, as long as it meant his freedom to do as he will against all comers. Another liberalism, the one that engages our attention beginning in the second half of the twentieth century, is egalitarian liberalism: Whatever liberty exists must exist for all. This idea was heresy for many of the most prominent "liberal" statesmen and philosophers of the earlier ages: Jefferson, Blackstone, Constant, Bentham, Smith, de Tocqueville all thought otherwise. Of course it was not new to history, said the historian David Brion Davis, that the freedom and independence of some men depend[ed] on the coerced labor of others. What distinguished American colonists was their magnificent effrontery. They rejoiced to find their ideals of freedom and equality reflected in the actual social order, but resolutely denied that the social order rested on a "mudsill" of slavery, as Southerners would later acknowledge.[21]

In a recent work, Domenico Losurdo asserts that these nonegalitarian thinkers (and others who justified slavery) were liberals because they identified a "private sphere" as one in which the state had no legitimate power to meddle, hence whatever happened there was the natural operation of the liberty that all had. But what they overlooked, among other things, were not only the faulty factual premises on which they rested their beliefs about slaves, women, and the working classes but also, and importantly, the large network of laws that propped up the power of the wealthy and well-born to ensure their dominance. It was a "private sphere" only because the law made it one, and even then, only partially private, at that. Take but a cursory look at the slave codes in the American colonies and later the Southern states to understand how incoherent their theory was, at least measured against a standard of liberty. Quite aside from the fundamental illiberalism of slavery itself were the many ways in which the law propped it up, against the liberty even of the slave-holders themselves. A slave was held to be property over whom the master could exercise absolute power—indeed, the master could discipline a slave even to death—but he was forbidden from having sexual relations with his slaves, from teaching them to read and write, or even, in Georgia at least, from allowing slaves the use of paper and pens.[22] To dampen the possibility of slave revolts, in 1836 the postmaster general refused to permit publications critical of slavery to circulate in the mail.[23] These laws, which might seem aimed at slaves, were in reality "for the eyes and ears of slaveowners.... It was the white man who was *required* to punish his runaways, prevent assemblages of slaves, enforce the curfews, sit on the special courts, and ride the patrols."[24] In the American South before the Civil War, legislatures had the power to mitigate the harsh treatment of slaves (even if they rarely used it), so it was not that some naturally arising private sphere disabled the protective power of the government.[25]

We are, thankfully, beyond all that.[26] Some notion of equality is fundamental to any kind of liberalism—the harm principle must be impartial between persons and at an absolute minimum each person must have an equal right to express its meaning by voting. Otherwise there can be no assurance that the open issues to be resolved under the harm principle have been subject to all the interests at stake. But as fundamental as is the right to vote, it by no means exhausts the criterion of equality. A full theory is beyond my scope (indeed, some have even suggested it is beyond anyone's scope).[27] The difficulty is that, as has been understood since the time of Aristotle, equality cannot mean treating every person in literally the same manner, for people's differences will entitle them to be treated differently. Equality can demand only that people be treated the same when they are in relevant respects the same.[28] In Dworkin's terms, people are entitled to be treated as equals, but not necessarily to equal treatment.[29] Since, as we have seen, the harm principle permits the state to choose a rule of decision when interests conflict, a particular rule will determine the respect in which people will be held to be different. It is the rule, in other words, that determines in what manner people are to be treated equally; it is not a principle of equality that determines how the line should be drawn. For example, to decide between the conflicting interests of a homeowner to view the outdoors and of a neighbor to erect a structure that would block the view, a rule of equality, in the sense of treating them equally, cannot settle the issue. The state must decide on other grounds which interest to prefer.

Nevertheless, there is one respect in which a principle of equality can determine the limits of state action, and that is in respect to the distribution of *political* goods and services. When the state decides to provide a service permitted under the harm principle—police protection, say—the only relevant difference among people is whether or not they are citizens or residents of the district within which the service will be provided. A policy that would deny police protection to members of one race or religious sect violates the equality principle because it would amount to the state's exalting one person or group of people over another, preferring one set of ends to another, a preference that would undercut the equality every person has to participate in the political process that makes the harm principle concrete in particular circumstances. Likewise, the same applies when the state makes available certain political goods.

A political good is a legal power by which the state authorizes people to act—for example, to testify and to be sued. Since people are free to act except in ways that are harmful, it may seem an anomaly to suppose that we do not have such powers unless they are first promulgated or endowed by the state. But a political good is different from an economic good produced by individuals and valued through the market. Only the state can produce political goods because apart from the state these goods are meaningless. It makes no sense to talk about whether one can be sued in the absence of courts.

But what kind of a good is it that its absence is a deprivation of liberty? If political liberty inheres in negative freedom, then the presence or absence of a good should have no bearing on a person's liberty. The poor may be unable to achieve as much as the wealthy, but they remain at liberty to try.[30] But because political and economic goods differ fundamentally, a person lacking a legal power loses liberty. For example, if I may not be sued in court, other people will be unwilling to enter into contracts with me. My liberty to contract is directly impinged, not because I am untrustworthy or uncreditworthy, but solely because the state refuses to recognize me as a jurisprudential entity, as having "legalworthiness." Liberty is the power to act without legal restraint; the state's refusing me a power is a legal restraint because a power is that which enables me to act. If the state refuses to let me vote (denying me legal power to cast a ballot), I have no liberty to make formal political choices. I am free to the extent that the state recognizes my legal power to act. So by definition depriving people of political goods, unlike other kinds of goods, impairs or thwarts their exercise of political liberty.

We take for granted the empowering quality of political goods, noticing them at all usually only by their absence. Slavery was a political condition of unfreedom not merely because slaves were subject to the control of others but because they were denied what we today understand as basic "civil rights." A succinct statement of these rights is contained in the federal Civil Rights Act of 1866:

> All persons within the jurisdiction of the United States shall have the same right in every State and Territory to make and enforce contracts, to sue, be parties, give evidence, and to the full and equal benefit of all laws and proceedings for the security of persons and property as is enjoyed by white citizens, and shall be subject to like punishment, pains, penalties, taxes, licenses, and exactions of every kind, and to no other. [Likewise, all citizens] shall have the same right, in every State and Territory, as is enjoyed by white citizens thereof, to inherit, purchase, lease, sell, hold, and convey real and personal property.[31]

Without the political goods named in the Civil Rights Act, the former slaves remained unfree in a significant *political* sense.[32]

Feinberg observes that the lack of a legal power is not an infringement of liberty in the context of the modern state's refusal to enforce a contract to enter into slavery: "The state simply refuses to offer, as a kind of service, a mechanism for creating legal obligations of the appropriate kind."[33] This surely sounds correct: How could it interfere with my liberty for the state to refuse to enforce a contract in which I give away my liberty? But the *content* of the contract obscures the *meaning* of the state's refusal to enforce it. In denying enforcement, the state does not merely refuse the parties a service; it denies them a basic liberty, the liberty of having their consent honored. Much of what we hold most valuable comes to us only through the cooperation of others. If liberty inheres in gratuitous but not contractual modes of cooperation the range of our power to act would shrivel. Lacking a car, I am unfree to travel in a practical but not political sense; but lacking a mechanism to guarantee me the car I *purchased*, I am deprived of the liberty to make choices about how to travel. When the state refuses to uphold my contract, it is denying me that to which I have a right, affecting me just as if in the first place it had pointed a finger at automobile dealers and said, "you are forbidden to sell a car to that man." I cannot complain that I lack liberty if I do not have the *means* to buy a car, but I do not see how it is anything other than a lack of liberty if I do not have a *right* to purchase a car. I can always try to get money to buy a car, but from whom, if not the state, can I get a power to enforce a contract?

Legal empowerment, then, is a kind of liberty—certainly legal disempowerment is a loss of liberty. So if I am free to buy or sell a car but forbidden from *enforceably* selling you my services in perpetuity, my liberty has been diminished.[34] The state may not deny or impede my liberty to seek my ends and leave you free to seek yours—that is, discriminate—unless to prevent a harm. The state is justified in refusing its contract mechanism, therefore, not because denying enforceability is not an infringement of liberty but because enforcing a slavery contract would implicate the state in causing a serious harm (to prevent which the state may, under the harm principle, interfere with liberty).[35]

This point is perhaps easier to see in the case of homosexual and bigamous marriages. "Homosexual couples and bigamous trios might complain that their *liberty* is infringed [by the state's refusal to recognize such marriages as legal], but such a complaint would not be convincing," says Feinberg. For the state has merely failed to provide a service: "[T]he law's failure to provide legal devices that enable two people of the same sex, or two people of one sex and one of the other, to be legal spouses, does not prevent people in these combinations from cohabiting on intimate terms."[36] But the law's failure *does* prevent these people from using the law to underwrite certain obligations permitted to heterosexual couples, for example, the right to inherit property if one of them dies intestate—and to proclaim to the world a relationship equal in status to that of a heterosexual marriage. In the days when antimiscegenation laws forbade interracial marriage, no one supposed that they were other than liberty-restricting. If as a white man I am, as we say, "free" to marry only white women, then I am necessarily unfree with respect to women of other races (and they with me).[37] So with homosexual or bigamous marriages: the state's refusal is liberty-infringing to this extent: I am at liberty, in the most profound sense of the word, to marry one person but not another (or others). In restricting the liberty of some, the state is expressly choosing one way of life over another, placing its imprimatur on one kind of personal end and not another, as the Supreme Court did in 1878 when it sustained a federal law banning polygamy in the Utah Territory.[38] The only justification for denying a legal power on a discriminatory basis is that the discrimination itself prevents harm; and as chapter 10 makes clear, the "harm" of homosexual marriages is not cognizable under the harm principle.

Bigamous marriages present a different problem. If it is the case, as seems likely, that many bigamous marriages are secret (two of the spouses in the trio being unaware of each other's existence), the fraud will permit redress. Feinberg finds no plausible reason under the harm principle to criminalize bigamy, because he finds civil remedies sufficient (the double wives or, presumably in rarer cases, the double husbands can sue for the injury occasioned by the fraud). From my perspective, it does not matter whether the state disapproves of bigamy civilly or criminally, since in either event the state is intervening. But since the fraud is very often not detected until the damage is done, criminal sanctions might deter some from engaging in the deceptive act in the first place.[39]

I conclude that the harm principle necessarily incorporates a principle of equality. Discriminating between different people in the administration of a law is justifiable if the relevant difference is necessary to prevent a harm, but not otherwise. The equality principle requires the state to make benefits and detriments equally applicable to people of different races, religions, and national origins and, for many purposes, to men and women. Whether sex difference and certain other differences among people, including disability and sexual orientation, are relevant bases on which to legislate to deter certain actual harms is today a hugely contested question that cannot be worked through here. Under the harm principle, the resolution depends in identifying harms that would flow from the application of a law that disregarded the arguably relevant differences. Once again, it is harm that determines the relevance of the difference; the relevance of the difference according to some nonharm criterion cannot provide the basis for the legislature to act.

Principle of Procedural Fairness

Our liberty must always be in jeopardy if the state were allowed arbitrarily to finger a particular person as the cause of harm. If I have not committed harm, the state may not invade my liberty, even to provide an "object lesson" to others. Scapegoating is not a liberal principle. That the intervention must bear some causal connection to the harm sought to be prevented or redressed is encapsulated in an effectiveness criterion—the penal legislation must "probably be effective in preventing (eliminating, reducing) harm."[40] It would not be effective if the procedures for determining whether the defendant was the actual wrongdoer were likely to lead to a false conclusion. If the police may torture people until they confess, there will be few who will not confess to crimes they did not commit when targeted for a beating. So to escape such illicit interferences with our liberty perpetrated by a rogue state, the harm principle must be interpreted to require a set of procedures that will ensure an accurate determination that the person whose liberty is infringed deserves to have it infringed *because* he is the one who has committed the harm in question.

In the context of law that punishes or compensates after the fact on the basis of a particular set of events shown to have been brought about by a particular defendant, these rules are among those with which we are familiar in the Bill of Rights. Procedural fairness includes the right to an impartial fact-finder, to confront the accuser, and to be represented by counsel, the violation of each of which might tend to impair the accuracy of the verdict.[41] An additional and singularly important procedural protection is reliance on evidence and rational and scientific proof of facts, not on feelings and the intensity and ubiquity of belief and testimony that are widespread in our culture but inaccessible to testing.[42] Marina Warner tells of a report in *The Times* of London that a property developer in Perthshire, Scotland, had been prevented from breaking the ground for some houses on land he had acquired because there was a fairy stone standing on it. Local people were seriously protesting against its removal. Telephone calls, council meetings, and newspaper interviews confirmed the determination of the objectors: the rock was ancient, it covered the entrance to a fairy fort or hill, and it was extremely unlucky to move any such cromlechs, menhirs, or other ancient monuments because the fairies would be upset ... and take their revenge. The *Times* reporters joked, dubbing the locals' beliefs "MacFeng shui." They quoted the chairman of the local council with responsibility for granting planning permission: "'I believe in fairies,' she said, 'But I can't be sure they live under that rock.' For her, the rock had historical and sacred importance because it was connected to the Picts and their kings had been crowned there." The builder's bulldozers were stopped; since then, there has been no more news from St. Fillian's Perthshire.[43]

A city council and a municipal code might reasonably decide to order a developer to abandon a project because a site has historical importance,[44] but the harm principle cannot tolerate a proceeding in which testimony about a "fairy stone" would be considered relevant to the outcome.

Procedural rights are harm-preventing in the conventional sense that they help thwart those who would railroad an unpopular defendant. In that sense, they evince a basic respect for persons, even those suspected of having acted wrongly and injuriously. But that is not the only sense in which procedural regularity and procedural rights deter harm. Even more importantly, they serve as a bulwark against the initiation of groundless prosecutions. Procedural rights are important not only because they permit people to defend themselves meaningfully, but because they prevent the innocent from having to do so.[45]

Outside the context of an adversary procedure, the problem of fairness is more complex and less amenable to well-defined procedural rules. To minimize an aggregative harm, the state will burden the doing of an act that in itself is harmless—for example, speeding. In this context, it is impossible to demonstrate through a set of procedural rules that each person against whom it is employed would have done a harm but for the rule, since the very point of the rule is to avert harm that will result only statistically from the mass of individual acts. Some speeders would have caused harm, others would not, and not knowing which the law curbs every person's right to speed. The only standard governing such a law is that of rationality. There must be, in the common constitutional phrase, a "rational connection" between the harm and the method chosen to prevent it. This rational basis or relationship between harm and law is a fundamental aspect of the general requirement of due process. As the Supreme Court put it in a leading case in 1934: "the law shall not be unreasonable, arbitrary or capricious, and ... the means selected shall have a real and substantial relation to the object sought to be obtained."[46] A rule that prohibited speeding by people driving only subcompact cars would run afoul of the principle of procedural fairness. Since larger cars would cause as much damage as small cars (and it is unlikely that the evidence would show that small cars are responsible for more accidents when speeding), the thing prohibited would not minimize the risk that is the ground for the prohibition.

Redressing Harm

One major reason for state intervention is to redress harms that have already occurred. The state may impose criminal penalties on the wrongdoer. In practically all cases warranting criminal punishment, the defendant will have knowingly and intentionally committed unlawful acts.[47] The state may also provide a forum in which a harmed person may seek recompense. In these cases, the defendant may or may not have committed the acts intentionally or knowingly and may or may not be a wrongdoer in the strong sense.[48] Punishing usually means imposing jail terms or monetary fines, although the availability of probation and community service gives sentencing judges a range of finely graded penalties. Civil remedies usually entail monetary compensation. A more rarely used form of redress is public shaming and humiliation, often associated with the old practice of being placed in the stock or pillory. Shaming has resurfaced recently in some states in requirements that sex offenders be named in a public registry, though such a requirement is more likely to be viewed as deterrence than redress. Indeed, each type of redress is simultaneously a method of deterrence or prevention, since each pledges the possibility of distress to anyone who violates the legal command that gives rise to the right of redress. In saying "do not murder" the law is promising punishment should murder be committed. Likewise, tort law shapes the legal environment in which people act: The threat of damage awards deters some behaviors and conditions others (for example, over many decades corporate spending on product safety research has increased in response to the perception of the rise in product liability suits).[49]

To preserve the widest liberty, the principle of least intrusion suggests that the state should avoid criminal process whenever "other means ... [are] equally effective at no greater cost to other values." But what other means are available and whether they will be equally effective is largely an empirical question. American law leaves deterrence and redress of negligent acts almost exclusively to tort law, but the crime of "negligent homicide" is well accepted and the rise in punitive damage awards suggest that twin sanctions cannot be ruled out. There is no abstract reason against using criminal sanctions as adjuncts to civil remedies. Consider, for example, Feinberg's suggestion that the state should not criminalize the making of a slavery contract between consenting parties: "Entering into a slavery contract is not in this and other civilized countries the name of a *crime*. The state simply refuses to offer, as a kind of service, a mechanism for creating legal obligations of the appropriate kind."⁵⁰ But the state does criminalize peonage (the holding of a person in servitude), whether by contract or otherwise. There is no logical reason that the harm principle cannot permit the state to criminalize the making of such contracts to prevent people from fraudulently forcing others into slavery—for example, by tricking the unfortunate "slaves" into thinking that they had an enforceable obligation to remain in peonage.

That the harm principle does not compel the state to remediate suggests the need for guidelines—"mediating maxims"⁵¹—to determine when deterrence and redress are appropriate. Similarly, under a "prudential consideration,"⁵² the state should consider, in setting the limits of redress, not merely the *legitimacy* of allowing redress but the *wisdom* or *prudence* of permitting regulators to do so. There is no philosophically principled means of determining when a particular class of harms or wrongs should be remediable: Once it is conceded that the state may act, the complex calculus of how best to proceed is not for the philosopher but for the people and their political institutions.

Aggregative Harms

I add a few words here about risk simply to round out the discussion of the methods the state may use to deal with it. When we speak of risk we mean that the harm has not yet occurred, so the conventional approaches to redress are beside the point. That is why suits by plaintiffs to enjoin risky activity are likely to be unavailing unless the harm is empirically shown to have a high probability of befalling the plaintiff from well-known causes (the proverbial example, again, is the neighbor playing with dynamite). A suit seeking to enjoin a purely speculative risk will normally be dismissed. Such a suit is one in which the probability that the plaintiff will be harmed is unknown or low and in which the probability of the event's occurring is equally unknown or low, even if the harm would be devastating should it actually occur. An example was the suit (ultimately dismissed) to bar the United States from orbiting the space shuttle on the grounds that it was carrying a space probe loaded with plutonium that would be highly toxic if it fell to earth. (A later, more timely concern was over the possibility that the startup of the European Center for Nuclear Research's Large Hadron Collider near Geneva might have created a black hole that would swallow the earth. If you're reading this, it didn't happen.)⁵³

A common class of risk is that of harm that could result from aggregating a type of activity, any instance of which is not harmful in itself. One example of an aggregative harm, presented in chapter 3, is driving on the roads. A single driver or even a few drivers are unlikely to cause harm, but for some critical mass of drivers, accidents are inevitable. The harm principle does not require the state to wait until particular accidents occur. Redress for harms already suffered is not the only form of intervention allowed. The state may take steps to reduce the number of accidents by providing rules of the road. Violations of these rules are thus criminalized, not because the actions are primarily harmful but because these "derivative crimes" will provide drivers with an incentive to act in ways that will reduce and even minimize the underlying harm. In addition to enacting rights-of-way, speed limits, and stop requirements, the state may license drivers, register automobiles, and mandate safety inspections; it may also impose higher penalties for certain types of unsafe driving (e.g., while intoxicated).

The realm of aggregative harm requires the state to pay particular attention to the principle of least intrusion, lest the legislature move up the ladder of generality and impinge on all activity. Consider the argument that murder is an aggregative harm: If you put enough people together long enough, some of them will kill others. Criminalizing wrongful killing, runs the argument, does not prevent murder,[54] so if we really wish to prevent murders we should predict who might commit them and then preventively detain them—either jail them or make them wear a tracking device and monitor their activities. But that would be a reductio ad absurdum. Why not jail us all? Preventive detention turns the harm principle on its head, forfeiting all liberty in liberty's name.

Accumulative Harms

Some harms become worrisome when many people engage in activities that are only minimally injurious or intrusive, considered one by one. For reasons already discussed, a private lawsuit will be inadequate: the victim cannot tie his injury to a particular person, the harm may be slowly progressing so that at any given instant a lawsuit would run afoul of the maxim *de minimis non curat lex* (the law does not bother itself with trifles), or there may be no satisfactory judicial remedy (a court cannot effectively instruct a defendant engaged in the normal activities of life "not to pollute"). One solution is to enact a regulatory scheme allocating ranges of allowable pollution to active polluters or to impose costs on activities not currently "charged" for polluting (since air is a "free good" no one pays for dirtying it without legislative intervention). The state will usually find it necessary to supplement the regulatory apparatus with an array of criminal laws and civil claims through which either the state itself or other parties can be empowered to prosecute, seek fines and compensation, and enjoin particular activities.

In dealing with accumulative harms the state is not limited to these usual forms of intervention. It may be more prudent, because cheaper, to tax and spend to create social programs that will divert destructive energies to more beneficial outlets than to wait until harms occur and then prosecute. One study offered evidence that recreation and training programs can reduce some types of crime more cheaply than prosecuting. That is the conclusion that "a growing number of mayors and judges, most of them Republicans" drew about efforts to prosecute street crime in California.[55] A *Los Angeles Times* study of a "three-strikes-you're-out" California law mandating long prison sentences for a third felony conviction "found that the law is taking a harsher toll on California's justice system than on its criminals":

> Third-time defendants who face the prospect of 25 years to life, as the law demands, are no longer willing to enter into [plea bargains] that used to settle 90% of all felony cases. Instead, they prefer to sit in county jail, awaiting trial. The result is a swelling jail population, a mushrooming court docket, and endless trial delays. To stem the tide, prosecutors are ignoring new "strikes," and judges are reducing felonies to misdemeanors. The result: just 1 in 6 eligible defendants has been packed off to prison for the 25-year minimum.[56]

If the state can prevent some crimes from being committed and train people to lead productive lives, nothing in the harm principle compels the state instead to spend more money prosecuting offenses after they have been committed. The harm principle permits anticipation, prevention, and diversion as well as after-the-fact responses like prosecution, punishment, and restitution.

Regulation versus Litigation: The Case for Licensing

In his well-known book *Capitalism and Freedom*, Milton Friedman argued against occupational licensing on the grounds that licensing deprives people of a fundamental liberty to engage in productive activities and that it inevitably leads to professional monopolies that restrict supply and raise prices.[57] That licensing has these economic effects and that the power to license is widely abused by existing governments I have no doubt.[58] But that it deprives people of a fundamental liberty is much more open to question.

As discussed in chapter 6, a fertile source of harm today is the exercise of expertise. Lay clients cannot anticipate or avoid damage that specialists whom they consult might force them to suffer. To deter and redress such harm, the state may bind experts to a fiduciary ethic of care for those to whom they minister. In the realm of redress, the fiduciary ethic means that in a suit for damages (for medical malpractice, say), the expert will be held to a standard higher than that of ordinary negligence. Without discussing the standard itself, Friedman assumed that the only legitimate way the state could deal with harm that unlicensed practitioners might cause is to open the courts to claims of malpractice. Unlike some conservatives, he freely admitted that "one of the protections of the individual citizen against incompetence is protection against fraud and the ability to bring suit in the court against malpractice."[59]

Suppose doctors were not licensed. Anyone could practice medicine (of course the state could always punish quacks for lying about their credentials; no one has the right falsely to claim a medical degree). Some number of patients would be harmed by the inadequate methods and knowledge of the unskilled and untutored quacks who would be permitted to practice, presumably a larger number of patients than are harmed by doctors under the prevailing licensing scheme. The only relief for these patients that Friedman would permit is a suit in the courts. Friedman is oblivious to the intangible nature of many harms, perhaps assuming, as some economists do, that anything for which we can seek redress may be quantified and monetized (so that if a patient suffers pain from malpractice he will be adequately compensated by a sum of money). In apparently assuming a one-to-one correspondence between actual harm and a legal verdict for money damages, he ignores the significant practical and evidentiary difficulties of proving any case. In fact, it is plausible to assume that in a regime of freedom for quackery many more patients would be injured and be uncompensated by malpractice than under the present system in which only education and experience entitle a doctor to practice.[60]

But as Friedman tells the story, the problem of injury would not *ultimately* be significant, for had licensing never existed the market would have developed means by which patients could sort quacks from knowledgeable doctors, essentially through an invisible hand by which different forms and places of practice would acquire reputations that would signal quality differences to lay patients. This is a *long-run* explanation, and it is unconvincing. People live in the here-and-now and reasonably expect protection from harms that befall them. The long-run explanation is at bottom an antiliberal one: It asserts that people *in the future* would benefit from the forms of practice that might develop if practice is left unhindered now, and so the state should refrain from exercising its power. But as chapter 9 considers at greater length, sacrificing people now by encouraging (or not preventing) harms to them so that people later may reap the benefits is a policy that libertarians reject in every other context.[61]

Confronted by a rising technical sophistication and a widening arena in which quacks could commit harms, it is both legitimate and prudent for the state to enact a policy that will (largely) eliminate a class of harms at the outset. The harm principle does not preclude the state from choosing to view the spread of unregulated medical practice as an aggregative harm (some people out of the mass of practitioners will cause harm) and to single out a particular characteristic (lack of knowledge and training) for prohibition. To wait until each case of harm materializes is to condemn many people to irremediable harm and suffering. None of this is to say that the licensing philosophy or methods the states actually use today are efficient, sound, or even designed to achieve a deterrent purpose. But it is within the state's authority (if not always its competence) to take action against both risks and after-the-fact harms simultaneously, by prohibiting outright some potential sources of the harm and remitting harms that result from useful activities to the scrutiny of a court. That some disadvantage will ensue from the prohibition (if there were no licensing, inexperienced, non-M.D. "doctors" might charge low-income patients lower prices than "real" doctors) is to say nothing more than that in employing a prudential consideration, the state must balance competing benefits and drawbacks (just as it does in allowing private malpractice suits—for if *these* suits were disallowed, the price of an office visit and treatment would presumably fall as well).[62] Nor does licensing and related regulation need to be all or nothing: Various intermediate forms of practice, as exist for some professions, could be developed so that certain procedures could be performed by those who had less expensive training and who could perform the service for less than what the highest-credentialed specialist would charge.

In choosing licensing to supplement a scheme of private redress to deal with malpractice, the state has not exhausted all modes of intervention. It could even more actively choose to specify the affirmative steps that physicians should take in treating particular ailments—what federal and many state governments do today in effect in listing which medical techniques will be eligible for reimbursement. This much more textured, detailed regulation is consistent with the harm principle, but might fail the prudential consideration, since regulations tend to harden and thus can impede the flexibility that science and practice require to progress. But it is too much to say, a priori, that a liberal state has no legitimate grounds to take actions designed to reduce identifiable types of harms to large classes of people. It is usually cheaper to close the barn door than to send out a rescue party.

A separate question is whether a regulatory scheme that bars unlicensed practitioners is paternalistic. If a customer or client wishes to avail herself of the services of such a person in return for lower fees, should she not make that judgment for herself? Should not her consent obviate the state's concern? For if not, what could the concern be but that it is not in her interest to proceed? And isn't that paternalism? I shall return to these questions in chapter 9.

8

What Who?

Why Who?

Delimiting the powers of government will avail us nothing if the government refuses to be bound by the limits established. To legitimate government, to realize a state in which the ideal is manifest and actually practiced, we must worry not only about *what* the governors may do but also about *who* they may be. The harm principle centers on the What—the point beyond which government may not tread. But the *measure* of legitimacy is ultimately useful only if it is accompanied by a *mechanism* of legitimacy. *Who* should rule is the "great Question"[1] that Locke said has disturbed mankind in all ages past. The harm principle will be only an intellectual curiosity if it cannot answer the question properly.

Until very near the present age, Mill noted, people had always thought "it a necessity of nature that their governors should be an independent power, opposed in interest to themselves."[2] Liberty would come either by constraining the ruler or by appointing a ruler whose interests coincided with those of the governed. Today it is a commonplace that liberty flourishes only in a regime both constrained and democratic. Not everyone agrees, however, that liberty depends on the nature of rulership. Isaiah Berlin argued, for instance, that negative liberty and democratic institutions are not logically connected:

> Liberty [in the negative] sense is principally concerned with the area of control, not with its source. Just as a democracy may, in fact, deprive the individual citizen of a great many liberties which he might have in some other form of societies so it is perfectly conceivable that a liberal minded despot would allow his subjects a large measure of personal freedom. . . . Freedom in this sense is not, at any rate logically, connected with democracy or self-government. Self-government may, on the whole, provide a better guarantee of the preservation of civil liberties than other regimes, and has been defended as such by libertarians. But there is no necessary connection between individual liberty

and democratic rule. The answer to the question "Who governs me?" is logically distinct from the question "How far does government interfere with me?"[3]

Hobbes argued that the despotic sovereign would not try to harm his subjects because his strength comes from the people's vigor. The sovereign's office, Hobbes said, is to protect

> the *safety of the people* ... [and] by Safety here, is not meant a bare Preservation but also all other Contentments of life, which every man by lawfull Industry, without danger, or hurt to the Commonwealth, shall acquire to himselfe.... The safety of the People, requireth further, from him, or them that have the Soveraign Power, that Justice be equally administred to all degrees of People; that is, that as well the rich, and mighty, as poor and obscure persons, may be righted of the injuries done them.[4]

These arguments assume that a "liberal despot" is possible. The term implies a sovereign without self-interest or with a self-interest that depends on satisfying the interests of the populace. But in the first place the populace consists of people with varying self-interests, and in the second, rulers are not machines but human beings, with their own desires and interests. More so than a multiplicity of rulers, a single ruler will confuse his own desires with those of his nation. Locke derided the idea that people would be sufficiently protected from individual predators if they would but place their fate in the hands of an absolute ruler: "This is to think that Men are so foolish that they take care to avoid what Mischiefs may be done them by *Pole-Cats,* or *Foxes,* but are content, nay think it Safety, to be devoured by *Lions*."[5] Believing in the possibility of the liberal despot is like believing in a populace of saints: The former assumes away liberty as the latter assumes away harm.

Yet paradoxically many theorists of the What continue to assume the plausibility of a liberal despot.[6] One of the most remarkable aspects of Robert Nozick's derivation of the minimal state is his silence about the state's governors.[7] Nozick writes as though protective associations would be some sort of computers. Solving problems through a set of prerecorded instructions, they may be subject to programming errors but they would not be natively malicious or in business to satisfy themselves. To these neutral agencies the people yield their own power to determine the fairness of the associations' proceedings, as Hobbes's subjects yielded to a king. This anti-statist writer ironically trusts heavily in the goodwill of the rulers. Only by constructing a ruler programmed to cause no harm can the dilemma of the overreaching state be solved. The programmed state would be forced to adhere to its minimal functions.

But people are not programmable, and a minimal state with monopoly power would, in the absence of an external control, sooner or later go rogue. When the dominant protective association morphs into the state, the people seem to lose forever the power to input the algorithm (a strangely Hobbesian argument for a libertarian to make). But if they do lose this power, the people forfeit the liberty to control the threat of injury. For an agency run by human beings beyond any power but their own self-control may always adopt rules that unfairly enhance the position of governors to the detriment of clients. Nozick offers no reason to believe that the original intent of the parties to the contract and the successor state's original obligations would be honored. In Nozick's world the dominant agency achieves what it thinks is fair solely because it has the clout to enforce its will. Missing is any demonstration that the transition to statehood would or could preserve rules that would be fair. Indeed, Nozick fails even to address the problem of whether the dominant protective agency would "turn" on its subscribers. Against Leviathan there is no appeal. The anarchist might justifiably complain that Nozick has succeeded only in replacing individual transgressors with a large and invincible one.[8] On balance, the anarchist would say, usurpation of people's rights is bound to occur; better, therefore, that the state not exist at all.

Nozick might have retorted that the minimal state has no incentive to usurp because it has so little power. But that is true only in the safety of his pages. In a state of nature in which people harm one another, Nozick has argued, something like a minimal state would emerge. Whether it performs well or ill is a risk that always accompanies power. If you object that the minimal state, being at the whim of an autocrat or an elite or a mob, might choose unfair rules (transgressing the original postulate that it protect property "and so on"), then I will (he might have continued) set forth those things that no state may morally undertake to do. But Nozick cannot delineate the rules that a minimal state is morally entitled to enforce.[9] This inability does not stem from any oversight on Nozick's part. It is built into his premises—and the premises of any like theory. Invisible-hand theories can show why political institutions exist but cannot guarantee legitimacy when the state arises because, as we have seen, the What is indeterminate. The metes and bounds of the harm principle must be drawn and redrawn as changing times and conditions require. Who controls the endless negotiation is therefore central to the problem of legitimacy.

Democracy and the Harm Principle

Ultimate holders of political power can be found, analytically, in relatively few categories: monarchs, aristocrats, stakeholders with property, experts, or the people as a whole.[10] I shall waste no words on the first two alternatives, since it is patent that the "liberal despot" renders the harm principle insecure, for reasons already discussed. The other categories deserve a closer look.

Stakeholders: Ownership and Independence as the Basis of Political Power

Until recent times, only an "independent" person—defined as one who possesses a certain sort of property—was thought fit to sit in the legislature or to cast a ballot. Four related arguments, not always disentangled, were pressed against enfranchising the poor and the dependent: (1) People dependent on others tend to absorb the worldview of the people on whom they depend and thus will not cast independent votes. (2) Toiling at rude work unfits workers to make important decisions. (3) Citizenship depends on having a property stake in the community. (4) The poor will inevitably steal from the rich by taxing them.

1. *Against dependence.* Many of these objections were urged during and after the seventeenth-century English civil war. Cromwell and his party of Independents argued that only those with landed estates should have the franchise. "If there be anything at all that is a foundation of liberty it is this, that those who shall choose the lawmakers shall be men freed from dependence upon others," said Cromwell's ally Henry Ireton.[11] He believed that members of trading corporations and owners of freehold property producing 40 shillings a year were alone entitled to vote. The Independents excluded shopkeepers, artisans, tradesmen, farmers who worked land leased for a term of years (even if the term was 99 years or 999 years), apprentices, servants, and beggars (as well as criminals, minors, and women). The progressive Levellers, a more radical group of small businessmen, wished to broaden the franchise considerably. They would have included anyone who retained the right to his own labor. Because self-employed shopkeepers, artisans, and a few others did not depend on someone else for a living, the Levellers proposed a political role for them in the commonwealth. But neither the Independents nor the Levellers acceded to the argument, advanced by some, that the rude sorts who depended on a salary or like remuneration should also be enfranchised. The wage-earner, the servant, the beggar, women—all were dependent on others; none could be trusted.[12]

2. *Toiling at rude work disqualifies.* Only "gentlemen" at leisure are in a position to choose wisely. As Burke said in the late eighteenth century:

> The occupation of a hairdresser, or of a working tallow chandler cannot be a matter of honor to any person ... to say nothing of a number of other more servile employments. ... The state suffers oppression if such as they ... are permitted to rule.[13]

3. *Control limited to those with an ownership interest.* Many revolutionaries in the United States voiced the sentiment that government of the nation should be entrusted to those who own it. The state, they claimed, is like a joint-stock company; only those with a property stake in the business should be entitled to control.[14] The

poor have no interest in property save to steal it. Hence enfranchising the poor is to cede property, not preserve it.[15]

4. *Danger of placing taxing power in hands of the poor.* A fourth argument closely paralleled the third. Since taxation is an important power, the enfranchised poor would in effect commit larceny through taxation to provide for themselves at the expense of the rich. As late as 1861, Mill himself argued in *Representative Government* that

> the assembly which votes the taxes, either general or local, should be elected exclusively by those who pay something towards the taxes imposed. Those who pay no taxes, disposing by their votes of other people's money, have every motive to be lavish, and none to economize.[16]

But the fallacy in all these arguments is the crabbed understanding of the stakes in a liberal polity. Under the harm principle, it is interests that are at stake, not any single one of them. In any event, the definition of property to which the propertied gave credence, even in the seventeenth century, was far more constricted than it needed to be. Locke did not confine the sense of property to physical possessions. He included life, liberty, and, most significantly, the labor of which every average person is capable. Hence people poor in physical possessions are not poor in property. Moreover, raising taxes is not the only issue governments are called upon to decide. You might as well say that a person without an automobile may not vote because legislatures are empowered to enact speed limits and pedestrians would have "every motive" to be miserly in letting stalwart motorists go about their way. You might as well hold that the poor have no stake in defining the law of larceny because they possess too little to be stolen or because they suffer less than the rich when they lose an article insignificant to a wealthy person. And you might as well understand that if the worry is about disproportionate government expenditures not tied to a motive to conserve, the wealthy have a far greater stake than the poor in spending lavishly on protection because they have so much more to secure (and a far greater motive to vote down safeguards against crimes by the propertied, like insider trading, and creation of financial instruments that they alone control). Property is not protected by disenfranchising those without "significant" amounts of it, but by recognizing that property itself is an interest among the many that deserve primary protection under the harm principle. All have a stake in it. All must have a role in vivifying it.

Expertise as the Basis of Political Power

Arguments for the legitimacy of expert rulers have an ancient lineage traceable to Plato, who in *The Republic* assumed "that good government is nothing but a matter of knowledge and that knowledge is always the possession of a class of experts, like the practice of medicine. . . . most men [being] . . . permanently in the relation to their rulers of a patient to his physician."[17] This assumption, that all public problems will yield to technical skills, has proved exceptionally durable, a hardy perennial of political justification. In 1962 the president of the United States told the graduating classes of Yale University:

> You are part of the world, and you must participate . . . in the solution of the problems that pour upon us, requiring the most sophisticated and technical judgment. . . . The central domestic problems of our time . . . relate not to basic clashes of philosophy or ideology, but to ways and means of reaching common goals—to research for sophisticated solutions to complex and obstinate issues. . . . What is at stake in our economic decisions today is not some grand warfare of rival ideologies which will sweep the country with passion but the practical management of a modern society.[18]

President Kennedy was largely mistaken (and his confusion was perhaps a portent of both foreign disaster yet to come and of the "grand [ideological] warfare" that wracks us to this day), because he failed to distinguish between technique and ends.

As we understand the term today, an "expert" is one who commands a body of knowledge and a technique for solving a class of problems or arriving at a goal already given. The more expansive its claim to knowledge, the greater the danger that a particular specialty will embrace questions that it is ill-prepared to answer. The tendency to claim expertise beyond the limits of technique may be manifested in two ways: the transposition of technique (by a person who mistakenly supposes his expertise in one technique can solve problems that require other specialized techniques); and the transposition of ends (by a person who is appointed on the basis of his skill in one technique to make judgments in matters about the propriety of human ends and the good). The transposition of technique is amusingly illustrated by a lesser work of Georg F. W. Hegel. In his *Dissertation on the Orbits of the Planets*, Hegel "proved" philosophically in 1801 that a planet could not exist between the orbits of Mars and Jupiter—and published his judgment a few months *after* the first asteroids had been discovered there.[19] The cure for this sort of mistake is a more acute understanding of the nature of phenomena subject to investigation and the proper use of other methods in that investigation. The problem of the transposition of ends is not so easily cured, for in leaping altogether outside the possibility of technique, the expert leaves behind the very possibility of expertise itself, as Harold J. Laski memorably chronicled:

> Lord Kelvin was a great physicist, and his discoveries in cable-laying were of supreme importance to its development; but when he sought to act as a director of a cable-laying company, his complete inability to

judge men resulted in serious financial loss.... Mr. Henry Ford is obviously a business man of genius; but, equally obviously, his table talk upon themes outside his special sphere reveals a mentality which is mediocre in the extreme.... Because a man is an expert on medieval French history, that does not make him the best judge of the disposition of the Saar Valley in 1919. Because a man is a brilliant prison doctor, that does not make him the person who ought to determine the principles of a prison code. The skill of a great soldier does not entitle him to decide upon the scale of a military armament; just as no anthropologist, simply as an anthropologist, would be a fitting governor for a colonial territory administered by native races.[20]

The abandonment of technique is often at best only dimly understood. Nobel laureate S. E. Luria, for example, noted three critical problems for which biologists have (wrongly) undertaken to provide solutions, in part because of public pressure that they do so. They are being asked

> to assume responsibility for new approaches to the management of our environment; ... to save and redirect the future of the human race by improving experimentally the heredity of mankind—presumably by selecting the meek or eliminating the violent; ... [and in connection with the current controversy over the genetic basis of intelligence, to provide a means for getting] the most out of each person according to his or her ability.[21]

None of these problems, as important as they may be, Luria insisted, is biological, though a "proper" solution of each requires some biological understanding. The problems are, rather, political. How to organize environmental priorities, how to eliminate social causes of crime, and how to provide proper education from the earliest ages are all problems that require social valuation for solution; they are not problems the solution to which is possessed in the technique of a single class (or many classes) of experts. Thus a physician has techniques for curing illness or reducing pain. You do not properly instruct the doctor on how to treat your symptoms if you wish to rid yourself of the ailment. But nothing in the expert's training in a specialized technique makes him also expert in deciding whether a person or group of persons should seek the ends he is trained to reach. Physicians may prescribe painkillers but it is for the patient to decide how to balance the reduction of pain against the risk of addiction to pain pills, or even treatment against death itself.[22]

The confusion between technique and ends in the political realm persists. Agreeing with President Kennedy, Philip N. Hauser, a president of the American Sociological Association, once declared that

[i]n approaching revision of the law to conform with contemporary realities, it is desirable to recognize that neither a "conservative" nor a "liberal" approach is relevant. The "conservative" has been correctly defined as a person who worships dead radicals; and the "liberal" as a chap whose feet are firmly planted in mid-air. The intuitive reactions of neither the conservative nor the liberal will adequately provide solutions for contemporary problems. What is required is a twentieth century approach— an engineering approach; that is, the resolution of problems through the application of knowledge, not a conservative or liberal approach.[23]

But governing is not bridge building. If the best way of fording a particular river is to cross a bridge, it is best for engineers to design and build it. A well-defined (that is, a determinate) end cannot be reached through political means. We do not set a ship adrift and expect it by wind, or by vote of the passengers on which direction to sail, to reach a set of plotted coordinates on the charts. But how best to choose the coordinates themselves—that is, how to pick our destination—is an entirely different question. To ask a civil engineer what to do may get us a bridge across the river, but that does not tell us on which side we should settle. The appropriate level of accident risk on the highways is not the determinate outcome of any conceivable expert knowledge. No expert can as an expert tell us the optimum level, though it would be foolish to refuse to consult with traffic experts to assess the consequences of setting the risk (via a speed limit, for example) at one level or another. The indeterminacy of the harm principle is an indeterminacy of ends. We employ the harm principle to provide every person with the possibility of seeking the good, but the harm principle requires that every person, in turn, participate in shaping its contours. To defer to experts is to defeat its very purpose.[24]

Citizenship as the Basis for Political Power

As we saw in chapters 2 and 3, the harm principle requires an authoritative law-making body—a legislature—to declare the contours of harm and risk of harm in the various circumstances of life. It should require no extended argument to establish two further implications: (1) citizenship as the basis for exercising political power under the harm principle, and (2) a ban on any attempt to delegate the legislature's law-making power elsewhere. The very indeterminacy that requires choices over a range of policies validates the people as a whole as decision maker, since there is no principled means to distinguish one person's stake from any other's in the choices left open by the harm principle. Weighting one person's vote over another's is to prefer the good of that person over another's. It is also to prejudge the very question to be decided. Precluding one person's vote on the grounds that his contrary, irresponsible, or uninformed view will taint the legislative decision is to decide in advance what the proper outcome should be. But the only proper outcome is the one that comes out.

Nevertheless, only on relatively rare occasions do the people themselves choose policies and laws directly. Of necessity the people are limited to selecting representatives to whom authority is delegated to make the actual choices. Representatives are legally free to decide as they choose. Though polls can reveal voter preferences on particular issues, polling provides no guidance on most issues. No political system can provide a candidate for each possible set of positions because the number of alternatives is incalculably high and would require an astronomical number of candidates at the national level if the voter were truly to have a choice in voting for a candidate who embraced the world exactly as he saw it.[25] Necessarily, therefore, the tendency is to blur issues or to group issues into clusters or attitudes. No one is chosen on the basis of promises about situations not yet developed or about more than a few existing articulated problems. Often, in fact, candidates will promise to achieve mutually contradictory goals (lower taxes, reduced deficit, more services).

The result is that only fitfully, when a particular yes-or-no issue catches widespread public attention, is indeterminacy under the harm principle resolved by the voting public. The lack of representation on the range of issues and the relative inability of people to judge matters outside their immediate ken can lead the state to divide into clusters of increasingly independent communities, reflected in interest-group pluralism—decisions for those who can afford to lobby harried legislators.[26] Even if the community were not divided in this way, the free rider problem would block many forms of legislation though most or even perhaps all might desire a particular policy or collective good.[27]

The problems of democratic representation are outside my scope. I can but note that from the perspective of the harm principle, the three most pressing problems yet to be solved are (1) obstacles to registration and voting, for unless people find it possible to vote, the outcome will not reflect the whole people's choice;[28] (2) the cost of campaigning, for unless candidates can be freed from raising the huge sums required to run or having their messages swamped, whether mounting challenges or defending their seats, there is little likelihood that views to which cash does not attach can effectively challenge those to which it does;[29] and (3) the barrier to public involvement in the writing and promulgation of regulations. That we do not formally restrict office-holding to particular experts does not dispose of the problem. A major difficulty for administration of the harm principle in complex industrial democracies is that we have tendered significant power to "expert" bureaucratic agencies that are rarely given significant guidance by the political branches and that are even more rarely open to participation by the people generally. When the people have no regular means of weighing in on the goals that regulatory agencies pursue, the legitimacy of the harm principle is in jeopardy. The delegation of law-making power to the bureaucratic state is a substantial issue for liberalism, and one that often goes unrecognized or is simply brushed aside.[30]

Restraints on Government Power

Even if legislators profess allegiance to the harm principle, their power is necessarily open-ended. Why are we obliged to obey the laws they enact to which we do not consent? The answer is that consent is irrelevant if the exercise of governmental power is restrained by impartial procedures that produce general outcomes. Obligation to abide by the rules follows from our relation to fellow citizens. If the state acts legitimately, a person who says, "Why am I obligated to do as it commands?" is like the person who asks, "Why must I speak the predominant language to be understood? It's unfair!" Fairness, to paraphrase Mae West, has nothing to do with it. The predominant language simply is, and there are consequences to not following it. Likewise, the state *is*, and if it acts *legitimately*, then it is right that there be consequences of flouting its decrees.

The rules of procedural legitimacy cannot be confined to "correct" interpretations of the harm principle, since these interpretations are not deducible but have moral force only because they are enacted by a legitimate state. By "interpretations" of the harm principle, I mean choices it allows—for example, establishing a tax code, determining the boundaries of criminal conduct, or setting rules of intestacy. I do not mean to imply that a legitimate state, simply for being procedurally sound, may then *disregard* the harm principle. Many types of legislative enactments are impermissible under the harm principle—for example, paternalistic policies (chapter 9) would be illegitimate outcomes of even a legitimate legislative process. Legitimacy, then, requires adherence both to the harm principle and to certain institutional forms and norms.

The practical effect of representative democracy is to place vast discretion in elected officials. To curb that discretion, we must find some means of restraining the power they exercise. In one-to-one transactions and relationships, people are constrained in part by some knowledge of the relationship itself and of the probable consequences of what they are doing. If they err in a serious way and cause harm, they will likely be held accountable, and that knowledge tends to keep them in check. Not so in government. As governmental power grows and officials become more remote from the people over whom they govern, it becomes harder and harder to trace the consequences of their actions. Moreover, most legal systems immunize officials from being sued personally, so that they are ultimately responsible only to those who appointed them or to the electorate. But getting elected (or being defeated) will have very little to do with much of the potential damage of which legislatures are capable. So damage will inevitably ensue for which there is, generally, no redress, unless the government is constrained in various other ways before the damage can be done. The list of institutional forms and norms that follows is no doubt familiar and incomplete, but it suggests the types of restraints that must necessarily be implemented for the harm principle to become a living reality.

Restraints Preserved in a Constitution

Suppose I ask my wife to wake me tomorrow morning at 11. I tell her that because I will be staying up quite late to finish this chapter, which I must reread before delivering to my editor at noon, I will no doubt be tired and even cranky. I forewarn her that I probably will mumble for her to leave me alone. This evening I'm anticipating my likely reaction in the morning and beseeching her to disregard whatever I say on being awakened. The rule to follow, I tell her, is the one I am announcing now. When she wakes me the next morning, I have had, as prophesied, only a few hours of sleep, am indeed tired and cranky, and do countermand my request of the evening before. "Go away," I say, putting my head under the pillow. I hope, in some foggy part of my brain, that she will respect this injunction, like Mammy Yokum's "Ah has spoken."

Which of the two "mes" is she to respect: the one from twelve hours ago or the one from twelve seconds ago? In garden-variety legislation the second in time of two conflicting statutes governs. But a later statute does not trump an earlier, superior constitution. And we may imagine my instructions in that light. A constitution is a framework for government that, in the sense used here, cannot easily be overridden by normal legislative process, so that its procedural and substantive constraints on government will endure unless persistent and pervasive dissatisfaction prompt a supermajority to override the disfavored constitutional ground rule. In constraining the government, a constitution promotes compliance with the harm principle in two essential ways: first, by blocking the government from exercising certain powers, it reduces the possibility that government will itself cause harm; and second, in narrowing the field of action, it resists the diffusion of government power and directs public attention, resources, and energy to those problems that need government scrutiny and action under the harm principle. A constitution that resists casual attempts to sideline its safeguards, when an ephemeral majority would prefer to dispense with them because of a case at hand, can ensure that government devote its force and intellect to solving problems rather than defending itself when every new issue arises. If my wife did not take seriously my instructions from the night before, she would waste her time and mine in trying to persuade me that my earlier instructions were sounder than my muttered disavowal, and she would have less patience and energy to roust me from my slumbers.[31] Beyond the general principle that a constitution must preserve itself against revisions prompted by momentary passions and transient majorities, several other forms and constraints are likely necessary to guarantee, as much as possible, fidelity to the harm principle.

Separation of Powers

"The accumulation of all powers, legislative, executive, and judiciary, in the same hands ... may justly be pronounced the very definition of tyranny," James Madison famously wrote in defending the Constitution.[32] Against the tyrant there is no redress; dividing the powers of government checks the power of government itself to do harm and reduces the tyranny of self-exemption. Rulers who combine executive and legislative power, said Locke, "may exempt themselves from Obedience to the Laws they make, and suit the Law, both in its making and execution, to their own private advantage."[33] That the harm principle might wither in the face of undivided power does not necessarily mandate constitutional divisions: What is formally required in the U.S. Constitution (that the same person may not simultaneously hold federal legislative and executive offices) is not a requirement in parliamentary systems (the executive departments in Great Britain consist of members of the British Parliament, for example). And the division of powers between central and regional or state governments varies widely among the liberal democracies. I will not dwell on the many policy issues, as significant as they are, that are rooted in the concept and pause only to note that many of the noisiest modern political arguments about the legitimacy of government policies do not concern governmental performance under the harm principle. They are disputes, rather, over the appropriate branch or agency or level of government to accomplish certain objectives. Although party conservatives and liberals quarrel over the appropriate place on the continuum of local to national government to place a mechanism for enacting particular policies, they usually argue less about the propriety of government intervention than about efficiency, efficacy, and constituency of "self government."[34] The conflict between the federal government and California over the sale of marijuana (Congress forbids the sale of marijuana for any purpose and California permits its sale for medical uses) poses interesting issues of federalism and Constitutional law but no issue under the harm principle, since both agree that the drug may be regulated.[35] (The drug debate does reverse the usual bias of conservatives for local control and liberals for national legislation.) But the wisdom of public policy, a perennial debate, is not the same as the legitimacy of public policy-making, the central concern of the harm principle.

Laws Applied Equally to All, Including Lawmakers

Tyranny is no less apparent when lawmakers are unshackled by their own laws than when they are free to exercise all governmental powers. Law is the harm principle applied; exempting lawmakers and other government officials from its commands creates a privileged class immune from accountability. This principle against self-exemption is essentially the idea of the rule of law: "The first condition of free government is government not by the arbitrary determination of the ruler, but by fixed rules of law, to which the ruler himself is subject."[36] In the United States, equal application of the law is disregarded in various ways: Congress frequently enacts laws applicable, for example, to all employers except itself.[37] The rule of law is frequently evaded in small or subtle ways—for instance, when a prosecutor refuses to apply the law to prominent citizens,[38] when an official purports to suspend laws that block enforcement of other policies,[39] or when the law is written in the form of standards rather than rules and then delegated to agencies to enforce, creating virtually unreviewable discretion to apply the law unequally.[40] Nevertheless, the ban on self-exemption can be a powerful control over the power to legislate under the harm principle given the line-drawing problem and the indeterminacy of many public-policy measures. Justice Antonin Scalia has suggested that such a ban is built into the Equal Protection Clause. It is

> what protects us, for example, from being assessed a tax of 100% of our income above the subsistence level, from being forbidden to drive cars, or from being required to send our children to school for 10 hours a day, none of which horribles are categorically prohibited by the Constitution. Our salvation is the Equal Protection Clause, which requires the democratic majority to accept for themselves and their loved ones what they impose on you and me.[41]

Nondelegation of Legislative Power

When the legislature delegates to others its power to enact law, government is only remotely in the hands of the people, if at all. Delegation transforms democratic government into government by experts (no one argues any longer that legislative power should be delegated to kings or nobles, though many people argue that it should be delegated to individual presidents, who mostly redelegate in turn to presumed experts). Delegation sometimes is inevitable, for some policies depend on findings of fact before they can be implemented. For example, the president might be delegated the power to extend most-favored-nation status to another country but only if it frees political prisoners. It blinks reality to suppose that Congress could enact such a law for each country only after investigating the facts in each instance. This sort of delegation is acceptable because the delegation is accompanied by a standard under which the delegate must operate: The president may not grant most-favored-nation status to any country he chooses but only to those meeting the legal criteria. But the people's power to fill in the harm principle is blocked almost completely when the legislature engages in standardless delegation that grants the delegate power to formulate policy itself—for example, granting power to a highway commission to set the speed limit "as the commission shall see fit." Then the people will have lost their voice in declaring the appropriate rule of the road or in influencing the legislature in striking the proper balance between liberty and risk. Nor will they have ceded their power to a neutral Nozickian legislator but often to particular interests, whose good will be exalted above that of many others, as the "regulatory capture" literature suggests.[42] A small but revealing example is that of a letter Attorney General Richard Olney wrote in 1894 to the president of the Burlington

Railroad responding to a complaint that the Interstate Commerce Commission would ruin its business:

> The Commission is or can be made of great use to the railroads. It satisfies the public clamor for supervision of the railroads, at the same time that the supervision is almost entirely nominal. Furthermore, the older such a commission gets to be, the more inclined it will be to take the ... railroad view of things. ... The better course is not to abolish the Commission but to utilize it.[43]

The Supreme Court acknowledges the nondelegation principle only in theory, and delegated policy-making at both the federal and state levels is one of the major impediments to the people's oversight of the harm principle in the United States.[44]

Frequent Elections and Universal Suffrage

Whatever the difficulties of dictating legislative outcomes through voting, they are compounded when elections are infrequent. Whether elections must be held at stated times, as is the American practice, or may be scheduled by the government within a range established by law, as is the British practice, probably makes no significant difference. What counts is a system in which legislators remember that they are representatives who may be turned out of office, not members of a ruling class. It follows that no policy is necessarily permanent; the harm principle knows no rule of finality. Majority rule cannot be justified unless today's losers may become tomorrow's winners. Voting must be open to all, else the formal equality criterion is defeated and the harm principle cannot fairly be made determinate in those instances in which choices must be made.

Freedom of Speech and Press

Voting is not the only means by which to anchor laws to the will of the electorate. Indeed, if voting were the only means by which the people could exercise any control or influence over the government, it is doubtful that there could be more than feeble public direction. Public policy requires vigorous public discussion, which only a principle of free speech can secure.[45]

A Note on Rights

The harm principle is not constitutionalized; that is, the state is not obliged by the principle itself to declare any particular harm or way of harming a matter that must be addressed by legislation or subject to judicial or other legal redress (as noted in chapter 1, the harm principle is modest).[46] In carrying out its functions under the harm principle, the liberal state nevertheless recognizes a host of rights, some enshrined in the Constitution itself, some matters of statutory or judicial declaration. These are, then, obligations of the state but not of the harm principle. The state commits itself to observing such rights, and to enforcing them against violators, both as restraints on the state in accordance with and as a straightforward application of the harm principle. Rights in this sense do not violate the original understanding that the harm principle does not necessarily maximize, minimize, or prioritize.

Other Constitutional Restraints

As chapter 7 indicates, several distinct principles, many of them constitutionally enshrined, are necessary to limit interventions under the harm principle (principles of proportionality, equality, least intrusion, retroactivity, and procedural fairness).[47] No doubt there are arguments for still other principles, although many independently stated constitutional restrictions in the U.S. Constitution might fairly be interpreted as special cases of the more general requirements for procedural fairness and separation of powers (for example, the rule against bill of attainders).[48] Since I do not pretend this to be a work of constitutional exegesis, it will serve no purpose to enunciate all such restraints that might fairly be inferred from a concern both to prevent the government itself from causing harm and to motivate it to tackle the work entrusted to it. But one further and different sort of potential restraint does merit separate explanation: why the harm principle itself should not be constitutionalized.

Against Constitutionalizing the Harm Principle

Why not "constitutionalize" the harm principle—enshrine it, that is, in a prohibitory clause in the Constitution itself? Other provisions of the Constitution explicitly instruct the government to refrain from regulating certain activities, importantly the First Amendment's ban on laws against freedom of speech, press, and religion. Would we not realize a liberal state more fully if the Constitution declared that "neither the United States nor any state shall enact any law that neither deters nor redresses a wrongful setback to interest"? The answer must surely be that we would not, for such a provision would merely transfer the problems of interpreting the harm principle and filling in its interstices from the legislatures to the courts, much as the Supreme Court, beginning in the 1890s, arrogated to itself for forty years the power to delineate the bounds of economic decision-making during the heyday of economic due process.[49] Yet from time to time proposals to constitutionalize the harm principle surface, and a brief inspection may prove instructive. One was a proposal some years ago for a constitutional "Happiness Amendment." I cite it not for its intellectual rigor but for the breadth of its coverage, to see what difficulties await any attempt to remove the harm principle from legislative hands. The full text of the proposed amendment follows:

> Any citizen eligible to vote in a Federal election shall have standing to bring a claim in a Federal court of appropriate jurisdiction challenging any act of a person whose acts threaten to cause or are causing substantial harm to the safety or happiness of a consequential number of people.
>
> The Court may grant such relief as it deems appropriate and may award reasonable costs of litigation, including attorney's fees.
>
> "Person" includes any individual, governmental entity (including any department or agency), or nongovernmental entity (including any unincorporated association, corporation, or partnership).
>
> "Happiness" means the rights of citizens to fundamental justice, fundamental liberties, fundamental fairness, and the perpetuation and protection of environmental quality.
>
> "Fundamental justice" includes, but is not limited to, the principles of "distributive" justice to the extent that any governmental entity, by legislation or otherwise, establishes barriers or lessens the opportunities of citizens to share in the entitlements, wealth, and resources of the United States on an equitable basis.[50]

Its authors, a sophisticated journalist and an experienced lawyer, termed this proposal an "accountability" amendment to overcome the failure of public institutions to guard us from dangers created by the private sector. The idea beguiled its proponents; indeed, they rhapsodized over its implications, concluding that "it is the most promising, the most supple, and, in the light of our American heritage, the most philosophically and pragmatically right instrument available."[51]

Unfortunately, they fell prey to the Nozickian fallacy of the neutral lawmaker. Their case rests on the assumption that the courts can succeed whenever legislatures fail. Tracing through the labyrinth, we see that under this Amendment a court could award damages for harm to happiness, defined as the right to fundamental justice, defined in turn as fundamental liberties or the principles of distributive justice, further defined as an equitable share in the wealth of the United States. What is fair, free, or just would be constantly subject to revision by agencies (courts) ultimately unaccountable to the people (the very problem that the authors were seeking to overcome). And since this new power would have constitutional status, ordinary majorities could not reverse the courts' judgment. Further constitutional amendments would be necessary to undo judicial error.

The list of potential difficulties is long; I note only a few here. If Congress voted money for expensive medical care for people suffering from cancer while providing none for people with heart disease, could a court rule that the law discriminated unfairly against the latter group? If Congress voted to finance universal health care but omitted funds for extremely expensive life-prolonging devices, would it have discriminated unfairly against the poverty-stricken aged without financial means of obtaining such treatment privately? If Congress barred private expenditures on these expensive life-prolonging devices, would that provision violate a fundamental liberty? Would a court be empowered to enjoin hospitals from performing abortions on the ground that they threaten substantial harm to a consequential number of the unborn? Would a different court, instead, think itself empowered to force a hospital to perform abortions on demand on the ground that to fail to do so would be to cause unhappiness (as defined) to both the born and unborn? Might the earnest pedestrian-plaintiff be entitled to an injunction against automobile driving because of the threat to health and safety? And would a court entertain a suit to rewrite the tax laws (always ready for a thorough overhaul, we can all agree) on the ground that as presently worded they interfere with the principles of distributive justice? In short, constitutionalizing even the limited notion of threatened harm to safety would be to put uncontrollable power in the wrong Who.[52]

Another illustration of the difficulty of constitutionalizing the harm principle is the well-known argument of Christopher D. Stone that lawyers ought to be permitted to intervene in lawsuits on behalf of trees, rivers, and other natural objects to protect their "interests."[53] The notion is both seductive and puzzling. If someone or something is being harmed, it seems elementary that that someone or something should be allowed to plead a case. But under the harm principle, only people have interests. To hold that trees have an interest could mean only that they have an interest in remaining in forests. It would be odd to suppose that they might also have an interest in being part of your front door or the paper on which I am printing my manuscript. So to give trees judicial standing—that is, to permit arbitrarily selected lawyers to speak for their interests—is simply to open the court to an argument that we would be better off as a society keeping the trees where they are than to permit an opposing use. The courtroom argument, then, would not be about the trees' welfare but about our own, about whether we would be better off preserving the particular natural resource or using it.

Putting such a case in court shortchanges the democratic process, however, because it eliminates (or disregards) the judgment of the people—expressed in legislative enactment—that some interests do not warrant protection, or at least, that the balance must be struck the other way. If a law required a government agency to think long and hard before letting a land developer clear a forest, it would be useful (at least as a convenient fiction) to permit lawyers to represent before the agency the putative interest of the forest in remaining whole. In that situation, legal standing for the forest is nothing more than a mechanism by which to vindicate the legislative declaration that the forests should be preserved.

In the absence of such legislation, however, conceding power to a court to enjoin the land developer's interference with the forest's "right" to be preserved is to cede all power to courts to define harm. If courts could make such judgments for forests, they could also rule on behalf of any "entity" capable of being named: all future generations, the Sunbelt states, all people with a low IQ, ethnic minorities (or majorities), scholarship students, unemployed actors. To grant courts inherent power to decide whether such inchoate groupings in some sense have been harmed by the act of another would drain the harm principle of any utility. Such a doctrine would permit a holding that any change in position or status of any person or group is a harm for which recovery should be allowed—and that any act contributing to such a change is legally actionable. All brakes would be off.

These suggestions for judicial intervention are confused, I suggest, because their advocates fail to appreciate that whereas redress for individual harms may be vindicated in court, community or social harms depend in the first instance on legislative enactment declaring policy—that is, resolving the *conflict* between warring interests, none of which is, in the abstract, wrong. In a book bewailing Americans' obstinate refusal to think in social terms, Mary Ann Glendon furnishes a telling example of this confusion. "A kind of blind spot," she writes,

> seems to float across our political vision where the communal and social, as distinct from individual or strictly economic, dimensions of a problem are concerned. In a leading environmental-law decision, the Supreme Court held that the Sierra Club had no standing to argue for preservation of federal parkland as a *shared* natural resource. The only way the association could remain in court was to establish that particular *individuals* would be harmed by the recreational development proposal it was challenging.[54]

But if federal parkland is to be preserved as a shared natural resource, Congress must first say so. To hold otherwise is to say that I may claim an interest in having everyone else share my interest in preserving the park. The harm principle cannot stretch so far.[55] *My* interest may certainly be thwarted if the trees are felled, if the noise renders my home inhabitable, if the loss of the park damages the environment. But I do not have an enforceable interest in your thinking the same way. Shared interests may be vindicated in court only if the community that shares that interest has first declared it to be so. The harm principle as a whole, then, cannot be constitutionalized in any meaningful sense, because it encompasses choices that may properly be made only by all those affected by the outcome.

To this point we have seen that the harm principle is capacious: It justifies a state that can deal with a vast range of complexities thrown up by an interdependent, forceful, churning population. Much that someone might wish to do is subject to the harm principle's reach. But we began with the premise that a harm principle is useful in no small part to guarantee a private space in which you and I can be free from meddlesome outsiders. The question to which we now turn is how to identify the personal domain sufficiently to bar the state from subordinating a person's interests to the state's conception of what those interests should be.

9

Paternalism and the Timeline

Self-Regarding and Other-Regarding Behavior

A state designed to protect each person from harm in the sense so far defined cannot dictate how people should live their lives. You may believe in the maxim "early to bed, early to rise" but you may not compel me to turn the lights out by your clock. Even if I would become "healthy, wealthy, and wise" by taking your advice, you have at most, Mill said, a good reason for remonstrating or reasoning with me or persuading or entreating me, but not any reason for forcing me against my will. Paternalism for adults is no business of the state: It ought not limit or interfere with a person's liberty for his own good.[1]

There are five major arguments against paternalism:

1. Whatever may be a person's good, that person knows it better than anyone else; the state is more likely than the individual to err in determining the appropriate end.
2. The state is likely also to err in determining appropriate means to an end (it assumes that if person A takes action X it will be against his interest Y, but this assumption may be false).[2]
3. Legislating a concern for one form of good (health, life) would deny a person the freedom to do things that would advance another good that, in his judgment, outweighs the legislated good (impairing health by being the subject of a medical experiment, taking two jobs to send children to college, going to war, learning to skydive).
4. Autonomy is itself a good: It is always better to choose than have the choice made.[3] Determining when a person's autonomy should be outweighed by other considerations is so daunting an undertaking that it is best to treat autonomy as an integral part of well-being.
5. People should not always be saved from foolish mistakes but must be free to *make* mistakes, even foolish ones, since otherwise they could never learn. The

sensible parent refrains from sparing the child every possibility of failure; carrying the child to keep it from falling will produce a child who can never walk.[4]

In validating these arguments, two problems emerge. First, even though people may know their own ends better than anyone else, they do not necessarily understand the facts that shape the means they adopt in seeking their ends; and second, opposing paternalism in the abstract tells us nothing about how to recognize a paternalistic law or policy in practice.[5] Many policies that appear paternalistic are not. Some critics suppose, for example, that it is paternalistic for the state to require warning labels on dangerous products such as cigarettes. It is unclear why they think so. The labeling requirement imposes a burden on the manufacturer to prevent harm to customers; it does not force the smoker to do anything.[6] In what follows, the task is largely to distinguish legitimate from paternalistic prohibitions; doing so often requires that we attend to the difficulty of knowing the dangers that lurk.

At its most general, the problem is to determine whether an act affects only the person with respect to whom a law forbidding it would be paternalistic. Does the law aim at that part of conduct "which merely concerns himself"?[7] If so, says Mill, then the law is illegitimate. Some argue that that is an impossible line to draw because others invariably have a stake in the harm a person may inflict on himself. When a Westchester County (New York) executive in 2005 proposed regulating wireless computer networks of businesses, bloggers blasted his proposal as paternalistic because it would compel companies to install firewalls (like requiring "for my own good, . . . self-locking doors on my house to help protect me from something," one blogger complained). But the purpose of the requirement was to protect customer information, not businesses, from hackers.[8] A law barring you from playing with dynamite is intended to prevent you from blowing up your neighbors, not yourself. If, in the classic example, I refuse to wear a motorcycle helmet and am thrown onto my head on the highway, my children may be thrown onto public relief and the public will bear the cost of scraping me from the road.

Examples of purely self-regarding conduct, intended to overcome this objection, require considerable tidying to be credible, since drinking and smoking and like conduct that some wish to ban or severely constrain obviously are not confined in their effects to the solitary imbiber or inhaler. So to leave something to the argument against repression, the sanitized example becomes highly idealistic. Consider

> a hard working bachelor who habitually spends his evening hours drinking himself into a stupor, which he then sleeps off, rising fresh in the morning to put in another hard day's work. . . . He has no family; he drinks alone and sets no direct example; he is not prevented from discharging any of his public duties; he creates no substantial risk of harm to the interests of other individuals.[9]

Such examples are scarce in reality: For every hard-working bachelor who always drinks alone and safely at home, many other oafs have dependent families and drive while intoxicated (or texting). Laws aim at the generality: It would be difficult to exempt self-regarding cases from other-regarding instances at which the law is directed. Even late sleeping is not purely self-regarding, unless the sleeper, wealthy or retired, stays abed routinely. The sleep-deprived employee will likely do an inferior job once he arrives at work.

A general answer to this difficulty is to follow Feinberg in "presupposi[ng] ... that there is no necessity that public harm be caused in sufficient degree to implicate the harm principle whenever an individual deliberately injures himself or assumes a high risk of doing so." For if we cannot draw a line "between other-regarding behavior and conduct that is primarily and directly self-regarding and only indirectly and remotely, therefore trivially, other-regarding," then every risky act is a potential harm, no law is paternalistic, and our freedom to seek our own good is in peril.[10]

We can often draw the line by invoking the principle of least intrusion.[11] The problem of the Sleepy Worker, for example, is essentially that of aggregative harm.[12] Most people who go to bed late will probably pose no danger to anyone. But if enough people deprive themselves of too much sleep, some among them will cause harm. To prevent these sorts of harms, a resolute lawmaker might think to impose a national bedtime. Under the principle of least intrusion a national bedtime would be impermissible, however, since it would cast too wide a net. Not everyone works the same hours or requires the same amount of sleep. In any event there is a much more tailored solution: Let the employer reprimand or fire the Sleepy Worker who happens to be delinquent or deficient. That is an ample remedy, and it provides substantial incentive for the Sleepy Worker to do what is best for him and for the employer. In other words, going to sleep late does not *cause* harm to the employer (it is too far back along the causal chain). The employer's beef is not sleeplessness but sloppy performance for whatever reason—the Sleepy Worker might be failing to do the job well for many reasons that to the employer would look exactly the same. For example, the employee may not be concentrating on work because (a) he is worried about his sick mother; (b) he is newly in love; (c) the job bores him; (d) he is eating poorly; (e) he is ill; (f) he is on drugs; (g) he is thinking about his much more exciting hobby; (h) he is depressed because his baseball team keeps losing; (i) he is planning a bank robbery to pay off a gambling debt, and so on. In short, the principle of least intrusion helps us to distinguish self- from other-regarding actions: The other-regarding aspect of the Sleepy Worker's behavior can be sufficiently controlled without recourse to liberty-limiting paternalism. What is left over must be the self-regarding aspect of conduct only. To legislate against it is to act paternalistically. In the sections that follow, I weigh the claims that various laws or common understandings are paternalistic and therefore inconsistent with the harm principle.

Consent to Risks

One familiar argument is that health and safety laws are paternalistic because they forbid consumers, workers, hobbyists, athletes, and others voluntarily to assume risks. This was the argument, for example, of the bakery owners in *Lochner v. New York*—in legally limiting the hours that bakers could work, the state was deciding for each worker what was in his best interest.[13] But the peculiarity of this argument is that the bakers themselves never urged it. The hours-limitation law was in their interest; Lochner himself was not a baker but a bakery shop owner. The purpose of the law was not to *impose* a particular good on a class of unwilling recipients but to *enable* them to achieve a collective end.[14]

Likewise, pure food and drug laws are straightforward applications of the harm principle (barring producers from selling harmful substances to others), not policies that deny zealots the chance to gamble their health in return for the pleasures of ingesting a particular compound. It is odd to say that one has a "liberty" to buy something with a poisonous ingredient, since no one has an intrinsic right to have a product made by someone else in any particular way. The liberty infringed is the producer's, not the consumer's. Is it a legitimate liberty interest to add deleterious substances to a product that will likely harm others? The harm principle says no. This also answers Milton Friedman's argument that occupational licensing is paternalistic:

> Individuals, it is said, are incapable of choosing their own servants adequately, their own physician or plumber or barber. In order for a man to choose a physician intelligently, he would have to be a physician himself. Most of us, it is said, are therefore incompetent and we must be protected against our own ignorance. This amounts to saying that we in our capacity as voters must protect ourselves in our capacity as consumers against our own ignorance, by seeing to it that people are not served by incompetent physicians or plumbers or barbers.[15]

But Friedman nowhere refutes the factual premise of our ignorance because the premise is quite true.[16] So in prescribing qualifications and standards for professionals, the state is not so much protecting us from choosing to run the risk of seeking out a quack (it is not, after all, that from consulting with an unqualified expert we get a thrill akin to mountain climbing or eating fatty potato chips), but seeking to reduce the actual harm that the unqualified would likely cause.

An apparently stronger argument for the strict anti-paternalist is that the impure-food enthusiast (or the devotee of the undereducated doctor) seeks cheapness, not pleasure. A manufacturing process that rigorously screens out impurities costs more, so by imposing safety standards on manufacturers (or educational qualifications on professionals), the state is mandating higher-priced foods, drugs, and professional care to the detriment of those who would pay less or cannot afford to pay more. But harm prevention always imposes costs: How much people should be required to pay for protection is quintessentially a question for legislators to resolve. If the costs are too high for some people to bear, then there can be no principled objection to the state's making available some allowance to cover the regulation's incremental cost.

Of course, not every regulatory scheme benefits the class for whom it is said to be intended. A bare claim of protection from harm does not make it so, and many such programs connive at undermining protection for those who most need it. That legislative agendas can be manipulated is a cause to reprimand officials and reform the law, not to abolish the harm principle.[17]

Persistent critics might respond that even a well-designed set of prohibitory regulations interferes with their liberty to contract for substances that they wish to have. Conceding the impropriety of stuffing food with dangerous substances sold to an unsuspecting public (or of a badly wired home that cannot easily be inspected), they argue that if they could *consent* to the purchase, then the prohibition is paternalistic. The answer depends on the nature of the substance being sold. Consider a dangerous diet pill tricked out in sugary sweetness and packaged attractively, except for the label: "Warning: This Stuff Will Probably Kill You." A safety agency may evaluate whether the label sufficiently alerts consumers to actual risks. It would be paternalistic for the state to prohibit the sale of properly labeled useful poisons on the ground that people could not be trusted to use them correctly (just as it would be paternalistic to stop the sale of kitchen knives because people might cut themselves). But the hypothesized adulterated foodstuff is not being sold as a poison; it is being marketed (except for a contradictory warning) as safe for eating. With such opportunism the harm principle is more than adequate to deal.

The argument for access to contraband thus boils down to a claim for substances that either (1) are safe but useless or else (2) are dangerous and marketed as such. A substance that falls into the first category is the apricot pit, notorious for decades when marketed as a cancer cure under the name "laetrile." Whether to ban the *claim* that laetrile can cure cancer depends on the empirical evidence.[18] The state may act against fraud and medical dangers, so if the Food and Drug Administration mistakenly bans a substance it may be denounced for scientific ineptness but not for paternalism. When the question is whose experts are to be trusted, the agency must ultimately prevail, as long as it acts reasonably against an actual threat. If, on the other hand, the agency knows that the contentious substance is not dangerous but wishes to ban it merely because it is not useful, the prohibition is paternalistic. If a person desires to avail himself of a hope, no matter how forlorn, that the stuff really is efficacious, then as long as he is adequately informed that competent opinion believes the "drug" to be useless, there can be no principled, nonpaternalistic ground to prevent him from obtaining it. To prevent trickery, the agency could prohibit the stuff from being labeled or advertised as a means of effecting a cure. It might even forbid drugstores from stocking it on their shelves (although this latter prohibition skirts close to the paternalistic line). But it ought not to prevent a grower or manufacturer from selling apricots or pits, labeled as such and nothing more.[19]

A substance in the second category—dangerous and labeled as such—presents a different problem. As a general rule, dangerous substances with beneficial uses ought not be kept off the market, as long as sufficient warnings are affixed and they can be safely contained and transported. But the state does bar some dangerous substances—for example, nonprescription, addictive drugs—and the question is whether the prohibition is paternalistic. So it might seem. Heroin and cocaine are not advertised or sold as medicinal.[20] But the objection to the sale of these drugs is not merely that false benefits might be claimed, since the state is prohibiting their sale even if they were to be packaged in boxes with the skull-and-crossbones and labeled "Warning—Extremely Dangerous, Quickly Addictive, and Possibly Fatal." The major reason for the prohibition is the addictive property of these drugs, which are sold not merely to adults capable of understanding addiction but also to children who we may presume do not appreciate the risks. In other words, for a substantial part of the population to whom the drugs would be distributed, consent could not be presumed. Moreover, it is extremely improbable to suppose that many adults fully understand the risks they are running by taking these drugs. And the fact of addiction means that continued use is less than fully voluntary and drastically reduces the incentives of drug takers to complain of the continuing harm being done by those who have addicted them. It is only voluntariness and consent to risks or harm that make a ban on use paternalistic. But a law that says "It's illegal to sell drugs *unless* you've properly warned your customer" would be unworkable, because the administrative burden of ensuring that the warning was given or effective is too great to bear.

Is it permissible for the state to deny adjudicatory relief from a general law to a particular person because of administrative inconvenience, including high cost? Feinberg gives an example of someone who wants a dangerous drug that will injure him physically. Acting under a general law, the doctor has refused to prescribe it. The would-be buyer is "a mystic whose drug-induced grand trances produce liver damage, and who thinks of 'physical health' as a distraction, and not part of his personal interest at all." Since the law is written generally, he has "no recourse but to conform, unless he could request a special administrative hearing from an equity board—an excellent idea where it is not too cumbersome and expensive."[21] An "equity board" or an "Anti-Paternalism Review Board" (APRB) is surely open to the state to create. There can be no principled objection to the state's attempt to calibrate its regulatory mechanism, if the taxpayers thought the effort worthwhile, even though the spectacle might prove unedifying. Visualize thousands (perhaps millions) of people lining up in shopping malls where the APRB regional offices might locate, to hear petitions from those who wished to prove that they were fully informed of the dangers of drug-taking but that they weighed their private pleasures over the likelihood of sickness or early death. (Would it be legitimate for the APRB to inquire how parents on drugs would care for their children or to demand they post a bond?) To prevent the regional offices from becoming mere rubber-stamps for exceptions to the drug laws (or excuses for extortion from the administrative or judicial officials), the APRB might impose onerous procedural requirements—lawyers, doctors' certificates, posting of bonds, for example—so that only the wealthy could afford access to the tribunals. That might be a sufficient source of grievance that the entire apparatus would collapse.

But all that said, there is good reason to question current American drug policy. If it is loosely justified by claims about the addictive qualities of drugs and their potential consequences, it is also frequently incoherent because it lumps substances with widely varying effects and offers reasons for doing so that do not stand up to scrutiny. The topic is too large even to attempt a summary of the claims and counterclaims, arguments and counterarguments. Here I can merely note some obvious difficulties.[22]

First, the very definition of a "drug" is contested. The most commonly used statutory definition is "any substance other than food which by its chemical nature affects the structure or function of the living organism."[23] By that definition, not merely marijuana, cocaine, heroin, amphetamines, PCP, LSD, and ecstasy are drugs, but so too are tobacco, caffeine, and herbs, among many other substances (including alcohol, if by the definition quoted, it is not a "food," itself an ambiguous term). Yet taking some of these substances will land you in jail and turning down others will cause people to look askance.

Second, the commonly criminalized drugs have different physical and mental effects. Some are highly addictive; some not. Some may do long-term damage to the taker (though perhaps no more so than alcohol or tobacco taken long-term); others may do little or no damage. A few, like PCP, may cause immediate danger to others by provoking rage in the user; most will not. Some, like marijuana, have medicinal effects; others do not. Many can impair judgment so that, like alcohol, a ban on their use under certain circumstances (driving) is obviously justifiable. Yet many of the psychotropic drugs are banned as a group as if they all had the same properties and posed the same dangers.

Third, several reasons for banning drugs are inconsistent with our policies toward other substances and activities that pose similar or greater dangers. The risk of disease and death from alcohol and tobacco far exceeds those from using the banned psychotropics. It is difficult, for example, to square the ferocious rejection, at least by the federal government, of medicinal use of marijuana and the medicinal use of licit drugs like Ritalin (with effects similar to cocaine) that can be easily enough abused.

Fourth, public policy generally discounts the recreational use of currently illicit drugs, even those with relatively low risk of danger to anyone, even though we rarely require people to justify other risky recreational activities: snowboarding, skydiving, skiing. A scholar of American drug policy, Douglas N. Husak, observes that the government does not defend its inconsistent refusal "to tolerate any level of risk when drug use is recreational" and its tolerance for people taking "enormous risks when they engage in recreational activities that do *not* involve the use of drugs."[24]

So it seems likely that though the ban on the use of various drugs is not paternalistic by the mere fact of their being outlawed, aspects of our current helter-skelter drug policies find their ultimate justification in a paternalism that a liberal society ought to avoid. And the existence of the ban on drugs raises the separate question whether fully informed people should be prevented from voluntarily risking serious injury or even death to pursue thrills. Assume that the legitimate objection to legalizing drug-taking hinges largely on drugs' addictive property. Other injurious conduct in which people willingly engage are not biologically addictive. These include riding motorcycles on major highways, surfing on huge waves, performing in a circus high-wire act, and engaging in high-risk sports such as boxing and mountain climbing. Assume that aficionados understand the risks, that the circus performer has not been duped onto the trapeze. Are laws that prohibit or regulate these activities paternalistic? Outright prohibition is paternalistic, if there is no danger (or no undue danger) to others. Some time ago a Consumer Product Safety Commission working paper carped on the dangers of snowmobiles, in language that might have been taken to justify an outright ban:

> Racing becomes a temptation and leads to collisions with other moving vehicles.... Dominating the environment may be a daredevil attitude on the part of many operators. The spirit of adventure guides drivers into uncharted fields and woods. Night riding is viewed as thrilling.[25]

Regulating what others find thrilling because mere thrills are not weighty enough to count against the risks is a perfect expression of the paternalistic spirit. But regulations designed to reduce dangers to others or intended to compensate for the likelihood that people do not in fact fully appreciate the dangers into which they are placing themselves are quite another story. So regulations governing the composition of motorcycle helmets, boxing gloves, and safety nets are unexceptionable. And even a requirement that riders, boxers, or trapeze performers use safety devices may be justified on the narrow ground that the risk of failing to wear a helmet or to use a safety net will impose direct costs on others—to clean up the mess and cover hospital charges, now nearing $100 million nationwide for the treatment of injuries to helmetless riders.[26]

A still broader answer is that the harm imposed on the rest of us by a refusal to wear helmets is a form of "moral extortion," since no one would leave a battered cyclist to die in his own blood on the highway:

> The resolute anti-paternalist stance that these victims of their own folly should be allowed to "pay the price" because "they asked for it" and knew

what they were doing, sounds hard-edged and cruel after the fact of their injuries.... In other cases where a voluntary chooser was allowed to dig his own hole and then "got in too deep" to escape when he changed his mind... we are then entitled to resent being put in the cruel dilemma of allowing continued suffering or else paying an unfair cost to allay it. In that case we might seek protection *for ourselves* from such moral extortion by passing a law against the voluntary risk-taking of others that subjects us to it.... But in the case of the motorcyclist with the smashed head, the harm is often irreversible, and the "psychic costs" already incurred irreparably.[27]

The difficulty with this argument is that the "harm" of "moral extortion" does not fit comfortably within the type of interests embraced by the harm principle. The spectacle of the dying motorist is offensive but it does not set back our interests (except in the ways already discussed and separately covered by the harm principle, therefore). It is merely that we are profoundly revolted by the idea that someone could "take advantage" of us in this way. If the motorist had decided instead to jump out of an airplane to his certain death over the ocean, so that we would never see the body, our umbrage though perhaps not our horror might be much less. It is the *sight* of the corpse that is disturbing, but we are not otherwise affected. Indeed, when we do not view the corpses but merely read about them, we are much more inclined to shrug. "What concern is it of ours," we ask, "if someone wants to kill himself?"

Just such a problem for the anti-paternalist is the much-discussed example of the gladiatorial contest posed by Irving Kristol as a counter to liberal confidence that all forms of "self-expression" should be allowed. Kristol supposed that everyone would agree that the state may legitimately ban such a contest in Yankee Stadium under the rules of the ancient Roman Colosseum—that is to say, with no rules, a fight to the death.[28] Although Kristol posed the contest as a problem of moralism, that is, as a general evil (see chapter 10), it also puts to the test the liberal's willingness to let freely consenting adults reap the consequences of their bargains. If gladiators consented to battle to the death in front of a paying audience, on what basis other than paternalism (or moralism) may the state intrude? Feinberg observes that "it is objectively regrettable (to put it mildly) that several hundred thousand adults should derive great pleasure from gory bloodshed, human suffering, and the sight of savage cruelty."[29] But if the gladiators agree, he says that it is paternalistic, without more, to stop the fight.

One commentator argues that the gladiator problem can be resolved by adding to the harm criterion another one, the criterion of human dignity. Dignity is violated when a person objectifies another, "den[ying] the victim the basic respect to which every person is entitled just by virtue of being a human being, no matter where he lives or to what cultural group he belongs." A fight to the death is "unacceptable not only because of the potential for death and injury ... and the indignity of turning human death into a show, but also because the benefits they produce (entertainment for the spectators and a chance to strike it rich for the participants) are quite frivolous compared to the quantity and quality of the harm involved."[30] But as used, the concept of dignity is ambiguous. Dignity, the gladiator might argue, lies in his right to exhibit courage and strength and by dying rather than suffering defeat when challenged. To permit himself to be saved short of death or to be denied the opportunity to demonstrate strength and courage may deprive him of the very dignity the state asserts it is protecting. Dignity, on this view, is respecting a person's freely chosen ends.

Of course it is always open to the state to require a punctilious monitoring system to ensure that the gladiators have freely consented and to establish ground rules for the protection of spectators. The authorities might also justify steep financial charges to the promoters or even an outright ban because of administrative impossibility if the mayhem that attends many European soccer matches were to infect the gladiatorial contests to such a degree that policing would bankrupt the municipality, cause a steep increase in local taxes, or be unequal to the task of maintaining order. But those difficulties aside, fidelity to the ideal that a person's ends are not for the state to determine or command leaves the gladiators free to square off.[31]

To prevent someone from taking this kind of risk on the grounds that it is unseemly, profoundly disturbing, or morally horrifying, when no other interest of ours is at stake, is essentially to say that we do not wish to live in a community in which such things are possible, just as we might not wish to live in a community in which people are free to do other horrifying things, like cross-dressing, or dancing, or attending the wrong church. Presumably we do wish to live in a community, however, in which a courageous medical researcher is prepared to risk his life on an untested serum because he has faith in his methods and because the payoff would be high if his serum works. But the only essential distinction between a fearless researcher and a daredevil cyclist or a gladiator prepared to die is that we approve the purpose (good of humanity, chance at Nobel Prize) of the researcher's risk and disapprove of the cyclist's or gladiator's purpose (cheap thrills or honor and riches). And that is a distinction the liberal ought not be prepared to make.[32]

Consent to Harms

In 1990 the U.S. Supreme Court signaled for the first time that we may each have an enforceable constitutional right to die by refusing "lifesaving hydration and nutrition."[33] Seven years later the same court rejected a right to assisted suicide, even to spare a dying person further suffering.[34] Are laws that prevent us from taking our own lives, or engaging others to help us, paternalistic?

Put in the form of a hypothetical question, in which we can specify the conditions precisely, the answer is yes. If I truly consent to be killed, liberalism should permit the execution. But most people would rightly hesitate. This is an example of a FAKE (facts are known exactly) argument[35]—a hypothetical example can give no assurances of its facts in the real world. How do we know that the "victim" was willing? If we permit the killer to do his job by obtaining consent, what are the risks that this exception to the law against homicide will inflict sufficient psychological damage that the next time he will kill without consent or that he will hear consent where there was none? In other words, a hypothetical story, succinctly told in a line or riddle, advances the argument but little, if at all.

The principal nonpaternalistic (or "soft paternalist") reason for laws against mercy killing is, then, the difficulty of proving consent and voluntariness. Anyone might restrain another from crossing an unsafe bridge, Mill said, if "there were no time to warn him of his danger, ... without any real infringement of his liberty; for liberty consists in doing what one desires, and he does not desire to fall into the river."[36] The state might reasonably suppose that because the penalty for being wrong is so extreme and final in the case of self-elected death it ought always pull the person back from the edge.

Feinberg agrees that the difficulty of ensuring "full, free, and informed" consent is a commonsense reason for rejecting a claim of consent by the victim to excuse harming him. But he speculates without much discussion that there must be a better reason for rejecting it, since "the voluntariness of an act of consenting [should not be] any harder to determine than the voluntariness of any other kind of act, for example the act of shooting oneself or the act of smoking a cigarette."[37] The comparison is unconvincing. Here it is useful to consider the distinction between an act that injures another whether or not the victim consents and an act that is injurious only without consent. Killing is an injury, whether or not it is murder (that is, whether or not wrongful). But if I permit you to use my car, you have not harmed me at all when you drive off in it. The injury—an act of larceny that deprives me of my car—occurs only if I do not consent, just as sex between consenting adults is not harmful, but without consent is rape.[38] Whenever we question a person caught doing something injurious that he might wish to do on selfish grounds (kill a rival, steal his possessions), it will always be problematic to provide a consent loophole. The incentive of the second party to avoid responsibility means that the issue of determining the voluntariness or reality of the other's consent will be difficult, because creative people have more ways to fake consent than does a person who is harming himself. (If you are committing suicide, you just go ahead and do it; you don't usually try to fool someone, because you don't need to "get away with it"). Moreover, if consent in the two-party situation is allowed, the incidence of sham consent will likely rise, since presumably more people will want to hurt others than will wish to hurt themselves. This increase may overburden the system. It will certainly cost it more. In any event, we ought more sensibly to be willing to reject Paternalism of the First Kind (interfering with what I'm doing to myself) than Paternalism of the Second Kind (interfering with harm to myself requiring another's cooperation).

Nevertheless, Feinberg suggests, this uncertainty could be handled practically at home, if the criminal law were amended to place the burden on the defendant to prove the excuse of "mercy killing," just as it now rests on defendants to show self-defense. Feinberg says it would be difficult to envision mercy killing occurring in a hospital—we don't want people walking into hospital rooms with guns. However, if the law were changed a mercy-killing business might develop, and it would be aided by statutory requirements of acceptable proof—for example, a notarized letter (or a videotape) stating the patient's consent, three witnesses, a doctor's testimony that the person was competent when the request was made. Whether we would take this trouble depends on whether we think we can develop sufficient institutional means to carry out the policy flawlessly, relatively cheaply, and efficiently. For as Feinberg notes of a plan that would excuse mercy killing of someone suffering from a "painful terminal illness":

> That means that an earlier conditional consent will not do.... The reliable witnesses have to be rounded up and ready to observe the formal request after the pain has already become severe, and this may create practical difficulties for the humane killer, since there may be little time between the advent of the severe pain and the disappearance of "competence." The suffering may threaten to continue indefinitely after competence has gone, giving the humane comforter no alternative to permitting it to continue or making himself subject to a murder charge.[39]

Many theoretical solutions founder on practical problems, and if practical problems are serious enough, theory itself may need to reject the proffered alternative, plan, or policy.

In the so-called philosophers' brief to the Supreme Court in the 1997 assisted-suicide cases, six eminent philosophers, including Dworkin, Rawls, and Nozick, insisted that to deny terminally ill patients "in agonizing pain or otherwise doomed to an existence they regard as intolerable" the right to demonstrate that their desire to die is "informed, stable, and fully free" the state must necessarily rely on "a religious or ethical conviction about the value or meaning of life itself,"[40] a position they argued the state could not be permitted to assert against a constitutional interest in individual liberty. The Court unanimously rejected their arguments, pointing to a dearth of any historical tradition that would justify a claim to "self-sovereignty" under these circumstances. The ruling did not turn on the claim that the state was relying on a particular version of the good, and it seems reasonable to conclude that it need not have, because nonpaternalistic reasons are available.[41] Case studies of two jurisdictions in which physician-assisted suicide and euthanasia are permitted suggest the force of those reasons.

In 1984 the Netherlands became the first country to legalize assisted suicide and euthanasia, at least in limited forms (expanded in 2001). The legislative scheme imposed a number of requirements on physicians playing an active role in the deaths of their patients, including reporting obligations. There is evidence that in a significant number of cases Dutch physicians do not report their euthanasia patients to the authorities as required. About 40 percent of general practitioners said the rule requiring them to consult with at least one other physician was "not very important," though the consultation requirement was aimed at ensuring that physicians not overlook at least obvious signs that suicide patients were being pressured into dying. One student of the issue concludes from these and much other data and survey results that "the ultimate justification for assisted suicide and euthanasia does not really seem to be about patient autonomy or suffering at the end of the day, but increasingly, a physician's subjective assessment about the patient's quality of life."[42]

The Oregon assisted-suicide law, enacted in 1993 and implemented in 1997, is different, but it has its share of difficulties. Among other things, it does not require particular sorts of specialists to be the prescribing physicians nor does it require physicians to be present when the patient commits suicide, and it is particularly lacking in confidential reporting so that records of noncompliance with the statutory rules are next to impossible to compile.[43] Unlike Dutch practice, American physicians rarely have long-standing relationships with patients: Oregon statistics show that in 2002 the median length of the relationship between doctor and patient seeking assisted suicide was eleven weeks; in some cases it was "days or hours."[44] The evidence also suggests that in a significant number of cases, inadequate pain control was a motivating factor, yet many treating physicians lacked experience in pain management, and relatively few referred patients seeking suicide assistance to doctors who specialize in pain control. Still other studies suggest at least the possibility that many patients seeking suicide assistance are suffering from treatable depression; some are worried about being financial burdens on their families; and referrals to doctors in many cases are to those working for HMOs that could have a conflict of interest, since it is cheaper to dispense a medication that will kill a patient than to treat the patient for depression or other symptoms over the long haul.

Data also show that minority groups are much less likely to receive adequate treatment across a range of diseases, including palliative care. The American Bar Association recommended against legalizing any form of euthanasia, noting that equal treatment for vulnerable patients, given the current health care system in the United States, "is illusory and, indeed, dangerous for the thousands of Americans who have no or inadequate access to quality health and long-term care services."[45] Available data also indicate that American women are less well medicated for pain than American men, and the Dutch experience shows physicians more willing to honor women's requests for assisted suicide than men's. While the numbers do not establish that women would feel more pressure to accept death, the data raise troubling questions.[46] Similar discrepancies in disease treatment and pain management show up in comparisons of aging and younger and wealthy and poorer patients. As an Oregon worker's group noted:

The average cost of drugs needed to terminate a life is ten dollars, making it a financially attractive alternative to long term treatment of patients with serious illnesses. Within this rubric we cannot condone legalizing physician-assisted suicide as a so-called choice for a patient who—isolated, alone, living in constant fear of or actually suffering the effects of not being able to obtain treatment due to their poverty—is pushed to the brink and comes to see suicide as a way out of that avoidable pain and suffering. In this context, to not cover basic medical treatment, but to authorize physician-assisted suicide is a form of murder.[47]

Whether it is possible to draft a law that would avoid all these traps (or that would be available only for the very wealthy) is a large question—certainly too large for this book—but without an answer it is unfair to conclude that a ban on physician-assisted suicide and euthanasia is paternalistic.

Banning Permanent Deprivations of Liberty

It is paternalistic to bar people from agreeing to deprive themselves of liberty to act in certain ways for fixed periods of time or even, in some circumstances, for all time. We consent to bind ourselves and restrict our liberty every time we make a contract, for then we obligate ourselves to do that which we would otherwise have every right to refuse to do and which no one could legitimately impose upon us to do. The very utility of liberty is to make choices. Making them may restrict our liberty when and where the choice applies.[48]

That we may choose to give up our liberty in a limited sphere for a limited time seems altogether different in kind from giving up *complete* liberty for all time, as in a contract to be enslaved by another. Mill rejected slavery contracts on the ground that in the name of liberty a person may not alienate his own liberty.[49] But Mill's explanation is unpersuasive, for a person might desire some very much greater good than his own liberty. If you can decide to *die* for your country or your loved ones, why may you not give your liberty for them, or for some other great purpose that being enslaved might secure?

One answer we have already seen: that to ensure bona fide consent, the law could require a huge laundry list of warnings that the would-be slave would be required to sign and have witnessed, including all the things that the slaveholder would be legally empowered to do (beatings, starvation, etc.). The list might be so long and so worded that it might be supposed no one, having once read and understood it, would ever sign it. The state might go even further and presumptively refuse to enforce a slavery contract because of the inherent untrustworthiness of the consent:

> Given the uncertain quality of evidence on [the question of voluntariness], and the strong general presumption of nonvoluntariness, the state might be justified simply in presuming nonvoluntariness conclusively in every case as the least risky course. Some rational bargain-makers might be unfairly restrained under this policy, but on the alternative policy, even more people, perhaps, would become unjustly (mistakenly) enslaved, so that the evil prevented by the absolute prohibition would be greater than the occasional evil permitted.[50]

Indeed, not merely the consent but the slave-owner's obligation is problematic. We may assume that no one would lightly enter into such a contract and so the owner's promised payment will be quite high—perhaps to care for the slave's children for the rest of their lives. By what means can the slave ensure that this promise will be carried out? The state should be justifiably skeptical that the owner would live up to his promise. Possibly a bond of sufficient magnitude would guarantee the children's perpetual care, but other promises might be impossible to secure with tangible collateral, and so the state might conclude that promises of this type must be banned.

A stronger nonpaternalistic argument against enforcing a slavery agreement can be built on a crucial distinction between two types of consent: "completed consent" (by which I agree to do something at a single moment or that has a unique consequence; e.g., paying money, completing an assignment) and "continuing consent" (by which I agree that something may happen as long as my consent continues). Some objects over which we bargain require continuing consent. It is not enough that I once consented; for the relationship or contract or requirement to be valid and meaningful, I must continually consent. You agree to marry me, but I cannot compel the marriage if you change your mind. When arrangements are bound by continuing consent, it is a harm to require the arrangement to continue when the consent ends. With completed consent, it is a harm for one party to negate or revoke consent later. Continuing consent is intimately related to what we mean by our own good. If continuing consent were not required, the slave would have no assurance that the bargain would be honored. By refusing to enforce the contract, the state does not bar the "slave" from submitting to the "owner": He can submit as long as he cares to, and only by that continuing consent can he ensure that the consideration for which he bargained will be paid.

Custom and Paternalism

Chess is a game of customary rules: We cannot point to any particular moment the game was conceived, but specific rules do exist, and we might not call it chess if knights moved straight. A particular group of chess players could change the rules of their game, either to see what happens or, knowing what would happen, because they prefer it. In time, we might say they were playing Modified Chess to distinguish it from Real Chess. If Modified Chess became wildly popular, we might forget what Real Chess was, and the modified game would become standard. But the state could have no interest in changing the rules, since no one is harmed by the custom. It would be paternalistic for the legislature to decree that henceforth chess is to be played by randomizing the starting position of the nonpawn pieces, because it would be more exciting and hence "better" for the players.[51]

Some games, on the other hand, induce harmful practices, and the state may regulate the competition to prevent them, even though the regulation may appear to operate against the athlete willing to bear the risk of side effects. An obvious example is the athlete who takes steroids to enhance his chances of winning. Left unregulated, steroid use would soon harden into custom, since competitive pressure would compel others to take them and run the same risks of injury. So a law against steroid use prevents a harm to everyone, even though no one is compelled to run the race or play the game. The law against steroids is different from the more usual paternalistic rule—for example, No Alcohol Because It's Bad for You—because drinking needs no competition. The harm in drinking is caused by the person who will suffer it (and in banning it the state is saving you from yourself). But in the steroid case, the harm is caused by other people whose use forces the victim to use it too. In other words, the harm is not in individual risk of physical abuse, but in the inability of *other* athletes to run a race free from steroid risk altogether. The behavior of one group of people forces the behavior on another, and this (nongovernmental) coercion is what the state seeks to stop.[52]

Suppose a small group of people belong to a club that venerates the ability to consume large quantities of liquor, even though members get blindingly drunk and wake up with horrible hangovers each morning. Would the state be entitled to step in and say Do Not Drink, to prevent each person from being forced by social norms within the club from having to do so? That we would be inclined to think not, because no member is compelled to join and no member is likely to lose status outside the club if he resigned, suggests that the scope of the state's power to intervene depends on the actual social context: How powerful is the cultural force or pressure to conform to a harmful activity?[53]

When the force of custom in the larger society is such that living by a social convention is harmful, the harm principle justifies state intervention. A classic example of a harmful custom eliminated by law is that of dueling.[54] The duel was an ancient custom by which a man could avenge dishonor to his name or family. What was bad about it? Besides the social or public interest in ending all forms of bloodshed with accompanying costs (of medical insurance, social security payouts, funeral arrangements, family deprivation, street cleanup, police time, etc.), an individual who could be drawn into a duel might have a strong interest in avoiding it. On its face, dueling was consensual: No one was forced *by law* to duel. But so strong was the custom among certain strata of society, so overwhelming was the pressure of public sentiment, that when the gauntlet was thrown down in response to even an imagined provocation, the challenger rarely refused the duel because the loss of face and public humiliation would have been too great. The custom put the dueler in a vise, forcing on him a choice of harms: to life or limb if the challenge was accepted, to one's place in society if it was refused.[55] In this sense the custom had the force of law: It coerced a reluctant swordsman into accepting a challenge, whether justly issued or not. So even though the state was not implicated in the duel (it did not enforce the challenge or "agreement" to duel), it would be inaccurate to say that by outlawing the duel the state is prohibiting two consenting adults from engaging in swordplay, any more than to say that the state interferes with consenting adults today by prohibiting one person from pointing a gun at another, since the pointing is likely to elicit alarm from the other and possibly quicker retaliation if the pointer is armed. Rather, the state is in effect *repealing* a customary law that had an extremely deleterious consequence for large numbers of people (beyond the immediate parties, dueling led to violence that spilled out into the larger society).[56]

The curbs on custom encountered in this section were pseudo-paternalistic because it appeared (falsely) that both parties consented to the risk of harm that might flow from following the custom. But since the duelers were not acting voluntarily, a law that prohibited them from engaging in harmful conduct is not paternalistic but merely an application of the harm principle.[57] Not every enactment to counter the harmful effect of widespread custom will appear in this light. Some customs are deleterious because they prohibit people from engaging freely with each other—just the opposite of "forced" consent, they block true consent from being sought or obtained. The objection to state interference with such customs I consider in chapter 10 in connection with racial (and related forms of) discrimination.[58] Antidiscrimination laws are not paternalistic because they are enacted neither to prevent the discriminator from harming himself nor to make him a better person. They are enacted to prevent harm to others.

Some Notes on Exploitation

Laws such as those against usury, "unconscionable" contracts of other sorts, and medical research on prisoners are designed to prevent "exploitation," commonly defined as taking an unfair advantage of someone's weakness, gullibility, or bad luck. In the sense pertinent to paternalism, the disadvantaged person was not put in dire straits by the exploiter but rather was found there. The exploiter takes advantage of the situation, though he had no role in bringing about the exploited person's plight. If he did, then the case is much different. Holding a man underwater and demanding money to rescue him is a form of extortion that is obviously punishable under the harm principle. But if a man is down on his luck and desperately needs an infusion of cash to stave off the bill collectors, is it paternalistic for the state to deny him the opportunity to borrow money at an exorbitant rate, if that is the only rate at which anyone might be willing to lend him the money? To argue that the exploiter is acting in an unconscionable way (in a manner highly or grossly unfair, repulsive, repugnant, or immoral) does not answer the charge of paternalism, since we are assuming that the usurer's offer is genuine, that the money is at risk, and that he will not retaliate if the cash-starved borrower walks away from the deal. Assuming uncoerced consent, on what liberal ground may the state interfere?

One answer may be the wholly practical one that nothing is lost by outlawing exploitation: The person who happens by in a boat or with a fistful of cash could either forgo the proposed transaction or ask a reasonable compensation in return, compensation that would have been accepted from anyone else not in such exigent circumstances. What then is lost but the exploitation? But this answer may not satisfy the person exploited. For one thing, in many exploitive situations the suffering person would not obtain relief but for the possibility of an exploitive return. Regular banks do not lend at regular interest to those with terrible credit ratings. The lure of exploitive gain might lead some to patrol the waters in rowboats and thus rescue people who would otherwise certainly have drowned. For another thing, a general law against "exploitation" or "unconscionable" dealings cedes virtually unreviewable power to courts or agencies to make ad hoc decisions case by case.

A different kind of answer may suffice for a limited range of cases. If there is a duty to rescue, that duty will be sufficient to overcome the claim to an exploitive reward, since the failure to rescue is itself a harm against which the state may act.[59] But the duty to rescue encompasses at best a tiny class of cases, symbolized by the drowning victim: The duty arises only if the rescuer happens to be immediately nearby the victim when the need for rescue arises and only if he would incur virtually no risk or cost in undertaking the rescue.

Still another kind of response to the claim that it is illegitimate to interfere with the noncoercive exploiter, a response we have repeatedly encountered, is the inherent uncertainty of real situations—the difficulty of ascertaining in the real world whether consent was genuine, that is, informed and uncoerced. The usurer may disguise the actual rate of interest, and the state may therefore have a legitimate interest in prompting full disclosure. The state will also have an interest in ensuring that the collection methods employed by the "loan shark" are not themselves harmful. To the protests of the collector who insists that his debtor was fully informed and readily consented to have his legs broken, and that banning such method is therefore paternalistic, the state may respond as it did to the bakery owners in chapter 4.[60]

The illusion of certainty is a principal reason for disallowing prisoners to offer themselves as subjects for medical experimentation. In the real world of prisons, it may be impossible to ensure that a prisoner will not have been coerced into "volunteering," possibly even by so subtle a method as a frown from a guard threatening harsh treatment later: "[W]henever there is such great disparity in the power of the parties, the opportunity and indeed, temptation, to coercion is always present."[61] There is also a danger that a prisoner without adequate information would be tricked into consenting. This problem is more easily solved, since the state can mandate disclosure forms and proof that disclosure was adequately made. That it is not paternalistic per se to bar experimentation on prisoners does not establish, however, that it is *never* paternalistic to do so: Practical judgments can be made only in the world. To conclude that a prisoner (or anyone else) is incapable of possessing the informed desire to cooperate with experimenters is a denial of the very possibility of autonomy, paternalism of the worst sort.

A different sort of argument for upholding laws against exploitation is that permitting it weakens people's altruism. Consider Feinberg's example of the Lecherous Millionaire, who promises to pay for a child's expensive operation if the mother agrees to sleep with him. If he understands that the courts will not enforce his contract he may allow himself to feel a sense of humanity and pay for the operation gratis. But he may also simply walk away.[62] Whether or not the offer is coercive, however, he has enlarged the mother's freedom (assuming that he did not make the child sick or stand in the way of others coming to the rescue). If the mother turns down the millionaire she is in no worse a position than if his offer had never been made.[63] The courts might refuse to enforce the contract if the mother was shrewd enough to promise to bestow her favors after the child's operation; she would argue that enforcement would be akin to rape, since she no longer consents (in effect, she would have exploited the exploiter). On the other hand, if she succumbed to her benefactor beforehand, the bargain seems to preclude a charge of rape, since she could have walked away, and it also seems enforceable, or else the millionaire would have succeeded in preying on her twice over. The real answer to exploitation cases of this sort is that they are hypothetical, and the usual problems of proof would make them grist for the pages of philosophers but not of the court reports.

Whether a contract can be sufficiently unconscionable to avoid the charge of paternalism if a court refuses to enforce it depends on the reason for calling it unconscionable. No simple formula is possible. If it is unconscionable because one party was misled or because the exploiter knowingly took advantage of the other party's ignorance, then there has been no genuine consent. Neither the cab driver nor the passenger have reason to complain if the law requires posting truthful information about fares; the driver who inflates his fare for the stranded motorist has no case if the passenger refuses to pay the excess. The case for intervention is much less clear if a dedicated believer in astrology pays a soothsayer to have the future foretold and later complains that the predictions were a bit off the mark. The difference is that the astrologer, unless he guaranteed a result, did not supply his client with objectively false and disadvantageous information. Although they play on the true believer's gullibility, soothsayers do not create beliefs but merely satisfy existing wants. The client is not initially complaining; he got what he paid for, and it would be paternalism to forbid the fortune-teller from satisfying the want. There remains a point beyond which the fortune-teller's fee may become unconscionable; for example, charging a person her life savings in return for "very important news about the future." In such an instance, the probability will be high that the fortune-teller will have actively misled the "mark"; overbearing misrepresentation requires the charlatan to make restitution.

One form of an ostensibly unconscionable contract is the so-called contract of adhesion, in which unequal bargaining power permits the stronger party to dictate unfavorable terms to the weaker party, usually through a boilerplate contract presented to the customer on a take-it-or-leave-it basis.[64] If the boilerplate contains a waiver of liability for any ensuing harm caused by the seller, it is not paternalistic for the state to refuse to enforce the waiver. This kind of clause in effect requires the customer to declare that he will not invoke the harm principle. The seller will argue that at worst the sales contract is noncoercively exploitive: No one forced the customer to make the purchase. But we have seen this argument before,[65] and it is invalid for the same reasons as before: We cannot assume knowledge of risk in a world of such complexity. Only if it can be shown that the parties fairly bargained over exactly that issue should a waiver of liability be upheld (as would happen, for example, if I were to tell you that my car is old and unreliable, so I'm selling it "as is," and you have the opportunity to have a mechanic inspect it before purchase). Many exploitive offers may be noncoercive, hence it would be paternalistic to refuse to enforce them, but it is never paternalistic to refuse to enforce an exploitive waiver of the harm principle itself—for it cannot be supposed that a wronged customer would oppose the state's stepping in.

A recurring form of exploitation is blackmail, a threat to release damaging information about someone to third parties unless the blackmailer is paid for his silence. Assuming that the blackmailer came by the information lawfully (he did not tap a phone or break into a home), he would violate no law in conveying the facts to the police or to the victim's spouse. Richard Posner suggests that the "real puzzle" of blackmail is that in its most common form it is a type of private law enforcement, since by paying to keep the information from the police, the blackmailed person in effect pays a fine for his illegal activities.[66] Although criminalizing blackmail might seem to spare the "victim" his just deserts, since the police may never learn of his wrongdoing, it is not paternalistic to make blackmail a crime. The "fine" the victim pays may be out of any proportion to the offense he is hoping to keep private; that lack of proportionality was one of Locke's central reasons for confining punishment to the law rather than opening it to the unfettered judgment of those who are wronged. Moreover, ignoring blackmail might provide an incentive to people to snoop in the affairs of others, threaten privacy, and create a climate of fear that people's legitimate secrets might be exposed or that false claims would be bruited about.

Self-Binding

An individual may seek to enforce his sense now of what is good for him against his anticipated sense at a future time of some other, even opposite, good. Discussing "alternating preferences," Thomas Schelling catalogued a number of (mostly) mental states that give rise to these alternatives: not fully alert (still sleepy, hence immune to the alarm clock you confidently set the night before); overstimulated or exhilarated (including success and relief—so influenced, you buy a child a costly present that you would not have contemplated before you were relieved of some anxiety); passion or infatuation ("marry[ing] in haste and repent[ing] at leisure"); captivation (engrossing yourself in a movie or a book instead of doing what you should); phobias, panic, and extreme terror (failing to act in a situation that, considered dispassionately when not terrorized, you ought to do to save yourself); appetite (the desire for goods or acts that you know, perhaps even when you are consuming or doing them, are bad for you); and perseverance or procrastination (the New Year's resolution that you quit at the end of the first week). Like Ulysses, we all know tricks that can help overcome the future weak self: For example, you refuse to buy yourself liquor or cigarettes so you can't turn to them in a moment of weakness. Contracts in general bind a future self. But there are limits on what may be contractually provided for. As Schelling notes: "In America I cannot go to a fat farm, a non-smoking resort, or an exercise camp and legally bind the management to hold me when I ask to get out."[67] May the liberal state assist us in our fight against our weaker nature by binding us from doing bad things to ourselves?

In the story of the donkey riders in the state of nature, we encountered in chapter 2 one way to consider the problem of state regulation of risk.[68] I might consider it rational to resign to the state my responsibility to keep up with safety developments and allow it to tell me what to do or refrain from doing for my own protection.[69] Gutmann and Thompson, who forthrightly insist that the state may enact paternalistic laws for some purposes, suggest that we could view helmet regulations and the like as rules "that citizens have imposed on themselves to protect themselves against future temptations."[70] The argument seems to be that such rules are not paternalistic in the formal sense because they are not imposed on us for our own good *without our consent*. But that is to substitute democratic rule for liberalism. A majority may have consented on behalf of the motorcyclist, but she may not agree, and it is *her* consent that counts. So if the state's assistance is in the form of prohibiting us from engaging in self-regarding activity, the answer is that with which we began: The liberal state may not treat us paternalistically. I may be unable to resist high-fat foods that keep me overweight, but the state ought not ban otherwise harmless foods (or harmless in moderation) simply because people are known to overindulge.

But not all assistance takes the form of an outright ban. By expanding or contracting the reach of political goods, the state may nonpaternalistically help us avoid what may appear to be self-caused harm. In some instances, for example, the law builds in delay as a means of recalibrating one's desire; Schelling mentions the bureaucratic rule that marriage licenses can "be issued only during daytime hours."[71] More widespread are state consumer-protection laws that require a "cooling off" period, during which a customer may unilaterally rescind a contract for the purchase of goods or services. This device is not paternalistic but an inexpensive means of avoiding garden-variety fraud and overbearing sales pressure. In a calmer moment, the customer may think through what he was told and reassess whether he really needs the goods or services, whether the price and terms are reasonable, and whether he can afford them. Such laws provide remedies for harmful behavior to a much broader group far more cheaply than an after-the-fact hearing, while not prohibiting customers from proceeding if they choose.

Some contracts can be used with opposite effect. Even if you cannot ask the state to make others keep you imprisoned, there are places you can bind not to let you back in. For example, New Jersey has established through its Casino Control Commission a "self-exclusion list," through which casinos may agree to deny entrance to gamblers who place themselves on the list and who change their minds. The agency has upheld the list against a gambler's desire to be a recidivist, wherever the casino is located, even if it is at an out-of-state casino chain.[72]

The Timeline

The anti-paternalist requires the state to refrain from acting against harm to self; it may intervene only to prevent harm to others. But do "others" include those long gone or not yet born? For the liberal, says one critic, "the three-dimensionality of time has collapsed into the present, and morally only the claims—present or future—of those alive are taken into account."[73] In a significant sense, the liberal does repudiate the past-oriented vision of the conservative and the future-oriented vision of the radical utopian. The liberal rejects state-enforced ancestor worship— requirements that bind us to the traditions of our forebears. Indeed, liberalism provided an escape from such notions. Likewise, an important strand of liberal thought disclaims concern for the future, holding that only the living count because the unborn do not have interests to be set back. Isaiah Berlin approves Bentham's remark:

> Individual interests are the only real interests . . . can it be conceived that there are men so absurd as to . . . prefer the man who is not to him who is; to torment the living, under pretence of promoting the happiness of them who are not born, and who may never be born?[74]

Berlin comments that "this passage is at the heart of the empirical, as against the metaphysical, view of politics" and that a pluralistic approach to values is "more humane" than that of the "system builders" who "deprive men, in the name of some remote, or incoherent, ideal, of much that they have found to be indispensable to their life as unpredictably self-transforming human beings."[75] Liberal skepticism toward the position that the state may legitimately concern itself with claims by others than those who are right here, right now, understandably stems from the brutality of dictatorships that claim utopian abstractions such as "future mankind" to justify crimes against present mankind.

The critique of this position relies on the commonplace that we cannot avoid acting on behalf of those yet to come. Anthony Arblaster derides Bentham's position, insisting that

> of course men and women *are* frequently "so absurd as to . . . prefer the man who is not to him who is." Every family that saves money or means to provide for as yet unborn children or grandchildren is guilty of this absurdity. So is the man who spends money and effort planting trees whose sight and shade he will never live to enjoy. So are states and societies which tax and levy the living in order to build homes, schools and hospitals for future generations, or operate pension schemes for an old age which many of the contributors to the scheme may never attain. And most people would think it almost criminally negligent of the state *not* to make such provision.[76]

But the examples are disingenuous. Most can be explained as proceeding from an impulse to benefit or avoid harm in some way to those here and now. That I *may* not live to see a pension does not mean I should be improvident or risk burdening my children. Though I may never enjoy the tree I may be confident that my children will. The state does not build schools that stand empty for decades awaiting a generation yet unborn—these institutions are built for those who can now use them. Even wars, which Arblaster views as fought for the sake of a "future advantage,"[77] are obviously fought (defensively) for the security of those now living. We dislike the thought of nuclear weapons blowing up the world not only because the human race will remain unborn but because those now living will die.

Dictatorships aside, the major problem with grounding a policy on reducing or eliminating harm to future generations is that it will usually be wholly speculative whether our failure to take action will set back their interest.[78] Ronald Dworkin raises the problem of people who wish to preserve a beautiful mountainside from the proposed depredations of strip coal mining. Dworkin's liberal believes

> that the conquest of unspoilt terrain by the consumer economy is self-fueling and irreversible, and that this process will make a way of life that has been desired and found satisfying in the past unavailable to future generations, and indeed to the future of those who now seem unaware of its appeal. He fears that this way of life will become unknown, so that the process is not neutral amongst competing ideas of the good life, but in fact destructive of the very possibility of some of these.[79]

The problem with Dworkin's position is this: We can say either that it is up to each generation (at every legislative session) to decide whether to permit strip mining or preserve the mountain, since this is a choice between conflicting interests and uses, so that even if we decide to keep the terrain intact our descendants could alter the balance; or we must say that it is inherently necessary, akin to a law of nature, to preserve the mountain "unspoilt," since if our descendants cannot cut it down either then no one ever can. But the latter alternative makes no sense, since the argument about one part of the terrain must apply likewise to all other parts of the terrain, and by parity of reasoning no development at all would ever be permissible. There is no way to deduce a natural law of preservation; at stake is a proper balance between conflicting values, and the actual balance must always be for the people who are around to make it, not for philosophers to dictate in the abstract for all time.

Moreover, to justify state interference with people's activities solely to forestall harm to future generations will almost always cause distress to us now. Consider, in this light, the following apocryphal story. Suppose that in 1876, during the national Centennial Celebration, Congress had begun to worry about the mounting possibility that the unchecked use of increasingly powerful technologies would seriously undermine and might potentially destroy the possibility of the good life. It created a new agency, the Federal Quality of Life Commission (FQLC), which was empowered to modify, control, restrain, prohibit, or otherwise regulate the use of any technology not in the public interest, having due regard for the benefits of technology, for the national commitment to productivity, and for public health and safety. The FQLC, our story continues, assembled a staff of lawyers, economists, engineers, and scientists, and even signed up one or two historians of science, not a discipline that had theretofore played any noticeable role in governmental proceedings.

After some desultory years, during which time the FQLC was intensely criticized for its lethargy, inaction, and even, on one occasion, for selling out the public (in a still-secret series of negotiations that permitted Alexander Graham Bell to proceed with his fledgling company), a new commission chairman looked for an issue that would make his reputation. He found it in a strange new contraption: the horseless carriage. (Inexplicably, railroads had been exempted from the commission's original charter. Some said the exemption was justifiable because railroading was an established technology—no one referred to "iron horses" any more and, after all, trains only traveled along predetermined tracks. Other people muttered darkly that the real explanation was a secret "deal" that would lead to Rutherford B. Hayes's peculiar election later that year.)

In any event, a farsighted staff report in the 1890s drafted by the commission's newest professional, the chief sociologist, reached a dismaying conclusion. The new form of transport, the automobile, as it was beginning to be called, would, if the commission did not intervene, fundamentally disrupt the traditional pattern of American life and cause serious injuries. Among the predictions were these:

1. The most efficient means of constructing automobiles would be the mass assembly line in large factories. Their use would demoralize an immense part of the American labor force, because thousands, maybe hundreds of thousands,

of workers would become mere "appendages of machines," as was already too true in other industries about which the commission could speak with some authority.

2. Economies of scale would in time to come give the corporations that manufacture the devices vast assets and considerable revenues. The resulting influence might seriously undermine democratic legislatures.

3. The automobile would provide a convenient means by which to go not merely from home to office or grocer but from town to town; and this implied several things. Population centers might shift beyond the city, spawning new types of communities that would abandon the cities to the poor and urbanize the countryside, despoiling the rural way of life. Intercity and interstate travel would require large public expenditures on highway construction that would needlessly compete with railroads and that would also require a network of thousands upon thousands of vendors of gasoline, since the automobile could not, like the train, carry its own fuel supply. In turn, this would prompt large investment in potentially lucrative oil fields and spawn another industrial class with a potentially corrupting political influence and might even involve the nation in foreign political adventures contrary to the spirit of our best traditions.

4. The increased use of automobiles would endanger health and safety. Riding around in flimsy vehicles not well anchored to the ground at speeds that might eventually exceed 15 miles per hour could cause an assortment of bodily injuries that would add significantly to the nation's medical bills and might even spark a move toward socialized medicine. Moreover, since the automobile is not rooted to a track, the danger of mechanical or human error would lead to gruesome carnage on the public roads, leaving households destitute if the income-provider met an untimely death (surely women would never operate so dangerous a contraption). The ensuing litigation would place the courts under an intolerable strain, making it impossible for men with honest suits to find a judicial ear to whom to complain.

And so on. Therefore, the FQLC staff proposed, the development of the automobile must be banned. That concluded, the staff could turn its attention to another alarming prospect: the electrification of the nation.[80]

The obvious point is that the decision now to forestall some distant potential disaster by barring us from undertaking presently nonharmful activities will likely choke off as much good as evil. To say that the automobile has done great damage and that therefore it should have been banned is to assume that the damage to particular people, here and now, for whom remedies might be in order, would not have occurred in some other form if the entire future course had been altered. Justifying state action on the basis of harm to future generations, not anchored to harm to people now living, would give a wholly open-ended power to the government that no logic could contain. Harm to others must be harm to others among us.

That does not mean, however, that the harm must be fully materialized before the state may act. Suppose we learn somehow that a certain manufacturing process will punch a hole in the ozone layer but that it will be 300 years before the hole is large enough to do any serious damage. May we stop it now? This is simply an exaggerated (and suspect[81]) example of an accumulative harm: The state need not wait until the buildup is ferocious.

May the state, then, never act on behalf of future generations? Arblaster notes that "virtually any modern government is expected, and therefore obliged, to make some provision for future generations, and thus to transgress Bentham's rule, by imposing some degree of privation on the living."[82] But the distinction between present and future is not clearly defined. In a significant sense, there is no present, since all our actions are aimed at states of being yet to come. But there is a distinction between present and future people, and when the government provides for the present of future generations it is almost invariably making provision as well for the future of present people. We do not construct museums to house our culture that will stand empty until some unborn future generation appears. We do not preserve purely for the sake of great-great-grandchildren no one now alive will ever know.

It is possible, I suppose, to imagine some sorts of government expenditures that arguably are intended solely for the sake of unborn generations.[83] Arblaster suggested the planting of trees—imagine the decision to replant at public expense a forest that will not come to maturity for 200 years. But it is difficult to see how even such reforestation would have no significant payoff until then. One reason for maintaining and rebuilding forests is preserving the earth's natural ecosystem, and the decision to reforest safeguards that land from polluting activities and refreshes the ecosystem as the trees grow, an activity that will benefit us now, or soon. Other possible future-oriented-only activities are "pure" exploration or cleanups. We might decide to send a crew of astronauts to a newly discovered planet that it will take 200 years to reach, so that the mission will yield no possible benefit to us. We might want to fund basic medical research, which might have no expected immediate payoff. Or we might decide to clean up a river so filthy that the best estimate is that it will be a century before it again becomes clean and useful. But the range of activities is narrow for which it is plausible even to suggest only long-term effects, and none of these interferes with our liberty in the name of preventing harm in the long run (stopping us from dumping toxic wastes into the river is aimed at preventing further harm now). Moreover, it does not seem sensible to view even these activities as *solely* oriented toward future human beings. Building the interplanetary rocket and medical research may yield significant benefits right now, and it is unlikely that we personally will realize no benefits from antipollution efforts, even the large-scale efforts needed to reverse global warming and to deal with radioactive wastes. In short, the fear that liberalism will not permit us to think about our descendants is mistaken in a practical sense. The liberal balks only at the totalitarian premise that we may be ordered to act to our detriment to bring about a wholly speculative good to some distant future epoch.

Soft Paternalism as Liberty Limiting

Soft paternalism, as Feinberg defines it and as the term has been used here, is the power to interfere with someone if his choice to harm himself is not voluntary, either because he was coerced or because he has certain sorts of faulty knowledge.[84] Mill took essentially this position in agreeing that when there is no time to warn it is always permissible to stop a person from doing unforeseen harm to himself. But soft paternalism, Feinberg concludes, is "not exactly a liberty-limiting principle":

> It does not purport to guide the legislator to the kinds of reasons that can support proposed *criminal* legislation. In fact it legitimizes certain private and public interferences with liberty so that they may *not* be prevented by the criminal law. Thus in effect it has the form of a negative principle for the legislator. It tells him that a certain class of alleged justifying reasons are *not* valid. It is *not* an acceptable reason in support of proposed criminal legislation that it is necessary to prevent the sorts of interferences soft paternalism permits. Interfering with an apparently demented suicide attempt, for example, should *not* be a crime.[85]

In the civil sense, however, soft paternalism *is* a liberty-limiting principle. It permits the state to establish various institutions to deal with harm that people may unknowingly inflict on themselves. Indeed, this soft paternalism principle is indispensable to various sorts of liberty-limiting policies of the modern state. At the very least, it permits the state to inspect and warn citizens of hazards endemic to the modern world. The state need not station a crossing guard at every unsafe bridge, but it may certainly post a sign and it may just as certainly repair bridges or require them to be repaired. This is just another way of saying that the state may act to forestall injuries the responsibility for which cannot necessarily be pinned to particular persons, especially the victim. Many of the affirmative institutions of the state, then, can be justified by this notion of soft paternalism: "to prevent persons from harming themselves nonvoluntarily... is a good reason for much non-punitive state interference with liberty: denying applications, invalidating contracts, issuing temporary restraining orders, imposing civil commitment, and so on."[86] But this interference is limited to actual harms. The principle of soft paternalism does not permit the state to intrude in our lives to prevent mere wrongdoing, even knowing wrongdoing, if the wrong is not itself harmful, as the next chapter makes clear.

10

Harm to Norms

People do all sorts of things that others prefer they not do. Protesters complain that people defy God's commandments, have deviant sex, make and view pornography, hire women for men's jobs, hire women for any job, refuse to hire women for any job, engage in interracial relationships, teach evolution, gamble, burn the flag, speak the wrong language, marry whom they should not, eat forbidden food, dance lasciviously, build aesthetically displeasing homes, wear risqué clothing, denigrate people they detest, express contempt for duly elected leaders, conspicuously consume, speak profanely, and flaunt their perversities. Among other things. Objectors view these behaviors as evils and say they should be subject to legislative prohibition even though they may harm no one. This view is often called "legal moralism," but the term is a misnomer, since it extends to conduct beyond the realm of morality as it is usually understood.[1] Broadly stated, the objection to these sorts of nonharmful conduct is that they violate religious, moral, social, or communal norms.

In a sense, legal moralism is the reverse of legal paternalism. The paternalist demands that you do something good for you (or refrain from something bad for you). The moralist demands that you do something good for him or for someone else (or again, refrain from something bad). Under the harm principle, the state may act to deal with harms caused by one or more people against one or more others; otherwise, not. A central feature of the harm principle, then, is that the state may not impose on others one person's (or one group of persons') belief about the good life.

Some sorts of conduct that people view as necessities of a tradition do not rise to the degree of universality that would prompt their proponents to seek to force the rest of us to conform to them. A particular religious or ethnic community may be committed to wearing a distinct type of clothing, for example, but would not ask the legislature to compel us to dress as they do. Its members do not view your wearing traditional clothing as good for them or your failing to wear it as a harm to them.[2] In other words, they have no interest in what clothing you wear. But there is a range of other acts that many people do suppose gives them an interest in your conformity. Their claim is not that they wish to impose the Good on you for your sake but for theirs—or even for the sake of the Good itself. If you do not pursue good they will be unable to pursue it themselves, or they or the world at large will in some way be sufficiently affected, even if not harmed, that it is right that you be made to abide by their norms.

There is no single overarching claim or argument that norms should be legislatively preserved and protected. I group various claims and arguments under the heading "harm to norms," recognizing that the term is allusive and not strictly accurate. The effect on norms condemned by legal moralists is actually a "pseudo harm," since only the interests of people can be harmed. Though it is convenient to label a single category—norms—for the cluster of problems that moralism raises, the issues are difficult to classify according to a simple principle or to range on a continuum of behavior or consequences. Among other things, we will be concerned with claims about acts that provoke the wrath of God, destroy a community or weaken its social bonds, undermine or change cultural traditions, and debase morality. In thinking through these claims, we need to distinguish what are often conflated: the type of act that causes the effect (for example, immorality, violation of a religious commandment or a social convention, personally revolting conduct); who is affected (for example, God, the community, one or more persons as individuals); and the type of claimed effect (for example, destruction of a community, felt personal distress, weakening or overthrow of custom, debasement of the community's "moral tone," actual harm). In general, I organize the discussion by types of acts rather than by groups affected or claimed effects, though these are often difficult to disentangle. It is the burden of this chapter to argue that there can be no general harm to norms except in the sense that the interests of many individuals are set back by an action or conduct that affects them all in a common or related way and that it is illiberal for the state to intervene in people's affairs when the claimed wrongdoing is harmless.

Expectations and the Externality Constraint

The general answer to the claims of legal moralism lies in what I shall call the "externality constraint." Most of my interests, and no doubt yours, are for things that I (or you) want to have or do or be. You want to sleep late, get a new job, learn the trumpet, be well-respected, live a holy life. These wants are internal to their holder: You may not succeed in satisfying them, but they concern your own interests. Some interests, however, are external: They are wants or preferences for other people's wants and cannot be satisfied unless someone else undertakes or refrains from an act. Ordinarily I do not have a stake in other people's wants or preferences—I cannot demand that you do something just because it would be good for me. I would be happy if you enjoyed the books I like to read, but I can only wish for it, not command it. If my book is stolen I, but not you, have been harmed, even though you had hoped to borrow it, and you grieve with me over its loss. Mr. X hopes that Ms. Y will marry him (and it would be to his good), but he has no cause to complain if she decides to marry Mr. Z. Under some circumstances, I may have an interest in your actions, because you contracted with me to undertake them or because we have a special relationship. In those circumstances, your wrongful failure to act accordingly sets back my interest and constitutes a redressable harm. So much, we have already seen, is implied by the harm principle.[3]

But, say its detractors, that is just the problem. Either a class of harms has been overlooked or we need greater protection than the harm principle affords. Certain types of conduct ought to be banned, runs the argument, simply because they violate one or more norms—of morality, civilized conduct, social convention, or historical tradition. (I note, again, that the legal moralist's argument is not confined to claims about morality; similar claims are made about breaches of other sorts of norms, as we will see.)

As the term was defined in chapter 3, people have interests in states of being that will enable them to realize their goals, short- or long-term. I have an interest in health because when I am ill I am less able to do what I want or need to do to achieve my ends. But to have an external interest in someone else's interests can and often will lead to general unresolvable conflicts. Say that X has an interest in Y's being his friend. May X prevent Y from leaving town to avoid losing benefits of the friendship? If X can have an external interest in Y so can Z. Suppose Z, who lives elsewhere, also has an interest in Y's friendship. Who wins in the fight between X and Z, assuming no special relationships beyond the friendship that would be undermined? If X could have such an interest in Y's interests, then Y is essentially a slave to X, for what is slavery but one person's right to control and dispose of another's interests.[4]

The safer course is to grant that we are often doomed to disappointment by the failure of people to live up to our hopes and that we have no enforceable rights to our expectations unless they are embodied in an explicit contract or inferred from an interaction that amounts to a mutual agreement to be bound. This conclusion is the externality constraint—that no one has a superior enforceable *external* interest in the interest of another. Or, to state it otherwise, it is illegitimate to interfere with another person when the interest one has in the other's conduct can be expressed solely by the assertion "that's not how *I* would choose *you* to behave" or "that's not how *I* would choose *you* to live your life," even if the reason for the statement is that you are acting immorally. (By immoral, I mean to exclude conduct or a state of being that is not harmful under the harm principle. Obviously, one can have an interest in another's not assaulting or stealing from him, conduct that is both immoral and harmful.) The externality constraint holds that in the absence of your consent or a need to prevent harm, it is improper to legislate a rule that would embrace the norm "My good requires you to do or refrain from doing X." The liberal state, then, must be neutral only toward internal preferences for the good; it may, indeed it should, refuse to permit one person from enforcing an external preference for behavior by another.[5]

Some commentators argue that the externality constraint should be porous. Richard J. Arneson has suggested that it is unnecessary to distinguish rigidly between external interests (my interest in your not dancing) and internal or personal interests (my interest in not dancing myself) so as always to exclude external interests in a conflict with personal interests. Personal should always trump external, Arneson says, when the only content to the external interest is a "non-self-interested preference" (for example, simply to prefer that people not dance; "I want it" is not a sufficient reason for state action). However, Arneson is prepared to give some weight to self-interested external preferences "included within the agent's conception of what would make her life go better." It is unclear whether this proposition is an advance, since Arneson's phrase might also apply simply to the "I want it" school; "I want it" could be the equivalent of "my life will be better knowing that people don't dance." Arneson compares the desires of

> some persons [who] want to live out a hippie life-style and other persons [who] wish to live in a neighborhood that is oriented to more traditional families. Both aims (I say) are perfectly legitimate, and, depending on circumstances, I would not wish to rule out giving either interest the force of law.... What I wish to reject is any version of liberalism like Feinberg's that would seek to solve such problems by discounting interests like the interest of the villagers in maintaining a family-oriented tone to their community as in principle an illicit reason for legislation.[6]

But if the interests of villagers in maintaining a "family-oriented tone" could trump the interests of individuals who choose to live together, it is difficult to see how to limit the scope of any claims to external interests.

Responding to this concern that denying the distinction between external and personal interests "would open the floodgates to all manner of illiberal restriction of individual freedom," Arneson denies "that all concern for personal autonomy evaporates once one decides that external interests can be legitimate grounds for criminal prohibition." He believes that rejecting the distinction will not lead to "a bigoted majority in a democratic society ruthlessly using state power to persecute a despised minority who merely wish to practice nonstandard behaviors that are central to their religion or way of life."[7]

His example, oddly, is prejudice against homosexual behavior. At least until very recently, social policy throughout the United States embodied precisely this form of bigotry. Arneson says that "concerns that could supply good reasons for criminal prohibition . . . will not include antihomosexual phobias and the like" for several reasons. One is that the "preference" against homosexuality "would not survive rational scrutiny with full information.... The desire of a homosexual to engage in preferred forms of sex and avoid unwanted celibacy would surely withstand critical reflection."[8] But that is an empirical statement and seems incorrect about the world as we know it. We can patiently explain to a person on a park bench the reason that homosexuality does not hurt him and back up our claims with all the latest data, and yet he will say: "I hear what you say, it's still wrong, and I want it stopped," just as villagers want the hippie commune banned, not because hippies have more cars (they have none), not because they are disease-infected (they are clean), not because they use drugs (that's illegal anyway), but just because "they set the wrong tone and therefore we want them out of our neighborhood."

Another reason, Arneson says, for supposing that recognizing external interests in policy-making will not yield "antihomosexual phobias and the like" is that we should exclude "malicious preferences, desires that aim at the frustration of the well-being of others, from the set of concerns that would legitimately influence policy.... The desire to live out a nonheterosexual sex life according to one's strong inclinations is nonmalicious."[9] But so it might be said about laws against hippie communes in the neighborhood: The desire of unrelated persons to live a communal life according to their strong inclinations is surely not malicious either. In any event, the desire of the moralist to ban homosexuality (or hippies) need not be aimed at frustrating the well-being of others. The moralist may deeply regret that his opposition to gays and lesbians will cause them distress; his opposition is due, rather, to his desire to avoid living among those he believes to be immoral people.

A third reason, says Arneson, for not fearing that the community will give in to "antihomosexual phobias and the like" is that the policymaker, if fair, would amplify "the satisfactions of the worse off" (presumably homosexuals[10]) over those of the well-off (the broader society).[11] But the position of the homosexual seems not to differ from that of the hippies who desire to live together. Any group to be constrained can say, "We're worse off, since you don't like us and want to constrain us, therefore you can't constrain us." Against whom or what, then, would the legislature be permitted to act?

Arneson offers the example of a community that strongly opposes bestiality, though a few people might have a mild but not intense desire to engage in it. Arneson says it "is extreme" to insist that personal autonomy must trump the strong desires of the community to ban bestiality, even if only one person in the community has a low-ranking desire to engage in it:

> One can allow external preferences to count in the calculation that determines acceptable state policy without forsaking a reasonable deference to personal autonomy—letting individuals live their lives as they choose so long as the interests of others are not thereby seriously adversely affected.[12]

That seems to mean, then, that the community could not ban bestiality if lots of people were intensely interested in engaging in sex with animals. If almost no one will consort with animals, you may ban the practice; if lots of people intensely desire to and will do so, you may not! In any event, nothing in this last account of allowing intense external preferences to determine policy would preclude a community from banning homosexuality, for example.[13]

Finally, Arneson suggests that granting the community scope to ban some practices on moral grounds (that is, to allow external interests to trump internal ones) will not unduly restrict liberty because people could always live elsewhere. Concerns about community

> tend to be local in scope. I care more about what happens in my neighborhood or town than about events on the other side of the country.... Hence a plausible communitarian case for restriction of personal liberty will most often recommend local restrictions, which means that the restriction of liberty is limited. Those whose freedom is curtailed still have the option to conduct themselves in their preferred way in the next neighborhood, or town, or over the county or state line.[14]

This makes sense only hypothetically. If a particular practice is sufficiently reviled in the larger community (county, state, nation) so that a majority against it exists in every locality, it is impossible to understand how the minority group will secure freedom to engage in strongly felt desires by moving elsewhere. If Chicago eschews homosexuality, so might Evanston and Wilmette—or Illinois. If Austin abjures blasphemy so might Dripping Springs and Wimberley—or Texas. If Berkeley bans barbecuing, so might Kensington and El Cerrito—or California. It is the same argument that tells the minority sect to take "your filthy habits" and go elsewhere. Whatever else it is, it cannot be justified on any liberal principle.[15]

The moralist's answer consists of two classes of propositions, not necessarily connected or carefully distinguished. In general, though, depending on the norm and circumstance in question, the moralist insists that violating a norm will have deleterious effects, including, in some instances, actual harm (which may be to individuals, groups, or the community as a whole), or will result in an evil state of affairs. In the next sections, I examine some of these claims.

Disobeying Religious Commandments: Provoking the Wrath of God

Suppose we discovered that God was threatening to destroy our community because so many of its residents engage in vile and wicked acts. To a marauding general demanding that we change our behavior we might say, "Nuts, we'd rather fight, for who are you to tell us how to behave?" But that retort is futile against God. If we wish to survive we had best behave ourselves. It would be a foolish political theory that denied Sodom and Gomorrah's rulers power to force compliance with

God's laws.[16] Widespread violations of religious commandments might thus be the source of actual harm to human life; indeed, the gravest sorts of setbacks to interest that we could possibly experience.

The difficulty with this argument is that it depends on an account of causation that liberalism cannot accept. Suppose A strikes B, blackening his eye. Our conventional view is that A has harmed B because his striking caused the blackening. If it turned out, however, that A's arm flung out because C pushed him from behind and A instinctively tried to steady himself, we might no longer attribute the harm to A but to C, and the cause might now be said to rest with C (or perhaps with both A and C). This is a scientific account of causation. But in some societies with a wholly different notion of causation, evil actions are never committed by people but by witches and demons: A did not fling his arm out (that is, did not intend to); a demon flung it out for him.

In a liberal society, black eyes are prevented by installing safety equipment on machinery and by enacting and enforcing laws against battery. In a witch-saturated community, however, safety equipment will be unavailing, since witches can always outwit human contrivance. To forestall harm in that community, therefore, it will be necessary to placate witches—for instance, by requiring every household to burn incense, incant ritual pleas, or make appropriate sacrifices. Success, just as in a scientific community, can be measured in the decline of injuries. If injuries do not decline, the presumption can only be that the placatory strategy was insufficient. Time, therefore, to redouble or refine the community's efforts by widening the search for and increasing the punishments of those who did not burn incense, say the prayers, or roast the goat. In this society, it is nonsense to suppose that liberalism is a wise policy. Letting each person define his own good (especially the crank at the end of town who does not believe in witches) may well be to send the community to its doom.[17]

To proponents of witchcraft or biblical wrath-of-God adherents, liberalism responds by refusing to credit the fear that God will destroy us when the state has not brought sinners into line. And this, for two related but separate reasons. First, liberalism requires a scientific explanation of cause, which by definition excludes supernatural accounts. So-called spectral evidence (auras, talking cats, and the like, supposedly seen by the benighted young accusers of the seventeenth-century Salem witches), has no place in court, as even some of the Salem judges ultimately acknowledged.[18] Second, there is no objective method to choose among the many offers of knowledge about which rules are witches' rules (or God's rules). To select one is to privilege one account of the good over others. The liberal state may not enforce religious commandments against certain acts, when the *sole* reason for objecting to the behavior is that it violates a religious commandment. That is the lesson of the religious wars that sparked what Mark Lilla has called the Great Separation of church and state.[19]

Toleration is therefore a policy that inherently prescribes a limit to the definition of harm. A person who is genuinely and even profoundly disturbed (aggrieved, upset, alarmed, frightened, panicked, even terrified) that others in his midst are by their thoughts or actions provoking God to smite the whole community has neither right to redress against the provocateurs nor a claim on the state to prohibit their conduct for that reason alone.[20] This conclusion is not one drawn only by liberals. Robert E. George, a leading perfectionist critic of liberalism, who views religion as an ultimate human good that government, in various ways, may support, agrees that government "should never attempt to coerce religious belief and practice."[21] Religious commandments must reside in their own sphere, independent of state machinery, promising the good for those who would choose it.

Prohibiting Immoral Conduct

George argues against legal moralism in the realm of religious commandments because religion is a good only when it is freely chosen. But he comes to the opposite conclusion about "legal enforcement of moral obligations," even though, like religion, moral goods "can be realized only in and by freely chosen acts (or omissions)" and not from "fear of punishment." He declares that there may be "a benefit... realized or harm prevented when laws deter people from immoral acts."[22] In George's view, the benefit is just that people may be spared committing the immorality. I examine that proposition shortly, but I begin with the seemingly more tractable claim that deterring immorality prevents harm.

Immorality as Harm to Community

The paradigmatic immorality-as-harm argument is Patrick Devlin's celebrated 1958 Maccabaean Lecture in Jurisprudence, "The Enforcement of Morals."[23] Devlin took on the Wolfenden Report, issued the year before, recommending that Britain decriminalize homosexual practices between consenting adults. Devlin's thesis, baldly stated, was this: Morality is the glue that bonds people into society, and when the glue dries out the society disintegrates.

> [S]ociety means a community of ideas; without shared ideas on politics, morals, and ethics no society can exist. Each one of us has ideas about what is good and what is evil; they cannot be kept private from the society in which we live. If men and women try to create a society in which there is no fundamental agreement about good and evil they will fail; if, having based it on common agreement, the agreement goes, the society will disintegrate. For society is not something that is kept together physically; it is held by the invisible bonds of common thought. If the bonds were too far relaxed the members would drift apart. A common morality is part of the bondage. The bondage is part of the price of society and mankind, which needs society, must pay its price.[24]

Devlin was quite insistent that preserving morality through law is the key to preserving society against disintegration, though he offered no proof, relying instead on unverified assertions—for example, "history shows that the loosening of moral bonds is often the first stage of disintegration."[25] The claim is that certain "inherently immoral" acts

> because they are ... the object of a certain kind of consensus, ... must be forbidden by law, not to prevent any wrongful harms they might cause directly, but simply to enforce the consensus, contingent and local though it may be, for that consensus is part of the social bond that unites us as a community, and we will all suffer irreparable harm if the bond breaks.[26]

If proven, this claim is sufficient to state a reason for public intervention under the harm principle, since all people require some community in which to recognize themselves as persons and to accomplish their ends. We recognize this requirement immediately in the plight of a person exiled to a desert island or to another society that speaks a different language, lives by different customs, and longs for different ideals from those of his home. To exile is assuredly to harm. So it is clear that I have a stake in the community, and a threatened destruction of the community is obviously a harm that the state may legitimately prevent. But it does not follow that an unforced change in a social consensus against particular conduct will cause society to crumble.

In Devlin's view, social disintegration may be triggered by indulgences in immoral acts or violation of taboos. It is the feeling of "intolerance, indignation, and disgust" for the act in question that legitimates the prohibition: "We should ask ourselves in the first instance whether, looking at it calmly and dispassionately, we regard it as a vice so abominable that its mere presence is an offence."[27] We might well wonder how a vice regarded as abominable might ever be looked at calmly and dispassionately, whether calmness must precede the finding of abomination or is merely a recommendation to the fact-finder to keep his head in the face of so much "horror."

Devlin supports his proposition through the metaphor of subversion: "The suppression of vice is as much the law's business as the suppression of subversive activities; it is no more possible to define a sphere of private morality than it is to define one of private subversive activity."[28] But the subversion analogy is faulty, on two counts. First, as H. L. A. Hart pointed out, private and consenting homosexuality is not seditious behavior; it does not connote perfidy, disloyalty, or betrayal.[29] Second, it *is* possible to define a sphere of "private subversive activity," at least in the sense in which it would be analogous to the concept of a sphere of private morality that Devlin condemned. We do acknowledge a private arena in which people are permitted to stand and challenge the state and society, through the expression of political and social opinions, challenges that have often prompted deep change. Yet we do not suppose that the community transformed is the community disintegrated, as long as people may go about their lives with expectations that they will be protected against real harms, as earlier defined.

The real difficulty of Devlin's position is not only that he eschewed any objective theory of morality but also that in the end he did not care whether the acts legislated against are actually immoral. Devlin recognized an act as sufficiently abominable to be damned only because certain people say so.[30] Like the good jurist who knows no truth but the judgments of juries, Devlin hung the outcome on a (fictitious) procedure, not on a substantive account. "Immorality," said Devlin, "for the purpose of the law, is what every right-minded person is presumed to consider to be immoral." Who is this right-minded person? Devlin defined him as "the reasonable man," "the man in the street," "the man in the Clapham omnibus," "the man in the jury box." Contradicting himself, Devlin argued that this reasonable man "is not to be confused with the rational man" for "he is not expected to reason about anything and his judgement may be largely a matter of feeling."[31] The calm and dispassionate analysis of the practice is now dispensed with. For Devlin, Hart famously said, "a practice is immoral if the thought of it makes the man on the Clapham omnibus sick."[32] So though one would like to reason with bus riders, it is hard to know how to do so, at least as long as they sit in the jury box. In any event, said Devlin, we need not do so.

Immorality reduced to feelings is no predictor of that without which society will not stand. To point to an often-cited example of an "abomination" that does not easily fit within the "morals" camp: "A prohibition against . . . interracial couples' appearing together in public could be justified on the basis of the horror aroused in the breasts of racists at the very sight."[33] In the nineteenth century, large segments of the population felt extreme loathing, disgust, and revulsion at the thought that a minority race might be allowed to mingle freely on socially equal terms with the white race. What defense against Devlin's argument could abolitionists mount to a legislature that enacted a law criminalizing manumission?[34] On Devlin's thesis, mandatory continued enslavement would be perfectly permissible. But that is the reductio ad absurdum, for the only immorality under those circumstances is enslavement itself. Devlin's thesis allows no possibility that the majority itself could be wrong:

> [T]he morals which underlie the law must be derived from the sense of right and wrong which resides in the community as a whole; it does not matter whence the community of thought comes, whether from one body of doctrine or another or from the knowledge of good and evil which no man is without. If the reasonable man believes that a practice is immoral and believes also—no matter whether the belief is right or wrong, so be it that it is honest and dispassionate—that no right-minded

member of his society could think otherwise, then for the purpose of the law it is immoral.[35]

In short, Devlin is declaring that if directed at a social prejudice that is held strongly enough, might makes right.[36] George holds that this failure to grapple with the truth of claims about morality invalidated Devlin's argument and showed that his

> version of legal moralism presents the real threat of tyranny.... Devlin's willingness to permit—indeed to *require*—the suppression of innocent or even honorable liberties (on the basis that mere prejudices are strongly held) means, by contrast, that no civil liberty is safe from infringement nor is any individual or minority protected from oppression.[37]

But even were we to accept Devlin's account, might makes right only if necessary to the continued existence of the society in which live the people whose moral consensus it is. It remains to be shown that the failure to provide legal backing to morality will inevitably or even potentially disintegrate the community. Devlin said so but gave no reason to believe so: "The law must protect also the institutions and the community of ideas, political and moral, without which people cannot live together."[38]

The most obvious fallacy is Devlin's equating a single convention with the string that, if pulled, will unravel all. What evidence will establish that the act that Devlin was prepared to see prohibited—homosexuality—weakens the bonds of society? Perhaps the argument is that family bonds will dissolve if it gets around that people are permitted to be homosexual, because more and more people will resign their heterosexuality. But that is a peculiar argument, to say the least. Sexual orientation, presumably, is not a matter of choice. My knowledge that Bert and Ernie go to bed together will scarcely induce me, a confirmed heterosexual, to seek out their pleasures.[39]

George suggests that Devlin has been widely misunderstood. He did not suppose, George says, that failing to enforce moral norms would lead to a breakdown of social *order*. Rather, it would lead to a loss of society, in the sense that people would no longer be "integrally related," even if they continue to live peacefully side by side (much as a couple whose marriage has disintegrated might continue to talk to each other civilly and even live in the same house, though not as a married couple).[40] This is, as George says, essentially the communitarian thesis, and is considered in the next section. But the point remains obscure and is stated sufficiently abstractly that it resists empirical verification. Which societies can anyone point to that are "integrally related," and when has the failure to legislatively enforce a moral norm (not aimed at preventing harm) been shown to have led to a community that coexisted "unintegrally"? Will legal acceptance of homosexual acts dissolve the "integral relations" of the citizenry? We do have some evidence. Homosexuality has been outlawed in many societies from time immemorial. But in many of those places and times the law was rarely enforced, certainly in recent years not sufficiently to make anyone wary of it. Consequently, even before the Supreme Court struck down such laws,[41] it was as though we had no law. In what manner, then, is society disintegrating? In the United States (and Great Britain) the failure to enforce and the eventual voiding of such laws may be partly responsible for the increasing acceptance of homosexuality. But that is scarcely evidence that we can no longer integrally relate to each other. What has weakened is not our social ties but the revulsion, if not the moral code. The disappearance of laws banning homosexual acts has stirred controversy, but it is hard to detect that our affective ties are weaker than they were before the Supreme Court spoke.[42]

Banning Actual Immorality

Actual Immorality and Community

To overcome the deficiency in Devlin's argument, the legal moralist hypothesizes that some conduct or states of being are truly immoral—not just objects of intense distaste or disgust. The moralist asserts that he has an interest in your doing something or refraining from doing something that is neither contractually required nor tortious and that ought not, but for its immorality, be proscribed.

This argument has two strands. The first is the same as Devlin's, with the added proviso that what is to be legislatively banned or regulated must in fact be immoral. George argues that various forms of immorality are harmful to various social institutions. He asserts, for example,

> that moral decay has profoundly damaged the morally valuable institutions of marriage and the family, and has, indeed, largely undercut the understandings of the human person, marriage, and the family, that are presupposed by the very idea of sexual immorality and by the ideals of chastity and fidelity which give family life its full sense and viability.

In denying that public morality is a public good, modern culture creates "public harm" to the "institutions of marriage and the family," which "have plainly been weakened in cultures in which large numbers of people have come to understand themselves as 'satisfaction seekers' who, if they happen to desire it, may resort more or less freely to promiscuity, pornographic fantasies, prostitution, and drugs." The weakening of society's "moral ecology" is a consequence, George says, of failing to support the "central tradition" of morality handed down by, among others, Aristotle and Aquinas. A "sound morals law" may help to "prevent people from habituating themselves to corrupting vices" that victimize so many.[43]

These claims are forcefully asserted but come without evidence. That marriage in many modern societies has different patterns or fails more often than in highly traditional societies scarcely demonstrates that the change is a consequence of the retreat of law. (Nor does a lower divorce rate or fewer single-parent families support the conclusion that legal regulation, in keeping the divorce rate low, was ever responsive to a host of other moral concerns about relations within the family or the effect of those relations on the children.) If the proposition is that children, for example, are actually harmed by divorcing parents, then the argument is no longer that the state must support a "moral ecology" but that it should investigate ways, consistent with the harm principle, to make parents responsible.

An immediate problem for the moralist is demonstrating that any particular act or state of being actually is immoral. Both the law and religion have authoritative machinery behind it. Legal codes and regulations emerge from state agencies, and courts determine meaning when necessary. Religious commandments take their validity, within their own sphere, from the authoritative texts to which their adherents subscribe and, in certain religions, from accepted religious leaders and their councils. There is no comparable authoritative source for determining whether particular conduct violates an operative moral code to which individuals, much less the state, should pay heed. More than we might like to think, our knowledge of immorality comes straight from our ability to shudder (and the shudder, and the quickness with which we often reach moral judgments, may be hardwired, according to mounting data from neurological and allied research).[44] Clive Bell, reflecting on his own aversions, cautioned against confusing immorality and a feeling of revulsion:

> The laws against incest are typical examples of gross intolerance. Most of us feel a sharp physical reaction—something like a shudder—at the idea of connections of this sort; and these reactions we are apt to mistake for profound ethical judgments. I know all about this feeling of disgust and disapprobation because I feel it, not only for incest and things of that sort, but for cheese. To me the sight of cheese is offensive, the smell shocking, the mere thought disturbing and vexatious: to see people eating it revolts my whole being to its depths and undermines my sense of human dignity. Yet reason tells me that the eating of cheese is no sin. Reason forbids me to mistake a physical reaction for a moral judgment, which is what every other part of my nature longs to do. Reason overrides prejudice. The essence of intolerance is the exalting of prejudices into principles, and the imposing of them on other people.[45]

Writing from the natural law tradition, George supposes that ultimately morality comes from reason, as Bell himself suggests, in understanding that he need not rely on his innate emotional reactions but can supersede them by thought. The reason of natural law comes from a "central tradition," as George has it, "an argument extended through time" and extended, refined, and modified by all those who have participated over the centuries.[46] Ultimately, then, morality comes from community, from the evolved understanding of value that people share—although of course it does not follow that what people share is actually moral. Many exalted thinkers, including Aristotle, a founder of a natural law tradition, long shared an ideal of slavery, but we have come at last to understand that slavery is not only wrong everywhere, but harmful. In any event, the argument that the source of moral value comes from community, which may legislate to maintain it, even if the particular acts aimed at are not harmful, is central to what in recent years has become known as communitarianism, and I defer further discussion to that section.[47]

Actual Immorality and Personal Distress

The second strand of argument about the harm of actual immorality is that in being confronted by it, or even in knowing that it is occurring, people can be repulsed, offended, or incapacitated. Unlike the more conventional sorts of injuries that fall within the harm principle's purview, the form of immorality now under question is an act that would not cause injury to those who do not conceive it to be immoral. It is presumed injurious only because the "victim" perceives its immorality. A person injured in a car accident suffers the injuries regardless of whether he supposes that the driver who hit him acted morally. Only the Puritan, who abjures dancing, for example, would feel distress at the notion that others' feet are gliding along the floor. Since injuries in the form of mental and physical distress are embraceable within the harm principle, why (assuming we get beyond the question of demonstrating the immorality of the acts) should acts causing them not be fit subjects of legislation?

There are two types of cases to which this particular claim of harm from immoral conduct can apply: private acts that occur generally but not within the personal experience of the complainant (e.g., dancing in private ballrooms), and acts that are public, directly perceived by the proponent of legal prohibition (for example, public nudity). I begin with the category of private acts.

Private Immoral Acts. At first blush, such acts do not seem to restrain the moralist from pursuing his interests. May he not go about his life as if dancers, for example, do not exist at all? The moralist answers that it is the knowledge that they do exist and are frolicking about that invades his interest. Here, an example from Daniel C. Dennett about a person's "belief environment" makes the point:

> I have a farm in Maine, and I love the fact that there are bears and coyotes living in my woods. I very seldom see them or even see signs of their presence, but I just like knowing that they are there, and would be very unhappy to learn that they had left....
>
> These are facts of a special sort. They are facts that are important to us simply because one part of the environment that matters to us is our belief environment. And since we are not easily gulled into continuing to believe propositions after the support for them has evaporated, it matters

to us that the beliefs be *true*, even when we won't ourselves see any direct evidence for them.[48]

So, too, the moralist's claim: His interest is in living in a community in which people do not dance and in knowing that it is a dance-free community.[49] But since he is not personally compelled to dance, he can have an interest in a belief environment in which others do not dance only by having an interest in others' interests; that is, an interest in how other people go about their lives.

The answer to all this we have already seen: Under the externality constraint, the claim necessarily falls outside the harm principle. It may be worth repeating to stress that the consequence of disregarding the externality constraint is incoherence. One person has an interest in another's not dancing, but another has an interest in ballet as a deeply moral exaltation of human capacity and art, without which the human spirit would be immeasurably impoverished.

A recent claim by six southwestern Indian tribes against the government's use of artificial snow on a public mountain suggests that such issues are not wholly theoretical. Humphrey's Peak is one of the several San Francisco Peaks situated in the Coconino National Forest in northern Arizona. The U.S. Forest Service issued a special use permit for the Snowbowl ski area, located on Humphrey's Peak. Snowbowl occupies about one percent of the combined Peaks' area. In 2002 the government approved a plan to upgrade the skiing facility, allowing it to make artificial snow from recycled wastewater so that the facility's operations would not be interrupted by variable snowfall. (The wastewater is also used for fire prevention.) The tribes sued to block the use. They conduct religious ceremonies on the Peaks, which their tradition teaches are alive. The tribes claimed neither physical interference in their ceremonies or in the natural surroundings nor coercion by the government to alter their religious practices. Rather, they asserted that the presence of the recycled rainwater, in the court's words, is "offensive to [their] religious sensibilities" and affects their "subjective spiritual fulfillment." In ruling against their claim, a federal appeals court held that these facts did not constitute a substantial burden on their free exercise of religion:

> Were it otherwise, any action the federal government were to take, including action on its own land, would be subject to the personalized oversight of millions of citizens. Each citizen would hold an individual veto to prohibit the government action solely because it offends his religious beliefs, sensibilities, or tastes, or fails to satisfy his religious desires. Further, giving one religious sect a veto over the use of public park land would deprive others of the right to use what is, by definition, land that belongs to everyone.[50]

The court did not doubt the sincerity of the religious beliefs. In other words, we may assume, for purposes of the argument here, the validity of the religious rules under which the tribes sought relief. The claim of a moral rule, unanchored in any authoritative text, has all the less cogency in avoiding the externality constraint.

The legal moralist persists, now asserting that the legislator may prohibit the immoral conduct because the immoral actor has given the moralist an interest in the immoralist's acting morally. How might such an interest arise? One plausible explanation is that it could arise through an expectation, either individually or socially aroused. The classic form of expectation is that created by a consciously negotiated contract. Not every expectation need arise in that way, however. As Lon L. Fuller has suggested, an obligation to behave in a certain way arises through "a stabilization of interactional expectancies ... so that the parties have come to guide their conduct toward one another by these expectancies." Fuller gives this example:

> My neighbor might for years have risen every morning precisely at eight, yet no one would think that this settled practice could create any obligation toward me unless it entered into some coordination of our activities, as it might if I had come to depend on him to drive me to work in his car.[51]

Just how stable or interactional the expectancy must be to constitute an enforceable obligation is a large question. For our purposes, it is enough to observe that few interactions short of an actual contract would give rise to an expectation, much less an enforceable obligation.

Suppose your favorite basketball player, call him Michael Jordan, decides to quit the game and take up baseball, at which he plainly does not excel. May you force him back to basketball or keep him from baseball? May anyone? Suppose that early in his career Jordan had announced in a televised interview that from gratitude to his many fans he intended to perfect his skills and to play the game until the end of his days. Your delight in this pronouncement prompted you to watch his games religiously thereafter. Further suppose that another fan who actually met Jordan told his hero that seeing him play was "truly inspiring" and that Jordan had responded: "It's fans like you who give me strength and I promise that I will never let you down." On the strength of this remark (and direct eye contact), the fan attended every game, only to see his hopes dashed when Jordan turned his fancy to baseball. If on the basis of these promises fans could force Jordan to continue playing, or bar him from playing baseball, or recover damages for their "loss," then a single misstep could be fatal to one's plans or ambitions. A person could be condemned ever after to do that about which he has changed his mind, on the strength of a claimed expectation aroused in someone else by an overly optimistic exclamation made in an emotional moment. If that were a criterion for state intervention, we would all be vulnerable to slips of the tongue, confusion, and mistakes. It is possible that Jordan's teammates would develop an expectation of continued play but even they, merely from his general statements, would have no grounds to force him to stay. Enforceable claims of moral conduct on the basis of an interactional expectancy fare no better. That someone has lived her life without dancing, that she has told her neighbor across the hall that she opposes dancing and that she will always refrain from dancing, does not obligate her to resist the impulse when she realizes after an artistic awakening that she has been hugely mistaken.[52]

I suggested above that an expectation that would anchor your interest in my acting morally might arise in two ways. The first—a personal expectation bred from the actions of another—is insufficient, I have concluded, in the absence of interaction that is or amounts to a contract (including a special relationship such as that between parents and children). A second form of expectation, though, might arise from the evolution of social practices encapsulated in what we generally call social norms. These are rooted in a community's practices and are not disposable, like a set of garden club bylaws. Even if the externality constraint prevents the moralist from claiming a general interest in other people's interests, the very existence of pervasive norms suggests a community-wide expectation that they will be observed. This argument thus slides into the communitarian claim that the state may enforce a community's social norms, which, to repeat, I consider in the next major section.

Public Immoral Acts: Visual Blight and Offensive Displays. There is a class of actions arguably harmful only when carried out in public or, as it were, only when displayed in the community. A common example is nudity. No one could sensibly insist that the bare act of being undressed in the privacy of one's home is harmful to anyone, but publicly disporting oneself in the buff will lead to embarrassed stares and a ride in a police car. The objection to such public exhibitions is not particularly that they are immoral but that they constitute nuisances. Feinberg applies the offense principle to public nudity and related displays. In its nonnormative sense, an offense refers to "any or all of a miscellany of disliked mental states (disgust, shame, hurt, anxiety)."[53] Normatively, offense is an offensive state brought on wrongfully by others. Although offenses are less serious than harms, they are nevertheless inconveniences, and, says Feinberg, the offense principle warrants the state in protecting us from the traps, though transient, imposed by some forms of offensive conduct. To illustrate the range of offenses that may arguably be prohibited, Feinberg offers a celebrated bus ride, in which the passengers engage in thirty-one forms of behavior at many of which, perhaps most, any reader is guaranteed to shudder. Within these thirty-one stories, Feinberg discerns six classes of offensive conduct—that which (a) affronts the senses; (b) disgusts and revolts; (c) shocks moral, religious, or patriotic sensibilities; (d) creates shame, embarrassment, or anxiety; (e) annoys, bores, or frustrates; and (f) causes fear, resentment, humiliation, or anger.[54] My point is not to summarize his examples of putative offenses but to consider briefly what it is about their public nature that arguably permits the state to regulate.

The short answer is that they are distractions that interfere with our ability to move in a crowded world. To chance upon a nude person or other unsavory sights[55] on the street corner in plain sight, the argument runs, slows us down and distracts us from our business. These encounters are, in effect, "unattractive nuisances." They are unattractive not because they are necessarily immoral but because it is simply factually true that we widely share a distress reaction to these sights. To avoid them, the state recognizes our collective interest in a public space free of such distractions.

The state's power to regulate is limited, in Feinberg's telling, however, by a variety of counterconsiderations. Some offenses are more serious than others, measured not only by the gravity of the offense but by the reasonableness of the offending conduct. Seriousness of the offense is ascertained by standards that measure the magnitude of the offense (intensity, duration, and extent), whether the offense is reasonably avoidable or was voluntarily incurred, and whether the viewer was abnormally susceptible to offense.[56] Reasonableness is measured by the importance of the conduct to the actor himself, the social value of the act, whether the actor has alternative available times or places to act, the actor's motive (conscientiousness vs. spite), and the nature of the locality in which the act took place.[57] The complex calculus that this multitude of factors requires yields little that can be generalized. An interracial couple holding hands might distract some people more than would a naked person walking alongside them, but it seems unarguable that the state may halt at most only the nudist (since to ban the interracial couple from holding hands is to violate the equality criterion: Such a law presumably does not ban holding hands in public, only interracial hand-holding).

Some acts covered by the offense principle might for slightly different reasons fall within the harm principle proper. Some distractions could be extremely dangerous in traffic, for example, and we should always be concerned over the exposure of children to sights that might be specially harmful to the immature mind. For these reasons, quite aside from the offense principle, there may be a legally cognizable collective or shared interest in regulating the public space in which we all at times interact.

The offense principle may seem intuitively plausible, but it bristles with difficulties. The possibility of a shared interest in the public space runs into the same limitations that affect the state's power to preserve the community against disintegration claimed to be caused by private immorality. Unless our distress is biologically determined (not every society objects to public nudity, for example), the claim of a widespread revulsion over one activity or another may simply return us to Devlin's dilemmas.[58]

For the state to preserve the character of our environment there must be an actual harm or offense amounting to a nuisance. A classic example of the problem is the growing tendency of many communities to enforce aesthetic zoning codes that dictate the appearance of homes and other buildings, often mandating shapes, sizes, materials, and colors. These codes, one writer says, are grounded in

> a public expectation as to how a man's property should *look*. . . . The law [is] enacting a will for visual continuity that can have no other legitimate

origin than in the vested power of the state, conceived not as a means to individual freedom, but as the expression of social consciousness. Such a law becomes legitimate only if we abandon the individualistic picture of human nature.[59]

Precisely so. Appearance codes that arise from mutual covenants of neighboring property owners to maintain the value of their property are unobjectionable because they reflect a collective interest individually determined. It may be in the interest of an entire town, or people in a section of a town, to preserve their property, but the legislated requirement that each person do so cannot be understood as an instrument of harm prevention. The problem is that there is no analogue to the private space that renders nonoffensive the conduct that is offensive only because seen in public. The person who wishes to lie around nude can always retreat into his home, but the home itself has no place to which it can retreat. It is always on display. To declare a particular building a "historic landmark" and bar the owner from altering it without permission of a public agency is to demand that one person dedicate his property to the purposes of another, and that seems a quintessential violation of the original premise: using one person's possessions as a means to others' ends. Some buildings might be so aberrant (in height, in iridescent sheen, in blocking a view, in naturally occurring noise from a wind-tunnel effect) that the state is justified in requiring alterations to prevent the actual harm that flows from their aberrant qualities. But regulating one person's property to preserve the character of the community seems no more defensible than regulating one person's conduct to do likewise.

This conclusion, it is worth noting, nicely illustrates liberalism's divide from communitarianism: Many people will find value in a town with a certain look and will despair if that look cannot be maintained. They will say that they are harmed. But they are not. They are disappointed, unhappy that things have changed. Liberalism permits change. It cannot provide an outcome acceptable to all. No set of principles can.[60]

Harmless Immorality

I note, without extended discussion, a final claim of legal moralism—that immorality is inherently wrong (in the sense of evil, debased, shameful) and should be subject to legislative proscription for no further reason. With any claim of harm or even effect on others off the table, I do not see how the argument could be sustained except by conceding the entire ground to the antiliberal. It is circular to argue that pure immorality disconnected from harm to anyone—for example, "impure" unexpressed thoughts and certain other rarefied possibilities[61]—nevertheless harms my expectation that people will conform to some absolute moral norm, since it must first be demonstrated that I have a right to expect people to behave according to that norm. Subjecting to legislative prohibition an inherent immorality that causes no harm but is said to be in essence flatly evil provides the state with power to determine each person's good. Many governments do so, but not liberal ones.

The Communitarian Challenge to Liberalism
Community as Source of Value

Devlin's case for criminalizing immorality is one strand of a set of related arguments known in recent years as "communitarianism." Though its principles are notoriously elusive, as many commentators have pointed out,[62] in general communitarians proclaim the paramount importance of community in determining the metes and bounds of human activity.[63] They contrast the selfishness that they say liberalism engenders with a public interest or a common good that attending to community would promote, ignoring or forgetting that it was the clash between contending versions of the common good that launched liberalism in the first place, to provide surcease from endless war and breathing room from the stifling closeness of an implacable social order.[64]

One aspect of the communitarian claim is curiously individualistic. Because people derive their identity from the norms of the community, whatever impairs the functioning of those norms will harm the constituent members of the community. As a recent critic sums it up: "One strand of modern communitarianism has been the claim that the identity of the moral agent is constituted by social institutions of the community of which she is a member. . . . A member cannot disengage from her community without a serious loss of self."[65] This proposition has been most famously put in a formulation by Alasdair MacIntyre:

> I am someone's son or daughter, someone else's cousin or uncle; I am a citizen of this or that city, a member of this or that guild or profession. I belong to this clan, this tribe, this nation. Hence what is good for me has to be the good for one who inhabits these roles . . . the key question for men is not about their own authorship; I can only answer the question "What am I to do?" if I can answer the prior question of "what story or stories do I find myself a part?"[66]

But this formulation has little explanatory power for the sorts of claims that communitarians might wish to make about propping up community norms by law. MacIntyre's formulation suggests that a particular woman in a traditional family must sacrifice her desires and ambitions to the family's expectations for her brother. Communitarians may argue that in stepping outside her socially constituted identity to take a job or move away she harms herself, but they do not advance beyond liberalism's insistence that the choice is hers. If obligation stems from the sentiment of attachment that arises through being formed by a community, a person who later identifies with another community or a different norm will have no less a sense of obligation. It has often been remarked that the convert is a fiercer loyalist to the new community's tradition than those who are born to it and who need not flashily display its adornments since their grounding in it is well known. At any rate, what's being fought over is not the communal obligations that are culturally or socially felt by "one who inhabits these roles," since if they are felt nothing more is needed. What's at stake is whether the state may legally bind to the norms and traditions of the community people who do not inhabit these roles. Communitarian "theory," if such it be, presumably must require that the law force members to adhere to tradition, so that the community will persist, for otherwise all that is left is liberalism.[67]

Consider some implications—for example, what place will women occupy in a society that bows to a communitarian vision? May the state ban contraception the better to ensure that women will more often and in greater numbers undertake their obvious role in the moral community? Deny egalitarian impulses by permitting men to be paid more to minimize women's working for a living? Eliminate divorce outright or leave it as a sole option for men? Prohibit interfaith marriages? Interracial ones? To preserve a community, would the state have power to ban proselytizing by "foreign" faiths? Could the state ban expressions of racial harmony to maintain a racist community?[68] Seemingly so, yet communitarians seem to back away at just these points. MacIntyre, for instance, after fiercely denouncing the modernity that he equates with liberalism, offers as the sum of human purpose not the acceptance of one's communal inheritance, or the state's power to dictate it, but the search for meaning that any liberal might propose: "The good life for man is the life spent in seeking the good life for man."[69]

A separate and more comprehensive communitarian claim is that since the most significant capacities of human beings are social and can be exercised only in society the state must necessarily be empowered to preserve it. To preserve society is to recognize it as the source of the principles of justice and to enact its norms in legislation. Right and wrong are not to be derived from abstract philosophical principles but discerned somehow from the shared understanding of the community. The communitarian holds that a particular practice is wrong because we disapprove it, not that we should disapprove it because it is wrong.[70] But as Stephen Holmes has noted, "The weakness of this reasoning lies in the tacit assumption that the characteristically human capacities that cannot be exercised except in society are necessarily praiseworthy."[71] To legally compel (or criminalize) a practice solely because it does (or does not) comport with our shared understanding risks tethering ourselves to widely held superstitions, prejudices, and follies, sorry examples of which are replete in the historical record: Why should societies warrant survival that saw slaves as unworthy or incapable of freedom, women as creatures to be confined to the home, people of different races as incompetent to mingle, heretics as unfit to live, or adherents to other faiths as pariahs? Patience, cooperation, neighborliness, fair play, and patriotism may be communally learned virtues worth fostering, but on what basis then could a communitarian state deny the communal understanding of race and sex prejudice, ethnic hostility, and religious fanaticism? Lynching flourished in tightly bound traditional communities of racists who conspired with the police, lied to the public, winked at juries, and overlooked the facts. These were not selves prior to their ends;[72] these were personalities formed by the community that ran roughshod over dissenters and turned on those who expressed even a sympathy for the disfavored among them. Slave patrols in the pre–Civil War South traveled to individual plantations to ensure conformity to the harsh code of total dominion over slaves, overriding the inclinations of owners who might be more lenient because they wished to be and because the formal law said they could be.[73] Genocide is not carried out by atomistic individuals, and most terrorists are not lone gunmen; they maim and kill in the name of a community. What limitation in theory blocks a warrior band from assaulting and killing a neighboring tribe under the true conviction that the aggression is "in accordance with our customs"?[74] What is there in communitarianism that would bar collective guilt and punishment for the crimes of individual perpetrators?[75] That many people share a belief, that the belief is embedded in a community's folkways, does not make it true or valuable.[76]

The companion claim, that the state must attend more to the common good of the community than to the individual good of each person, is no more substantial. (In essence, this is the claim that the community serves not only as the source of principles of justice but also as the model for their content. In other words, principles of a just order must not be whatever a community happens to value, since the community could have bad values; rather, the principles must themselves be communal.) The argument runs that citizens will reject the state's demands as illegitimate unless, in the words of Charles Taylor, there is a "common form of life ... seen as a supremely important good, so that its continuance and flourishing matters to the citizen for its own sake and not just instrumentally to their several individual goods or as the sum total of these individual goods."[77]

Communitarians point to very few historical examples of societies purportedly dedicated to a politics of the common good and a shared view of a common way of life. And, as Will Kymlicka points out, they are hopelessly faulty examples. One, the New England town government, excluded "women, atheists, Indians and the propertyless." Are there shared ends that, in Kymlicka's words, will "serve as the basis for a politics of the common good which will be legitimate to all groups in society"? Kymlicka says that Sandel and Taylor, two of the leading contemporary communitarians, "give no examples of such ends, perhaps because there are none."[78]

The claim that liberalism itself is a harm to the community, that there cannot be social order without unity, is not new to the communitarians of the late twentieth century. It has always been the hymn of antiliberals. In the sixteenth-century preliberal Elizabethan worldview, as one tract put it, "[W]e must agree in religion, we must serve but one master, one body will have but one head.... The nobles must be of one belief, of one faith, of one religion; they must all agree upon one head. The gentlemen will follow; the commons cannot tarry long behind."[79] Writing in *Vanity Fair* in 1921, G. K. Chesterton proclaimed:

> Modern society is intrinsically insecure because it is based on the notion that all men will do the same thing for different reasons.... To expect that all men for all time will go on thinking different things, and yet doing the same things, is a doubtful speculation. It is not founding society on a communion, or even on a convention, but rather on a coincidence. Four men may meet under the same lamp post; one to paint it pea green as part of a great municipal reform; one to read his breviary in the light of it; one to embrace it with accidental ardour in a fit of alcoholic enthusiasm; and the last merely because the pea-green post is a conspicuous point of rendezvous with his young lady. But to expect this to happen night after night for an interminable period is unwise.[80]

Chesterton bewailed the "present ... contrary condition of being externally similar and internally torn asunder." He too wished for a common creed as the securest basis of internal order. But, as Charles Frankel later warned, "giving men the same ultimate ends and the same sound statement of belief [would not] really guarantee that they would meet amicably at their pea green lamp post." How can imposing a common belief "guarantee that men will employ the same means to reach these ends, or that they will interpret the words of this philosophy in the same way?" To guarantee agreement on a statement of ultimate faith requires "an agreed-on institution which can enforce a single interpretation of that faith."[81] Which faith will give us peace and unity in our everyday lives? Chesterton proclaimed that "spiritual unity will either never return, or it will return with the return of the creed for which Christmas stands." But, of course, not even Christians agree on matters of faith,[82] and it was their murderous attempts at unity that prompted political thinkers to perceive the possibility of social order in diversity.

Communitarianism's real quarrel is with pluralism, not liberalism. It wants a unity it cannot have and with a lack of which it wishes not to cope. The communitarian fallacy is the supposition that if people are not united on ultimate ends they cannot unite on any ends. There are two errors here, Frankel wrote. One is "overintellectualizing human behavior." People "do not have to love the same ultimate good to live at peace with one another; good manners will do the job perfectly well." Moreover, most of the time people will get along because they do not let single, "ultimate" values sidetrack them into unremitting hostility; they compromise, rather, because they "have other values besides those that are in dispute."[83] Even if four people congregate under the lamp post for different reasons and discover, when they meet, that they do not like each other and will not join in spiritual union, they may still develop a common interest in that corner. They may all want it well illuminated, for example, and may happily form a pressure group to see that this is done, so that the painter can paint well, the monk read his breviary more easily, the drinker keep from bumping his head, and the young lover from accosting the wrong girl.... [They] do not have to agree on the same ultimate ends in order to co-operate willingly on a common project.[84]

The state does not need to earn legitimacy by enforcing a common set of ultimate ends. The unifying common good of a political community is, rather, the invitation to all to participate in an enterprise that works to secure the freedom to seek the good as each conceives it.

The communitarian argument contains three further defects worth noting. First, communitarians often ignore many forms of community that, consistent with liberalism, do provide a unifying good for their members. Michael Sandel argues, for example, that the state must enforce a social morality to combat the intolerance that "flourishes most where forms of life are dislocated, roots unsettled, traditions undone." Adrift in such a world, individuals lie "vulnerable to the mass politics of totalitarian solutions."[85] But his argument is largely ahistorical, if not also a non sequitur, a captive of the faulty presupposition that liberal society consists solely of selfish individuals whose struggles rip apart social traditions and who then, isolated and alone, resign themselves to Leviathan.[86] But that is not how freedom is lost. The totalitarian revolutionary, perhaps empowered by sudden natural cataclysms or economic disasters, dissolves a society's intermediate communities and binds individuals to a single state-enforced path, often in the name of an imagined tradition. Liberal societies guard against this danger by supporting a robust freedom of association and explicitly protecting the people's right to establish and join smaller communities too numerous to list or count (neighborhoods, schools, churches, civic associations, political parties, rescue committees, alumni groups, athletic teams, sports clubs, recreational groups, offices and other workplaces, chambers of commerce, craft associations, fraternal organizations, and all the rest). The liberal state wards off totalitarian impulses by encouraging a diversity of norms and institutions and preserving each person's power to engage in practices in association with others unmolested by those who are simply revolted by nonharmful traditions alien to them. If totalitarianism ultimately fills political space emptied of pluralistic customs and institutions, it makes no sense to view a state-enforced morality as a substitute for that lost pluralism. The legal moralist argues that morality is worth preserving, that the immoralities that constitute its violation are evils to be suppressed, and that, in a community of diverse opinions (else why would this even be an issue?), the majority must rule. But why should minorities feel allegiance to such a state? Why should a communitarian wish to abolish self-constituting communities? As Richard Wollheim has put it: "The identity, and the continuity, of a society resides not in the common possession of a single morality but in the mutual toleration of different moralities."[87]

Second, communitarians neglect the capacity of these communities, like the larger community, to police themselves. Consider one such community—a sports team. It's easy enough to see that a team's goal—winning the game—is a common end of its members, and that a team is more than a "mere association of individuals."[88] A true team is not an association that holds a meeting and sends out a newsletter to subscribers. It is, if it is working well, a psychological unity in which the common interest may run counter to individual interests, but in which the individuals nevertheless devote themselves to that common interest, hence the commonsense notion of "teamwork." A particular basketball player might prefer to sink the most baskets in a game, but his overriding interest is winning the game, and playing for the team means passing the ball to someone else when that is a more likely way of scoring on the play. A team member who plays selfishly and unproductively will be cut from the team, despite his individual interest in remaining on it, not because the state enforces the norm of winning but because the team does. Similarly, the language community: Above all, language is a social practice, created, spoken, and changed by communities, but no one (except, apparently, the French) proposes that the state intrude to freeze the language by fixing the vocabulary and discarding words and phrases incompatible with the linguistic custom.[89]

In important ways, the general social community has the same authority.[90] If a common tradition is as important to society as communitarians claim, then it will regulate most behavior on its own. If it fails to maintain the people's fealty, if people deviate from it, and others follow them, why should it command respect? If a taboo against dancing erodes, and society now kicks up its heels, what has changed that needed protection? If it is still the same society, then the disappearance of a moral norm was irrelevant to it. If it is a different society, on what basis can we mourn its disappearance? What is this particular society that it deserves to "live," independent of the people who constituted it and who, we may suppose, did not die or come to some other harm when Elvis came to town?[91]

The communitarian thesis looks in the wrong direction: It is not social but political disintegration we need fear. The state may protect the machinery by which people are empowered to seek their good, but it ought not prevent people from changing their minds about what that good is (nothing prevents the protesting Puritan from declining the invitation to the dance, whatever his neighbors are doing). The state may seek to preserve itself, but it should not freeze into place the customs and traditions that the community has made and that it can unmake.

A third defect in the communitarian arguments of the late twentieth and early twenty-first centuries is their failure to progress beyond hazy pronouncements of abstract principle. Details of the community norms to be restored are never made clear; the significance or consequence of "community" as a communitarian term is always left vague; the methods and limits of communitarian politics are not spelled out. Many commentators have noted this skittishness. "Communitarians find loathsome," says Nancy L. Rosenblum,

> preoccupation with rights, most of all, and a dreary, adversarial system of justice; also, rampant commercialism and arid utilitarianism. Their aversions are plain. But they are disinclined to propose alternatives. Community is more often an invocation than a reference to specific political forms. It is not just that the parameters of community are vague, its character at the most general level is undefined.

This nebulousness, says Stephen Holmes, "is not an incidental feature of communitarianism, moreover; it is an essential one." Communitarians "never provide sufficient detail about the national political institutions they favor to allow us to compare the advantages and disadvantages of illiberal community with the vices and virtues of the liberal societies we know."[92]

Civic Republicanism

Another strand of modern communitarianism is civic republicanism. The republican believes "not simply that the good must be pursued through politics (which still does not state what it is), but that the content of the human good is active citizenship in a virtuous political community."[93] But that definition does not seem to provide liberalism's benefits or correct its putative defects. If human good is simply active citizenship, then civic republicanism would permit those in power to ban disliked religious observances or prohibit interracial marriage. If "virtuous political community" excludes these and other forms of discrimination, where do those values come from? The "republican community does not argue the ... claim that the good is whatever your community values, but rather the substantive moral claim that the good involves *living in and as* a political community."[94] But this claim does not seem to advance much beyond liberalism, which, after all, permits active citizenship but does not command it. Civic republicanism cannot cure what it sees as liberalism's political defects by abandoning liberalism's essential limits, though whether it stands for anything more than tinkering with political institutions (in the United States they certainly need reform) still remains to be seen.[95]

In his major work on civic republicanism, *Democracy's Discontent*, Michael Sandel takes to task the "procedural republic" that he says liberalism has spawned, "the priority of fair procedures over particular ends" (a position that I have largely staked out in this book). It has led people, he claims, to fear "for the loss of self-government and the erosion of community." He contrasts this dominant political theory, as he sees it, with civic republicanism, his preferred alternative, which he defines as not merely a "sharing in self-government" but "deliberating with fellow citizens about the common good and helping to shape the destiny of the political community."

When citizens come together to debate public policy, they are carrying out the highest calling and only in so doing is it possible to preserve our freedom. The liberalism of unencumbered selves "lacks the civic resources to sustain self-government"; it "cannot secure the liberty it promises, because it cannot inspire the sense of community and civic engagement that liberty requires."[96] But this view is mistaken, and on two grounds. One, which I consider in the next chapter, is an ambiguity in such terms as "highest end" and "the good life." The other mistake, which derives from the first, is the belief that because the liberal posits a good that the state may not declare, there is no motive or reason for liberal selves to engage with each other in the political arena.

In offering a contrast between liberal and republican views of civic engagement, Sandel says that the liberal supports freedom of speech "so that people may be free to form their own opinions and choose their own ends." But the liberal cannot, he asserts (and by implication the republican can), "support it on grounds that a life of political discussion is inherently worthier than a life unconcerned with public affairs, or on the grounds that free speech will increase the general welfare."[97] But the liberal certainly must agree that without freedom of speech the general welfare would be severely circumscribed. Whether concern for public affairs is or is not a liberal belief depends on sorting out the ambiguity in "a life." If by "a life unconcerned with public affairs" Sandel means a way of life or a culture, then of course the liberal not only can but must support the proposition. The liberal would draw the line only at supposing that it must hold true for any particular person ("a" life). As I have sought to demonstrate throughout, *the civic conversation over policy choices is essential. The harm principle is not a machine programmed to crank out rules on its own: It is a tool that the public and its legislators must use to seek the proper and best ends of the state.* In the most interesting and important cases, harm is not self-defining. That is why everyone is entitled to the franchise, and why freedom of speech is guaranteed, so that the essential conversation can be carried on robustly throughout the populace to determine the direction, means, and ends of the state. So Sandel's prime goal of civic republicanism—that we must participate in political association—is precisely what liberals hold (or ought to hold) central to their own beliefs as well.

I have already noted the significance of the long-run trend from natural systems to human systems.[98] Increasing numbers of people are no longer compelled to scratch out a living day to day; we have become free to do other things. But that freedom is not itself free. It comes at a price. For to achieve the freedom from drudgery we have necessarily to rely on the human systems that have substituted for nature and to play our part in them, and these systems require our constant attention. As the quip usually attributed to Oscar Wilde has it: "The trouble with socialism is that it takes up too many evenings." Though we need not spend hours every day tilling the soil or foraging for food (or avoiding wild predators), we are not free to act as we will. We must maintain the new systems that feed us, clothe us, house us, protect us, and provide us employment and purpose and keep them safe for us. Our energies thus move from the natural realm to the human realm, from nature to culture and politics. Liberalism does not seek somehow to rise above this task, because it cannot. Liberalism does not renounce civic engagement. Political engagement is as essential to liberalism as it is to civic republicanism. The quarrel is not over the necessity of participation but the subject of the debate, to which I return in the next and last chapter.

Modern-day communitarians seem to endorse Edmund Burke's belief that "Parliament is not a *congress* of ambassadors from different and hostile interests, which interests each must maintain, as an agent and advocate against other agents and advocates; but Parliament is a *deliberative* assembly of *one* nation, with *one* interest, that of the whole." Say that liberalism permits a politics of mutual bribery, campaign contributions for subsidies, and tax breaks: What would change when a political majority in a communitarian regime brought even *more* areas under public rule? Neither Burke, nor the communitarians, nor the civic republicans have a theory for making the legislature deliberative in his sense.[99]

The incompleteness of communitarianism is not surprising. It is of a piece with Rousseau's mischief in supposing, without saying how, that real people could pick out a genuine "general will"—the collective, unitary good of the community—from the expressed separate wills of all those who constitute it. But imagining utopia, or worse, believing that it once existed, puts us all at risk, for it tricks us into looking past the sinkholes that menace our every step and into seeing safeguards that are not there.[100]

Multiculturalism and Group Rights

A seemingly more narrow form of communitarianism has emerged in the politics of multiculturalism. If the community at large cannot become a unified whole, perhaps specific traditions within it can maintain their forms. May particular minority groups in liberal democratic cultures be exempted from laws and policies that are said to impair or erode the minority way of life? May the state enact laws that bind members of the minority group to the group's folkways?[101]

These questions might have affirmative answers because of an ambiguity in the liberal notion of equal respect. Charles Taylor has pointed to two forms of liberalism, which he labeled the *politics of universalism* and *the politics of difference*. Universalism sees each citizen as equivalent: Equal respect for each person requires that differences among people be disregarded when considering basic liberal rights such as freedom of speech and the right (and obligation) to attend school. The politics of difference holds that ignoring differences between people, insofar as they themselves view the differences as significant, violates equal respect. For example, universalism would require all schoolchildren to attend public schools conducted in the majority language; a difference-based regime would not only permit but require schoolchildren of the minority culture to attend separate schools in their own language.[102]

An often-cited example of an attempt to buttress a minority culture by *mandating* separateness is the Canadian approach to multiculturalism.[103] Quebec has declared itself a "distinct society," maintaining by law its francophone culture. French-speaking citizens and immigrants are not permitted to send their children to English-speaking schools. All firms with more than fifty employees must conduct their business in French. Commercial signage must be in French exclusively (though this provision was struck down, in theory, as unconstitutional). By the lights of a universalist liberalism, these laws are clearly discriminatory. They apply not only to English-speaking immigrants who happen to live in Quebec but also to French-speaking Canadians who might wish to send their children to English-speaking schools, despite the majority's desire to preserve French culture. A relatively rare instance in the United States of *exemption* from majority culture played out in the case of *Wisconsin v. Yoder*, in which, recall, the Supreme Court upheld the religious and parental claims of the Old Order Amish community to have their children excused at the age of fourteen from the state's mandatory school-attendance policy, which required attendance for all schoolchildren through age sixteen.[104]

Which is the worse discrimination—to be told what you must do because of your presumed identity in a particular culture? Or to suffer the possibility that in the long run the culture will die out because under the banner of universalist rights, rules that might preserve it (e.g., mandatory attendance at separate schools) may not be enforced against group members? If it is permissible to recognize and preserve the language of other cultures, should not the same approach apply to religious rituals as well? If the religious culture of a "distinct society" is, say, animist, must its members be required to attend animist ceremonies or be forbidden from attending a Catholic Church? Should proselytizing be banned?[105] May women be required by law to adhere to a dress code promulgated by religious or tribal leaders?[106] If preserving the culture is paramount, should it not also be permissible to override the claims of free speech and prohibit members of the culture from engaging in heresy or speaking out, even in subtle ways (as determined by the religious leader or the minister of culture), against the values of the culture?

The paradox of a universalist rights theory that arguably discriminates by failing to recognize difference lies in corrupting the word "discrimination." If it is discriminatory to say to each person "you may speak which language or practice which religion you wish," when a group's cultural leaders say that group norms deny its "adherents" such a choice, then we have come to a logical and political impasse. In the name of not privileging universalism, group leaders (rarely democratically chosen) will then be privileged above the choices that might be made by those to whom they minister. Of course, a society may not be committed to liberalism, but if it is, it fails that commitment by winking at, if not actively promoting, illiberal rules. To allow particularists to co-opt the language of harm ("to prevent harm to a cultural way of life, i.e., to preserve the good life, the state must permit particular individuals to impose a collective choice to supersede the choices that other particular individuals would make") is simply to deny liberalism at its core. In the name of the good life, leaders of the "distinct society" may mutilate women,[107] kill dissenters,[108] and direct the lives of all their "followers." Preventing harm to individuals is replaced by preserving folkways. To do so in a multiculturalist country, particular groups will tend to close themselves off from the larger society, some, like social black holes, becoming tightly bound cults.

Taylor suggests the possibility of a middle path.[109] The problem, however, as Taylor acknowledges, is that there can be no clear line between "fundamental rights" and practices necessary to "cultural survival." Should American prosecutors back away from trying to stamp out the plural-marriage system of an entrenched minority in Utah and elsewhere? Should the machinery of government be lent to Catholic prelates who can use all the help they can get to protect their parishioners from modern forms of birth control? If tribal communities may not be forced to speak English, may they be forced to speak the old languages instead? Should the expert judgments of shamans be given equal weight to those of Western physicians? Should the teaching of evolution be banned from schools that fundamentalist Protestant children attend? And what distinguishes a legitimate minority group from those with pretensions to a way of life? Should Tony Soprano, his family, and associates be permitted to settle things their own way, the old way, free of the bothersome oversight of police and prosecutors?

Taylor does not say. "In the nature of things," he concedes, "compromise is close to impossible" on some issues: "one either forbids murder or allows it." What, then, does it mean to say that we ought to "let cultures defend themselves, within reasonable bounds," by permitting "collective ends ... as legitimate considerations in judicial review, or for other purposes of major social policy"?[110] K. Anthony Appiah has responded that to require those whose identities spring from a particular culture to buttress practices of that culture may mean that communicants will be forced into scripts. To be "recognized" as, for example, a black man may require not just toleration but "to be respected *as a Black*"; a gay man "*as a homosexual.*" But to force such modes of recognition may impel the individual, against his own personal understanding, to "organize [his] life around [his] 'race' or [his] sexuality.... Between the politics of recognition and the politics of compulsion, there is no bright line."[111]

The claim for multicultural rights is not limited to a group's right to exempt itself from the law or to commit the law to its own ends. In addition to breathing room around the line separating fundamental rights from nonconforming practices, many committed multiculturalists want recognition of the equal value of the minority culture. For example, Bhikhu Parekh says: "The liberal is in theory committed to equal respect for persons. Since human beings are culturally embedded, respect for them entails respect for their cultures and ways of life."[112] This claim poses a quandary: A believer in equal respect must, by respecting each person, respect that person's norms, and must show that respect not only by recognizing and approving those norms but also by supporting them, including norms that may not themselves reflect a concern for equal respect (for example, a religious tradition that subjugates women to men). But this contradiction is entirely in the eyes of the critic. Why must respect for persons translate to respect for everything they stand for? Must the state aid the adherent's church in killing heretics in the name of equal respect? What of respect for the heretic? The way out of this paradox is simple: Equal respect for a person does not entail political support for all the positions that he holds. One can care for people without agreeing with or even caring about their cultural traditions. The state need not aid others in committing harm simply because these individuals define harm in a different way. As we have seen, it is the state that defines harm, not individuals or groups within society.[113]

A liberal state may consistently support distinct cultural communities in many ways—most importantly, by rejecting demands that the majority's way of life be imposed on everyone and by recognizing each person's right to adhere to the norms of particular cultures. But it is the members' rights to belong that are paramount, not the cultures' continued vitality if unsupported by their participants' voluntary commitments. It may be valuable that the planet contain a multitude of cultural traditions, but not at the cost of forcing adherence against the will of those who are seen as members. While there is undoubtedly a loss in the recent extinction of thousands of the world's languages, the abstract value of a plenitude of tongues ought not be paid by forcing the native speakers of each one, or their children, to refrain from learning and speaking other languages. The liberal state must provide legal refuge for members of minority traditions who choose to exit.

Harms by Community: Association and Equality

The liberal opposition to communitarianism may prove problematic for ending discrimination based on immutable characteristics like race, sex, ethnicity, or the religion of one's forebears. The bigot seems to have a telling retort to the demand that he deal or associate with people of different races and ethnicities. "You may deplore my beliefs," he might say; "you might even suppose that my refusal to have anything to do with these people is immoral, but you have just finished saying that the state may not act against immoralities per se, that the state should leave traditions alone. That is legal moralism. To require me to deal with or serve certain people against my wishes is to exalt their desire for how I behave over mine, and you have said the externality constraint prohibits the state from giving weight to such a preference. If it is improper for me to legislate against their presence, must it not also be improper for them to legislatively force themselves upon me? If you favor diversity, you must leave me free to follow my own inclinations and to associate only with those whom

I find congenial. All else is tyranny." This argument has many forms of expression. Milton Friedman has put it two ways:

> I deplore what seem to me the prejudice and narrowness of outlook of those whose tastes differ from mine [in respect to the color of a man's skin or the religion of his parents] and I think the less of them for it. But in a society based on free discussion, the appropriate recourse is for me to seek to persuade them that their tastes are bad and that they should change their views and their behavior, not to use coercive power to enforce my tastes and attitudes on others.[114]
>
> The ACLU will fight to the death to protect the right of a racist to preach on a street corner the doctrine of racial segregation. But it will favor putting him in jail if he acts on his principles by refusing to hire a Negro for a particular job.[115]

It is unnecessary to assume that the proponent of discrimination is a pathological bigot. He may be quite civil in meeting on vacation with dissimilar others and might conceivably even vote for them in elections to political office (or at least not object to their election). He may concede that mandatory segregation laws are untenable.[116] Nevertheless, in wanting to preserve his race or "culture," he refuses to hire, work with, or rent to people of the "wrong" race, religion, ethnicity, or sexual orientation. What case can be made for outlawing private discrimination in housing, the job market, public accommodations, and the like?

The answer lies in the force of custom that I earlier suggested was a sufficient reason to legislate against dueling.[117] Custom imprisons people as a bug in amber; it freezes them; it stereotypes them. Through custom we act unthinkingly in formulaic, ritual ways. Sometimes custom is good because it serves efficiency; sometimes it is evil because it is harmful to particular people. The custom that supported dueling did so by harming the person who refused to accept the challenge. A legal prohibition against it, I concluded, is not paternalistic, because the custom acted as a coercive force against an unwilling participant. Likewise, I suggest, a legal prohibition against private acts of discrimination is not moralistic, for custom now acts often (perhaps even usually) coercively against the discriminators themselves.[118] So entrenched are such prejudices that anyone seeking to deal with a disfavored person as an equal is likely to find himself as ostracized by his community as was the person in an honor-drenched society who balked at accepting a challenge to duel.[119]

The binding force of this custom was the central point of the trial in Harper Lee's *To Kill a Mockingbird*. A young woman kissed a black handyman, presumably on the way to seducing him. But her father chanced to see the kiss and savagely beat her. To explain away the beating, the girl falsely accused the handyman of having violated her. Addressing the jury, the defendant's lawyer, Atticus Finch, attempted to dispel the force of the searing prejudice that he knew would incline the jury to convict, despite the gross improbability of the testimony they had heard from everyone but the defendant. The girl, said Finch of the chief prosecution witness,

> has committed no crime, she has merely broken a rigid and time-honored code of our society, a code so severe that whoever breaks it is hounded from our midst as unfit to live with.... She knew full well the enormity of her offense, but because her desires were stronger than the code she was breaking, she persisted in breaking it.... She [then] did something every child has done—she tried to put the evidence of her offense away from her.... She must destroy the evidence of her offense.... What did she do? She tempted a Negro. She was white, and she tempted a Negro. She did something that in our society is unspeakable: she kissed a black man. Not an old Uncle, but a strong young Negro man. No code mattered to her before she broke it, but it came crashing down on her afterwards.[120]

So severe was the code that despite Finch's plea that the jury be fair-minded and do its duty, the citizens were no less constrained by it, and they returned a guilty verdict. To be sure, Finch's speech is literature, not history, but literature that more eloquently than most historical accounts[121] reveals a truth that cannot be denied about the impact of that particular custom on people's behavior.

A custom with so much coercive force should be viewed as no less binding than the law itself—as law, in fact.[122] A set of antidiscrimination laws, then, amounts to a change in the law, a repeal of the old mores and establishment of new ones.[123] No doubt many fair-minded people would not have acted in so discriminatory a manner had there been no code to fetter them. For them, legally enforceable policies against discrimination might be welcomed, not as paternalism (the law is not trying to make them better people) nor as moralism (the law is not trying to enforce a morality on unwilling recipients) but as a means both of allowing them to do what is morally right and, more significantly perhaps, to avoid actual harm to both the traditional victims of discrimination and to those who despise the custom but feel its force.

That discrimination is harmful it seems supererogatory to demonstrate. Even the dullest intellect today must hear Justice Henry B. Brown's well-known words from *Plessy v. Ferguson*, upholding the doctrine of "separate but equal," as utterly unconvincing and self-serving racism. The Court majority, he said,

> consider[s] the underlying fallacy of the plaintiff's argument to consist in the assumption that the enforced separation of the two races stamps the colored race with a badge of inferiority. If this be so, it is not by reason of anything found in the act, but solely because the colored race chooses to put that construction upon it.[124]

Brown neglected to mention that enforced separation came always at the behest of white legislative majorities and meant that the entire white world, the dominant culture, the source of wealth, invention, and opportunities, would be materially closed to the "colored race," impairing their interests in education, commerce, jobs, and the opportunity to participate in the culture of the nation. Even so simple an act as riding on a train with a white person, to discuss whatever was to be discussed, was closed to the black person. It is this forced disconnection from the surrounding society and the badge of inferiority that is implied by it that constitutes the harm.[125] As Emile Durkheim suggested, the harm from such a disconnection can even lead to suicide.[126] The self is fragile and may fall apart if not connected to society. The state ought to do something to foster the connection, at least by prohibiting others from conspiring to keep an entire group from connecting. On this view, then, in barring such practices as private demands for segregation and refusals to deal on the basis of race, the state is adhering to the harm principle in striking straightforwardly at harmful practices.

That the state may outlaw significant areas of private racial discrimination does not mean that every choice that hinges on race, religion, or ethnicity is subject to state interference. The principle prescribes its own limit: It is the force of custom, we may assume, that prevented whites from serving blacks and other minorities in places declared "open to the public" and from hiring in circumstances in which the recruiting net was cast over an entire potential workforce identified on the basis of skills relevant to the job. Some refusals to deal, however, are intimate and do not hinge on the force of custom but on purely personal preferences, even though an older custom may have shaped those preferences. The line is fuzzy, but it presumably must be drawn wherever and however we differentiate between public and private relations. Whom I invite to share my friendship can be no business of the state, for my familiar relations are an important part of my personal ends.[127] That is why the suggestion that intimate relations be regulated seems perverse and illiberal—for example, the "personal advertisements" in many newspapers and magazines in which advertisers declare their preferences by race and sex.[128]

Dissatisfied with fracture, moralists and communitarians devoutly wish for a common and universal meaning. They want unification. Nor is the union of people sufficient; they also want everyone to recognize the rightness of a united whole. Lacking a way of wishing out loud for a common religion to regain the ground, communitarians seek it in the sociological realm. But they have no program for imposing this longing, and they are rightly fearful of the state's substitute for cheering a football team on—an army and a navy, my country right or wrong, especially, or perhaps only, when on the field of battle. The problem that they properly acknowledge, because, as they say, it is not their problem, but all of ours, is the ancient one—how to unite the warring dimensions of the human psyche, how to give us happiness and repose in a world that seemingly offers only mystery and emptiness. Communitarians, or some of them at any rate, cannot abide a society in which different people accept different meanings, because they do not suppose human beings can make their own authentic meaning. If not from God, meaning must come from the communal tradition. But what is so far on offer has not proved reassuring: Therapy does not "cure" the problem at the root of the human psyche; a common religion lies beyond the likelihood of belief or of agreement; philosophy and science at best can give us only very partial answers. On this account we are at an impasse, and the liberal solution has been to agree to ask the questions, in respectful harmony, if possible, with everyone else. No questions are ruled out, no answers are imposed within. It has been the burden of this book to show that the most sensible condition for seeking after the truth that all profess to want is a liberal political order that offers as much equal ground to the quest as any political order is likely to give.

11

Liberalism Redressed

The pieces of liberalism's "one very simple principle" are now at hand, and at least loosely assembled. Fit together, they show liberalism to be a capacious doctrine that provides a comprehensive rationale and a textured set of means to accomplish what we ought to want from a political theory—and the government it describes. In particular, the harm principle does far more work than most people have supposed. Not only does it provide a toolkit for dealing with daily disturbances, it is sufficiently robust and nuanced to permit government to alleviate human suffering without sacrificing a broad liberty for each individual to seek the good life as he or she conceives it. Liberal principles also provide for institutions and practices that make it possible to achieve these ambitions in the world as we know it. Liberalism is responsive, moreover, to the many jeremiads leveled against it over the years. I express these responses as conclusions, without attempting to restate the case that has been the subject of the preceding chapters.[1]

Liberalism is respectful of people.[2] It is impartial in its dealings with its citizens and assumes the political equality of all. It serves humanity's dual nature by balancing regimentation and license, communal norms and unfettered personality. It supports liberty for all, both to discuss and vote on matters properly of public concern and to pursue private ends in matters outside its domain.

Liberalism accepts self-interest as necessary but not sufficient to the human good. By acknowledging the universal motivation of self-interest, it is realistic and respectful without being utopian. It rests at bottom not on a slavish acceptance of bare self-interest but on the nuanced principle that people may pursue their interests as long as they do not harm others. It gives play to self-interest not as selfish egoism but as an antidote to the embrace of irrational passions that historically brought communities to ruin and condemned most people to impoverished lives because their interests were seen as less important than those of their betters. Liberals need neither assume that people are rational calculators of their own interests nor conclude that the rejection of that assumption implies a government that may substitute its judgment for judgments that each of us may make.

Liberalism is a middle way that acknowledges its own limits. It does not hold power to decide every human question or resolve every matter of human concern.

A liberal constitution relieves the public over the short run, in which immediate political decisions must be made from risking repeal of its basic principles at the hands of overwrought and transient majorities, while allowing change that proves itself necessary over the longer run. Liberal constitutionalism not only limits the means through which the state may act to accomplish its ends but also withdraws from its purview contentious issues that have only ever been resolved bloodily and that, we have come to learn, can far more safely be left to people, individually or in groups, apart from the compulsions of law.

Despite, or more likely because of, its limitations, the liberal state has power to achieve its ends and even increases the chances that political outcomes will be superior to those of states with unlimited power. By publicly withdrawing some matters from the political conversation, it permits citizens and officials to concentrate on issues that require political resolution and avoids both the hostilities provoked by endless disputation and the paralysis that ultimately stifles and destroys states that supervise every sort of human interaction. But contrary to the claims of those who see liberalism as weak, in withdrawing its writ from some objectives, the liberal state does not forsake the necessary power to accomplish its legitimate political ends. It retains a wide range of legal, institutional, administrative, and political techniques, including the power to tax, criminalize, regulate, adjudicate, remonstrate, and establish programs to cope with and ameliorate the harms that disrupt people's pursuit of their own best ends.

Liberal government aims to preserve the rule of law, from which no privileged class, including the leadership, is exempt. The liberal state is not arbitrary. To ensure that public officials are beholden to citizens and not vice versa, citizens of a liberal state must have a place to stand that provides distance and independence from the government. This it accomplishes in part by prizing the stability and diffusion of property. The state strives to contain power that may be used to dislodge property unilaterally from its owners, while underwriting institutions that permit property, land, and labor to be fairly traded.

In the public realm, citizens are political and civic equals. That is a measure of liberalism's respect for persons, but so too is its respect for persons' differences, so that people are not forced into straitjackets in the social and economic realms. Liberalism propounds an equality of opportunity, not an equality of results.

Liberalism need not forsake those who appear to be down and out. It has ample theoretical resources to attend to people's welfare needs. The state may see to those who are, or are likely to be, destitute, hungry, homeless, unemployed, unhealthy, and uneducated. Though liberalism speaks the language of equality of opportunity, it need neither construe equality or opportunity in a narrow, miserly way nor resist the call that some part of society's product be redistributed to those in need.

Liberalism is conscious of and concerned at all times about the possibility of achieving human good. Through constitutional principles and public policies, it supports the myriad ways in which people work together in their searches for proper human ends. To permit people to realize these ends, the state deliberately refrains from enforcing a single or even a range of goods that are politically determined. Its restraint is due not to a weak-kneed relativism or subjective disdain for the good but from a hard-headed and historically informed understanding that the world is irretrievably pluralistic and that only dissatisfaction and rebellion can come from imposing a common, nonpolitical good, even one that a large majority implores the state to make manifest in law. The common good that liberalism espouses is the maintenance of a political community in which people may live in mutual respect in the search for what is good for them and in forbearing to impose that good on others.

Farewell to *Zoon Politikon*: Value beyond the State

Michael Sandel, one of the most prominent left-wing critics of liberalism, asserts that liberalism's creation of the "procedural republic" violates our essential nature. Citing Aristotle, he says: "It is only as participants in political association that we can realize our nature and fulfill our highest ends."[3] At the center of this ancient claim lies a significant ambiguity. No doubt it is true that we cannot realize our highest ends without government and without participating in its control. But our highest ends do not have to be the ends of government or the ends proclaimed by government or the act of participating. In asserting that a human being is *zoon politikon*, Aristotle evidently believed or is most often taken to believe that that is all that humankind is: Man is above all and *only* a political animal. Liberalism asserts something quite different: Human beings are, among other things, political beings, who gain strength in political association, but that is not all that they are, nor need a particular person share in some common end to achieve his ultimate good.

Sandel's civic republicanism rests on the ambiguity of the "concern" it has for human undertakings:

> Unlike the ancient conception, liberal political theory does not see political life as concerned with the highest human ends or with the moral excellence of its citizens. Rather than promote a particular conception of the good life, liberal political theory insists on toleration, fair procedures, and respect for individual rights—values that respect people's freedom to choose their own values. But this raises a difficult question. If liberal ideals cannot be defended in the name of the highest human good, then in what does their moral basis consist?[4]

But liberalism *does* see political life as *concerned with* the highest human ends. It strives to make them possible. It simply disagrees that the *state* must come to declare a particular conception of the good life. Nor does liberalism eschew moral excellence.

A citizenry without civic virtue would cause the political arena to collapse. Liberalism does not deny the need for morality. What it does deny, rather, is that morality necessary for political life must be congruent with particular religious or other cultural traditions. Liberal ideals may quite specifically "be defended in the name of the highest human good": Without them, large numbers of people cannot hope to aspire to it. "Toleration and freedom and fairness" are indeed values, and the liberal defense of them is not a relativist defense, as Sandel grudgingly recognizes.[5]

Sandel says that central to liberalism is a self capable of choice and that this liberalism must therefore be opposed "to any view that regards us as obligated to fulfill ends we have not chosen—ends given by nature or God, for example, or by our identities as members of families, peoples, cultures, or traditions."[6] Again, this claim is ambiguous. Liberals can agree that any number of people, despite an inclination to do otherwise, will feel morally obligated, for example, to support their parents, to take on a job to help their families, or to accompany their families in sabbath devotions. The liberal would say that they chose to do so. Sandel appears to duck the question whether the civic republican state could justify imposing the moral obligation as a legal one. I may feel duty-bound to attend my family's church, but no civic republican, I take it, would mandate that I do so.

Sandel points to the decision that Robert E. Lee made at the outbreak of the Civil War. Until then, he had served as an officer in the Union army opposed to secession. Yet when the war came, "Lee concluded that his obligation to Virginia outweighed his obligation to the Union: 'With all my devotion to the Union, I have not been able to make up my mind to raise my hand against my relatives, my children, my home.'" Sandel appreciates "the poignance of Lee's predicament [his "*moral* dilemma"] without necessarily approving of the choice he made." Even for Sandel, then, Lee *chose*. (Is it an irony that Sandel speaks warmly of Lee's moral struggle, even while disapproving the choice? Is that a liberal impulse trying to spring free?) A few pages later, Sandel decries what he sees as liberalism's need "to separate the case for toleration from any judgment about the moral worth of the practices being tolerated." Has he not done just that in his apparent sympathy with Lee's dilemma?[7]

In all of this, the central fallacy is the assumption that the common good must be a good that is common. Some part of the common good is a good in common—most important, the liberal state itself, with institutional norms and practices that seek to reduce and redress the harm and risk of harm that confront us. Within that arena, the liberal should surely accept the proposition that security lies in the public's robust participation. But beyond that arena lies a zone of neutrality into which the state ought not intrude. To object that neutrality in this zone is not itself neutral misses the point. Opponents of neutrality have no better place to stand. If neutrality fails, if we cannot abstain from an official position on the good beyond a harm-free condition, then the only alternative is to choose someone's conception of the good. All other conceptions must fall also.

The Great Separation[8] sidesteps the problem: It is not the job of politics and the state to resolve all problems, settle all disagreements, or provide an overarching order to all things ("Evolution accounts for . . ." "The road to salvation is . . ." "The best baseball team is . . ." "You really ought to study to become a . . ." "It's not your place to . . ."). We do not need political machinery to force us to act or to construct answers to the mysteries of the universe and the perplexities of our culture. We seek answers from much better qualified people or from institutional processes: scientists, historians, priests, baseball playoffs, parents, friends, you, and me.

This restriction on the state's scope is often misunderstood (almost willfully at times, it seems), and not only by communitarians who are just outside the liberal camp. Thus, the conservative essayist G. K. Chesterton declaimed: "The modern man says, 'Let us leave all these arbitrary standards and embrace liberty.' This is, logically rendered, 'Let us not decide what is good, but let it be considered good not to decide it.'"[9] Antiliberals take Chesterton a step farther, accusing liberalism of being infected by an insidious relativism: a collective shrugging of the shoulders that asserts since we ought not decide between versions of the good, any possible end is as good as any other—pushpin is as good as poetry, in Bentham's adage. If liberals really do say that, then they deserve the scorn they often get—and the way of life the state might then properly decree. For who in his right mind would declare that "my objective is to have no objective, my end is to have no end, my good is to remain neutral toward all goods"? Whose philosophy of life compels him to pray each day: "Oh Lord, save me from ever having to think about the good"? The liberal does not believe it is good not to decide what is good: That is a terrible choice, if it is even a choice at all. So that cannot be, and indeed is not, what liberalism asserts. The liberal believes, instead, that no ultimate good can be decided by vote.[10]

Politics as a means to the good life answers the complaint that liberal neutrality merely disguises its intentions and actually aims at forcing people to constantly uproot their lives by reexamining their choices. The liberal state frees people to live with doubt but does not direct them to abandon faith. Those who wish to avoid the quest may stay at home in whatever cultural tradition is available. If we deny that the proper objective for the state is to help the individual achieve his or her own objectives, then everyone must worry about living in a society the politics of which is likely to require people to live badly. Whoever is in charge is overwhelmingly likely to be wrong in the policies implemented to help the citizenry strive for the good. That isn't a mathematical proposition, simply a commonsense one: There already are too many versions of the good to usefully count. The opposite of liberalism is not your good but someone else's, for if the state's writ ran to all things, you would not likely be ensconced in your own tradition. Liberalism is a political understanding about how people in the same society can secure different ends—put more pointedly, about how you can prevent me from dictating yours.

To protest that political liberalism does not attend to ultimate goods, leaving it, rather, in the hands of each of us, is a little like complaining that my cardiologist is interested only in the state of my arteries and not of my manuscript. I seek her advice about my health, but I do not need her opinion on the merits of my work. That the First Amendment denies the state power to ban the expression of an idea does not mean that you or I need to voice it. The failure to grasp this commonplace distinction between state and society plays out in a host of misunderstandings about political life. A clear, and surprising, example was the complaint of Gilbert Highet, the mid-twentieth-century Columbia University classicist and judge of the Book of the Month Club, who took book publishers to task for opposing book censorship even as they practiced it themselves:

> [I]n practice, most of the opponents of censorship do not believe in the indiscriminate utterance and publication of all knowledge without exception. (It is odd to hear a publisher bitterly complaining of restrictions imposed on him by a law or an organization, and then saying quite sincerely "There were half a dozen books offered to me last year which I simply refused to touch.")[11]

That a particular publisher might find a book or idea distasteful and thus refuse it is scarcely an argument that the state should censor it for all of us.

In other words, the state remains quiet so that you may speak up. This conception of neutrality shrinks the state (to use a spatial metaphor that is frequent though not entirely apt). It sees the state as one form of social organization among many, with particular, and often quite significant powers, but not to be employed in pursuing everything that people may suppose valuable.[12] The liberal political realm provides the order necessary for each of us, separately or with others, to try to live the life we seek, without involving itself in the merits of our choices. A state is for making and enforcing rules about certain sorts of things, so that a church, a card game, a hospital, a language, a business enterprise, or a service organization can serve other purposes and seek to accomplish them by other means. For the state to be an instrumental good it must be a good instrument. It strives to ensure, or ought to, in all the ways open to it, that you do not end up a victim of my ends.

The Passive Nobility of Liberalism

Some voices, past and present, object that even if all of the foregoing is true, liberalism as so described is pallid and thin, insufficient to excite people to their fullest capacities or to exert themselves to create what is noble and heroic. Friedrich Nietzsche condemned liberalism for enshrining "as the fundamental principle of society" the need "to refrain mutually from injury," for it must lead "to dissolution and decay" by shackling the strong man and reining in his will to power.[13] In a similar vein, Allan Bloom charged that in seeking to avoid the bad rather than approach the good, rejecting Aristotle's call to "mak[e] men good and doers of noble deeds," liberalism leads to paleness, to "the diminishing of men's attachment to their vision of happiness in favor of mere life and the pursuit of the means of maintaining life." The desired community is "one without tension, without guilt (except for those who do not go along), without longing, without great sacrifices or great risks, one made for men's idle wishes."[14]

These charges are wildly overblown, if not altogether false. It takes no extended discussion to remember that whatever Nietzsche might have meant by the will to power, the attempt of those who sought to put their will above all nearly wrecked the world. Bloom's impatient account of at least one sort of liberal theory lacks in veracity what it contains in literary flair. He failed to mention that in making men "good and doers of noble deeds" the state often makes men good and dead and their families slaves. Neither does it stand up to investigation to suppose that a state wedded to the harm principle will somehow abolish longing, tension, risk-taking, and the willingness to sacrifice. Nietzsche and Bloom, like so many others for whom philosophy is the only reality, have mistaken exuberance for politics and ambition for the state, ignoring the evidence that we have multiple commitments that can motivate us to act nobly and seek goodness outside the political realm.

Communitarians offer a separate critique of liberalism's claims. They indict liberalism for its preoccupation with justice, that is, with principles and rules that spell out the legal connections and relations of persons in the community. Presupposing a higher form of human association, communitarians argue that "justice is a remedial virtue, a response to some defect in community, some incompleteness in the development of community, which can and should be overcome. Justice, far from being the first virtue of social institutions, is something that the truly good community has no need for."[15] But the contention that "[if] people responded spontaneously to the needs of others out of love or shared goals, then there would be no need to claim one's rights"[16] is doubly mistaken. Much rides, as always, on an "if." *If* a few rulers had slaves genetically bred to serve them happily, those lucky few would congratulate themselves on the virtue of a society that could rise above justice. *If* we each responded with all others' needs in mind we could no doubt all relax. Or, as Madison put it more succinctly, "if men were angels, no government would be necessary."[17]

But we are not angels and cannot be. Government is necessary. A world of angels, not merely moral but omniscient, a world without friction, is not our world. Nor have we a way to make it so. Even those who purport to share a single vision of the good are often at each other's throats (consider all the nonliberal states that have collapsed, to the utter sorrow and ruin or near ruin of the societies they had been ruling). Many have supposed otherwise. Herbert Spencer expressed a seemingly commonsense notion that government is necessary as an external restraint only as long as internal restraints are missing:

> But the diminution of external restraint can take place only at the same rate as the increase of internal restraint. Conduct has to be ruled either from without or from within. If the rule from within is not efficient, there *must* exist a supplementary rule from without. If, on the other hand, all men are properly ruled from within, government becomes needless, and all men are perfectly free. Now the chief faculty of self-rule being the moral sense..., the degree of freedom in their institutions which any given people can bear will be proportionate to the diffusion of this moral sense among them. And only when its influence greatly predominates can so large an installment of freedom as a democracy become possible.[18]

But even in Spencer's time it was simplistic and mistaken to believe that the moral sense is sufficient internal constraint and that if only the state were permitted to create a virtuous citizenry the need for government would diminish accordingly. It is pure fantasy to suppose that attending solicitously to each other, from the best of motives, would permit us to rise above all conflict and harm, avoiding the need for rights and law. Aggregative and accumulative harms cannot be controlled by an application of the moral sense, as we know from many homely examples; for instance, our failure to voluntarily conserve energy through sincere appeals to adjust our thermostats. Andre Malraux is said to have once "asked a Communist who was describing the perfect life of the future, 'What about the man who is run over by a tram?' The answer was, 'In the perfect tramway system of the future there will be no accidents.'"[19] But perfect systems cannot exist, and accidents will always bedevil us. So even if we all were angels, the problem of defining injury persists. Government, the agency for doing so, is necessary not merely now but permanently. Despite fond hopes and bold predictions, the state will not wither away, not because our very participation in it is our highest end but because without it we cannot adequately contain the relentless collisions that diminish our chances of realizing our good, however defined.

Those melancholy facts belie the romantic lament that liberal statesmanship and arid reasoning have brought us to a pallid politics lacking in ambition, nobility, or pursuit of the good. True, a liberal state frowns on freelance knights, swords at the ready, with ambitions to conquer the ground and establish a new regime. True, liberalism looks askance at clerical claims that God has ordained the state to the rule of divines, even, or especially, one who has just received instructions from God earlier in the morning. Liberal states tend to oppose swashbucklers who would corner the market in basic commodities or any other good. And liberalism does not suppose that the people are entitled to whatever a majority of them happens to want.

But all that still leaves plenty to do. The harm principle begets a liberalism that is indeterminate in its practical policies. The liberalism of the harm principle is not contained in a handbook of harm prevention. There is no prescriptive manual to which we can all turn for determinate answers. There is no principle that because we wish to purify the environment we must reduce chemical pollution to one part per trillion or that because we wish to alleviate human suffering we must do whatever it takes to cut in half (or pick your own fraction) the number of people living in poverty. But these real problems are among the appropriate ones to solve. The proper debate between liberals and conservatives ought not be over the legitimacy of government but over the degree of harm we should tolerate and the means we should choose to reduce it and repair its effects.

That the harm principle lacks clear prescriptions seems to bother some critics,[20] but as we have seen, indeterminateness is an essential characteristic. Because it cannot minimize harm or maximize freedom in any quantitative (or even, likely, qualitative) way, voters and policy-makers must necessarily confront a dizzying array of choices. Few if any of these choices come in binary pairs such that one is right and the other wrong. Local rules vary from place to place, within the same liberal society and between liberal societies, not because one populace has a better notion than the others but simply because, as Brian Barry has put it, "this is the way we do things here."[21] It is no reproach to liberalism that people enact ordinances that differ from place to place, since people value things, and assess the hierarchy of harms and their costs of prevention, in different ways.

Liberalism is indeterminate also in a closely related sense: It does not and cannot promise to prevent deep-seated, fundamental change. Liberalism permits (and, many would presumably argue, welcomes and encourages) social and economic changes: new technologies, new casts of mind, new tempers and moods, new cultural meanings. It must therefore set new balances as the facts on the ground are changed by the onrush of events. Human history does not stand still in liberal communities: The human pageant is not fixed but malleable and variegated. To those who wish for timeless verities, it is this lack of promise that perhaps most fuels a widespread discomfort with liberal values. Liberalism liberates, and the freedom to act can be unsettling and even jarring. But it scarcely makes sense to decry the liberal state and the society it supports as a pallid place bereft of ambition or a sense of nobility.

Is liberalism possible? The question is far more pretentious than the answer. We know that it is possible because many societies today are living some variant of it. The harm principle, we must finally conclude, generates a set of political principles that not surprisingly resemble those on which many democracies are more or less based. It is not surprising because, to repeat what a biographer of John Stuart Mill has said, the harm principle "is so forcibly and memorably argued that it has passed into the public philosophy of all the great Western democracies."[22] But it has passed into constitutions and political practices mostly as abstractions, as I have just noted, and there is much in all the great liberal democracies that remains illiberal.

Millian Moments: Is the Harm Principle at Work in the Real World?

It is a fair question in a work of theory whether the principles discussed are a force in the world beyond the book. I offer here a brief intimation that the harm principle is a touchstone for resolving major policy problems, despite the apparent shellacking suffered by politicians perceived as liberals at the grassroots during the past three decades and more. For one thing, the major liberal innovations of the past century remain largely operational: workers' compensation, Social Security, Medicare, equal voting rights, antidiscrimination legislation, governance of the market, product safety laws, and environmental protection, among many others.

Perhaps more significant are the justifications for attempting to repeal liberal policies. For example, although a major ground of the opposition to abortion rights is its immorality, there are signs that opponents are seeking to demonstrate that it is also harmful. One claim is that the fetus feels pain; this was not an argument associated with early opposition to *Roe v. Wade*. Hostility to pornography was once rooted in its immorality, but beginning in the 1980s there were various attempts to demonstrate judicially, so far unsuccessfully, that pornography harms women and is discriminatory to boot. A very recent attempt to ban violent video games failed in the Supreme Court, in part because the Court could find no evidence, given how the law was written, that the legislature was aiming at actual harm; the glaring loopholes in the law suggested that the legislators were merely expressing their moral disapproval of the games. In 1965 the Court in *Griswold v. Connecticut* struck down an anticontraceptive law on the grounds (though the Court did not quite put it this way) that the ban on condom sales was responsive to nothing that could be called harmful. Nearly four decades later, and following much the same logic, the Court in *Lawrence v. Texas* struck down a ban on private homosexual conduct, disavowing the claim that the law may ban what does not actually harm someone. Relatedly, a significant aspect of the current debate over same-sex marriage is whether it is harmful to children.[23]

Less persuasive, perhaps, but nevertheless highly suggestive, is the reaction in the United States of some Republican politicians to problems that Democratic politicians seek to subject to regulation. Conservatives who once might have opposed various proposals on the ground that the government has no legitimate claim to exercise such power now insist, instead, that the object of the power (that is, the problem being confronted) isn't real—hence, for example, the almost frenzied denial of global warming.[24] The old oppositional impulse has faded. Objection to the power of government to thwart, prevent, deter, address, or redress harm increasingly appears to be a losing game. To avoid the power of government, then, requires avoiding the problem that it is asserted government must confront. I do not mean to imply that Republicans are the only sinners in trying to avoid the harm principle.

Many Democrats, who may be eager to accept the harm rationale in proposing legislation, are much more loathe to concede the countervailing harm that reform might bring; some also mistakenly suppose that the government *must* tackle anything that someone labels a harm.

There is some evidence, too, that liberal justification of laws repealing crimes against morality need not, as had been predicted, lead at best to a "fragile toleration" of practices that the dominant majority had widely reviled. Sandel asserted in 1996 that the liberal case for legalizing homosexuality, that each person should be free to choose his form of sexual intimacy,

> leaves wholly unchallenged the adverse views of homosexuality itself. But unless those views can be plausibly addressed, even a court ruling in their favor is unlikely to win for homosexuals more than a thin and fragile toleration. A fuller respect would require, if not admiration, at least some appreciation of the lives homosexuals live. But such appreciation is unlikely to be cultivated by a legal and political discourse conducted in terms of autonomy rights alone.[25]

In the fifteen years since he wrote those lines, much has happened. The Supreme Court's 2003 ruling in *Lawrence*, overturning laws prohibiting homosexual conduct on precisely the liberal lines that Sandel deplored, has led to dramatic social changes. Same-sex marriage, barely on the horizon in 1996, now exists in six states, with various other forms of union protected in many other states—seemingly more than "a thin and fragile toleration." The military's "Don't Ask, Don't Tell" uneasy compromise on homosexuals enlisting and serving in uniform has been repealed. "Don't Ask, Don't Tell" was not a liberal policy but, if anything, a communitarian one, a placatory gesture to the military community's disquiet. It, not the liberal repeal, was "a thin and fragile toleration" for people who were, after all, seeking a communitarian good, to serve their country.

These examples may all be the merest wisps in the wind, but they do suggest that the wind is blowing.

Facing Up to Harm

We suffer today from a vastly incomplete and often incoherent account of harm in all its manifestations. One of the most significant political fault-lines in American society, and perhaps in many other societies as well, is that which divides those who think in political party terms over the meaning and seriousness of the risks we face and the harms that might ensue. Conservative Republicans (there are of course many shadings of belief within all the parties) suffer from a disposition to understate, overlook, and temporize about the reality of harmful and risky conduct. They are, for example, less likely to believe that harm will result from unfettered markets or to detect harms when they occur; that is why conservatives champion the cause of doctors and corporations who bewail the cost of malpractice and product liability insurance, and why they are more likely to believe that the plaintiff is prevaricating than suffering harm. It is why antiliberals mock and distort the facts of what occurs by assigning cute (and often loaded) names to cases rather than talking about their details.[26] Liberal Democrats, contrarily, tend in the other direction, frequently overstating the extent of potential harms and underestimating the sometimes deleterious effects of prevention and redress on the very people they aim to help.[27]

To avoid the hand of government, conservatives often deny that harm occurs; to seek to eradicate harm, liberals forget that a heavy hand can cause as much. That government may legitimately address the problem of harm does not mean that its practitioners do so intelligently or efficiently. Large-scale administrative agencies told to serve "the public interest" can become sluggish, hidebound, loathe to innovate, motivated to serve their own convenience, and captive to groups that prey on them with sizable capital resources. Shibboleths about harmful levels of taxation can force otherwise intelligent policymakers to take leave of their senses. But the list of contradictions and incoherent policies bred by "practical" politics is far too long for a final chapter (or any chapter) in a book such as this. This is not a history of harm or of the attitudes that lie along a political continuum of thinking about harm. That history, and an accompanying analysis of the modern capacity to inflict harm and to find efficient ways to reduce it, must be undertaken elsewhere.

We need to seek consensus on harm. It will not be an easy task, because it will require all of us to move beyond the platitudes that give us comfort. We must question whether the trend toward "total redress" that began in the second half of the twentieth century is sustainable, at least through the conventional institutional and legal devices on which we tend to rely.[28] It is also possible that we have moved to an era of such technological power and interdependence that even if we wished to redress them some harms can no longer be corrected by ordinary means. How does one remedy the bombing of the World Trade Center? Or the befouling of an ecosystem when a tanker run aground (or an underwater oil well blowout) releases millions of gallons of oil? Or the defrauding of a banking system in which hundreds of billions of dollars evaporate? Or the vanishing of pensions for thousands of people in the collapse of a giant energy company? Or the sudden deflating of a real estate bubble that crashes the worldwide economy?

In thinking through the conditions that surround and threaten us, we need to question whether we are individually equipped to pick out what is harmful and to reason sensibly about workable policies for dealing with it. A growing psychological literature suggests that commonsense notions of harm are often wrong for a variety of important psychological reasons: The cues that we use to make sense of the world are often faulty and do not point in the direction that we take them to. Moreover, our beliefs even about what counts as evidence and what counts as harm depend crucially on cultural outlook, and the claim of neutral reasons for adopting a certain policy against a specific type of harm may fail to convince those of different cultural persuasions.[29] But these problems are not specific to a particular outlook or group of people, and they will not disappear if an antiliberal attitude were somehow to be enshrined in a democratic state.

What are the prospects for a society that cherishes a liberalism built on the harm principle, a society that daily confronts the opposing pull of jungle and zoo? None of us can foretell the future. We face perils at every turn, and it continues to be the human responsibility to dedicate our political resources to reducing them, even if they cannot be wholly eradicated. But it seems a reasonable conclusion that a community dedicated to human betterment can flourish only when all are permitted to participate in its construction, that harms will diminish and opportunities will grow only when a core of individuality is respected in every person, and that a liberal order is the only likely means of approaching, if not achieving, all our disparate ends.

Appendix

FOUR LIBERAL PREMISES AND THEIR PROBLEMS

At one time or another, and sometimes simultaneously, four principles in particular have been advanced as central to the quest to derive powers and limits of the state: (1) *Consent*: The state is legitimate to the extent that people have consented to its reach and methods. (2) *Dialogue*: Legitimate political power can be understood as the outcome of a conversation among the people. (3) *Equality:* Liberal commitments are justified to the extent that they hold the state to respect the equality of all. (4) *Neutrality:* A liberal state is one that maintains official neutrality toward the good.

In this appendix, I suggest that each of these four principles is more complex and controversial than needed and in any event reduces to, converges on, or collapses into the others. Moreover, though each captures an important aspect of the liberal approach to politics, the work of each principle can be accomplished much less controversially and more conventionally by the harm principle. In what follows I do not presume to present an account close to the full theories as they have been explored by political theorists, for there is no single version of any of them, and the writings about each are voluminous. None of what follows will satisfy the specialists, and no doubt the brevity of my descriptions forces me to omit what specialists would take as essential elements or qualifications. My aim is simply to suggest the difficulties in each and to offer reasons for believing that there is a simpler alternative.

The Consent Premise

It is a commonplace that consent justifies political power. Governments, the Declaration of Independence declared, "deriv[e] their just powers from the consent of the governed." We accept the premise, stated this broadly (and its implication that if we consent we are obliged to obey the law), for if all consent who is left to complain? But on closer inspection it is a cheap trick, since consent just isn't given. States historically have emerged in stages and without the people's agreement.[1] To make sense, consent-based theories must solve three problems:

1. The people to be consulted must have a set of ground rules, a parliamentary procedure, for deliberating among themselves, since the content of the social contract will depend on discussion, and possibly negotiation, rather than on experiment.
2. Deliberations must produce fundamental rules, principles, and institutions (the commitments) to which the people will be asked to consent.
3. The parties must be shown to have unanimously endorsed the commitments.

The seventeenth- and eighteenth-century social contract theorists were aware of these problems, and they sought but did not find ways of solving them. They did not have a theory of dialogue, a plan for deliberation. They could not show that a particular set of substantive commitments would emerge (that is why Hobbes's citizens could produce an absolute sovereignty and Locke's a parliamentary system). Moreover, they could guarantee neither the unanimity of the founding generation nor, beyond them, consent by those who followed. Notoriously, to solve this last problem, Locke proposed that people give "tacit" consent, but it was a half-hearted and implausible claim: A person is presumed to have consented to the state in which he finds himself just by "barely traveling freely on the highway" or by continuing to live there (even if "lodging only for a week").[2] The problem, as Don Herzog has noted, is that if a conception of tacit consent is plausible, it is likely to be too thin, as Locke's surely is, to "generate an obligation" to be bound by what the state decrees.[3]

Seeking to avoid these difficulties, John Rawls, modernizing the social contract device, proposed not real but only "rational" consent. To avoid the first and third problems he brought to the conference table, in what he called the "original position," not flesh-and-blood people but disembodied wraiths, each shrouded in a "veil of ignorance." They are shorn of all knowledge about their place in society, class position, social status, and "fortune in the distribution of natural assets and abilities," like intelligence and strength, nor do they "know their conceptions of the good or their special psychological propensities."[4] Let's call them "ignorant savants." But the savants are no longer people deliberating or consenting, for they are all the same, and they collapse into a single person.[5] Hence there is no need for discussion, and "unanimity" is guaranteed. Rawls still needs to solve the second problem—he must deliver the actual principles. But instead of looking to the actual deliberations of real people, Rawls can substitute himself. He needs a rational argument but not a theory of discourse, since no one can interrupt him in his own book. But his solution is spun out only after a lengthy and complex argument with many moving parts. One reason for doubting Rawls's derivation of the principles of justice is that, as even he admits, they can be altered by "filtering" the veil of ignorance in different ways—for example, increasing or decreasing the savants' risk-averseness by letting in more or less knowledge of themselves or the world.[6] Whatever he has produced, it is unclear why the result should be considered a social contract or why we should agree with the substantive principles that Rawls teases out. Indeed, many serious critics do not.[7]

In either case, then, whether of actual people or ignorant savants, consent does not stand on its own as bedrock. More is needed—in the first instance, at least a set of ground rules for carrying on a conversation that might lead to consent and, in the second, a vast apparatus of argumentative moves. Each approach, moreover, seems to assume that people in the foundational bargaining are to be treated equally. Rawls says that in seeking "the most appropriate conception of justice" citizens must be "regarded as free and equal."[8] Presumably a similar criterion would be applied to a social contract parley among real people, or else it would first be necessary to spell out a reason for treating them unequally. So a Consent Premise to the problem of political power appears to require that other potential premises be worked out first.[9]

The Consent Premise has an additional difficulty (as already noted). Since its metaphor is a people consenting to establish a state, it would serve as foundational only in the first generation. How could it bind later generations, who have no opportunity to consent? Various answers have been given, and the point need not detain us. For Rawls, the next generations do not pose a problem since only rational consent is required, and each next person would, when placed behind the veil, become an ignorant savant and agree to what had been decided. For other social contractarians, Locke's conception of tacit consent would serve as well, or as poorly, since it was designed to legitimize the state for succeeding generations. The problem remains as significant, or insignificant, as the problem that attends consent in the first generation. If that problem could be solved, presumably this too could be. (In thinking through why the Constitution would bind later generations, James Madison held that people who have the power to amend the Constitution but refrain from doing so have sufficiently demonstrated consent to the regime.[10])

A separate "consent of the governed" theory holds that legitimate government depends on citizens consenting to each enactment of government. In its pure form, plebiscitary democracy, it is no more possible than traditional social contract theory. The substitute, majoritarian representative democracy, is of course the attempt to build consent into the operations of government. In that sense, it is part of the liberal commitments. But it cannot itself be foundational because it is completely impracticable. For one thing, as Herzog notes, it is next to impossible to know whether people actually are consenting or to what they might be consenting when they vote for or against a candidate: Perhaps a vote for one person is actually a vote against his opponent and not consent to a candidate's platform. Perhaps a voter stays home on election day because he is happy with conditions, and so a nonvote is nonetheless consent.[11] Moreover, it is impossible to express consent to every bill that will pass through (or be blocked in) the legislative chambers. There are too many issues to register consent by voting for (or against) a representative. The possibility of consenting is even more attenuated for actions of courts and administrative agencies. At best, consent or rejection can effect only changes in direction.[12]

So it appears that we cannot collect the consent of actual people to a form and practice of government, that from consent alone we cannot derive legitimate principles, or that the principles claimed to be legitimate do not result from the deliberation of real people. Universal consent either is absent or it is hypothesized. In either case it does not exist.

Instead of gussying up the Consent Premise in a vain attempt to make it workable, I suggest that if people everywhere were asked to declare the most important function of the government to which they would consent, they would put it that the government should attempt to stop people from harming each other. The Consent Premise holds that a rule, institution, or practice is legitimate if all consent. One way to read that proposition is that the rule, institution, or practice is taken to be morally correct only because no one complains. But another way to read it is that consent bestows substantive legitimacy—that consent makes right. If so, then the failure of the Consent Premise means, on its own terms, that state action is illegitimate because people have not consented to it. Insofar as state activities are coercive they may be taken as harmful. If it is wrong for the state, through its agents, to coerce, then it seems to follow that it would be equally wrong for any person to coerce, and thereby harm, another. We must also then conclude that each person may legitimately attempt to resist the harmdoer. To demand absolute autonomy—it is wrong for anyone to interfere with anything I choose to do, regardless of why or what I choose—subjects its proponent to a version of Cartesian skepticism: If I doubt the validity of any moral judgment I cannot simultaneously assert moral judgments of my own. To say that no one may properly interfere with or coerce me, regardless of the cause, is already to talk about rights.[13] To argue that there are moral limits to what a person may do to me entails at least the morality of some sort of defense against interference. Now if I may defend myself against unwarranted interference, then it may be merely a series of details to assign to someone else, including a set of political institutions, the right and power to prevent the same unwarranted interference.[14] Otherwise we must paradoxically conclude that it is wrong to attempt to prevent people from wronging, that is, harming, each other.[15]

So it is probable that what would receive universal assent is the proposition that the state may act in appropriate ways to deal with those who cause harm. This chain of reasoning is essentially Locke's construction of the social contract[16] (which gets a closer look in chapter 2). It may be that it is also Rawls's. The first principle of justice to which his argument leads is this: "Each person is to have an equal right to the most extensive total system of equal basic liberties compatible with a similar system of liberty for all."[17] It is conceivable—I do not parse the intricacies of his first principle—that it boils down to this: "Do no harm."

The Dialogue Premise

Dialogue is indispensable to every human. We are all conversationalists, and those who cannot communicate with others are condemned to living a less full life. Some (cloistered monks) may seek silence, but even that mode of life is supported by the communicative efforts of others. Dialogue in general is not peculiar, therefore, to any particular political theory, but its use and forms do depend on political purposes and will vary across different theoretical approaches.

The foundational claim is that through a type of conversation, political commitments can be legitimated. The Dialogue Premise recognizes the need for actual people to talk things through. It holds that not merely acceptance but legitimacy itself depends on discussion: "The legitimacy of laws rests on the persuasiveness of the reasons that can be garnered for those laws. Domination is transformed into self-rule when citizens are convinced in a free and equal conversation that the limits placed upon them are not chains but self-imposed limits for good reasons."[18] But it is not always clear whether the dialogue proposed is intended for a constitutional convention or for everyday politics. Noting that even were we to agree with them, abstract philosophical principles such as those of Rawls and others must always be fleshed out in real life, Amy Gutmann and Dennis Thompson propose a "deliberative democracy," a form of reasoning, called reciprocity, about moral disagreements "to reach mutually acceptable decisions." Dialogue of this sort, they say, is for "middle democracy," the realm of actual politics in "any setting in which citizens come together on a regular basis to reach collective decisions about public issues."[19] As indispensable as deliberation is for democratic politics, the nuanced process they recommend is not foundational. It may help citizens beyond the impasse of moral disagreement, but it does not establish in the first instance the legitimacy of political commitments. It is, rather, one of them.

How can dialogue be structured to yield legitimacy of our basic institutions? There are two contrasting models: constrained and unconstrained. The former limits the deliberating citizens in topics and modes of reasoning. Rawls, for example, would restrict savants "to presently accepted general beliefs and forms of reasoning found in common sense, and the methods and conclusions of science when these are not controversial"[20] (though his approach is not really talk at all, as we have seen). Charles E. Larmore proposes "a universal norm of rational dialogue": When the parties disagree about a basic belief, "each should prescind from the beliefs that the other rejects," and retreat to neutral ground.[21] Bruce A. Ackerman would also constrain the dialogue of his citizens by imposing a rule of neutrality that precludes relying on notions of the good or the superiority of persons. But these and related models block a range of potential answers to fundamental questions, though they do not necessarily generate the same conclusions. Rawls's approach yields a set of basic principles; Ackerman's neutrality premise permits his fanciful discussants to talk endlessly. But whatever the model, constrained dialogue is not full dialogue, and it restricts the conclusions as well. "Excluding from debate what is today deeply contested assumes a fixity and permanence to the constellation of disputes and differences of opinion which just happen to prevail today. To limit the discursive agenda to 'plain truths now widely accepted' is to preempt deep social and political criticism" of them.[22] In the end, constrained dialogue is rigged: The discourse required to produce an agreeable set of commitments suppresses conversation that some of the speakers might wish to have.[23]

The unconstrained model, associated with the writings of Jürgen Habermas, is found in the "ideal speech situation." It proposes a wide-open public conversation, unlimited in content or duration. Participants in the ideal speech situation "must have an equal chance to initiate and to continue communication," with no limitations imposed on assertions, explanations, desires, feelings, or recommendations.[24] From this unconstrained public debate the participants will construct the fundamental rules of justice. This basic notion has spawned many models, ranging from foundational to middle democracy. I do not seek to catalog or summarize them but simply to note difficulties in the use of discourse theory as foundational.[25]

Circularity problems are apparent. Begin with the ground rules. Michael Walzer says that ideal speech "presuppose[s] some institutional arrangements, but what institutional arrangements are morally preferable is one of the things that the conversation is supposed to decide."[26] Discourse theories assume that all are to be treated equally and with respect in joining the public discussion. So behind the foundational premise of discourse lies a different premise, equality. But real-world inequalities would block any real society from even remotely approaching the norm of discourse open to all. This problem leads Nancy Fraser to conclude that "[a] necessary condition for participatory parity is that systemic social inequalities be eliminated."[27] So to eliminate systemic inequalities requires a prior knowledge of how to redistribute justly, and justice, in the discourse theorist's view, can come only by first having the conversation. As Simone Chambers puts it: "[W]e must find a way of talking with each other as equals about the elimination of systemic inequality before we can eliminate it."[28]

Still other problems lurk in the call for unconstrained and universal participation. Some citizens may resist broadcasting their deepest personal feelings and reasons through a public microphone. Many would be wary of "render[ing] themselves transparent to others," as J. Donald Moon points out: Dreading disapproval, feeling pressed to conform, fearing loss of autonomy and intimacy if stripped of privacy, they might "withhold or even dissimulate their beliefs and feelings."[29] Other citizens would be unable to speak effectively: "assemblies have a habit of rewarding smooth talkers, and the common desire for recognition in public life routinely induces a preference for victory through clever speech that overwhelms the cooperative search for mutual accommodation and the principled search for truth."[30]

Though Habermas claims the ideal speech situation is structured to be real, the speakers will not deliver or hear real conversation, because they must avoid the mistakes that come from gathering knowledge in our haphazard, trial-and-error fashion. Somehow, in ways never spelled out, the speakers must be given an accurate account of the world as it is, unhampered by prejudice, bias, mistake, ignorance, and difference of opinion, and the account must be the same for all. Why should we suppose that to be possible? Any authoritative view of the nature of human institutions (the market, the political order, and the relationship between them) would, Walzer notes, depend on "a single set of historical and sociological 'facts.' But whoever made [the speakers] such a present would thereby determine the resolution of the debate, and that resolution would determine, in turn, the shape of whatever agreement they reached about, say, distributive justice."[31] The speakers speak, but they do not negotiate or compromise, and they speak with the unrealistic expectation of ending in consensus (all who would be affected by the norms to be developed would accept them). In the real world, conversations of this magnitude end usually in confusion or disagreement, from lack of time, exhaustion, ennui, or boredom, or with the desire to pick up the conversation later, in another direction, even if the original speakers thought the topic exhausted and completed. Moreover, in the real world, it is sometimes necessary to interrupt, sometimes to listen silently to a monologue (a lecture or speech), and sometimes to have access to a monologue that people may look at later (a book to which other books may reply in due course). None of these things can be guaranteed to yield a fixed understanding that all will accept. Indeed, in a world of different viewpoints, understandings, analyses of evidence, and methods, and unconstrained by all the limitations of ordinary life, it is unlikely that any conversation will yield anything but more debate. And according to the discourse theorists, if somehow the speakers got beyond all that and reached resolution, the outcome, no matter how noxious, would be the political commitments by which all would have to live. An ideal speech situation requires that the discussants respect liberty and equality going in, but they are not bound to honor either coming out.[32] To avoid knuckling under to the fiery oratory of utopians and dictators, the speech "situation" can only be ideal, not real. In short, the problem with a dialogue theory as an answer to political legitimacy is that it is wholly circular: The very mechanism intended to determine what rules to follow and through what institutional means they will be enforced requires that the rules and institutions already be designed.

The Equality Premise

Even though liberalism is usually thought to be a philosophy of liberty, most liberal theories begin, as forethought, with the idea that what matters first is equality—everybody to count for one, nobody for more than one, in Bentham's well-worn phrase. Rawls concurs: His elaborate setup is intended to "represent equality."[33] The leading modern proponent of the premise is Ronald Dworkin, who says that "[n]o government is legitimate that does not show equal concern for the fate of all those citizens over whom it claims dominion and from whom it claims allegiance."[34] Will Kymlicka takes the view that "every plausible political theory has the same ultimate value, which is equality [—meaning] ... treating people 'as equals.' ... [E]galitarian theories require that the government treat its citizens with equal consideration; each citizen is entitled to equal concern and respect."[35] But the apparent priority of equality is not as significant as it may appear, and for three reasons.

First, liberal philosophies begin with equality because ideas of *in*equality are far more numerous and far harder to justify. Suppose, for example, we sought to generate our political commitments using this Prime Rule: The decision maker shall be "he who is best." How would we determine who that person is until we have rules for doing so? But the rules for doing so must first be announced under our Prime Rule, by He Who Is Best. We encounter again an unresolvable circularity. If we let our intuition or our feelings tell us who is best, even feelings informed by consequentialist reasons (a sober, educated, fair-minded person is a better decision-maker than a beer-swilling unschooled lout), then we avoid the circularity. But no rational account will allow us to use our intuition because any such initial claim is arbitrary. That, discourse theorists say, is why the answer must be found by conversation designed to reach agreement, though, as noted above, for the same rational reason, the conversation assumes the equality of all speakers.

A second, and deeper, problem of equality as foundational is that the concept of equality seems to rest on a different premise. Because a person's ends, as values, are not provably "correct" or "incorrect" from facts in the world, it seems impossible to show why the state should prefer one end to another without endorsing a set of values that not all may share. Hence the claim that each person should be treated with equal respect. By this view, it is neutrality that is foundational, not equality.[36]

A third problem is that an equality premise does not determine an outcome. Those who would begin with a norm of, say, equal respect, can disagree bitterly over what it entails. The antiliberal with a specific view of the good avoids this problem. For him, equal respect means leading everyone to the same end, no matter the protest, since respect entails taking seriously the need to help each person achieve the good.[37] This approach is closed to the liberal, who needs a different principle to decide how or even whether to give effect to the political practice of equality. As Amartya K. Sen has noted:

> [A] characteristic of virtually all the approaches to the ethics of social arrangements that have stood the test of time is to want equality of *something*—something that has an important place in the particular theory. Not only do income-egalitarians ... demand equal incomes, and welfare egalitarians ask for equal welfare levels, but also classical utilitarians insist on equal weights on the utilities of all, and pure libertarians demand equality with respect to an entire class of rights and liberties. They are all "egalitarians" in some essential way.[38]

An initial premise of equality, in other words, does not determine what sort of equality should be realized in the real world.

Herbert Spencer in the 1850s wished to equalize maximum liberty: "Every man has freedom to do all that he wills, provided he infringes not the equal freedom of any other man."[39] So too argues the much more sophisticated modern libertarianism of Robert Nozick (discussed in chapter 2). Hobbes, to the contrary, despite his premise of initial equality, proceeded to minimize freedom equally. Rawls's famous "difference principle" holds that material inequalities in the real world are justifiable but only if arranged "to the greatest benefit of the least advantaged"—inequality for a purpose.[40] Walzer espouses what he terms "complex equality," the idea that various spheres of distribution (such as politics, wealth, employment) have norms that should be respected and that the state should serve to prevent a distribution in one sphere from dominating a distribution in another (for example, wealth influencing elections and officeholding).[41] In his account, there is no single overarching equality to maintain.

Modern theories rooted in equality can be quite complicated—for example, Dworkin's. Creating his own fictional world (an uninhabited desert island on which people washed up on shore conduct an ingenious series of auctions of the island's resources), Dworkin argues for a complex form of redistribution of resources measured not by absolute outcome but by the value of the resources to their possessors. Dworkin's equality requires a host of institutions: He specifies a "baseline liberty/constraint system" that dictates how a person may use the resources that he wins in the auction. To assure that people will be equally respected and have equal resources, society must "select the baseline system that gives most plausibility to the claim that an auction from that baseline treats people with equal concern." What sorts of things does this baseline system comprise? People must be provided "with enough physical security and enough control over their own property to allow them to make and carry out their plans and projects," and the system must guarantee at least these fundamental liberties: "rights to freedom of conscience, commitment, speech, and religion, and to freedom of choice in matters touching central or important aspects of an agent's personal life, like employment, family arrangements, sexual privacy, and medical treatment."[42] He does manage, therefore, to derive many of the liberal commitments from his initial premise of equality, but the path is difficult to follow, and the auction that appears to offer a means of realizing equality works only hypothetically[43] and with unrealistic assumptions (for example, that each person knows at the time of the auction not only how he wishes to live his life but also the facts about his choices that would vindicate his bid). In the end, his argument may even rest, crucially, on a more basic principle—liberty—that is not derived from equality. Dworkin says that once the baseline is established, "liberty and equality cannot conflict, as two fundamental political virtues, because equality cannot even be defined except by assuming liberty in place, and cannot be improved, even in the real world, by policies that compromise the value of liberty."[44]

Rawls asserts that since the life situations into which people are born (distribution of talents, physical handicaps) are morally arbitrary, others more advantaged should be barred from complaining about being asked to help out those in need.[45] Rawls denies that people "deserve" the attributes with which each was born and concludes that justice requires overcoming the undersupply of (a good) family and (useful) talents by taking from those with an oversupply.[46] Dworkin similarly insists that the state may redistribute the social product to redress inequalities resulting from natural endowment, though not, he says, those resulting from ambition.

But it is unclear why *because* people do not deserve their initial attributes, the less well endowed have a claim against those more well endowed. If I do not deserve my endowments, why do others? Why are other people (through the state) entitled to appropriate their value? Should a tax on talents be levied whether or not their possessor exercises them? If only talents put to work could be taxed, a pianist with large hands and singular brain wiring might forsake his musical ability and the chance of lucrative concert performances to seek earnings by pursuing an occupation for which he is not talented in the hopes of earning untaxed income, depriving society, if not the pianist, of his music. But if talents could be taxed merely by being possessed, assuming there were a way to measure the worth of fallow talent,[47] power to redress morally arbitrary inequalities would be unbounded. It would, as William A. Galston argues, permit a state to thwart or even eliminate desert altogether, by suppressing the fruits of an individual's "ability, effort, and self-denial" in striving to realize his conception of the good.[48]

Even if we ignore the problem of reassigning (the value of) morally arbitrary talent, a different and probably unresolvable practical problem remains: how to discern the part of our undeserved attributes to be redistributed and how to redistribute. Who can say which native characteristic disadvantages me and which spurs me to achieve? K. Anthony Appiah criticizes Dworkin on just these grounds: It is unclear whether a particular circumstance is an undeserved talent or a facet (what Dworkin calls a "parameter") of our lives that pushes us toward some goal. For some people who are deaf, for example, deafness is not a handicap but a condition that leads them to live their lives in a certain way; they would (and do) refuse "corrective" treatment. What then is undeserved for which redistribution, even were it possible, should be undertaken? Under Dworkin's master principle, society should strive "to make people's impersonal resources [i.e., their wealth and property] sensitive to their choices but insensitive to their circumstances." In other words, and to put the matter only generally, a person is entitled to keep what wealth he has amassed to the degree that it has come to him as a result of his choosing to work hard and sacrifice other possibilities for it, but not to the degree that it has come to him because of such circumstances as his innate talents. But part of choosing is the ambition that one harbors, and why should we suppose that ambition is purely a matter of will? People are presumably born with (or acculturated to) different degrees of ambition, just as they have different ranges of talent. Some people, we might say, have a talent for ambition. So even assuming it were possible to sensitively reallocate to others by distinguishing that to which a person is fairly entitled from that which is unfairly accorded by the "birth lottery," it is unclear that there is any principled way to know what it is that is fairly attributable to our inherent makeup or propensities and what it is that we have somehow individually added to them.[49]

Despite the breadth of many claims for material redistribution, the promise of the Equality Premise is in another sense narrow. The remedies for inequality are almost always monetized. But money rarely compensates well for inequalities other than an imbalance of wealth or goods obtainable in the marketplace. Actual equality often matters far more. But restoring someone to the equal position he should have is normally taken to be impossible. As Appiah says, Dworkin wants to "try to equalize the economic value of our talents, not (since we cannot) the talents themselves."[50] But suppose it were possible. Can the Equality Premise accommodate demands to equalize talents? Consider an athlete born with a physical handicap—for example, a body with no limbs below the knees. The birth lottery has quashed his chances, without assistance, to compete in Olympic track and field events, despite his fierce ambition to do so. Is he entitled to compensation for his thwarted desire? On what basis could it be measured? How could he prove the requisite ambition? Direct physical assistance might avoid the need to calculate a compensable award and to test for ambition. In 2008 Oscar Pistorius, partially legless, was at first refused permission to compete in the Olympics because officials said his prosthetic legs, carbon-fiber blades called Cheetahs, are "too efficient." Although he had been training for, competing in, and winning track meets (thus satisfying the ambition test), perhaps it was correct to deny him the use of a particular prosthetic that arguably gave him legs superior to those of muscle and bone. (In May 2008, an international court overruled the earlier ban, permitting him to attempt to qualify, though in the actual event he later failed.[51]) But the general problem persists. Does the Equality Premise require the state to invest in resources that would offset particular handicaps? In the coming republic of genetics, should the state encourage parents to augment their zygotes with souped-up physical attributes, or at least be required to repair bad genes, or should they be barred from tampering? At least some versions of the Equality Premise seem to encourage expectations that these inequalities should be redressed without providing any financial or political institutions for doing so.

The Neutrality Premise

"The distinctive liberal notion is that of the neutrality of the state," says Larmore in a clear statement of a widely held opinion.[52] But neutrality, like equality, is a murky concept.[53] And like equality, neutrality requires an object. Neutral about what? The usual object is variously described as "the good," people's ultimate ends, or comprehensive moral and philosophical views. So, for example, the state should not favor one religion over another by, for instance, subsidizing its church or minister, since doing so is to take sides. But the simplicity of an example hides conceptual complexities.

The Neutrality Premise has two strands: neutrality as an end and as a means.[54] Neutrality as an end prohibits the state from promoting or enforcing particular ways of life for two reasons: (1) because lacking an accepted measuring stick the state has no way of comparing the worth of one to another, and (2) if the state did compel people to adopt one way of life it would antagonize those whose ways of life would be disfavored, and thus disturb the very peace it was trying to achieve. Neutrality as a means has two quite different aspects. In each, the state takes for granted that there is an end to be served and adopts a policy of neutrality to attain it: (1) The good is individual autonomy, and to secure it the state must remain neutral toward other ways of life both to foster diverse traditions and to avoid discouraging an individual from developing and exercising the power to choose one of them. (Another end to be served might be that, contrary to those who argue for a single social order, the very existence of diversity in social and religious traditions benefits society as a whole.) (2) There is some other good—for example, salvation—but the state must remain neutral because coercing religious belief and practice subverts the unforced acceptance that is the basis for attaining it (this was Locke's argument in his essay on toleration).[55]

Critics charge that the Neutrality Premise fails for two reasons: It is a contradiction in terms, since the very defense of neutral liberalism is not neutral, and in any event neutrality is impossible to carry out. I shall consider each argument in turn. Neutrality contradicts itself because choice is not a universal good. If you prefer to deflect choice, having to choose may be frightening, even paralyzing. The terror of being free, of choosing how one shall live, of settling on *a* good or *the* good, may be too much to bear. In a society ordered by a single tradition, people avoid this psychological pressure, for the good is given and a general, and sometimes quite specific, way of life is prescribed. Security and comfort lie in following a custom or decision imposed from without and accepted as true. Faced with the dilemma whether to accept or reject choice, many people might flee freedom, either by surrendering to totalitarianism or even by committing suicide.[56] So the decision to let each person determine his own ends is not a neutral policy, but one with a specific concept of good—the good of choices arrived at autonomously. Hence the argument for neutrality is not itself neutral and is therefore internally inconsistent.[57]

The claim that neutrality is impossible to carry out rests on an argument about its terms. By making a choice, the argument goes, the state *by definition* has committed itself to one good rather than another—the end that will be carried out or promoted by the choice. Support for this argument seems to come easily in a multitude of examples. Consider this one, from Calvin Trillin:

You may be wondering why I haven't gotten around to discussing the question of whether or not female reporters have a right to be in the locker rooms of the National Football League. As it happens, I'm still trying to deal with a news report of several weeks ago that a Japanese construction company barred a female reporter from a tunnel completion ceremony because, in the words of the project supervisor, "the presence of women could anger the jealous Goddess of the Mountain."[58]

According to Larmore, neutral liberalism rules out "foster[ing] or implement[ing] any conception of the good life that some people reject" for otherwise it denies "the equal freedom that all persons should have to pursue their conception of the good life."[59] Here, the construction company rejected, on religious grounds, a conception of the good life in which women and men must be treated equally. Now assume the female reporter asserted a legal right against sex discrimination. In the United States, the Supreme Court presumably would say that the company's claim does not trump a general law forbidding discrimination on the basis of sex,[60] but if it is a genuinely religious claim the antidiscrimination law is not neutral.

The example may seem fanciful. In the weekday sense of the phrase, western cultures do not impute agency to "acts of God," except in a metaphorical sense (oddly, since in these acts God is seen as malevolent; we do not ordinarily apply the term to acts for which humans are responsible, like winning a game). But in many parts of Africa, even as nations seek to develop a western legal system, malevolent acts are frequently ascribed to human agency through the construct of witchcraft: "the practice of secretly using supernatural power for evil—in order to harm others or to help oneself at the expense of others."[61] Anyone in the United States who asserted such a claim would be summarily shown the courtroom door. The clash between outlooks is a growing problem, and it should remind us that hewing to scientific evidence, while rational, is not neutral, at least as the native cultures see it.[62]

Many other examples are closer to home. Gutmann and Thompson point to parents who want their children relieved from reading certain public school textbooks because of religious objections. "In this case two comprehensive moral views face each other in a standoff.... Neither exempting the children from the reading classes nor upholding the school board's right to require the children to use the textbooks is morally or politically neutral."[63] The schools could avoid the problem by withdrawing the offending texts, but the consequence would be to eviscerate liberal education, reducing learning to only that tiny corpus of knowledge to which no one objected.[64]

More generally, neutrality seems unable to deal with affinities some people have for bad things. In the usual sort of example, the sociopath, who sees good in an abhorrent way of life, would object to legal prohibitions against a preference for killing, maiming, and other destructive behaviors.

The answer to this critique of neutrality as impossible lies in one of many ambiguities in the concept of "the good." Defining the good as anything that people wish for or seek after forces all choices to be between goods, and it must then be true that the claim to neutrality is defeated. But not every human valuation need be included in the definition. We quite ordinarily view questions of right and wrong as lying on a different plane. Herzog takes Ackerman to task for failing to understand the difference. The denizens in Ackerman's fantasy world seek answers to pressing concerns through disputations in which neutrality is maintained by barring conversationalists from asserting that one person's conception of the good is better than another's or that one person is intrinsically superior to another. Herzog poses the problem of a shiftless person who has frittered away his assets and now, destitute, demands an equal share of an industrious worker's resources. Industrious responds that Shiftless is not "entitled" to it. Shiftless can only retort that Industrious violates neutrality rules in arguing that he deserves what he has accumulated more than Shiftless does, because it amounts to the claim that Industrious is better than Shiftless. But to equate a claim of right with an assertion that the holder is "better than" the other ultimately dissolves moral responsibility. That we could be led to such a conclusion suggests that something must be improper about our understanding of "better than" and "the good."[65]

We have circled back, I suggest, to the harm principle, into which the concept of neutrality collapses.[66] People may seek the good up to the point that doing so harms another. (The argument from harm may be the answer, also, to the conflict between the jealousy of the Mountain Goddess and the legal rule against discrimination.) It may seem that I am simply substituting one name for another. Certainly the meaning of harm is not self-evident, and as this book makes clear many of the problems with which the Neutrality Premise must wrestle reappear in different guise. But guise is important. The apparent impossibility of neutrality as practiced may be overcome by thinking through the limits of the state in terms of causing harm rather than seeking good.

For all their difficulties, each of the four liberal premises just examined—consent, dialogue, equality, and neutrality—is a part of liberalism's foundation. Stripped of philosophic finery, each may be a way of understanding the harm principle explored throughout the book. The harm principle not only seems to satisfy the requirements expressed in each of the four premises but also generates practices and institutions that are responsive to the concept of the self discussed in chapter 1. *Consent*: It seems intuitively correct that people would more readily consent to a government's undertaking to deal with the harms that surround them than anything else a government might do, in no small part because it is more straightforwardly a part of our everyday experience than the other premises offered as substitutes. *Dialogue*: To serve its purposes, the harm principle requires democratic discussion as the means of defining and carrying out its purposes. *Equality*: The harm principle obeys the requirement of equal respect; it does not single out people by their individual characteristics or irrelevant attributes. *Neutrality*: The harm principle strives, to the extent feasible under any single principle, to be impartial toward all nonharmful ways of living, to provide liberty, that is, for everyone. But a mere principle cannot work unaided or we could dispense with government altogether and write tracts on morality that would automatically guide proper behavior. To give it flesh (and muscle and bone, and heart and mind) the harm principle entails a constellation of institutions and practices. In testing it, we find few easy answers and many doubts. The harm principle may seem to straddle two sides of many questions. All that should not surprise, given the tension in which we find ourselves, squeezed between forces that threaten us with big bombs and Big Brother.

ACKNOWLEDGMENTS

This book is its own great-grandchild. Since such a preposterous claim deserves some justification, I offer the following evidence. In 1971, I answered an ad placed by the Phi Beta Kappa Society in the *New York Review of Books*, announcing a Bicentennial Fellowship Program to write a book on "the crisis in America." My brief proposal, that the continuing turmoil from the 1960s was rooted in our increasing inability to determine what should properly be public and what private, was one of seven awarded a Bicentennial grant the following year. I doubt that I had ever heard of John Rawls or understood how deeply rooted the philosophical problem was. I am indebted to the selection committee members: Ruth M. Adams, John Brademas, Ralph Ellison, Mason W. Gross, and John W. Ward, and to the Bicentennial Program director, Richard Schlatter, University Professor of History at Rutgers University, for his many kindnesses.

The original manuscript was written in 1973–1974, and thoroughly rewritten in 1977–1978. As it turned out, the revised manuscript was inadequate, and my dissatisfaction with it led me to enroll at Columbia University in 1983 to work toward a Ph.D. in political theory as a way of systematically confronting the arguments I had encountered in only a helter-skelter way in the 1970s.

At Columbia my greatest debt is to Professor Robert L. Amdur, who patiently helped a harried student during a dozen years of intermittent study. In particular, Bob has served as a sounding board for many of the ideas that ultimately made their way into this book and, perhaps more importantly, as a skeptic toward many other ideas that did not. I also thank Professor Kent Greenawalt for comments on a paper for his course on legal philosophy at Columbia Law School, a revised version of which forms part of the argument about the welfare problem in chapter 5, and for comments on my dissertation, the third completely reworked version of this book, in 1994–1995. A salute to Peggy Freund, late secretary to the Department of Political Science, who smoothed my way many times for more than a decade. Thanks, too, to the dissertation defense committee: Professors Vincent Blasi, Ira Katznelson, and Andrew Nathan (and also Professors Amdur and Greenawalt).

Several people said they would read one or another of the continuing revisions during the period 1995–2007. Warm thanks to the two who did: then Dean Joseph P. Tomain of the University of Cincinnati Law School and Judge Richard A. Posner. I record a special debt to Judge Posner, whom I did not know. In the late 1990s I mailed him without so much as a by-your-leave a copy of the third version, thinking that my subject might prove of interest to him. He read it, promptly and fully, and offered many helpful criticisms, as did Dean Tomain, leading to yet further revisions. I also sent a copy of the dissertation manuscript to Professor Joel Feinberg, who read at least portions of it and with whom I had a correspondence in the mid-1990s. We pledged to meet, in New York or Tucson, but alas, we never did.

At New York Law School, I am indebted to the late Dean Harry H. Wellington, who provided me with two summer research grants to pursue revisions in the late 1990s; to Paul Mastrangelo of the New York Law School Library, who for years has been supplying me with articles and other materials the need for which seemed always to arise on the cusp of a deadline; and to two student researchers, Al Amadio in the mid-1990s, for help in tracking down articles, and Elizabeth Silva, a third-year student in 2011, for her unflappable attention to my late-night emailed requests to plug gaps in the notes. Truly effusive thanks to Dean Richard A. Matasar, my friend and colleague for a dozen years, who released me from duties as associate dean for academic affairs and granted me a full year's sabbatical in 2007–2008 to rewrite the book for the fourth time. I am grateful to Bob Amdur and my colleague Professor Edward A. Purcell for providing me with extensive and acute comments on that manuscript.

After 2008 I continued to revise, particularly in 2011 in response to extended comments from two anonymous reviewers (and in 2012 from a third). Thanks to them and, at Oxford University Press, to my editor, David McBride, who saw the possibilities and never wavered; to Kay Kodner, for her exemplary copyediting; and to Leslie Johnson and the extended production crew.

In an entertaining foreword to *The New Industrial State*, John Kenneth Galbraith explained that his manuscript was the better for having been laid aside during the two years he spent as ambassador to India so that it could be largely rewritten on his return. "Let every writer," he said, "if he cannot arrange a tour as ambassador before publishing, at least take a long reflective holiday."[1] Reflecting for four decades, however, may be overdoing it. During those forty years, this book has been written wholesale four times, and overhauled a fifth, with additional, though more minor, retail revisions thereafter. If this book were computer software, it might be subtitled v.4.67. One brief portion has been published before, a part of chapter 2, under the title "The Relativity of Injury," in *Philosophy and Public Affairs*. I am grateful to Professor T. M. Scanlon for seeing to publication of the article, and, much more recently, to Thomas R. Vischi for helpful conversations about federal drug policy.

For forty-four years I have been blessed with the services of two of the finest literary agents in the business, Georges and Anne Borchardt, who have seen me through deals large and small. This one went on longer than anyone could ever have had any reason to suppose, and Anne and Georges remained stalwart and optimistic all along the way. To both, a career's gratitude.

My wife, Jo Shifrin, always deserves—and hereby gets—very special thanks, for her many indulgences on a daily basis, for her close reading of the entire manuscript more than once, and for her insistence that if she couldn't understand something it was my fault, in penance for which I was to scrub the prose until what remained spoke in language that she could follow; and with love for all the reasons that she alone knows.

I should also acknowledge an intermittent friendship with Allan Bloom, I as a very young college student, he (as I now reconstruct it) a very young professor. He played a crucial if delayed catalyst to my graduate study by insisting, during one long conversation in the early 1960s, that I should "take the next four years off and study Plato." The idea struck me then as absurd, and I never took him up on it, but though the thought lay dormant, it would not dissolve, and it nagged sufficiently to spur me on to Morningside Heights, where I nibbled the works of Plato and so many other political thinkers, studying at least some of what Bloom touted (as I was pleased to be able to tell him in person in the late 1980s). He did not live to see this book, and I rather suppose, rereading his scornful early attack on Rawlsian liberalism, that he would not have cared much for it.

Finally, I record my profound debt to Professor Charles E. Lindblom, who introduced me as an undergraduate fifty years ago not only to many of the questions raised here but also to the Great Conversation about them across the ages. He taught me early on something of the art of thinking hard and has remained a kindly and helpful, if distant, presence in my life for all this time. To him I gratefully dedicate this book.

Now at last it is time to let these pages escape the blinking cursor and slip away. Book, be fixed in print and bound in paper, and hear my borrowed parting sigh (from James Branch Cabell, the master American stylist of the early twentieth century):

> Depart, depart, my book! and live and die
> Dependent on the idle fantasy
> Of men who cannot view you, quite, as I.
> For I am fond, and willingly mistake
> My book to be the book I meant to make,
> And cannot judge you, for that phantom's sake.[2]

NOTES

Chapter 1

1. The phrase is Justice Benjamin N. Cardozo's in *Palko v. Connecticut*, 302 U.S. 319, 325 (1937).
2. Aristotle (1983, 3 [Book 1, 1252b30–1253a3]) held "that the state is a creation of nature, and that man is by nature a political animal." The state's highest purpose is to fulfill an objectively determinable good life. (1962, 4–5 [Book 1, chap. 2, 1094b5–10]; 34 [Book 2, chap. 1, 1103b2–7]; 1988, 63–65 [Book 3, chap. 9, 1280a7–1281a10]).
3. Rousseau (1978, 55 [Book I, chap. VII]).
4. All at once: Losurdo (2011, 188–191) makes the particular point of demonstrating that early liberals were deeply inconsistent, justifying inhumane and miserable living and working conditions of the masses (particularly slaves, women, and the working poor), because they defined such conditions as belonging to a private sphere that the state may not invade. Indeed, liberalism's most influential founder, John Locke (1910, §110), explicitly accepted slavery in South Carolina in "The Fundamental Constitutions of Carolina." For a discussion of Locke's views on slavery, see Farr (1986); Grant (1991, 67ff); Welchman (1995) (arguing that Locke meant to justify slavery).

    Completely: As Judith Shklar (1991, 22) chastises the overhasty generalizer: "[L]iberalism has been very rare both in theory and in practice in the last two hundred odd years, especially when we recall that the European world is not the only inhabited part of the globe." For histories of the different conceptions of liberalism, see, e.g., Holmes (1995); Johnston (1994); Manent (1994); Bellamy (1992); Arblaster (1986). Many dozens of other book-length accounts are available.
5. Cf. Appiah (2007, ix–x): "[W]e may have learned to think of these core elements of the liberal tradition as contested; so that, to put it crudely, liberals are not people who *agree* about the meaning of dignity, liberty, equality, individuality, toleration, and the rest, but are, rather, people who *argue* about their significance for political life. We may have learned, that is, that the liberal tradition—like all intellectual traditions—is not so much a body of doctrine as a set of debates.... My own suspicion is that ... what we now call the liberal tradition would look less like a body of ideas that developed through time and more like a collection of sources and interpretations of sources that we now find useful, looking backward, in articulating one influential philosophical view of politics." Alan Wolfe (2009, 25) says that liberalism "is not a software program that can spit out the answers to whatever questions we may have, nor is it a set of abstract principles or an inchoate bundle of well-meaning platitudes." Rather, it "is characterized by a set of dispositions toward the world that defines what kinds of creatures we are, establishes goals for us to reach, and lays down guidelines for the fairest ways to reach them."

6. Holmes (1993, 3–4).
7. Holmes (1995, 13–15, 27 ["self-exemption"]). See also Macedo (1991, 2, 80); Starr (2007, 23).
8. Two other lists: Berkowitz (1999, 4–5): "[E]ven as a political doctrine liberalism rests on the fundamental premise of the natural freedom and equality of all human beings. To establish and secure the personal freedom of all, the liberal tradition has articulated a set of characteristic themes including individual rights, consent, toleration, liberty of thought and discussion, self-interest rightly understood, the separation of the private from the public, and personal autonomy or the primacy of individual choice; and it has elaborated a characteristic set of political institutions including representative democracy, separation of governmental powers, and an independent judiciary." Wolfe (2009): (1) a disposition to grow (to develop); (2) a sympathy for equality; (3) a preference for realism (facts over romanticism and emotions); (4) an inclination to deliberate; (5) a commitment to tolerance, even for those who do not tolerate you; (6) an appreciation for openness; and (7) a taste for governance.
9. "The disparagement of 'liberalism' is not a passing fashion of the late 20th century. It is a recurring feature of Western political culture since at least the French Revolution." Holmes (1993, xi).
10. Pound (1939, 62). Of this phrase, Irving Howe (1977, 30) remarked four decades later that "there were, as it turned out, far worse things in the world than 'a mess of mush.'"
11. Harper (1969, 35).
12. MacIntyre (1984, 256).
13. Lukacs (2004, B9–10).
14. Unger (1975, 58).
15. Galston (1991, 42).
16. Mental disorder: Savage (2000); Godless: Coulter (2006); sin: Salvany (1994); evil: Hannity (2004); tragedy: van den Brink (2000); assault: Berryhill (1995); lacking common sense: Robertson (1993); fascist: Goldberg (2008); death: Dunn (2011); demonic: Coulter (2011); wanting liberty: Hannity (2002).
17. Taibbi (2007).
18. Shklar (1991, 21), Also: Dunn (1993, 29): "[I]n the case of liberalism . . ., it is by no means obvious what there is for us to concentrate our minds upon." Coleman (1992, 1): "It is impossible to characterize liberalism in either a comprehensive or an uncontroversial fashion. Sometimes liberalism is thought to identify a set of political or moral *values*, for example, autonomy, equality, or neutrality. Other times liberalism is identified with concrete political *rights* of the sort conferred on individuals in the U.S. Constitution: especially, freedom of expression, religion, and association. Yet other times it is thought to articulate a form or family of political *justifications* or constraints on justificatory strategies."
19. Geuss (2001, 69).
20. Isaiah Berlin (1969, 121) noted of the cognate concept "freedom" that historians of ideas have recorded "more than two hundred senses." He did not catalog the 200 meanings or provide references.
21. For a sense of liberalism as a public policy, party, partisan, or political label, see Brinkley (1998); Krugman (2007); Starr (2007); Wolfe (2009). For a sketch of how liberalism in this sense lost its political force as a distinct set of ideas, see Dworkin (1985, 181–186).
22. Utilitarianism (Douglas [1946, 71]): "Liberalism is a program that aims for the greatest good for the greatest number." Democracy (Pepper [1946, 71]: "[Liberalism] is really a synonym for democracy." Egalitarianism (Brooks [2008]): "[O]rthodox liberalism [is] a belief in using government to maximize equality." For an argument that liberalism and democracy are inconsistent, see Levine (1981).
23. Ryan (1995, 292–3). This same concept is expressed in various ways by many writers: Shklar (1991, 21): "Liberalism has only one overriding aim: to secure the political conditions that are necessary for the exercise of personal freedom." "Every adult should be able to make as many effective decisions without fear or favor about as many aspects of her or his life as is compatible with the like freedom of every other adult. That belief is the original and only

defensible meaning of liberalism." Berkowitz (1999, 189): "In the liberal tradition, personal freedom or individual liberty is originally understood in opposition to dependence on the arbitrary will of other human beings or submission to the rule of capricious laws."
24. Lukes (1971).
25. Decter (1976, 50).
26. Waldron (1987, 128).
27. Reiman (1994, 19–20).
28. Bowles (1946, 71).
29. According to Brinton (1953, 189).
30. Hirschman (1991).
31. Frankel (1976, 57).
32. Roberts (2008).
33. Revkin (2008).
34. The heartfelt plea was reported in Rucker (2009) and has been widely repeated and discussed: "At a recent town-hall meeting in suburban Simpsonville, a man stood up and told Rep. Robert Inglis (R–S.C.) to 'keep your government hands off my Medicare.' "I had to politely explain that, 'Actually, sir, your health care is being provided by the government,'" Inglis recalled. 'But he wasn't having any of it.'" See also Noah (2009).
35. Letwin (1998, ix).
36. Lawrence E. Cahoone (2002, 128) posits as the first tenet of conservatism that "endurance is validity. What endures, in so far as it endures, is valid." In Michael Oakeshott's classic metaphor, the state has no direction; its purpose is simply to endure: "In political activity, then, men sail a boundless and bottomless sea: there is neither harbour for shelter nor floor for anchorage, neither starting-place nor appointed destination. The enterprise is to keep afloat on an even keel: the sea is both friend and enemy, and the seamanship consists in using the resources of a traditional manner of behaviour in order to make a friend of every hostile occasion." Oakeshott (1991, 60).
37. Although the word may be modern, the theme is centrally rooted in the arguments of the classical liberals. John Locke (1983, 55) recognized in his essay on toleration that "the diversity of opinions ... cannot be avoided," even in the world that he knew in the late seventeenth century.
38. Mill (1970, 306). Hayek (1976, 37). Cf. a more poetic version in Auden (1966, 14):

> Some thirty inches from my nose
> The frontier of my Person goes;
> And all the untilled air between
> Is private *pagus* or demesne.

The spatial metaphor should not be expanded, as it were, to its borders. The "sphere" or "frontier" or "untilled air," like a house, or a room in a house, is not an absolute sanctuary. The real meaning of the principle is that though you are not free to do just anything within your own space, you are free to do certain things within *any* space.
39. Hart (1961, 190); Fuller (1964, 42); Hayek (1976, 36).
40. Locke (1965, 311 [chap. 2, §6]); Smith (1982, 82 [pt. II, § II, chap. 1]).
41. Jefferson (1961, 15), March 4, 1801. Cf. Jefferson's contemporary across the ocean, William Hazlitt (1933, 305): "[E]ach man's will is a sovereign law to itself; this can only hold in society as long as he does not meddle with others; but so long as he does not do this, the first principle retains its force."
42. Thomas (1985, 95).
43. Mill (1974, 135).
44. Lindblom (1990, 43). Consider how much easier it is to identify what we oppose than to conceptualize what we favor: "When equality became, with liberty and fraternity, one of the three great slogans of the French Revolution, it was not because people had a clear idea what it was they wanted equality of. What they knew for sure was what they were *against:* treating

45. Mill did not use the term *redress* or consider how or the degree to which the state may provide remedies for private wrongs. For problems specific to redress, see Lieberman (1981a; 1990, 99–115).
46. On the eighteenth-century British "Black Act," see Thompson (1975); Hay and Linebaugh (1975).
47. "The harm principle is unquestionably valid only as long as it is left entirely *vague*. Any specification of it, particularly of what is to count as 'other-regarding' and as harmful, generates trouble. All but the most trivial examples or applications are actually or potentially controversial." Cahoone (2002, 37). See also Holtug (2002) for a similar conclusion that various conceptions of harm are implausible. But see Donner (1991, 188–197).
48. Knowles (2001, 196). Cf. Volokh (1999, 1537): "The notion that wise, impartial, nonpartisan courts can and should protect our liberty against spurious though popular claims of harm is quite appealing. But after . . . seeing the difficulty—maybe the impossibility—of coming up with any general, principled theory of what constitutes harm (breach of contract? defamation? copyright infringement? monopolization? interference with another's patent monopoly? alienation of affections? annoying uses of residential property? insider trading?), I've reluctantly abandoned that particular hope."
49. Arneson (2000, 237).
50. A poem too widely anthologized to require further citation. Ernest Thayer, "Casey at the Bat: A Ballad Sung in the Year 1888," was first published in the *San Francisco Examiner* on June 3, 1888. Of course, the poem is silent about the aftermath, and Mrs. Casey, if there was such a lady, makes no appearance.
51. See, e.g., Mackie (1977, 125–148).
52. Rawls (1971, 3).
53. Ibid., 98.
54. Arneson (2000, 237). See also Fishkin (1983, 348–356) for an argument that ranking payoffs defeats other aspects of such theories.
55. The negative conception of freedom "is said to license the 'diabolical defence of Albania' against the charge of being a less free society than Britain, since the presence of severe restraints on religious practice in the former—and their absence in the latter—could thereby be forensically countered by pointing to the considerably fewer traffic restrictions in the former than in the latter." Steiner (1983, 80), quoting in turn from Taylor (1979, 183).
56. Hammond (1996, 13–35).
57. The claim that liberals erroneously rely on an unencumbered self is the subject of Sandel (1982). See also Taylor (1985, 187–210); Scruton (1980); Kekes (1997); Etzioni (1994). For a response to the supposition that accepting the self as encumbered would lead liberalism out of a false philosophy and into the arms of communitarianism, see Gardbaum (1992, 734n175): "The claim that rejection of the unencumbered self results in substantive political community is the central fallacy of Sandel's work." On communitarianism, see chapter 10.
58. One common statement of this claim: "All liberal philosophies start with some conception of the free autonomous individual in some mythical or hypothesized state of nature." Schroeder (1998, 502).
59. Bacon (1960, 122).
60. Aristotle assumed that "[t]he normal human being is not self-sufficient. Any being that is, and 'needs nothing from the state,' like a god, cannot be part of the community at all. Hence autonomy for the individual human being was not an ideal, because it was not seen as possible, let alone desirable. . . . For Aristotle it is axiomatic that the community is by its nature prior to the individual. For modern liberalism the opposite axiom holds good." Arblaster (1986, 22–23).

61. Hobbes (1981, 102 [pt. I, chap. 4]).
62. On "atomistic" individuals, see Taylor (1985).
63. Hobbes's theory ignored the reality of the wars that raged around him: These were not fought by isolated individuals but by thoroughly socialized human beings; communities were pitted against communities. See chapter 10, text at notes 70–76.
64. Hazlitt (1933, 305).
65. Inherent rights need a fuller explanation than that they are attached to something elemental. We do not assign rights to body parts or to the molecules that compose them—rights are not ascribed to things because they are "elementary." Rights are attributed to human beings for reasons having to do with individuality, not elementariness. There is no logical reason that an "elementary" entity may not be subordinated to some degree to the functioning of other such entities.
66. Spender (1975).
67. "As even developmental psychologists are beginning to recognize . . ., our cognitive development is always situated within a particular social context and constrained by specific social circumstances. Rather than a solitary individual developing in a vaccum [sic], the child is essentially a cognitive 'apprentice,' socially instructed by others." Zerubavel (1997, 15). See Vygotsky (1978); Luria (1976). See also Allport (1955); Bronfenbrenner (1979); Rubin (1980).
68. The neurological basis of the self—that is, how brain mechanisms create an autobiographical account of a person—is distinct from the question of the content of that autobiography, including its "internal" desires and beliefs, and the influence of others on its development. For one of the most comprehensive summaries of the literature and the problem of the self that comes to consciousness, see Dennett (1991, esp. chap. 13). See also Damasio (1994, 236–244); Damasio (2010); Pinker (2002); Kandel (2007); Gazzaniga (2008). That the self has a physical basis within an individual brain does not moot the issue debated by political theorists. Descartes' dualism theory, that mind is something other than the matter of the brain, has now been widely rejected, although it has had occasional defenders: see Koestler (1967); Pepper and Eccles (1977).
69. Walzer (2004, 93).
70. Mumford (1967, 46). Evolutionary psychologists: "An evolutionary perspective inevitably eluded Hobbes and Rousseau; less forgivably it still eludes some of their intellectual descendants. The philosopher John Rawls asks us to imagine how rational beings would come together and create a society from nothing, just as Rousseau imagined a solitary and self-sufficient proto-human. These were only thought-experiments, but they serve to remind us that there never was a 'before' society. Human society is derived from the society of *Homo erectus*, which is derived from the society of *Australopithecus*, which is derived from the society of a long-extinct missing link between humans and chimps, which in turn was derived from the society of the missing link between apes and monkeys, and so on, back to an eventual beginning as some sort of shrew-like animals that perhaps genuinely lived in Rousseauian solitude." Ridley (1998, 156–157). *Pace* Ridley, Roger D. Masters (1978, 6) points out that in *Discourse on the Origin of Inequality*, Rousseau "contains an evolutionary approach to human history which is all the more remarkable in that it was written fully a century before Darwin. . . . Indeed, Rousseau's contribution to evolutionary thought was so great that he has been called a founder of modern anthropology and sociology." See also Ridley (2011, chap. 2).
71. Burckhardt (1954, 100).
72. Lovejoy (1936, 59ff.).
73. De Tocqueville (1955, 96).
74. That said, there is growing evidence that some dispositions, mental states, social proclivities, emotional strengths, and even knowledge of the physical world are "hardwired" in the brain. Anyone who has ever raised two or more children knows that not all of how each child behaves can be explained by the common home and family that each shares. For a lively discussion of the growing field of cognitive developmental psychology and entertaining

examples of how psychologists tease out changes in the early blooming of the self, see Bloom (2005).
75. This idea has even crept onto the op-ed pages. The columnist David Brooks (2007) proclaimed: "There is no self that exists before society." What he meant is far from clear. He said that he was led to this belief by a theory that "emphasizes how profoundly we are shaped by relationships with others, but it's not one of those stifling, collectivist theories that puts the community above the individual," and he took to task both "Ayn Rand individualists" and "New Age narcissists." We are, he says, "embedded creatures."
76. Walzer (2004, 162).
77. Charles Taylor (1985, 189,197–198) ascribes to the social contractarians the view that atomistic individuals "are self-sufficient outside of society" and since that view is obviously untrue, a philosophy such as liberalism that resists the claim "that we ought to belong to or sustain society" must fail. It is unclear (to me) what the ambiguous notion of belonging to society means and what its implications are for the powers of a state. Whatever it means it is false that the social contractarians supposed individuals are self-sufficient outside society (why, then, would Hobbes suppose they needed a social contract?) and false also that liberalism opposes sustaining society.
78. Stephen Holmes (1991, 286n21) traces back to at least 1796 the claim, as he summarizes it, "that the social constitution of the individual logically entails that the edifice of liberal politics be razed and replaced by a system celebrating the supremacy of society over the individual."
79. Kymlicka (1991, 52). As Michael Walzer notes (1990, 21): "Contemporary liberals are not committed to a presocial self, but only to a self capable of reflecting critically on the values that have governed its socialization; and communitarian critics, who are doing exactly that, can hardly go on to claim that socialization is everything."
80. Quoted in Kotkin (2001, 69). By "here," the teenager means the Soviet Union.
81. Carried to its extreme, it resembles the argument Robin Fox (2001, 21) attributes to F. H. Bradley, who argued "that individuals do not exist, that the social is real and the individual the abstraction. Take away from any so-called individual everything contributed to his nature and person by society (starting with the genetic contribution of his parents, grandparents, and so forth) and what is left? Nothing." But that is like saying there is no present, because take away all that the past has contributed to the present and what is left? Nothing.
82. Durkheim (1973, 54, 231n4): "A verbal similarity has permitted the belief that 'individualism' necessarily derived from 'individual' and therefore egoistic feelings.... This is how it is possible, without contradiction, to be an individualist, all the while saying that the individual is more a product of society than its cause. It is because individualism itself is a social product just like all moralities and all religions."
83. Morris (1972). See also Frank (1999).
84. Cf. Cuddihy (1978, 44): "Classical Christianity had begun by severing the individual from his ethnic group and his family. 'The God of Christianity,' [Georg] Simmel wrote, 'is the God of the individual.... The individual stands before his God in absolute self-reliance.... For Antiquity and the ethnic world the picture seems quite different. The god of each closed group is its private god, who cares for it or punishes it; and the gods of other groups are accepted as equally real.'" Quoting Simmel (1959, 67).
85. Pirenne (1956, 51); Bryant (1968, 143). See also Hilton (1969).
86. In 1260 a French knight, "Louis Defeux, was wounded by a certain Thomas d'Ouzouer and proceeded against his assailant in court. The accused did not deny the fact, but he explained that he had himself been attacked some time before by a nephew of his victim. What offense, then, had he committed? Had he not, in conformity with the royal ordinances, waited forty days before taking his revenge—the time held to be necessary to warn one's kindred of the danger? Agreed, replied the knight; but what my nephew has done is no concern of mine. The argument availed him nothing, for the act of an individual involved all his kinsfolk. Such, at any rate, was the decision of the judges of the pious and peace-loving St. Louis. Blood thus

called for blood, and interminable quarrels arising from often futile causes set the hostile houses at each other's throats." Bloch (1961, 126–127). The idea of collective guilt has largely disappeared in the west, although in recent times it flared up briefly in the formal law. In *Korematsu v. United States*, 323 U.S. 214 (1944), in which the Court upheld the conviction of an American citizen of Japanese ancestry for failing to report to a detention center after the bombing of Pearl Harbor, Justice Frank Murphy declared in dissent: "To infer that examples of individual disloyalty prove group disloyalty and justify discriminatory action against the entire group is to deny that under our system of law individual guilt is the sole basis for deprivation of rights." Or, as Justice Robert H. Jackson put it, dissenting in the same case: "Guilt is personal and not inheritable." But the idea persists elsewhere. A notorious case of a community's right to seek revenge against an innocent person because of a family wrongdoer played out in Pakistan in 2002, when a Punjab village council ordered that a woman be gang-raped "as punishment after her younger brother was accused of illicit relations with a woman from a rival tribe." Masood (2005). The incident caused an international uproar. Pressed by the victim, Mukhtaran Bibi, and her lawyers, and international publicity, the government prosecuted the men accused of the rape, leading to several acquittals and a subsequent overturning of death sentences for those convicted. The Pakistan Supreme Court set aside the acquittals and ordered a new trial; eventually one of the rapists was reconvicted. The victim, Mukhtaran Bibi (now known as Mukhtar Mai), became internationally famous. See Mai (2007); Kristoff and WuDunn (2010); see also Diamond (2008).

87. "[J]ustice is a universal of all cultures. It is a tightrope that man walks, between his desire to fulfil his wishes, and his acknowledgement of social responsibility. No animal is faced with this dilemma: an animal is either social or solitary. Man alone aspires to be both in one, a social solitary." Bronowski (1973, 411). Once again, Durkheim (1973b, 149–163) was there first.

88. Cf. Conquest (2000, xv): "Above all, we must insist, as against the utopian concepts, that a tolerable order of things is one of a proper balance between the social and the individual: that human being is neither an ant nor a shark." This point is consistent with Jeremy Waldron's claim about the liberal position on "the relation between freedom and social order. Some philosophers say there is a definitional connection between freedom and social order: *real* freedom (sometimes, freedom for the *true* self) just *is* submission to and participation in the order of a good society. Others maintain that freedom is lost or the principle of liberty is violated whenever *any* rule of social order is enforced, no matter how well-grounded it is in the requirements of social life. Liberalism, it seems to me, repudiates both of these extreme positions." Waldron (1987, 131). Note also Feinberg (1988, 85): "Humans are essentially social, and their communities are structured associations of individuals, not super-individuals themselves. The individual is a social being through and through, and much of what we think of as essential in him is inconceivable without his relations (membership, belonging, allegiance, status, inherited culture, etc.). On the other hand, a social group is indeed nothing but a collection of individuals, not merely aggregated, but in often complex, sometimes hierarchical relations to one another. Any analysis of individuals and societies, then, that makes too stark a contrast between them, either by considering individuals as self-sufficient and 'logically prior,' or by treating groups as moral organisms, is radically deficient."

89. Wolfe (1999), critiquing Kekes (1997).

90. Raz (1988, 410, 412). Raz's theory of "competitive pluralistic moralities," ibid., 404, is complex and convoluted, and I do not consider it further beyond this note. He says at various points that autonomy in a morally pluralistic society requires tolerance, "within bounds," even of "bad or evil actions." Ibid., 403–404. But he does not tell us how to distinguish evil or bad actions that should be permitted to flourish from those that should not, namely "the morally bad and repugnant." One answer might be the harm principle, but Raz has it perform double, and likely contradictory, duty. He asserts that the harm principle derives from a primary "autonomy principle." Ibid., 425. That principle holds that "personal autonomy [is] an essential ingredient of the good life" and it "imposes duties on people to secure for all the

conditions of autonomy." Ibid., 415. But since coercing people in the name of autonomy is contradictory, "autonomy-based duties," therefore, "never justify coercion" unless there is harm. Ibid. But in the absence of harm, on what basis may the government provide a range of services financed by taxation, a duty implied by the autonomy principle (since governments must "provide the conditions of autonomy for people who lack them")? Ibid. Raz's response is two-fold: on the one hand, "sometimes failing to improve the situation of another is harming him [thus permitting the government] to use coercion both in order to stop people from actions which would diminish people's autonomy and in order to force them to take actions which are required to improve people's options and opportunities." Ibid., 416. On the other hand, "subsidiz[ing] certain activities, reward[ing] their pursuit, and advertis[ing] their availability," is merely encouraging those activities, not engaging in coercion. Ibid., 417. Aside from the potential contradiction, duties of that sort are likely wholly open-ended. The harm principle is no longer a limiting principle. An autonomous person might wish, for example, to sample various religions, an unattainable ambition in a society in which most of the world's religions have failed to take hold. May the government subsidize the building of various religious communities and their churches to provide "an adequate range of options and the opportunity to choose them"? Ibid., 418. How would the government be held to its moral duty? And what else would be expended from the fisc? Aside from the perplexity of viewing a governmental mandate as both a response to harm necessitating coercion and as a non-coercive encouragement, the argument that the state *must* aim toward protecting and enhancing the autonomy of every person seems controversial. I therefore return to the primacy of the harm principle, as less controversial and more readily understandable. Autonomy is an obvious byproduct of the harm principle, but it is not an open-ended good that the state may seek to enhance independent of harm.
91. Macedo (1991, 261).
92. The duality of human nature also dissolves the dichotomy that runs through much of political thought over the ages that man is either bad, in which case we need government to contain the evil, or man is good, in which case we can let people flourish and look to build nirvana. Summarizing one such view, Wolfe (2009, 36) says: "Thomas Sowell [1987] has argued that nearly all social theorists can be placed into one of two camps: those who hold that human nature is fundamentally bad and therefore in need of the constraints of firm laws and strong institutions, which Sowell identifies with conservatives such as himself; and those who believe it is fundamentally good and therefore compatible with utopian longings, a property of liberals and radicals." The dichotomy is false, and liberals need not foolishly look forward to withered states and blissful utopias. Man is neither only or always good or always or only bad. Man is both. Two saints, driving down the road, can still wind up in an accident.
93. Cahoone (2002, 130). A bit astonishingly, two pages later Cahoone instructs that conservatives are fundamentally "committed to the universal validity of a particular form of order, regardless of history, tradition, or culture, namely, that of modern *civil association*." Ibid., 132. Apparently that particular universal truth cannot be discovered; it just proclaims itself.
94. Fish (1994, 135, 137).
95. Ibid., 138. Fish's fallacy is the question-begging claim that those who step outside the party of reason will not be "tolerated." But in a liberal regime, they are. No one is telling leaders of cults, adherents to unscientific world views, or mainstream pious reverends who prefer simply to proclaim their faith that they must shut up. The airwaves and printed pages are full of their claims, demands, bromides, and dyspepsia. They talk to each other and seek converts. That they are not heeded by as many as they would like is not the fault of reason. Liberalism does not, because it could not, promise that every preference be translated into public policy.
96. For a recent argument about the universality of reason, see Lynch (2012). I note without discussion that the term is ambiguous. "Reason" can mean a way of thinking; a kind of explanation; a method of asking questions; a procedure for investigating; a set of starting assumptions about existence, causes, or methods of proof; a claim about sense data and perception; and much more.

97. Mass famines, for example, have accompanied the "reasoned" policies of corrupt thinkers on both the right and the left. See Conquest (1986); Dikötter (2010); Becker (1997); Woodham-Smith (1991).
98. Reasoned interpretation of religious texts is scarcely a modern idea. The Talmud is a compendium more than a millennium in the making. Catholic doctrine to this day relies on the reasoned theologizing of Aquinas nearly eight centuries ago. Benjamin Jowett (2000, 477–536) scandalized many when he suggested in 1860 in an essay "On the Interpretation of Scripture" that the Protestant Bible be understood through secular interpretive techniques, but today that premise is a commonplace.
99. On cognitive limitations, see Kahneman (2011); Trivers (2011).
100. Hayek (1979, 176): "If the Enlightenment has discovered that the role assigned to human reason in intelligent construction had been too small in the past, we are discovering that the task which our age is assigning to the rational construction of new institutions is far too big. What the age of rationalism—and modern positivism—has taught us to regard as senseless and meaningless formations due to accident or human caprice, turn out in many instances to be the foundations on which our capacity for rational thought rests. *Man is not and never will be the master of his fate; his very reason always progresses by leading him into the unknown and unforeseen where he learns new things.*" Cf. Vaclav Havel in a 1992 speech to the World Economic Forum (quoted in Hammond 1996, 79–80): "The modern era has been dominated by the culminating belief, expressed in different forms, that the world—and Being as such—is a wholly knowable system governed by a finite number of universal laws that man can grasp and rationally direct for his own benefit.... [It] gave rise to the proud belief that man, as the pinnacle of everything that exists, was capable of objectively describing, explaining and controlling everything that exists, and of possessing the one and only truth about the world.... It was ... an era in which the goal was to find a universal theory of the world, and thus a universal key to unlock its prosperity. Communism was the perverse extreme of this trend.... The fall of Communism can be regarded as a sign that modern thought—based on the premise that the world is objectively knowable, and that the knowledge so obtained can be absolutely generalized—has come to a final crisis.... The end of Communism is a serious warning to all mankind. It is a signal that the era of arrogant, absolutist reason is drawing to a close." Havel's rhetoric overruns facts and logic. Some people may have supposed the world is wholly knowable, but it is not the necessary or even probable conclusion to be drawn by those who espouse reason. No scientist believes that the world is "wholly knowable," not even Laplace, who suggested at best that it was knowable in principle. That some people became Communists, that they professed to believe that Marx had used scientific methods to reach inescapable conclusions, and that these translated into the economic and political systems of Soviet Communism, scarcely shows that it is reason's fault. Anyone can misuse reason, as anyone can misuse religion. One might just as well blame the Catholic religious tradition (I did not say institutional church traditions) for priestly sexual predation or the homilies of Jesus for the imbecility and insensitivity of the Rev. Fred Phelps. For the fact is that Communism was an ideology preached by relatively few and it lasted as long as it did because it was enshrined in a police state. On Phelps, see Alvarez (2006); Hagerty (2011)
101. I refer, of course, to the last page of Orwell (1949) before the fictional appendix.
102. Herzog (1989, 216). Franck (1999, 125).
103. See Wolin (2004) for glimpses of intellectuals who betrayed their reason both as supporters of fascism and as those who seem to have forgotten its lessons.
104. Holmes (1963, 5).
105. Bierce (1958, 24) mordantly distinguished the "Conservative, [a] statesman who is enamored of existing evils, ... from the Liberal, who wishes to replace them with others."
106. Rawls (1993, 217). Rawls answers his own question: "Our exercise of political power is proper and hence justifiable only when it is exercised in accordance with a constitution the essentials of which all citizens may reasonably be expected to endorse in the light of principles and ideals acceptable to them as reasonable and rational." Ibid. Rawls also asserts that a

well-ordered society satisfies three publicity conditions, one of which is that the "full justification of the public conception of justice" is publicly known. Ibid., 67. This is a breathtaking requirement if that full justification means anything like understanding the reasoning that Rawls himself undertakes to create a theory of political liberalism, for the argument he presents is intricately convoluted and rambling, difficult at best to the initiate and virtually unreadable by anyone who has not been immersed in political theory. Even if they attempt it, reasonable people are not likely to make their way through the turgid prose of Rawls; they have better things to do. That for forty years specialists have been debating and faulting the principles, that even Rawls himself backed away in *Political Liberalism* from what he earlier proposed as universal principles of justice in *A Theory of Justice*, suggests the utter implausibility of the idea that legitimacy depends on complex principles being accepted by all, even if modified by the word "reasonable."
107. Solomon (1995, 2).
108. Waldron (1987, 134–135).

Chapter 2

1. Morris (1967, ix).
2. E.g., Weldon (1953); Van Dyke (1960); Sabine and Thorson (1973); Connolly (1983); Miller (1991); Honderich (1995); Audi (1995). I suggested adding "harm" as an entry in the forthcoming multivolume *The Blackwell Encyclopedia of Political Thought*, but the editors appear to have rejected the suggestion (though "risk" and "suffering" are included, as of May 2012).
3. Rawls (1971, 450) refers to harm or injury (not indexed) apparently only in this context: "To have a complaint against the conduct and belief of others [in justice as fairness] we must show that their actions injure us." Rawls here is comparing injury to the feelings of moral revulsion that may sweep across "the larger part of society" that abhors "certain religious or sexual practices" which it regards "as an abomination." Rawls also speaks (213) of the "government's right to maintain public order and security" as "an enabling right," and considers the possibility that liberty of conscience may be limited "when there is a reasonable expectation that not doing so will damage the public order which the government should maintain," but he does not discuss the contours of public order or security. His concern is with the kind of knowledge that the government may accept as demonstrating the certainty or imminence of "consequences for the security of public order"; on the nature and gravity of insecurity and disorder Rawls is silent.
4. Writing from the jurisprudential perspective, Roscoe Pound agreed that nothing inherent in the categories of liability corresponds to any theoretical concern about defining injury or harm. These concepts, as applied, are historically, not theoretically, derived: "When lawyers began to generalize and to frame conscious theories, the crude beginnings of liability in a duty to compound for insult or affront to man or gods or politically organized society, lest they be moved to vengeance, became liability to answer for injuries caused by oneself or done by persons or things in one's power and liability for certain promises made in solemn form. Thus arises a twofold basis for liability—the duty to repair injury and the duty to carry out formal undertakings—which has persisted in subsequent theory. *But the resulting categories of delict and contract do not represent any inherent requirement of legal thinking. They are historical products*" (Pound [1937], 428; emphasis supplied). This understanding long predates Pound. In adopting Article IV of the Declaration of the Rights of Man on August 26, 1789, the French National Assembly concisely stated the general view that what is harmful is not of philosophic but of conventional legal interest: "Liberty consists in the power to do anything that does not injure others; thus, the exercise of the natural rights of every man has only such limits as assure to other members of society the enjoyment of the same rights. These limits can only be determined by law." Quoted in Hobhouse (1994, 29).
5. Burke (1969, 150–151).
6. Machiavelli (1974, 278 [Book Two, 2]).

7. Locke (1967, 257 [chap. XI, §106]).
8. Charleston, S.C., *Gazette*, September 26, 1775, quoted in Wood (1972, 63); Adams quoted in Wood (1972, 63).
9. This was the mistake that Mill (1974, 128 [chap. 1, ¶3]) noted: "As the struggle proceeded for making the ruling power emanate from the periodical choice of the ruled, some persons began to think that too much importance had been attached to the limitation of the power itself. *That* (it might seem) was a resource against rulers whose interests were habitually opposed to those of the people. What was now wanted was, that the rulers should be identified with the people; that their interest and will should be the interest and will of the nation. The nation did not need to be protected against its will. There was no fear of its tyrannising over itself."
10. Jostle: Smith (1982, 83 [Part II, §2, chap. 2, ¶1]). Smith (1937, 669 [Book V, chap. 1, Pt. II]) also declared that "the second duty of the sovereign [—the first is national defense—is] that of protecting, as far as possible, every member of society from the injustice or oppression of every other member of it." Smith (1982, 79 [Part II, §2, chap. 1, ¶1]) distinguished the virtue of beneficence, which cannot be forced, from the virtue of justice, "the observance [of which] is not left to the freedom of our own wills, which may be extorted by force, and of which the violation exposes to resentment, and consequently to punishment.... [T]he violation of justice is injury: it does real and positive hurt to some particular persons, from motives which are disapproved of." He pointed to three general categories of injustice, the commission of which entitle society and the victim to exact "vengeance and punishment": (a) murder and physical injuries; (b) theft and other interferences with possessions; and (c) denial of "what are called ... [a man's] personal rights, or what is due to him from the promises of others" (ibid., 84 [Part III, §2, chap. 2, ¶2]). Similarly, much later Hayek (1978), 109, held that "the limitation of all coercion to the enforcement of general rules of just conduct was the fundamental principle of classical liberalism, or, I would almost say, its definition of liberty" but he does not provide details of the fudge word *just*.
11. Smith (1978, 489).
12. Locke (1965b, 311 [chap. 3, §6]; 314 [§11]; 316 [§13]; 396 [§§ 124–126]). That Locke supposed he was deriving political principles from "natural rights" need not detain us. I note it primarily because Robert Nozick follows his convention to derive a set of principles that he claims give us a minimal state (see next section). Locke, at least, does not so much derive principles as state them. In effect, he starts with a harm principle, though a crude and unformed one. That is why a natural rights premise was not included in the examination of liberal premises in chapter 1.
13. Locke (1965b, 308 [§3]).
14. Ibid., 399 [§131]; emphasis in the original.
15. It might seem that Locke did in fact specify the content of the public good to which the laws must be devoted: protecting property. Although scattered passages leave Locke open to a charge of ambiguity, the better conclusion is that he does not use "property" to signify any narrow sense of actual possessions exclusively. Rather, as he says, men "unite for the mutual *Preservation* of their Lives, Liberties and Estates, which I call by the general Name, *Property*." And the "great and *chief end* therefore, of Mens uniting into Commonwealths, and putting themselves under Government, *is the Preservation of their Property*" (ibid., 395 [§123, §124]). This broader conception of property leaves indeterminate the public good to which legislation must be devoted. Moreover, as discussed in "The Relativity of Property" in this chapter (also see the text after note 47 in chapter 3), even the narrow conception of property is inescapably indeterminate.
16. Nozick (1974, ix). In this section I deal primarily with Nozick's claim "that any more extensive state [than a minimal one] will violate persons' rights not to do certain things, and is unjustified." Ibid. In later sections (see chapters 6 and 9) I deal with "two noteworthy implications [which] are that the state may not use its coercive apparatus for the purpose of getting some citizens to aid others, or in order to prohibit activities to people for their *own*

good or protection." Ibid. The remainder of this chapter derives substantially from Lieberman (1977).
17. The foregoing is a most abbreviated summary of an argument that occupies Nozick for 125 pages.
18. Ian Shapiro (1986, 289) says that it is absurd to suppose we must justify the presence or activity of government, rather than the absence or inactivity of government. One response that theorists who "derive" states from first principles might offer (certainly Nozick could offer) is that in setting limitations on the power of government, the theorist is doing just what Shapiro suggests: The proposition that a government may act only up to some limits provides the justification for absence or inactivity beyond those limits.
19. See Lorenz (1952); Bleibtreau (1968).
20. For more on this point, see chapter 8.
21. Nozick (1974, 141) does not dwell on the problem of uncertain knowledge, though in oblique fashion, he acknowledges it only to (apparently) dismiss it. "To have rested the case for the state on the denial" of an assumption that a set of principles exists that is acceptable, unambiguous, clearly understandable, and complete "would have left the hope that the future progress of humanity (and moral philosophy) might yield such agreement, and so might undercut the rationale for the state." This amounts to saying that the hope that we may one day learn to harness nuclear fusion might induce people right now to abandon oil and coal to supply our energy needs. The state is necessary for two reasons discussed below in this chapter: We do not possess the requisite certainty today and it is impossible ever to achieve it.
22. Marriage and family relations were subject to canonical, not secular, authorities. But not even secular legal institutions were unified in a single political structure. In England in the seventeenth century, Chief Justice Coke discerned no less than fifteen separate legal systems that functioned more or less autonomously, and it was common for a court of one type, jealous of its prerogatives, to order a court of another type to cease hearing a particular case. These are spelled out in Coke (1979).
23. Not so easy at that. Every society outlaws murder but the acts of killing that constitute murder vary from culture to culture and age to age. As I was first writing this section, the newspaper brought the outraged voices of editorialists decrying a Maryland judge who sentenced a man to only eighteen months for killing his wife on finding her in bed with another man. At sentencing the judge said: "I seriously wonder how many men married, five, four years would have the strength to walk away without inflicting some corporal punishment." (Quindlen [1994]).
24. The clients have read their Hobbes (1981, 186 [Book I, chap. 13]).
25. The promulgation of legislative rules following adjudicative hearings has a basis in the anthropological literature. See, e.g., the story of a Cheyenne warrior whose horse was borrowed without permission. The Cheyenne chiefs first discussed the issue as a "case," inviting both the owner and the friend who borrowed the horse. Settling the case, the chiefs then announced their resolution as a rule to be applied in the future. See Llewellyn and Hoebel (1941, 127); Hoebel (1954, 24).
26. The prospectus is not the only regulation open to the protective association of which Nozick would presumably disapprove. Although Nozick expressly forswears paternalism, the protective association could certainly perform this "service" bilaterally for its clients. Suppose I offer to pay my association a premium for protection not merely from others but from myself, a service that seems reasonable when I realize how complicated the world is and how many things there are that could injure me about which I have little or no knowledge. So I insist that the association look out for me. Because this is a noncoerced agreement, my rights have not been violated. Suppose now that the Association's office of Paternal Regulations, having much experience in these matters, counsels me that for the best protection I should enter into an irrevocable contract. Otherwise, just when the association is about to force me to do (or refrain from doing) something for my own good, I might terminate the contract, thereby defeating the purpose of the deal. Like Ulysses insisting he be kept tied to the mast as his

vessel passed the Sirens, no matter how much he begged to be released, the Association suggests I consent now to be bound to respect self-protective regulations later. I agree and am handed a rule book that directs me first of all to wear a helmet whenever I ride my donkey. The rule states I can be fined for failing to wear my helmet under these and associated conditions. Now so far this regulation binds only people who have agreed to abide by it—indeed, only those who have even agreed to pay extra for this protection. But the protective association, as it gradually became the dominant agency, might enforce the rule against nonconsenters too, since the cost and effort of sorting out in the middle of traffic who is and who is not a consenter might be too high for the association to bear. To those who complain that they are being forced to wear a helmet for their own good, the dominant association, now the minimal state, might respond that although it is true their rights are being "technically" violated, nevertheless they are receiving adequate compensation—in the form of the greater safety that attaches to being forced to abide by the rule! See chapter 9, text at notes 26–27.

27. Birrell (1899, 10–11).
28. Ibid.
29. *Slaughterhouse Cases*, 83 U.S. (16 Wall.) 36 (1873). I have idealized the facts. In the real case, the evidence, which the Supreme Court ignored, seemed clearly to suggest that the surviving slaughterhouse bribed the legislature to obtain its monopoly.
30. There is no necessary connection between property rights in the United States Constitution and natural property rights such as are implicit in the strong version of them to which Nozick holds. The Supreme Court from the 1890s to the 1930s could have been correct about the Constitution and wrong about natural rights: Whether the Constitution incorporates Locke's or anyone else's theory of natural rights is an entirely different matter. The story is offered here as analogy only.
31. Commons (1957, chap. 2).
32. Thus in 1898 the Court ruled that valid railroad rate regulation depended upon a company's earning a "fair" rate of return on the value of its land. *Smyth v. Ames*, 169 U.S. 466 (1898). This was the "fair value fallacy": The value of land was dependent on the rates that railroads had been able to charge before the imposition of rate regulation. Hale (1952, 462ff.). If just compensation requires giving back to a company the value of what had been limited by a regulation called forth because the rate was exorbitant, then regulation would be self-defeating. Yet so it was held for more than forty years until the Supreme Court finally returned in 1940 to the position it had announced in *Slaughterhouse* in 1873. See *Federal Power Commission v. Hope Natural Gas Co.*, 320 U.S. 59 (1940).
33. One typical preindustrial conflict arose when farm animals strayed across the fields and trampled crops of other farmers. On whom should the liability for damage to crops fall? The British rule was that the owner of the animals was liable to fence in his animals; the American rule, owing to different circumstances, was that the crop farmer must fence out his neighbor's animals. See *Seeley v. Peters*, 10 Ill. 130 (1848). But no a priori natural law spelled out the appropriate conclusion that the courts were bound to follow: It was, rather, the state that provided the rule.
34. Horwitz (1977, 36).
35. Cf. Nozick (1974, 163): "The socialist society would have to forbid capitalist acts between consenting adults."
36. See chapter 4, text at note 42.

Chapter 3

1. Jeremy Bentham, "Anarchical Fallacies," in Waldron (1987b, 53).
2. The carelessness of such a reading is discussed in Ten (1980, chap. 2). For "concerns": Mill (1974, 135 [chap. 1, ¶9]). For "affects": ibid., 137 (chap. 1, ¶12).
3. "We take then our point of departure from the fact that human acts have consequences upon others, that some of these consequences are perceived, and that their perception leads to

subsequent effort to control action so as to secure some consequences and avoid others. . . . [These] consequences are of two kinds, those which affect the persons directly engaged in a transaction, and those which affect others beyond those immediately concerned. In this distinction we find the germ of the distinction between the private and the public. When indirect consequences are recognized and there is effort to regulate them, something having the traits of a state comes into existence. When the consequences of an action are confined, or are thought to be confined, mainly to the persons directly engaged in it, the transaction is a private one" (Dewey [1927, 12–13]).

4. Gleick (1987, 8). The idea that each person affects all others has been labeled the "Donne effect." See Vining (1978, 32), noting Justice Blackmun's reference to John Donne's line "No man is an island" in *Sierra Club v. Morton*, 405 U.S. 727, 760n2 (1972) (Blackmun, dissenting).

5. The assertion of power to control such effects is not, in fact, alien to American politics. In an important case construing Congress's constitutional power to regulate commerce, the Supreme Court once upheld a fine levied against a farmer who, in excess of an allotment under the Agricultural Adjustment Act, grew a small amount of extra wheat to feed to his own livestock; the Court reasoned that even though his excess wheat was consumed on the farm, that wheat competed with wheat that he otherwise would have had to buy, and hence had an effect on the market price for wheat. *Wickard v. Filburn*, 317 U.S. 111 (1942).

6. "Directly": Mill (1974, 137 [chap. 1, ¶12]); "primarily": ibid., 185 (chap. 3, ¶1).

7. Bentham (1948, 2–3, 24, 29).

8. The utilitarian is not confined to a calculus of pain and pleasure. But the problem of open-endedness is not solved by substituting happiness and unhappiness, likes and dislikes, utility and disutility, or any other similar pairing.

9. Feinberg (1984, 1985, 1986, 1988).

10. See Ten (1980). A summary of the argument that Mill intended the harm principle to apply to interests rather than people is in Donner (1991, 188–197).

11. Feinberg (1984, 26). Feinberg's Offense Principle says: "It is always a good reason in support of a proposed criminal prohibition that it is probably necessary to prevent serious offense to persons other than the actor and would probably be an effective means to that end if enacted." In what immediately follows, I focus on Feinberg's understanding of harm, postponing consideration of offense to chapter 11 and a succeeding volume. Feinberg recognizes a third liberty-limiting principle, the Soft Paternalism Principle, but it is more accurate to understand it as an application of the harm principle than as a principle of paternalism. I postpone discussion of this principle to chapter 9.

12. Mill does not limit himself to the criminal law; he discusses problems of taxation and regulation, for instance. But because he is silent about the problems of redress through a system of private law, confining the state to criminal law may well have been the major part of Mill's supposition about the extent of the harm principle's application. Feinberg concedes that his argument is sometimes inconsistent in concluding that a certain kind of conduct ought not be criminalized (hence not be considered a harm) but that it nevertheless might be dealt with by the government through alternative means, such as taxing. For example, he concludes that a criminal ban on smoking would be paternalistic but that taxing cigarette use would be permissible. He suggests two reasons for the distinction: Generally, criminal law is far more coercive than other governmental means of affecting conduct, and alternatives such as taxation may succeed in causing a "dangerous activity to pay its fair share of the considerable social costs." Feinberg (1984, 25). I think Feinberg's argument is inconsistent, for if the activity is dangerous, and may be taxed to compensate for social costs, then it is also harmful and so a criminal ban is not paternalistic. Writing before the widespread shift in American attitudes about smoking (volume 1 was written in the early 1980s), it is possible that Feinberg did not anticipate targeted bans on smoking (e.g., in the workplace) in which the rationale is explicitly that secondary smoke causes injury to others.

13. As I worked on an earlier version of this book, I queried Feinberg about his decision to restrict the harm principle to the criminal law. Why did he not broaden it to embrace all state action, as Mill evidently did? His response: "The one negative comment common to most readers and many reviewers of *The Moral Limits* is that I was too confined to the criminal law, that I should have developed and defended a theory to distinguish the punitive function of criminal law from the compensatory function of the law of torts, in particular. That is, between private and public law—*your* concern. Often these critics ask me why—for heaven sakes—I didn't do that, and my only honest (accurate) reply is that I didn't think of it!" Letter to the author from Joel Feinberg, October 10, 1994.
14. Feinberg (1984, 36).
15. Ibid., 31–64. I emphasize that here, as throughout the discussion of Feinberg's harm principle, I skim the surface of a very rich intellectual stew. Feinberg's subtleties, interesting examples and counterexamples, and analytical prowess are too extended to treat in a single volume.
16. "In this category are the interests in the continuance for a foreseeable interval of one's life, and the interests in one's body, the absence of absorbing pain and suffering or grotesque disfigurement, minimal intellectual acuity, emotional stability, the absence of groundless anxieties and resentments, the capacity to engage normally in social intercourse and to enjoy and maintain friendships, at least minimal income and financial security, a tolerable social and physical environment, and a certain amount of freedom from interference and coercion." Feinberg (1984, 37).
17. Ibid.
18. Ibid., 43.
19. Ibid., 44.
20. Feinberg (1984, 111) rules out an actor's claim to "morally disreputable interests": "If there are any interests in causing pain and suffering for their own sakes, for example, such interests cannot be the grounds of claims against others." Hence, no one can claim a "right" to inflict pain simply because he has an "interest" in doing so. Feinberg offers no reason beyond the intuitively obvious one for excluding morally disreputable interests; he simply postulates it. The explanation, I think, must be sought in the distinction between external and internal interests in the behavior of others. This point is covered at greater length in chapter 10.
21. A New York City Legal Aid Society handbook for lawyers working in the family courts lays out an astonishing variety of cases that have led to both acquittals and conviction. "In one case, inflicting cuts and bruises on a child was deemed 'excessive corporal punishment,' amounting to neglect, the most basic and frequently charged form of child mistreatment. But in another case, shaking a child and causing her to hit her head on the pavement was ruled allowable. Hitting a 9-year-old with the buckle end of a purse strap for leaving his 2-year-old sister alone in a room was acceptable. Hitting a child with a belt for lying on the floor, kicking a table and peeling paint off a wall was not." Newman and Kaufman (2008).
22. Feinberg (1984, 45).
23. Ibid., 51.
24. The real answer to the Epicurean's dilemma is that given his focal aims it is exceedingly unlikely he would willingly endure the pain and offense that filing a lawsuit would provoke. Or, as Feinberg (1984, 51) notes: "The Epicurean, if he is true to his creed, has acquired his own disciplined immunities. He will not let himself be hurt by his ill treatment at the hands of others, especially by the noncriminal conduct of others under a code derived from the harm principle as applied to standard interests."
25. Arthur Ripstein (2006, 242) has argued that the harm principle is inadequate to the task at just this point because it does not deal with cases of harmless wrongdoing. If your watch is none the worse for wear, if you did not miss it because you did not know it was gone, and if it is now back in your possession, your interest may not have been set back but you were nonetheless wronged because someone used your property without permission. As an alternative to the harm principle, he proposes a "sovereignty principle," which bars the doing of

something without the other person's consent in a form that "dominates" the other (using one's person or property for some unconsented purpose). It is unclear whether the sovereignty principle is anything more than a subtle modification of the harm principle and whether it brings its own theoretical problems. Almost all of the conduct that Ripstein says would be dealt with by the sovereignty principle would also be covered by the harm principle. The cases that would not are almost all sufficiently exotic (like the example of the watch) that the supposed inability of the harm principle to deal with them would not disturb our sense that it is robust enough to deal with the cases that count. Moreover, Ripstein explicitly declares that the sovereignty principle is a principle "governing *private* interactions," and "does not need to be hostile to *public* purposes" (242, emphasis in original). If the state may deal with matters not covered by the sovereignty principle by enacting legislation under an undefined concept of public purpose, it is likely that the force of the sovereignty principle's requirement of consent would be wholly undercut.

26. Although Feinberg's definition of setback appears straightforward, it has at least one unexpected consequence: It suggests that the traditional American law of conspiracy violates the harm principle. Under the usual rule, any two or more people who in the course of planning an unlawful activity take a single step to further their plan are guilty of conspiracy. (Some conspiracy statutes do not require that an overt act be performed. For example, under the New York penal law, "a person is guilty of conspiracy in the first degree when, with intent that conduct constituting a class A felony be performed, he, being over eighteen years of age, agrees with one or more persons under sixteen years of age to engage in or cause the performance of such conduct." N.Y. Penal Law § 105.17 (McKinney 2011). For a good discussion of the knowledge requirement, see Judge Learned Hand's majority opinion in *U.S. v. Falcone*, 109 F.2d 579 (2d Cir. 1940). See also Katyal (2003, 1309); Sarnoff (2011, 671–672). Suppose three friends decide to rob a bank. They discuss a plan one evening, and the next morning one of them shops at a hardware store for gloves and a crowbar, tools essential to the heist. If the goods were bought before anyone disavowed the plan, all are guilty of conspiracy, even though at that stage it is difficult to see how any interest has been set back. The bank has an interest in security and freedom of customers and employees from anxiety, but since no one connected with the bank knew anything about the plan, no one could have been in fear. Feinberg (1984, 20) discusses several so-called derivative or backup crimes—acts of disobedience to the system of justice, made punishable to enforce compliance with the system's commands; e.g., contempt of court for failing to carry out a judicial order. Other derivative crimes are tax and draft evasion, practicing medicine without a license, "and perhaps perjury, bribery, bail-jumping and escape from prison." It may be that conspiracy is, like these, a derivative crime, and therefore the state may properly intervene at some stage before the actual crime is carried out, to protect the public interest—that is, the interest of each of us—in the security of our property by minimizing the number of actual attempts against property.

27. As Feinberg (1984, 63) notes, it would be a severe practical problem for the state to apportion its protection to the gravity of the harm, and in any event prosecuting the unlucky thief who makes off with small change "does not interfere with the normal everyday exercise of individual liberty." In that connection, Feinberg (1984, 10) insists at the beginning of his work that no single liberty-limiting principle states conditions that are either necessary or sufficient for state intervention: There may be some other reason for limiting liberty than the one proposed in the harm principle, as indeed he later says in describing his separate offense principle, and some other reason for not limiting liberty, as he explains in chaps. 5 and 6 in discussing mediating maxims (for example, the crime is too trivial or a civil approach may be more sensible). That a harm principle governing criminal law may not state a sufficient condition says nothing about state action to limit liberty generally; a harm principle governing the whole range of state action does state a sufficient condition to engage governmental machinery. But for Mill the harm principle certainly does state a necessary condition, since it is the *sole* criterion for judging the legitimacy of state interference, and for that reason, Feinberg generally seems to treat it as necessary, despite his formal disavowal.

28. Holtug (2002, 368–373). Holtug does not analyze the harm principle in Feinberg's terms, so his terminology differs from how I characterize the problem in the text. It may be that if he were to view the sorts of problems he raises from the perspective of the Feinberg criteria, many of them would dissolve.
29. Ibid., 369.
30. Feinberg (1984, 109ff.).
31. Ibid., 111.
32. This problem is the subject of Feinberg (1988). Also, see the text at notes 36–39 in this chapter for a brief discussion of "harmless wrongdoing" in a context divorced from traditional concern about whether the underlying action is immoral.
33. Feinberg (1984, 111, 112). By "sick and wicked" interests, Feinberg refers to "[c]ertain kinds of morally disreputable interests [that] can be ruled out, straightaway, as possible grounds for valid moral claims. If there are any interests in causing pain and suffering for their own sakes, for example, such interests cannot be the grounds of claims against others."
34. This appears to be the answer to Larry Alexander (2005, 325), who says that "Feinberg has little to say about what distinguishes wrongful from nonwrongful harming or offending. For example, he does not contribute to the debate over whether negligently caused harm is 'wrongfully' caused or whether one who goes into business solely to bankrupt a competitor or who erects a 'spite fence' on his own property has 'wrongfully' harmed his intended victim." Feinberg did not suppose he needed to because his context was limited, as noted, to criminal law.
35. I disregard the difficulties of such crimes as manslaughter: reckless indifference to the likely consequences of an action, resulting in death. It is not strictly necessary for every crime to have a deliberate intent; but all crimes do incorporate some notion of culpability, some strong sense of foreseeability—if the defendant had been *thinking about* what he was doing, he would have realized that it was quite likely to lead to a serious injury.
36. Feinberg (1984, 20, 63).
37. This issue is discussed in detail in Lieberman (1973, 161–167, 274–280).
38. *Schlesinger v. Reservists Committee to Stop the War*, 418 U.S. 208 (1974).
39. Standing is a much vexed issue of federal jurisprudence. When a court denies standing it is saying that a litigant does not have a sufficient stake in the matter to give the argument about it the requisite particularity to ensure that in hearing the case the court will engage in more than an academic exercise. A failure of standing is usually tantamount to saying that the litigant has not been harmed by whatever he is complaining about. In this case, the Court refused to acknowledge that a citizen has an interest, no matter how dilute, in the proper functioning of government. The Court's refusal to be drawn into the controversy reflected its antipathy toward deciding citizen suits raising what it considers abstract constitutional questions. However, the suit over the Incompatibility Clause was not abstract at all, but quite sharply raised a fundamental question by the most relevantly interested parties—citizens demanding that their government live up to its fundamental constitutional obligations. Quite aside from the justiciability of the claim, nothing in the harm principle precludes a constitutional rule that an officeholder must have attained a certain age.
40. *Frothingham v. Mellon*, 262 U.S. 447 (1923). Indeed, when the question arose whether a spending program violated a *direct* prohibition of the Constitution, namely the Establishment Clause, a later Court granted standing to contest. *Flast v. Cohen*, 392 U.S. 83 (1968).
41. Wrongful conception, sometimes also known as wrongful birth, is the claim that a child born in a subpar condition (retarded, diseased, illegitimate) was harmed and wronged by the act of conceiving it, as was alleged, for example, in *Williams v. New York*, 18 N.Y.2d 481, 233 N.E.2d 343 (1966), in which the plaintiff's mother, a mentally deficient patient in a state institution, was raped by an attendant.
42. Feinberg (1984, 102). When Feinberg wrote, wrongful conception was mostly a philosophical curiosity, rarely arising in court. I suspect that much worse is yet to come to test our understanding of the harm principle. One has only to contemplate the possibility of genetic

engineering: Wanting your child to be blond and blue-eyed (or not) is perhaps of no consequence, but giving your child four arms is of every consequence, and it is only the beginning of what we can imagine, and if we can imagine it, can it be far behind? For more recent discussions, see Fredericks (1993); Mason (2007); Priaulx (2007).
43. Feinberg (1985, 3).
44. For example, Feinberg (1988, 271) argues that a tort action might be preferable to criminal law in some circumstances simply because it is less intrusive: "In principle then it is morally legitimate to criminalize threats to withhold favorable information as blackmail. But there is no real need to go so far if adequate civil remedies are provided. Court orders to produce the evidence are surely a more economical intrusion on private liberty." He also notes in several places that a civil law preventing people from enforcing their evil contracts is a surer way of avoiding and redressing a wrong than a criminal prosecution; e.g., Feinberg (1986, 15, 71–72).
45. Actually, there is a context in which it makes some sense to talk this way. The very premise of liberalism is that the state should not choose the good because there is a less intrusive, better way of arriving at it, namely the unhindered choice of each person acting privately; likewise, the premise of the economic market is that the free choice of buyers and sellers will yield an efficient result that the state could not manage. But it makes no sense to say that the state should defer to these same networks of unconstrained free choices to redress and deter harms when it is these very networks that produce the harm.
46. Feinberg (1988, 253).
47. Feinberg (1984, 36). Again, I emphasize that Feinberg means by this claim about the harm principle to limit the use of criminal law. He does not intend, and that is my point, to rule out interventions against nonwrongful harms as long as they are not dealt with by the criminal process. Indeed, he deals with just such interventions in Feinberg (1984, chaps. 5 and 6).
48. Feinberg (1984, 203).
49. Ibid., 191ff.
50. As the puerile but potent slogan of the gun lobby goes: "Guns don't kill; people do." However, see Polsby (1994, 58); Zimring (2003). Polsby asserts that "gun-control laws don't work," making it more difficult for legitimate users, even as "illicit markets easily adapt to whatever difficulties a free society throws in their way."
51. In 2008 and 2010, the Supreme Court held for the first time that the Second Amendment confers an individual right, enforceable against both the states and federal government. *District of Columbia v. Heller*, 554 U.S. 570 (2008); *McDonald v. City of Chicago, Illinois*, 130 S.Ct. 3020 (2010). Although the Court struck down a flat ban on keeping handguns in the home, it explicitly acknowledged that the right is not absolute and left open the possibility of continuing bans on sales to certain classes of people, of certain sorts of weapons, and carrying them in certain places.
52. The question of effective regulatory policy is separate, of course, from the question whether any particular policy is consistent with the constitutional requirements of the Second Amendment. In any event, the problem of aggregative harms is pervasive. In 1993 the Consumer Product Safety Commission ordered that all disposable cigarette lighters be child-proofed because children start more than 5,000 residential fires a year, leading to 150 deaths and 1,500 injuries. To reduce the number of fires started by someone else, the order requiring manufacturers to spend more money than they otherwise would have had to spend is neither paternalistic nor punitive; rather, it is aimed at the aggregative harm that arises from improperly supervised children. "Lighters" (1993).
53. Mill (1974, 221 [chap. 4, ¶19]).
54. Ibid.
55. See Sunstein (2005). For an assessment and critique of Sunstein's approach, see Mandel and Tathii (2006).
56. Philosophers know the accumulation problem as the sorites paradox or the paradox of the heap. When does the addition of sufficient units to the pile of things being accumulated

constitute a heap (or accumulation) of them? One grain of sand is not a heap, but then neither are two grains, and so on, so that there cannot be a heap. Understandably, policy-makers, impatient with logical puzzles, need not be detained by this paradox. They may simply look at the accumulation, at whatever point the consequences become (or can be anticipated to become) sufficiently troubling, and decide to legislate a solution to deal with whatever has accumulated.

57. Feinberg (1984, 231).
58. As Brian Barry (1965, 198) summarizes Rousseau's explanation of this principle: "Rousseau does not deny that it may be in your interest to *break* a law which benefits you *qua* member of the community; all he says is that it is certainly in your interests to *vote* for it, and that if you have voted in favour of a certain punishment for a certain crime you have no business to complain if your wish for a certain general policy is applied to you in a particular case."
59. A principal complaint about litigation today in the United States is that we are stretching beyond sensible limits to find *particular* persons to hold accountable for accumulative harms. But the answer, often rejected by the complainers, is that if the accountable persons are so diffuse that it is injudicious to pin personal responsibility on particular people, then we must seek a different remedy (e.g., direct regulation). The real issue is not whether we suffer harm, or whether state intervention is legitimate, but what the nature of that intervention, the remedy, should be. See Lieberman (1990).
60. Even in criminal cases, the issue of causation is difficult. A general analysis of causation can fill volumes. See, e.g., Hart and Honoré (1985). I sidestep the problem because my concern is not to discuss specific cases but simply to indicate that different types of harm will require different theories of causation.

Chapter 4

1. On earthquakes, see Shrady (2008).
2. Kennedy (1994), reviewing Kearns (1994).
3. Actually it masks two ambiguities. The other arises from the terms in which the question is usually put: Are these social forces beyond *our* control; is there nothing *we* can do about it? If the question is whether a single individual can counter the tide of history, the answer is almost surely that he cannot. Even the "hero in history" cannot effect any change he wills, and there are few such heroes. See Hook (1955). But this consideration does not mean that *we*, collectively, might not be able to direct our affairs more satisfactorily than letting things drift.
4. The question in all such cases is whether human agency is somehow mixed in the natural occurrence. If the boat was badly built, so that a sturdier one might have withstood the foreseeable gale, a remediable harm may well have been caused by human beings. See chapter 5 on the problem of public provisioning of welfare and benefits.
5. Smith (1937, 14 [Book I, chap. 2]).
6. On the harmony thesis, see generally Hirschman (1977).
7. Cf. Edmund Burke (1969, 271), who noted the "innumerable servile, degrading, unseemly, unmanly, and often most unwholesome and pestiferous occupations to which by the social economy so many wretches are inevitably doomed." Some invisible hand!
8. Hammond and Hammond (1968, 29). The Hammonds' studies have been severely criticized. F. A. Hayek labels as the "one supreme myth" the "legend of the deterioration of the position of the working classes in consequence of the rise of capitalism." See Hayek (1963, 9–10), who cites studies to suggest that the Hammonds were wrong to assert that standards of income and welfare declined from the eighteenth to the early nineteenth century, and even points to an admission by the Hammonds themselves that later data establish that earnings increased during this period. Hammond and Hammond (1947, 15). I cite the Hammonds here not for the proposition that conditions worsened but for observations of how bad things in fact were.

9. Ibid., 17.
10. Marx and Engels (1978, 479).
11. Townsend (1971, 35–36).
12. Mandeville (1970, 294). Arblaster (1986, 174–175) comments: "Mandeville's very candour exposes a double standard at the heart of his argument. For while the high incomes and lavish spending of the rich will stimulate production, similar practices by the 'multitude of Laborious Poor' are by no means to be encouraged. Society is to consist of an elite of consumers supported by a great mass of producers."
13. President of Royal Society quoted in Hammond and Hammond (1968, 49).
14. The best short account of Malthus and Ricardo is still Heilbroner (1980, chap. 4); see also Lekachman (1959, chaps. 6–7).
15. Spencer (1970, 339–340). The quoted passage is Spencer's argument against sanitation laws; for his identical argument against poor laws, see 288ff. Richard Hofstadter (1955, 41) summarizes his arguments. Though I have characterized Spencer as arguing that life or death is "deserved," his words are, I concede, a bit cryptic. He never expressly argued that life and death are moral deserts, but his statement that it is "well" that people live or die seems more than a biological conclusion which, then, would be but a tautology. In a draft of this book, I occasionally called Spencer and others "social Darwinists," but my colleague Edward A. Purcell urged me to abandon this usage because "there were very few true 'social Darwinists' and the rhetoric that seems to be 'social Darwinist' is not for the most part really 'Darwinist' at all." Personal communication (n.d.). For more on this point, which is not necessary to the argument I am pressing, see, in addition to Hofstadter, Bannister (1955); Persons (1956, 160–266).
16. Hammond and Hammond (1968, 172).
17. Holmes (1963, 76).
18. Hayek (1976, 38).
19. Shklar (1990, 80).
20. Hayek (1976, 37).
21. "Primum non nocere"—first, do no harm—commonly thought to be the first dictum of medical ethics does not in fact appear in the Hippocratic oath; the phrase evidently comes from Galen. But a form of it appears in the ancient oath and in the oath that most physicians swear upon entering the profession. While even within the world of medicine the rule is not free from ambiguity, its basic meaning derives from a context that is missing from the field of social interaction generally. The rule commands the doctor to heal or at least relieve the patient. It does not require the doctor to consider how an evil person might harm others once the doctor has effected a cure.
22. Portions of this section derive from Lieberman (1981a, 10–12) and (1990, 105).
23. See Macfarlane (1970); Thomas (1971); Kors and Peters (2001); Simmons (1974); Geschiere (1997); Ashforth (2005).
24. The closest the common law came to permitting suits against nature was the concept of deodand, the forfeiture to the crown of animals or even inanimate things that killed a human being. "In the oldest records," say Pollock and Maitland (1968, 2:474n4), "we see no attempt to distinguish the cases in which the dead man was negligent from those in which no fault could be imputed to him, and the large number of deodands collected in every eyre suggests that many horses and boats bore the guilt which should have been ascribed to beer."
25. Polanyi (1944).
26. Cf. Wolfe (2009, 90): "Once culture replaces nature, in short, everyone becomes dependent on each other, and because of that, everyone deserves the support of everyone else."
27. See, generally, Haskell (1977, esp. chaps. 2, 11).
28. Quoted in Holbrook (1954, 34–35).
29. Rousseau (1964, 96).
30. Niebuhr quoted in Carr (1941, 203).
31. Ross (1907, 9).
32. Commager (1950, 332–333).

33. On the market as a general coordinating system, see Lindblom (2001, 1977).
34. Hirschman (1991, 7).
35. "The jeopardy thesis argues that the cost of the proposed change or reform is too high as it endangers some previous, precious accomplishment." Ibid.
36. Murray (1984, 9).
37. Hayek (1944, 1960, 1973, 1976, 1979).
38. Arblaster (1986, 285).
39. I do not mean to imply that the output of American legislatures is invariably liberal, in the sense of harm preventing and redressing. We live, after all, in a society that is only partially liberal, and often antiliberal.
40. The choice lies in the moral realm, not in the physical or historical realm. Feinberg (1984, 121) notes that a hotly "debated issue among jurisprudential writers is how we are to distinguish *the* cause of a harm from the welter of events that are acknowledged causal factors. Put from the opposite vantage point, the question is how we are to identify the consequences of a given act of wrongdoing. A given act can have effects radiating out to great distances in space and echoing through the corridors of time for centuries. There may be an infinite number of ways in which the world will be different because this act was done and not another. Yet clearly not all of these future effects can be charged to the act in question as its consequences, no more than the act itself is the consequence of every prior event but for which it would not have been done. The making of singular causal judgments in the interest of such practical purposes as imputations of responsibility obviously requires that infinite causal chains, both past and future, be severed abruptly."
41. See Horwitz (1977, 114–116).
42. Ibid., 44.
43. Mill (1974, 227 [chap. 5]).
44. Feinberg (1984, 36). A similar argument was presented to the Supreme Court in 1837. A toll bridge company argued that a charter granted it by the state to construct a bridge was a legal monopoly, and that a later charter to a competing company building a toll-free bridge must be revoked. The Court disagreed. *Charles River Bridge Co. v. Warren River Bridge*, 36 U.S. (11 Pet.) 420 (1837).
45. Feinberg (1984, 31).
46. The idea that the state can enhance its power to govern effectively by limiting its reach is a major theme of Stephen Holmes's analysis of liberalism (1995, chap. 4).
47. The centralization of power and the consequent sapping of responsibility can reach absurd heights. Roy A. Medvedev (1975, 125) provided a brilliant example: "Not long ago in Moscow an Old Communist, who had participated at many party congresses, died. His friends and comrades, also veteran party members, brought an obituary to *Pravda* signed by all of them. A member of the editorial board responsible for such things was at a loss what to do—he himself was unable to decide whether or not the deceased came into the category of persons about whom it was permissible to write in *Pravda*. In order to settle this 'problem,' he had to telephone the Central Committee, which gave him permission to publish. But then there arose a new, no less fundamental uncertainty. How should the obituary be signed—with the surnames of the friends of the deceased or without any names at all, using instead the standard anonymous formula, 'a group of comrades'? Here again this editor of *Pravda* did not have sufficient authority to make a decision. Once more he had to call the Central Committee and talk at great length with an official of the apparat (it was decided not to include the signatures)."
48. The example is described in detail in Porter and van der Linde (1995, 125). Malcolm Gladwell (1997, 49) quotes Porter and van der Linde: "The belief that companies will pick up on profitable opportunities without a regulatory push makes a false assumption about competitive reality—namely, that all profitable opportunities for innovation have already been discovered, that all managers have perfect information about them, and that organizational incentives are aligned with innovating. In fact, in the real world, managers often have highly incomplete information and limited time and attention."

49. Huxley (1896, 36–37).
50. See, e.g., Stewart Macaulay (1963, 55).
51. The reasons are spelled out in more detail in chapters 5 and 6.
52. Smith (1937, 128–129, 429, 460).
53. Coleman (1992, 435).
54. The collapse of the stock market in the fall of 2008, signaling the "Great Recession," prompted the Bush administration to come running to Congress for authority to deal with the crisis in ways that mocked its pretensions of fidelity to "free market" hands-off policies. Even the most deeply committed libertarians, in particular, former Federal Reserve chairman Alan Greenspan, confessed error and conceded the necessity of government intervention. See Andrews (2008).
55. Constant quoted in Arblaster (1986, 233). For a discussion of Constant, see Holmes (1984); see also Manent (1994, chap. 8).
56. Hayek (1976, 37). Hayek attributes this understanding to Hume and Kant.
57. Woodham-Smith (1991).
58. Nozick (1974, ix).
59. Hobhouse (1994, 70). Hobhouse's essay appeared originally in 1911. For other classic progressive responses, see Addams (1910); Frankfurter (1930).
60. The employers also argue that the governor's proposed legislation is paternalistic. About that they are incorrect, as chapter 9 explains. G.A. Cohen (1987, 65) argues that a worker can be simultaneously forced to take on hazardous work and free to do so. The intricate argument was devoted to explaining how both right-wingers, who claim that the worker was free to decline, and left-wingers, who assert that the worker was coerced, could both be correct. Much of the argument is a play on words (or a plea to use words correctly), for Cohen notes that the worker is free to take on the job he is forced into, "even if, as is usually true, I do not do it freely."
61. See Feinberg (1986, 247).
62. Feinberg (1984, chap. 4). I am paraphrasing the argument broadly.
63. For more on duty to rescue, see chapters 5 and 6.
64. T. H. Huxley (1893, 192–193) once wrote: "If some great power would agree to make me always think what is true and do what is right, on condition of being turned into a sort of clock and wound up every morning before I got out of bed, I should instantly close with the offer. The only freedom I care about is the freedom to do right; the freedom to do wrong I am ready to part with on the cheapest terms to anyone who will take it of me." One commentator says that these words "prove [Huxley], great and liberal though he was, a readymade and willing citizen of Plato's Republic." Christopher Morris (1967, 45). Not necessarily. Let's continue the story. Suppose Huxley had answered a knock at the door to discover a strange figure with a fringe of light about his brow, who informed Huxley that the stranger had read Huxley's *cri de coeur*, that he was delighted to have been summoned to the eminent author's abode, and that, inasmuch as he was the Great Power come at last, Huxley should prepare to have the key inserted and be wound up. We can imagine Huxley inviting the stranger in for tea and questioning him minutely, only to conclude that his claim is unproved and thus to bid him good day without becoming a clock.
65. The picture of the owner rowing around with a notary at his side is, I hope it will be agreed, too fanciful even for these fanciful speculations—one might just as well say: "Well, but suppose *God told* the judge that the owner was telling the truth."
66. The Supreme Court told the story in its much lambasted 5–4 decision in *Lochner v. New York*, 198 U.S. 45 (1905).
67. This must be their claim. If an owner admitted that he could afford to provide better conditions but simply wished not to do so (or we had strong reason to believe that he was lying when he denied that he could afford the cost), then the state could justify weighing more heavily the interest of the workers in their health and safety than the interest of the owner in refusing to improve conditions.

68. Hobhouse (1994, 42–43) argued that "in the field that has been in question the contention is that one party is not willing. The bargain is a forced bargain. The weaker man consents as one slipping over a precipice might consent to give all his fortune to one who will throw him a rope on no other terms. This is not true consent. True consent is free consent, and full freedom of consent implies equality on the part of both parties to the bargain. Just as government first secured the elements of freedom for all when it prevented the physically stronger man from slaying, beating, despoiling his neighbours, so it secures a larger measure of freedom for all by every restriction which it imposes with a view to preventing one man from making any use of his advantages to the disadvantage of others."
69. Mill (1970, 314 [Book V, chap. 11, §7]; 329–330 [Book V, chap. 11, §12]). In exactly the same year, Alexis de Tocqueville equated regulation of working hours with "despotism" and said that "nothing authorizes the state to interfere in industry." Quoted in Losurdo (2011, 196).
70. In general, see Nove (1992), Bardhan and Roemer (1993), Roemer (1994), Weil (1996), Ollman (1998), Schweickart (1996, 2002), Bockman (2011).
71. Mill (1970, 118–143, 141 [Book IV, chap. 7]).
72. For a brief comparative analysis of market socialism, both as an aspect of capitalist systems and as an entire system, see Lindblom (1977, 95–97, 112–114, 339–343). For Yugoslavia, in particular, Dirlam and Plummer (1973). For China, Weil (1996), Garrick (2012), Hsu (2007).
73. Roemer (1994); Schweickart quotation from Ollman (1998, 18).
74. Schweickart, in Ollman (1998, 18). His basic economic model is set out in Schweickart (1996, 69–77).
75. Ollman (1998, 18).
76. Schweickart (1996, 184–193).
77. Ibid., 282. Schweickart (2002, 173–177) offers some mitigation for the harsh effects of his four laws, though it is unclear from his short analysis whether his proposals would meet constitutional standards, let alone the economic and psychological effects of a socialist takeover.

Chapter 5

1. On classical liberal arguments for welfare, see Stephen Holmes (1995, 247–265).
2. Hobbes (1981, 387 [Book II, chap. 30]).
3. Locke (1965b, 329 [chap. 5 §27]; 1965a, 206 [chap. 4 §42]).
4. Smith (1937, 79).
5. Burke quoted from *Thoughts and Details on Scarcity* in Macpherson (1980, 56, 59).
6. Herbert Spencer (1970, 288).
7. On the potato famine, see Woodham-Smith (1991).
8. Paine (1995, 6–7).
9. See Paine (1995, 625ff [Part II, chap. V]).
10. Arblaster (1986, 230).
11. Mill, laissez-faire: (1970, 314 [Book V, chap. 11, §7]); charity: (ibid., 333–336 [§13]); crime: (ibid., 335). On this last point, Stephen Holmes (1995, 253) comments: "In effect, welfare support is a payment to the indigent for refraining from crimes (against the rich, among others). If criminals who are apprehended are given food and shelter, then how, for safety's sake, can the noncriminal poor be guaranteed any less?"
12. Hobhouse (1994, 76–77, 86–90); Moon (1993, 129); Tawney (1961); Kymlicka (1990, 75). On Rawls and Dworkin, see the Appendix. Rawls (1971, 302) begins with a right to liberty and constructs a secondary "difference principle" that calls for "social and economic inequalities . . . to be arranged so that they are . . . to the greatest benefit of the least advantaged." Dworkin (1985, 203) begins explicitly with a right to equality: "[Liberalism's] constitutive morality provides that human beings must be treated as equals by their government,

not because there is no right and wrong in political morality, but because that is what is right." On failure of government: Wellman (1982, 134).
13. Nozick (1974, 168). Nozick considers redistribution "from the perspective of an entitlement theory," which I explore below as an analogue of the harm principle.
14. Hayek (1979, 55). Although Hayek consistently maintained the need for a social "safety net," he never defended his position, which remained an ad hoc judgment throughout his works.
15. Fried (1987, 101).
16. Lomasky (1990, 128).
17. The dichotomy between "negative" and "positive" is a staple of the political literature in the context of freedom. As described by Isaiah Berlin (1969, 122, 131) in his well-known essay "Two Concepts of Liberty," one is "said to be [negatively] free to the degree to which no man or body of men interferes with my activity.... You lack political liberty or freedom only if you are prevented from attaining a goal by human beings. Mere incapacity to attain a goal is not lack of political freedom." Positive freedom, by contrast, "derives from the wish on the part of the individual to be his own master." The concept of positive liberty is dangerous, Berlin declared, because it can be used to justify coercing people to achieve their "true" or "higher" freedom. But, as Gerald MacCallum (1972, 176) pointed out in an essay a few years after Berlin published his, freedom is a triadic relationship and can always be expressed in the formula X is free from Y to do Z: "Whenever the freedom of some agent or agents is in question, it is always freedom from some constraint or restriction on, interference with, or barrier to doing, not doing, becoming, or not becoming something." Nevertheless, the concept of negative and positive rights seems to play a useful role in thinking through the application of the harm principle to social provisioning.
18. Herbert Spencer (1970, 279) made the point in a homespun way: "The notion..., that everyone has a right to a maintenance out of the soil, leaves those who adopt it in an awkward predicament.... [A]sk for some precise definition of it; inquire, 'What is a maintenance?' They are dumb. 'Is it,' say you, 'potatoes and salt, with rags and a mud cabin? Or is it bread and bacon in a two-roomed cottage? Will a joint on Sundays suffice? Or does the demand include meat and malt liquor daily? Will tea, coffee, and tobacco be expected? And if so, how many ounces of each? Are bare walls and brick floors all that is needed? Or must there be carpets and paper hangings? Are shoes considered essential? Or will the Scotch practice be approved? Shall the clothing be of fustian? If not, of what quality must the broadcloth be? In short, just point out where, between the two extremes of starvation and luxury, this something called a maintenance lies.' Again they are dumb."
19. Fried (1978, 108).
20. Plant (1991, 269).
21. Fried (1978, 110).
22. Ibid., 113.
23. Plant (1978, 270).
24. Mill (1974b, 309).
25. Donner (1991, 173–174).
26. Feinberg (1984, 109): "Every person has a claim both against other individuals and against the state to force performance from others of what is my due, or to protect me, by threat of punishment, from unwarranted interference from other individuals. My legal claim not to be punched in the nose has this double character: it is a claim against all other citizens to their noninterference and a claim against the state to its protection."
27. That I do not have a claim-right against the state to enforce my negative right against being harmed means only that the state must first recognize negative rights as legal entitlements. There is no natural law of torts or crimes: Through its various agencies the state must declare them (as the common law courts do) or enact them (as legislatures do). Once established, it then of course makes sense to think of a right against being assaulted, say, as a right that I may demand the state enforce. This principle is well-established in criminal law: No one has a right to have a malefactor tried; prosecutors have discretion whether to indict. In civil law, we

generally view the courts as obligated to hear our cases; they do not normally have discretion to decline to hear a complaint if jurisdictional prerequisites are met.
28. For a detailed justification of taxes in liberal states, see Holmes and Sunstein (1999).
29. Nozick (1974, 153ff.).
30. Ibid., 161.
31. Both quotations, ibid.
32. Ibid., 151.
33. Ibid.
34. By implication at least, Nozick says a good deal about the rules of justice in transfer, and in one passage discusses justice in acquisition according to Locke (174–182). But he is forthrightly silent about the rules of rectification; indeed, he says that he does "not know of a thorough or theoretically sophisticated treatment" of the issues involved in a theory of rectification (152). As I suggest, a "pure theory of rectification" is impossible.
35. The idea of knowing and free consent includes the notion that the transferee was not tricked by a promise of assets or performance that was later breached. As Susan Moller Okin (1989, 79–88) makes clear, Nozick's principle of justice in acquisition is seriously deficient because it cannot avoid the conclusion, once you get down to cases, that every mother owns her children. But that contradicts his most basic point, that every person has rights. To protect children from just this conclusion, something far more than a minimal state will be necessary. See the section "Children and Families" in this chapter.
36. You do not need to be a Marxist to agree with at least the thrust of Marx's conclusion that "conquest, enslavement, robbery, murder, in short, force," have played a part (Marx said "the greatest part") in the accumulation of property. Marx (1977, 874). A stunning example of the failure of rectification built into the foundations of the state is what happened as the Soviet Union was imploding in 1991. As party apparatchiks deserted the Soviet government and took up residence in the Russian government, they stole, plundered, and looted vast amounts of the "people's" assets. Kotkin (2001).
37. Historically, tradition or custom substituted for literacy and written records, and these are a poor substitute for more rigorous notions of justice. "Every act, especially if it was repeated three or four times, was likely to be transformed into a precedent—even if in the first instance it had been exceptional or even frankly unlawful. In the ninth century, when one day there was a shortage of wine in the royal cellars at Ver, the monks of Saint-Denis were asked to supply the two hundred hogsheads required. This contribution was thenceforward claimed from them as of right every year, and it required an imperial charter to abolish it." Bloch (1961, 114).
38. De Tocqueville (1955, 61–62).
39. Nozick (1974, 231).
40. In the complex reality of the historical world, an argument might be offered that it is unlikely a society rich enough to afford welfare payments was wholly innocent of harmful wrongs done these people. It would, of course, have to be a very complicated argument and despite strong anti-immigrant sentiments that aliens (particularly illegal aliens) are not entitled to welfare assistance, the practical difficulties of proof would likely lead back to an administrable criterion such as poverty, rather than moral desert.
41. I note without resolving a particular difficulty in viewing welfare as a principle of compensatory justice. The problem of compensation requires an answer to two related questions: (1) Who is entitled to be compensated? and (2) Who must pay the compensation? Like almost everyone who writes about this problem, I have focused on the first question and ignored the second. But it is incorrect to assume that the answer to the first question provides the answer to the second. Since we are not sure who has been victimized by past acts of injustice, it makes sense, I have argued, to adopt welfare programs as an approximation to the principle of rectification. But welfare must be paid for, and an issue of fairness on the other side remains. If we must be fair to those who will be receiving, we should be no less fair to those who will be giving. Surely there are some people in society who we can say with confidence

have not exploited or acted unjustly toward the least well off, just as there are some people who we can confidently suppose have not benefited from any of the injustices that we are trying to rectify. For example, a recently arrived wealthy immigrant or a very hard-working person who began life poor may have cheated none who are in the class of welfare recipients. But the argument against trying to carve out a class of "morally irreproachable" persons from a general tax law is the vast impracticability and expense of doing so. What administrative machinery would determine those who belong to groups that either committed or benefited from some violation of a rule of justice in acquisition or transfer? Just as to prevent an aggregative harm the state may limit the liberty of all, even those who would cause no harm by, say, speeding, so the state may require all who are wealthy enough to be taxed to bear the cost of providing for those who are least well off; in effect, a principle of "aggregative compensation." Many of these issues are explored in works on "reparative justice." But they generally treat a particular form of historical injustice, such as slavery, toward particular groups of people whose descendants are ostensibly identified by group characteristics, such as race, rather than consider individuals whose ancestors happen to have been harmed without recompense in any one of innumerable ways. For an acute look at many of these difficulties, see Thompson (2002).

42. Beginning in early 2008, a national debate raged over whether to provide relief for those who have lost or were about to lose their homes to foreclosure resulting from the collapse of the housing market. It seems clear both that many unwary people were essentially tricked into signing dangerous mortgage instruments and that many others were simply greedy and have been hurt by their own stupidity or greed. Sorting between these claims is a task for adroit policy-making, but the difficulty does not make illegitimate legislative attempt to ease the crisis.

43. Terry (1994).

44. Such were the arguments in several high-profile corporate support programs during the past three decades, ranging from the Chrysler bailout, debated in the fall of 1979 and signed in January 1980 (in which the government was a co-signer and guarantor but did not put up the money needed to rescue the ailing automaker), to the massive federal bailout of automobile companies, banks, and other financial institutions, beginning in 2008 when the stock market crashed and the country slid into deep recession.

45. Hayek (1979, 55) argues essentially this. Providing a social minimum is necessary in a society "in which the individual no longer has specific claims on the members of the particular small group into which he was born. A system which aims at tempting large numbers to leave the relative security which the membership in the small group has given would probably soon produce great discontent and violent reaction when those who have first enjoyed its benefits find themselves without help when, through no fault of their own, their capacity to earn a living ceases."

46. Nozick (1974, 169).

47. Ibid., 172.

48. Nozick justifies compulsory taxation by demonstrating the obligation of subscribers to the dominant protection agency to compensate nonsubscribers who lose the opportunity to engage in self-help remedies when the dominant agency assumes a monopoly of coercive force. Ibid., 24–25, 114–115.

49. Donner (1991, 176–177). The argument is not Donner's own belief but her characterization of it, to which she provides responses.

50. To cite only one of countless examples, 10,000 of the 70,000 Chinese deaths in the wake of a devastating earthquake in Sichuan Province in May 2008 were caused by faulty construction of schools. The scale of suffering was immeasurably compounded by grievous mistakes, intentional and negligent, from the highest levels of policy to the workers' construction practices. Put aside that China is not a liberal society, it would hardly be sensible to suppose that private assistance could save people on the scale of the disaster that confronted those in the affected areas. Jacobs (2008).

Notes to Pages 112–119   301

51. Steinberg (2000, 33, 97, 66).
52. Ibid., 33–42, 47–68.
53. Different generations will point to their own dimly remembered examples: the malformation of Thalidomide babies in the late 1950s, the Love Canal deformities that came to light in the late 1970s, and the continuing course of genetic problems stemming from the 1986 meltdown at Chernobyl.
54. Cf. the stories of government bungling and "conspiracy" with private actors in covering up the causes of natural disasters, in Steinberg (2000) with the successful outcome of several New Deal programs, told in Leighninger (2007).
55. The benefits Smith had in mind were "works ... for facilitating the commerce of the society," including "good roads, bridges, navigable canals, harbours, &c." and public education. Smith (1937, 681ff. [public works]; 7616ff. [education of youth]).
56. Mill (1974, 136 [chap. 1, ¶11]).
57. Mill (1970, 150–151 [Book V, chap. 1]).
58. Stephen (1991, 61).
59. Feinberg (1989, 315). This argument assumes that taxation is equivalent to a loss of liberty. But as explained in the text at notes 46–49, the mere fact of taxation is consistent with the harm principle, and so the objection to public goods under the harm principle must ultimately rest more on the project than on its cost.
60. Again, Feinberg can afford the concession, because for him the harm principle explains the limits of criminal law, not the limits of all state activity. The problem is more acute when resting on Mill's asserted principle in *On Liberty*.
61. Cf. the argument in chapter 7, text at notes 40–46, for basing democratic procedural regularity on the harm principle itself.
62. So, for example, libraries directly support the government itself by holding and cataloging records essential to government operations: laws, regulations, reports of court decisions, investigative reports, and the like. Broader libraries, collecting the books, periodicals, and printed ephemera of the nation's publishers, may be directly useful to the government, too, insofar as officials need access to the writings that constitute and explain the society in which it operates, but they are also justifiable as places in which citizens can go for like purposes to undertake a study of government, its operations, and the matters to which people may conclude it ought, or ought not, attend. So too, though perhaps the case is a bit more attenuated, collections of art and artifacts in museums. For one argument favoring public support of the arts, see Dworkin (1985, 221–233). Other major projects—space travel, basic physics research—may be explained as related to national security and defense, or may, rather, simply be undertakings that someone would very much like to do, with the assistance of a cooperative member of Congress with a penchant for earmarks. I leave the classification of these and many other projects for another day.
63. Mill (1974, 147, 148).
64. Once again, I emphasize that what can be shown is the cogency of *some* contract rules under the harm principle, not any *particular set* of contract rules. I do not suppose that every section of the Uniform Commercial Code or the *Restatement of Contracts* is directly explicable under the harm principle. But it need not be. What the harm principle endorses is the idea of a contracts code. For a general history of changes in the law of contracts, see Atiyah (1979).
65. Beyond primary rules, the state inevitably must supplement the code books with rules designed to implement and enforce them, including prohibition of derivative crimes, acts that must be sanctioned if the commands of the law are to be enforced.
66. Of course a public fire department might be wholly justified by the need to deal with negligence and put down arson, a project fully consonant with the harm principle. And as already noted in the text after note 50 in this chapter, fire protection is justifiable on welfare grounds.
67. As Feinberg (1984, 129) puts it: "If a general duty to rescue in some circumstances may be imposed on the public then there will be no principled way of drawing the line between aid

in unanticipated emergencies near at hand, and aid to starving paupers or the distant needy who cannot be saved without extreme inconvenience, unfair sacrifice, or unreasonable risk."
68. Ibid., 170.
69. See text after note 50 in this chapter.
70. Compare to Judith Shklar's quite different sense that "when we can alleviate suffering, whatever its cause, it is passively unjust to stand by and do nothing. It is not the origin of injury, but the possibility of preventing and reducing its costs, that allows us to judge whether there was or was not unjustifiable passivity in the face of disaster" (1990, 81).
71. The distinct problem of the state's relation to future generations beyond our children and grandchildren is considered in chapter 9.
72. By what right do parents bring children into the world? The biblical injunction to be fruitful is not philosophically binding nor is an argument from biology. Does the impossibility of seeking the unborn's consent mean that the decision to conceive is morally tainted? What kind of a thing is existence that a nonexisting person could have a right to it? Nozick (1974, 38) suggests, without necessarily endorsing, the argument that "to exist for a while is better than never to exist at all" but that is a theory of what is good, not a theory of what is right. Kant held that a person may never be used solely for another's ends. Are children conceived as ends in themselves or as objects of pride for their parents, as workers, as comfort in a parent's old age, or as carriers of immortality? (Hear Gabe Pressman, the New York television commentator, ruminating a generation ago on the meaning of his son's birth when Pressman was sixty, in what must be the funniest statement of the proposition ever made: "Now that I'm older and wiser, I realize immortality is the most important thing about life, and that you probably achieve it best through children"; quoted in Klemesrud [1985]). Is it as an end in itself that a child is conceived to carry on the family name or even the human race itself? Perhaps it is possible to skirt the issue of a right to existence by denying the claim of harm in having been born (the unborn, obviously, never complain). Feinberg (1984, 102) says of a claim that a doctor's negligence resulted in the birth of a child with serious defects: "To be harmed is to be put in a worse condition than one would otherwise be in . . ., but if the negligent act had not occurred, [the person] would not have existed at all. The creation of an initial condition is not the worsening of a prior condition; therefore it is not a harm, no matter how harmful it is."
73. Recall the problem of defining the line between corporal punishment and abuse in chapter 3, note 21. If a child is abandoned, the state must have the authority to take the child in and find a suitable means of raising it to adulthood, regardless of the cause of abandonment. The death of parents may not be their fault, but there seems no way around the conclusion that the setback to the interest of the orphan is wrongful for purposes of the harm principle and likewise, but more obviously, for the child who is abandoned. Many libertarians—including apparently Nozick (1974, 265)—hold that private agencies can deal with such problems. The superiority of private to public activity is an old concept. Long ago, Justice Holmes (1961, 77) asserted that "universal insurance, if desired, can be better and more cheaply accomplished by private enterprise." But the discussion here is not about whether private agencies could do the job or even do it better, but about what would happen if they did not. The state acts legitimately in setting the ground rules and even administering orphanages, regardless of who else might act or do it better.
74. Feinberg (1986, 326). See also Feinberg (1980); Laslett (1992, 24–47).
75. The positions of Locke and other Enlightenment figures are taken from Gay (1977, 518–522). In "An Essay on Charity and Charity Schools," added to *The Fable of the Bees* in 1723, Mandeville (1970, 294, 320) said: "To make the Society Happy and People Easy under the meanest Circumstances, it is requisite that great numbers of them should be Ignorant as well as Poor." And "By bringing them up in Ignorance, . . . we shall have made . . . Labor cheap [and] we must infallibly out-sell our Neighbours."
76. Mill (1974, 239).
77. Cf. Simone Chambers (1996, 183): "In the past, much of liberal theory has focused on the fairest way to mediate, channel, organize, and aggregate competing and divergent interests

and beliefs. Interests and beliefs themselves were taken as given, as in a sense, belonging to the person and not to be questioned. What we are seeing is a shift in focus from the coordination of interests and beliefs that are taken as given, to the generation of interests and beliefs that are understood as malleable. The *formation* of individual interests, beliefs, and values has replaced the *competition* among individual interests, beliefs and values as a central theme in liberal theory."

78. "[F]reedom ... does not occur spontaneously or arise necessarily; it is created and maintained by human beings, and to actualize it, citizens and officeholders must exercise a range of basic virtues. Moreover, because of the limitations which liberalism places on the state, liberal regimes depend on virtues that they cannot, left to their own devices, summon easily or cultivate vigorously. Liberalism's dependence on even a modest degree of virtue can be embarrassing because liberalism must restrain itself from taking all the necessary steps to insure that citizens will develop the virtues necessary to sustain it." Berkowitz (1999, 189–190).

79. Tennessee case: *Mozert v. Hawkins*, 827 F.2d 1058 (6th Cir. 1987) (freedom of religion); Alabama case: *Smith v. Board of School Commissioners*, 827 F.2d 684 (11th Cir. 1987) (establishment).

80. Gill (2001, 22).

81. *Wisconsin v. Yoder*, 406 U.S. 205 (1972). By removing their children from the temptation and knowledge that might come from education beyond the eighth grade, the parents wished to avoid alienating them from their farming community, living in which they held to be essential to their salvation. The majority concluded that harm to the children had not been shown, though it is unclear what sort of evidence would make out such a demonstration. Significantly, the children themselves were not asked to express their wishes about opting out of school. Dissenters contested the majority's conclusion about the community's ability to provide a "successful" life, a term not well-defined or deeply explored.

82. Cf. Gutmann and Thompson (1996, 63–69), who argue that parents have no right to exempt their children from having to read and confront secular textbooks because everyone must learn to listen and discuss issues in terms accessible to all. Galston (2002b, 19ff.) disagrees: Letting some parents exempt some children from some classes would not "significantly impair the development of democratic citizens." But the effect of exemptions, one might suppose, depends on the circumstances. Being exempted from a class in logic might have no bearing on good citizenship, whereas exempting students from a class on American civics or history might well. See also Gutmann (1982, 261–277); and Gutmann (1987).

83. Kymlicka (1990, 267).

84. In an article examining the civic virtue necessary to democratic government, Linda C. McClain (2001, 1665–1666) argues for a deeper understanding of the need to foster sex equality as "a core element in a conception of civic virtue in a good society." But she recognizes "that there are significant constitutional principles and prudential considerations, such as a respect for pluralism and the value of civil society serving as a buffer against the state, that argue against government compelling families to organize themselves according to one uniform vision of what sex equality requires." Galston (1991, 254–255) flatly denies the state any power to intervene. But both agree that the state must involve itself in civic education.

85. Sandel (1982, 28–35).

86. Okin (1989, 32). Indeed, one might wonder why the family member should not strive to be just toward those for whom he affects a deep and long-lasting love. Why is justice not a part of love, if by justice we mean eschewing cruelty, dominion, and unfairness? "If [families] normally operate in accordance with spontaneous feelings of love and generosity, but provide justice to their members when, as circumstances of justice arise, it is needed, then they are just and better than just. But if they do not provide justice when their members have reason to ask it of them, then despite their generosity and affection, they are worse." Ibid.

87. Ibid., 171.

Chapter 6

1. Hayek (1976, 36). I note, without further analysis, the likelihood that the federal health care individual mandate that Americans purchase insurance (upheld in *National Federation of Independent Business v. Sebelius*, 567 U.S. ___ [2012]) is justifiable under the harm principle, if not the Commerce Clause. Those arguing against its constitutionality contend that Congress may not require citizens to "act" (buy insurance), but the notion of derivative legislation developed in chapter 3 (see text at note 36) seems intuitively applicable to a requirement designed to prevent a free-rider problem, like penalizing those who do not pay their taxes. For a brief statement of this position, see Tomasky (2012).
2. *Bailey v. Alabama*, 219 U.S. 219 (1911).
3. *Butler v. Perry*, 240 U.S. 328 (1916) (conscripted labor for road maintenance); *Arver v. U.S.* 245 U.S. 366 (1918) (military draft).
4. Mill (1974, 136 [chap. 1, ¶11]).
5. Indeed, when the land is the source of the harm, just compensation is unnecessary. For example, the Supreme Court upheld a Virginia law that permitted the state to destroy, without compensation to the owners, all red cedar trees within a certain distance of apple orchards if they were carrying a communicable plant disease called cedar rust. *Miller v. Schoene*, 276 U.S. 272 (1928). In some cases, land may be seized to redress harms; for example, to prevent environmental damage by averting construction on a fragile shoreline. *Lucas v. South Carolina Coastal Council*, 505 U.S. 1003 (1992).
6. See the text at note 16 in chapter 3.
7. A similar argument will support the affirmative obligation to comply with a summons or subpoena to testify in court or before other official bodies. The requirement to tell what you know, when asked as part of an official inquiry or other proceeding, derives from the state's undisputed power to enact those regulations that enable it to conduct necessary investigations. That some liberal democracies dispense with juries is no argument against jury service; it is well within the harm principle to mandate the jury system.
8. Perhaps. Arguably, military service is, like jury service, uniquely necessary to preserve the state. Even though a potential inductee does not wrongfully set back an interest of another— it is the enemy that does that—the state needs a practical means to repel invaders who mean to harm many and destroy the state. But it is unclear how far this argument might go: Could the state draft people to become police and firefighters on the same grounds? Or is the distinction that localized domestic violence and fires do not threaten the state's very existence?
9. Feinberg (1986, 21–23).
10. Macaulay (1897, 495, 496–497), quoted in Feinberg (1984, 152, 154–155).
11. Michael Lind (2005, 17) writes: "[W]hile republican liberals have no trouble justifying the sacrifice of individual wealth, freedom, or even life in defense of the greater good of the republican citizenry, individualist liberals find it impossible to explain how someone who dies for his country is dying for his own liberty or well-being. This problem, which individualist liberalism of the modern center-left kind shares with libertarianism, is often evaded by borrowing the rhetoric of the quite different republican liberal tradition [for example, by quoting President Roosevelt asking for "personal sacrifice" during World War II] . . . to patch a gaping hole that not even the most imaginative redefinition of personal freedom can cover." But it is unnecessary to redefine personal freedom, since a duty to rescue, or an obligation that the state imposes to maintain itself, is sufficient to justify the draft, without having to pretend that the soldier who dies for his country has died for his own liberty. And of course it was not a liberal who failed to ask for sacrifice by the country at large during the years of the Iraq war, nor a liberal who eliminated the draft in 1972.
12. The argument is essentially that lawyers are a public utility and should be required to demonstrate that their actions have contributed to the public good. One statement of this view is in Marks, Leswing, and Fortinsky (1972, chap. 14). A sophisticated argument is Luban (1988, 282–289). In May 2012, New York State Court of Appeals Chief Judge Jonathan Lippmann

announced that the court, by fiat, would impose a fifty-hour pro bono obligation on law school students as a condition of being admitted to practice law in the state. The Court refrained from requiring members of the bar to devote any hours to such endeavors, even though, unlike those still in school, practitioners presumably actually know how to represent clients. Lippmann justified the mandate by noting the need to "demonstrate in a very tangible way . . . commitment to the ideals of our great profession." He was silent about the utility of having actual lawyers demonstrate that same commitment. He also refrained from considering whether the obligation to help those who cannot afford legal services actually lies on the whole community, which it should finance through general tax revenues. Spector (2012).

13. On licensing, see Gellhorn (1956); Lieberman (1970); Young (1987); Rottenberg (1980). And see chapter 7, "Regulation versus Litigation: The Case for Licensing."
14. Thalidomide (a morning sickness pill sold between 1957 and 1961, said to have caused as many as 20,000 severe birth defects worldwide); Bhopal (a gas leak in 1984 at a Union Carbide plant in India caused 8,000 deaths and nearly 560,000 injuries); Chernobyl (a 1986 explosion at a nuclear power plant in Ukraine released radioactive contaminants across Russia and Europe, causing possibly hundreds of thousands of cancer deaths since); Exxon Valdez (in 1989 an Exxon oil tanker hit a reef in Alaska and spilled millions of gallons of oil, the worst oil spill in U.S. waters until 2010); Deepwater Horizon (also known as the BP oil spill, the largest marine oil spill in history, began in April 2010, when an underwater explosion opened a wellhead, releasing 5 million barrels' worth of oil into the Gulf of Mexico, contaminating hundreds of miles of shoreline and seriously injuring marine life and befouling deepwater, shore, and marshland).
15. According to Centers for Disease Control, more than 443,000 deaths annually in the United States are attributable to cigarette smoking. http://www.cdc.gov/tobacco/data_statistics/tables/health/attrdeaths/index.htm (accessed May 20, 2012).
16. Muller (1971, 91).
17. Machan (1983, 280).
18. Belloc (1977).
19. The remainder of this section derives largely from Lieberman (1981a, 35–40).
20. Friedman (1973, 261).
21. Horwitz (1977, 86–87).
22. "[T]here is wanting the only element which distinguishes voluntary acts from spasmodic muscular contractions as a ground of liability. . . . [There has not been] an opportunity of choice with reference to the consequences complained of—a chance to guard against the result which has come to pass. A choice which entails a concealed consequence is as to that consequence no choice." Holmes (1961, 76).
23. Horwitz (1977, 99).
24. *Ryan v. New York Central R. R. Co.*, 35 N.Y. 210 (1866).
25. Prosser (1964, 924).
26. Friedman (1973, 422).
27. Richard A. Posner (1972, 73) argued in an early and classic law and economics article that the negligence law of the late nineteenth century compensated victims relatively fully and was designed to achieve an "efficient (cost justified) level of accidents and safety." Many others have disputed these claims; for a short summary, see Purcell (1992, 256–262).
28. Ibid., 424.
29. Spencer in fact never married.
30. The setting, but not the argument, from Thomson (1983, 137).
31. Spencer (1970, 339–340).
32. Spencer did insist, in decrying the institution of poor laws, that "[t]he poverty of the incapable, the distresses that come upon the imprudent, the starvation of the idle, and those shoulderings aside of the weak by the strong, which leave so many 'in shallows and in miseries,' are the decrees of a large, far-seeing benevolence." Ibid., 289. But he never progressed beyond his generalizations to indicate whether concepts such as imprudence have substantive meaning

other than as a name for one cause of suffering. Many distresses might be described as having been caused by some sort of imprudence (being run over by a horse might have resulted, under this argument, from the imprudence of the pedestrian, who prudently should have stayed in bed), but that is a useless definition, for it amounts to inferring imprudence from the distress rather than tracing the distress from the imprudence. The term thus can be neither limited nor distinguished from its opposite, except by checking to see whether its presumed consequence exists, a logical trick that denies the possibility of suffering befalling a prudent person (a rich person whose silver is stolen must thus have imprudently failed to safeguard against the theft). On this theory, no government at all is necessary, a proposition that Spencer did not accept. Compare the nice comment of Will Kymlicka: "To say that all forms of injustice are forms of exploitation is not to gain an insight but to lose a word." Kymlicka (1990, 180).
33. *R. v. Jones*, 91 Eng. Rep. 330 (1703).
34. Feinberg (1986, 287).
35. Hofstadter (1955, 89).
36. Marx (1978, 160).
37. Kelman (1974, 88).
38. Writing at the turn of the twentieth century and prognosticating about the turn of the twenty-first century, T. Baron Russell (1906, 239) supposed that the growing capacity of education would permit food laws and the like to be repealed: "Now it would be a highly perilous measure to abolish, at a stroke, all protective legislation against adulterated or impoverished foods. We have built up a social condition in which every man think himself entitled to be protected against such frauds. But in a community which has been taught to take care of itself, and protect itself against frauds by its own intelligence, such protections would be retrograde and injurious." He may have been right to predict greater education, but he altogether missed the growth of specialization that would outstrip any general education.
39. See the text at notes 47–48 in chapter 3.
40. *MacPherson v. Buick Motor Co.*, 217 N.Y. 382, 111 N.E. 1050 (1916).
41. The hugely variegated circumstances of the world require judgment case by case. From the fact that X burned a pile of leaves on his property next door to his neighbor Y, it does not follow that X caused Y harm (Y's argument is that his house would not have burned had X not burned the leaves). The jump from initial condition to ultimate outcome omits all sorts of intervening relations: Z may have taken a pile of those burning leaves and put them against Y's house; a gust of unexpected and strong wind may have blown the fire against all reasonable expectations or historical experience onto Y's house. These are matters that must be worked out by the legal system; that the courts answer wrongly in a particular case does not mean that the state acts illegitimately in enforcing the law of torts. See, generally, Hart and Honoré (1985). Note that many of the reforms of the tort system during the first three-quarters of the twentieth century have been sharply limited or even reversed during the past three decades; see, generally, Henderson and Twerski (2011); "Common Sense" (1996, 1782); Priest (1992, 704–705); Rabin (1992, 710–711).
42. A common example was that of the keeper of wild animals. If they escaped, even if it was not his fault, he was responsible for the damage they caused.
43. Milton Friedman has condemned occupational licensing of professionals on the grounds that it is "strictly paternalistic." I deal briefly with the argument against protecting ourselves from experts by licensing in chapter 9; see the text at note 15. The problem of imbalance or asymmetries of knowledge has been developed in the relatively new field of information economics. For some of the classic papers, see Stiglitz (2009).
44. A term introduced in Lieberman (1981a, 20).
45. *Kansas v. Mayes*, 531 P.2d 102 (Ka. 1975).
46. This was partially the view of Louis D. Brandeis (1914, 323–234); it is advanced comprehensively in Luban (1988, 169–174).

Chapter 7

1. The inquiry here is about the limits of the fourth and fifth components of the harm principle. See the text after note 44 in chapter 1.
2. Locke (1965b, 312 [chap. 2, §7], 315 [§12]). Locke states expressly that the Law of Nature is "as intelligible and plain to a rational Creature, and a Studier of that Law, as the positive Laws of Common-wealths, nay possibly plainer"; but he seems inescapably in these passages to include within that law and intelligibility, the "measures of punishment."
3. Mill (1974, 137 [chap. 1, ¶12]).
4. Feinberg (1984, 26).
5. It is the compliance requirement that is essential, not the nomenclature. A fishing "license" is not a license in this sense but a means of collecting a tax, since the ordinance imposes no requirement beyond paying a fee to obtain a piece of paper that will keep the fish and game warden at bay.
6. Mill (1974, 234 [chap. V, ¶9]).
7. *Sonzinsky v. United States*, 300 U.S. 506 (1937).
8. *United States Postal Service v. Council of Greenburgh Civic Assn.*, 453 U.S. 114 (1981).
9. As Locke (1974, 314 [chap. 2, §11]) insisted, the private right of action is fundamental: The magistrate may remit punishment for the common good, but may not remit "the satisfaction due to any private Man, for the damage he has received."
10. Punishment serves both deterrent and redress functions: The state must sanction criminal behavior for the law credibly to serve as a deterrent, but the purpose of punishment is not exhausted in that service. Friedrich Nietzsche (1989, 63) suggested that originally the recompense for a harm was simply the infliction of pain on someone, giving the victim a kind of pleasure: "Throughout the greater part of human history punishment was *not* imposed *because* one held the wrongdoer responsible for his deed, thus *not* on the presupposition that only the guilty one should be punished: rather, as parents still punish their children, from anger at some harm or injury, vented on the one who caused it—but this anger is held in check and modified by the idea that every injury has its *equivalent* and can actually be paid back, even if only through the *pain* of the culprit."
11. Exodus 21:24.
12. As Ted Honderich (1971, 27, 28) notes: "A murderer might in this sense be said to deserve execution. What a man who commits rape or breach of promise deserves, in this sense, is a question which leaves room for reflection." Moreover, since "the distress of a penalty and the culpability of an offender are not commensurable," it is impossible to know how to fit punishments to culpability "equivalently."
13. "Blacking" referred to a means of disguising one's face in the commission of a crime. See Thompson (1975, 22–23). Without parliamentary discussion, the law, enacted in 1723, appeared to take aim at poaching of game in national forests and elsewhere, but it covered so much ground that it amounted to a complete criminal code and turned relatively minor infractions into capital crimes.
14. Feinberg (1984, 63).
15. Of course it is not *compelled* by the harm principle to do so. The district attorney quite likely will be reluctant to press charges against the ten-year-old who swipes a bar of candy, and he will be more likely to press charges against a ten-year-old who points a gun at the store manager and demands the contents of the cash register than the twenty-year-old who steals the candy. My only point here is that he is not *required* to do so.
16. Our liberty is not all of a piece; there are several different kinds of liberty that, subject to the harm principle, everyone ought to enjoy. Here are six:

    1. liberty to take action at all (i.e., freedom from physical restraint, such as being jailed);
    2. liberty to do particular things (i.e., freedom from prohibitions, such as those contained in the criminal law, against our acting in particular ways);

3. liberty to possess property (i.e., freedom from a taking of our property to give to someone else, as, primarily, through taxation, and directly by seizure);
4. liberty not to act (i.e., freedom from a compulsion to act or do a particular thing, for example, to rescue);
5. liberty to contract (i.e., freedom from a defeat of our expectations of how others will act);
6. liberty to think and speak (i.e., freedom from interference with the formation and communication of our ideas).

The state may abridge Liberty 1 by putting a criminal in jail but not, to be proportional, direct that once he gets out he must give a week's pay to every starving child who lives in his town (abridgement of Liberties 3 and 4) or forfeit his right to speak to his neighbors (abridgement of Liberty 6).

17. An interesting example of a trivial case that got out of hand just because it was prosecuted was the theft of $20 worth of ice cream that netted a seventeen-year-old black youth with no prior record a three-year prison sentence in Georgia. A national uproar forced the state's Board of Pardons and Parole to commute the sentence to two years' probation in 1993. Smothers (1993).
18. See Rawls (1971, 42–43).
19. See the text at note 55 in chapter 1. To hold otherwise would require the state to tax as feasible and spend what it raises on harm prevention and redress until it either ran out of money or ran out of harms.
20. The retroactivity principle, expressed constitutionally in the United States in the Ex Post Facto Clause, speaks only of loss of liberty, so as it has been interpreted it does not bar such things as retroactive tax assessments, since these are orders to pay in the future on the basis of a different calculation of the tax owed and not penalties for past actions. *Brushaber v. Union Pacific Railroad Co.*, 240 U.S. 1 (1916); *United States v. Darusmont*, 449 U.S. 292 (1981). The retroactivity principle is not free from all doubt. For example, the Supreme Court has declared, shockingly in my view, that a legal alien resident of the United States may be deported for an act that was lawful at the time committed; *Harisiades v. Shaughnessy*, 342 U.S. 580 (1952); *Lehmann v. United States ex rel. Carson*, 353 U.S. 685 (1957).
21. Davis (1975, 261); see also Davis (1966, 391ff.) and Tomlins (2010).
22. Losurdo (2011, 97–101).
23. Foner (1998, 85).
24. Jordan (1977, 108).
25. Tushnet (2003, 31). In one of the most notorious cases dealing with the power of Southern masters over their slaves, *State v. Mann*, 13 N.C. (2 Devereux) 263 (1830), the North Carolina supreme court refused to permit even a local jury to meddle with this "private" power. Justice Thomas Ruffin dismissed an assault and battery conviction of one John Mann in Chowan County, who "shot at and wounded" for "some small offense" a slave he had hired from her master. A local jury had convicted Mann on finding that the punishment he inflicted "was cruel and unwarrantable and disproportionate to" the slave's offense. Ruffin declared that the duty of the slave is to obey, and "such obedience is the consequence only of uncontrolled authority over the body. There is nothing else which can operate to produce the effect. The power of the master must be absolute to render the submission of the slave perfect." That was a much more tyrannical power than the British monarchs had over their subjects.
26. Nor is it only liberals who have accepted an egalitarian premise. In 1954, when the Supreme Court in *Brown v. Board of Education*, 347 U.S. 483 (1954), jettisoned the nonegalitarian racial rule of "separate but equal," many sober critics disagreed, pointing to what they said was clear evidence that the framers of the Fourteenth Amendment, in which the Equal Protection Clause appears, did not intend the clause to prohibit segregated schooling. In 1990, in a patronage case, Justice Antonin Scalia dissented from the Court's overturning a "long tradition of open, widespread, and unchallenged use that dates back to the beginning of the Republic," as long as the patronage practice in question is "not expressly prohibited by the

text of the Bill of Rights." Justice John Paul Stevens responded that by that standard, "the constitutional attack on racial discrimination would, of course, have been doomed to failure." Scalia retorted that tradition gives content only to *"ambiguous"* constitutional text, and "no tradition can supersede" the Equal Protection Clause, which leaves "no room for doubt that laws treating people differently because of their race are invalid." But many thought the clause highly ambiguous, and many more did not doubt that it permitted segregation. When a tradition-minded justice can no longer find ambiguity in a legal text that forty years earlier was highly controversial, the triumph of at least racial (and by implication other forms of) egalitarianism seems assured.

27. See Westen (1982); William Cohen (1985). But see Dworkin (2000).
28. Aristotle (1988, 69–70 [1282b22–1283a30]).
29. Dworkin (1985, 190) distinguishes between treating people equally, in the sense of equal distribution of resources, and equal treatment. "Sometimes treating people equally is the only way to treat them as equals; but sometimes not. Suppose a limited amount of emergency relief is available for two equally populous areas injured by floods; treating the citizens of both areas as equals requires giving more aid to the more seriously devastated area rather than splitting the available funds equally." See "The Equality Premise" in the Appendix.
30. Feinberg (1986, 71) seems to agree with this general analysis: "A legal disability consequent on the state's failure to produce a service (or confer a 'legal power') is not the same as a legal duty to desist enforced by the threat of punishment for disobedience. How can one 'disobey' the nonpossession of a legal power?"
31. Civil Rights Act of 1866, today codified in 42 *United States Code* §§1981, 1982.
32. This understanding was the catalyst for the Fourteenth Amendment's Equal Protection Clause, when the Civil Rights Act ran into constitutional difficulty.
33. Feinberg (1986, 71).
34. The would-be slave owner is deprived of the freedom to make a contract for the thing he most desires in the world: absolute power over another human being. And the would-be slave is also deprived of something of value, the *enforceable* ability to sell himself into temporary or permanent *actual* slavery. That would be worth more than an unenforceable "contractual" power. The nonenforceable contract, after all, is nothing more than an agreement to be a slave for as long as the slave wishes to be, and no longer. The archetypical Hollywood casting director is more likely to give a starring part in his next picture to the beauty who promises herself irrevocably to him for the night than to the starlet who says she'll come to his room but reserves the right to depart without notice.
35. I consider slavery contracts in the text at note 49 in chapter 9.
36. Both quotations, Feinberg (1986, 71).
37. The state law struck down in *Loving v. Virginia*, 388 U.S. 1 (1967), in which the Supreme Court invalidated antimiscegenation laws nationwide, prohibited whites from marrying any nonwhites (except descendants of Pocahontas). But it left nonwhites free to marry as they pleased: "Negroes, Orientals, and any other racial class" except whites could intermarry. It is not merely a metaphoric sense in which the racially discriminatory definition of marriage could be said to have restricted the liberty of all.
38. *Reynolds v. United States*, 98 U.S. 145 (1878).
39. As Feinberg (1986, 265–267) recognizes in the case of fraudulent bigamy against the second wife. What of nonsecret bigamous marriages or open polygamous marriages? Other considerations, such as the children's welfare, and the ownership of property, will come into play, and I need not work through all the problems and ramifications here. Even if we were to conclude that the case for harm is unproven, the state could still insist on a written disclosure that provides binding answers to the range of issues that would be presented in such cases. Mandatory prenuptial agreements of this sort might well serve to reduce the number of such legalized arrangements.
40. Feinberg (1984, 26).

41. Ensuring accuracy is not the only function of some of the provisions, to be sure. But they do serve as a check on spurious results. Other constitutional rights usually thought of as part of procedural fairness are aimed less at guaranteeing accurate results than at curbing the power of the state to interfere excessively with liberty. For example, the Fourth Amendment right to be secure in one's possessions is intended to keep the state from intruding on a person's privacy unless it has probable cause to believe that the papers or other artifacts to be found would materially aid in establishing guilt. The Fifth Amendment right against double jeopardy is designed to prevent a person from losing liberty while responding to repeated prosecutions and from living in fear that such an ordeal may never end.
42. For a lively discussion of the roots of the turn against evidence in popular culture, see Kaminer (1999, chaps. 3, 5, 6). See also Manjoo (2008); Specter (2009).
43. Warner, "Introduction" to Kirk (2007, vii–viii).
44. But see the brief discussion in the text after note 59 in chapter 10, about the problem of landmarking historical sites already privately owned.
45. See Lieberman (1981b, 695).
46. *Nebbia v. New York*, 291 U.S. 502 (1934). Over the years, the Supreme Court's pronouncements on what constitutes a "rational" connection between harm and rule for constitutional purposes have often been dubious. See, for illustration and discussion of the difficulty of the Court's scrutiny standards, *City of Cleburne v. Cleburne Living Center*, 473 U.S. 432 (1985). The point at issue here is not whether the Court is correct in its reading of rationality but that the legislator should be bound by the requirement.
47. The usual criterion is knowingly and intentionally committing an act, not knowledge that the act has been outlawed. People often commit acts ignorant that the law prohibits them from doing so; their ignorance, as the saying has it, is no excuse. But when they are ignorant of certain facts, their act may be excusable. If I take your car, reasonably thinking under the circumstances that it is mine, I have not intended to deprive you of your property and am not, therefore, guilty of larceny.
48. See the text after note 45 in chapter 3.
49. See, e.g., Viscusi and Hersch (1990).
50. Feinberg (1984, 26; 1986, 71).
51. Feinberg (1984, 187ff., 215–217, 243–245).
52. Lieberman (1990).
53. Space shuttle: Broad (1989); Large Hadron Collider: Overbye (2008).
54. But criminalizing wrongful killing greatly reduces its incidence. It is as much a fallacy to argue that a law is unsuccessful because people violate it as it is to argue that a law is unnecessary because no one violates it. What people might do in the absence of law is always the issue.
55. 1994 study: National Recreation and Park Association (1994). Judges and mayors: Smolowe (1994).
56. The *Los Angeles Times* study is Colvin and Rohrlich (1994); Spiegel (1994); the quotation is from a summary in Smolowe (1994). See also Butterfield (1995).
57. Friedman (1962, 137–160).
58. See Lieberman (1970); Young (1987). Winston (2011).
59. Friedman (1962, 157). Friedman did not consider the costs and inefficiencies of the civil litigation system, the difficulties of proof, and the system's reliance on the fallibility of human judgment under conditions of insufficient information and psychological uncertainties of assessing testimony and even documentary evidence. For Friedman, the system seemed to be a generally costless machine for arriving at accurate determinations of value lost and the amount to be recovered in restitution, especially in cases of malpractice in which the judge or jury must translate human suffering, which might have been prevented if sole reliance had not been on after-the-fact litigation, into dollars.
60. Friedman does discuss the litigation problem to the extent of offering the eccentric notion that licensing actually makes it more difficult for patients to win lawsuits: His argument is that

licensing somehow fosters medical associations, which in turn conspire to deny privileges in hospitals to physicians who testify against fellow physicians. Many studies have verified the existence of this widespread practice; see, for example, Gross (1966, 120). But it is difficult to see how licensing has contributed to it. Hospital privileges are independent of licensing, and the creation of medical associations was not a response to occupational licensing. In Friedman's regime, degreed doctors might be willing to testify against quacks (they would certainly have a competitive reason to do so) and so the problem of establishing the quack's negligence might be less than establishing that of an M.D., but that is scarcely determinative or the only impediment to winning a lawsuit.

61. Whether and how long it would take non-M.D. "doctors" to acquire their various reputations is an empirical question. The state might well conclude that the "fit" between reputation and skill would not in the best of circumstances be perfect, so that a need to license remained.
62. There is, of course, a huge literature on the relationship of medical malpractice litigation and the cost of medical treatment. A comprehensive recent analysis is Sloan and Chepke (2008). Also see the report of the Harvard Medical Practice Study, Brennan (2004).

Chapter 8

1. Locke (1965a, 257 [chap. XI, §106]).
2. Mill (1974, 127).
3. Berlin (1969, 129–130).
4. Hobbes (1981, 376, 385 [chap. 30]).
5. Locke (1965b, 372 [chap. VII, §93]).
6. The next pages on Nozick derive from Lieberman (1977, 65–67).
7. For the derivation of the minimal state, see "Nozick and the Relativity of Harm" in chapter 2.
8. Cf. the celebrated passage in Augustine's *City of God*: "In the absence of justice, what is sovereignty but organized brigandage. For, what are bands of brigands but petty kingdoms? They also are groups of men, under the rule of a leader, bound together by a common agreement, dividing their booty according to a settled principle. If this band of criminals, by recruiting more criminals, acquires enough power to occupy regions, to capture cities, and to subdue whole populations, then it can with fuller right assume the title of kingdom, which in the public estimation is conferred upon it, not by the renunciation of greed, but by the increase of impunity." Augustine (1985, 88–89). As Herbert A. Deane (1963, 129 [Book 4, chap. 4]) describes Augustine's claim, it sounds rather like Nozick's protective association: "[T]he king is distinguished from the robber not by the absence of wickedness or cupidity but rather by his exalted position, his impunity, and his acceptance by the group over which he rules."
9. See the text after note 19 in chapter 2.
10. Some other categories have been advanced from time to time—for example, the educated. Mill (1975, 278) argued that only those who can "read, write, and I will add, perform the common operations of arithmetic" should be entitled to vote. But because elementary education can be largely achieved in modern societies, and because the extent to which it cannot would lead me too far afield, I refrain in what follows from considering education as a possible criterion for selecting eligible voters.
11. Ireton quoted in Macpherson (1964, 128).
12. Intelligence and learning were irrelevant. "[I]n the cautious enfranchisement of the propertied middle class," Robert Heilbroner (1995, 62) reports, "even the prosperous Adam Smith did not possess the financial qualifications to entitle him to vote."
13. Burke (1969, 138).
14. The idea that the franchise should rest on a person's having some monetary stake in the community continued symbolically in the United States until 1964, when the Twenty-Fourth Amendment abolished the poll tax.
15. This belief was reflected in the Constitution, most particularly in the clause reserving to Congress the power to enact bankruptcy laws, thus reducing the likelihood that popular

assemblies in the states would enact debt relief or otherwise make it difficult for creditors to recover their loans. Another fear was that if the poor have the vote, then the rich will simply buy their votes. Hence only the rich can be independent, and only the independent can be virtuous.

16. Mill (1975, 279). Mill's proposal to deny the franchise to those who do not pay taxes is naive even on its own terms, at least as we have come to understand taxation. For the very wealthy are adroit at avoiding taxes, and the incidence of taxation may fall more heavily on the relatively less well off. In this opinion, though, Mill was close to the sentiments of Adam Smith (1978, 489), who in his *Lectures on Jurisprudence* in the 1760s held that government is the safeguard of the rich against the poor: "Law and government, too, seem to propose no other object but this, they secure the individual who has enlarged his property, that he may peaceably enjoy the fruits of it." Likewise, said Smith: "Laws and government may be considered in this and indeed in every case as a combination of the rich to oppress the poor, and preserve to themselves the inequality of goods which would otherwise be soon destroyed by the attacks of the poor, who if not hindered by the government would soon reduce the others to an equality with themselves by open violence." Ibid., 208.
17. Sabine and Thorson (1973, 64).
18. Kennedy (1963, 475, 470–471, 473).
19. Hegel's *Dissertation* is noted in Clarke (1975, 116–117). An analogous example is provided by Bishop George Berkeley, who in a tract little read today, *Siris, a Chain of Philosophical Reflections and Enquiries on the Virtues of Tar Water*, advocated tar water as a cure-all for "scurvy, hysteria, hypochondriacal disorders, plague, erysilepelas, all disorders of the urinary passages, gout, gangrene, and the bloody flux." Berkeley quoted in Jameson (1961, 32).
20. Laski (1925, 8).
21. S. E. Luria (1974).
22. In 1954 Justice Robert H. Jackson was told that if he did not drastically curtail his strenuous work habits, a heart attack, likely fatal, would result. Leaving the Supreme Court and relegating himself to an inactive life did not attract him: Six months later he died as predicted. See "Proceedings" (1955, xxix).
23. Hauser (1976, 28).
24. A particularly potent claim to govern in the modern world is that of religious leaders, but insofar as they assert authority to rule, it is because of their expertise in the norms of the religion, by which in such countries the citizenry is bound to subscribe. What makes them experts is an issue internal to the faith, not to the state. Often, the antiliberal claim of moral authority to govern is simply that they believe themselves to have it. Peter Galison unearthed this example: "It is on record that a small religious body once adopted two resolutions as a declaration of its faith. The first was, *Resolved,* That the saints should govern the earth. Second, *Resolved,* That *we* are the saints." Galison (2003, 125), quoting Allen (1883, 6).
25. Assuming a dozen independent issues on which either a yes or no position could be taken, there are 4,096 different combinations of positions. Assume three dozen such issues and the total is a staggering 68,719,476,760 candidates necessary to express each possible set of positions. But of course in our world there are thousands of issues in national campaigns (consider all the shadings and degrees between the extremes of any one issue), and the total is too large to calculate. With only 333 issues, the number is more than 1 followed by 100 zeros. The formula is given by 2^n, where n = the number of issues.
26. The bibliography of interest-group pluralism is much too large to summarize here. But two relatively early works seriously questioning the premise that the "public interest" is realized in the complex vector of political decisions wrought by interest-group lobbying and legislative log-rolling are still worth noting: Kariel (1961); Lowi (1969). See also Lindblom (1977, chap. 13); Farber and Frickey (1991).
27. This is the problem of collective action: "The larger the group, the farther it will fall short of providing an optimal amount of a collective good." Olson (1971, 35). Moreover, Arrow's Theorem suggests that a system of democratic representation entails choices that are ultimately

incoherent and that group voting can never reach a stable and authentic consensus: If we prefer A to B and B to C the final choice might not be A over C. See Arrow (1963); MacKay (1980); Farber and Frickey (1991, chap. 2). For a well-known critique of the resulting rational-choice literature, see Green and Shapiro (1994).

28. See, for example, *Crawford v. Marion County Election Board*, 553 U.S. 181 (2008), for part of the debate on what may be a trend of state legislatures to make voter registration more difficult. For the suggestion that tightening registration laws is a partisan effort, see Alvarez (2011); Savage (2011).

29. In the 2008 national elections, the presidential race cost nearly $1.7 billion, nearly twice the amount spent only four years earlier. The total cost for all national races exceeded $5 billion. See, generally, Magleby (2011). In 2010 the Supreme Court rolled back several precedents and overturned various federal statutes aimed at curbing the influence of campaign contributions on federal elections. *Citizens United v. Federal Election Commission*, 130 S.Ct. 876 (2010).

30. Space alone precludes further discussion of the problem of expertise. The subject has a substantial literature. Though some of his examples are dated, still one of the most lucid explorations of this theme is Price (1965); see also Turner (2003), Fischer (1990) and, for a much more curmudgeonly and opinionated view, Saul (1992). For a counterview, see Mashaw (1999). For more on delegation, see "Nondelegation of Legislative Power" in this chapter.

31. As Stephen Holmes (1995, 102) notes, "[T]he idea that state capacities can be sharply increased by strategic limitations on power turns out to be a fundamental premise of liberal-democratic thought."

32. Madison, *Federalist* No. 47, in Rossiter (1961, 301).

33. Locke (1965b, 410 [chap. 12,§143]). "In other words, the separation of powers heightens the possibility that the perspective of the ordinary citizen, subject to the law, will be represented within the lawmaking process. It increases the likelihood that legislation will serve 'the good of the whole' and not just the private advantage of a few lawmakers." Holmes (1995, 166).

34. On localism vs. nationalism, see Rosenblum (1998, 279–281).

35. For a brief discussion of drug regulation and paternalism, see the text after note 19 in chapter 9.

36. Hobhouse (1994, 11). Or as Thomas Paine put it: "In America, *the law is king*. For as in absolute governments the King is law, so in free countries the law *ought* to be king; and there ought to be no other." Paine (1995, 98). Stephen Holmes (1995, 27) refers to this as the principle of self-exemption.

37. For example, sex-discrimination laws; see *Davis v. Passman*, 442 U.S. 228 (1979). Not until 1995 did Congress end its exemption from general discrimination and workplace laws. Gray (1995). See Grassley (1998). A very recent controversy over whether members of Congress are immune from insider trading laws, see Schweizer (2011) and Henning (2011), led Congress to enact and President Obama to sign a measure outlawing some forms of trading on knowledge gained by virtue of holding congressional office (Pear 2012).

38. A biographer of Justice John Marshall Harlan tells the story of his service on the staff of Emory Buckner, U.S. Attorney in Manhattan in 1925. Faithful to his charge of prosecuting Volstead Act violations, Buckner, "shortly after taking office[,] ... poured the contents of his ample cellar of bootleg wine and whiskey down the drain—much to the consternation of Harlan and other staffers, who suggested, to no avail, that he simply leave his cellar unlocked, permitting his valued stock to be 'stolen.'" Yarbrough (1992, 17). Buckner evidently felt no remorse over violating the law except as a law-enforcement official, and Harlan, remorse only that his boss was to that degree law-abiding.

39. Liptak (2008)

40. A rule takes the form: "No one under 21 may drink." A standard takes the form: "No one may drink who is immature." See Kennedy (1976). I do not mean to suggest that standards can or should be avoided in law-making. They are frequently quite useful, but the broader and vaguer they are, the more power the government has to fit its enforcement to the parties before it.

41. *Cruzan v. Director*, Missouri Dept. of Health, 497 U.S. 261, 300 (1990).
42. Often the regulating agencies will draw their memberships, partial or entire, from the group or industry to be regulated. For example, California law "seats representatives of polluters on the Water Pollution Control Board. The milk laws put the producers on the board that determines the distribution and price levels of milk." Stone (1975, 95). On regulatory capture, see Stigler (1971, 1975); Kariel (1961); Lowi (1969); Noll (1971); Lazarus (1974); Wilson (1980, 1989); Laffont and Tirole (1991); Shuck (1981); Bagley and Revesz (2006); Shapiro and Steinzor (2008); Morrissey (2011) (to get the FBI off their backs, online poker sites are seeking "to legalize, regulate and tax online poker").
43. Olney, quoted in Lazarus (1974, 20). The Interstate Commerce Commission, the first such federal regulatory agency, was abolished a century later, in 1995, with its few remaining functions scattered to other agencies. In 1973 the Interior Secretary Rogers C. B. Morton told a group of oil industry executives at the White House that the Office of Oil and Gas, a partial predecessor of the Department of Energy, "is an institution . . . designed to be your institution, and to help you in any way it can. . . . Our mission is to serve you, not regulate you. We try to avoid it." Quoted in Mintz and Cohen (1976, 227).
44. The doctrine that Congress may not delegate its powers is apparently constitutionally binding by virtue of the command in Article I, §1, that "all legislative power herein granted shall be vested in a Congress." The Supreme Court last overturned a delegation of law-making authority two generations ago in 1935 in *A. L. A. Schechter Poultry Corp. v. United States*, 95 U.S. 495 (1935) (holding the National Industrial Recovery Administration unconstitutional). For arguments favoring delegation, see Attorney General's Committee (1941); Lowi (1969); Stewart (1975); Mashaw (1985). For an argument against much modern delegation of legislative power, see Schoenbrod (1993). A serious challenge to delegated rule-making arose in a 2001 Supreme Court case in which some had held out hope that the nondelegation doctrine would be reinvigorated. At stake was a law directing the Environmental Protection Agency to set standards "the attainment and maintenance of which in the judgment of the Administrator, . . . and allowing an adequate margin of safety, are requisite to protect the public health." Their hopes were dashed when the Supreme Court unanimously upheld the law. *Whitman v. American Trucking Associations, Inc.*, 531 U.S. 457 (2001).
45. This principle is so significant for controlling the government and has so many topics and subtopics that I defer discussion to a later book, to be titled *Speech Matters*.
46. On the modesty of the harm principle, see the text at notes 47–56 in chapter 1. On constitutionalizing the harm principle, see the last section of this chapter.
47. See "General Limiting Principles of Intervention" in chapter 7.
48. Article I, §9.
49. For a short discussion, see Lieberman (1987, 336–343).
50. Mintz and Cohen (1976, 579) (footnotes omitted).
51. Ibid., 617.
52. The argument over the extent of judicial power to control legislative actions is too complex and extended to be dealt with here and in its details is beside my point, since the argument concerns the nature of the constitutional relation between legislature and judiciary in the American scheme. For the position that the power should be narrowly construed, see Ely (1980); for a quite different position, see Tushnet (1988).
53. Stone (1972, 1985).
54. Glendon (1991, 112). The case was *Sierra Club v. Morton*, 405 U.S. 727 (1972).
55. See "Expectations and the Externality Constraint" in chapter 10.

Chapter 9

1. Mill (1974, 135 [chap. 1, ¶9]). Mill says that the state may not interfere with a person because it will be better for him, or make him happier, or because others would find it wise or right to do so. Andrew Levine (1981, 115) points out that Mill omits to say that harm to

oneself cannot be a ground for interference. Levine reads that omission as highly significant: as "an implicit, and very likely unconscious, acknowledgment of the ultimately arbitrary character of excluding consideration of harm to oneself. Mill needs that exclusion, however, if the appeal to harm is to work to delineate the scope of the liberal component [i.e., harm is the dividing line between the public sphere where interference is tolerated and the private sphere where it is not]. But whatever makes the prevention of harm to others a plausible ground for allowing interference seems to hold as well for harm to oneself. Thus the exclusion of harm to oneself, however crucial for Mill's efforts to develop a substantive liberalism, apparently cannot be justified." "Seems to hold as well" is not a strong argument. In fact it is not an argument, but a passing observation. Aside from whatever motivated Mill, unconsciously or not, to omit "harm" from his list of reasons that do not overcome the prohibition against interference, harm seems to be wholly included in Mill's exclusion of interference for reasons of wisdom or rightness.

2. This assertion is controversial. There is mounting evidence that people are often not the best judges of the means to their own ends, though that does not determine the case. See, e.g., Kahneman (2011); Trivers (2011); Chabris and Simons (2010); Schulz (2010); Lehrer (2008, 91); Kida (2006); Rachlinski (2002–2003).

3. Cf. Mill (1974, 187–188 [chap. 3, ¶4]): "He who lets the world, or his own portion of it, choose his plan of life for him, has no need of any other faculty than the ape-like one of imitation. He who chooses his plan for himself, employs all his faculties. He must use observation to see, reasoning and judgment to foresee, activity to gather materials for decision, discrimination to decide, and when he has decided, firmness and self-control to hold to his deliberate decision.... It is possible that he might be guided in some good path, and kept out of harm's way, without any of these things. But what will be his comparative worth as a human being? It really is of importance, not only what men do, but also what manner of men they are that do it." Also see Feinberg (1986, 58–60), on the relationship between autonomy and a person's good. That choice is always good is far from universally accepted; it is explicitly denied by perfectionists, for whom the good way of life is knowable.

4. As Feinberg (1986, 62) puts it: "There must be a right to err, to be mistaken, to decide foolishly, to take big risks, if there is to be any meaningful self-rule; without it, the whole idea of *de jure* autonomy begins to unravel." For an engaging essay on harm to self, see Portman (2004).

5. Feinberg (1986, 8, 9, 12, 14) distinguishes various forms of paternalism, which I summarize in this note. Since the burden of this chapter is to determine when apparently paternalistic rules are not in fact so, I do not make much of the distinctions noted here: (1) The *require-forbid* distinction: "Some paternalistic coercive laws *require*, while others *forbid* certain kinds of behavior." (2) The *mixed-unmixed* distinction: "Unmixed paternalistic laws have no motive or reason other than preventing self-harm or consented-to harm from others." Mixed laws are those justified partly to prevent people from harming or consenting to harm to themselves "and partly for other reasons, for example, the desire to protect still other persons, or the general public." (3) The *harm-benefit* distinction: There is a difference between laws that aim to prevent harm from befalling a person (legal paternalism proper or "harm-preventing paternalism") and laws that seek to benefit him (positive paternalism, "extreme paternalism," or "benefit-promoting paternalism"). (4) *Single-party case vs. two-party case:* The single-party ("direct") cases include "laws prohibiting suicide, self-mutilation, and drug use." Two-party cases ("laws prohibiting euthanasia, dueling, and drug sales") "are paternalistic when one party's request for (or consent to) the action of a second party does not give the second party license to do what the first party wants (or is willing) to have done. If the second party nevertheless carries out his agreement then *he* has violated the law and will be punished." (5) The *soft vs. hard paternalism* distinction: "hard paternalism" is what Feinberg labels the Principle of Legal Paternalism (paternalism proper: preventing self-regarding harmful conduct for a person's own good). "Soft paternalism holds that the state has the right to prevent self-regarding harmful conduct (so far it *looks* "paternalistic") *when but only when*

that conduct is substantially nonvoluntary, or when temporary intervention is necessary to establish whether it is voluntary or not." Now ordinarily soft paternalism is not paternalism at all, although in certain one-party cases it may seem so: We might interfere with someone who was drunk on the grounds that he did not know what he was doing. Since this is not interfering with the liberty of *someone else* who is threatening harm, it does not easily fall within the harm principle. Hence, Feinberg concludes, "the only morally valid liberty-limiting principles" are the harm principle, the offense principle, and the principle of soft paternalism.

6. Lively (1983, 149). That a cost may be imposed on the consumer is inescapable (paying marginally more, perhaps, for the printing of the warning on a package label). One way or the other government taxes of necessity; imposing an extra cost does not make the thing on which the public money is expended a paternalist act. Another example: Hart (1963, 31–33) argued that the inadmissibility of a victim's consent as a defense to an assault charge is a paternalistic rule. But if a victim's consent would lead to dismissal of the charge, does not that provide the thug with a strong incentive to threaten the victim to state her consent after the fact? In that light, the rule against admissibility is a harm-prevention rule, not a paternalistic one.
7. Mill (1974, 135 [chap. 1, ¶9]).
8. West (2005).
9. Feinberg (1986, 56).
10. Both quotations from ibid., 22. Robert Paul Wolff (1968, 24–25) suggests that the distinction Mill drew between self-regarding and other-regarding conduct is not useful on Mill's terms because Mill insists that his defense of liberty is a utilitarian one, and on utilitarian terms, any interest that one person has in another must be permitted to weigh in the balance. "The root of the problem is that Mill treats the distinction between the inner and outer spheres as a matter of *fact*, whereas it is a matter of *rights* or *norms*. Self-regarding actions are those which only the individual himself has a *right* to concern himself with; his interests are the only interests which can legitimately be invoked in any moral evaluation. External or other-regarding actions are just those in which other persons have a rightful interest."
11. See "Principle of Least Intrusion" in chapter 7.
12. See "Aggregative Harms and the Problem of Risk" in chapter 3.
13. *Lochner v. New York*, 198 U.S. 45 (1905). See the text at notes 58–69 in chapter 4. For an excavation of *Lochner* and a contrarian view of almost everything that the case is said to stand for, see Bernstein (2011), reviewed in "Recent Book" (2012).
14. As Feinberg (1986, 20) puts the point: "When most of the people subject to a coercive rule approve of the rule, and it is legislated (interpreted, applied by courts, defended in argument, understood to function) *for their sakes*, and not for the purpose of imposing safety or prudence on the unwilling minority ('against their will'), then the rationale of the rule is *not* paternalistic. In that case we can attribute to it as its 'purpose' the *enablement* of the majority to achieve a collective good, and not, except incidentally as an unintended byproduct, the enforcement of prudence on the minority. Depending on the collective good involved, the costs and benefits, and the comparative sizes of the majority and minority, the statute may be fair or unfair, wise or unwise, but in either case it will not be 'paternalistic.'"
15. Friedman (1962, 148).
16. See the text at notes 33–38 in chapter 6; see also Turner (2003). The premise is not true for every occupation or even for every aspect of occupations that are currently licensed. That the state may protect patients, clients, and consumers from the harm that can come at the hands of quacks and incompetents does not mean that legislatures regulate only those occupations that pose such dangers. Legislatures are notoriously suckered by occupational groups posing no particular danger into giving them a licensing monopoly, and they all too often grant exclusive power to a licensed group to undertake certain tasks that do not require licensing. See, generally, Lieberman (1970), Rottenberg (1980), Luban (1988), Brint (1994), Kritzer (2002).
17. Regulatory schemes often create what Ivan Illich (1973, 39) dubbed "radical monopolies": rules that prohibit competing technologies, materials, and workers. Illich cited a Mexican program intended to secure proper housing for the lower class. The government mandated

standards for homes: "These standards were intended to protect the little man who purchases a house from exploitation by the industry producing it. Paradoxically, these same standards deprived many more people of the traditional opportunity to house themselves. The code specifies minimum requirements that a man who builds his own house in his spare time cannot meet."

18. Cohn (1981). Laetrile marketing has been called "the slickest, most sophisticated, and certainly the most remunerative cancer quack promotion in medical history" (Lerner 1981, 91). See Bausell (2009); Ernst and Singh (2008). On the FDA's fight against laetrile, see Meyers (1991, 325–329).

19. Feinberg (1988, 186–187) suggests that the "primary case against legalization" of laetrile is the "argument from exploitation": Drug companies and others would make immense profits, even though not at the expense of anyone's rights. "Yet some parties will be turning to their own advantage the misery and desperation of others, achieving a gain for themselves only because of others' misfortunes. That is a form of parasitism that tends to offend the objective observer, whether ultimately justifiable or not. It is not pleasant to behold the strong and healthy making their living off the desperate hopes of the powerless." But if no one is harmed, why should it be banned? Those who persist in wanting to ban the sale have a nagging suspicion (very likely warranted) that the temptation to make those large profits will probably keep the seller or manufacturer from disclosing all the evidence that the stuff is worthless. So the real problem is misleading claims and lack of appropriate warnings; those huge profits would come only from advertising the substance as a "sensational" cure, and *that* could be prevented.

20. Again, I ignore the empirical argument about whether some addictive drugs should be prescribed in medical settings, such as painkillers, for example. Many substances are prescribed for such purposes that are dangerous if misused, so it is a nice question whether the legalizing of some now-proscribed drugs for medical use would make illicit use more widespread (the legislature might fear that doctors might in effect be "bribed" into "prescribing" marijuana and harsher drugs). But these are empirical questions, not questions of legitimacy.

21. Feinberg (1986, 128).
22. I base much of the following brief discussion on Husak and de Marneffe (2005).
23. Ibid., 14–15.
24. Ibid., 85–88.
25. Quoted in Kelman (1974, 162).
26. A broader answer, at least for motorcycle helmets (and possibly by analogy for safety nets), is that they minimize the risks that riders will cause accidents involving others by preventing the cyclist from losing control should gravel or other loose debris be kicked up and block the cyclist's vision. Some state courts in the late 1960s invalidated such laws on the grounds that the *particular* regulations did not serve the stated purpose; see *American Motorcycle Assn v. Davids*, 158 N.W.2d 72 (Mich., 1968); *People v. Fries*, 42 Ill.2d 446, 250 N.E.2d 149 (1969); *State v. Betts*, 21 Ohio Misc. 175, 252 N.E.2d 866 (Mun. Ct., 1969). But the judges seem to have been willfully obtuse in failing to grant the legislatures the usual loose connection between the end and means chosen, as other courts chose to do; see, for example, upholding the constitutionality of helmet laws, *Everhardt v. City of New Orleans*, 253 La.285, 217 S.2d 400 (1968), *appeal dismissed and cert. denied* 395 U.S. 212 (1969); *Rhode Island ex rel. Colvin v. Lombardi*, 241 A.2d 625 (R.I., 1968); *Commonwealth v. Howie*, 238 N.E.2d 373 (Mass., 1968). In any event it would not be difficult to write a regulation requiring helmets that would be aimed precisely at the stated evil of harm to others. See Royalty (1969). Many helmet laws were repealed during the 1980s and 1990s, though the trend now seems to be reversing again. Atwood (2008, 273–280; on medical costs, 280–281). For more recent discussions, see also Schuster (2004); Neiman (2008).

27. Feinberg (1986, 140–141).
28. The example was proposed by Kristol (1971), and is discussed at some length in Feinberg (1988, 128–133, 328–331).

29. Feinberg (1988, 329).
30. Bergelson (2007, 165, 218, 228).
31. One answer to Kristol may be to look more minutely at what would be entailed by following the fight rules. It seems clear that the scenario specified by Kristol is unrealistic even in the imaginary world of his hypothetical. There would have to be rules of some sort, because if the fight were wholly without them, one fighter could call in an air strike or simply arrive with a long-range weapon and annihilate his opponent on the spot (like Indiana Jones from a distance shooting a turbaned assassin brandishing a large sword in *Raiders of the Lost Ark*). The organizers would not want to showcase or risk the spectators' ire a one-second knockout. So rules would be established. Only certain weapons? Only certain moves? But a fight with rules means the possibility of cheating, and since restitution after the fact for violation of the rules is a practical impossibility, the state could regulate, including banning such fights altogether, on the nonpaternalist ground that there is no other effective way to prevent one or both fighters from breaking the rules. In the real world, the closest thing to Kristol's fight to the death is "mixed martial arts" (MMA), unlawful in New York and Connecticut but legally recognized elsewhere in the United States. Its major promoter, Ultimate Fighting Championship, bans eye gouging, biting, "groin attacks, heel kicks to the kidney, and throat strikes." Zwick (2012, 8).
32. The debate over the gladiator problem continues. For one view that the anti-paternalist position is mistaken in the case of consent to actual injuries to the person, see Postema (2005, 315–318), and for a brief response, Alexander (2005, 331).
33. *Cruzan v. Director, Missouri Dept. of Health*, 497 U.S. 261 (1990).
34. *Vacco v. Quill*, 521 U.S. 793 (1997) (rejecting an equal protection challenge); *Washington v. Glucksberg*, 521 U.S. 702 (1997) (rejecting a due process challenge).
35. On FAKE arguments, see the text after note 63 in chapter 4.
36. Mill (1974, 229 [chap. V, ¶5]).
37. Feinberg (1988, 213).
38. The argument is spelled out in Bergelson (2007, 210).
39. Feinberg (1986, 350–351) notes that he is following an idea of Rachels (1978, 61–63); he suggests other practical difficulties as well.
40. Dworkin (1997, 43). The other signatories were Thomas Nagel, Thomas Scanlon, and Judith Jarvis Thomson.
41. The argument that there are more prosaic, though still fundamentally important, reasons for rejecting assisted suicide than adhering to a religious conviction is pursued vigorously in Weithman (1999).
42. Gorsuch (2006, 113–114).
43. Ibid., 118.
44. Ibid., 122.
45. Ibid., 126.
46. Weithman (1999, 570).
47. Jones (2007, 190), quoting from a pamphlet of the Friends of Seasonal and Service Workers in Portland. Nor is that the only worry. As another commentator has noted: "The legalization of euthanasia or assisted suicide also raises important worries about possible harms to those who do not choose either. The most common fears are that the medical care offered to terminally ill patients might explicitly or tacitly be reduced, that incentives to develop better palliative treatments might diminish, that some people might mistakenly be left to die or be killed, that patients might inappropriately be pressured to choose death, and that some might intentionally be killed against their wishes if illegal killings can more easily be hidden." Rakowski (2004, 261n4).
48. An example of a legitimate agreement to refrain from an action for all time is the sale of a trademark or corporate name, the seller agreeing never to compete under that or a similar name.
49. "By selling himself for a slave, he abdicates his liberty; he forgoes any future use of it beyond that single act. He therefore defeats, in his own case, the very purpose which is the

50. Feinberg (1986, 79).
51. There are many variants of chess. One that has received considerable attention since 1996 is Fischer Random Chess or Chess960, which involves placing the nonpawn pieces in the primary position in random order for each game. It takes its name from the 960 possible starting positions. See, e.g., McClain (2007); Poulson (2005).
52. Feinberg (1988, 317). This approach applies equally to circus performers who wish to dispense with nets.
53. For example, a custom of playing Russian roulette within a teenage gang culture might well warrant state intervention, even though the custom is localized in this single community.
54. See Feinberg (1984, 220–221; 1986, 18–20).
55. Alexander Hamilton wrote in a letter the evening before his fatal encounter with Aaron Burr "that 'what men of the world denominate honor' made it impossible for him to 'decline the call.' ... If Hamilton ignored the challenge, Burr would 'post' him—that is, publish his refusal in the newspapers—and his political career would be effectively ruined. ... Hamilton and Burr belonged to a class for whom no public offense could go unchallenged even if one felt no personal outrage." Krystal (2007, 80). What exactly is it that feels compelling to the reluctant duelist? He fears the social opprobrium, the sneer of his peer, the bad words that people of his class will utter about him behind his back and that will lead his family to suffer. But that is akin to a well-recognized harm, the harm of slander. Analogously, the argument is that a ban on dueling prevents the spread of a kind of slander, of harmful social opprobrium. And note that the custom does not direct harm to only the one against whom the gauntlet is thrown: The challenger might be equally reluctant but feel compelled to issue the invitation to redress his honor only because of the shame that he would incur were he to appear to avoid the opportunity to challenge his nemesis in the first place. That appears to be the situation in which the Duke of Wellington, then prime minister of England, found himself in 1829, when he was charged, during the course of his successful efforts in persuading Parliament to enact the Catholic Relief Act (permitting Catholics to sit in Parliament for the first time in 150 years), with selling out England to the Pope. Taking this as base libel by his accuser, George William Finch-Hatton, tenth Earl of Winchilsea, the Duke felt honor-bound to challenge him to a duel when Winchilsea refused to apologize beforehand. As Kwame Anthony Appiah (2011, 12) puts it in an engaging chapter on the death of the duel, "dueling was contrary to Wellington's own inclinations, to civil law and to Christian teaching, and, so it might seem, to political prudence." That dueling had been unlawful for decades suggests the force of the custom. Appiah concludes that dueling finally died, in mid-nineteenth-century England, laughed out of existence, as "lower orders," "mere tradesmen," fancied that they should duel for slights to them, thus dealing a death blow to the practice among the upper class, which could no longer see honor in following a practice taken up by their inferiors.
56. Moreover, such consent as could be inferred was probably not informed. Because the code was customary and not enacted, it was never clear what the boundaries were: which kinds of insults were "legitimate" provocations and which were merely pretexts. So in outlawing duels, the state was also outlawing a major source of "law" violations by those who abused the custom to exact private revenge for imagined slights and grievances.
57. Although the dueling case is, I think, a straightforward application of the principle that the state may repeal customs that produce harm, I concede that the contours of this principle are ill-defined. As noted, the "custom" of private club members' drinking themselves blind is probably not one that can be legislated against under the harm principle, since custom does not require anyone to join the club and the opprobrium if one were to fail to drink or to quit is probably not very great. However, the more the custom has permeated society generally and the more serious the harm that ensues, the sounder the argument that the state may regulate or even eliminate it under the harm principle.

58. See "Harms by Community: Association and Equality" in chapter 10.
59. See text after note 9 in chapter 6.
60. See text after note 58 in chapter 4.
61. Feinberg (1986, 260).
62. Richard M. Titmuss (1971, 245, 246, 239) argues that in the case of blood supply "the commercialization of blood and donor relationships represses the expression of altruism," wastes blood, costs more than in voluntary systems, increases medical risks (because donors-for-pay more likely lie about diseases from which they suffer), and reduces rather than expands options: "[P]rivate market systems in the United States and other countries... deprive men of their freedom to choose to give or not to give." But Titmuss may simply have erred: Kenneth J. Arrow (1972, 350) has suggested that Titmuss is wrong both in his theoretical explanations and his empirical evidence. Some of Arrow's expressions of doubt are, in turn, discredited by Peter Singer (1973, 312–319). Be that as it may, Titmuss's arena of investigation into the relationship between commerce and altruism is narrow. Although it is possible that paying for blood will deter altruists from donating their blood for free, the traffic in blood is quite unlike most other exchanges; moreover, the example is not parallel to many other forms of exploitation in which the claim is not that the market should be abolished to foster altruism but that the amount charged in an existing market should be regulated. Herbert Spencer (1970, 286) interestingly made a cognate argument in objecting to state-funded poor relief on the ground that it would narrow the option of private charity, "In truth there could hardly be found a more efficient device for restraining men from each other and decreasing their fellow feeling than this system of state almsgiving. Being kind by proxy! Could anything be more blighting to the finer instincts?"
63. Feinberg (1986, 229–233) discusses this problem in the context of sorting out the coerciveness of the millionaire's offer and concludes that this is a "freedom-enhancing coercive offer."
64. See Rakoff (1983); Trebilcock (1993, 118ff.).
65. See text after note 17 in chapter 6.
66. Posner (1996, 41). Of course, not every object of blackmail is unlawful; sometimes the blackmailer threatens to expose merely embarrassing or deeply upsetting facts that the victim would not wish revealed.
67. Schelling (1987, 172–175, 180).
68. See chapter 2, note 26.
69. This same argument from an economic perspective is given in Kelman (1983, 217–248).
70. Gutmann and Thompson (1996, 264).
71. Schelling (1996, 182).
72. Mulvihill (2007).
73. Parekh (1972, 83).
74. Bentham quoted in Berlin (1969, 171).
75. Ibid.
76. Arblaster (1986, 52).
77. Ibid., 53.
78. An interesting example of the problem of state action justified to prevent harm to future generations comes from an unlikely source—the science fiction of Isaac Asimov, inventor of the term "robotics." Asimov imagined the robot (read: the state) as the servant of human beings. Under the Three Laws of Robotics, first discussed explicitly in 1942, a robot may be told what to do (the legislature enacts rules for government to follow, or for each of us to follow) but not, under the First Law, when those orders would cause harm to human beings: "A robot may not injure a human being, or, through inaction, allow a human being to come to harm." Suppose an order to save one person would put another in jeopardy. In Asimov's stories, this conflict usually led the robot's "positronic" brain to melt down. But late in his series, Asimov developed a Fourth Law, called the Zeroth Law. This law is peculiar, since it enables a robot to exalt "mankind" over an individual person, permitting harm to the individual if necessary to preserve mankind. In Asimov's hands the robot was always a good and

wise servant of mankind; Asimov never spelled out the totalitarian implications of this Zeroth Law. But the conundrum he raised—real harm to a particular person here and now vs. a widespread, though only potential, harm of a different sort to those in the distant future—shows how even the most well-intentioned servant of mankind can do serious harm. Asimov worked out his four laws in dozens of stories and articles and four novels over more than four decades. The stories and articles are collected in Asimov (1990); the Zeroth Law is described in Asmiov (1985).

79. Dworkin (1985, 141). Dworkin's liberalism does not rest on the harm principle but on a complex notion of equality, though an equality grounded in the basic notion that the government may not choose among conceptions of the good.

80. Such a commission is, of course, wholly apocryphal. Who would propose such a monstrosity? Cf. Unger (2004, 453), suggesting the logic of a reformist fourth branch of government empowered to systematically intervene in all of society: "Its activities embrace, potentially, every aspect of social life and every function of all the other powers in the state. If the other powers could not resist and invade the jurisdiction of this corrective agency, it would become the overriding authority in the state." Unger calls it evil, while postulating it as a corrective to the paralysis of checks and balances. It is surely no coincidence that a quarter-century later, Unger wangled a position running a new Brazilian ministry, originally called the Secretariat for Long-Term Actions, later changed to the Ministry of Strategic Affairs. Unlike his philosophical fantasy, this ministry does not speak for the state. In 2008, Unger said that "I have the only position in the government that is about everything, except for the position of the president. He has all the power, and I have none." See Romano (2008).

81. How would we know that the damage would be manifest three centuries hence, that it would not become palpable long before that, or that the ozone layer would not be harmed now?

82. Arblaster (1986, 53). See, generally, Laslett and Fishkin (1992). See also Gutmann and Thompson (1996, 155–164, 162) for the suggestion that a deliberative process can help influence a longer-range view, and that procedural devices, such as a "future generations impact statement" and bestowing honors and recognition on "citizens and public officials whose actions show exceptional concern for future generations," could harness the "love of fame after death" that "could extend the temporal horizons of the democratic process."

83. I lay to one side here the obvious point that *nothing* the government does, no expenditure it makes, is without effect in the present, if for no other reason than that any long-term program involves payrolls that benefit the living. But the objective is to search out a motive for these expenditures rooted solely in preventing harm to future people, and so it cannot be a justification of any such program that it is providing work for those now living.

84. "Soft paternalism holds that the state has the right to prevent self-regarding harmful conduct... *when but only when* that conduct is substantially nonvoluntary, or when temporary intervention is necessary to establish whether it is voluntary or not." Feinberg (1986, 12).

85. Ibid., 14–15.

86. Ibid.

Chapter 10

1. Feinberg (1988, 8–9) discerns two nonparallel axes of moralism, which he labels *strict-broad* and *pure-impure*. Strict moralism deals with inherent morality, morality in the objective sense, universal morality, independent of any social convention or belief about it. Broad moralism concerns morality that is anchored in a particular society's conventions. Pure moralism constitutes moral evils independent of any harm they may cause. Impure moralism is the realm of evils that are said to be ultimately harmful to society as a whole. When these axes are crossed, a fourfold set of moralisms emerges, two of which are independent of harm in any sense and two of which are rooted in harm as the justification for legislation. More particularly, Feinberg defines the four strands of moralism as follows: "The *pure legal moralist in the strict sense* demands that the law prevent and/or punish inherent immoralities even when

they are harmless (because voluntary and consented to) and unoffending (because not forced on the attention of unwilling observers)." "*Pure moralism in the broad sense* certifies as a reason for criminalization the need to prevent a free-floating evil other than objective immorality as such." "*Impure moralism in the strict sense* argues for criminal legislation against 'inherent immoralities,' not as free-floating evils but as events or states of affairs which in virtue of their coarsening effect on those who participate in or observe them, or their power of suggestion to others, will produce—albeit indirectly—immense harm over the long run." "Finally, *impure moralism in the broad sense* argues for intervention by the criminal law to prevent a free-floating evil other than inherent immorality, but gives as its ultimate legitimizing reason the need to prevent the harm or offense incidentally associated with or produced by that evil." Among the latter harms: people with deficient character and the loss of great art and music from declining standards.

2. Nor, to round out the possibilities, do they consider it a harm to them that you don their traditional garb or a good to them that you do not. The argument has been pressed by some cultural communities that outsiders who imitate a community's traditions harm its members. For example, in the 1990s adherents of the New Age movement in the American West began adopting American Indian rituals. "But many Indian tribes and organizations, far from being flattered by the imitators, have denounced the movement as cultural robbery. 'This is the final phase of genocide,' says John Lavelle, a Santee Sioux who is the director of the center for Support and Protection of Indian Religions and Indigenous Traditions. 'First whites took the land and all that was physical. Now they're going after what is intangible.' The National Congress of American Indians this month approved a 'declaration of war' against those they accuse of exploiting sacred rituals, citing 'non-Indian "wannabes," hucksters, cultists, commercial profiteers and self-styled New Age shamans.'" Johnston (1993, A1).

3. See chapter 3, "Wrongful Harmdoing: Harm as Wrongful Setback to Interest."

4. One source of support for the exclusion of external interests might be found in a claim of Ronald Dworkin (1976, 272–278; 1985, 359–372) that in assessing which social policies would yield the greatest net social satisfaction, the government may count only personal, not external, preferences. For example, a racist's personal desire to live in a particular neighborhood should be counted, but not his desire that members of other racial groups not have houses there. Including both in the calculation would be a form of illegitimate "double counting," Dworkin says, because it would take account of an implicit personal preference to live in a single-race neighborhood as well as an almost identical external preference that other racial groups not live there. H. L. A. Hart (1983, 213–219) rejects the double counting argument for reasons which need not be summarized here (though on the face of it the argument does seem weak since utilitarians do not take account of the *content* of preferences but merely sum their number and intensity). But in the end, Dworkin's reason for excluding external preferences does not apply to the claim I make about the externality constraint. Dworkin is attacking utilitarianism, or a form of it, which requires preferences or desires to be aggregated. But the harm principle does not aggregate (or it need not). From the perspective of the harm principle, external interests are not excluded because to count them would be to violate an egalitarian principle against double counting but because doing so would often be giving weight to a desire to harm. Note, also, that utilitarianism permits counting incompatible preferences and the argument against double counting does not depend on any objection to the inconsistencies among preferences. But to count external interests under the harm principle would lead to all sorts of unresolvable issues stemming from the existence of incompatible external interests held by others.

5. Feinberg (1988, 61) puts this point somewhat differently: "When two persons each have interests in how one of them lives his life, the interests of the one whose life it is are the more important." Feinberg grants that "one person can have a genuine interest in the private life of another of an 'external' sort, for example an interest that he have 'correct values' as an end in itself." I think this statement mistaken, for it suggests the possibility that a circumstance could arise in which the external interest of the other person is more important than the internal

6. Arneson (1990, 368, 381, 379). Arneson seems to be taking a leaf from Dworkin's playbook in arguing that some sorts of external interests, masquerading as personal interests, be accorded weight. Dworkin (1975, 236) characterized some personal preferences as "parasitic upon external preferences"; that is, a white student who prefers studying with other whites is, "except in very rare cases," playing on "racist convictions" or "contempt for blacks as a group." Dworkin would not count a personal preference parasitic on an external preference that fails to treat the other with equal respect (that is, "preferences . . . affected by prejudice"). Dworkin notes that personal and external preferences can be "so inextricably tied together . . . that no practical test for measuring preferences will be able to discriminate the personal and external elements in any individual's overall preference." Under those circumstances, Dworkin would sniff the prejudice and discount the preference. Arneson seems less disposed to do so. He accepts, for example, a claim to wish to live in a neighborhood with a "family-oriented tone" as a personal interest, rather than as one parasitic on an external interest in hippies not living in a particular way. Whether or not such considerations make sense under utilitarianism, they would make the harm principle unworkable. See note 4 above.
7. Ibid., 379.
8. Ibid., 381–382.
9. Ibid., 381.
10. As Arneson says (ibid.): "Laws that would destroy or greatly reduce some people's chances of a happy sex life in a society that puts great emphasis on sexual fulfillment as an element of the good life mark out a portion of the citizenry for lifelong disadvantage in a way that fair welfare-maximizing, with its strong commitment to preference satisfaction egalitarianism, must repudiate."
11. Ibid., 381–382.
12. Ibid., 382.
13. Bestiality might be proscribable under the harm principle directly, if we were to assimilate animals as "others" so that we could deter at least certain kinds of harms directly. See Franklin (2006).
14. Arneson (1990, 382).
15. I concede that this issue is partly empirical. If a person truly had options, we might feel less squeamish about inviting him to pack up or accept laws against violations of norms. But relocating, too, is burdensome. In any event, it seems reasonably clear that many prejudices are deeply held and would operate nationally.
16. The story of Sodom and Gomorrah is told in Genesis, Chapters 18 and 19.
17. For an engaging satire of the clash between the legal systems of cultures grounded in science and the supernatural, see Menen (1949). A political theory of witchcraft is not an idle fancy. In 1580 Jean Bodin "published his distressing and all too influential book on demonology, *De la démonomanie des sorciers*, in which he described at great length the passion of witches for evil forces and the way by which they should be detected and punished." Franklin (1992, xi). For contemporary African political problems with witchcraft, see Geschiere (1997, 22); Ashforth (2005, 10, 17). Nor is this sort of thinking confined to cultures far removed from our own. An American religious agitator, Fred Phelps, and his ragtag Westboro Baptist Church of Topeka, Kansas (parishioners of which are almost entirely members of Phelps's family), have noisily claimed, for example, that U.S. soldiers have died in Iraq as God's punishment for American failure to stamp out homosexuality. The church's well-publicized demonstrations at funerals of U.S. soldiers who died in war abroad led to a multi-million-dollar verdict in a mental distress case filed by the father of one such soldier, culminating in a Supreme Court ruling that the demonstrations are protected by the First Amendment: *Snyder v. Phelps*, 131 S.Ct. 1207 (2011).

18. On spectral evidence, see Hoffer (1997, 78–80).
19. The Great Separation: Lilla (2007). See also Barry (2012). The proponent of a wrath-of-God harm actually faces a third obvious difficulty: how to tell which particular act is provoking the divine displeasure. Fred Phelps says God kills American soldiers because America tolerates homosexuality. A senior Iranian cleric asserts that God sends earthquakes because many women dress immodestly. Associated Press (2010). Notoriously, Jerry Falwell said three days after the terrorist attacks on September 11, 2001, that America made God "mad" because it has been "throwing God out of the public square" with the aid of the American Civil Liberties Union and the federal court system, among others. Harris (2001). It requires no original wit to wonder whether God is rather more annoyed at the arrogant certitude of those who dare speak in his name.
20. A more difficult situation arises, though, when the act complained of on religious grounds is aimed at a particular person. Suppose a certain cultural group "reasonably" fears the practice of voodoo (not that the belief is well-founded in any scientific sense of causation but merely that the group has a historical, genuine religious belief in the efficacy of the practice). Adherents believe that an experienced voodoo practitioner can put people under spells that will set back their interests (and we may assume that the belief itself leaves one on whom a spell is placed in a psychologically injured state). May the state yield to the importuning of voodoo victims and prohibit its practice? The anxiety-ridden will insist that all voodoo be barred, since the bare knowledge that someone somewhere can pay a practitioner a fee for a curse as a reprisal against an enemy is enough to arouse the greatest fears. Abstractly, such conduct seems to fall within the purview of the harm principle. If the practice is part of an established religious tradition, then on the very ground just established (toleration for the practice of religion), voodoo cannot be held abstractly as a wrong. (The problem of the authenticity of the religion is a difficult one that I do not explore here. To be faithful to the spirit of toleration, it should not matter whether a religious belief is grounded in a tradition thousands of years old or sprang up yesterday, as long as it is a genuine belief. There is some slight authority in American constitutional law for the position that the age of the tradition might matter; see *Wisconsin v. Yoder*, 406 U.S. 205 [1972]. But the better approach, I think, is to see the tradition as supplying a form of evidence of genuineness that would be lacking in the claim that someone "just last night" heard from God that he must perform some unspeakably upsetting act.) The conclusion that voodoo is not a wrong is consistent with the rule that the state may not upset a decree of religious excommunication, despite its import in the life of the (former) communicant. *Kedroff v. St. Nicholas Cathedral of Russian Orthodox Church*, 344 U.S. 94 (1952); *Serbian Eastern Orthodox Diocese for the U.S. & Canada v. Milivojevich*, 426 U.S. 696 (1976). Anxiety is distressing and at times debilitating, but all sorts of acts make us anxious that it would be unwise to countermand for that reason. But the bare knowledge that voodoo is being practiced is different from the knowledge that voodoo is being practiced against *me*. The distinction between generalized practices and practices aimed at a particular person is significant for the harm principle: Whereas a general religious practice is not wrongful, a practice that is undertaken for the sole purpose of hounding me might be. Here a further distinction is necessary. Just as excommunication is necessarily aimed *at* a particular person, voodoo, if aimed at a sinner as part of the religious ritual, is not open to question by the state. But a person who yells curses and makes a show of summoning demonic forces, repeatedly and directly aimed at a particular person *for the purpose of* doing that person an injury, and not as part of an established religious practice, is subject to state intercession. These considerations are not, alas, merely theoretical; see Burnett (2009).
21. George (1995, 226).
22. Ibid.
23. The speech is reprinted as "Morals and the Criminal Law," Devlin (1965, chap. 1).
24. Ibid., 10.
25. Ibid., 13.
26. Feinberg (1988, 139).

27. Devlin (1965, 17).
28. Ibid., 13–14.
29. Hart (1971, 52–53).
30. The moralist, at bottom, fails to distinguish between the majority's *disapproval* of an action and the *effect* of that action other than the disapproval. The harm principle cannot be so broad as to include disapproval, for then every whim or fancy, every imagined insult, every disliked difference, or even disliked similarity, would be grist for state intervention, for putting down by the king or priest or majority. So for someone to say "your very *face* affronts me" is not to say that he is harmed by the presence of the bearer of that face in the community.
31. Quotations in this and previous three sentences from Devlin (1965, 15).
32. Hart (1971, 54).
33. Grey (1983, 15).
34. To be fair, Devlin (1965, 16, 18) did not hold that the merest whisper of outrage justifies a criminal law. He proposed three "elastic" principles: (1) "toleration of the maximum individual freedom that is consistent with the integrity of society"; (2) "in any new matter of morals the law should be slow to act"; (3) "as far as possible privacy should be respected." Nevertheless, the general *principle* that Devlin espouses is the primacy of the legislature to act against immorality that has no definition other than the degree to which it arouses indignation.
35. Ibid., 22–23.
36. The thesis of might (or votes) makes right would make it impossible rationally to choose between the mossbacks who say: "I abhor gays' holding hands," and the politically correct twenty-first-century modern who retorts: "And I abhor your uptight, non-hip, repressed, narrow-minded approach to life. You make me sick and it's *you* who ought to be shut up."
37. George (1995, 78).
38. Devlin (1965, 22).
39. Devlin evidently thought homosexuality *is* a matter of choice. Whether, had he known different, he would have dropped his argument is anyone's guess, but the argument as presented does not seem to stand or fall on the voluntariness of the choice. Regardless of why people engage in homosexuality, the people in Devlin's society were repulsed by it and hence, in terms of the argument, it would remain subject to being outlawed. A different argument for the disintegration thesis with respect to homosexuality is that society would be impossible without families and that the loosening of sexual mores contributes to a weakening of the family bond. But it is unclear how outlawing homosexuality could be thought to affect family bonds, since homosexual couples increasingly have determined to create families. At most, the family bond argument provides justification for tighter enforcement of laws against such sexual misconduct as adultery. But the argument must still pass empirical tests: First, it is at least possible that adulteries over which a discreet silence is maintained *contribute* to family stability, by removing the pressure that the philandering spouse might otherwise feel to divorce. Second, growing sexual permissiveness among the young might ultimately encourage family bonds. As one sociologist has concluded: "Contrary to fears at the time, the [sexual] revolution of youth in the 1920s was not a revolt against the family. In fact, the family was becoming a more central part of life, as expectations for happiness and fulfillment through marriage reached new heights. The 'glorification of sex' was an aspect of 'the sexualization of marriage.' The new ideal of companionate marriage emphasized the sexual side of marriage as part of a more intimate personal relationship between husband and wife. Dating and petting permitted young people to explore their compatibility with a variety of partners." Skolnick (1991, 46). Third, if the family is endangered, the peril may be far removed from sexual license. Christopher Lasch (1979, 9) argued, for example, that capitalism and the "integrating tendencies of modern industrial society" have led to familial atrophy. Fourth, as feminists have argued, the family that the traditionalists wish to maintain were (and are) repressive institutions that have covered up abuse, taught misogyny, and failed to care fully for every member, on the whole keeping women from achieving anything close to the full lives of which each is capable, so that women in society

as a whole will be less harmed if the nature of the family bond changes and becomes more egalitarian. Okin (1989).
40. George (1995, 65–71).
41. *Lawrence v. Texas*, 539 U.S. 558 (2003), struck down laws banning homosexual acts between consenting adults in private.
42. A different sort of case has been presented by the constitutionalizing of a right to abortion in the United States. That refusal to condemn by law the violation of what many view as profoundly immoral has led to intense controversy, and some might suppose that the revulsion millions of people have felt about abortion practices in the United States after *Roe v. Wade* show the possibility that even social bonds can be snapped by a failure to uphold a common morality. Abortion rights have undeniably led to social disorder in various places at various times. But this example is significantly distinguishable from the problem of homosexuality. Unlike the claims about homosexual conduct, abortion involves people in what is arguably actual harming. The debate has been over whether the fetus is or ought to be considered a person; hence the outcry by millions of those opposed that abortion is murder. The debate over abortion, in other words, focuses in the eyes of its detractors on the state's willingness to countenance the killing of other people by large numbers of women and their cooperating physicians and medical staffs. The state's failure to bar significant harm might much more understandably lead to a weakening of the social bonds. But in this case the underlying philosophical argument is different, since under the harm principle no one can doubt the state's legitimate power to act. Debates over the nature of harm and the persons affected are part of normal liberal politics, and every society must consider as part of the political calculus to what degree any particular resolution of such issues will cause a rupture in people's willingness to remain together.
43. George (1995, 36–37, 37, 227). George is both a legal moralist and a paternalist: He favors morals legislation both to prevent harm to others and also, and in some ways more importantly, to one who is tempted to be immoral. The law "provides a person whose reason and will may be overwhelmed by powerful temptation . . . with a countervailing motive not to succumb to the tempting vice." Ibid., 227.
44. See Hauser (2007). "The central idea," Hauser says, is that "we evolved a moral instinct, a capacity that naturally grows within each child, designed to generate rapid judgments about what is morally right or wrong based on an unconscious grammar of action." Ibid., xvii.
45. Bell (1947, 80–81).
46. George (1995, 19), following Berlin (1991, 24).
47. Whether natural law is universal, as opposed to a more local morality rooted in a community's traditions (the basic principle of communitarianism), I leave undiscussed.
48. Dennett (1991, 452).
49. Cf. Robert H. Bork (1991, 123–124): "Knowledge that an activity is taking place is a harm to those who find it profoundly immoral. . . . Moral outrage is a sufficient ground for prohibitory legislation." Bork's assertion seems to imply either that he agrees with Devlin's analysis that might makes right (who else but a majority of like-minded outraged moralists could enact the law?) or that he would agree with, say, the Coalition for Pigs, that on the strength of strong religious traditions and the absolute moral nausea felt by adherents of those traditions, the state may order me to refrain from exercising my craving for bacon with my eggs.
50. *Navajo Nation v. United States Forest Service*, 535 F.3d 1058, 1063–1064 (9th Cir. 2008), *cert. den.* 556 U.S. 1281 (2009).
51. Fuller (1971, 180–181).
52. Even a contract to desist could not serve in the long run to defeat her change of mind. At most, presumably, the new dancing enthusiast would be obliged to refund whatever compensation she took from the neighbor to refrain from dancing. We could impose facts on the example that might seem to obligate the repentant nondancer. Suppose her neighbor informed her that she was moving in to the next-door apartment on the express condition that she refrain from dancing, and she agreed. The neighbor would then have an interest in

the other's interest in not dancing. To repudiate the agreement now would defeat that interest. But the example is now so loaded with fine conditions that it no longer resembles the claims about moral expectations in the world outside the apartment building. At worst, the neighbor might force the new dancer to move; she could not bar her from dancing elsewhere.

53. Feinberg (1985, 1).
54. Ibid., 10–13.
55. For example, a sign touting the culinary delights of eating human flesh and heralding our town as the cannibal capital of the world; from ibid., 70–71. See Postema (1987, 435).
56. Feinberg (1985, 35). Thus in *Cohen v. California*, 403 U.S. 15 (1971), the Supreme Court held that wearing an embroidered jacket reading "Fuck the Draft" in the Los Angeles County Courthouse could not serve as the basis of a charge of disturbing the peace, under the First Amendment, since, among other reasons, people could avert their eyes.
57. Feinberg (1985, 44).
58. Precisely on this ground, Alexander (2011) presses the argument that regulating aesthetics of the neighborhood is a form of legal moralism and therefore those who approve aesthetic regulation are legal moralists. It is not clear to me whether the claim holds—that is, that one who approves regulating the appearance of public spaces is necessarily operating outside the harm principle. If a city-owned restaurant chooses not to serve green butter (perfectly healthy but mixed with coloring) because it fears patrons will recoil, that's not a moral calculation but an economic one. The question, then, is whether some aesthetic choices create harms. How? Is it valid to say that public surroundings can affect property value, which is an interest that may be publicly protected? The argument is that people in a community each have an interest in maintaining the tax base of their town. Otherwise, people may flee, depressing the housing market, and tourists may decline to visit if the architectural vista changes in too significant a way. To preserve the visual character of the community (to maintain a particular "look" or to rid itself of unsightly vistas) the legislature may find it necessary to enact a code to prevent financial erosion; without appropriate finances, the state would be unable to carry out its various public missions. The state could purchase the property and put the burden on taxpayers to preserve their community, but since it is for a public purpose, it may regulate through zoning, as it regulates so much else. Whether the argument proves too much, I leave for another time. (For example, what is the response to the claim that property values also decline when the "wrong" person moves in next door and so the state may steer certain people to another part of town or refuse them entry altogether? The appropriate answer may be that property values can be trumped by the equality criterion, but I leave this problem to another day.)
59. Scruton (1980, 74).
60. But see the counterargument in note 58 above.
61. Feinberg (1984, 21–25) proposes the following as candidates for "free-floating evils," that is, morally wrong acts that do no harm to anyone: violations of taboos, discreet and harmless conventional immoralities (private sexual acts), religiously tabooed practices, moral corruption of another (or oneself), evil thoughts, impure thoughts, wanton and capricious squashing of small animals or flowers in the wild, and extinction of a species. The last on his list is controversial, more so perhaps than when Feinberg wrote. Intentional extinction of some species may cause considerable harm to people's lives by interfering with the community's ecology.
62. See, for example, Buchanan (1989, 853): "It is fair to say that the eloquence and rhetorical power of communitarian writers frequently exceed their ability to expound their theses clearly and to make the logical structure of their arguments manifest." To the same effect, Posner (1990, 414–419). See also commentators quoted on the third defect of the communitarian argument in note 92 below.
63. For a summary of the principal communitarian positions, see Kymlicka (1995a, 366–378). For more extended treatments, see Holmes (1993, chaps. 4–7); Rosenbloom (1989). Principal texts are Sandel (1982); MacIntyre (1984, 1988); Taylor (1985); Bellah (1985); Etzioni (1994). See also: Bell (1993); Mulhall and Swift (1996); Delaney (1994); Tam (1998); Phillips (1993); Friedman (1994).

64. Cf. Holmes (1995, 268): "The starting point for liberalism is not the atomistic individual, but the conflicts that ensue when differently socialized individuals, immersed in contrasting creeds, customs, and affective attachments, clumsily rub shoulders and attempt to coexist." See also Lilla (2007).
65. Knowles (2001, 116).
66. Alasdair MacIntyre (1984, 204–205). This notion, that a person's identity derives from a specific tradition and that there is nothing universal in each of us by virtue of our hereditary origin as Homo sapiens, resembles the claims of Joseph-Marie de Maistre (1974, 97), conservative proponent of the Counter-Enlightenment, who memorably wrote that "[t]here is no such thing in the world as *man*. In my life I have seen Frenchmen, Italians, Russians, and so on. I even know, thanks to Montesquieu, that one can be Persian. But as for *man*, I declare I've never encountered him. If he exists, I don't know about it." But that claim is false almost on its face, and it is certainly false as we understand matters today. To say that because people are culturally shaped, that because they identify with nationality and other traditions, they share no commonality beneath the cultural overlay is, crudely, like saying that there is no such thing as a computer, generally, because each machine has a brand on it (Dell, Mac, HP, Lenovo) and because their screens display different software faces to the casual viewer. Or that there's no such thing as language generally, because I have heard only French, or Italian, or Russian spoken, not language.
67. If the claim is that other people must be directed to follow communal norms to prevent distress to the person who is trying to inhabit her social role (without the cooperation of others, her expectations of a meaningful life may be interrupted or destroyed), the answer should by now be clear. To pin people to a social norm is to say nothing more than that the person seeking to maintain her "place" in society wishes to have an interest in others' interests, and that is barred by the externality constraint.
68. "In one southern city the censorship board thus ruled 'obscene' a movie which showed black and white children playing together in a school yard." Abraham and Perry (1998, 201). This reference cites erroneously to a newspaper account that does not mention the event. In 1947, Lloyd T. Binford, arch censor of film for three decades in Memphis, Tennessee, banned the 1947 movie *Curley* because it showed black and white children fraternizing in the same school. "Memphis Bars Negro Children at Play in Film" (1947); see Strub (2007); Finger (n.d.). Consider also these letters to the editor of *Life* magazine in 1942, responding to a story about Paul Robeson's starring as "the first Negro in America to play Othello." "Life Goes to a Performance of Othello" (1942, 83). One correspondent from Houston said succinctly that the article "where the Negro and whites are in the same play, is more than I can stomach. What in the hell is this country coming to?" The other letter writer, from Covington, Kentucky, pointed to "the horrible, indelible, undeniable and terrifying fact that there are white men with so little respect for themselves that they would cause to be printed the picture of a Negro man with his arm around a white woman in a love scene." Letters to the Editors (1942, 11).
69. MacIntyre (1984, 219).
70. Communitarians in this sense follow Devlin's reasoning, not George's.
71. Stephen Holmes (1991, 232). Cf. Freud (1959, 10–11): "When individuals come together in a group all their individual inhibitions fall away and all the cruel, brutal and destructive instincts, which lie dormant in individuals as relics of a primitive epoch, are stirred up to free gratification."
72. See text at note 57 in chapter 1.
73. As Tushnet (2003, 51) notes: "Legal historian Sally Hadden [2001] has explored in great detail Wyatt-Brown's primary example [of Southerners being expected to adhere to a code rather than being able to do whatever they wanted because the law said they could]: masters who tried to make their plantations 'the prime center of group loyalty' by keeping out the slave patrols that the community used to ensure that slaves were properly docile. In the end, Hadden shows, masters' resistance was overcome, because the proper regard of the community was essential to the preservation of the very honor that the masters sought to demonstrate."

74. See the account of the Maori attack on the Moriori peoples in Diamond (1997, 53ff.).
75. As noted in chapter 1, note 86, a village council in Pakistan's Punjab Province ordered a woman gang-raped "as punishment after her younger brother was accused of illicit relations with a woman from a rival tribe." Masood (2005). Should a cultural community's deep-seated tradition outweigh due process? How does communitarian theory prevent such a punishment?
76. Again, I note without examining the moralist's problem of proof. Who is the authoritative expositor of the community's morality? If it is the legislator, then what prevents legislators from expressing their personal predilections as substitutes for the community's moral notions? And how can we decide that what the community shuns is immorality or something that it simply regards with distaste? For example, was it the Michigan community's sense of morality that prohibited women from working as bartenders (see *Goesaert v. Cleary*, 335 U.S. 464 [1948])? Was it a moral code that led to bans on interracial marriage? Dworkin examines four examples of reasons that people sometimes incorrectly advance as a "moral position": prejudice, personal emotional reaction, rationalization (reliance on false and implausible "facts"), and parroting (reliance on others' opinions). These are often the basis for an advocate's conclusion that a practice should be outlawed as immoral, but such reasoning is faulty and should be rejected, Dworkin argues (1976, 248–253). In assessing a community's claims, do we take a poll? What would the poll ask? Do we ask only "right-thinking people," as it is sometimes phrased; in other words, should we substitute experts (religious leaders? ethicists? philosophy instructors?) for the citizenry? Do we compare texts? One writer proposes as a "mode of justification" a mode of "immanent critique.... We abstract from a given culture its primary principles and use those to reflect upon the actual practices of that society. Values are context bound, rather than transcendental, and can be discovered by a process of ideological archeology." Moody (1994, 99) is unclear on who appoints the archeologists and who trains them. As we saw, Devlin avoided this serious problem by expressly disavowing any need to probe the reasonable man's reasoning: It was enough that he wished a behavior to be outlawed.
77. Taylor (1986, 215), quoted in Kymlicka (1995a, 374).
78. Kymlicka (1995a, 375).
79. Speaking in 1989, Michael Walzer (1990, 6) compared communitarianism to pleated pants: "transient but certain to return." The modern communitarian argument flared from the early 1980s through the mid-1990s and then seemed to burn out. It is now (in 2012) quiescent, in part because it was shown to be, as it had accused liberalism of being, incoherent. It was also too vague to constitute a political theory, and its adherents did not descend below their plane of high abstraction to give it content. Mainly for these reasons, my discussion is briefer than it might have been had this book been published fifteen years earlier. Elizabethan tract: Morison (1984), quoted in Herzog (1989, 43).
80. Chesterton (1921).
81. Frankel (1956, 80).
82. As I was working on this point, in March 2008, I chanced, while driving, to be tuned to a Delaware radio station on which a woman was recounting an appraisal of the ideas of the Rev. Billy Graham. She said she was following along pretty well until she realized he was suggesting that one can be baptized "spiritually," that is, she said, without "being immersed." Where, she wondered, did the Bible allow that? It's crucial to baptism, she said, her voice becoming heated, that there be water. Does political theology permit a water-free baptism? Require it? Prohibit it? Legislatures once fought over such things. Left to politics, the odds are not so much that the state will get it wrong but that society will be fragmented even worse, not unified, by the attempt to get it at all.
83. Frankel (1956, 82).
84. Ibid., 83. Frankel was perhaps more sanguine than many, a half-century later, about the possibility of social cohesion in a pluralistic society. A current manifestation of this age-old problem is in India, where, Martha C. Nussbaum (2007a) reports, violent clashes between Hindus and Muslims in Gujarat indicate "that in a thriving democracy, many individuals are

unable to live with others who are different, on terms of mutual respect and amity. They seek total domination as the only road to security and pride." See also Nussbaum (2007b).
85. Sandel (1984, 7).
86. In effect, this critique turns on its head the story that Hobbes told, that the human world began with atomistic, ego-driven, selfish individuals who need to be tamed. The modern communitarian accuses liberalism not of beginning but ending there. But historically, it was not individual against individual who fought the bitter religious wars of the sixteenth and seventeenth centuries. It was a clash between pluralistic cultures, between communities, not between individuals. The problem for individuals was how to get out of the way. The war of all against all was a war of community against community, not man against man.
87. Wollheim (1959, 38), quoted in Golding (1975, 65).
88. As Allen Buchanan (1989, 856–857) summarizes it, the communitarian claim is that "a genuine community is not a mere association of individuals. Members of a community have common ends, not merely congruent private interests, and these are conceived of and valued as common ends by the members."
89. I exaggerate slightly. Daniel Defoe, in an essay published in 1697, proposed an academy to root out pernicious changes to the language: Its work "should be to ... polish and refine the English tongue, and advance the so much neglected faculty of correct language, to establish purity and propriety of style, and to purge it from all the irregular additions that ignorance and affectation have introduced. . . . The reputation of this [academy] would be enough to make them the allowed judges of style and language; and no author would have the impudence to coin without their authority. Custom, which is now our best authority for words, would always have its original here, and not be allowed without it. There should be no more occasion to search for derivations and constructions, and it would be as criminal then to coin words as money" (Defoe [1894, 139–141]). The French Academy has long tried to police the French language, with increasingly less success. See, e.g., Simons (1994); Wiley (1967). For a list of other language "regulators," see http://www.aboutlanguageschools.com/regulators/ (accessed November 17, 2011).
90. Whether a geographic community or a general society is a community in the communitarian sense is a separate and interesting question that I need not address. Communities consciously constituted by their members to serve a purpose, like a basketball team or an orchestra, have the communal purpose for which they are formed. Individuals have purposes, and the state has a purpose, as an instrument to permit people to live in peace and to safeguard their attempts to fulfill their purposes. But it is unclear (to me) whether a more general community has a purpose apart from its members' or what that purpose might be. Whatever it might be, it is not well addressed in the communitarian literature. See Simpson (1994).
91. If the "good of community" cannot be approached from the perspective of individual members—i.e., if it is incorrect to argue that individuals may choose whether to continue to participate in the community for their sake and its sake, because this is to take the individual's side over the community's—then the conclusion to be drawn is that any given community is a good in itself; it is good *for that community* (for the world?) that it exists. What can that mean? That there be a group of people who hold to certain views, continue certain practices, state certain opinions, live in certain ways? Why should it matter whether one day the annual parade no longer takes place, or if people cease to come to church in the numbers they once did? These things can, of course, matter to individuals—I can be disappointed, even crushed, if the "old neighborhood" haunts vanish, if the ways of a people disappear; unsettling changes by their very nature can affect me profoundly—but that is to consider the problem from the individual's perspective. Why should it matter to the community itself? Is it just that it is unfortunate when the world loses some of its diversity, as it does when an ancient language dies out with the shrinking population of an ancient society? Or is it like an argument that roads must be built for the sake, not of individual drivers, but of the traffic itself?
92. Rosenblum (1989, 215); Holmes (1993, 178). See also Gutmann (1985, 319–320): "The communitarian critics want us to live in Salem, but not to believe in witches. Or human

rights.... [It makes no] theoretical sense to assume away the conflicts among competing ends—such as the conflict between communal standards of sexual morality and individual sexual preference—that give rise to the characteristic liberal concern for rights. In so doing, the critics avoid discussing how morally to resolve our conflicts and therefore fail to provide us with a political theory relevant to our world."

93. Gardbaum (1992, 725). See, generally, Symposium (1988). While this manuscript was in the hands of the copyeditor, I came across Philip Pettit's *Republicanism* (Pettit 1997). By "republicanism," Pettit proposes that the central good to be pursued is that of non-domination. He compares non-domination with "noninterference," which is the idea that he supposes lies at the center of liberalism. In his account, republicanism is superior because a liberal state that does not interfere with its citizens would still tolerate acts of domination by those in the private realm against their "inferiors" (husbands against wives, employers against employees, etc.). Although it is in many ways an ingenious account, Pettit rarely moves beyond abstractions, which make it difficult to tell what policies a republican state so defined could pursue, as he concedes. Ibid., 147. Moreover, his definition of liberalism is not sufficiently nuanced. Liberalism is not simply a state that does not interfere; it can interfere heavily if necessary to put down harmful activities, which might well include acts of domination. In the end, it is possible, perhaps even likely, that the republican state he envisions is the liberal state that I describe. He comes close to saying so: "The republic is a state that is forced to track the common interests of its citizens"; it may not "tak[e] account of goods that are not presumptive matters of citizen *interest*, ... [nor take] account of good that are not matters of *recognizable* interest ... [or] that are not matters of *common* interest. Thus it outlaws the perfectionist state that espouses some alleged good without regard to citizen interests. It outlaws the paternalistic state that fails to take account of people's perceptions of their interests. And, most conspicuously of all, it outlaws the state that takes account of the recognizable interests of some individual or group other than the citizens as a whole." Ibid., 290-291. In any event, Pettit's republicanism is apparently not that of "mainstream" civic republicanism.

94. Gardbaum (1995, 729).

95. Shapiro (1986, 296-297): "Many of the new communitarian writers appear to assume that community is synonymous with republican community, and that this notion should be opposed, at a very high level of generality, to the neo-Kantian liberalism of Rawls, Nozick, and their progeny. Advocates of this view should keep in mind, however, that republicanism as an ideology has also proven itself serviceable to social and political repression, both historically and in the contemporary world, and that to embrace it as an abstract ideal is to say little useful from the point of view of articulating a viable alternative political ideology. Those interested in advancing this debate should shift it to a lower level of abstraction and seek to supply substantive content to the various communitarian proposals they advocate."

96. Sandel (1996, 4, 3, 5, 6).

97. Ibid., 10.

98. See text at note 22 in chapter 4.

99. Burke's Speech to the Electors of Bristol quoted in Stephen Macedo (1991, 118). Gordon Wood (1993, 250-251) reminds us that the failure to articulate a means of achieving a disinterested public good is not a new question; it reaches back to the beginning of the American republic. In the 1780s, "the state legislatures could scarcely fulfill what many revolutionaries in 1776 had assumed was their republican responsibility to promote a unitary public interest distinguishable from the private and parochial interests of people. By the 1780s it was obvious to many that 'a spirit of *locality*' was destroying 'the aggregate interests of the community.' ... Washington, for one, quickly realized that to expect ordinary people, such 'as compose the bulk of an Army,' to be 'influenced by any other principles than those of Interest, is to look for what never did, and I fear never will happen.' Even most officers could not be expected to sacrifice their private interests and their families for the sake of their country ... In short, the Anti-Federalists were saying that liberally educated gentlemen were no more capable than ordinary people of classical republican disinterestedness and virtue and that

consequently there was no one in the society equipped to promote an exclusive public interest that was distinguishable from the private interests of people." See also Herzog (1986, 487, 484): "Critics of liberalism are fond of charging liberalism with being perniciously incomplete. Liberals, they tell us, refuse to hold up any authoritative conception of the good life; liberals think that all that matters is survival, or the gratification of appetites. Liberals have an easy rejoinder: Politics is now one social setting among many, so individuals can pursue the good life in other social settings. To say that politics shouldn't be about the good life isn't to say that the good life doesn't matter. The accusation seems better directed against republicans. That we should share commitments may sound inviting; it might be nice to live in a community with others who shared your deepest commitments.... But which commitments should we share?" And: "We might move to quash gay rights, or keep women in traditional roles, thinking that the increased freedom of either group threatens social order and community. These options are unpleasant, no doubt; but we need a theoretical account of how we are to build a politics of civic virtue in the United States."

100. The attentive reader may have noticed that I have omitted one major class of activity. That class comprises the principal means by which humans interact in the world: the expression, depiction, and communication of ideas, opinions, and feelings. Unconstrained speech can cause direct harm—for example, incitement that sparks an unruly crowd to loot and maim—and the expression of both opinion and facts widely and daily can offend listeners. Yet for the most part we leave speech unfettered, even though, over time, it can be highly subversive, prompting revolutionary changes in the culture. Many suppose that culture should be regarded as more dear a possession than the particular artifacts valued within or by it, for it is the culture that gives them their meaning. Yet we legally protect these artifacts against theft or destruction, because they are essential to individual human lives, while allowing speech that may transform the culture in which the artifacts have meaning. I omit these two issues, speech that causes harm and the offense that people take from freedom of speech in its widest meaning, not because they are insignificant—obviously they are of the greatest significance—but because they are too important and complex to be considered adequately in a single book. I hope to return to them in succeeding volumes, which I have tentatively titled *Speech Matters* and *Taking Offense*.

101. The politics of multiculturalism is a large topic and I consider it only briefly here. More extended accounts can be found in Magnet (2005), Brown (2003), Galston (2002a), Barry (2001), Kymlicka (1989, 1995b, 1995c), and Gutmann (1994).

102. As Taylor (1994, 43) puts it, the "two modes of politics, then, both based on the notion of equal respect, come into conflict. For one, the principle of equal respect requires that we treat people in a difference-blind fashion. The fundamental intuition that humans command this respect focuses on what is the same in all. For the other, we have to recognize and even foster particularity. The reproach the first makes to the second is just that it violates the principle of nondiscrimination. The reproach the second makes to the first is that it negates identity by forcing people into a homogeneous mold that is untrue to them. This would be bad enough if the mold were itself neutral—nobody's mold in particular. But the complaint generally goes further. The claim is that the supposedly neutral set of difference-blind principles of the politics of equal dignity is in fact a reflection of one hegemonic culture. As it turns out, then, only the minority or suppressed cultures are being forced to take an alien form. Consequently, the supposedly fair and difference-blind society is not only inhuman (because suppressing identities) but also, in a subtle and unconscious way, itself highly discriminatory." It is unclear why Taylor does not consider that a politics of universalism can permit dissenters to choose to be educated in their native languages; the possibilities need not be between two polarizing and exclusive regimes.

103. I draw this narrative of the Quebec experience from Taylor, ibid.

104. See text at note 81 in chapter 5.

105. In nonliberal Malaysia, Muslims "are subject to separate laws on inheritance and marriage and must marry within the faith." The nation's highest court refused to permit a Muslim

woman to convert to Catholicism and remove "the word Islam from her identity card to marry her Catholic fiancé." To do so, the court ruled, a Muslim religious court must first consent. Fuller (2007).

106. In some parts of India, conservative pressure has forced women in universities and elsewhere to dress according to a strictly religious code; rapes and other crimes committed against them are excused when they failed to wear the proper clothing. Neelakantan (2006).

107. See, e.g., Walker and Parmar (1993).

108. An Afghan Muslim man who converted to Christianity faced the death penalty because under the civil law, Islam is the "supreme law," and under the religious code, conversion is a sin punishable by death. Munadi and Hauser (2006). The official reason for releasing him in the particular case was that the investigation lasted beyond its legal limit, but there were also questions about the man's mental stability and the likelihood that he held dual citizenship.

109. Taylor (1994, 60–61) sees "other models of liberal society" that do not insist on "uniform application of the rules defining [fundamental] rights, without exception" and that are open to collective goals. These other models "do call for the invariant defense of *certain* rights, of course. There would be no question of cultural differences determining the application of habeas corpus, for example. But they distinguish these fundamental rights from the broad range of immunities and presumptions of uniform treatment that have sprung up in modern cultures of judicial review. They are willing to weigh the importance of certain forms of uniform treatment against the importance of cultural survival, and opt sometimes in favor of the latter. They are thus in the end not procedural models of liberalism, but are grounded very much on judgments about what makes a good life—judgments in which the integrity of cultures has an important place."

110. Ibid., 63, 64.

111. Appiah (1994, 161, 162, 163). The argument that people should be respected as members of groups, rather than as individuals, seems unlikely to lead to a wholesome outcome. Nancy Fraser (1986, 428) says that we must deal with people politically from "the standpoint of the '*collective concrete other*,'" which is to say that we should encounter others "less as unique individuals than as members of groups or collectivities with culturally specific identities, solidarities and forms of life." And under "the most general ethical force of this orientation ... we owe each other behavior such that each is confirmed as a being with specific collective identifications and solidarities." Even if it were meaningful, to sort out all possible "specific collective identifications and solidarities" would be impossible, and the press of time would quickly pigeonhole most of us into sterile and hypothetical categories that would imprison us: Would female professionals be classified as belonging to a cultural group who do housework? Would gay golfers be classified by sexual orientation or as athletes? Would national origin, language group, and religion serve to balkanize us as we attempt to show respect for one another in this "orientation"? See Moon (1993, 180ff.) for a fuller discussion.

112. Parekh (1994, 13), quoted in Barry (2001, 127).

113. Taylor (1994, 66, 68–69) forthrightly acknowledges the problematic nature of the conclusion that many wish to draw from the premise that we owe equal respect to all cultures, namely, that all cultures are in fact of "equal worth." Taylor labels as a presumption "that all human cultures that have animated whole societies over some considerable stretch of time have something important to say to all human beings." But the raw demand bristles with difficulties: "It makes sense to demand as a matter of right that we approach the study of certain cultures with a presumption of their value.... But it can't make sense to demand as a matter of right that we come up with a final concluding judgment that their value is great, or equal to others'. That is, if the judgment of value is to register something independent of our own wills and desires, it cannot be dictated by a principle of ethics. On examination, either we will find something of great value in culture C, or we will not. But it makes no more sense to demand that we do so than it does to demand that we find the earth round or flat, the temperature of the air hot or cold."

114. Friedman (1962, 111). Friedman's position seems almost willfully perverse. He suggests (110) that the harm from discrimination is done to the discriminator: "The man who objects

to buying from or working alongside a Negro ... thereby limits his [own] range of choice. He will generally have to pay a higher price for what he buys or receive a lower return for his work."
115. Ibid., 114–115.
116. See "Equality Principle" in chapter 7.
117. See text at notes 54–56 in chapter 9.
118. The custom against which the law acted in the dueling example in chapter 9 forced a person to "accept" the risk of harm against his will; the custom against which the law acts in this chapter forced a person to act to cause harm against his will.
119. Here I depart from Feinberg's less nuanced view that the state should avoid folkways: "What liberalism *is* committed to saying about tradition is that the state should leave community traditions alone, neither restrict them nor enforce them. Rather it should let communities work out their own historic courses, write their own stories, find their own pattern of evolution, conduct their own argument (without force) with dissidents and reformers. That is not only the state role that is *just* for all (as the liberal emphasizes); it is also the best way for the traditions themselves to flourish." Feinberg (1988, 97).
120. Lee (1960, 206).
121. Historical accounts abound. Any standard history of the civil rights movement in the United States amply records the strength of the custom and the ostracism of those seeking reform; see, for example, Branch (1988); Garrow (1986); Woodward (1974).
122. The Supreme Court has essentially denied this proposition in a narrow context in a case construing a federal civil rights law, 42 United States Code §1983, that permits private damage suits for violations of constitutional rights by people acting "under color of law" or by virtue of a "custom, or usage, of any State." The claim was against private restaurant owners who refused to seat black patrons. Justice Harlan's majority opinion concluded that the latter phrase "requires state involvement and is not simply a practice that reflects long-standing social habits." *Adickes v. S. H. Kress & Co.*, 398 U.S. 144, 166 (1970). Rather, custom "must have the force of law by virtue of the persistent practices of state officials" (at 167). In dissent, Justice Brennan insisted that the term "means custom of the people of a State, not custom of state officials" (at 231)—"a widespread and longstanding practice, commonly regarded as prescribing norms for conduct, and backed by sanctions" (at 224), even though "not backed by the force of the state" (at 225). *Adickes* was a matter of statutory construction, and does not stand for the proposition that Congress is debarred from directly legislating against a custom that results in widespread discrimination on the basis of race. As a matter of constitutional law, Congress clearly may do so. *Jones v. Alfred H. Mayer Co.*, 392 U.S. 409 (1968) (under the Thirteenth Amendment, Congress may prohibit discrimination in the sale of private homes); *Heart of Atlanta Motel v. United States*, 379 U.S. 241 (1964) (under the Commerce Clause, Congress may enact public accommodations laws outlawing racial discrimination in renting hotel rooms). I am arguing that the harm principle, likewise, will permit a legislature to overturn custom in this sense when the effect of the custom is to cause harm.
123. Friedman (1962, 118) expresses the old saw that "we should not be so naïve as to suppose that deep-seated values and beliefs can be uprooted in short measure by law." But it seems inescapable that enforced law can uproot, or importantly contribute to the uprooting of, even deep-seated values and beliefs over time; the history of much of the past half-century in America would have to be denied were it otherwise.
124. *Plessy v. Ferguson*, 163 U.S. 537, 550 (1896).
125. Will Kymlicka (1991, 145) has suggested that by itself separation is not necessarily an evil. The "aboriginal peoples of North America ... value their separation from the mainstream life and culture of North America. Separation is not always perceived as a 'badge of inferiority.'" But the problem confronted here is not separation per se, but *enforced* segregation by the dominant group, which I believe would be universally understood as a badge of inferiority.
126. Simpson (1951, 14).
127. There will necessarily be a fuzzy boundary too between familiar or intimate friendships and relationships that arise in sole proprietorships and small businesses. The state might wish to

err on the side of the intimate relationship, by extending the right to associate, free from public interference, to small businesses. On the other hand, since it seems unlikely that anyone would protest to the point of suing over someone's refusal to be his friend, demands for equality in business relationships would not, in fact, be about intimate relationships that belong entirely to the field of private relations. This general point was central to Justice Lewis F. Powell's concurring opinion in *Runyun v. McCrary*, 427 U.S. 160, 187–189 (1976), raising the question whether §1981 of the federal civil rights statutes can constitutionally ban exclusion of applicants to a private school solely on the basis of race. Powell agreed that it did.

128. "Racial Steering" (1994), arguing that advertisements such as "seeking white female" or "black male," etc., "creates harms that should be weighed against its worth" and finding its worth wanting.

Chapter 11

1. In this short summary I follow some of the themes, though not the method or historical summary, of Stephen Holmes (1995). On self-interest, see his chap. 2. On restraints and limitations, see his chaps. 4, 5, and 7.
2. Again, I note that throughout I am speaking of liberalism as a coherent and political theory, not as a political party or as a description of how any particular government actually acts.
3. Sandel (1996, 6, 7).
4. Ibid., 7–8.
5. Ibid., 10.
6. Ibid., 12.
7. Ibid., 15, 19–20, quoting Freeman (1934, 443).
8. Lilla (2007).
9. Chesterton (1905, 33).
10. Dworkin takes to task Mark Tushnet for expressing such views. Tushnet conceded as "caricature" his description of classical liberalism as one of "autonomous ... isolated islands of individuality." Tushnet (1983, 783ff.). Dworkin (1986, 440n19) says that the description is "more a forgery."
11. Highet (1954, 81).
12. Cf. Herzog (1989, 171–175).
13. Nietzsche (1907, 225–226 [§259]), quoted and discussed in Holmes (1993, 235–236).
14. Bloom (1975, 654, 653, 653, 662). Bloom's diatribe was aimed exclusively at Rawls's account of liberalism in *A Theory of Justice*, but Bloom's language seems to embrace much of the liberalism that the harm principle produces.
15. Kymlicka (1991, 113).
16. This is Kymlicka's characterization of Michael Sandel's claim. Kymlicka (1995a, 367).
17. Madison (1961, 322).
18. Spencer (1970, 216).
19. Malraux quoted in Conquest (2000, 35–36). In an impassioned essay written one year before his death, Leo Tolstoy (1948, 53) exhorted his readers to "destroy governments" by the simple expedient of withholding funds and service (as soldiers). All governments, Tolstoy exclaimed (echoing Augustine), are frauds and robbers. And the security of the people? "[I]n Christendom there is no need to protect the peoples, one from another."
20. See, e.g., Wagner (1994, 104).
21. Barry (2001, 284–291).
22. Thomas (1985, 95).
23. Fetal pain: See Miller (2010). A 2005 Senate bill that did not pass declared that the "[f]ederal government [has an] interest in reducing the number of events in which great pain is inflicted on sentient creatures" and concluded that it is a "medical fact [that] ... unborn infants.. can feel pain ... even more intense than that of newborn infants." Unborn Child Pain Awareness Act, S. 51, 109th Cong., 1st Sess., §2(7) (2005) (available at http://www.gpo.gov/fdsys/

pkg/BILLS-109s51is/pdf/BILLS-109s51is.pdf [accessed November 17, 2011]); see also Nebraska's Pain-Capable Unborn Child Protection Act, §5, Nebraska Revised Statutes §28-3.102–111 (2011); Unborn Child Pain Awareness/Prevention Act, 63 Oklahoma Statutes Annotated §1-738.6–1.739.17 (2011). Pornography harmful and discriminatory: Dworkin and MacKinnon (1988); MacKinnon (1993); Butler (1997, 74–75); MacKinnon and Dworkin (1998). Violent video games case: *Brown v. Entertainment Merchants Ass'n.*, 131 S.Ct. 2729 (2011). *Griswold v. Connecticut*, 381 U.S. 479 (1965). *Lawrence v. Texas*, 539 U.S. 558 (2003). Harm to children: see Sullivan (2004).

24. The impulse to deny reality is a spreading phenomenon and is not necessarily limited to politicians seeking to avoid legislation. See, for example, Manjoo (2008); Specter (2009).
25. Sandel (1996, 107).
26. A common reflection of this tendency is the misuse and distortion of the facts in cases that become notorious. For example, in the common understanding of the "hot coffee" case, in 1994 Stella Liebeck won millions of dollars from an Albuquerque, New Mexico, jury for managing to spill hot coffee that she had just purchased at a McDonald's restaurant, implying that the courts are acting moronically in permitting such a judgment to stand, since everyone knows that coffee is hot. In fact, the coffee was superheated, the plaintiff's burns were extensive, and McDonald's had had hundreds of earlier complaints about just this problem. See Cain (2007) (available online at http://www.jtexconsumerlaw.com/V11N1/Coffee.pdf) (accessed November 17, 2011). HBO premiered a documentary on the case on June 27, 2011, featuring vivid photos of the burns; see: http://www.hotcoffeethemovie.com/default.asp (accessed November 17, 2011).
27. For example, it is a common complaint that regulations are often excessively picky and achieve relatively little, but compel costly outlays to lawyers, accountants, and others to assist in compliance. See, e.g., Howard (1994).
28. On total redress, see Lieberman (1981a, 31–32).
29. See Rachlinski (2002–2003); Kahan (2007).

Appendix

1. See, for example, Strayer (1970). Ratification of the United States Constitution is a rare historical instance in which the people were consulted. The Framers were clear that to be operative this document beginning "We, the People" had to be actually ratified by the people. In establishing procedures to choose delegates to the ratification conventions, several states waived their usual property qualifications for voting; New York "invited all free adult male citizens to vote." Amar (2005, 7). But that left unfree males and all women, and in any event, New York was the state most open to an expanded electorate. See also Shapiro (2005, 21–22, and chap. 1) on the problem of discerning whether consent is authentic.
2. Locke (1965b, 392 [§ 119]).
3. Herzog (1989, 185).
4. Rawls (1971, 12).
5. Ibid., 139.
6. Rawls (1971, 20) essentially admits that through a process he calls "reflective equilibrium" he is doing just that.
7. The literature on Rawls is, of course, voluminous, and I do not aim to summarize any of it. For a critique of the veil of ignorance published shortly after the original *Theory of Justice*, see Barry (1973, chap. 2); and the three essays in Part I of Daniels (1974). See also Kukathas and Pettit (1990) and references cited; Hirshman (1994) and references cited.
8. Rawls (1993, 3).
9. Bruce A. Ackerman (1980, 196) claims that his consent theory is different from Rawls's hypothetical consent in which individuals are denuded of any self-identity and from the imaginary consent of the original social contractarians. He claims that "ideal theory focuses upon the *explicit* agreements made by flesh and blood people on the basis of their particular

insights into the concrete opportunities that social life affords them." But his scheme works if at all only because of a claimed "perfect technology of justice" and a hypothetical "Commander" with no self-identity who seeks a single answer to every question asked: "Are you offering a proof of your claim with a reason other than 'I am better than you'?" and all in the context of a request for a single product, "manna," by people who are only hypothetically real as they attempt to found a new society off earth. At best, we seem to face a choice between imaginary participants in the real world or putatively real participants in an imaginary world (actually, puppets in both). Some choice.

10. Thomas Jefferson thought that a "living generation" can bind only itself. Stephen Holmes (1995, 157) suggests the practical difficulty: "To require the express consent of every generation to the constitutional framework (or of every individual to majority rule) would introduce an element of nervous hysteria into the heart of democratic politics, weakening its capacity to resolve conflicts and aggregate diverse interests without violence." Without a theory of tacit consent, Madison said, it would be impossible to accept the legitimacy of "the rule by which the majority decides for the whole." Madison (1981, 24) quoted in Holmes, ibid.

11. Herzog (1989, chap. 6).

12. Ibid., 203–205, suggests that consent of the governed can be seen in the "responsiveness" of the government to the people. While, as noted in the text, this is an important component of the liberal institutional commitments (representative government that must listen to the people, more or less, more often than now and then), it does not get at the problem of majorities' disinclination to permit some ways of life that the majority repudiates as bad.

13. The reductio ad absurdum of this argument is summed up in a "manifesto" that Mary Midgley (1993, 3) says she "once heard someone lay down in an argument about the duty of toleration"—to wit: "But surely it's always wrong to make moral judgements?"

14. This is the burden of Part I of Nozick (1974), discussed in chapter 2.

15. In the Crito (49–50), Socrates argues for a proposition that sounds close to affirming this apparent fallacy. Socrates says that he takes as a premise "that it is never right either to act unjustly, or to repay injustice with injustice, or to avenge ourselves on any man who harms us, by harming him in return." This proposition Socrates then uses to bolster his claim that it would be unjust to disobey the verdict of the Athenians that he must drink the hemlock, because the law, even if wrong, must be obeyed. What saves Socrates' argument from the anarchist fallacy is that Plato begins from quite contrary premises: not that the state may never interfere with us, no matter what we have done, but rather that the state is prior to and sets the boundaries of our lives. When Plato, in *The Laws* (Book 9, 880b–881d), backs away from the perfectionist republic, he also backs away from his earlier conclusion. Plato "thought that when a young thug beats up an old man, the able-bodied persons who do not interfere are just as guilty as the attacker." Shklar (1990, 41).

16. Simone Chambers (1996, 23) argues that Locke was not a contractarian at all: "Locke, when speaking about moral authority, is not a contractarian but a natural rights theorist. Locke does not use contract as a procedural test of right action, nor does he apply it to the traditional area of justice. The rules that regulate right action and just exchange already exist in the state of nature. It could be argued that if we were perfectly rational, we would choose to follow natural laws, but what makes them just is their having been sanctioned by God, not our having consented to them." But there may be little difference between the two positions, for the problem, which Locke readily admits, is that we do not know how to apply the laws of nature or necessarily discern them in the particular case. That means that the social contract is the political device by which people consent to the legislature's judgments (or the courts') about what the right rule is in the circumstances. So rather than a procedure to *devise* the rule, it's a procedure to *discover* the rule. Indeed, for centuries British jurists denied that they were altering or creating the law; even Parliament was assumed merely to be declaring what the law had always been, to be restoring the ancient law to an abused people. See Kern (1970, 164–166). Not until 1966 did the House of Lords, the highest British court,

explicitly concede that it had power to overrule its prior decisions, though it had been doing so for centuries. See Cross and Ham (1991, 104ff.).
17. Rawls (1971, 302).
18. Chambers (1996, 7).
19. Gutmann and Thompson (1996, 1, 12).
20. Rawls (1993, 224). Strictly, the true constraint is the veil of ignorance, through which Rawls filters in and blocks from entering the knowledge he thinks appropriate to the conversation.
21. Larmore (1987, 53).
22. Chambers (1986, 75). See also Greenawalt (1988).
23. Moon (1993, 96).
24. Benhabib (1989, 150).
25. For a brief description of Habermas's theory, see Rosenfeld (1995).
26. Walzer (1989–90, 185).
27. Fraser (1993, 121).
28. Chambers (1996, 207).
29. Moon (1993, 92).
30. Berkowitz (1999, 180).
31. Walzer (1989–90, 194). The points in this paragraph are a very short summary of his argument.
32. Gutmann and Thompson (1996, 17).
33. Rawls (1971, 19): "The parties in the original position are equal. That is, all have the same rights in the procedure for choosing principles.... Obviously the purpose of these conditions is to represent equality between human beings as moral persons, as creatures having a conception of their good and capable of a sense of justice. The basis of equality is taken to be similarity in these two respects."
34. Dworkin (2000, 1). Dworkin has consistently sounded this theme. Thus: "Government must treat those whom it governs with ... equal concern and respect" (1976, 272–273). Jeremy Waldron says that Dworkin "insists that liberals are more deeply committed to an ideal of equality than to any ideal of liberty" and that that the liberal commitments to various freedoms (e.g., religious belief, speech, etc.) "are all derivative from a fundamental commitment to equality of concern and respect." Waldron (1987a, 130), pointing to Dworkin's essay "Liberalism" in Dworkin (1985, 181–204).
35. Kymlicka (1990, 4).
36. Dworkin (1985, 203) says that skepticism about theories of the good does not underwrite his account of liberalism—namely, that the state must treat people as equals. Liberalism's "constitutive morality provides that human beings must be treated as equals by their government, not because there is no right and wrong in political morality, but because that is what is right." Dworkin goes on to say that what follows from that starting point is that government must be neutral on questions of the good life (ibid., 191). But it is unclear why that follows ineluctably. If we had a way of sorting out good from bad ways of life, why should we hesitate in telling those who follow the bad ways that they must desist and, if they refuse, to force them to? In fact, as is plainly the case, we do just that by invoking the harm principle to prohibit harmful exercises of various persons' beliefs about the good (serial killers', for example). If we are not, then, obliged to accept people's pursuit of their ways of life simply because we must treat them as equals, it seems to follow that our reluctance to regulate other, nonharmful ways of life stems from our inability to agree on a yardstick.
37. See, e.g., George (1995, chap. 3).
38. Sen (1992, ix).
39. Spencer (1970, 95).
40. Rawls (1971, 302).
41. Walzer (1983).
42. The discussion in this paragraph is based on Appiah (2001, 65). The quotations are from Dworkin (2000, 143, 148, 149, 127).

43. Among other things, because the auction is a once-and-forever occurrence, it cannot deal with the problem of generations. As Appiah (2001, 66) notes, "It is a central fact of our moral lives that we enter history one at a time." Because there is no such thing as a "tacit auction," Dworkin's premise is even shakier than that of the social contractarians, who at least could point with a wink to some conduct of later generations as signifying consent.
44. Dworkin (2000, 182).
45. Rawls (1971, 15, 103ff.).
46. See Galston (1991, 161–162). As Will Kymlicka (1990, 106) has summed up (without endorsing the argument): "People who are born naturally disadvantaged have a legitimate claim on those with advantages, and the naturally advantaged have a moral obligation to the disadvantaged."
47. Suppose a child with obvious musical or athletic talent refuses to commit herself to the amount of practice requisite to drawing an income from its exercise, forgoing before the talent ever matured the prospect of concert performances or tennis competitions. Would the raw but undeveloped talent be taxable, in part to force those with particular talents to exercise them? How should someone be taxed who "wastes" his talent, for example, by teaching mathematics when he could have earned large sums working for a Wall Street firm?
48. Galston (1991, 161).
49. The argument in this paragraph is drawn from Appiah (2001, 64); the quotation is from Dworkin (2000, 323).
50. Appiah (2001, 67).
51. Too efficient: Gibbs (2008). Overruled: Robinson and Schwarz (2008). To qualify, runners must show that they can better certain times for each event. Failed to qualify: Robinson (2008). As this book goes to press, he is said to be likely to qualify for the 2012 London summer Olympics. Sokolove (2012). At birth, Pistorius lacked fibula in both legs, and his feet were defective; at eleven months, his legs were amputated below the knee.
52. Larmore (1987, 42).
53. To illustrate, I note, without further discussion, several definitions offered by Raz (1988). He differentiates "principled neutrality" ("To be neutral . . . is to do one's best to help or hinder the various parties concerned in an equal degree") from "by-product neutrality" ("Persons [are] neutral if they can affect the fortunes of the parties and if they affect the fortunes of all the parties equally regardless of their reasons for so doing") (113). He also distinguishes between not taking an action that will assist in leading to or supporting a conception of the Good and not *justifying* an action on the grounds that it will promote the Good (135–136) (Raz characterizes the latter as "the exclusion of ideals"). Raz also specifies three "interpretations of political neutrality": "1. No political action may be undertaken or justified on the ground that it promotes an idea of the good nor on the ground that it enables individuals to pursue an ideal of the good. 2. No political action may be undertaken if it makes a difference to the likelihood that a person will endorse one conception of the good or another, or to his chances of realizing his conception of the good, unless other actions are undertaken which cancel out such effects. 3. One of the main goals of governmental authority, . . . is to ensure for all persons an equal ability to pursue in their lives and promote in their societies any ideal of the good of their choosing" (114–115).
54. See, generally, Gardbaum (1991, 1355–1358).
55. Locke (1983).
56. Totalitarianism: Fromm (1941). Suicide: As one of his editors summarizes one of Emile Durkheim's principal findings: "The stronger the forces throwing the individual onto his own resources, the greater the suicide-rate in the society in which this occurs." Simpson (1951, 14).
57. As one critic put it: "The chief difficulty with the principle of neutrality is that only liberals find it convincing. No non-liberal could countenance placing all positions on an equal footing in the manner its proponents desire. Neutrality turns out to be dependent on a more constitutive liberal moral belief such as autonomy and the existence of a reasonably homogenous moral community." Bellamy (1992, 240).

58. Trillin (1996, 54).
59. Larmore (1987, 46).
60. *Employment Division v. Smith*, 494 U.S. 872 (1990).
61. Tebbe (2007, 190): "A witch is a human being who secretly uses supernatural power for the purpose of harming others. Occult aggression is always believed to be caused by another human being acting out of malevolence. Belief in the occult therefore gives ordinary misfortune a moral significance: Once hardship is attributed to sorcery, it is transformed from something senseless into the meaningful result of human volition. Witchcraft, in other words, is seen to cause not simply *suffering*, which can result from a natural disaster or an illness, but *harm*, understood as the product of intentional action. Consequently, sorcery is perceived to be unjust in much the same way as physical violence."
62. Anyone in a U.S. courtroom today. But for earlier times, see Boyer and Nissenbaum (1974); Hill (1995); Demos (1982); Starkey (1989); Notestein (1968); Barstow (1994). For studies of the modern African experience with witchcraft, see Geschiere (1997, 22); Ashforth (2005, 10, 17).
63. Gutmann and Thomson (1996, 64–65).
64. See Moon (1993, 64–66) for the same problem arising out of family relations.
65. Herzog (1989, 151–156). "I may grant you that your conception of the good is at least as good as mine and grant you further that you're at least as good as I am. But I may go on to say, quite coherently, that my principle of right, whatever it is, is better than yours." Ibid., 155.
66. Ackerman (1980, 84) does not index harm and mentions it only in passing to suggest that causing harm "impos[es] illiberal relations on others." More directly, Ackerman's neutrality rules appear to converge on the harm principle. Suppose that a weak neighbor is quarreling over a sadist's continued attempts to torture him. The script might run as follows:

> WEAK NEIGHBOR: Sadist is torturing me. He must be compelled to stop his incessant attacks.
>
> COMMANDER: Why do you say that?
>
> WEAK NEIGHBOR: Because I don't like it.
>
> COMMANDER: That is not a reason. To comply with the subsidiary principles that The Lord Ackerman has given us [see the Completeness Rule, ibid., 35)], we would have to consult you every time a question arises to see whether you like the proposed answer.
>
> WEAK NEIGHBOR: I didn't mean that exactly. I meant that torture is not good for me.
>
> SADIST: That sounds like an argument that violates the Neutrality Principle: You are asserting a reason that appears to be rooted in your conception of the Good.
>
> WEAK NEIGHBOR: I don't know how else to say it. The torture hurts, so it's not good for me.
>
> COMMANDER: Sadist, what do you say to that?
>
> SADIST: It is just as I have said, Commander. Weak Neighbor is merely complaining that what I do violates his sense of what is good. And as you unfailingly tell us, "No reason is a good reason if it requires the power holder to assert: (a) that his conception of the good is better than that asserted by any of his fellow citizens, *or* (b) that, regardless of his conception of the good, he is intrinsically superior to one or more of his fellow citizens." [Ibid., 11]
>
> COMMANDER: But who is the power holder here?
>
> SADIST: Why, Weak Neighbor, of course; he wishes to stop me by invoking your authority.
>
> COMMANDER: No, I don't think so. Weak Neighbor is complaining about the power that you wield over him. It is you who must justify your continued torture of him.
>
> SADIST: Why, that's simple; it's because I like—
>
> COMMANDER: Careful now. You surely cannot say that you like to torture people, that it is good for you. Aren't you arguing that your conception of the good is better than Weak Neighbor's?

SADIST: But he is arguing likewise. For you to bar me from torturing him means that you are accepting his good instead of mine. If he is at least as good as I am, I am at least as good as he is. We seem to be at an impasse.

COMMANDER: No, I don't think so. He is asserting that you are harming him. One who seeks to justify harming another is essentially arguing that the injured party is inferior to the attacker.

SADIST: If you bar me from harming him, then you are barring everyone from harming anyone else. What you are really saying, I take it, is that the answer to the question whether the exercise of power by one person over another asserts the superiority of the power wielder depends on whether the power wielder is in some sense harming the other person.

COMMANDER: Yes.

SADIST: Then the Neutrality Principle boils down to the Harm Principle.

COMMANDER: Perhaps that is so.

SADIST: But what, then, is harm?

WEAK NEIGHBOR: Go back to page three, Sadist, and read on.

Acknowledgments

1. Galbraith (1967, ix).
2. Cabell, "At Outset" (1916, 21).

REFERENCES

Abraham, Henry J., and Barbara A. Perry. 1998. *Freedom and the Court.* 7th ed. New York: Oxford University Press.
Ackerman, Bruce. 1980. *Social Justice in the Liberal State.* New Haven: Yale University Press.
Addams, Jane. 1910. *Twenty Years at Hull-House.* New York: Macmillan.
Alexander, Larry. 2005. "When Are We Rightfully Aggrieved?" *Legal Theory* 11, no. 3: 325–332.
———. 2010. "Plastic Trees and Gladiators: Liberalism and Aesthetic Regulation." *Legal Theory* 16, no. 3: 77–90.
Allen, William F. 1883. *Report on Subject of National Standard Time Made to the General and Southern Railroad. Time Conventions.* New York: National Railway Publishing.
Allport, Gordon W. 1955. *Becoming: Basic Considerations for a Psychology of Personality.* New Haven: Yale University Press.
Alvarez, Lizette. 2006. "Outrage at Funeral Protests Pushes Lawmakers to Act." *New York Times,* April 17, A14.
———. 2011. "GOP Legislatures Move to Tighten Rules on Voting." *New York Times,* May 29, A1.
Amar, Akhil Reed. 2005. *America's Constitution: A Biography.* New York: Random House.
Andrews, Edmund L. 2008. "Greenspan Concedes Error on Regulation." *New York Times,* October 24, B1.
Appiah, K. Anthony. 1994. "Identity, Authenticity, Survival: Multicultural Societies and Social Reproduction." In *Multiculturalism,* ed. Amy Gutmann. Princeton: Princeton University Press.
———. 2001. "Equality of What?" *New York Review of Books,* April 26, 63–68.
———. 2007. *The Ethics of Identity.* Princeton: Princeton University Press.
———. 2011. *The Honor Code.* New York: W. W. Norton.
Arblaster, Anthony. 1986. *The Rise and Decline of Western Liberalism.* Oxford: Basil Blackwell.
Aristotle. 1962. *Nicomachean Ethics.* Trans. Martin Ostwald. Indianapolis: Bobbs-Merrill Educational Publishing.
———. 1988. *The Politics.* Ed. Stephen Everson and trans. Jonathan Barnes. New York: Cambridge University Press.
Arneson, Richard J. 1990. "Liberalism, Freedom, and Community." *Ethics* 100, no. 2: 368–385.
———. 2000. "Rawls versus Utilitarianism in the Light of *Political Liberalism.*" In *The Idea of a Political Liberalism,* ed. Victoria Davison and Clark Wolf. Lanham, Md.: Rowman & Littlefield.
Arrow, Kenneth J. 1963 (1951). *Social Choice and Individual Values.* 2nd ed. New Haven: Yale University Press.
———. 1972. "Gifts and Exchanges." *Philosophy and Public Affairs* 1, no. 4: 343–362.
Ashforth, Adam. 2005. *Witchcraft, Violence, and Democracy.* Chicago: University of Chicago Press.
Asimov, Isaac. 1985. *Robots and Empire.* New York: Doubleday.

———. 1990. *Robot Visions*. New York: ROC/Penguin.
Associated Press. 2010. "Iran: Fashion That Moves the Earth." *New York Times*, April 19, A11.
Atiyah, P. S. 1979. *The Rise and Fall of Freedom of Contract*. Oxford: Clarendon Press.
Attorney General's Committee on Administrative Procedure. 1941. Administrative Procedure in Government Agencies, S. Doc. No. 8, 77th Cong., 1st Sess.
Atwood, Denise A. 2008. "Riding Helmetless: Personal Freedom or Societal Burden?" *Phoenix Law Review* 1: 269–292.
Auden, W. H. 1966. *About the House*. London: Faber.
Audi, Robert. 1995. *The Cambridge Dictionary of Philosophy*. New York: Cambridge University Press.
Augustine. 1958. *City of God*. Ed., Vernon J. Bourke. Garden City, N.Y.: Image Books.
Bacon, Francis. 1960. *The New Organon*. Ed. Fulton H. Anderson. New York: Macmillan.
Bagley, Nicholas, and Richard L. Revesz. 2006. "Centralized Oversight of the Regulatory State." *Columbia Law Review* 106, no. 6: 1260–1329.
Bardhan, Pranab K., and John E. Roemer. 1993. *Market Socialism: The Current Debate*. New York: Oxford University Press.
Bannister, Robert C. 1955. *Social Darwinism: Science and Myth in Anglo-American Social Thought*. Boston: Beacon Press.
Barry, Brian. 1965. *Political Argument*. London: Routledge & Kegan Paul.
———. 1973. *The Liberal Theory of Justice*. Oxford: Clarendon Press.
———. 2001. *Culture and Equality*. Cambridge, Mass.: Harvard University Press.
Barry, John M. 2012. *Roger Williams and the Creation of the American Soul: Church, State, and the Birth of Liberty*. New York: Viking.
Barstow, Anne Llewellyn. 1994. *Witchcraze: A New History of the European Witch Hunts*. New York: HarperCollins.
Bausell, R. Barker. 2009. *Snake Oil Science: The Truth about Complementary and Alternative Medicine*. New York: Oxford University Press.
Becker, Jasper. 1997. *Hungry Ghosts: China's Secret Famine*. New York: Free Press.
Bell, Clive. 1947 (1928). *Civilization*. Middlesex, U.K.: Penguin.
Bell, Daniel. 1995. *Communitarianism and Its Critics*. Oxford: Clarendon Press.
Bellah, Robert N., Richard Madsen, William M. Sullivan, Ann Swidler, and Stephen M. Tipton. 1985. *Habits of the Heart*. Berkeley: University of California Press.
Bellamy, Richard. 1992. *Liberalism and Modern Society*. University Park: Pennsylvania State University Press.
Belloc, Hilaire. 1977. *The Servile State*. Ed. Robert Nisbet. Indianapolis: Liberty Classics.
Benhabib, Seyla. 1989. "Liberal Dialogue." In *Liberalism and the Moral Life*, ed. Nancy L. Rosenblum. Cambridge, Mass.: Harvard University Press.
Bentham, Jeremy. 1948. *An Introduction to the Principles of Morals and Legislation*. New York: Hafner.
Bergelson, Vera. 2007. "The Right to Be Hurt: Testing the Boundaries of Consent." *George Washington Law Review* 75, no. 2: 165–236.
Berkowitz, Peter. 1999. *Virtue and the Making of Modern Liberalism*. Princeton: Princeton University Press.
Berlin, Isaiah. 1969. *Four Essays on Liberty*. New York: Oxford University Press.
———. 1991. *The Crooked Timber of Humanity: Chapters in the History of Ideas*. New York: Alfred A. Knopf.
Bernstein, David E. 2011. *Rehabilitating Lochner: Defending Individual Rights against Progressive Reform*. Chicago: University of Chicago Press.
Berryhill, Dale A. 1995. *The Assault: Liberalism's Attack on Religion, Freedom, and Democracy*. Lafayette, La.: Vital Issues Press.
Bierce, Ambrose. 1958. *The Devil's Dictionary*. New York: Dover.
Birrell, Augustine. 1899. *Seven Lectures on the Law and History of Copyright in Books*. London: Cassell.
Bleibtreau, John N. 1968. *The Parable of the Beast*. New York: Macmillan.
Bloch, Marc. 1961. *Feudal Society*. Vol. 1. Chicago: University of Chicago Press.
Bloom, Allan. 1974. "Justice: John Rawls vs. the Tradition of Political Philosophy." *American Political Science Review* 69, no. 2: 648–662.

Bloom, Paul. 2005. *Descartes' Baby: How the Science of Child Development Explains What Makes Us Human*. New York: Basic Books.
Bockman, Johanna. 2011. *Markets in the Name of Socialism: The Left-Wing Origins of Neoliberalism*. Stanford: Stanford University Press.
Bork, Robert H. 1991. *The Tempting of America: The Political Seduction of the Law*. New York: Touchstone/Simon & Schuster.
Bowles, Chester. 1946. "Nine Definitions of Liberalism." *New Republic*, July 22.
Boyer, Paul, and Stephen Nissenbaum. 1974. *Salem Possessed: The Social Origins of Witchcraft*. Cambridge, Mass.: Harvard University Press.
Branch, Taylor. 1988. *Parting the Waters: America in the King Years 1954–63*. New York: Simon & Schuster.
Brandeis, Louis D. 1914. *Business—A Profession*. Boston: Small, Maynard.
Brennan, T. A., L. L. Leape, N. M. Laird et al. 2004. "Incidence of Adverse Events of Negligence in Hospitalized Patients: Results of the Harvard Medical Practice Study." *Quality Safety Health Care* 13, no. 2: 145–152.
Brinkley, Alan. 1998. *Liberalism and Its Discontents*. Cambridge, Mass.: Harvard University Press.
Brint, Steven. 1994. *In an Age of Experts: The Changing Role of Professionals in Politics and Public Life*. Princeton: Princeton University Press.
Brinton, Crane. 1953. *The Shaping of the Modern Mind*. New York: Mentor.
Broad, William J. 1989. "Suit Calls Space Probe Cancer Threat." *New York Times*, September 29, 10.
Bronfenbrenner, Urie. 1979. *The Ecology of Human Development*. Cambridge, Mass.: Harvard University Press.
Bronowski, Jacob. 1973. *The Ascent of Man*. Boston: Little, Brown.
Brooks, David. 2007. "A Partnership of Minds." *New York Times*, July 20, A23.
———. 2008. "Ceding the Center." *New York Times*, October 26, 14wk.
Brown, Michael F. 2003. *Who Owns Native Culture?* Cambridge, Mass.: Harvard University Press.
Bryant, Arthur. 1968. *The Medieval Foundations of England*. New York: Collier.
Buchanan, Allen E. 1989. "Assessing the Communitarian Critique of Liberalism." *Ethics* 99, no. 4: 853–882.
Burckhardt, Jacob. 1954. *The Civilization of the Renaissance in Italy*. New York: Modern Library.
Burke, Edmund. 1969 (1790). *Reflections on the Revolution in France*. Ed. Conor Cruise O'Brien. Baltimore: Penguin.
Burnett, Victoria. 2009. "Spain Links Voodoo to Forced-Prostitution Case." *New York Times*, May 23, A7.
Butler, Judith. 1997. *Excitable Speech: A Politics of the Performative*. New York: Routledge.
Butterfield, Fox. 1995. "California's Courts Clogging under Its 'Three Strikes' Law." *New York Times*, March 23, A1.
Cabell, James Branch. 1916. *From the Hidden Way: Dizain des Échos*. New York: Robert McBride.
Cahoone, Lawrence E. 2002. *Civil Society: The Conservative Meaning of Liberal Politics*. Malden: Blackwell.
Cain, Kevin G. 2007. "And Now the Rest of the Story ... the McDonald's Coffee Lawsuit." *Journal of Consumer and Commercial Law* 11: 15–18.
Carr, E. H. 1941. *The Twenty Years' Crisis*. London: Macmillan.
Chabris, Christopher, and Daniel Simons. 2010. *The Invisible Gorilla and Other Ways Our Intuitions Deceive Us*. New York: Crown.
Chambers, Simone. 1996. *Reasonable Democracy*. Ithaca, N.Y.: Cornell University Press.
Chesterton, Gilbert K. 1905. *Heretics*. New York: John Lane.
———. 1921. "The Mad Hatter and the Sane Householder." *Vanity Fair*, January, 54.
Clarke, Arthur C. 1975. *Technology and the Frontiers of Knowledge*. New York: Doubleday.
Cohen, G. A. 1987. "Are Disadvantaged Workers Who Take Hazardous Jobs Forced to Take Hazardous Jobs?" In *Moral Rights in the Workplace*, ed. Gertrude Ezorsky and James W. Nickel. Albany: State University of New York Press.
Cohen, William. 1985. "Is Equal Protection Like Oakland? Equality as a Surrogate for Other Rights." *Tulane Law Review* 59, no. 4: 884–909.

Cohn, Victor. 1981. "Laetrile Flunks Test, Is Found As Effective As 'No Treatment.'" *Washington Post*, May 1, A3.
Coke, Edward. 1979 (1644). *The Fourth Part of the Institutes of the Laws of England concerning the Jurisdiction of Courts*. New York: Garland.
Coleman, Jules. 1992. *Risks and Wrongs*. New York: Cambridge University Press.
Colvin, Richard Lee, and Ted Rohrlich, 1994. "Courts Toss Curveballs to '3 Strikes.'" *Los Angeles Times*, October 23, A1.
Commager, Henry Steele. 1950. *The American Mind*. New Haven: Yale University Press.
Commons, John R. 1957. *The Legal Foundations of Capitalism*. Madison: University of Wisconsin Press.
"'Common Sense' Legislation: The Birth of Neoclassical Tort Reform." 1996. *Harvard Law Review* 109, no. 7: 1765–1782.
Connolly, William E. 1983. *The Terms of Political Discourse*. 2d ed. Princeton: Princeton University Press.
Conquest, Robert. 1986. *Harvest of Sorrow: Soviet Collectivization and the Terror-Famine*. New York: Oxford University Press.
———. 2000. *Reflections on a Ravaged Century*. New York: W. W. Norton.
Coulter, Ann. 2006. *Godless: The Church of Liberalism*. New York: Crown Forum.
———. 2011. *Demonic: How the Liberal Mob Is Endangering America*. New York: Crown Forum.
Cross, R., and J. Ham. 1991. *Precedent in English Law*. 4th ed. London: Oxford University Press.
Cuddihy, John Murray. 1978. *No Offense: Civil Religion and Protestant Taste*. New York: Seabury Press.
Damasio, Antonio R. 1994. *Descartes' Error: Emotion, Reason, and the Human Brain*. New York: G. P. Putnam's Sons.
———. 2010. *Self Comes to Mind: Constructing the Conscious Brain*. New York: Pantheon Books.
Daniels, Norman, ed. 1974. *Reading Rawls: Critical Studies of A Theory of Justice*. New York: Basic Books.
Davis, David Brion. 1966. *The Problem of Slavery in Western Culture*. Ithaca, N.Y.: Cornell University Press.
———. 1975. *The Problem of Slavery in the Age of Revolution 1770–1823*. Ithaca, N.Y.: Cornell University Press.
Deane, Herbert A. 1963. *The Political and Social Ideas of St. Augustine*. New York: Columbia University Press.
Decter, Midge. 1976. "What Is a Liberal—Who Is a Conservative?" *Commentary* 62, no. 3: 50.
Defoe, Daniel. 1894. *An Essay upon Projects*. London: Cassell.
Delaney, C.F., ed. 1994. *The Liberalism-Communitarianism Debate*. Lanham, Md.: Rowman & Littlefield.
Demos, John. 1982. *Entertaining Satan: Witchcraft and the Culture of Early New England*. New York: Oxford University Press.
Dennett, Daniel C. 1991. *Consciousness Explained*. Boston: Little, Brown.
Devlin, Patrick. 1965. *The Enforcement of Morals*. London: Oxford University Press.
Dewey, John. 1927. *The Public and Its Problems*. Denver: Alan Swallow.
Diamond, Jared. 1997. *Guns, Germs, and Steel*. New York: W. W. Norton.
———. 2008. "Vengeance Is Ours." *New Yorker*, April 21, 74–87.
Dikötter, Frank. 2010. *Mao's Great Famine*. New York: Walker.
Dirlam, Joel B., and James L. Plummer. 1973. *An Introduction to the Yugoslav Economy*. Columbus, Ohio: Charles E. Merrill.
Donner, Wendy. 1991. *The Liberal Self: John Stuart Mill's Moral and Political Philosophy*. Ithaca, N.Y.: Cornell University Press.
Douglas, Paul. 1946. "Nine Definitions of Liberalism." *New Republic*, July 22.
Dunn, John. 1993. *Western Political Theory in the Face of the Future*. New York: Cambridge University Press.

Dunn, J. R. 2011. *Death by Liberalism*. New York: Broadside Books.
Durkheim, Emile. 1973a (1898). "Individualism and the Intellectuals." In *Emile Durkheim on Morality and Society*, ed. Robert N. Bellah. Chicago: University of Chicago Press.
———. 1973b (1914). "The Dualism of Human Nature and Its Social Conditions." In *Emile Durkheim on Morality and Society*, ed. Robert N. Bellah. Chicago: University of Chicago Press.
Dworkin, Andrea, and Catharine A. MacKinnon. 1988. *Pornography and Civil Rights: A New Day for Women's Equality*. Durham, N.C.: Organizing Against Pornography.
Dworkin, Ronald. 1976. *Taking Rights Seriously*. Cambridge, Mass.: Harvard University Press.
———. 1985. *A Matter of Principle*. Cambridge, Mass.: Harvard University Press.
———. 1986. *Law's Empire*. Cambridge, Mass.: Belknap Press of Harvard University Press.
———. 1997. "Assisted Suicide: The Philosophers' Brief." *New York Review of Books*, March 27, 41–47.
———. 2000. *Sovereign Virtue: The Theory and Practice of Equality*. Cambridge, Mass.: Harvard University Press.
Ely, John Hart. 1980. *Democracy and Distrust: A Theory of Judicial Review*. Cambridge, Mass.: Harvard University Press.
Ernst, Edzard, and Simon Singh. 2008. *Trick or Treatment: The Undeniable Facts about Alternative Medicine*. New York: W. W. Norton.
Etzioni, Amitai. 1994. *The Spirit of Community*. New York: Touchstone.
Farber, Daniel A., and Philip P. Frickey. 1991. *Law and Public Choice: A Critical Introduction*. Chicago: University of Chicago Press.
Farr, James. 1986. "'So Vile and Miserable an Estate': The Problem of Slavery in Locke's Political Thought," *Political Theory*, 14(2):263–289.
Feinberg, Joel. 1980. "The Child's Right to an Open Future." In *Whose Child? Children's Rights, Parental Authority, and State Power*, ed. William Aiken and Hugo LaFollette. Totowa, N.J.: Rowman & Littlefield.
———. 1984. *The Moral Limits of the Criminal Law*. Vol. 1: *Harm to Others*. New York: Oxford University Press.
———. 1985. *The Moral Limits of the Criminal Law*. Vol. 2: *Offense to Others*. New York: Oxford University Press.
———. 1986. *The Moral Limits of the Criminal Law*. Vol. 3: *Harm to Self*. New York: Oxford University Press.
———. 1988. *The Moral Limits of the Criminal Law*. Vol. 4: *Harmless Wrongdoing*. New York: Oxford University Press.
Finger, Michael. n.d. "Banned in Memphis." Memphis Flyer Online, www.memphisflyer.com/memphis/Content?oid=oid%3A42950 (accessed October 27, 2011).
Fischer, Frank. 1990. *Technocracy and the Politics of Expertise*. Newbury Park, Calif.: Sage.
Fish, Stanley. 1994. "Liberalism Does Not Exist." In *There's No Such Thing as Free Speech and It's a Good Thing Too*. New York: Oxford University Press.
Fishkin, James S. 1983. "Can There Be a Neutral Theory of Justice?" *Ethics* 93, no. 2: 348–356.
Foner, Eric. 1998. *The Story of American Freedom*. New York. W. W. Norton.
Fox, Robin. 2001. "Human Nature and Human Rights." *Harper's*, April 19.
Franck, Thomas M. 1999. *The Empowered Self*. New York: Oxford University Press.
Frankel, Charles. 1956. *The Case for Modern Man*. New York: Harper and Brothers.
Frankel, Max. 1976. "What Is a Liberal—Who Is a Conservative?" *Commentary* 62, no. 3: 57.
Frankfurter, Felix. 1930. *The Public and Its Government*. New Haven: Yale University Press.
Franklin, Julian H., ed. 1992. "Introduction." In Jean Bodin, *On Sovereignty*. New York: Cambridge University Press.
———. 2006. *Animal Rights and Moral Philosophy*. New York: Columbia University Press.
Fraser, Nancy. 1986. "Toward a Discourse Ethic of Solidarity." *Praxis International* 5, no. 4: 425–429.

———. 1993. "Rethinking the Public Sphere: A Contribution to the Critique of Actually Existing Democracy." In *Habermas and the Public Sphere*, ed. Craig Calhoun. Cambridge, Mass.: MIT Press.
Fredericks, Arnold R. 1993. *Jurisprudence and Human Births*. Washington, D.C.: Abbe Publication Association.
Freeman, Douglas Southall. 1934. *R. E. Lee*. New York; Charles Scribner's Sons.
Freud, Sigmund. 1959 (1923). *Group Psychology and the Analysis of the Ego*, ed. James Strachey. New York: W. W. Norton.
Fried, Charles. 1978. *Right and Wrong*. Cambridge, Mass.: Harvard University Press.
———. 1987. "Is Liberty Possible?" In *Liberty, Equality, and the Law*, ed. Sterling M. McMurrin. Salt Lake City: University of Utah Press.
Friedman, Jeffrey, ed. 1994. "Communitarianism," *Critical Review* 8, no. 2: 159–340.
Friedman, Lawrence M. 1973. *A History of American Law*. New York: Simon & Schuster.
Friedman, Milton. 1962. *Capitalism and Freedom*. Chicago: University of Chicago Press.
Fromm, Erich. 1941. *Escape from Freedom*. New York: Holt, Rinehart & Winston.
Fuller, Lon L. 1964. *The Morality of Law*. New Haven: Yale University Press.
———. 1971. "Human Interaction and the Law." In *The Rule of Law*, ed. Robert Paul Wolff. New York: Simon & Schuster.
Fuller, Thomas. 2007. "Malaysia's Highest Court Refuses to Honor a Muslim's Conversion." *New York Times*, May 31, A7.
Galbraith, John Kenneth. 1967. *The New Industrial State*. Boston: Houghton Mifflin.
Galison, Peter. 2003. *Einstein's Clocks, Poincaré's Maps*. New York: W. W. Norton, 2003.
Galston, William A. 1991. *Liberal Purposes*. New York: Cambridge University Press.
———. 2002a. *Liberal Pluralism*. Cambridge: Cambridge University Press.
———. 2002b. "Expressive Freedom of Association in a Liberal Pluralist State." *Responsive Community* 12, no. 3: 13–26.
Gardbaum, Stephen A. 1991. "Why the Liberal State Can Promote Moral Ideals after All." *Harvard Law Review* 104, no. 6: 1350–1371.
———. 1992. "Law, Politics, and the Claims of Community." *Michigan Law Review* 90, no. 4: 685–760.
Garrick, John, ed. 2012. *Law and Policy for China's Market Socialism*. New York: Routledge.
Garrow, David. 1986. *Bearing the Cross: Martin Luther King, Jr., and the Southern Christian Leadership Conference*. New York: William Morrow.
Gay, Peter. 1977. *The Enlightenment: An Interpretation*. New York: W. W. Norton.
Gazzaniga, Michael S. 2008. *Human*. New York: Ecco.
Gellhorn, Walter. 1956. *Individual Freedom and Governmental Restraints*. Baton Rouge: Louisiana State University Press.
George, Robert E. 1995. *Making Men Moral*. Oxford: Clarendon Press.
Geschiere, Peter. 1997. *The Modernity of Witchcraft: Politics and the Occult in Postcolonial Africa*. Charlottesville: University Press of Virginia.
Geuss, Raymond. 2001. *History and Illusion in Politics*. New York: Cambridge University Press.
Gibbs, Nancy. 2008. "Cool Running." *Time*, January 28, 116.
Gill, Emily R. 2001. "Neutrality, Autonomy, and the Liberal State." *Responsive Community* 11, no. 3: 15–24.
Gladwell, Malcolm. 1997. "Just Ask for It." *New Yorker*, April 7, 49.
Gleick, James. 1987. *Chaos*. New York: Viking.
Glendon, Mary Ann. 1991. *Rights Talk, The Impoverishment of Political Discourse*. New York: Free Press.
Goldberg, Jonah. 2008. *Liberal Fascism: The Secret History of the American Left from Mussolini to the Politics of Meaning*. New York: Doubleday.
Golding, Martin P. 1975. *Philosophy of Law*. Englewood Cliffs, N.J.: Prentice-Hall.
Goodwin, Doris Kearns. 1994. *No Ordinary Time*. New York: Simon & Schuster.
Gorsuch, Neil M. 2006. *The Future of Assisted Suicide and Euthanasia*. Princeton: Princeton University Press.

Grant, Ruth W. 1991. *John Locke's Liberalism*. Chicago: University of Chicago Press.
Grassley, Charles, with Jennifer Shaw Schmidt. "Practicing What We Preach: A Legislative History of Congressional Accountability." *Harvard Journal on Legislation* 35, no. 1: 33–49.
Gray, Jerry. "Congress Approves Measure Extending Work Laws to Itself." *New York Times*, January 18, A1.
Green, Donald P., and Ian Shapiro. 1994. *Pathologies of Rational Choice Theory: A Critique of Applications in Political Science*. New Haven: Yale University Press.
Greenawalt, Kent. 1988. *Religious Convictions and Political Choice*. New York: Oxford University Press.
Grey, Thomas C. 1983. *The Legal Enforcement of Morality*. New York: Alfred A. Knopf.
Gross, Martin. 1966. *The Doctors*. New York: Random House.
Gutmann, Amy. 1982. "What's the Use of Going to School? The Problem of Education in Utilitarianism and Rights Theories." In *Utilitarianism and Beyond*, ed. Amartya Sen and Bernard Williams. New York: Cambridge University Press.
———. 1985. "Communitarian Critics of Liberalism." *Philosophy and Public Affairs* 14, no. 3: 308–322.
———. 1987. *Democratic Education*. Princeton: Princeton University Press.
———, ed. 1994. *Multiculturalism*. Princeton: Princeton University Press.
Gutmann, Amy, and Dennis Thompson. 1996. *Democracy and Disagreement*. Cambridge, Mass.: Belknap Press of Harvard University Press.
Hadden, Sally E. 2001. *Slave Patrols: Law and Violence in Virginia and the Carolinas*. Cambridge, Mass.: Harvard University Press.
Hagerty, Barbara Bradley. 2011. "A Peek Inside the Westboro Baptist Church," http://www.npr.org/2011/03/02/134198937/a-peek-inside-the-westboro-baptist-church (accessed November 17, 2011).
Hale, Robert L. 1952. *Freedom through Power: Public Control of Private Governing Power*. New York: Columbia University Press.
Hammond, J. L., and Barbara Hammond. 1947. *The Bleak Age*. Rev. ed. London: Pelican Books.
———. 1968 (1917). *The Town Labourer*. New York: Doubleday Anchor.
Hammond, Kenneth R. 1996. *Human Judgment and Social Policy*. New York: Oxford University Press.
Hannity, Sean. 2002. *Let Freedom Ring: Winning the War of Liberty over Liberalism*. New York: Regan Books.
———. 2004. *Deliver Us from Evil: Defeating Terrorism, Despotism, and Liberalism*. New York: William Morrow.
Harper, Alan D. 1969. *The Politics of Loyalty: The White House and the Communist Issue, 1946–1952*. Westport, Conn.: Greenwood.
Harris, John F. 2001. "God Gave U.S. 'What We Deserve,' Falwell Says." *Washington Post*, September 14, C03.
Hart, H. L. A. 1961. *The Concept of Law*. New York: Oxford University Press.
———. 1963. *Law, Liberty and Morality*. New York: Oxford University Press.
———. 1971. "Immorality and Treason." In *Morality and the Law*, ed. Richard A. Wasserstrom. Belmont, Calif.: Wadsworth.
———. 1983. *Essays in Jurisprudence and Philosophy*. Oxford: Clarendon Press.
Hart, H. L. A., and Tony Honoré. 1985. *Causation in the Law*. 2d ed. New York: Oxford University Press.
Haskell, Thomas L. 1977. *The Emergence of Professional Science: The American Social Science Association and the Nineteenth-Century Crisis of Authority*. Urbana: University of Illinois Press.
Hauser, Marc D. 2007. *Moral Minds: The Nature of Right and Wrong*. New York: Harper Perennial.
Hauser, Philip M. 1976. "Demographic Changes and the Legal System." In *Law and the American Future*, ed. Murray L. Schwartz. New York: Columbia University Press.
Hay, Douglas, and Peter Linebaugh et al. 1975. *Albion's Fatal Tree: Crime and Society in Eighteenth-Century England*. New York: Pantheon Books.

Hayek, Friedrich A. 1944. *The Road to Serfdom*. Chicago: University of Chicago Press.
———. 1960. *The Constitution of Liberty*. Chicago: University of Chicago Press.
———. 1963. *Capitalism and the Historians*. Chicago: Phoenix Books.
———. 1973. *Rules and Order*. Chicago: University of Chicago Press.
———. 1976. *The Mirage of Social Justice*. Chicago: University of Chicago Press.
———. 1978. *New Studies in Philosophy, Politics, Economics and the History of Ideas*. Chicago: University of Chicago Press.
———. 1979. *The Political Order of a Free People*. Chicago: University of Chicago Press.
Hazlitt, William. 1933. In *Complete Works*, ed. P. P. Howe. Vol. 19. London: Dent.
Heilbroner, Robert L. 1980. *The Worldly Philosophers*. 5th ed. New York: Simon & Schuster.
———. 1995. *Visions of the Future: The Distant Past, Yesterday, Today, and Tomorrow*. New York: Oxford University Press and the New York Public Library.
Henderson, James A., Jr., and Aaron D. Twerski. 2011. *Products Liability: Problems and Process*. 7th ed. New York: Aspen.
Henning, Peter T. 2011. "Murky Signals for Congress on Insider Trading." http://dealbook.nytimes.com/2011/11/25/murky-signals-for-congress-on-insider-trading/ (accessed on November 27, 2011).
Herzog, Don. 1986. "Some Questions for Republicans." *Political Theory* 14, no. 3: 487.
———. 1989. *Happy Slaves: A Critique of Consent Theories*. Chicago: University of Chicago Press.
Highet, Gilbert. 1954. *Man's Unconquerable Mind*. New York: Columbia University Press.
Hill, Frances. 1995. *A Delusion of Satan: The Full Story of the Salem Witch Trials*. New York: Doubleday.
Hilton, R. H. 1969. *The Decline of Serfdom in Medieval England*. London: Macmillan.
Hirschman, Albert O. 1977. *The Passions and the Interests: Political Arguments for Capitalism before Its Triumph*. Princeton: Princeton University Press.
———. 1991. *The Rhetoric of Reaction*. Cambridge, Mass.: Belknap Press of Harvard University Press.
Hirshman, Linda R. 1994. "Is the Original Position Inherently Male-Superior?" *Columbia Law Review* 94, no. 6: 1860–1881.
Hobbes, Thomas. 1981 (1651). *Leviathan*, ed. C. B. Macpherson. New York: Penguin.
Hobhouse, L. T. 1994. In *Liberalism and Other Writings*, ed. James Meadowcroft. New York: Cambridge University Press.
Hoebel, E. Adamson. 1954. *The Law of Primitive Man*. Cambridge, Mass.: Harvard University Press.
Hoffer, Peter Charles. 1997. *The Salem Witchcraft Trials*. Lawrence: University Press of Kansas.
Hofstadter, Richard. 1955. *Social Darwinism in American Life*. Rev. ed. Boston: Beacon Press.
Holbrook, Stewart H. 1954. *The Age of the Moguls*. Garden City, N.Y.: Doubleday.
Holmes, Oliver Wendell, Jr. 1963 (1881). *The Common Law*, ed. Mark DeWolfe Howe. Boston: Little-Brown.
Holmes, Stephen. 1984. *Benjamin Constant and the Making of Modern Liberalism*. New Haven: Yale University Press.
———. 1991. "The Permanent Structure of Antiliberal Thought." In *Liberalism and the Moral Life*, ed. Nancy L. Rosenblum. Cambridge, Mass.: Harvard University Press.
———. 1993. *The Anatomy of Antiliberalism*. Cambridge, Mass.: Harvard University Press.
———. 1995. *Passions and Constraint*. Chicago: University of Chicago Press.
Holmes, Stephen, and Cass R. Sunstein. 1999. *The Cost of Rights: Why Liberty Depends on Taxes*. New York: W. W. Norton.
Holtug, Nils. 2002. "The Harm Principle." *Ethical Theory and Moral Practice* 5, no. 4: 357–389.
Honderich, Ted. 1971. *Punishment, the Supposed Justifications*. New York: Penguin Books.
———, ed. 1995. *The Oxford Companion to Philosophy*. New York: Oxford University Press.
Hook, Sidney. 1955. *The Hero in History*. Boston: Beacon Press.
Horwitz, Morton J. 1977. *The Transformation of American Law, 1780–1860*. Cambridge, Mass.: Harvard University Press.

Howard, Philip K. 1994. *The Death of Common Sense: How Law Is Suffocating America*. New York: Random House.
Howe, Irving. 1977. "Socialism and Liberalism: Articles of Conciliation?" *Dissent* 24, no. 1: 22–35.
Hsu, Carolyn L. 2007. *Creating Market Socialism: How Ordinary People Are Shaping Class and Status in China*. Durham, N.C.: Duke University Press.
Husak, Douglas, and Peter de Marneffe. 2005. *The Legalization of Drugs*. New York: Cambridge University Press.
Huxley, T. H. 1893. "On Descartes' Discourse." In *Method and Results*. London: Macmillan.
———. 1896. *Evolution and Ethics and Other Essays*. New York: D. Appleton.
Illich, Ivan. 1973. *Tools for Conviviality*. New York: Harper & Row.
Jacobs, Andrew. "Parent's Grief Turns to Rage at Chinese Officials." *New York Times*, May 28, A1.
Jameson, Eric. 1961. *The Natural History of Quackery*. Springfield, Ill.: C. C. Thomas.
Jefferson, Thomas. 1961. *Inaugural Addresses of the Presidents of the United States*. House Doc. No. 218, 87th Cong., 1st Sess. Washington, D.C.: U.S. Government Printing Office.
Johnston, David. 1993. "Spiritual Seekers Borrow Indians' Ways." *New York Times*, December 27, A1.
Johnston, David. 1994. *The Idea of a Liberal Theory*. Princeton: Princeton University Press.
Jones, Robert P. 2007. *Liberalism's Troubled Search for Equality: Religion and Cultural Bias in the Oregon Physician-Assisted Suicide Debate*. Notre Dame, Ind.: University of Notre Dame Press.
Jowett, Benjamin. 2000 (1860). "On the Interpretation of Scripture." In *Essays and Reviews: The 1860 Text and Its Reading*, ed. Victor Shea and William Whitla. Charlottesville: University Press of Virginia.
Kahan, Dan M. 2007. "The Cognitively Illiberal State." *Stanford Law Review* 60, no. 1: 115–154.
Kahneman, Daniel. 2011. *Thinking Fast and Slow*. New York: Farrar, Straus & Giroux.
Kaminer, Wendy. 1999. *Sleeping with Extra-Terrestrials: The Rise of Irrationalism and Perils of Piety*. New York: Vintage Books.
Kandel, Erich R. 2007. *In Search of Memory: The Emergence of a New Science of Mind*. New York: W. W. Norton.
Kariel, Henry S. 1961. *The Decline of American Pluralism*. Stanford: Stanford University Press.
Katyal, Neal Kumar. 2003. "Conspiracy Theory." *Yale Law Journal* 112, no. 6: 1307–1398.
Kekes, John. 1997. *Against Liberalism*. Ithaca, N.Y.: Cornell University Press.
Kelman, Steven. 1974. "Regulation by the Numbers—a report on the Consumer Product Safety Commission." *The Public Interest* 36 (Summer): 88.
———. 1983. "Regulation and Paternalism." In *Rights and Regulation*, ed. Tibor R. Machan and M. Bruce Johnson. San Francisco: Pacific Institute for Public Policy Research.
Kennedy, David M. 1994. "Affairs both Foreign and Domestic." *New York Times Book Review*, September 11, 9.
Kennedy, Duncan. 1976. "Form and Substance in Private Law Adjudication." *Harvard Law Review* 89, no. 8: 1685–1778.
Kennedy, John F. 1963. "Commencement Address at Yale University." In *Public Papers of the Presidents of the United States, John F. Kennedy, 1962*. Washington, D.C.: U.S. Government Printing Office.
Kern, Fritz. 1970. *Kingship and Law in the Middle Ages*. New York: Harper Torchbooks.
Kida, Thomas. 2006. *Don't Believe Everything You Think: The Six Basic Mistakes We Make in Thinking*. Amherst, N.Y.: Prometheus Books.
Kirk, Robert. 2007. *The Secret Commonwealth*. New York: New York Review Books.
Klemesrud, Judy. 1985. "Older Fathers: Become a Parent after 50." *New York Times*, January 7, B8.
Knowles, Dudley. 2001. *Political Philosophy*. Montreal: McGill-Queen's University Press.
Koestler, Arthur. 1967. *The Ghost in the Machine*. New York: Random House.
Kors, Alan Charles, and Edward Peters, eds. 2001. *Witchcraft in Europe, 400–1700*. 2d ed. Philadelphia: University of Pennsylvania Press.
Kotkin, Stephen. 2001. *Armageddon Averted: The Soviet Collapse 1970–2000*. New York: Oxford University Press.

Kristoff, Nicholas D., and Sheryl WuDunn. 2010. *Halt the Sky: Turning Oppression into Opportunity for Women Worldwide.* New York: Vintage Books.

Kristol, Irving. 1971. "Pornography, Obscenity, and the Case for Censorship." *New York Times Magazine*, March 28, 24.

Kritzer, Herbert M. 2002. "The Future Role of 'Law Workers': Rethinking the Forms of Legal Practice and the Scope of Legal Education." *Arizona Law Review* 44, no. 4: 917–938.

Krugman, Paul. 2007. *The Conscience of a Liberal.* New York: W. W. Norton.

Krystal, Arthur. 2007. "En Garde!" *New Yorker*, March 19, 80.

Kukathas, Chandran, and Philip Pettit. 1990. *Rawls, A Theory of Justice and Its Critics.* Stanford: Stanford University Press.

Kymlicka, Will. 1990. *Contemporary Political Philosophy.* New York: Oxford University Press.

———. 1991. *Liberalism, Community, and Culture.* New York: Clarendon Press.

———. 1995a. "Community." In *A Companion to Contemporary Political Philosophy*, ed. Robert E. Goodin and Philip Pettit. Cambridge: Blackwell.

———. 1995b. *Multicultural Citizenship.* New York: Oxford University Press.

———, ed. 1995c. *The Rights of Minority Cultures.* New York: Oxford University Press.

Laffont, J. J., and J. Tirole. 1991. "The Politics of Government Decision-Making: A Theory of Regulatory Capture." *Quarterly Journal of Economics* 106, no. 4: 1089–1127.

Larmore, Charles. 1987. *Patterns of Moral Complexity.* New York: Cambridge University Press.

Lasch, Christopher. 1979. *The Culture of Narcissism.* New York: W. W. Norton.

Laski, Harold J. 1925. *The Limitations of the Expert.* London: Fabian Society.

Laslett, Peter. 1992. "Is There a Generational Contract?" In *Justice between Age Groups and Generations*, ed. Peter Laslett and James S. Fishkin. New Haven: Yale University Press.

Lazarus, Simon. 1974. *The Genteel Populists.* New York: Holt, Rinehart & Winston.

Lee, Harper. 1960. *To Kill a Mockingbird.* New York: Popular Library.

Leighninger, Robert D., Jr. 2007. *Long-Range Public Investment: The Forgotten Legacy of the New Deal.* Columbia: University of South Carolina Press.

Lekachman, Robert. 1959. *A History of Economic Ideas.* New York: McGraw Hill.

Lerner, Irving J. 1981. "A Lesson in Cancer Quackery." *CA: A Cancer Journal for Clinicians* 31, no. 2: 91–95.

Letwin, Shirley Robin. 1998. *The Pursuit of Certainty.* Indianapolis: Liberty Fund.

Letters to the Editors. 1942. *Life Magazine*, September 21, 2–11.

Levine, Andrew. 1981. *Liberal Democracy: A Critique of Its Theory.* New York: Columbia University Press.

Lieberman, Jethro K. 1970. *The Tyranny of the Experts.* New York: Walker.

———. 1972. *How the Government Breaks the Law.* New York: Stein and Day.

———. 1977. "The Relativity of Injuries." *Philosophy and Public Affairs* 7, no. 1: 60–73.

———. 1981a. *The Litigious Society.* New York: Basic Books.

———. 1981b. "Review of Marvin E. Frankel, Partisan Justice." *New York Law School Law Review* 27, no. 2: 695–697.

———. 1987. *The Enduring Constitution.* New York: Harper & Row.

———. 1990. "Toward a Theory of Injury." In *Pernicious Ideas and Costly Consequences: The Intellectual Roots of the Tort Crisis*, Jacqueline R. Denning et al. Washington, D.C.: National Legal Center for the Public Interest.

"Life Goes to a Performance of Othello." 1942. *Life Magazine*, August 31, 82–85.

"Lighters Required to Be Child-Proof," 1993. *New York Times*, June 9, A25.

Lilla, Mark. 2007. *The Stillborn God.* New York: Alfred A. Knopf.

Lind, Michael. 2005. "How Should Liberals Think about Liberty?" *Washington Monthly*, May, 17.

Lindblom, Charles E. 1977. *Politics and Markets: The World's Political-Economic Systems.* New York: Basic Books.

———. 1990. *Inquiry and Change.* New Haven: Yale University Press.

———. 2001. *The Market System.* New Haven: Yale University Press.

Liptak, Adam. 2008. "Power to Build Border Fence Is Above All U.S. Law, for Now." *New York Times*, April 8, A1.
Lively, Jack. 1983. "Paternalism." In *Of Liberty*, ed. A. Phillips Griffiths. Cambridge: Cambridge University Press.
Llewellyn, Karl N., and E. A. Hoebel. 1941. *The Cheyenne Way*. Norman: University of Oklahoma Press.
Locke, John. 1910 (1670). "The Fundamental Constitutions of Carolina." In *Select Charters and Other Documents Illustrative of American History 1606–1775*, ed. William MacDonald. London: Macmillan.
———. 1965a (1690). *First Treatise*. In *Two Treatises of Government*, ed. Peter Laslett. New York: New American Library.
———. 1965b (1690). *Second Treatise*. In *Two Treatises of Government*, ed. Peter Laslett. New York: New American Library.
———. 1983 (1689). *A Letter Concerning Toleration*. Ed. James H. Tully. Indianapolis: Hackett.
Lomasky, Loren E. 1990. *Persons, Rights, and the Moral Community*. New York: Oxford University Press.
Lorenz, Konrad Z. 1952. *King Solomon's Ring*. New York: T. Y. Crowell.
Losurdo, Domenico. 2011. *Liberalism: A Counter-History*. Trans. Gregory Elliott. London: Verso.
Lovejoy, Arthur O. 1936. *The Great Chain of Being*. Cambridge, Mass.: Harvard University Press.
Lowi, Theodore W. 1969. *The End of Liberalism*. New York: W. W. Norton.
Luban, David. 1988. *Lawyers and Justice*. Princeton: Princeton University Press.
Lukacs, John. 2004. "The Triumph and Collapse of Liberalism." *Chronicle Review* 51, December 10, 39.
Lukes, Steve. 1971. *Individualism*. New York: Harper Torchbooks.
Luria, Alexander R. 1976. *Cognitive Development: Its Cultural and Social Foundations*. Cambridge, Mass.: Harvard University Press.
Luria, S. E. 1974. "What Can Biologists Solve?" *New York Review of Books*, February 7, 27.
Lynch, Michael P. 2012. *In Praise of Reason*. Cambridge, Mass.: MIT Press.
Macaulay, Stewart. 1963. "Non-Contractual Relations in Business: A Preliminary Study." *American Sociological Review* 28: 55.
Macaulay, Thomas Babington. 1897. "Notes on the Indian Penal Code." In *Works*, ed. Hannah More Macaulay Trevelyan. Vol. 7. New York: Longmans, Green.
MacCallum, Gerald C., Jr. 1972. "Negative and Positive Freedom." In *Philosophy, Politics and Society*, ed. Peter Laslett, W. G. Runciman, and Quentin Skinner. 4th series. Oxford: Basil Blackwell.
Macedo, Stephen. 1991. *Liberal Virtues*. New York: Oxford University Press.
Macfarlane, A. D. J. 1970. *Witchcraft in Tudor and Stuart England*. New York: Harper Torchbook.
Machan, Tibor R. 1983. "The Petty Tyranny of Government Regulation." In *Rights and Regulation*, ed. Tibor R. Machan and M. Bruce Johnson. Cambridge: Ballinger.
Machiavelli, Niccolò. 1974. *The Discourses*. Trans. Leslie J. Walker. New York: Penguin.
MacIntyre, Alasdair. 1984. *After Virtue*. 2d ed. Notre Dame, Ind.: University of Notre Dame Press.
———. 1988. *Whose Justice? Which Rationality?* Notre Dame, Ind.: University of Notre Dame Press.
MacKay, Alfred F. 1980. *Arrow's Theorem: The Paradox of Social Choice*. New Haven: Yale University Press.
Mackie, J. L. 1977. *Ethics: Inventing Right and Wrong*. New York: Penguin.
MacKinnon, Catharine A. 1993. *Only Words*. Cambridge, Mass.: Harvard University Press.
MacKinnon, Catharine A., and Andrea Dworkin, eds. 1998. *In Harm's Way: The Pornography Civil Rights Hearings*. Cambridge, Mass.: Harvard University Press.
Macpherson, C. B. 1964. *The Political Theory of Possessive Individualism*. New York: Oxford University Press.
———. 1980. *Burke*. New York: Oxford University Press.
Madison, James. 1961. No. 51. In *Federalist Papers*, ed. Clinton Rossiter. New York: Mentor Books.
———. 1981. *The Papers of James Madison*, ed. Charles Hobson and Robert Rutland. Vol. 13. Charlottesville: University Press of Virginia.

Magleby, David B. 2011. *Financing the 2008 Election*. Washington, D.C.: Brookings Institution Press.
Magnet, Joseph Eliot. 2005. *Litigating Aboriginal Culture*. Edmonton: Juriliber.
Mai, Mukhtar. 2007. *In the Name of Honor: A Memoir*. New York: Washington Square Press.
Maistre, Joseph-Marie de. 1974 (1797). *Considerations on France*. Trans. R. Lebrun. Montreal: McGill-Queen's University Press.
Mandel, Gregory N., and James Tho Tathii. 2006. "Cost-Benefit Analysis versus the Precautionary Principle: Beyond Cass Sunstein's *Laws of Fear*." *Illinois Law Review* 2006, no. 5: 1037–1079.
Mandeville, Bernard. 1970 (1714). *The Fable of the Bees*. Ed. Philip Harth. New York: Penguin.
Manent, Pierre. 1994. *An Intellectual History of Liberalism*. Princeton: Princeton Univ. Press.
Manjoo, Farhad. 2008. *True Enough: Learning to Live in a Post-Fact Society*. New York: John Wiley.
Marks, F. Raymond, Kirk Leswing, and Barbara A. Fortinsky. 1972. *The Lawyer, the Public and Professional Responsibility*. Chicago: American Bar Foundation.
Marx, Karl. 1977. *Capital*. Trans. Ben Fowkes. New York: Vintage Books.
———. 1978. "The German Ideology: Part I." In *The Marx-Engels Reader*, ed. Robert C. Tucker. 2d ed. New York: W. W. Norton.
Marx, Karl, and Friedrich Engels. 1978 (1848). "The Manifesto of the Communist Party." In *The Marx-Engels Reader*, ed. Robert C. Tucker. 2d ed. New York: W. W. Norton.
Mashaw, Jerry L. 1985. "Prodelegation: Why Administrators Should Make Political Decisions." *Journal of Law Economics and Organization* 1, no. 1: 81–100.
———. 1999. *Greed, Chaos, and Government: Using Public Choice to Improve Public Law*. New Haven: Yale University Press.
Mason, J. K. 2007. *The Troubled Pregnancy: Legal Wrongs and Rights in Reproduction*. Cambridge: Cambridge University Press.
Masood, Salman. 2005. "Pakistan's High Court Suspends Acquittals in Village Gang Rape." *New York Times*, June 29, A3.
Masters, Roger D., ed. 1978. "Introduction." In Jean-Jacques Rousseau, *On the Social Contract*. New York: St. Martin's Press.
McClain, Dylan Loeb. 2007. "Giraffes, Viziers, and Wizards: Variations on the Old Game." *New York Times*, August 19, A29.
McClain, Linda C. 2001. "The Domain of Civic Virtue in a Good Society: Families, Schools, and Sex Equality." *Fordham Law Review* 69, no. 5: 1617–1666.
Medvedev, Roy A. 1975. *On Socialist Democracy*. New York: Alfred A. Knopf.
"Memphis Bars Negro Children at Play in Film." 1947. *Chicago Daily Tribune*, September 20, 12.
Menen, Aubrey. 1949. *The Prevalence of Witches*. New York: Charles Scribner's Sons.
Midgley, Mary. 1993. *Can't We Make Moral Judgements?* New York: St. Martin's Press.
Mill, John Stuart. 1970 (1848). In *Principles of Political Economy*, ed. Donald Winch. New York: Penguin.
———. 1974a (1859). *On Liberty*. In *Utilitarianism and Other Writings*, ed. Mary Warnock. New York: New American Library.
———. 1974b (1861). *Utilitarianism*. In *Utilitarianism and Other Writings*, ed. Mary Warnock. New York: New American Library.
———. 1975 (1861). *Considerations on Representative Government*, in *Three Essays*. New York: Oxford University Press.
Miller, David, ed. 1991. *The Blackwell Encyclopaedia of Political Thought*. Cambridge, Mass.: Blackwell Reference.
Miller, Jennifer M. 2010. "Understanding Fetal Pain: How Changed Circumstances Demand a Legal Response." *Cumberland Law Review* 40, no. 2: 463–497.
Mintz, Morton, and Jerry S. Cohen. 1976. *Power Inc*. New York: Viking Press.
Moody, Thomas. 1994. "Some Comparisons between Liberalism and an Eccentric Communitarianism." In *The Liberalism-Communitarian Debate*, ed. C. F. Delaney. Lanham, Md.: Rowman & Littlefield.
Moon, J. Donald. 1993. *Constructing Community: Moral Pluralism and Tragic Conflicts*. Princeton: Princeton University Press.

Morison, Sir Richard. 1984 (1536). In *Humanist Scholarship and Public Order: Two Tracts against the Pilgrimage of Grace*, ed. David Sandler Berkowitz. Washington, D.C.: Folger Shakespeare Library.
Morris, Christopher. 1967. *Western Political Philosophy*. New York: Basic Books.
Morris, Colin. 1972. *The Discovery of the Individual 1050–1200*. New York: Harper Torchbooks.
Morrissey, Janet. 2011. "Poker Inc. to Uncle Sam: Shut Up and Deal." *New York Times*, October 9, BU1.
Mulhall, Stephen, and Adam Swift. 1996. *Liberals and Communitarians*. 2d ed. Cambridge: Blackwell.
Mulvihill, Geoff. 2007. "Self-Banned Gambler Can't Get Back In." *Washington Post*, January 18: http://www.washingtonpost.com/wp-dyn/content/article/2007/01/18/AR2007011800371_pf.html (accessed May 20, 2012).
Muller, Herbert J. 1971. *The Children of Frankenstein*. Bloomington: University of Indiana Press.
Mumford, Lewis. 1967. *Technics and Human Development*. New York: Harcourt Brace.
Munadi, Saltan M., and Christine Hauser. 2006. "Afghan Convert to Christianity Is Released, Officials Say." *New York Times*, March 28, A3.
Murray, Charles. 1984. *Losing Ground: America's Social Policy 1950–1980*. New York: Basic Books.
Myers, Beth E. 1991. "The Food and Drug Administration's Experimental Drug Approval System: Is It Good for Your Health?" *Houston Law Review* 28, no. 1: 309–336.
National Recreation and Park Association. 1994. "Beyond 'Fun and Games,' Emerging Roles of Public Recreation." Arlington, Va.: National Recreation and Park Association.
Neelakantan, Shailaja. 2006. "In India, Conservatives Want Women under Wraps." *Chronicle of Higher Education*, May 26, A47.
Neiman, Melissa. 2008. "Motorcycle Helmet Laws: The Facts, What Can Be Done to Jump-Start Helmet Use and Ways to Cut Damages." *Journal of Health Care Law and Policy* 11, no. 2: 215–248.
Newman, Andy, and Leslie Kaufman. 2008. "Murder Case Tests Limits on Parents' Right to Hit." *New York Times*, January 20, 33.
Nietzsche, Friedrich. 1907 (1886). *Beyond Good and Evil*. Trans. Helen Zimmern. New York: Macmillan.
———. 1989 (1887). *On the Genealogy of Morals*. Ed. Walter Kaufmann. New York: Vintage Books.
Noah, Timothy. 2009. "The Medicare-Isn't-Government Meme." *Slate*, August 5 (available at http://www.slate.com/articles/news_and_politics/prescriptions/2009/08/the_medicareisntgovernment_meme.html) (accessed September 3, 2011).
Noll, Roger G. 1971. *Reforming Regulation, An Evaluation of the Ash Council Proposals*. Washington, D.C.: Brookings Institution.
Notestein, Wallace. 1968 (1911). *A History of Witchcraft in England*. New York: Thomas Y. Crowell.
Nove, Alec. 1992. *The Economics of Feasible Socialism Revisited*. New York: Routledge.
Nozick, Robert. 1974. *Anarchy, State, and Utopia*. New York: Basic Books.
Nussbaum, Martha C. 2007a. "Fears for Democracy in India." *Chronicle of Higher Education*, May 18, B8.
———. 2007b. *The Clash Within: Democracy, Religious, Violence, and India's Future*. Cambridge, Mass.: Belknap Press of Harvard University Press.
Oakeshott, Michael. 1991. "Political Education." In *Rationalism in Politics and Other Essays*. New and expanded ed. Indianapolis: Liberty Press.
Okin, Susan Moller. 1989. *Justice, Gender, and the Family*. New York: Basic Books.
Ollman, Bertell, ed. 1998. *Market Socialism: The Debate among Socialists*. New York: Routledge.
Olson, Mancur. 1971. *The Logic of Collective Action: Public Goods and the Theory of Groups*. New York: Schocken Books.
Orwell, George. 1949. *1984*. New York: Harcourt, Brace.
Overbye, Dennis. 2008a. "Gauging a Collider's Odds of Creating a Black Hole." *New York Times*, April 15, F2.
———. 2008b. "Suit to Halt Big Collider in Europe Is Dismissed." *New York Times*, September 30, A21.
Paine, Thomas. 1995. *Collected Writings*, ed. Eric Foner. New York: Library of America.

Parekh, Bhikhu. 1972. "Liberalism and Morality." In *The Morality of Politics*, ed. Bhikhu Parekh and R. N. Berki. London: Allen & Unwin.
———. 1994. "Superior People: The Narrowness of Liberalism from Mill to Rawls." *Times Literary Supplement*, February 25, 13–16.
Pear, Robert. 2012. "The Caucus; Obama Signs Ban on Insider Trading." *New York Times*, April 5, A14.
Pepper, Claude. 1946. "Nine Definitions of Liberalism." *New Republic*, July 26.
Pepper, Karl R., and John C. Eccles. 1977. *The Self and Its Brain*. New York: Springer.
Persons, Stow, ed. 1956. *Evolutionary Thought in America*. New York: George Braziller.
Pettit, Philip. 1997. *Republicanism: A Theory of Freedom and Government*. New York: Oxford University Press.
Phillips, Derek L. 1993. *Looking Backward: A Critical Appraisal of Communitarian Thought*. Princeton: Princeton University Press.
Pinker, Steven. 2002. *The Blank Slate: The Modern Denial of Human Nature*. New York: Viking.
Pirenne, Henri. 1956. *Economic and Social History of Medieval Europe*. New York: Harvest Books.
Plant, Raymond. 1991. *Modern Political Thought*. Oxford: Basil Blackwell.
Polanyi, Karl. 1944. *The Great Transformation*. Boston: Beacon Press.
Pollock, Frederick, and Frederic William Maitland. 1968. *The History of English Law*. Cambridge: Cambridge University Press.
Polsby, Daniel D. 1994. "The False Promise of Gun Control." *Atlantic Monthly*, March, 57.
Porter, Michael, and Claas van der Linde. 1995. "Green and Competitive: Ending the Stalemate." *Harvard Business Review* (September–October): 120–134.
Portman, John. 2004. *Bad for Us: The Lure of Self Harm*. Boston: Beacon Press.
Posner, Richard A. 1972. "A Theory of Negligence," *Journal of Law and Economics* 1, no. 1: 29–96.
———. 1990. *Problems of Jurisprudence*. Cambridge, Mass.: Harvard University Press.
———. 1996. "The Immoralist." *New Republic*, July 15 and 22, 38.
Postema, Gerald J. 1987. "Collective Evils, Harms, and the Law." *Ethics* 97, no. 2: 414–440.
———. 2005. "Politics Is about the Grievance: Feinberg on the Legal Enforcement of Morals." *Legal Theory* 11, no. 3: 293–323.
Poulson, Kevin. 2005. "Unorthodox Chess from an Odd Mind," *Wired*, July 19: http://www.wired.com/culture/lifestyle/news/2005/07/68227?currentPage=all# (accessed September 1, 2011).
Pound, Ezra. 1939. *ABCs of Economics*. New York: New Directions.
Pound, Roscoe. 1937. "Liability." In *Encyclopedia of the Social Sciences*. New York: Macmillan.
Priaulx, Nicolette. 2007. *The Harm Paradox, Tort Law and the Unwanted Child in an Era of Choice*. London: Taylor & Francis.
Price, Don K. 1965. *The Scientific Estate*. Cambridge, Mass.: Belknap Press of Harvard University Press.
Priest, George L. 1992. "The Inevitability of Tort Reform." *Valparaiso University Law Review* 26, no. 3: 701–707.
"Proceedings in the Supreme Court of the United States in Memory of Mr. Justice Jackson." 1955. *U.S. Reports* 349: xxvii–li.
Prosser, William. 1964. *Handbook on the Law of Torts*. 3rd ed. St. Paul, Minn.: West.
Purcell, Edward A. 1992. *Litigation and Inequality: Federal Diversity Jurisdiction in Industrial America, 1870–1958*. New York: Oxford University Press.
Quindlen, Anna. 1994. "Same Old Math." *New York Times*, October 22, 23.
Rabin, Robert L. "The Politics of Tort Reform." *Valparaiso University Law Review* 26, no. 3: 709–716.
Rachels, James. 1978. "Euthanasia." In *Matters of Life and Death*, ed. Tom Regan. New York: Random House.
Rachlinski, Jeffrey. 2002–2003. "The Uncertain Psychological Case for Paternalism." *Northwestern University Law Review* 97, no. 3: 1165–1225.
"Racial Steering in the Romantic Marketplace." 1994. *Harvard Law Review* 107, no. 4: 877–894.

Rakoff, Todd D. 1983. "Contracts of Adhesion: An Essay in Reconstruction." *Harvard Law Review* 96, no. 6: 1173–1284.
Rakowski, Eric. 2004. "Reverence for Life and the Limits of State Power." In *Dworkin and His Critics*, ed. Justine Burley. Malden, Mass.: Blackwell.
Rawls, John. 1971. *A Theory of Justice*. Cambridge, Mass.: Harvard University Press.
———. 1993. *Political Liberalism*. New York: Columbia University Press.
Raz, Joseph. 1988. *The Morality of Freedom*. Oxford: Clarendon Press.
"Recent Book." 2012. *Harvard Law Review* 125, no. 4: 1120–1128.
Reiman, Jeffrey. 1994. "Liberalism and Its Critics." In *The Liberalism-Communitarianism Debate*, ed. C. F. Delaney. Lanham, Md.: Rowman & Littlefield.
Revkin, Andrew C. 2008. "Skeptics on Human Climate Impact Seize on Cold Spell." *New York Times*, March 2, 18.
Ridley, Matt. 1998. *The Origins of Virtue*. New York: Penguin.
———. 2011. *The Rational Optimist*. New York: Harper Perennial.
Ripstein, Arthur. 2006. "Beyond the Harm Principle," *Philosophy & Public Affairs* 34, no. 3: 215–245.
Roberts, Sam. 2008. "The Mighty Political Legacy of William F. Buckley Jr." *New York Times*, March 1, B2.
Robertson, Pat. 1993. *The Fall of Liberalism and the Rise of Common Sense*. Nashville: W Publishing Group.
Robinson, Joshua. 2008. "Pistorius Left Off South African Olympic Team." *New York Times*, July 19, D1.
Robinson, Joshua, and Alan Schwarz. 2008. "Olympic Dream Stays Alive, on Synthetic Legs." *New York Times*, May 17, A1.
Roemer, John. 1994. *A Future for Socialism*. Cambridge, Mass.: Harvard University Press.
Romano, Carlin. 2008. "Boss Nova: Harvard Law's Roberto Unger Takes on the Future of Brazil." *Chronicle Review*, June 6, B10.
Rosenblum, Nancy L., ed. 1989. *Liberalism and the Moral Life*. Cambridge, Mass.: Harvard University Press.
———. 1998. "Fusion Republicanism." In *Debating Democracy's Discontent*, ed. Anita L. Allen and Milton C. Regan Jr. New York: Oxford University Press.
Rosenfeld, Michel. 1995. "Law as Discourse: Bridging the Gap between Democracy and Rights." *Harvard Law Review* 108, no. 5: 1163–1189.
Ross, E. A. 1907. *Sin and Society*. Boston: Houghton Mifflin.
Rossiter, Clinton, ed. 1961. *The Federalist Papers*. New York: New American Library.
Rottenberg, Simon, ed. 1980. *Occupational Licensure and Regulation*. Washington, D.C.: American Enterprise Institute.
Rousseau, Jean-Jacques. 1964. *The First and Second Discourses*. Ed. Roger D. Masters. New York: St. Martin's Press.
———. 1978. *On the Social Contract*. Ed. Roger D. Masters. New York: St. Martin's Press.
Royalty, Kenneth M. 1969. "Motorcycle Helmets and the Constitutionality of Self-Protective Legislation." *Ohio State Law Journal* 30, no. 2: 355–381.
Rubin, Zick. 1980. *Children's Friendships*. Cambridge, Mass.: Harvard University Press.
Rucker, Philip. 2009. "S.C. Senator Is a Voice of Reform Opposition; DeMint a Champion of Conservatives." *Washington Post*, July 28, A1.
Russell, T. Baron. 1906. *A Hundred Years Hence: The Expectations of an Optimist*. Chicago: A. C. McClurg.
Ryan, Alan. 1995. "Liberalism." In *A Companion to Contemporary Political Philosophy*, ed. Robert E. Goodin and Philip Pettit. Cambridge: Blackwell.
Sabine, George H., and Thomas L. Thorson. 1973. *A History of Political Theory*. 4th ed. Fort Worth: Holt, Reinhart & Winston.
Salvany, Don Felix Sarda Y. 1994. *Liberalism Is a Sin*. Rockford, Ill.: Tan Books.
Sandel, Michael J. 1982. *Liberalism and the Limits of Justice*. New York: Cambridge University Press.

———. 1984. "Introduction." In *Liberalism and Its Critics*, ed. Michael J. Sandel. New York: New York University Press.

———. 1996. *Democracy's Discontent: America in Search of a Public Philosophy*. Cambridge, Mass.: Belknap Press of Harvard University Press.

Sarnoff, Julia N. 2011. "Federal Criminal Conspiracy." *American Criminal Law Review* 48, no. 2: 663–696.

Saul, John Ralston. 1992. *Voltaire's Bastards: The Dictatorship of Reason in the West*. New York: Free Press.

Savage, David G. 2011. "Election Laws Tightening in GOP-Run States." *Los Angeles Times*, October 30:http://www.latimes.com/news/nationworld/nation/la-na-vote-florida-20111031,0,196273.story (accessed November 5, 2011).

Savage, Michael. 2000. *Liberalism Is a Mental Disorder*. Nashville: Thomas Nelson.

Schelling, Thomas. 1987. "Ethics, Law, and Self-Command." In *Liberty, Equality, and the Law*, ed. Sterling M. McMurrin. Salt Lake City: University of Utah Press.

Schoenbrod, David. 1993. *Power without Responsibility: How Congress Abuses People through Delegation*. New Haven: Yale University Press.

Schroeder, Jeanne L. 1998. "The End of the Market: A Psychoanalysis of Law and Economics." *Harvard Law Review* 112, no. 2: 483–558.

Schuck, Peter H. 1981. "Book Review of *The Politics of Regulation*." *Yale Law Journal* 90, no. 3: 702–725.

Schulz, Kathryn. 2010. *Being Wrong: Adventures in the Margin of Error*. New York: Ecco.

Schuster, John W. 2004. "Riding without a Helmet: Liability, Social Efficiency, and the More Perfect Wisconsin Compromise to Motorcycle Helmet Liability." *Iowa Law Review* 89, no. 4: 1391–1418.

Schweickart, David. 1996. *Against Capitalism*. Boulder, Col.: Westview Press.

———. 2002. *After Capitalism*. Lanham, Md.: Rowman & Littlefield.

Schweizer, Peter. 2011. *Throw Them All Out*. Boston: Houghton Mifflin Harcourt.

Scruton, Roger. 1980. *The Meaning of Conservatism*. London: Macmillan.

Sen, Amartya K. 1992. *Inequality Re-Examined*. Oxford: Clarendon Press.

Shapiro, Ian. 1986. *The Evolution of Rights in Liberal Theory*. New York: Cambridge University Press.

———. 2005. *The Flight from Reality in the Human Sciences*. Princeton: Princeton University Press.

Shapiro, Sidney, and Rena Steinzor. 2008. "Capture, Accountability, and Regulatory Metrics." *Texas Law Review* 86, no. 7: 1741–1785.

Shklar, Judith. 1990. *The Faces of Injustice*. New Haven: Yale University Press.

———. 1991. "The Liberalism of Fear." In *Liberalism and the Moral Life*, ed. Nancy L. Rosenblum. Cambridge, Mass.: Harvard University Press.

Shrady, Nicholas. 2008. *The Last Day: Wrath, Ruin, and Reason in the Great Lisbon Earthquake of 1755*. New York: Viking Press.

Simmel, Georg. 1959. *The Sociology of Religion*. Trans. Curt Rosenthal. New York: Philosophical Library.

Simmons, Marc. 1974. *Witchcraft in the Southwest: Spanish and Indian Supernaturalism on the Rio Grande*. Lincoln: University of Nebraska Press.

Simons, Marlise. 1994. "Ban Englizh? French Bicker on Barricades." *New York Times*, March 15, A1.

Simpson, George, ed. 1951. "The Aetiology of Suicide." In Emile Durkheim, *Suicide*. New York: Free Press.

Simpson, Peter. 1994. "Liberalism, State, and Community." *Critical Review* 8, no. 2: 159–173.

Singer, Peter. 1973. "Altruism and Commerce: A Defense of Titmuss against Arrow." *Philosophy and Public Affairs* 2, no. 3: 312–319.

Skolnick, Arlene. 1991. *Embattled Paradise, The American Family in an Age of Uncertainty*. New York: Basic Books.

Sloan, Frank A., and Lindsey N. Chepke. 2008. *Medical Malpractice*. Cambridge, Mass.: MIT Press.

Smith, Adam. 1937. *Wealth of Nations*. New York: Modern Library.

———. 1978. *Lectures on Jurisprudence*. Ed. R. L. Meek, D. D. Raphael, and P. G. Stein. Oxford: Oxford University Press.

———. 1982. *The Theory of Moral Sentiments*. Ed. D. D. Raphael and A. L. Macfie. Indianapolis: Liberty Classics.
Smolowe, Jill. 1994. "Going Soft on Crime." *Time*, November 14, 63.
Smothers, Ronald. 1993. "Georgia Panel Eases Sentence of Youth in Ice Cream Theft." *New York Times*, September 21, A16.
Sokolove, Michael. 2012. "The Fast Life." *New York Times Magazine*, January 22, 28.
Solomon, Robert C. 1995. *A Passion for Justice*. Lanham, Md.: Rowman & Littlefield.
Sowell, Thomas. 1987. *A Conflict of Visions: Ideological Origins of Political Struggles*. New York: William Morrow.
Specter, Michael. 2009. *Denialism*. New York: Penguin Press.
Spector, Joseph. 2012. "Pro Bono Work Will Be Required to Pass N.Y. Bar," *USA Today*, May 20, 2012, http://www.usatoday.com/news/nation/story/2012-05-02/new-york-pro-bono-required/54699318/1 (accessed May 20, 2012).
Spencer, Herbert. 1970 (1851). *Social Statics*. New York: Robert Schalkenbach Foundation.
Spender, Stephen. 1975. "The Multiple Sins of Human Nature," *New York Times*, January 4:23.
Spiegel, Claire. 1994. "'3 Strikes' Loophole Can Give Offenders a Break." *Los Angeles Times*, October 24, A1.
Starkey, Marion L. 1989 (1949). *The Devil in Massachusetts*. New York: Anchor Books.
Starr, Paul. 2007. *Freedom's Power*. New York: Basic Books.
Steinberg, Ted. 2000. *Acts of God: The Unnatural History of Natural Disaster in America*. New York: Oxford University Press.
Steiner, Hillel. 1983. "How Free: Computing Personal Liberty." In *Of Liberty*, ed. A. Phillips Griffiths. Cambridge: Cambridge University Press.
Stephen, James Fitzjames. 1991. *Liberty, Equality, and Fraternity*. Chicago: University of Chicago Press.
Stewart, Richard B. 1975. "The Reformation of American Administrative Law." *Harvard Law Review* 88, no. 8: 1669–1813.
Stigler, George J. 1971. "The Theory of Economic Regulation." *Bell Journal of Economics and Management Science* 2: 3–21.
———. 1975. *The Citizen and the State, Essays on Regulation*. Chicago: University of Chicago Press.
Stiglitz, Joseph E. 2009. *Selected Works*. Vol. 1, *Information and Economic Analysis*. New York: Oxford University Press.
Stone, Christopher D. 1972. "Should Trees Have Standing?" *Southern California Law Review* 45: 450–501.
———. 1975. *Where the Law Ends*. New York: Harper & Row.
———. 1985. "Should Trees Have Standing Revisited: How Far Will Law and Morals Reach? A Pluralist Perspective." *Southern California Law Review* 59, no. 1: 1–154.
Strayer, Joseph R. 1970. *On the Medieval Origins of the Modern State*. Princeton: Princeton University Press.
Strub, Whitney. 2007. "Black and White and Banned All Over: Race, Censorship and Obscenity in Postwar Memphis." *Journal of Social History* 40, no. 3: 685–715.
Sullivan, Andrew, ed. 2004. *Same-Sex Marriage: Pro and Con—A Reader*. Rev. ed. New York: Vintage Books.
Sunstein, Cass. 2005. *Laws of Fear: Beyond the Precautionary Principle*. Cambridge University Press.
Symposium on Republicanism. 1988. *Yale Law Journal* 97, no. 8: 493–1723.
Taibbi, Matt. 2007. "The American Left's Silly Victim Complex." Originally at www.adbusters.org/the_magazine/include/print.php?id=271; http://what-is-is.blogspot.com/2007/08/taibbi-biggest-problem-with-liberalism.html (accessed October 16, 2011).
Tam, Henry. 1998. *Communitarianism*. New York: New York University Press.
Tawney, R. H. 1961 (1931). *Equality*. 4th rev. ed. New York: Capricorn Books.
Taylor, Charles. 1979. "What's Wrong with Negative Liberty." In *The Idea of Freedom: Essays in Honour of Isaiah Berlin*, ed. Alan Ryan. Oxford: Oxford University Press.

———. 1985. "Atomism." In *Philosophy and the Human Sciences: Philosophical Papers 2*. New York: Cambridge University Press.

———. 1986. "Alternative Futures: Legitimacy, Identity, and Alienation in Late Twentieth Century Canada." In *Constitutionalism, Citizenship and Society in Canada*, ed. A. Cairns and C. Williams. Toronto: University of Toronto Press.

———. 1994. "The Politics of Recognition." In *Multiculturalism*, ed. Amy Gutmann. Princeton: Princeton University Press.

Tebbe, Nelson. 2007. "Witchcraft and Statecraft: Liberal Democracy in Africa." *Georgetown Law Journal* 96, no. 1: 183–236.

Ten, C. L. 1980. *Mill on Liberty*. New York: Oxford University Press.

Terry, Don. 1994. "Basketball at Midnight: 'Hope' on a Summer Eve." *New York Times*, August 19, A18.

Thomas, Keith. 1971. *Religion and the Decline of Magic*. New York: Charles Scribner's Sons.

Thomas, William. 1985. *Mill*. New York: Oxford University Press.

Thompson, E. P. 1975. *Whigs and Hunters: The Origin of the Black Act*. New York: Pantheon.

Thompson, Janna. 2002. *Taking Responsibility for the Past: Reparation and Historical Justice*. Cambridge, U.K.: Polity Press.

Thomson, Judith Jarvis. 1983. "Some Questions about Government Regulation of Behavior." In *Rights and Regulation*, ed. Tibor R. Machan and M. Bruce Johnson. Cambridge, Mass.: Ballinger.

Titmuss, Richard M. 1971. *The Gift Relationship: From Human Blood to Social Policy*. New York: Pantheon.

Tocqueville, Alexis de. 1955 (1858). *The Old Regime and the French Revolution*. Trans. Stuart Gilbert. New York: Doubleday Anchor.

Tolstoy, Leo. 1948 (1900). *The Slavery of Our Times*. Trans. Maude Aylmer. London: Porcupine Press.

Tomasky, Michael. 2012. "Did Liberals Screw Obamacare?" *The Daily Beast*. March 28, http://www.thedailybeast.com/articles/2012/03/28/michael-tomasky-asks-did-liberals-screw-obamacare.html (accessed on March 29, 2012).

Tomlins, Christopher. 2010. *Freedom Bound: Law, Labor, and Civic Identity in Colonizing English America, 1580–1865*. New York: Cambridge University Press.

Townsend, Joseph. 1971 (1786). *A Dissertation on the Poor Laws by a Well-Wisher to Mankind*. Berkeley: University of California Press.

Trebilcock, Michael J. 1993. *The Limits of Freedom of Contract*. Cambridge, Mass.: Harvard University Press.

Trillin, Calvin. 1996. *Too Soon to Tell*. New York: Warner Books.

Trivers, Robert. 2011. *The Folly of Fools: The Logic of Deceit and Self-Deception in Human Life*. New York: Basic Books.

Turner, Stephen P. 2003. *Liberal Democracy 3.0: Civil Society in an Age of Experts*. Sherman Oaks, Calif: Sage.

Tushnet, Mark. 1983. "Following the Rules Laid Down: A Critique of Interpretivism and Neutral Principles." *Harvard Law Review* 96, no. 4: 781–827.

———. 1988. *Red, White, and Blue: A Critical Analysis of Constitutional Law*. Cambridge, Mass.: Harvard University Press.

———. 2003. *Slave Law in the American South*. Lawrence: University Press of Kansas.

Unger, Roberto Mangabeira. 1975. *Knowledge and Politics*. New York: Free Press.

———. 2004. *False Necessity*. London: Verso.

van den Brinck, Bert. 2000. *The Tragedy of Liberalism*. Albany: State University of New York Press.

Van Dyke, Vernon. 1960. *Political Science: A Philosophical Analysis*. Stanford: Stanford University Press.

Vining, Joseph. 1978. *Legal Identity: The Coming of Age of Public Law*. New Haven: Yale University Press.

Viscusi, W. Kip, and Joni Hersch. 1990. "The Market Response to Product Safety Litigation." *Journal of Regulatory Economics* 2, no. 3: 215–230.

Volokh, Eugene. 1999. "A Common-Law Model for Religious Exemptions." *U.C.L.A. Law Review* 46, no. 5: 1465–1566.

Vygotsky, Lev S. 1978. *Mind in Society: The Development of Higher Psychological Processes.* Cambridge, Mass.: Harvard University Press.
Wagner, David M. 1994. "Alasdair MacIntyre: Recovering the Rationality of Traditions." In *Liberalism at the Crossroads*, ed. Christopher Wolfe and John Hittinger. Lanham, Md.: Rowman & Littlefield.
Waldron, Jeremy. 1987a. "Theoretical Foundations of Liberalism." *Philosophical Quarterly* 37, n.o. 147: 127–150.
———, ed. 1987b. *Nonsense upon Stilts: Bentham, Burke, and Marx on the Rights of Man.* New York: Methuen.
Walker, Alice, and Pratibha Parmar. 1993. *Warrior Marks: Female Genital Mutilation and the Sexual Binding of Women.* New York: Harcourt Brace.
Walzer, Michael. 1983. *Spheres of Justice: An Essay on Pluralism and Equality.* New York: Basic Books.
———. 1989–90. "A Critique of Philosophical Conversation." *Philosophical Forum* 21, nos. 1–2: 182–196.
———. 1990. "The Communitarian Critique of Liberalism." *Political Theory* 18, no. 1: 6–23.
———. 2004. *Politics and Passion.* New Haven: Yale University Press.
Weil, Robert. 1996. *Red Cat White Cat: China and the Contradictions of "Market Socialism."* New York: Monthly Review Press.
Weithman, Paul J. 1999. "Of Assisted Suicide and 'The Philosophers' Brief.'" *Ethics* 109, no. 3: 548–578.
Welchman, Jennifer. 1995. "Locke on Slavery and Inalienable Rights." *Canadian Journal of Philosophy* 25, no. 1: 67–81.
Weldon, T. D. 1953. *The Vocabulary of Politics.* Baltimore: Penguin.
Wellman, Carl. 1982. *Welfare Rights.* Totowa, N.J.: Rowman & Allanheld.
West, Debra. 2005. "Cross Westchester: We Said Wireless, Not Clueless." *New York Times*, November 20, 2 (Westchester).
Westen, Peter. 1982. "The Empty Idea of Equality." *Harvard Law Review* 95, no. 3: 537–596.
Wiley, W. L. 1967. *The Formal French.* Cambridge, Mass.: Harvard University Press.
Wilson, James Q., ed. 1980. *The Politics of Regulation.* New York: Basic Books.
———. 1989. *Bureaucracy: What Government Agencies Do and Why They Do It.* New York: Basic Books.
Winston, Clifford, Robert W. Crandall, and Vikram Maheshri. 2011. *First Thing We Do, Let's De-Regulate All the Lawyers.* Washington, D.C.: Brookings Institution Press.
Wolfe, Alan. 1999. "The Revolution That Never Was," *New Republic*, June 7, 36–37.
———. 2009. *The Future of Liberalism.* New York: Alfred A. Knopf.
Wolff, Robert Paul. 1968. *The Poverty of Liberalism.* Boston: Beacon Press.
Wolin, Richard. 2004. *The Seduction of Unreason: The Intellectual Romance with Fascism from Nietzsche to Postmodernism.* Princeton: Princeton University Press.
Wollheim, Richard. 1959. "Crime, Sin, and Mr. Justice Devlin." *Encounter*, November, 38.
Wood, Gordon S. 1972. *The Creation of the American Republic, 1776–1789.* New York: W. W. Norton.
———. 1993. *The Radicalism of the American Revolution.* New York: Vintage.
Woodham-Smith, Cecil. 1991 (1962). *The Great Hunger: Ireland 1845–1849.* New York: Penguin.
Woodward, C. Vann. 1974. *The Strange Career of Jim Crow.* 3rd rev. ed. New York: Oxford University Press.
Yarbrough, Tinsley E. 1992. *John Marshall Harlan, Great Dissenter of the Warren Court.* New York: Oxford University Press.
Young, S. David. 1987. *The Rule of Experts.* Washington, D.C.: Cato Institute.
Zerubavel, Eviatar. 1997. *Social Mindscapes.* Cambridge, Mass.: Harvard University Press.
Zimring, Franklin E. 2003. "Continuity and Change in the American Gun Debate." In *Evaluating Gun Policy: Effects on Crime and Violence*, ed. Jens Ludwig and Philip J. Cook. Washington, D.C.: Brookings.
Zwick, Jesse. 2012. "No Holds Barred." *New Republic*, June 7, 7–8.

INDEX

A. L. A. Schechter Poultry Corp. v. U. S., 314n44
abortion, 326n42
accident victims, loss suffered by, 73, 134, 136
accumulative harm. *See* harm, accumulative
Ackerman, Bruce A., 259, 268, 336n9, 340n66
act of God, 132–133, 267
Adams, John, 31
addiction, 168, 185
addictive substances, 131, 185–187, 317n20
Adickes v. S. H. Kress & Co., 334n122
aesthetics, regulation of, 223–225, 327n58
affirmative obligations, 127–142
aggregative harm. *See* harm, aggregative
alcohol, regulation of, 65–66
American Bar Association, 192
ancient lights, 44
ancient usage, 80
antitrust, 85
Appiah, Anthony K., 275n5, 278n44, 339n43
  critique of Dworkin, 264–265
  on dueling, 319n55
  on identity, 236
Aquinas, 218, 283n98
Arblaster, Anthony, 202, 205, 278n60, 294n12
Aristotle, 150, 218, 220, 244, 248, 278n60
Arneson, Richard J., 210–212, 323nn6, 10
Arrow, Kenneth J., 320n62
Arrow's theorem, 312n27
artificial snow, 221
Asimov, Isaac, 320n78
assisted suicide, 191–193
association, freedom of, 230
assumption of risk, 135
attractive nuisance, 119 (*see also* unattractive nuisance)
Auden, W. H., 277n38
automobile, development of, 203–204
autonomous self, 19–25, 135, 138, 278n58, 282n90, 335n10

autonomy, 190, 252, 258, 266, 281n90
  and community claims, 210–211
  and negative rights, 101
  and paternalism, 180, 198

Bacon, Francis, 20
badge of inferiority, 239–240, 334n125
Bailey v. Alabama, 304n2
bakers, working conditions of, 88–92
baptism, 329n82
bargaining power, imbalance of, 92
baseline, 53, 82, 90, 263
belief environment, 220
Bell, Alexander Graham, 203
Bell, Clive, 219
Belloc, Hilaire, 132, 136
Bentham, Jeremy, 47, 48, 149, 201, 202, 205, 246, 261
Berkeley, George, 312n19
Berlin, Isaiah, 162, 201, 276n20, 298n17
bestiality, 211–212
Bibi, Mukhtaran, 281n86
Bierce, Ambrose, 28, 283n105
bigamy, 153, 309n39
Birrell, Augustine, 42
birth lottery, 265
Black Act, 147, 148
blacking, 307n13
blackmail, 199
Blackstone, William, 149
Bloom, Allan, 247, 248, 273
blood supply, 320n62
Bodin, Jean, 323n17
bookselling, 42
Bork, Robert H., 326n49
Bowles, Chester, 5
Bronowski, Jacob, 24, 281n87
Brooks, David, 276n22, 280n75
Brown, Henry B., 239–240
Brown v. Board of Education, 308n26

Brushaber v. Union Pac. R. R. Co., 308n20
Buckley, Christopher, 6
Buckley, William F. Jr., 6
Burckhardt, Jacob, 21, 22
Burke, Edmund, 26, 30, 98, 165, 234, 293n7
Burr, Aaron, 319n55
Butler v. Perry, 304n3
butterfly effect, 47

Cabell, James Branch, 273
Cardozo, Benjamin N., 138–139
Casey at the Bat, 17, 278n50
Casino Control Commission, 201
causation, 66–68, 213, 306n41
  in market, 69–75
caveat emptor, 132, 136, 157, 140
central planning, 82–84, 93
certainty. *See* uncertainty
Chamberlain, Wilt, 104
charity, 97–100
Charles River Bridge Co. v. Warren River Bridge, 295n44
cheese, revulsion to, 219
chess, 194–195
Chesterton, G. K., 229, 246
Cheyenne adjudication, 286n25
child labor, 70–71
Christianity, 30, 72, 280n84
citizenship, 169–171
City of Cleburne v. Cleburne Living Center, 310n46
civic republicanism, 232–234, 244, 331nn93, 95
civic virtue, 245, 303n84, 332n99
civil association, 282n93
civil remedies, 59–62, 253
Civil Rights Act of 1866, 152
Coconino National Forest, 221
coercion, 51, 89, 91, 114, 132, 195, 197, 221, 282n90, 285n10, 289n16, 296n60
Cohen, G. A., 296n60
Cohen v. California, 327n56
collective concrete other, 333n111
Commager, Henry Steele, 78
common good, 5, 33, 244, 245, 307n9, 332n99
  (*see also* good)
  claims to by communitarians, 226, 228, 230, 232
Commons, John R., 44
Communist obituary, 295n47
communitarian thesis, 217
communitarianism, 226–234, 248
community
  harms to, 179, 212–214, 214–218, 226–241
  harms by, 237–240
  vs. individual, 19–25, 210–212, 280n82
compensatory justice, 108, 299n41
competition, 55, 80–82, 89, 93, 95, 195
  harms, 80–82
complex equality, 263

conscription, 128
consent, 15
  completed and continuing, 194
  of governed, 257
  to harms, 189–193
  by later generations, 257
  premise, 255–258
  to risks, 183–189
  tacit, 256, 257, 337n10
conservatives, 98, 173, 246, 277n36, 333n106
  against autonomy, 24
  attitude to harm, 250–253
  compared to liberals, 6–7, 169, 201, 283n105
  core belief, 282n93
  on human nature, 24, 282n92, 328n66
  and litigation, 159
  on misuse of reason, 25
conspiracy law, 290n26
Constant, Benjamin, 85, 149
Constitution
  need for, 172
  violation of as harmless, 58–59
constitutionalizing the harm principle, 175, 176–179
Consumer Product Safety Commission, 187, 292n52
contempt of court, 57
contract law, 54, 84–85, 117
  adhesion in, 199
  self-binding, 199–201
  unconscionability in, 197–198
contributory negligence, 135
cooling off period, 200
copyright, 42
corporal punishment, 51, 289n21, 302n73
corporation, as person, 87
Crawford v. Marion County Election Board, 313n28
criminal vs. civil, 59–62, 119, 288n12
critical thinking, challenges to, 122–123
Cromwell, Oliver, 165
Cruzan v. Director, 318n33
custom, 75–78, 194–196, 238

dam construction, 118
Davis, David Brion, 149–150
Deane, Herbert A., 311n8
Declaration of Independence, 255
Declaration of the Rights of Man, 284n4
Defoe, Daniel, 330n89
delegation of legislative power, 170, 174–175
democratic despotism, 31
Dennett, Daniel C., 220
deodand, 294n24
derivative crime, 57–59
Devlin, Patrick, 224, 226, 325n39, 328n70, 329n76
  on protecting morality by law, 214–218, 325n34

dialogue, 15–16
dialogue premise, 259–261
difference principle, 263, 297n12
dignity, 188–189
discrimination, 108, 125, 153, 232, 235, 251, 313n37
  based on immutable characteristics, 237–240, 334n122
  based on sex, 267–268
  by Congress, 332n102
  under Fourteenth Amendment, 309n26
  as harmful, 196, 333n114
District of Columbia v. Heller, 292n51
Donne effect, 288n4
dress code, 207–208
drug, meaning of, 186
drug regulation, 19, 132, 146, 173, 182, 317nn19, 20
  paternalism and, 183–187, 315n5
dueling, 195–196, 238, 315n5, 319nn55, 57, 334n118
Duke of Wellington, 319n55
Durkheim, Emile, 23, 240, 280n82, 339n56
duty
  to act, 127–142
  positive and negative, 127
  to rescue, 90, 118–120, 129–131, 197
Dworkin, Ronald, 202, 321n79, 329n76, 335n10, 338n36
  and auction of resources, 263, 339n43
  on equality premise, 261–265, 297n12
  on external preferences, 322n4, 323n6
  philosophers' brief and, 191
  as redistributionist, 99
  on treating people as equals, 151, 309n29, 338n34

earthquake, 300n50
education, right to, 4, 40, 72, 98, 99, 111, 120–126, 168, 240, 303nn81, 84
efficiency, 83, 85, 108, 138, 173, 238
egalitarian liberalism, 149–154
Eighteenth Amendment, 65
elections, 4, 13, 175, 238, 263, 313n29
eminent domain, 128
employment harm, 88–92
Employment Division v. Smith, 340n60
Enlightenment, 121, 283n100
entitlement theory, 103–108
Epicureans, 51, 289n24
equal respect. *See* equality of respect
equal treatment. *See* equality of treatment
equality, 99, 103, 124–125, 242–243, 276n22, 297nn68, 12, 321n79, 335n127. *See also* complex equality
  and antidiscrimination laws, 237–240
  definitional problems of, 277n44
  and dialogue, 260–261

criterion, 16, 175, 224, 327n58
  in original position, 338n33
  premise, 261–265
  principle, 14–16, 149–154, 176, 276n8, 327n58
  of respect, 16, 234, 243, 236–237, 262, 268, 323n6, 332n102, 333n113
  sex equality, 303n84
  of treatment, 33, 151, 192, 309n29, 338n34
euthanasia, 191–193
evidence, 36, 41, 82, 123, 152, 221, 248, 261, 324n20
  costs of, 310n59
  of facts, 7, 65, 108, 158, 184, 194, 217–218, 251, 303n81
  scientifically accessible, 4, 14, 37, 90–91, 154, 253, 261, 267
  spectral, 213
existence, right to, 302n72
expectations, 61, 74, 308n16, 325n39, 327n52
  in contract law, 117
  and the externality constraint, 208–212, 265, 328n67
  formation of, 222–223
expertise, 166–169
exploitation, 196–199
external preferences, 209, 210, 211, 212, 323n6
  (*see also* interest in another's interest)
  double counting, 322n4
externality constraint, 222, 223, 237, 328n67
  (*see also* interest in another's interest)
  defined, 208–212

facts, turning away from, 26, 90, 154, 181, 253, 262, 276n8, 329n76, 336n26 (*see also* evidence)
fairy stone, 155
FAKE argument, 90, 190
family relations
  decay of, 217–219, 303n86, 325n39
  government intrusion into, 120–126, 286n22
  individual submerged in, 5, 21–23, 75, 280n84, 281n86
  and legal duties, 127
  role of, 226–227, 279n74
famine, 72, 75, 88, 98, 283n97
Federal Power Commission v. Hope Natural Gas, 287n32
Federal Quality of Life Commission, 203–204
Feinberg, Joel
  on bigamy, 309n39
  on causation, 295n40
  on competition, 80
  on duty to rescue, 90, 119, 301n67
  on Epicureans, 289n24
  on exploitation, 317n19
  on folkways, 334n119
  and garrison threshold, 129

Feinberg, Joel (*continued*)
   and harm principle, 48–67, 288n12, 289n13, 290n26–27, 291n34, 292n44, 298n26
   on harmed condition, 82, 302n72
   on individual as social being, 281n88
   on interest in another's interest, 322n5
   and lecherous millionaire, 198
   on legal power, 152–153, 309n30
   on mercy killing, 190–191
   on moralism, 321n1, 327n61
   on morally disreputable interests, 289n20, 291n33
   and offense principle, 223–224, 288n11
   and principle of least intrusion, 143
   on paternalism, 182, 185, 188, 206, 315n5, 316n14, 321n84
   on public goods, 114–115
   on slavery contract, 156
fellow-servant rule, 135
fetal pain, 335n23
fiduciary ethic, 139–142
Finch, Atticus, 238–239
Fish, Stanley, 25–26
Flast v. Cohen, 291n40
focal aims, 49
folkways, 228, 234, 236, 334n119
Food and Drug Administration, 184
fortune telling, 198
Frankel, Charles, 229, 329n84
Frankel, Max, 6
Fraser, Nancy, 260, 333n111
fraud, 39–41
free rider, 94, 114, 118, 129, 170
freedom, definitions of, 276n20
freedom of association, 230, 237–240
freedom of speech and press, 175, 332n100
Fried, Charles, 99–100
Friedman, Milton
   costs of litigation and, 310nn59, 60
   on discrimination, 238, 333n114, 334n123
   on malpractice, 160
   on occupational licensing, 159–160, 183
Frothingham v. Mellon, 291n40
Fuller, Lon L., 10, 222
futility thesis, 78
future generations, 6, 79, 179, 339n43
   bound by earlier generation, 257, 337n10
   education of, 120–121, 124
   harm to, 201–205, 320n78, 321n82

Galbraith, John Kenneth, 272
Galileo, 20
general will, 234
genetic change, 122, 168, 248, 265, 291n42
genetic defects, 112–113
George, Robert E., 214, 217, 218, 219, 326n43

Geuss, Raymond, 5
gladiatorial contest, 188–189
Glendon, Mary Ann, 179
global warming, 7, 205, 251
God
   instructions from, 90
   provoking wrath of, 212–214
Goesaert v. Cleary, 329n76
good, 10, 13. (*See also* political good; public goods)
   and autonomy, 281n90, 315n3
   common, 5, 33, 170, 214, 226, 228, 229–230, 231, 331n99
   of community, 330n91
   custom as, 238
   dialogue premise and, 259–261
   education in, 122
   equality premise and, 261–265, 338n33
   expert knowledge of, 167
   and externality constraint, 208–214
   focal aims as, 49
   as goal of state, 31, 32, 83, 131, 141, 191, 232–233, 236, 292n45, 321n79
   highest or ultimate, 3, 7, 8, 16, 24, 27, 30, 82, 193, 227
   instrumental, 45
   knowledge of behind the veil, 256
   life, 24, 202, 203, 207, 227, 233, 236, 242, 244, 246, 267, 275n2, 281n90, 323n10, 332n99, 333n109, 338n36
   moralism and, 207
   of nondomination, 331n93
   and neutrality, 14, 51, 169, 202, 266–268, 339n53
   and paternalism, 12, 180–183, 199, 200, 203–205
   pursuit of in private realm, 120–124, 242–249, 331n99
   skepticism of, 338n36
   social, 70
   universal theory of, 8, 29
   utilitarian notion of, 103
government
   delegation of power, 170, 174–175
   entrusted to citizens, 169–171
   experts claim to run, 166–169
   extent of, 14, 66, 172, 243, 286n18, 303n78, 313n31
   requirements to function, 115–116
   restraints on, 171–176
   stakeholders claim to power, 165–166
Great Separation, 213, 246
Great Transformation, 76
Greenspan, Alan, 296n54
Griswold v. Connecticut, 251
group guilt, 4, 23, 228, 281n86
group rights, 234–237, 333n111

Index 367

gun control, 64–65, 292n51
Gutmann, Amy, 200, 259, 267, 303n82, 321n82, 330n92

Habermas, Jürgen, 260
Hamilton, Alexander, 319n55
happiness amendment 176–179
Harisiades v. Shaughnessy, 308n20
Harlan, John Marshall, 313n38
harm
  accumulative, 66–68, 83, 110, 158–159, 249
  aggregative, 67, 83, 155, 157–158, 182, 249
  to community, 179, 214–218
  from competition, 80–82
  concept neglected, 29–32
  defined, 29–32, 49–57, 62–66, 284nn3, 4
  disassociated from actor, 66–68, 77–78
  to employment, 88–92
  as function of government to ameliorate, 8–9
  government control over, 10–13
  indeterminacy of, 32–33
  by market, 79–92
  to market, 84–85
  nonjusticiable, 58, 291n39
  to norms, 207–241
  not known a priori, 51
  preventing incipient, 117–118
  principle, and democracy, 164–170
  redressing, 156–159
  relativity of, 33–39
  remedies for, 143–161, 253
  state as final authority for defining, 38
  vs. misfortune, 12, 70, 73, 76, 81, 89, 103, 111–112, 134, 317n19, 340n61
harm principle, 7–14, 48–57, 138, 242, 254
  accumulative harms under, 66–68
  and aesthetics, 327n58
  affirmative obligations under, 128
  aggregative harms under, 62–66
  alternatives to, 14–16, 255–269
  and animals, 323n13
  and central planning, 82–85
  and children, 302n73
  competition under, 79–82
  and conspiracy law, 290n26
  and constitutional standing, 291n39
  constitutionalizing, 176–179, 326n42
  and contract law, 54, 84–85, 117, 301n64
  and custom, 319n57, 334n122
  elements of, 12
  education under, 120–126
  Feinberg's version, 48, 59, 115
  and fiduciary ethic, 139–142
  forms of intervention under, 143–161
  and health care, 304n1
  indeterminateness of, 248–250
  and intention to commit consequences, 132
  and jury service, 304n7
  and liberty, 307n16, 316n5
  and licensing, 131
  limited to criminal law, 288n12, 289n13, 292n47, 301n60
  Locke's version of, 285n12
  Mill's version of, 11–12, 59
  and market socialism, 91–95
  maximizing under, 18, 322n4
  and misfortune, 70, 111
  modesty of, 16–19
  negative and positive rights in, 101–103
  and negligence, 133
  and neutrality, 340n66
  and norms, 207, 209, 215, 219–220, 221, 224, 233, 240
  and offense, 325n30
  and paternalism, 180–206
  and proportionality, 60, 143, 147–148, 166, 199, 290n27, 307nn15–16
  Raz on, 281n90
  restraints against government required by, 170–176
  and rulership, 162–170
  and self-provisioning, 115–116
  compared to sovereignty principle, 289n25
  strong and weak versions, 59–62, 78
  and taxation, 101–103, 301n59
  timeline in, 201–205
  compared to utilitarianism, 18, 323n6
  as vague, 16–17, 278n47
  and voodoo, 324n20
  welfare assistance under, 101–103, 109
  at work in the real world, 251–252
  working conditions and, 87–89
harmed condition, 82
harmless immorality, 225–226
harmless wrongdoing, 57–59
harmony thesis, 70
Hart, H. L. A., 10, 215–216, 316n6, 322n4
Hauser, Philip N., 168
Hayek, Friedrich A., 283n100, 285n10, 293n8
  on jeopardy thesis, 78
  on negative rules, 10, 127–128
  on property, 86–87
  on safety net, 99, 298n14, 300n45
  on spontaneous order, 73–74
Hayes, Rutherford B., 203
Hazlitt, William, 20–21, 277n41
Hegel, Georg F. W., 167
Heilbroner, Robert, 311n12
helmet, wearing of, 181, 187, 200, 287n26, 317n26
Henry VIII, 27
Herzog, Don, 256, 257, 268, 332n99, 340n65
highest good. *See* good
Highet, Gilbert, 247

hippies, 210–211
Hippocratic Oath, 140, 294n21
Hirschman, Albert O., 78
historic landmark, 225
Hobbes, Thomas, 9, 16, 20, 84, 97, 163, 263
Hobhouse, Leonard T., 88–89, 99, 297n68
Holmes, Oliver Wendell Jr., 28, 73, 134, 136, 302n73, 305n22
Holmes, Stephen
　on communitarianism, 232
　on consent, 335n10
　on disparagement of liberalism, 280n78
　on liberal institutions, 4
　on limitations of state power, 313n31
　on society vs. individual, 227, 295n46, 328n64
　on welfare payments, 297n11
Holt, Chief Justice, 137
homosexuality, 55, 236, 323n17, 324n19, 325n39, 326n42
　as harm to community, 214–218
　laws against rejected, 251–252
　marriage, 153
　prejudice against, 210–212
Horwitz, Morton J., 80
hot coffee case, 336n26
House of Lords, power to overrule decisions, 337n16
Howe, Irving, 276n10
human agency, 47, 68, 73, 75–79, 92, 111, 267, 293n4
human being as individual, 4, 22–23, 228, 281n86 (*see also* self)
human nature, 21–25
　duality of, 281n87, 282n92
Hume, David, 84, 97
Humphrey's Peak, 221
Hurricane Katrina, 113
Husak, Douglas N., 186
Huxley, Thomas H., 84, 296n64

ideal speech situation, 260
identity, 226, 230, 235, 236, 328n66, 332n102, 336n9 (*see also* self)
ignorant savants, 256
immoral conduct, prohibition of, 214–226, 251, 322n1, 325n34, 329n76
Incompatibility Clause, 58
indeterminacy, 32–33, 49, 164, 249–250, 285n15
　of entitlement, 105–109
Indian rituals, 322n2
individual, 21 (*see also* self)
　atomistic, 20, 24, 228, 280n77, 328n64, 330n86
　derived from Christianity, 23, 280n84
　nonexistence of, 280n81
　shaped by community, 22–23
inequality, in health care, 192–193 (*see also* equality)
intent, as element of criminal law, 56–57

interdependence, 24, 37, 79, 111, 139, 179, 253
interest
　in another's interest, 50–51, 81–82, 209 (*see also* externality constraint)
　of Epicurean, 51
　of a person, 49–52
　setback to, 52–54
interests
　conflicts between, 51
　morally disreputable, 50, 289n20
Interstate Commerce Commission, 175
intervention
　forms of, 143–161
　limiting principles of, 147–156
　modes of, 144–146
　types of, 146–147
investment harm, 82–84
invisible hand technique, 34
Ireton, Henry, 165

Jackson, Robert H., 281n86, 312n22
Jefferson, Thomas, 11, 40, 149, 337n10
jeopardy thesis, 78, 295n35
Jones v. Alfred H. Mayer Co., 334n122
Jordan, Michael, 222
jury duty, 128–129

Kansas v. Mayes, 306n44
Kant, Immanuel, 97, 121, 302n72
Kedroff v. St. Nicholas Cathedral of Russian Orthodox Church, 324n20
Kekes, John, 24
Kennedy, David M., 69
Kennedy, John F., 167
Korematsu v. U. S., 281n86
Kristol, Irving, 188, 318n31
Kymlicka, Will, 99, 124, 228, 262, 306n32, 334n125, 339n46

laetrile, 184, 317nn18, 19
laissez-faire, 38, 72, 92, 99, 136, 139
land, obligations of, 86
language regulation, 330n89
Large Hadron Collider, 157
Larmore, Charles E., 259, 265, 267
Laski, Harold J., 167
Lavelle, John, 322n2
law, applied equally to all, 173–174, 313n37
Lawrence v. Texas, 251–252
lawsuits on behalf of trees, 178–179
lawyers, as public utility, 304n12
least intrusion, principle of, 148–149
lecherous millionaire, 198
Lee, Harper, 238
Lee, Robert E., 245
legal moralism, 207–226, 237, 327n58
legal power, 152

Index

Lehmann v. U. S. ex rel. Carson, 308n20
Letwin, Shirley Robin, 7
Levellers, 165
liberalism
  attacks on, 4–5
  commitments of, 4, 275n5, 276n8
  conception of human nature in, 19–25
  definitional difficulty of, 4, 276nn18, 22, 23
  despotic, 163
  extent of, 275n4
  as faith, 25–26
  ideas of, 3–7, 281n88
  inconsistency of founders of, 275n4
  as mess of mush, 4, 276n10
  norms of, 4
  paradox of, 79, 98–99
liberty, 31, 51, 83, 137
  and entitlement theory, 104–105
  maximizing, 18
  permissible interference with, 12, 24, 48–49, 55–60, 64–68, 113–115, 120, 128, 140, 143–161
  and rulers, 162–165, 174
  and paternalism, 180–206
  permanent deprivations of, 193
  community and, 212, 217, 233
  liberalism and, 242–254
  legal empowerment as essential to, 151–154
  types of, 307n16
  working conditions and, 89, 92
licensing, 60, 131, 145, 159–161, 183, 306n43, 310n60, 316n16
Liebeck, Stella, 336n26
Lilla, Mark, 213
limited liability, 87
Lindblom, Charles E., 12
Lippmann, Jonathan, 304n12
Lochner v. New York, 183
Locke, John, 9, 87, 143, 147, 173, 266
  on contracts, 84
  on education, 121
  on natural law, 11, 31–33, 44, 307n2
  and property, 86, 97, 166, 285n15
  on punishment, 307n9
  on rulers, 162–163
  on slavery, 275n4
  as social contractarian, 337n16
  on tacit consent, 256–257
  on toleration, 277n37
Lomasky, Loren E., 99
Losurdo, Domenico, 150, 275n4
Loving v. Virginia, 309n37
Lucas v. South Carolina Coastal Council, 304n5
Luria, S. E., 168

Macaulay, Thomas, 129–130, 140
MacCallum, Gerald, 298n17

Macedo, Stephen, 25
Machiavelli, Nicolò, 30–31
MacIntyre, Alasdair, 226–227
MacPherson v. Buick Motor Co., 306n40
Madison, James, 172, 248, 257, 337n10
Mai, Mukhtar, 281n86
Maistre, Joseph-Marie de, 328n66
malpractice, 159–161
Malraux, Andre, 249
Malthus, Thomas, 71–72
Mandeville, Bernard, 72, 302n75
market, 69–96
  as human agency, 75–79
  as natural force, 69–75
  redressable harms of, 79–92
  socialism, 93–95
marriage, 50, 194, 236, 286n22, 325n39
  bigamous, 153, 309n37
  failure of, 217, 218–219
  interracial, 216, 232, 309n37, 329n76, 332n105
  licenses, 200
  polygamous, 153, 309n39
  same-sex, 153, 251–252
Marx, Karl, 137, 283n100, 299n36
mass disasters, 131, 301n53, 305n14
maximin, 18
maximizing, 17–19, 176, 250
McDonald v. City of Chicago, 292n51
Medicare, 7, 277n34
Medvedev, Roy A., 295n47
merchants, right to patronage of customers, 45, 80
mercy killing, 191
middle democracy, 259
military service, 128–129
Mill, John Stuart, 9–10, 29, 128, 250
  on autonomy, 315n3
  on competition, 80
  on education, 121
  on extent of harm principle, 288n12
  harm principle and, 11–12, 17, 47, 48, 49, 59, 65, 278n45, 290n27
  on laissez-faire, 92, 99, 116
  on paternalism, 180–181, 190, 206, 314n1
  on proportionality, 143
  on public goods, 113–114, 118
  on rights, 101
  on rulers, 162, 285n9
  on rules, 116
  on slavery contracts, 193
  on taxation, 145
  on voters, 166, 311n10, 312n16
  on worker cooperatives, 93
Miller v. Schoene, 304n5
minimal state, 33–45, 79, 103, 163–164, 287n26, 299n35

mixed martial arts, 318n31
Moon, J. Donald, 99, 260
moral ecology, 218
moralism, types of, 321n1 (*see also* legal moralism)
morality, 57, 231, 239, 258, 269 (*see also* immoral conduct)
   and communal norms, 208, 214–217, 230, 245, 326n47, 329n76, 331n92
   as forbearance, 10
   and liberalism, 4, 297n12
   from reason, 218
   traditional, 86, 252, 321n1, 326n42
Morris, Christopher, 29
Mozert v. Hawkins, 303n79
multiculturalism, 234–237
Mumford, Lewis, 21
Murphy, Frank, 281n86
Murray, Charles, 78

national bedtime, 182
natural disasters, remedies for, 111–113
National Federation of Independent Business v. Sebelius, 304n1
natural force, market as, 69–75
natural law, 32, 44, 54, 72, 84, 203, 219–220, 287n33, 298n27, 337n16
natural rights, 29–47
natural systems vs. social systems, 76–78, 233
Navajo Nation v. U. S. Forest Service, 221
Nazis, 25
Nebbia v. New York, 310n46
negative duties, 10, 127
negative rights, 100–103, 151, 298n17
negligence, development of the law of, 133–139
Netherlands, right to die in, 191–192
neutrality
   Ackerman's, 340n66
   ambiguities of, 123–124
   and dialogue, 259
   and the good, 202, 245–247, 254, 338n36
   and equality, 262
   and external preferences, 209
   premise, 14, 16, 255, 265–268, 276n18, 339n57
   types of, 339n53
Newman, John Henry, 6
Niebuhr, Reinhold, 77
Nietzsche, Friedrich, 247, 248, 307n10
nondomination, 331n93
Nozick, Robert, 41, 63, 84, 88, 94, 99, 191, 263, 287n35, 302n72–73, 331n95
   entitlement theory of, 103–106, 108–110
   on rectification, 299n34
   theory of minimal state and, 33–39, 43–46, 285n16, 286n26
   theory of rulers and, 163–164
   on uncertainty 286n21
nudity, 223–224

nuisance, 119, 223–224
Nussbaum, Martha C., 329n84

offense, 51, 52, 60, 223–224, 288n11, 319n55, 322n1, 332n100
   principle, 48, 223, 224, 290n27, 316n5
   defined, 288n11
offensive conduct, 223 (*see also* offensiveness; offense)
offensive displays, 223–225
offensiveness, 51, 60, 188, 209, 221, 223–225
office held under the United States, 58
Okin, Susan Moller, 125, 299n35, 303n86
Old Order Amish, 123–124, 235
Olney, Richard, 174
Olympics, 265, 339n51
Oregon assisted suicide law, 192–193
others, meaning of, 201–205

Paine, Thomas, 98, 99, 313n36
Parekh, Bhiku, 236
patent lawyer, 140
paternalism, 180–201, 207
   custom and, 194–196
   and self-binding, 199–201, 286n26
   soft, 190, 206
   types of, 315n5
   and warning labels, 181
perfectionists, 24, 122, 214, 315n3, 331n93, 337n15
personal stake, 50
perversity thesis, 78–79
Pettit, Philip, 331n93
Phelps, Fred, 283n100, 323n17, 324n19
philosophers' brief, 191
Pistorius, Oscar, 265, 339n51
planning, of market, 82–84
Plessy v. Ferguson, 239
pluralism, 8, 38, 170, 229, 230, 303n84, 312n26
political animal, 7, 244, 275n2
political good, 151–154, 200–201
political theory, nature and complexity of, 17–19, 28
politics of difference, 234
poll tax, 311n14
pollution, 66–67, 158
polygamy, 153, 236
poor laws, 305n32
poor relief, 97–100
pornography, 251
positive rights, 100–103
Posner, Richard, 199, 305n27
Pound, Ezra, 4
Pound, Roscoe, 284n4
poverty, 71–73
power as paralyzing, 83, 243
Pressman, Gabe, 302n72

private. *See* public vs. private
privileges of lord of the manor, 27
privity, 138–139
procedural fairness, principle of, 154–156
procedural republic, 232, 244
production harm, 85–87
Prohibition, 65
projects, public funding of, 113–115, 301n62
property
    as natural right, 86
    redefinition of, 44–45
    relativity of, 41–46
    restrictions on, 85–87
    rules, 87
    taking of, 43–44
proportionality principle, 60, 143, 147–148, 166, 199, 290n27, 307nn15–16
protective association, 34–41, 42, 45, 63, 94, 163–164, 286n26
proximate cause, 135
public goods, 113–116, 118
public projects, 113–115, 301n62
public vs. private, 10
punishment, right to inflict, 32–33

racial discrimination. *See* discrimination
Rawls, John, 15, 28, 259
    on equality, 261–264
    on harm, 29
    on least advantaged, 18, 191
    on redistribution, 99, 108
    on social contract, 256–258
    on utilitarianism, 17
Raz, Joseph, 24, 281n90, 339n53
reason
    ambiguity of, 282n96
    as sin of liberalism, 25–28, 283n100
reasonableness, 224
rectification principle, 105–108
redistribution, 103–113
regulation vs. litigation, 159–161
regulatory capture, 174–175, 314n43
relativism, 244, 246
religious commandments, violations of, 212–214
religious wars, 27, 202, 213, 279n63, 330n86
republicanism. *See* civic republicanism
rescue, duty to, 90, 113–120, 129–131, 197
retroactivity, 149
Reynolds v. U. S., 309n38
Ricardo, David, 72
right to die, 189–193
rights, negative and positive, 100–103
risk, 174, 181
    and aggregative harms, 62–67, 157
    and bankruptcy, 87
    borne by buyers, 56
    and duty to rescue, 118–119

    and experts, 168–169
    as object of the harm principle, 40, 74, 160
    and special relationships, 132–139
robotics, 320n78
Roe v. Wade, 251
Roemer, John, 93
Rosenblum, Nancy L., 232
Ross, E. A., 77
Rousseau, Jean-Jacques, 4, 77, 121, 234, 279n70, 293n58
Royal Society, 72
Ruffin, Thomas, 308n25
rule
    of law, 33, 243
    making, 116–117
    vs. standard, 313n40
rulers, 31, 162–170
rules
    of conduct, 74
    of the road, 63–64
Runyan v. McCrary, 335n127
Russell, John, 98
Russell, T. Baron, 306n38
Ryan v. New York Central R. R. Co., 305n24

same-sex marriage, 153, 251–252
Sandel, Michael, 125, 228, 230, 232–233, 244–245, 252, 278n57
Scalia, Antonin, 174, 308n26
scapegoating, 154
Schelling, Thomas, 199–200
Schlesinger v. Reservists Committee to Stop the War, 291n38
schools, withdrawing children from, 123
    (*see also* education)
Schweickart, David, 94–95
scientific reductionism, 20
Seeley v. Peters, 287n33
self, 19–25, 240 (*see also* identity)
    binding, 199–201, 286n26
    exclusion list, 201
    neurological basis of, 279nn68, 74
    prior to its ends, 21–22, 278n60
    provisioning, 115–116
self-regarding conduct, 48, 181–182
Sen, Amartya K., 262
separation of powers, 172–173
Serbian Eastern Orthodox Diocese v. Milivojevich, 324n20
setback to interest, 49–57
    baseline of, 53–54
    wrongfulness of, 54–57
sex discrimination. *See* discrimination; family relations
Shakespeare, 18
Shklar, Judith, 5, 73, 275n4, 276n23, 302n70, 337n15

Singer, Peter, 320n62
situated self, 19
Slaughterhouse Cases, 287nn29, 32
slaughterhouses, 43–44
slave patrols, 228
slavery, 23, 108, 150
   and conscription, 128
   contracts, 152–153, 156–157, 193–194, 318n49
   as harmful, 220
   inconsistency of liberals toward, 150, 275n4
   nature of, 209
slaves
   genetically bred, 248
   patrols against, 227–228, 328n73
   poor as alternative to, 72–73
   power over, 308n25
Smith, Adam, 11, 31, 70, 85, 97, 113, 149, 285n10, 301n55, 312n16
Smith v. Board of School Commissioners, 303n79
Smith, Winston, 27
smoking
   curbs, 68, 181, 190, 288n12
   deaths, 305n15
Smyth v. Ames, 287n32
social contract, 15, 20, 25, 34, 46, 97, 256–258, 280n77, 336n9, 337n16
social Darwinism, 294n15
social disintegration, 214–218
social harm, 65, 214–218 (*see also* community, harms to)
social harmony, 70
social systems, control of, 75–79
social uncertainty principle, 105–109
socialism, 108 (*see also* market socialism)
socialist revolution, 94–95
socialization, 21
society, reconstruction of by reason, 25–28
Socrates, 337n15
soft paternalism, 190, 206
sorites paradox, 292n56
sovereignty principle, 289n25
space shuttle, 157
specialization, 76, 137
Spencer, Herbert, 136, 306n32
   contradictions of, 84, 305n29
   and laissez faire, 72, 98, 294n15
   on liberty, 263
   on necessity of government, 248–249
   on poor relief, 306n32, 320n62
   on public education, 121
   on welfare, 298n18
Spender, Stephen, 21
spontaneous order, 73–74, 78
standard of care, 135–136
standing, 58, 291n39
state, as final authority for defining harm, 38

state of nature, 42, 56, 200, 278n58
   in social contract theory, 20, 32, 143, 163, 337n16
   in Nozick's theory, 33–36, 38–41, 63, 164
   in reality, 21, 61
state of war, 20
state vs. society, 247
State v. Mann, 308n25
Stephen, James Fitzjames, 114
steroids, 195
Stevens, John Paul, 309n26
Stone, Christopher D., 178
strict liability, 133–134, 139, 141
suicide, 240, 266, 339n56
   assisted, 191–193
Supreme Court
   on closed communities, 123, 235
   on compulsory service, 128
   delegation doctrine of, 175
   on economic conditions, 92, 176, 287nn29, 30, 288n5
   on gun rights, 292n51
   on harm, 251
   on harmless wrongdoing, 58
   on homosexuality, 218, 252
   and reasonableness of law, 155–156
   on right to die, 189, 191
   on selecting a good, 153, 179
   on sex discrimination, 267
   on taxing power, 146
   on zoning, 43–44
survival of the fittest, 71–73

taboo, 215, 231, 327n61
tacit consent, 256, 257, 337n10
talent, undeserved, 264
Tawney, R. H., 99
tax evasion, 66
taxation
   legitimacy of, 102, 110, 145
   subsidizing public goods by, 114, 118
taxpayer injury, 58–59
Taylor, Charles, 228, 234, 236, 280n77, 332n102, 333n109, 333n113
teamwork, 231
terminal illness, 191
textbooks, secular, 122
Thirteenth Amendment, 128
Thompson, Dennis, 200, 259, 267, 303n82, 321n82
three-strikes law, 159
timeline, 201–205
Titmuss, Richard M., 320n62
Tocqueville, Alexis de, 22, 106, 149, 297n69
toleration, 231, 236, 324n20, 337n13
   as core of liberalism, 4, 244, 245, 275n5, 276n8
   as limit on definition of harm, 213
   necessary for religious salvation, 266
   as robust, 252

Tolstoy, Leo, 335n19
Townsend, Joseph, 71–72
tradition, 230–231, 241
  and assisted suicide, 191
  and liberalism, 5, 8, 10–11, 201
  and morality, 209, 218, 245
  multicultural, 234–237, 246
  natural law, 219–220
  and reason, 25–28
  supplanted by human systems, 75–76, 86
  undermining of, 207–210
  value stemming from, 226–228
Trillin, Calvin, 266
Tushnet, Mark, 335n10
tyranny, definition of, 172

U. S. v. Darusmont, 308n20
U. S. v. Falcone, 290n26
ultimate good. *See* good
unattractive nuisance, 223–224
  (*see also* attractive nuisance)
uncertainty
  and assisted suicide, 191
  of events, 86, 116, 197
  extent of, 19, 137
  about the good, 12
  and Nozick, 36, 38, 39–41, 286n21
  principle of social, 106–109
unemployment benefits, 110
unencumbered self, 19 (*see also* self)
Unger, Roberto M., 321n80
unintended consequences, 73–74, 79
universal suffrage, 175
universalism, 234
Ur Protective Association, 39–41
utilitarianism, 5, 17, 103, 232, 276n22, 322n4, 323n6

Vacco v. Quill, 318n34
video games, attempt to ban, 251
visual blight, 223–225

Volstead Act, 313n38
Voltaire, 121
voodoo, 324n20
voting, 150, 170, 175, 251, 258, 313n27, 336n1
  (*see also* elections)

Waldron, Jeremy, 281n88, 338n34
Walzer, Michael, 21, 260, 261, 263, 280n79, 329n79
Ward, Lester, 137
Warner, Marina, 154–155
warning labels, 56, 132, 181, 184–185, 193, 316n6, 317n19
welfare needs and benefits, 71–73, 103–113, 243
welfare policy, 97
West, Mae, 171
Whitman v. American Trucking Assn., 314n44
Wickard v. Filburn, 288n5
Wilde, Oscar, 233
Williams v. New York, 291n41
Wisconsin v. Yoder, 235, 303n81
witchcraft, 75, 213, 267, 323n17, 330n92, 340n61
Wolfe, Alan, 24, 275n5, 276n8, 282n92, 294n26
Wolfenden Report, 214
Wollheim, Richard, 230
worker cooperatives, 93
workers
  harmful conditions of, 88–92
  injuries to, 70–73
working class, subsistence payments to, 97–98
working conditions, 70, 88–92, 293n7–8
wrongdoing, harmless, 57–59
wrongful conception, 59, 291nn41–42
wrongful death, 136
wrongful setback to interest, 49–57

zoning, 43
zoon politikon, 7, 244